The City in Time and Space

This ambitious study treats urbanization and urbanism all over the world, and from the earliest times to the present. Professor Southall, a pioneer in the study of African cities, discusses the urban centres of ancient Sumeria, Greece and Rome, as well as medieval European cities, Chinese, Japanese, Islamic and Indic cities, colonial cities and the great metropolises of the twentieth century. Drawing on this historical and comparative perspective, he offers a fresh analysis of world urbanization in the contemporary period of globalization. The study emphasizes the enduring paradox of the city, which juxtaposes splendid cultural productions with the poverty and deprivation of the majority.

AIDAN SOUTHALL is Professor Emeritus of Anthropology at the University of Wisconsin. He has had a distinguished career as an Africanist and urban anthropologist spanning several decades, and has previously taught at universities in Africa and Britain.

The City in Time and Space

Aidan Southall

Professor Emeritus, University of Wisconsin, Madison

PUBLISHED BY THE PRESS SYNDICATE OF THE UNIVERSITY OF CAMBRIDGE
The Pitt Building, Trumpington Street, Cambridge CB2 1RU, United Kingdom

CAMBRIDGE UNIVERSITY PRESS
The Edinburgh Building, Cambridge CB2 2RU, UK
  http://www.cup.cam.ac.uk
40 West 20th Street, New York, NY 10011–4211, USA
  http://www.cup.org
10 Stamford Road, Oakleigh, Melbourne 3166, Australia

First published 1998

Printed in the United Kingdom at the University Press, Cambridge

Typeset in Plantin 10/12 pt   [SE]

A catalogue record for this book is available from the British Library

Library of Congress cataloguing in publication data

Southall, Aidan William.
  The city in time and space / Aidan Southall.
    p.   cm.
  Includes bibliographical references.
  ISBN 0 521 46211 8
  1. Cities and towns – History.   I. Title.
HT111.S63   1997
307.76′09–dc21   97–8671   CIP

ISBN 0 521 46211 8 hardback

I dedicate this book with love and gratitude to
JAMIDODI, who did the hardest work and
kept me going till I had finished it.

Contents

Illustrations

Acknowledgements

I am deeply grateful to my editor Jessica Kuper for her welcome clairvoyance in pressing me to revise and recreate the manuscript, for the great help received from the readers she chose and for guiding me through the various stages of publication.

I am grateful to Random House for permission to quote from pages 52–3 of *Power/Knowledge: Selected Interviews and Other Writings 1972–1977* by Michel Foucault, edited by Colin Gordon (New York: Pantheon, 1980) (this passage was taken from *Magazine littéraire*, 101, June 1975, reprinted as 'Le jeu du pouvoir', in D. Grison (ed.), *Politiques de la philosophie* (1976)); and for permission to quote from *Encyclopaedia Britannica*, 15th edition (1974), XIII: 1005–8.

The passage from Fernand Braudel, *Afterthoughts on Material Civilization and Capitalism* (1977) pages 6–7 is reprinted by permission of The Johns Hopkins University Press.

I wish to thank Dr J. Mellaart for permission to reproduce illustrations and plans of Çatal Hüyük; the Tourist Office of the City of Périgueux for an illustration of the old city and cathedral; the Mary Evans Picture Library for illustrations of Isfahan; H. Gutschow for the diagram of the Bhaktapur mandala; the Hong Kong Tourist Office for an illustration of the city; Rex Features, representatives of Sipa Press, for illustrations of Les Minguettes; and the Associated Press for the illustration of Grozny.

Introduction

Our objective is to display the city as a human achievement which appeared, spread and intensified over the last ten millennia. All the most admirable and desirable achievements have been intensified in the city, as have the worst horrors. The limitations of human expression and communication compel me to carve this mass of time and space into manageable, communicable portions, although every dissection violates reality. The theory of modes of production adumbrated by Marx is developed into a scheme of divisions which economically maximizes illumination and minimizes distortion.

The process of writing drummed in cumulatively the overwhelming sense that the fate of the majority of human beings has been continually glossed over and travestied, for the obvious reason that those providing the record had contrary interests which affected their selection and focus. The loftiest minds have thus been compromised.

Our basis of selection was to include all urban cultures which seemed to offer doors to progress in the well-being of humankind. In his sample Toynbee chose only 'some particular phase of each city's history that has been great in the sense that it has made a mark on the subsequent history of civilization' (1967:5). When an urban culture ceases to offer this I cease to follow it. Greek cities offered a new way in which a substantial minority achieved cultural enlightenment. Though it was at the expense of women and the majority of men its presentation offered aspirations to men and women which have never been lost. Christ's ministry is recorded mostly in the countryside, but the culmination and sequel had to be in the city. Song China seemed on the brink of a quantum leap towards new affluence which might have spread more widely, but momentum was lost. Current urban civilization has moved towards unprecedented heights of affluence and freedom for all, but almost at the point of achievement threatens self-destruction.

In this perspective we elaborate the theoretical framework and its dilemmas (chapter 1). Our selectivity focuses on pristine cities, the Asiatic mode of production in its earliest form, in Sumeria, China, the

1

Andes and Mexico (chapter 2); on cities of the Ancient mode of production in Greece and Rome (chapter 3); on medieval cities of the Feudal mode of production in Europe (chapter 4); on medieval cities of the Asiatic mode of production in the Sinic, Japanese, Islamic and Indic regions (chapter 5); on colonial and Third World cities as the dynamic bridge between medieval feudal and modern capitalist cities (chapter 6) and finally on the transformation of cities from the Feudal to the Capitalist mode of production in Europe and ultimately the world as a whole (chapter 7).

Emerging more strongly as construction of the book proceeded was realization of the centrality of movement of peoples and of cultural breakdowns to the transformation process in the mode of production, each constituting a change in the context and dynamics of urban life. The movement of peoples and breakdown of socio-cultural systems is documented: from the Asiatic to the Ancient, the Ancient to the Feudal and the Feudal to the Capitalist mode of production.

Though very strongly marked and perhaps more thoroughly studied, this was not distinctively a European phenomenon. The Japanese moved purposefully to borrow the urban culture they envied (though transforming it paradoxically in the process), in a way that the Germanic peoples lacked the organization to do vis-à-vis Rome. They thus almost artificially created a situation which led to breakdown and opportunistic feudalism in Japan. The Islamic movement swept away all the regimes and occupied all the cities of western Asia, North Africa and eastern Europe, in contempt rather than envy, but absorbed more from them than they realized. The Mughal Empire drew its urban culture from Iran, but achieved a territorial spread far greater than its source, as also did the European migrants to the Americas. The Europeans moved outwards after the Renaissance and Reformation in the persons of their adventurers and traders, in contempt rather than emulation of the peoples, cultures and cities they found. It was the outward movement which generated the internal breakdown and transformation, here a lengthy rather than cataclysmic process. In the Asiatic to Ancient to Feudal transitions it was culturally less sophisticated peoples who triggered the transition. In the Feudal to Capitalist transition it was, for the first time, a more internal process and more urban based. Movement and breakdown are dialectical complements of each other.

1 'Writing the city under crisis'

Chapter 1 recognizes the deepening urban crisis, rehearsed almost daily in press and media. It images the urban vista of the last ten millennia, the concentration of the best and worst in human potentiality. Major intellectual approaches and the dilemmas of anthropology in studying the city are discussed. The grand theme of the city is introduced and the theory of successive, dialectically related modes of production is spelled out as the chosen framework of presentation.

Prologue

To write about the city in the mid-nineties is to write under pressure of 'deepening crisis' (in our present day economies and societies) (Braudel, 1985, III:625). For anthropology, to which nothing human is alien, the city encapsulated human achievement and destiny. If the motive of history is to explain the present and the obligation of anthropology to empathize reflexively with the other, the last frontier of time and culture is daring to ask what we have learnt in the city to save our grandchildren from ultimate destruction.[1] The city concentrates the human experience and has taught some lessons although the future is not to be foretold. Braudel read clearly but broke off at the intractability of the social problem. We cannot hope that dominant groups will agree to hand over (Braudel, 1985, III:632). Marx dared to envisage a new human being, without whom his revolution could never succeed. If there is any new element in the situation it is the gravity of the crisis.

In his fascinating *Afterthoughts on Material Civilization and Capitalism* (1977) Braudel unwittingly summed up the anthropologists' view of the people in the city through the ages.

I began with daily life, with those aspects of life that control us without our even being aware of them: habit or, better yet, routine – those thousands of acts that flower and reach fruition without anyone's having made a decision, acts of which we are not even fully aware. I think mankind is more than waist deep in daily routine. Countless inherited acts, accumulated pell-mell and repeated time after time to this very day, become habits that help us live, imprison us, and make decisions for us throughout our lives. The acts are incentives, pulsion, patterns, ways

3

of acting and reacting that sometimes – more frequently than we might suspect –
go to the beginnings of mankind's history. Ancient, yet still alive, this multi-
centuried past flows into the present like the Amazon River pouring into the
Atlantic Ocean the vast flood of its cloudy waters. (1977:6–7)

The urban vista

Cities appeared some ten thousand years ago. The first cities had only a
few thousand inhabitants, but were, none the less, the largest population
concentrations of their time, just as are the metropolitan conurbations of
today, with their fifteen to twenty million populations, overlapping into
the continuous agglomeration of megalopolis and oecumenopolis. The
first cities were all city-states, but very few cities are city-states today.[2]
The dominant urban form is now the western industrial capitalist city, the
first to dominate, in a sense, the whole world. But the longest and largest
continuous urban cultural tradition is that of China. If there is anything in
common between such disparate manifestations, it must be a relative
factor. Despite the great diversity of cities in time and space, there is a
demonstrable thread of continuity through their dialectical transformations from earliest beginnings till today, as they have played an ever
greater part in human life (Toynbee, 1967:13).

All these cities, from the smallest to the largest, the earliest to the latest,
have been the greatest points of concentration and of increasing density in
their time and space:[3] a concentration of women and men and their social
relationships; of shelter, buildings and physical plant; of productive
resources, goods and services, consumption and exchange activities; of
wealth, power and energy; of information, communication and knowledge, intellectual training and even thought; of religion, ritual and ceremonial, of creative, aesthetic sensibility and innovative stimuli, all
necessarily correlated with parallel processes of the division of labour,
role differentiation and general specialization involving increasing
inequality and growth in co-ordination and hierarchy, aimed at increasing
efficiency and reduction of friction.

The first cities, and subsequently the greatest cities in any cultural or
politico-economic region, have given expression to the best and the worst
extremes of human potentiality. As concrete expressions of the
concentration of women and men, and always of the largest number of the
most creative and powerful women and men, they have displayed the
glories of urban art and architecture in temples, tombs and palaces, the
magnification of human energy in progressive mastery of the immediate
environment,[4] the splendid vistas of triumphal arches, colonnades and
avenues, the grandeur of monumental squares, processions and celebra-

tions, the beauty, utility and convenience of theatres, circuses, baths, markets, fountains and sewers, aqueducts, canals and drains,[5] but they have also been the scene of violence, crime, terrorism, torture, execution and massacre, the exploitation of urban workers and rural masses, the poor housed in squalid hovels or tenements, ridden with disease and early death, the spoliation of nature and the glorification of war, with resultant devastation.

In the past, the urban poor, like the rural poor, were taken for granted, as part of the divine plan. This is no longer so, but the poor are still very much with us, as Christ prophesied. Furthermore, widely influential urban theory has suggested that urbanization now threatens all whom it envelops, both rich and poor, with the danger of increasing impersonality and anomie. I reject this simplistic unilinear theory, along with the modernization theory which parallels it. Urbanization must refer to both the human as well as the material and technological aspects of the process, in their interaction. While the material and technological aspects of urbanization do threaten impersonality, the human components defend themselves vigorously against this, and could, in principle, even turn technological development away from this direction. However, in the Capitalist mode of production even the human use of technological development, especially in the electronic and communication explosion, threatens to increase exploitation and mask hegemony.

Intellectual approaches

There is no escape from the fact that our intellectual resources for analysing and understanding cities are predominantly recent and Euro-American, however much lip-service may be paid to Bottero, Vico and Bodin, to Ibn Khaldun and Ssu-ma-chi'ien. A major effort is required to transcend even unwitting ethnocentricism. The primary emphasis of history on detailed events entails unmanageable problems of bulk, the result of which is that western historians who attempt to focus outside the western world become locked in specialized regional blocs, as Orientalists, Sinologists, Islamicists, Africanists and so forth, subject to their own ethnocentric myopia. The Euro-American domination of world scholarship has to be accepted, for the moment, as an unfortunate but ineluctable counterpart of the parallel development of the material power and intellectual resources of the western world. But its dangers need to be recognized and constant attempts made to transcend them.

Anthropology is a suitable vehicle for such an effort, because it has always given a higher priority to the transcendence of ethnocentricism than any other discipline. Anthropological interest in cities is recent, but profound, though still not widely recognized or adequately theorized. The conventional restriction of anthropological interest to small-scale, isolated non-western and usually pre-state societies was both intellectually and practically untenable. In principle, anthropology has always claimed an interest in all things human, frequently invoking the Roman poet Terence in support.[6]

To fulfil this mission, anthropology has to bridge the gap which at present constitutes an irrational hiatus at its heart, between the knowledge of the beginnings of cities provided by anthropological archaeology, and the knowledge of what may be the end of cities as hitherto known, provided by contemporary urban anthropology. This hiatus of some three thousand years has been the province of historians, and anthropologists can only hope to bridge the gap by beginning to tackle the tremendous task of respectfully using historians[7] as anthropological informants and putting historical data to their own use.

We must not exaggerate the influence of cities in history, but seek to understand the varying part they have played as human concentrations in different periods, regions, cultures and political economies. Cities cannot be reified like actors on a stage, nor can comparisons be made by lifting cities out of context, or by lifting aspects of urban life out of context of the city as a whole. The history of cities is an integral part of the history of human affairs as a whole (Toynbee, 1967:14). The recent form of city, which has expanded so enormously, is reaching the end of the process of concentration as hitherto known, since the current information and communication revolution opens the possibility that the actual physical concentration of human bodies and of face-to-face relationships in dense urban agglomerations of ever vaster size may be becoming superfluous. For 99% of their history, cities have been walking cities for most people. Then for a brief century, more and more rapid means of bringing our bodies and their social interactions into proximity with one another were invented. Now even that may become increasingly superfluous as the remote transmission of sight and sound is substituted for that of bodies. But this has become the latest mechanism through which capitalist exploitation is maintained and increased.

The electronic explosion has carried the accelerating evolution of communications to a new dimension, from the rapid transport of physical bodies, which made feasible cities eighty miles across instead of the previous eight, to the transmission of voices and images almost instantaneously round the world. Rationally speaking, therefore, it is no longer people's bodies that have to be moved into central points of concentration, but only their voices and the images of their faces and actions, which suffice to concentrate their relationships on a new dimension at a higher density than before. This rational possibility may, however, be rejected, if political leaders, business executives and culture brokers insist on having hands to shake and secretaries to touch. Corporations are already banishing their production, distribution and bookkeeping activities to long, low, windowless buildings far from city centres, where land is cheap, yet continue to build ever denser clusters of the high rise, skyscraper headquarters of management and symbolic domination in downtown areas.

'Any society which has in it what we call "towns" or "cities" is in *all* aspects an urban society . . . "rural" refers only to a set of specialities of an urban society characterized by being linked (under any technology known) to specific geographical spaces' (Leeds, 1980). Recognizing the essential truth of this, one might have reservations about so absolute a claim, for earlier times, but it is becoming entirely true today. Not only is concentration no longer technologically necessary, nor is it sociologically necessary, in the technical sense. In late capitalist economies the influence of the city penetrates the remotest places to such an extent that they become in a sense urban and thus the antagonism of town and country seems to be transcended in the final absorption of the latter by the former. The deepest 'rural' countryside is now, in its primary function, an urban playground for the urban consumption of leisure, while the productive activities of agriculture, formerly considered by definition rural, have been mechanized, industrialized, monetized and commoditized and thus also urbanized.

No wonder that the 'urban question' has arisen, with the study of urban phenomena approximating the study of complex societies as a whole and the city losing its distinctness as an object of theoretical study and basis of disciplinary focus. Urban sociologists have also been much exercised by doubt as to whether any coherent body of problems and theories really exists which can properly be called urban sociology, just as urban anthropologists have constantly worried because their studies seemed to be *in* the city by purely common sense, conventional definitions of what the city is, rather than *of* the city in any viable conceptual and theoretical sense. Saunders concludes that 'a distinctive urban sociology cannot be developed in the context of advanced capitalist society . . . The city in contemporary capitalism does not itself constitute a theoretically significant area of study' (1986:15). Weber, Durkheim and Marx and Engels 'all came to the conclusion that the city in contemporary capitalism was not a theoretically specific object of analysis'. Saunders supposes that it was for this reason that urban sociology pays so little attention to what these founders actually said about cities, and pays attention rather to other parts of their work.

Although Castells played a major part in the downfall of theoretical urban sociology, he has subsequently attempted a bizarre resuscitation. Jettisoning his previous Marxist stance he has swung to the opposite extreme of substituting meaning for material causation in the context of total cultural relativism. 'A city', he says, 'is what a historical society decides a city will be. "Urban" is the social meaning assigned to a particular spatial form by a historically defined society' (1983:302). This is a redundant truism, necessarily known in all societies. It involves the abandonment of all comparison, although Castells himself seems still to indulge in it. It reverses the old adage 'actions speak louder than words'. Material relations are transmogrified into meaning, class struggle into experience. Medieval merchants did not struggle for urban freedoms, they simply *declared* the city a free space and *defined* the city as a market (1983:303). Yet he is not prepared to abandon the materialistic conflict, for he denounces social movements aimed at transforming meaning without being able to transform society. His pessimism is justified, but after promising a new theory of society, he arrives at a conclusion which can only be described as magical (Southall, Nas and Ansari, 1985:12–16). Though not a theoretically significant area of study, or specific object of analysis in the capitalist era, the city was none the less central to Marx's theory, for 'the foundation of every division of labour that is well developed, and brought about by the exchange of commodities, is the separation of town and country. It may be said that the whole economic history of society is summed up in the movement of this antithesis' (1967:352). In fact, Marx specified a different relation of the city to the society in each mode of production. It is this changing relation of city and society that I take as justification for the study of the city, and of urban anthropology.

Urban anthropologists have not realized that these dilemmas indeed express the theoretical conclusion that there are by common consent tumultuous happenings *in* the city, but no longer distinctive processes *of* the city, because urban life and events are conditioned and determined by processes and forces generated in the political economy and culture far transcending any urban or even national limits. The attempt to define the urban leads to contorted tautologies (Plotnicov, 1985:50–1). The unity lies in the wholeness of the total human experience of it, bounded at the beginning by the temporal immensities of the pre-urban era and at the end by the still impenetrable mysteries of the post-urban age. Cities have never been seriously and comprehensively looked at as a whole, so the nature of their unity has never been fully explored or perceived.

I base my approach to the city on the idea of concentration, but extend it beyond mere population to include its more profound social, cultural and politico-economic implications, since these are even more highly concentrated. I previously defined these on the basis of role relationships (1973:106), which are far more highly concentrated in cities than population as such, but the notion applies differentially to different general domains of role relationships, such as kinship, religious, political, economic (production) and recreation (consumption) – concentration applying in its most extreme form to the latter two. Concentration of social relationships in general defines the most fundamental character-istic common to cities in all time and space. The purpose of studying cities in this sense is to understand how the relationship of those concentrations to the rest of society has varied over time and space, and how these variations reflect the changing organization of urban concentrations and the organization of production and society as a whole.

Dilemmas of anthropology in studying the city

This runs counter to a very influential emphasis in current anthropology: the privileging of the short term over the long term. This is curious at a time when there is more serious anthropological interest in history than ever before, but it has been intrinsic to social anthropology for most of the century, since the fieldwork revolution began. The previous armchair anthropology was deeply concerned with longer issues, but in such a flawed manner as to make us still afraid of contamination, although those long-term issues will not leave us. The synchronic fieldwork thrust of anthropology is its most distinguished contribution and the fundamental perspective for all other problems, and it might surprise any anthropolo-gist to be accused of short-sightedness when the dominant reflexive para-digm demands sensitive awareness of the situation of others in its racial, ethnic, gender, economic and political world context, whose historical dimension is manifestly ineluctable. 'Our past is present in us as a project' (Fabian, 1983:93). But the intense and in itself worthwhile concentration on problems of the person marginalized long-term issues, although the very debate on degrees of individualism and self-consciousness in the still western anthropologist and her and his various worldwide others cannot avoid the world context of basic inequality and injustice, colonialism and exploitation, with their very long histories. Because their attention and interest are not focused in this direction, very sophisticated anthropolo-gists often perpetuate astonishingly naive statements. Thus it is suggested that social theory since the nineteenth century treated self-consciousness as an aberration (Cohen, 1992:221–41).

The problem of diachrony

Exploring and imparting meaning to any human phenomenon with a long history involves the differentiation of significant moments or ages in its diachronic unfolding. No descriptive account can include more than a minute percentage of the multitudinous stream of acts, events, occurrences through which a phenomenon has been manifested. Unless the basis of such severe selectivity is clarified, the validity of the account cannot be assessed. A descriptive account soon becomes unmanageably bulky and self-defeating, therefore inevitably incomplete and partial. A more systematic selective account is more meaningful and no more dangerous if the basis of selection is made clear. Any division into periods is artificial in magnifying discontinuities into clear-cut breaks, suggesting a nomothetic absoluteness where a polythetic relativity is a more plausible approach to reality (Needham, 1975). With this proviso accepted, comes the question of identifying the relative discontinuities deemed most significant.

All cultures possessed of means of recording (as well as others), have indulged in uncomplimentary characterization of those around them, involving notions of temporal as well as spatial differentiation. Thus when the Chinese some millennia ago arranged the human world in concentric squares (imperial domain; domain of nobility; domain of barbarian Sinification; domain of barbarian allies; and wild domain) they conflated space, time and politico-economic status. In the third domain the barbarians were in *process* of Sinification. The barbarian allies were clearly expected to graduate into this state, with wild barbarians following behind. When Tylor says few would dispute that the sequence Australian, Tahitian, Aztec, Chinese, Italian is the right order of culture, he does not even specify what period is in question. The vague categories of Savagery, Barbarism and Civilization and the Stone, Bronze and Iron Ages held sway from the eighteenth through the nineteenth century till elaborated to the point of absurdity by Morgan and thus retained by Engels, then ultimately refined by White, Sahlins and Service, the latter becoming the last standard bearer of the 'Band–Tribe–Chiefdom–State' formulation till he too succumbed to unanswerable criticism, by Morton Fried and others, taking refuge in the simple dichotomy between Egalitarian and Hierarchical, ironically echoing the original Primitive–Civilized pair.

The theory of modes of production worked out by Marx and Engels from the 1840s onward brings us on to a different level of thought, knowledge and analytical precision. Perhaps no theory has ever been subjected to such intense critical debate for so long, yet, as Thompson remarks, Marx is always in the process of being judged wanting, but always returning undaunted (1978:45). The theory has been little used by anthropologists during the last decades, when they temporarily lost interest in longer perspectives and were beguiled by the pleasures of the text. However, if they had a pre-eminent guru, it was surely Michel Foucault, who became an essential part of their armature and almost magical guarantee of postmodernity. Nevertheless, when accused of distancing himself from Marx, Foucault had this to say:

> I often quote concepts, texts and phrases from Marx, but without feeling obliged to add the authenticating label of a footnote with a laudatory phrase to accompany the quotation. As long as one does that, one is regarded as someone who knows and reveres Marx, and will be suitably honoured in the so-called Marxist journals. But I quote Marx without saying so, without quotation marks and because people are incapable of recognizing Marx's texts I am thought to be someone who does not quote Marx. When a physicist writes a work of physics, does he feel it necessary to quote Newton and Einstein? He uses them but does not need the quotation marks, the footnote and the eulogistic comment to prove how completely he is being faithful to the master's thought. And because other physicists know what Einstein did, what he discovered and proved, they can recognize him in what the physicist writes. It is impossible at the present time to write history without using a whole range of concepts directly or indirectly linked to Marx's thought and situating oneself within a horizon of thought which has been defined and described by Marx. One might even wonder what difference there could ultimately be between being a Marxist and being a historian. (1980:52–3)

Harvey constantly insists, throughout his analysis, on the continuing validity of the 'theoretical tools that Marx devised' (1990:188) and of 'the grasp of his historical materialist enquiry' (1990:328) and the 'metanarrative of capitalist development that Marx proposed' as the means of theorization. Many influential writers now favour a return to Marxist perspectives in order to combat the ruthless injustices of the new world order (sc. globalization).

'If, as Marx insisted, it takes an alienated individual to pursue the Enlightenment project with tenacity and coherence sufficient to bring us to some better future, then the loss of the alienated subject would seem to preclude the conscious construction of alternative social futures' (Harvey, 1993:54). 'Alienation of the subject is displaced by fragmentation of the subject.' 'Eschewing the idea of progress, postmodernism abandons all sense of historical continuity' (Harvey, 1990:54).

I look to the general idea of women and men in their productive relationship with nature, however simple or complex, or transformed, on the implicit assumption that in the long run the majority have sought to increase their productivity, and the groups which succeed in this have always achieved dominance. It is the idea which Marx developed into his theory of modes of production, an articulated combination of forces and relations of production, where the forces of production consist *essentially* of the mode of appropriation of nature by men and women, the relations of production being the system whereby the surplus product is extracted and distributed, consisting of property relations and the class order upholding and enforcing them. Mode of production theory is the theory of a trajectory, in which cities emerge as the ambiguous flower of the growing concentration and unequal distribution of production, power and people in human society, continuously increasing (from a global perspective), until in the Capitalist mode of production the contradictions, spread for the first time throughout the world, begin to build up to explosive proportions.

Current preoccupation with the individual prejudices anthropology and much general scholarship against Marxist thought. A prevalent approach to the problem of the individual and society is that, while each is the receiver of a cultural heritage, each must make this heritage their own, processing it through their mind and experience. (Indeed, some of Marx's most celebrated utterances were on this point.) As conditions change and individuals carry out this process differently, social and cultural change may occur. How far differences in processing arise from changes in external conditions and how far from individual initiative (surely some combination of both), remains debatable, but in contexts where culture and society appear to have changed very little over considerable periods of time, it seems as though the degree of individual differences in processing must either have been slight or have cancelled one another out. The latter seems plausible, taking account of character and personality differences as experienced and reported in societies of all types. Here the short- and long-term distinction is crucial, for in the latter, individual differences are of little significance to the extent that they cancelled one another out, but in the short term they are very important for the individuals concerned and of rich significance for the quality of cultural and social life, as, once again, Marx and Engels clearly recognized. It is arguable that major Marxist concepts are in some form unassailable in the long term, but can, if perhaps unwisely, be largely ignored in the short. It is necessary to remember that Marxist concepts are never approached impartially and hardly ever receive a fair hearing. They were strenuously perverted for seventy years in the Soviet Union and are today the object of persecution and repression in most countries, or more sophisticatedly dismissed with embarrassed disdain. To the extent that academics are all middle-class intellectuals, serious attention to Marxist thought involves a degree of masochism which is unlikely to be general.

Furthermore, it is important to remember with due modesty that human beings are always, half unwittingly, striving to increase their stature, and as ideas are clearly the most distinctive human product in our eyes, it is inevitable that we shall always be trying to exaggerate their importance in our affairs and destiny. Theories which elevate the influence of 'new' ideas are always therefore suspect. Theory builders also frequently ignore the difference between short and long term. Marx and Engels always insisted that the kind of economic determinism in which they believed was essentially long term and ultimate. In the short run a large place could be given to culture. This does not mean, however, that the production relationship, in its widest sense, exerts *no* determinative force in the short run. In offering his very gentle version of determinism, Thompson injects a very stark example: 'People starve: their survivors think in new ways about the market. People are imprisoned: in prison they meditate in new ways about the law' (1978:9). I hold, with Stephen Jay Gould (1986:54), that evolutionary science is fundamentally historical science, and I agree with Habermas that 'the key to the reconstruction of the history of the species is provided by the concept of mode of production . . . the criteria of social progress singled out by historical materialism as the development of the productive forces and the maturity of forms of intercourse can be systematically justified' (1979:12).

A recent attempt at a 'new' theory of political evolution omits economic factors altogether and again blames Marx for slighting the individual human being. Could this be Marx who said 'the chief defect of all previous materialism is that things, reality, sensuousness are conceived only in the form of the *object* or of *contemplation*, but not as sensuous human activity, practice, not subjectively'. Or again, 'the materialistic doctrine that men are products of circumstance and upbringing, and that, therefore, changed men are products of other circumstances and changed upbringing, forgets that *it is men* who change circumstances and that the educator must himself be educated'. 'The first premise of all human history is, of course, the existence of living human *individuals.*' 'The social structure and the state are continually evolving out of the life process of definite individuals . . . the study of actual life process and activity of the individual of each epoch . . . men are the producers of their conceptions, ideas, that is, real active men . . . (and of course) men make their own history' (Marx and Engels, 1976:35–6). The problem is that the concept of the individual is a social product the purpose of which is to mask relations that dominate people (Ouroussoff, 1993:281). 'So adept at understanding what makes illusions real for others, we are reluctant to analyse the illusions that create reality for us' (Ouroussoff, 1993:281).

The grand theme

The grand theme is the city itself, the central arena on which the fateful drama of human wealth and inequality has been played. The creation of the city involved a sharp rise in inequality, which alone made possible the splendid achievements in art and architecture and the vital innovations in the organization of human life which the city has brought. The emergence of the city concentrated wealth and the power of wealth, at first within the constraints of supernatural sanctions and religious worship and belief.

The city has always depended upon the tragic paradox that the glorious achievements enjoyed by the few depended on the subjection of the many, who actually produced them. Apparently it could not have been otherwise. Mobilizing and centralizing the productive forces meant that the goods and services previously enjoyed by all in relatively egalitarian, self-subsistent communities could be greatly multiplied and so invested in hitherto impossible production of more specialized goods and services, which were nevertheless only sufficient for a very few to enjoy as luxuries and to exchange for others impossible to supply locally.

The heart of the paradox was that those who stood to lose seem first to have welcomed and encouraged it, until they had created fetters from which they could not escape. This was the first and greatest instance of alienation and fetishism, whereby social action takes the form of the action of objects, which turn on the producers and rule them instead of being ruled by them.[8]

Godelier explained that domination and exploitation appeared first as an exchange of services and so won the consent of the dominated. These services rendered by the dominant group involved the invisible realities and forces controlling (in the thought of these people) the reproduction of the universe and of life (1978a:767). This process lay at the roots of the state as well as the city, which therefore necessarily arose together in the city-state, however much the process of city and state formation may have been syncopated in different sequences and speeds at certain times and places.

The drama of inequality has taken various forms and different levels of intensity and brutality, yet persisted inexorably till our own day, when it has become the most menacing and intractable problem of all great cities, embracing and exacerbating all the other scourges which afflict them and presenting both urban and national governments with their hardest challenge. The excesses of inequality in urban life have ebbed and flowed, and its management and complexion have varied in ways which mark the main phases in the unfolding of human destiny in the city from beginning to end.

The representation of these phases is the initial key. A descriptive account of pristine city-states, imperial capitals, Greco-Roman cities, medieval cities, pre-industrial Asiatic and American cities, colonial, Third World and modern industrial and post-industrial cities, or a more spatial-temporal Toynbean account of cities framed in the rise and fall of civilization, might be attractively familiar, but with low penetration.

My bodeful choice has been inspired by Marx, with a degree of (revisional) rethinking which formerly caused scandal but now scarcely earns attention. In sum Marx wrote 'the foundation of every division of labour that is well developed, and brought about by the exchange of commodities, is the separation of town and country. It may be said that the whole economic history of society is summed up in the movement of this antithesis' (1967:352). In 1859 he also wrote, 'In broad outlines Asiatic, ancient, feudal and modern bourgeois modes of production can be designated as progressive epochs in the formation of society' (Marx and Engels, 1969a:504). Without explicitly spelling them out, Marx suggested four contrasting dialectical relations of town and country, corresponding to these four 'progressive epochs'. These four relations form an alternation of two interlocking binary oppositions. The four relations also embody four dominant forms of property, which will each be considered in its context. It may seem overbold to sum up several millennia of urban phenomena in four such brief propositions. They are cited not for their completeness but for the intensity of their insight and their continuing inspiration, and will also be considered in their proper context.

In this chiasmal structure, a series of transformations in the relation of the city to the country corresponds to the transformation from one mode of production to another.

Phases

A   ASIATIC MODE: UNITY OF TOWN AND COUNTRY
B   ANCIENT MODE: RURALIZATION OF THE CITY
C   FEUDAL MODE: ANTAGONISM BETWEEN TOWN AND COUNTRY
D   CAPITALIST MODE: URBANIZATION OF THE COUNTRY (Marx, 1973)

Asiatic mode: unity of town and country

The first city-states, though unknown to Marx, conform to this prescription of indifferent unity of town and country in that there was no political, religious, institutional or administrative differentiation made between town and country. The territory of the embryonic city-state as it emerged was necessarily small, dominated physically and symbolically by the central city which subsumed it, controlling through ritual rather than political means. The temple controlled a large work force and significant parts of the productive land (which it had been instrumental in creating), but otherwise ordinary folk were left encapsulated in their traditional kin-based communities, through which tax-rent was collected.

The city-state gave powerful symbolic expression to supernatural beings and values, relating them closely to the ritual leaders who brought them into being. The urban concentration was essential to the effective deployment of religio-political symbolism and facilitated the production, display and trading of luxury objects and the consumption of agrarian surplus which made the city possible. The pristine city-states were the first instance of economic mobilization for luxury in addition to subsistence production. They were small but exquisite. In their early stages they were not warlike but controlled by the supernatural sanctions of the divine beings in which all believed, even if they were managed by a privileged elite. This was a relatively idyllic situation compared with the brutal exploitation practised by most rulers from that time to this. The integrated identity of the city and society was never repeated in so complete a fashion, even in the city-states of Greece or medieval Italy.

The favourable conjunction of circumstances in time and place led to the multiplication of city-states and growth of their populations, causing competition for resources and increasing conflict, demanding production and improvement of weaponry, with the organization of armies involving new leadership. Overall leadership thereby became more politicized. Fighting between city-states led to dominance of some over others. The politico-military leaders of dominant city-states, still reinforced by their charismatic powers and symbolic ritual identification with the city's well-being, struggled to extend their territories and the most successful built the first empires.

The pristine period from the emergence of the first city-states lasted for five or six millennia, from early Jericho, Çatal Hüyük and Uruk to the earliest imperial conquests of Akkad and Ur III. The rise of empires brought expansion to their capital cities, some of them even more splendid than the city-states, though hardly more brilliantly innovative than they. Regional and district towns and trading cities also developed. These first empires were multiple states, offering the conquerors great plunder, personal and communal enrichment, with mass labour of captives and slaves. The interests of the conquerors and their followings were enhanced, but apart from irregular tribute collection most of the conquered communities were left effectively autonomous. The first empires were expressions of vaulting ambition, which over-reached itself and soon crumbled, to be followed by numerous other attempts.

Thus the structural relation of ruler and ruled; land, production and tax-rent; central elite and outlying communities; charisma, suzerainty and sovereignty, remained essentially the same despite the change in emphasis and scale. Some later empires succeeded in expanding the political and administrative at the relative expense of ritual and religious action, especially China with its unprecedented development of systematically organized bureaucracy, although government remained imbued with ritual and symbolic behaviour and belief. The great variety of forms of the Asiatic mode prevailed for several millennia in the Old World and the New, the first radical transformation being the Ancient mode of production which developed in the Mediterranean, without replacing the Asiatic mode in most of Asia and the New World. The picture could be complicated without greatly clarifying the analysis, by arguing for variant modes of production for the Sinic, Indic, Islamic, mesoamerican and Andean versions of the Asiatic mode. Burton Stein defined the medieval Cola empire of South India as a segmentary state (1977, 1980) and it also fits Marx's characterization of the Asiatic mode of production (1973:472–4) and the detailed definition given by Gough in finding the Cola state an expression of the Asiatic mode of production until quite recent times (1981:113, 407).

Ancient mode: ruralization of the city

The Greek city, paradigmatically Athens, was run by the owners of rural land who were its chief resident citizens, hence Marx's aphorism: ruralization of the city. The Ancient mode was an almost miraculous jump in the direction of the rights of Man (but not Woman). Notoriously based upon a slave majority of workers, with women largely confined to domestic roles, the productive forces in the Greek city still remained too weak to provide a higher standard of living and thinking, for any but a small minority. Greek democracy can therefore be seen as a superlative achievement, or a sham, from different angles. It did allow unprecedented freedom of thought and action to this minority of men, whose thoughts and philosophies, poems, dramas, sculpture, architecture, mathematical and mechanical advances affect us still today.

Though the Greek genius seems superior intellectually and aesthetically, the city-state of the Romans and several other peoples moved in a similar direction. The Greeks faced the Persian threat fairly early, but not too early, so their heroic victories then allowed their genius to flourish in peace, apart from their own internecine quarrels. These eventually reduced them to political impotence, leaving their cultural achievements to flourish on their own, while Alexander, tutored in Athens by Aristotle, spread their city-state model throughout south-western Asia, where it flourished in its Hellenistic form. The Roman version grew in its own historical context, called from conquest to conquest, till republic turned into empire and the city-state model, subordinated to imperial needs, was used as an instrument of civilian rule and cultural assimilation, from Britain to Mesopotamia, within the expanding fence of the frontier legions.

Feudal mode: antagonism between town and country

More recent and better documented, the Feudal mode, even more clearly than the Ancient mode, arose from mass immigration into the site of the grand societal collapse and the initially destructive yet ultimately innovative attempts to plunder, salvage and build upon that situation. The imperial political economy disintegrated in the west and nothing could replace it, so multiple invasive political economies emerged and tried to occupy its space. They became dual societies expressing antagonism between town and country: kings and feudal nobles in political control of productive land and living in castles, merchants and craftsmen living in emergent urban communes, managing the production of goods and wealth. Why merchants now? Because they had developed under the Greeks and Romans as slaves, freedmen and foreigners previously outside society and were now inside and entirely free, for the city air was the essence of freedom. In Crete and Mycenae, Egypt or Babylon, the independent merchant could not be imagined. In the Far East the merchant developed separately (tenuously linked by the Silk Road), following a similar trajectory in practice, but not in ritual status. Now the independent merchants of Europe, increasingly wealthy and influential, struggled for complete control of the cities. Artisans and proletariat often supported them for their own personal and class freedom. Such class divisions and aspirations had never reached the level of action in any previous urban political economy.

Capitalist mode: urbanization of the country

Of the major elements in capitalism, some launched it, some confirmed it. Profit had long driven merchants to venture and risk, accelerating accumulation. Venice, Genoa and Amsterdam advanced European trade and finance at the end of the Middle Ages with multiple stimuli from the Renaissance and Reformation. Portugal and Spain spread tentacles of trade round the whole world for the first time, planting seeds of cities wherever they went, drawing on the superior skills of men from the Italian, German and Dutch cities. Portugal sought gold and silver but brought slaves, pepper, spices and many important new commercial plants. Spain mainly plundered gold and silver from the temples and palaces of the splendid mesoamerican and Andean cities, which they destroyed, and excavated mines where ores beckoned. Merchants and financiers from the European cities processed all this into their economies, causing a huge and sustained jump in capital accumulation. The Dutch cities came together as a nation to exploit global opportunities more effectively, while Britain and France mobilized their greater national potential to develop competitive worldwide trade networks, seizing colonies and capturing slaves. Internal economies were expanding through increasing specialization, improved crops, technology and land management, raising efficiency, and enclosing commons and peasant land, leaving destitute surplus labour to migrate to towns as industrial workers.

The combination of world trade network with imported raw materials and export markets, buoyant rural economy, accumulated capital and technical invention drove British textile manufacture to explosive expansion, inaugurating the industrial factory system. Private profit, global import–export and capital accumulation in a monetized commodity economic network, agrarian expansion, scientific knowledge and technical innovation generated the upsurge of power-driven machinery in textile manufacture, ushering in the Capitalist mode of production, in which large numbers of entrepreneurs make all the production and financial decisions, and buy labour power in a free market, where they can hire and fire workers who have nothing to offer but their labour power.

The incipient world trade network founded and peopled colonial cities as a subordinate form within the Capitalist mode, to channel exports and imports and exploit local people and economies wherever possible. These colonial cities and territories became the Third World of independent nation-states in the twentieth century, subaltern economies exploited rather than exploiting, in a system of unequal exchange imposed and maintained by the overwhelming power of the First World capitalist nations. The cynical theory was that the Third World cities and nations should catch up with the First World standards of living and productivity, but with all the dice loaded against them in a global economy where all the advantageous positions have already been taken, the gap has only widened, as the capitalist system moves on to higher levels of production and inequality in the information age. Marx's urbanization of the country becomes an inescapable global phenomenon.

Secondary themes

Migration and transition

The transition from one mode of production to another has been treated as a piece of automatic logic (Godelier, 1981), but I am determined to treat it in the empirical sense upon which Marx would have insisted, 'for the social structure and the state are continually evolving out of the life process of definite individuals . . . as they work under definite material limits, presuppositions and conditions independent of their will' (Marx and Engels, 1976:35–6). In the light of Marx's own principle, his classic statement of the process of transition (Marx and Engels, 1969a:503–4) cannot escape modification in the light of prolonged further analysis of the process of history. Marx's concise statement of the relative timing and sequence of the different elements in transition is unsustainable. That no social order perishes before all the productive forces for which there is room in it have developed, and that new, higher relations of production never appear before the material conditions of their existence have matured in the womb of the old society itself, would require extremely strained definitions of 'social order' and 'old society' to enable the statement to fit the facts. It is still too mechanically and naively conceived and transgresses Marx's own more profound statements of what history is. The pieces in play are not like chessmen, whose contours are precise, rigid and never changing, nor are their movements regular.

Nevertheless, there was in a valid sense a transition from the Asiatic mode to the Ancient mode in the eastern Mediterranean and there was a transition from the Ancient mode to the Feudal mode in western Europe. In both cases, the part played by *migration into the setting of societal collapse* cannot be ignored as the engine of transition and the carrier of the seeds from which, beyond prophecy, 'higher relations of production' would eventually appear. Migration may often seem a rural process, but all cities derive from it. Pregnant as is the womb metaphor, it is uncomfortably here that it resides. The first precondition was breakdown. The second, intimately linked, the arrival of new populations, partly responsible for the breakdown and, for the moment, of unquestionably lower cultural achievement, although they would through the complex unfolding of the dialectic of the situation, so far from mechanical interaction of a few simple and easily definable elements, eventually evolve higher relations of production. It is only with hindsight that one could argue for 'higher relations of production' (a somewhat relative matter anyway), in the Feudal mode. It was rather that the Feudal mode led on to the further transition, in which the movement of peoples took place in the opposite sense.

Rather than taking over and rising again like a phoenix from a situation of collapse, the causative movement of peoples was outward, to plunder diverse groups all over the world, and inward on return with the spoils of capital accumulation. Marx throws brilliant light on the transition, but it becomes focused only by altering the lenses in relation to one another (Southall, 1988b:79; Godelier, 1981).

Centralization and decentralization

It is argued that 'to reify the weak phases of the Sassanian, Byzantine or T'ang Chinese into a Feudal-like mode of production, and the strong phases of the same states into an Asiatic mode, wrongly separates into different modes of production oscillations within the continuum of a single mode' (Wolf, 1982:82). I counter that it is the Sassanian, Byzantine and T'ang regimes that are unduly reified here. The distinction between oscillation and continuum is arbitrary and essentializes the concept of mode of production. A more illuminating and workable analysis takes *decentralization* as an inherent tendency of feudal systems and *centralization* as an intrinsic aim of the formations expressing the Asiatic mode of production. This centralization is achieved principally on the ritual and symbolic dimension, which can only be given effective political expression in especially favourable sequences of development, as illustrated in more detail later. Periods of decentralization in China, which together lasted longer than the periods of centralization, cannot be dismissed as mere oscillations.

Merchants

Merchants have been an essential component of all towns and cities, without whom they could not exist. Their role and status have varied from one mode of production to another. Of all roles they are the most intrinsically urban. In the Asiatic mode of the first cities and empires, merchants were agents of the temple and the throne. They were not an autonomous group and had no significant aspirations of their own. Yet as long-distance traders by ship they must have been autonomous for considerable periods. They were certainly ready to seize opportunities, but remained at the mercy of the political elite, who were themselves tempted to find channels of participation in the profits of trade.

In the Ancient mode of production, overseas trade was the very source of the city's greatness, yet, seemingly against logic, trading was forbidden to citizens, who as landowners were tainted with nobility. Merchant and noble have been treated as incompatible essences in most cultures, merchants the opposite of noble, ignoble and polluting. The Greek and Roman Stratagem was for trade to be carried out on behalf of and often under the control of citizens, by non-citizens who could be citizens of other cities living in exile, or by slaves and freedmen. It was in cities of the Feudal mode of production that merchants came into their own, profiting from the inherently antagonistic and contradictory nature of the system. Despised as usual by nobles, they were as usual indispensable, but in addition, for the first time they found the opportunity of becoming dominant in their own communities and even driving the nobles out. Yet the most ineradicable characteristic of the merchants was the temptation and attraction of nobility. They had to emulate those who despised them and master the symbols of excellence most contradictory to their nature. The merchant city of the Feudal mode was to Weber the full and only realization of the city.

Merchants were the essential midwives to the Capitalist mode of production, magnified and transformed into industrialists and financiers. Wealth still procured nobility in time, but as the noble aristocratic upper class lost its traditional function, a certain second generation decadence and withdrawal was required to confer a disenfranchised nobility on heirs of merchant millions. Whereas in the Feudal mode merchants were only half dominant through antagonism of town and country, in the Capitalist mode they were unrivalled, especially in their merchant banker guise, which combined dominance with remarkable freedom of movement and manoeuvrability. As merchant bankers and industrial tycoons reach their pinnacles of wealth and have society largely at their feet, they still face the paradox that if they assume any formally leading position in the state, their flexibility is routinized and they become imbued with ritual and symbolic attributes and obligations which contradict their merchant logic.

2   Pristine cities

Chapter 2 deals with pristine cities, those which appeared first in any major world region, as distinctively innovative urban forms. They all expressed the Asiatic mode of production in its earliest, simplest form, developing from forms of the Kinship mode of production.

THE OLD WORLD

First signs

The pristine cities and earliest empires test our aspiration to frame the story of the city in a theoretical perspective. The logic of the data suggests concentration on Sumeria and China, with glances at striking cases: Jericho and Çatal Hüyük, and in the New World a complementary focus on Teotihuacan and the Maya, with passing glances at Andean valleys and highlands, Olmec and Monte Alban. The urban civilization of the Indus valley will be mentioned briefly, because little that is illuminating and uncontested can be said about it.

Doubtless many heroic attempts were made, few of which may ever be known to us. The astonishingly early settlements of the eighth millennium BC, at the 'walled oasis town' of Jericho, in Palestine; Hacilar and Çatal Hüyük in the Konya plain of south central Anatolia and Jarmo in the foothills east of the Tigris stand out before the successful establishment of continuous urban settlement. Jericho with its extraordinary spring in the midst of arid terrain seems to have attracted unusual settlement by mesolithic hunters in flimsy huts even in the tenth millennium and by the ninth produced a massive stone wall with at least one tower,[1] and round, domed, brick houses, which Kenyon (1957, 1981) claims as a town of 2,000 to 3,000 people, without pottery, but with the earliest wheat and barley known and perhaps the necessity of irrigation. New settlers in the eighth millennium produced more elaborate, many roomed rectangular houses, but still lacked pottery, and were followed by a long break in occupation. Hacilar was similarly abandoned after its early

CATAL HÜYÜK
BUILDING LEVEL VII

LEVEL VII
LEVEL VI

NOT EXCAVATED

NOT EXCAVATED

Plate 1 Çatal Hüyük

a The seventh- and early sixth-millennium levels show extremely dense contiguous settlement (no streets being required since access was from the roof) of rectangular houses and shrines, with two courtyards. The one acre excavated revealed over forty houses with from one to eight rooms, suggesting that the whole thirty-two-acre site contained a considerable population.

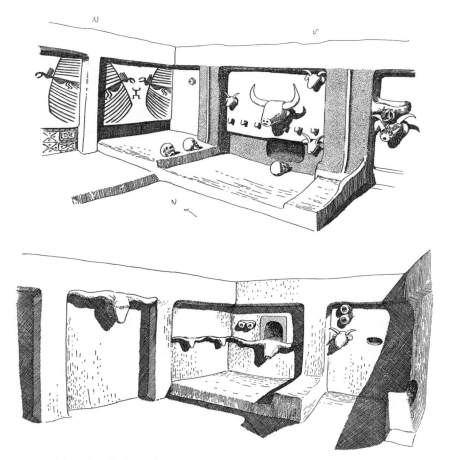

b and c Shrines show extraordinary religious and symbolic representational figures, in wall paintings and projections. Breasts are modelled in plaster, or moulded on wild animal skulls and jawbones, perhaps symbolizing the beginning and the end of life (Todd, 1976:51). Some breasts had the jaws of wild boar projecting from the nipples. Between a post and a bull's head a pair of pendulous women's breasts appeared, open at the nipple and painted red like the muzzle of a bull. From each protruded the beak of a griffon vulture (*gyps vulvus*) (Mellaart, 1967:126). Mellaart interpreted certain human figures as goddesses in a birth-giving position, some immediately above a plaster bull's head, suggesting the birth of such an animal from the female figure (Todd, 1976:51).

Both in parturition and nurture there seems to be a tight juxtaposition between female power, human or divine, and seemingly male and animal forces of aggression. These are the earliest known urban representations of humans and animals.

achievement of mud brick houses with plastered, burnished and painted interiors, but like Jericho no pottery. More amazingly, Çatal Hüyük later in the seventh millennium had a dense walled settlement covering thirty-two acres, with traces of mats and actual textiles and clay pots, amounting to a veritable neolithic town (Mellaart, 1967). Jarmo with its cluster of packed clay houses, wheat, barley, domestic goats, sheep, pigs and some-what later pottery, and its 3,000 year long continuous occupation, though 'inadequately excavated and still unpublished' (Mellaart, 1967:22), has seemed significant for the emergence of urban life because of its proxim-ity to the foothills from which the villagers may have descended into Mesopotamia to inaugurate the known epoch of continuous urban development. It is thought 'roughly contemporary with Jericho and Çatal Hüyük' (Adams, 1972:967).

Çatal Hüyük is particularly remarkable for the density of its rectangular buildings of sundried brick, rising up the slope in serried rows, with entry only through apertures in their flat beam and rush roofs, and for its pow-erful and original artistic forms. The profusion of manifestly symbolic decoration in certain rooms suggests that shrines occupied from one third to one sixth of all houses so far excavated, portraying an elaborate ritual and cognitive system of symbolic oppositions between nature and culture, female and male, life-giving fertility and savage destruction. The apparent mother goddess, sometimes represented in twin form, or even as a pair of leopards, is frequently giving birth to a horned bull, while breasts are modelled with the jaws and tusks of wild boars protruding from their gaping nipples. Rows of bulls' heads with extravagant horns decorate walls and benches. Polychrome wall paintings show intricate textile and *kilim* designs, hunting scenes, huge black vultures attacking headless human figures as if corpses exposed in Zoroastrian style, and actually a landscape of the city itself with a volcano erupting in the background (Mellaart, 1967:*passim*).

Sumeria

By the sixth millennium BC the rising alluvium of the Euphrates and Tigris, extending southward into the Persian Gulf, provided new land of potentially high fertility for human occupation. It would require very heavy labour but might eventually offer high returns. People moving down from the mountains, settled long before, or up from the desiccating south, created new sedentary communities, pioneering a new production regime balancing fishing, herding and agriculture based on simple, small-scale irrigation, 'transforming an inhospitable jungle-swamp into navig-able canals and irrigated fields' (Toynbee, 1967:14). Population and settlements multiplied and the high level of productivity permitted unprecedented density. These communities must have been at first egalitarian, producing ritual leaders without politically coercive powers, who represented the will and the need of the people in acting as channels of communication with deities believed capable of assuring the cosmic and climatic harmony and sense of well-being which all desired. The people wished to ensure the good-will of divine forces and to give thanks for it, which they could best do by offering gifts of the means of life through their accepted leaders. These offerings of consumable goods were presented to the deities, requiring special holy places to be set apart for the purpose, and after the unseen deities had consumed the offerings in their unseen fashion their material remains were shared and consumed by the people.

The original early fourth millennium temple at Eridu was an artificial terrace, perhaps against flooding, and extended eighty feet by forty, with an altar, offering table and façade decorated with niches. It remained the cult centre of the god Enki for two millennia as the same spot was gradually raised up into a prototypical ziggurat. All the major gods in the later pantheon originally had their chief sanctuaries in particular cities (Adams, 1966:129).

Some communities grew faster than others in population and wealth. Their holy places became more holy shrines, attracting allegiance from lesser centres round about. Those in charge of these shrines became more important leaders, their ritual functions as priests were elaborated and they became more specialized and more separated from agricultural and materially productive tasks, acquiring the status of divine kings, and also acquiring subordinate staff to assist them, all willingly supported by the people in recognition of their shared success. Over the centuries such temple staffs acquired vested interests of their own. It was their duty to enter into communion and communication with the supernatural forces and to relay their wishes and desires to the people. The temples grew ever larger, reflecting more abundant offerings from the rising productivity of larger, more skilled populations. Growing relations of exchange between neighbouring communities and cities, and with more and more distant places, accentuated this process, which was by no means always smooth, yet moved generally in this direction. Eridu also yielded boat remains, evidencing growth of water transport during the fourth millennium.

Disputes were settled between kin groups and also through mediation of ritual specialists of the temples, who could invoke increasingly irresistible sanctions from the supernatural beings they served. The relations within and between communities remained thus largely peaceful and no defensive fortifications were constructed or required. The numerous small sites in the vicinity of the emerging city-state of Uruk were all of less than ten hectares, though actually somewhat larger than they were subsequently. They were not clustered and showed no hierarchical arrangement in relation to Uruk.

During the fourth millennium, when some communities had already been developing for over a thousand years, conditions began to change more rapidly. Merchants were probably sailing the rivers and trading as far as the Persian Gulf, using cylinder seals to record their transactions. They were essentially agents of the temples.

With the encouragement of the temple staff and the blessing of the gods, the people had to build many large temples and their abundant offerings required further buildings for storage and new organizations for distribution. In certain fields the will of the temple staff imperceptibly acquired the force of command. The increasing numbers of servants required in temple service and maintenance could not only convey divinely ordained instructions but also see that they were carried out. Though primarily ritual, the temple system was at the same time the fundamental basis of the productive system, through the heavenly bodies who, apart from their divinity, provided the calendar, foretold the seasons and co-ordinated instructions for agricultural production with heavenly sanctioned authority and minute precision. Means of recording were essential and both numbering and writing systems were developing. By the end of the fourth millennium numbering systems were very precise, while writing was still rather rudimentary. Uruk had the indigenous sexagesimal system and also a decimal system which must have come from elsewhere. Usable written sources appeared later, for practical and commercial rather than ritual or magical purposes.

For centuries the major ceremonial centres had received a flow of prestations from the smaller towns and villages within their sphere of influence, in return for their major temple's blessing and assistance in both supernatural questions and matters of material production and exchange. Uruk became a large ceremonial centre, which must have exercised considerable influence over the smaller communities of the surrounding area, but there was still no formal element of coercive and centralized political control. The system was exactly that described under the rubric of the segmentary state (Southall, 1956a, 1988a and b; Stein, 1977, 1980) with ritual divine kingship but still within the parameters of the Kinship mode of production.

From about 3000 to 2500 BC the speed of change increased. The now powerful Uruk city-state was somehow able, by persuasion or compulsion, to bring within its new defensive walls most of the population of the surrounding small settlements, whose numbers dropped to a half and eventually only a ninth of what they had been. The complementary process was that the subordinate cities within Uruk city-state territory rose in numbers from two to four and finally eight. Uruk expanded by a whole order of magnitude to a population of 40,000–50,000. Walls were now built enclosing an area of 400 hectares, probably including some gardens and cultivation as well as the city proper. Such a large and dense population could no longer run its own affairs as an egalitarian community with voluntary leadership as it had 2,000 years before. The great size of the temple and its large production organization embodied a high degree of specialization. The need to maintain order and provide protection demanded organized manpower with ultimate means of coercion. More clearly political as well as economic functions were becoming differentiated. The temple remained a complex multi-functional institution, but its running gradually became more distinct from the supreme organization of administration under high officers of the state with large staff and servants, while the temple needed its own separate leadership organization and staff. The chief priest or priestess was now distinct from the divine king, although the latter was still supreme in the religious as well as secular sphere. (The king of England is head of the church but he is not archbishop of Canterbury.)

The divine kingship of a city like Uruk was a long but direct development over several millennia from the ritual leader of the earlier egalitarian community. He was still the supreme figurehead in the symbolic sense, terminologically confused if not equated with the deity itself. This was something quite different from and more profound than the crude personal declarations of divinity by later Akkadian and Babylonian rulers, or Roman emperors long after them. The king, his family, kin and high officers had not resisted the opportunity and temptation to mobilize political support, transform voluntary presentations into solid tribute, and mystical ownership of the soil into large estates with high productivity, as well as profitable commercial and maritime ventures throughout Sumeria and beyond.

Ur had earlier and denser settlements round it than Uruk, but it reached urban size later and was never more than one eighth the size of Uruk. Its rural sustaining area was smaller and poorer, and there was no transfer of population from hinterland to city as was the case with Uruk. By the time of Ur dominance at the end of the third millennium (2114–2004 BC) Uruk was smaller and population may have moved from city to city.

The situation of the city-state of Umma was similar to Ur but in size it was between Ur and Uruk. Umma's surroundings were little occupied most of the fourth millennium, then suddenly intensely settled after 3000

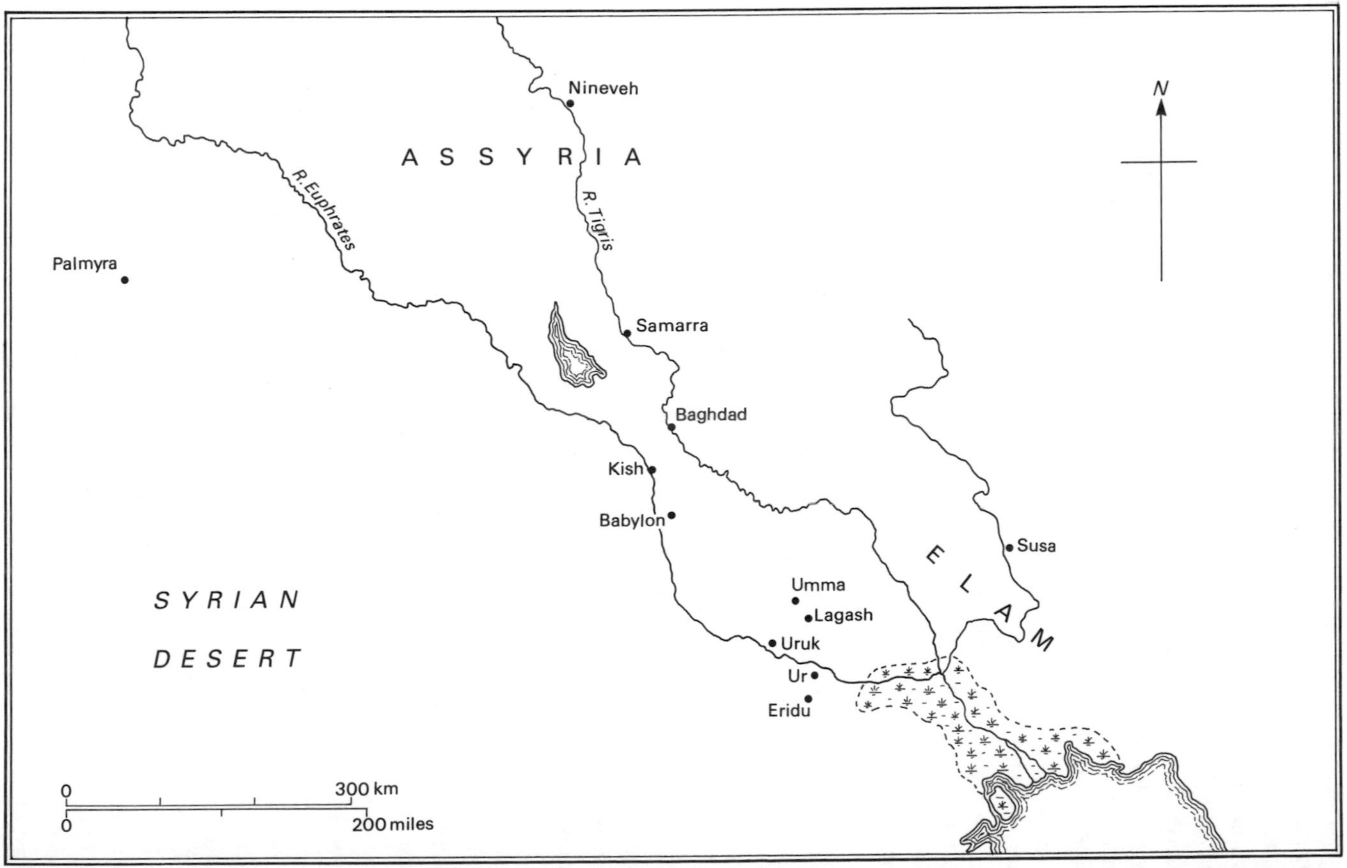

Map 1 Sumeria and Mesopotamia

BC with dense clusters of large towns, some almost adjacent to each other, but probably all absorbed into Umma city-state before 2500 BC. Uruk, Ur and Umma, as well as Eridu, were within a day's walk of one another and the divergence in their patterns of development is striking.

The Sumerian city-states, both capital and subordinate cities, had become very thick on the ground. Disputes over boundaries, land and personal quarrels were inevitable. For problems solved by ritual sanctions a thousand years before, imperative judicial processes, political coercion and armed action now seemed more effective methods. Once peaceful communities now entered upon an era of internecine strife. Perhaps they were still constrained by ritual conventions. The cities of Umma and Lagash fought over fertile border land and its produce for generations. Other rulers tried to mediate in vain. When the king of Umma attacked the king of Lagash, forced his head under the yoke and led him to the gate of the god Enlil at Nippur, something other than naked aggression was afoot.

Corporate patrilineal kin groups held most of the land. Marriage was monogamous and women had extensive rights in inheriting, managing and disposing of property, in ritual, trade and administration and as potential heads of families. Women slaves appeared in the fourth millennium and male slaves later. The temple of the major deity remained the largest institution in the state. Apart from its duty to glorify its deity and by reflection its ruler and city, it must receive, record, store, administer and redistribute the vast stocks of food and commodities contributed now without much option by the population or produced on its own estates. It must run these estates and their labour, which if they did not comprise all productive land, may have included as much as a third. Its agricultural workers, though not slaves, were bound to the land. The rest of the land was occupied by the estates of the royal family and high officers, or still under autonomous kin communities. There were also slaves, resulting from war, or grievous deprivation, but it was not a slave economy. Female slaves were devoted by their families, or by destitution, serving the temple and playing an important part in crafts and industries it ran, such as wool manufacture.

There was a very compact and centrally organized component in the economy, with large numbers of workers, even including state traders, receiving official rations, many having official allocations of land, with expected production quotas. By the late third millennium there was some buying, selling and leasing of land among increasing numbers of the elite. But the divine king was still the mystical owner of the soil, in the name of all, with the supreme duty to maintain the fertility and harmony of the realm. The majority of the population owned no land, having only usufruct as local community members.

The transformation we have described illustrates the growing contradictions between the earlier, more egalitarian and voluntaristic process of the Kinship mode of production and the more hegemonic, yet still segmentary process of the Asiatic mode of production.

Four thousand years later, Gough found the Cola state in South India still an example of the Asiatic mode (1981:113, 407), while also being a segmentary state in structure and process, as Stein had demonstrated (1977). Its capital city was still dominated by vast temples. City-states and later imperial states of the Asiatic mode were still segmentary in form, although they could mobilize much greater wealth at the centre, without being able to exercise more than a contingent suzerainty over peripheral units. But it was in the interests of the ruler, the central staff and local population alike to glorify the ruler and so glorify themselves. Consequently, the impression is conveyed that the pomp and circumstance of the ruler in his capital city reflected a centralized political control of his whole realm which never existed. Most historians have thus been misled. The narrative interpretation of Sumerian city-states which we have constructed could probably apply, *mutatis mutandis*, to other less well-documented areas of the emergence of pristine cities.

Marx was thinking of the great Asiatic states of medieval times, with their grandiose yet fragile capitals, which he derided as 'royal camps'. Of the Sumerian city-states he could know nothing, so it is remarkable that the model fits as well as it does, for pristine city-state was a form not then envisaged. The era of city-states has some distinctive features not encountered subsequently. There was a remarkable degree of concentration and intensity about the Sumerian cities, both physically and organizationally, expressing itself in rapid, innovative developments unparalleled for many centuries afterwards. They were precocious foretastes.

They had mastered the column, the arch, the vault and the dome by the early third millennium, not to mention pottery, the wheel, the cart, draft animals and advances in metallurgy. Their legal codes were less brutal than the more famous later ones of Hamurabi at Babylon. Their leading women were freer in dress and range of activity, as priestesses, estate managers and composers of songs and poems. The Sumerian language disappeared, but Sumerian literature, gods and heroes were remembered and celebrated long after they had gone. They laid the basis of their ecology and economy, their temple and city system, during times of relative peace. Their productivity and expansion reached a crescendo, perhaps inevitably, as they began more determinedly to destroy one another in war. So the curtain came down on their era with two attempts at imperialistic aggression and expansion, both of which soon failed, that of Sargon of Akkad and Third Dynasty Ur.

In 2350 BC Sargon of Akkad conquered the Sumerian city-states and established the first known 'empire', its capital as yet undiscovered. Former cup-bearer of the king of Kish, exposed at birth, reared by a gardener and beloved of the moon goddess Ishtar, Sargon's conquests spread far, supposedly capturing fifty kings, throwing down city walls and cleansing his weapons in the sea. He ruled for fifty-six years and was followed by several briefer reigns, but his empire crumbled in constant wars and rebellions. Empire was a matter of brief conquest and recognition of suzerainty, with irregular tribute but no sustained attempt at centralized administration, though many offices were filled with citizens of Akkad. Trade was, however, important as ships came from Bahrain and the Indus cities.

As Akkad declined, Third Dynasty Ur established forty provinces under its domination, former city-states, with governors appointed and sometimes hereditary (bearing the same title as the divine kings), with annual tribute negotiated by emissaries. Ur also took exports to Bahrain to exchange for copper and ivory from the east. Ur collapsed in much the same way as Akkad, after just over a century, in wasting wars and revolutions, famine and attacks by Elamites and Iranians.

The kings of Ur were buried together with their court officials, servants and women. Extraordinary treasures of gold, silver, bronze and semi-precious stones were found in these tombs, with exquisitely fashioned and richly adorned musical instruments, weapons, engravings, mosaics and statues.

Susa

The city-state of Susa's development over two crucial millennia explicitly documents the emergence of a segmentary state, though the account is limited to hypotheses on 'population growth, inter-regional exchange or "long-range" trade, and local craft production and exchange as single variable causes or prime movers' (Wright and Johnson, 1975:268). By the mid-fifth millennium the Susiana plain, some 200 kilometres north of Uruk and the Euphrates, but part of 'Greater Mesopotamia', already had a large population with no dominant centres. Before the end of the millennium Susa had been founded and covered about ten hectares, with over forty other surrounding sites averaging 1.2 hectares each, thus two distinct levels of settlements, a 'minimal administrative complexity'. Susa had a large central platform of mud brick supporting a number of elaborate buildings and store rooms with other large buildings around. Stamp seals have simple linear geometric designs and a few representing caprids and abstract cruciform or human figures (Wright and Johnson,

1975:273). By the early fourth millennium population (or site numbers) had fallen. There were only twenty-two small sites of the same average size as before, but several sites averaging five hectares, some of them 'dominating' (spatially) smaller villages and forming three or four disjointed clusters, Susa still remaining twice as large. There were signs of collapse and abandonment on the marginal plains, followed by new settlers with 'ceramics of highland affinity' (Wright and Johnson, 1975:275). By the mid-fourth millennium population had tripled to recover its early density, but was more concentrated, in fifty settlements of three size categories: villages averaging 1.4 hectares, smaller centres averaging 6.4 hectares and Susa 12 hectares.

By the criterion of 'specialized administrative activities', implying some hierarchy of control in decision making (Wright and Johnson, 1975:267) Susa had rapidly achieved statehood. Evidence suggests the distribution of ceramic items from central workshops in Susa and several subordinate centres to the numerous smaller settlements. This correlated with similar transitions in the mid-fourth millennium in Sumerian city-states such as Nippur, Niniveh and Uruk. Growth continued and Susa reached 25 hectares with fifty-four settlements in four size categories, but during the late fourth millennium there was a 'general decline in settled population', corresponding with a marked increase in Sumeria, which 'possibly resulted from interaction between different primary states in Greater Mesopotamia' (Wright and Johnson, 1975:276).

The city-state of Susa thus developed along a path similar to that of fourth millennium Uruk, though never reaching the vast scale of the latter in the third millennium. As in Sumeria, Susa was later caught up in the wars of the would-be imperialist phase, and only much later resuscitated as capital of the Persian Empire in its heyday.

Tepe Yahya

These pristine city-states arose in conjuncturally favourable ecological space–time niches, on the basis of long local development and internally generated stimulus without any major impact from any other human community. It is of vast significance that all pristine city-states developed through the opportunity of relatively peaceful endogenous growth and not as a result of war or conquest.

However, trade between autonomous city-states, once established, even at great distances, did become an important stimulus to further urbanization. The first known primary trading and commercial city-state was Tepe Yahya, half way between Mesopotamia and the Indus, more than 500 miles east of Susa and Ur, with Mohenjodaro equally far further east and Harappa another 400 miles north-west. Already a busy trade centre by about 3560 BC at about the time when Susa tripled in size and Uruk was a large ceremonial centre destined for explosive growth half a millennium later, Tepe Yahya was, from fifth millennium neolithic beginnings, a bronze age city with Proto-Elamite writing, mud brick buildings and varied artefacts (Lamberg-Karlovsky and Lamberg-Karlovsky, 1973). It was close to large deposits of soapstone, which it traded all over Sumeria and to Harappa. Pre-Harappan pottery was found at Tepe Yahya and a soapstone bowl found at Harappa was probably from there. Harappan-type seals and writing have been found in Mesopotamia, which may have followed the same route.

Development and efflorescence

Reflecting on the evolution of urban society in mesoamerica and Sumeria, Adams asks whether it can be approximated to the trajectory of the abrupt 'step' or the even 'ramp' (suggested by Braidwood and Willy, 1962:351) and concludes that the abrupt step or even ramp characterization applies to different aspects (1966:171): monumental architecture and artistic achievement to the former, and to the latter the 'emergence of increasingly autonomous, differentiated sectors of activity – socioeconomic classes; military, political and administrative elites; economic networks of tribute, trade and redistribution etc.'(1966:172). In the former aspects protoliterate Uruk and classic Teotihuacan (Mexico) 'both rise in one incredible burst to a plateau that was not demonstrably surpassed during the remainder of the sequence'(Braidwood and Willy, 1962:351). He sums up the sequence as from theocratic polities to militaristic polities to conquest states. In my interpretation these are stages in the transformation of segmentary states from the Kinship mode of production to the Asiatic mode of production. It seems as though the already long-established aesthetic and craft traditions and institutions of the pristine city-states may have proceeded to even higher levels of excellence early in the conquest state phase, fed by the windfall of new booty resources and the flush of victory. But as the early conquest states destroyed one another in rapid rise and fall, the artistic impulse was either overwhelmed or prostituted in fulsome adulation of the vainglorious figureheads of increasingly oppressive and exploitative regimes. So in a later context did the glories of Florentine painting and sculpture flow on for a while after the fall of the free city-state and the institution of a dependent, autocratic dukedom, before declining themselves.

Babylon

Babylon was the pre-eminent city which rose and endured through this turbulent era of the late third millennium, frequently destroyed and grandiosely rebuilt. It was so well placed on both banks of the middle Euphrates, right in the centre of matured or developing civilizations, that its wealthy merchants could not long be repressed, as every new regime needed them and pampered them afresh, till finally Alexander the Great, before dying in its royal palace, once again restored and confirmed the privileges for which they constantly strove. Here in a specially conducive though much tortured context, merchants emerged as a potential force in their own right, never dreaming of formal urban autonomy, but leaping at every favourable chance to catch the ear of the new conqueror flush with spoils demanding management, exchange and magnificent consumption. Later capital cities at Seleucia, Ctesiphon and Baghdad were avatars of Babylon (Toynbee, 1967:16).

Harappa

Harappa and Mohenjodaro, the colossal cities which are only the greatest among dozens of other pre-historic urban sites in the Indus valley and beyond, achieved their great size just at the point of the highest development in Sumeria, around 2300 BC, when its prosperous but now warring city-states were about to be engulfed in the destructive aggressions of Sargon and Ur. Certainly they were great commercial centres, with a writing system (undeciphered), ubiquitous emphasis on baths, great and small, water supply and drainage. Both had rectilinear street plans, with ramped, stepped 'citadel' mounds on the west, reminiscent of ziggurats, with no confirming ritual evidence, but huge granaries and supposedly ceremonial halls. Large courtyard houses lined the main streets with blank walls, stairs leading to flat roof or second storey, and also rows of one room quarters. All had bathroom or privy enclosures, with elaborate drainage through the thickness of walls out to the main street drains. Mass pottery was produced, cotton woven and dyed for the first time, cattle, camels and asses, bullock carts and boats were used; wheat, barley, rice, peas, sesame, dates and melons grown. The ithyphallic yoga figures, lingam motifs, lack of pins and profusion of bangles and nose ornaments; use of bulls, tigers and elephants in ceremonial art, all suggest continuities with later Hindu civilization. But the cities broke down and were abandoned before the time of the Aryan invasions. Whether the Harappan people were Dravidian Proto-Tamils, or descended from the highlands of Baluchistan as once guessed, remains undemonstrated. Did the Harappans come down from the hills, driven by ecological poverty and overpopulation, attracted by the possibility of exploiting the extraordinary fertility of the capricious and dangerous Indus floods at an epoch of ripe conjuncture, or were they just the slowly developing population of pre-Aryan Dravidian India, achieving a brief, spectacular prosperity before over-reaching themselves and then retreating before the Aryan invasion to become the Tamils of historic India?

Egypt

The prevalent view of Egypt as developing quite differently, from neolithic villages into kingdoms without a city-state phase, may result from archaeological difficulties in the Nile mud. The protodynastic city of Hierakonpolis in Upper Egypt may represent the end of the city-state period in the late fourth millennium BC. Hoffman suggests evidence for a drop in rainfall at this time, forcing population out of the fragile mixed dry farming, herding and hunting economy of the marginal park-savannah on the desert fringes, into greater dependence on the Nile alluvium, concentrating more population in and around Hierakonpolis, much as happened at Uruk with the onset of Mesopotamian civilization (1970:74). There is evidence of organized basin inundation and of rituals connected with irrigation performed by the protodynastic ruler. Growth and pressure of population may have led to inter-city warfare and eventual attempts at political unification of Egypt from the south, which culminated in the fusion of the Lower and Upper Kingdoms with their red and white crowns.

Certainly no agricultural villages of anything like the age of those in south-west Asia have yet been discovered in Egypt. Granted its extreme length and narrow width, the very ecology of Egypt was concentrating and stable, cutting short the development of city-state clusters of the Sumerian type. No pristine cities were preserved for posterity by changes of the river's course leaving them high and dry. The core cultivable areas have been worked for thousands of years. The appearance of cities in Egypt may have been as early as anywhere else, but our knowledge is mainly limited to the royal ceremonial and funeral monuments. However, the close identity of divinity, kingship and state makes it certain that Egyptian capital cities such as Heliopolis, Memphis, Hierakonpolis, or Thebes were closely oriented to the elaborate system of ritual and political symbols which received their highest expression in temples, tombs and palaces of kings, priests and nobles. Their extraordinary millennial stability was dramatically ruptured once, when the deviant fourteenth-century Pharaoh Akhenatton and Queen Nefertiti created the new city of

Amarna, 200 miles north of Thebes, for their outburst of monotheistic sun-worship, beautiful in its open-air freshness and vigorously naturalistic wall paintings, but doomed by neglect of empire, taxation and affairs of state to a bare dozen years' survival. Major breaks between dynasties facilitated politico-economic change as they did in China.

China

Four millennia of continuity in the world's longest and largest urban tradition makes the Chinese city a crucial test for theoretical interpretation. Chinese history has been represented as a long struggle to attain and recurringly to regain political unity, a cycle of consolidation, stabilization, stagnation and eventual fragmentation and chaos all over again (Hucker, 1975:16–17).

China's periods of unity gave expression to the Asiatic mode of production, at successive levels of growth and development, while periods of disunity and breakdown allowed for various expressions of the Feudal mode of production. In significant ways, the relationship of town and country, of cities to the rest of society varied accordingly. The Asiatic mode is essentially a centralizing process, while the essence of the Feudal mode is decentralization after breakdown. Chinese Marxists classified China as 'Slave Society' from the twenty-first to the fifth century BC (Xia, Shang and most of Zhou) and the rest of Chinese history as 'Feudal Society' (*Early China*, 1980:97). Bourgeois Sinologists have made various interpretations, for the most part applying the designation Feudal only to the Zhou dynasty.

'The Shang state was gruyère filled with non-Shang holes, rather than *tou-fu* solidly Shang throughout' (Keightley, 1979–80:26). Shang may have been just one – 'albeit the most powerful and literate one' – of a number of states in China in the middle of the second millennium BC, according to Chang, and even later (Keightley, 1979–80:28). Shang was a theocratic polity in which religion, politics and kinship were metaphysically fused (Keightley, 1979–80:29). The Shang realm consisted of a core area within which the power and wealth of the king and ruling class were concentrated, surrounded by more or less autonomous entities, some of which the king could on occasion command (though it is not clear that the commands were obeyed), others of which sometimes supported and fought for the king and at other times against him (Keightley, 1979–80), in other words, the Asiatic mode of production in its early segmentary state form (Southall, 1988b:74–9). The king went on royal progresses which combined hunting and inspection and involved a form of tax whereby groups visited provided sustenance to the king and his entourage, a refined version of the plunder mechanism (Keightley, 1986:64). The king was constantly involved in divination on every kind of matter, including the health and prosperity of the peripheral groups. He performed rituals and human sacrifices for the same purpose, including rain. He was clearly acting as priest and diviner most of the time. Although not using a Marxist concept, many other Sinologists support the same perspective: 'in earlier times the Shang culture area probably comprised a number of competing ceremonial centres, each of which exercised direct control over a limited terrain in its immediate vicinity, and exacted tribute from other centres and surrounding tracts of territory to the extent that its ruler was powerful enough to do so' (Wheatley, 1971:63). The situation has been compared to the kingdom of Sumer and Akkad, which was always 'a union of petty kingdoms controlled by the kings of the ruling race'(sic), never a centralized kingdom ruled by a single king and his officials (Creel, 1936:137). Hence the frequency of the title 'King of Kings' in so many pre-capitalist states of the Asiatic mode of production (Persia, Ethiopia, etc.).

Early China is thus compared to Sumeria, where the 'petty kingdoms' were city-states which had been under the control of temples and their high priests before more secular monarchies developed. So in China, recent excavations revealed large numbers of urban sites which must have been the capitals of city-states. The earliest beginnings now seem to reach back beyond Shang into the Xia dynasty, long regarded as legendary, but now apparently emerging from the mist (*Early China*, 1986:2).

The crucial Chinese pre-urban developments, though several millennia later, seem to have been more widespread than in early south-west Asia (Stover and Stover, 1976). Neolithic culture, of the fifth millennium BC, has been found in the valley of the Wei, largest tributary of the Yellow River, where the first cities were to appear two millennia later. Local millet and soya beans, wheat, cattle, sheep, goats and later the horse, transmitted from the west; pigs, dogs, chickens, ducks, geese, rice, yams and taro from southern China and south-east Asia. The hand-made pottery of the Far East is by far the most ancient in the world, appearing in Japan by the ninth millennium and in Taiwan and Thailand by the eighth.

Several lasting characteristics of Chinese cities are traced back to the neolithic: the southward orientation of houses, the longhouse style, already an elite form among the mass of half subterranean pit dwellings; walls of pounded earth, wheel-made pottery, becoming mass produced as in Sumeria and Indus, and tripods later reproduced in bronze (occurring as far west as Anatolia in the third millennium BC); recording by knotted strings (like the Inca *quipu*, later superseded by writing, which was distinctively Chinese, even if the idea stimulus appears further west, like scapulimancy linked with divination; weaving of textiles and the use of cowries as currency.

Early in the second millennium city-states developed in the middle of the Yellow River and Wei valleys, with rectangular pounded earth walls, astronomically oriented to the cardinal directions. Ancient texts show that the ritualization of the city, at best, imposed a moral and supernaturally sanctioned imperative upon rulers to use supreme power justly and benevolently for the welfare of all people, a pious principle mouthed and hypocritically claimed by all rulers since, despite growing inequalities in the distribution of wealth and the institutions of slavery and serfdom. At worst it was an opium for the people, to sanctify naked exploitation as in their best interests, or at any rate their ineluctable destiny. The dictum of the Book of Rites that 'the ritual does not extend down to the common people; punishments do not extend up to the great officers' is not reassuring.

The K'ao'kung Chi gives the specifications of the Zhou[2] capital as a square with sides of nine *li*, each side having three gates, traversed by nine meridional and nine latitudinal avenues, each of the former being nine chariot-tracks wide (Wheatley, 1971:411). This prescription is identical with that of a comparable date, but a much older urban tradition, in the Arthasastra design for Indian cities, which, even more remarkably, is similar to the actual ground plan of third millennium BC Mohenjodaro, according to Wheatley (1971:414), and to the city of Jerusalem as described by Ezekiel (48) and by St John (Revelation 21). Jerusalem is described as a square of equal sides, oriented to the cardinal points, with three gates in each.

The siting of cities was decided by geomancers, sometimes with awkward changes in their computations so that huge cities were switched from site to site two or three times within a few years of their founding. The geomancers worked on behalf of the ruler, who was visualized as establishing the cardinal orientation of the city himself.[3] It was 'laid out as an *imago mundi* with cosmogony as paradigmatic model' (Wheatley, 1971:417, 450). Microcosm paralleled macrocosm and heaven was virtually brought down to earth and embodied in the city 'as a sacred territory within the continuum of profane space'. Any irregularity in the representation of the celestial archetype was inauspicious and supposed to cause misfortune. 'Rites obviate disorder as dikes prevent inundation' (Li'Chi, quoted by Wheatley, 1971:418; Stover and Stover, 1976:31).

The central point was crucial to the whole process of orientation and was thus a quintessentially sacred focus of creative force, the point of closest communication between earth and heaven above and also with the underworld below. As axis of the world it has been symbolized in various cultures as a navel or umbilicus, column or pillar, vine, tree or other plant, rope or mountain. It was the place 'where the four seasons merge, where wind and rain are gathered in, where *yin and yang* are in harmony' (Wheatley, 1971:428).

The most important official buildings were ranged along the main processional north–south axis, always facing south. This processional way represented the celestial meridian.

The five points constituted by the 'pivot of the four quarters' appear not only in the ideal design of the city but also, as it happens, in the form of the Shang kingdom with its capital at the centre surrounded by the four districts themselves again named after the four cardinal points. The symbolic and conceptual centre of the city was not in its physical centre, but in the centre of its northern wall, facing south. The four in five model of the quincunx was yet further expressed in the imperial domain, surrounded by the four successive concentric squares (Stover and Stover, 1976:32).

The symbolic structure of the Chinese cosmological city has elements in common with many pristine urban traditions both in the Old and New Worlds. It is the unique combination of age, continuity and living literate tradition that imparts greater elaboration and detail to the Chinese version, physically embodied in Chang'an, 'the T'ang capital which approximates most closely of all Chinese cities to the canonical prescription' (Wheatley, 1971:411–14, 416–51). It relates nature to society and the cosmos, and the world to the state and the city, to the passage of time, to public and private social life and the parts and processes of the body. The Palace City in the centre of the north side occupied by the royal family faces the people's city to the south, as the ruler must always ritually face his vassals, looking from north to south as they face him prostrate from south to north. Thus Emperor and Palace alike face south, absorbing the light. The palace of the Crown Prince is on the east side, of spring and sowing; that of the Queen Dowager on the west side, of the autumn and harvest. So also in the domestic family house the master is on the north but moves towards the east (senior and left) and the mistress is on the south, moving towards the west (junior and right). At night both keep their heads to the north, their feet to the south. The city is the main stage on which the drama of life, public and private, for ruler and ruled, the state and the individual, is symbolically enacted.

Surrounding the Palace City to the south was the Imperial City, accommodating the main central government institutions, while again surrounding it on three sides and extending much further south was the capital city, the main city of the people. From the Palace City in the north the main processional, axial route, 500 feet wide, passed through the Imperial City and the people's city to the great south gate, dividing the whole into its eastern (left) and western (right) halves. Most official and wealthy households were on the left, while on the right was a much denser population including transients and camel caravans from the Great Silk Road. The eastern (left) Market was called the urban Market. The Ministries of the Left and of the Right were on their appropriate sides of the processional way.

The axis or umbilicus was thought of as the Pole Star representing the axis of the world, and casting no shadow at the summer solstice. For Confucius this symbolized the moral force of government. Such ideas appear in relation to the Ka'aba stone in the central mosque of the city of Mecca, in the Roman Forum, and in mesoamerica where the idea of asymmetry was basic and the axis was deflected from the centre. The Chinese axis pivot of the four quarters was also represented by the altar tumulus to the God of the soil in the capital city, made of blue-green earth on the east side to represent the cerulean dragon and the bursting spring vegetation; of red earth representing the Phoenix of summer on the south; white earth on the west representing the autumn harvest, war and metallic weapons, memory, regret and unaltered past mistakes; black earth on the north for damp winter and darkness; and yellow earth on top, the imperial colour, associated with the loess soil of the Yellow River valley which gave China its productive richness from the beginning (Wheatley, 1971:434–5; Stover and Stover, 1976:30). The axis was also physically related to the Kunlun Mountains and visualized in nine tiers, echoed in the nine convolutions of the conch shell and the nine tiers of Burmese and Thai pagodas. The Pole Star, axis of the world, was thought to be straight above Mount Meru in the Indian cosmic design, and above Mt Sumbu in Ural-Altaic thought and also above the Elburz Mountains in Iran.

When a new satellite city-state was formed, its ruler took with him a clod of earth from the king's altar (Wheatley, 1971:175) in the capital city to plant at the base of his new altar of the soil, west of his palace gate, in the same five symbolic colours: blue-green, red, white, black and yellow (Stover and Stover, 1972:42). East of the gate he erected the altar of his own ancestors, symbolizing his own increasing political independence.

The city walls stood for the boundary of the universe, established through the ritual potency of the ruler. Circumambulation of the city by the ruler at his coronation performed a similar function in Cambodia, Burma and ancient India.

Historic China passed through three distinguishable phases: in approximate terms, eight centuries of Shang development from the initial Kinship mode of production to the Asiatic mode of production in its loose, ritual form; nine centuries of Zhou variations on the Feudal mode of production and two millennia of developing bureaucratic mandarin China in the increasingly centralized form of the Asiatic mode of production (cf. Godelier's discussion 1978:229–30, 241–6). However, these two millennia were punctuated by longer and shorter breaks, in which varying regional and local conditions favoured further variations of the Feudal mode of production, viz. four centuries of Qin/Han with two short breaks of about eight and sixteen years; four and a half centuries' break of Feudal variations; one and a half centuries of Sui/T'ang including a ten-year break; two centuries of complete and partial break with further expression of Feudal mode of production; three centuries' of Northern and Southern Song, with the Asiatic mode of production in its most dynamic form, continued by almost a century of Yüan; half a century of Feudal break; two and a half centuries of Ming in Asiatic mode of production; half a century of Feudal break followed by two centuries of Qing, with Asiatic mode of production in intensified but involuted and finally disintegrating form, accompanied by increasing foreign pressure and intervention.

Yoruba

In the city of Ife (Bascom, 1969b:9–10), Sky God gave the God of Whiteness a chain, lump of soil in a snailshell and a five-toed chicken, saying 'go down and create the Earth'. He got drunk on the way and younger brother Oduduwa and Chameleon went on to the edge of heaven, let down the chain and climbed down, threw the soil upon the primeval waters and put the chicken on it. The chicken scratched at the soil, scattering it in all directions to the ends of the earth. Chameleon tested the firmness of the earth. Oduduwa stepped down on it and made his home where his sacred grove stands in Ile-Ife ('earth spreading') today.

Ile-Ife was the centre of the world. From Oduduwa, its first king, descended the kings and founders of the other Yoruba city-states and of Benin city with which Portuguese began to trade in the fifteenth century. The myth validates the quarters and markets of Ife. It is re-enacted annually. Dancers dressed as chickens scratch at the earth and a five-toed chicken is sacrificed for the Oni (king). Every diviner's chain of palmnuts tossed to diagnose his patients' oracle, echoes the chain (Bascom, 1969b; Apter, 1992). As in all pristine cities writing appears for ritual purposes.

Yoruba proceeded no further with it before European intervention. Oracles are calculated from poetically coded numerical combinations of eight or sixteen, 256 possibilities in all (16x16). The chain consists of eight half seed shells, or sixteen palmnuts. Sixteen major deities, compass points, Ife quarters, sons of Oduduwa founders of city-states, all reiterate the point.

City-state kings were secluded divine figures, appearing at rare rituals, faces hidden behind bead-fringed crowns. The palace was in the centre with the market opposite. The sectors of the lineages radiated outwards to the city wall. The heads and titled officers of the corporate, localized lineages provided the king's council. Beyond the walls each lineage's lands radiated out from its urban sector. Woodcarvers, bronze casters, calabash carvers, weavers, drum makers, leatherworkers, blacksmiths and carpenters were organized in craft guilds. Women ran market trade, men long-distance trade. Men cultivated, going from the city daily, living at their more distant fields for long periods as work required. All belonged to an urban-based lineage and essentially to the city in spirit through membership of its institutions and participation in its rituals, as loyalty to the ruler required.

All resided in large rectangular thatched compounds, facing inwards to the courtyard where most domestic activities occurred. They could contain as many as two thousand or as few as twenty. The classical plan resembled a wheel: the *oba*'s palace the hub, city walls the rim, the spokes a series of roads radiating from the palace, linking it to other centres, passing through sectors under sector chiefs with their compounds grouped round them. The central hill was the navel of the Yoruba universe, the *Oni*'s palace the umbilicus of the world (Krapf-Askari, 1969:30). Ancient Ife had seventeen sectors, one central, four in the cardinal points and three attached to each of these, combining the Yoruba sixteen with the structure of the Chinese quincunx. Eighty years ago the *Oni*'s palace had walls a yard thick at the base, a great gate house, richly sculptured doors and colonnaded verandahs, but it was already much decayed (Frobenius).

The Yoruba city-states exhibit many features similar to those of the city-states millennia before. They cannot be considered pristine innovators in a time capsule. They lived in a world which had changed beyond recognition from that of Uruk or Çatal Hüyük, each the leaders of their day, as the Yoruba were not. Yet, they were extraordinarily isolated by the Sahara Desert and the rain forest until the thirteenth or fourteenth century. They were creative innovators, as were the producers of the earlier Nok culture of northern Nigeria and the city-state of Jenne-Jeno in Mali, only recently revealed (McIntosh, 1995).

THE NEW WORLD

The Andes and Mexico

Middle America and the Andes also developed urban forms out of cere-monial centres. Several human groups, in conjuncturally favourable ecologies, advanced, not in unison or imitation, but in fearful and conflictful harmony, like some deep movement bursting through the surface at different places, different moments and in somewhat different forms. This risks putting in too teleological terms what is self-evident: these groups were, each in its own way, in a total sense, ready; they and the time were ripe.

The north Andean coasts of Ecuador and Peru favoured an exception-ally rich fishing and gathering economy by at least the third millennium BC. Indeed, it is claimed that coastal people in Peru began constructing large-scale, monumental architecture at that time. The second millen-nium saw cultivation in the deep valleys and canal irrigation, with cotton, gourds and chili coming from east of the Andes. Large settlements devel-oped in the first millennium, such as Chuquitanta and Aspero covering thirteen hectares. In the Casma valley a gigantic earth pyramid of 640 by 180 metres was constructed.

The city of Cuzco represented a puma (Rowe, 1963). It was conceptu-ally divided into quadrants, in turn divided into three sectors each and again subdivided into three, making nine sectors each and again sub-divided into three, making nine sectors in each quadrant, except the western with fourteen. Each basic triplet was supposed to consist of one of the three intermarrying classes, such that, with a cross-cousin marriage system, category A married category B producing category C. The total of forty-one sectors constituted lines radiating from the centre outwards beyond the city to some 400 sacred shrines, cared for by the sectors (Zuidema, 1964). A somewhat similar conceptual structure of ritual action is found at the city of Kashi (Varanasi) (Sinha and Saraswati, 1978:15–16).

The influence of the Andean capacity for intensive agriculture and permanent settlement spread far and may have reached Mexico. Given fragmentary evidence, these developments are consistent with the transi-tion from the Kinship mode of production to the Asiatic mode, with the emergence of city-states and then attempts at empire, as happened in the Old World some two millennia before.

In highland Mexico domesticated maize developed from the fourth to the first millennium, to become a super-crop in the lowlands also (Macneish, 1973). Many ceremonial centres developed, but at first without large permanent population, in the La Venta (Olmec), Monte Alban (Oaxaca) and Teotihuacan regions of the north-east coast, southern and central highlands respectively.

The high point of indigenous urbanization was in the first millennium AD. The colossus of Teotihuacan dominated the highlands and spread tentacles far beyond, in fine contrast to the dozens of major Maya cities, certainly much smaller, but architecturally no less spectacular. The Maya centres were long denied the title of cities, but accumulating data show them to have larger resident populations than previously thought.[4] Unquestionably they were impressive concentrations of monumental buildings – a common-sense notion of a city – but they also had low-density urban populations, involved in construction, maintenance and city-state rituals of the centre, as well as in agricultural production nearby. There were four cosmic directions, each with its colour, tree and bird. The heavens were thirteen layered, the underworld nine layered. The earth was conceived as a giant turtle floating in water with lilies and fish. The giant silk-cotton tree of abundance was the centre of the world from which the four directions radiated as the four processional thoroughfares of the city. They were represented by stone causeways at several sites. That they had only a ritual purpose shows that the Maya city-state was indeed the cosmos.

Maya city-states

The peer polity characteristics (Renfrew and Cherry, 1986) of the Maya city-states, with their maize agriculture, reflect a considerable spatial homogeneity. Lack of important local resource differences (apart from contrived exotica) failed to motivate warfare with any economic or territorial goals, leaving a low pressure towards state formation.

Divine shamanic kings reigned over the city-states and with their consorts were believed to conjure up and communicate with dead ancestors and supernatural beings, with whom they claimed co-essence (Freidel, 1992:3). Like Shiva, they 'danced the world', creating and maintaining it by acting out its cosmic rhythm. They demonstrated their sublime kingship by ferocious personal feats of bloodletting, trance-dances, masked pageants, human sacrifices and suicidal ball games in their ceremonial centres. In their extraordinary flamboyance, they even risked capture, together with their supernatural 'battle beast' companions, such as Sun Jaguar and Eighteen Rabbit Snake, as they performed warrior feats on their ritual frontiers and even in the sky (Freidel, 1992:5).

The intensity of belief, firing and fired in the agony of self-inflicted torments of physical torture and gory mutilation, in which all levels of the population seem to have been involved, could not but in turn generate an equally intense conviction of the validity of the fiercesome world they created. So terrible, and so consistent, a world of horror (as we see it) takes us beyond the normal dimensions of existence, beyond any banal, matter of fact contrast or division between imagination and reality, ruling class and citizen or peasant, beyond the capacity of mundane political analysis. The normal concept of cruelty seems inept and impotent. The evidence is that these city-states worked on the basis of competitive torture of both self and other, in which a labourer's life of unremitting toil stone-cutting, or constructing pyramids, palaces and temples, might have seemed a blissful release from the higher morality of self-immolation for the public good. They operated at a very high level of communal fervour. But it was fragile and subject to sudden collapse. Slaves and captives, whose hearts were torn out live, no doubt paid the highest price, but kings who slashed their flesh and nurtured the gods of all with their own blood could hardly be regarded simply as oppressive tyrants. Their self-sacrificial fury may have generated a kind of emulative devotion and loyalty of which we can have little ken.

Legitimacy of royal succession to kingship of the city-state was demonstrated by shamanic initiation to the status of supernatural, and by descent from historical founders and from gods, ritually manifested. The fine obsidian blades were primarily used for letting blood, the major medium for the construction of holy spirit. Bloodletting, which both nurtured the gods and opened the bleeding royal actor to trance communication with the supernatural, was equated with harvesting ripe corn. The royal rituals were more modestly replicated at all levels of Maya society down to the village. In some mysterious way, best captured by Godelier's insight (1978), Maya people, men, women, leaders, kings and gods, were all together encapsulated in this terrible magical world of ritual and belief, of which their cities were the glorification and the stage, so richly and endlessly elaborated as to convince. If they must seem to some excessive and obsessive, no wonder Marx applied the notion of false consciousness to such phenomena.

So wrapped up were all in constant prestations and spectacular performance that coercive political rule may hardly have been relevant. Ample land for swidden, and sometimes irrigated highly bred maize made subsistence production relatively unlaborious and abundant. Prestations and exchanges consisted largely of subsistence produce and exotic articles of ritual value such as feathers. Bitter warfare between kings and gods, partly imaginary and if partly real, mainly for captives to sacrifice, or factional strife among elites (Brumfiel and Fox, 1994), all had to be channelled into the same all-embracing ritual cosmological struggle harnessing the whole people. It cannot be harder to credit than the voluntary practices of jabbing spines through ear and penis, or drawing studded cords through the tongue.

These were city-states emerging from the Kinship mode of production to achieve a theocratic, ritual and segmentary form of the Asiatic mode, as their mobilization of production and labour, construction of splendid temples, tombs and stelae, devising and elaboration of calendars, numerical and astronomical, with mythologies recorded in advanced hieroglyphic logograms, richly suggest. There may have been a more military phase of competitive inter-city warfare and imperial ambitions, as elsewhere, preceding the downfall attributed to excessive population and ecological damage. In a contested issue, where space forbids elaboration of alternatives, I can only offer my reasoned choice.

Teotihuacan

By the second century BC Teotihuacan already covered six square kilometres with a population of about 30,000, with four specialized obsidian workshops and houses on stone foundations. Its rectangular grid pattern of fifty-seven metre blocks came to cover over twenty-two square kilometres with an estimated population of 125,000 by AD 200, having drawn into it 85% of the valley of Mexico. Its range of dominance spread farther than that of the later Aztec. It influenced the culture and economy of all mesoamerica before its decline, destruction and abandonment about AD 750. It was by far the largest pre-Colombian city, the first metropolis of the New World. Its ceremonial way ran roughly north and south, between the pyramids, larger but less lofty than that of Cheops. East–west avenues crossed, with a large market and major central temples, which were repeated on reduced scale at twenty-three temple complexes throughout the city. Main residential compounds were built in stone, with high, blank walls to the street and one storey rooms round patios facing a temple. There were over 2,000 such complexes, with some ethnic-occupational specialization suggested by the clustering of Oaxacans, Mayans, merchants, obsidian and pottery workshops. By AD 500 there were 400 craft workshops specialized in obsidian core-struck blades, chipped points and knives, with green obsidian workshops near the market and a hundred more specializing in ceramic, figurine, shell, lapidary, basalt, slate and ground stone work, with yet others in perishable materials such as feathers. There were many colourful murals both on temple walls and apartment interiors. Two thousand three hundred stone apartment compounds, accommodating up to a hundred people each, replaced former adobe houses of the majority population.

Foreigners seem to have lived near the periphery, as did the artisans, and labourers in less permanent structures, though many would have been servile members of the large, central compounds of the elite (Millon, 1973).

The extraordinary size of Teotihuacan, far larger than any other pristine city in the whole world, evokes bafflement and incredulity. It belongs to a qualitatively different dimension of its own. Crucial aspects of its structure and functioning as city and as polity remain speculative. We cannot fill in all possibilities and any choice may be faulty. It seems to have grown as a relatively peaceful theocratic polity, later developing military orders and eventually militaristic aspects which seem to have led to its downfall. There is nothing to suggest that its wide-ranging cultural dominance amounted to 'empire'. Though without peer or precedent, its overall structure and dynamics cannot plausibly have been other than those of a segmentary state with a highly ritualized political economy expressing the Asiatic mode of production.

As with the Maya, scholars often perceive rulers and gods as either equated or confused. Representation of gods in human form came after that of humans themselves, perhaps expressing the will of the latter to emphasize this equation. Perhaps it could be said of the late, militaristic phase, as it was of the far more militaristic Aztec, that war was ideologically aimed at securing captives for sacrifice, although massive booty was also obtained. Although the divine kings might be buried in sumptuous unexcavated tombs at the foot of the great pyramids, 'Burials vary from simple, unceremonious inclusions in construction fill to moderately well endowed tombs' (Adams, 1966:111). 'The largest of the great enclosures contained both ceremonial and residential structures', like Eanna's precinct at Uruk, but there are 'many smaller yet impressively large compounds which are lavishly decorated', suggesting a broad rather than a very narrow elite. In the absence of writing, numeral notations and possible glyphs served ritual rather than administrative purposes. The rain and lifegiving fertility god of the city, Tlaloc, is represented as jaguar, feathered serpent, butterfly, owl or shell. The incredible wealth of mural art suggests to Adams demoniac gods more remote and awesome than those of Mesopotamia, 'surely less human in their relations with one another or with man' (1966:124). However, the anthropologist may question whether it was not the mesoamerican concept of cosmic humanity rather than of divinity which differed.[5]

The basic enigma is how a city of such a size fed itself. It may have been first by simple drainage of swamp land and later small-scale canal irrigation from a limited number of springs, supplemented by the large supply of subsistence products which the city's impressive ritual-cosmological dominance brought to its great shrines from all around. Besides, the great market places (not required in the distributive systems of the more moderately sized Sumerian city-states) may have brought a large supply of foodstuffs for exchange with the vast volume of craft products in both practical and ritual demand and produced nowhere else but in the numerous workshops of the city.

Teotihuacan is so monstrously incomprehensible as a material phenomenon that it has prompted wild speculation and hypotheses without evidence (Kurtz and Nunley, 1993:761). There is a danger of interpreting the ritual, symbolic and sometimes phantasmagoric paraphernalia of divine kingship as mundane political reality. Uruk is the nearest analogy, displaying the same process of implosive expansion, perhaps with the same implications. Teotihuacan was only three times as big! This process seems to belong essentially to the special developmental circumstances of the pristine city-state, unless one should note a perverse analogy by reversal, in which impoverished Third World primate cities are drawing population out of the stagnating countryside to a state of unemployment, crime and drug consumption in the primate city.

It seems that where the first burst of pristine urbanization succeeded most, in both the Old World and the New, it did so in circumstances whereby it was able to demonstrate an irresistibly attractive and hitherto unknown way of life to its region, drawing an extraordinary majority of the population into itself. This imposed enormous strain on the city-state, above all to feed itself. But evidently it also spurred unprecedented efforts in production and trade which enabled the precocious metropolis to achieve its zenith and carry on for some centuries before a seemingly inevitable decline set in.

In the case of Uruk, Adams speculatively suggested internal tendencies towards consolidation of political leadership and external military threats (1972:739). The latter, however, could only have been from wandering nomads, or from other city-states, none of which was the equal of Uruk until later. Given the Teotihuacan parallel it is essential to consider further possible cultural forces of support (Kurtz and Nunley, 1993), an ideology of work, implanting 'those moral and ethical principles that publicly assert the social and cultural benefits of work by individuals and groups for a hypothetical commonweal' and which are persuasively inculcated into the consciousness of the people (1993:762–3). 'The textual inscription provided by Teotihuacan's art, architecture and artefact suggests its government was relatively successful in attaining a culturally hegemonic relationship with its population and was thus assured of the people's support from production *incentives* to generate sufficient surpluses to satisfy the needs of citizens, carry out its policies and support the ruling class'(1993:763). Such incentives are embedded in a set of social norms related to resources, values and time (Wallman, 1979:4–10).

Major support for the system arises from being socialized within it, or even coming into it with awe and wonder from the outside. In this state of society, mode of production, technology and cultural knowledge (and here the analogy with recent cultures understood in depth by anthropologists is not false), there was an imperative need for ritual, symbolic and hieratic certainty, to assure confidence in the fearful vagaries of daily life and guarantee belief in the ultimate relations of gods, divine kings and people, in the successful control and maintenance of fertility in crops, animals and humans, in victorious defence against malignant occult powers and in achievement of ecstasy of communion with the deities controlling earthly well-being as well as harmony with the immediate forces of nature and the ultimate forces of the universe. Translation of the chaotic and agonizing experiences of daily life and its pyschic terrors into the eternal harmony of the cosmic universe was an achievement of priceless value, for which the vast majority of the population were undoubtedly prepared to pay, if not with their lives (as was often the case), at least with the full energy of their productive forces. Here was the religious system of symbols 'which acts to establish powerful, pervasive, and long lasting moods and *motivations* in men [*sic*] by formulating conceptions of a general order of existence and clothing these conceptions with such an aura of factuality that the moods and *motivations* seem uniquely realistic' (Geertz, 1966:4).

There is no country in the world where the natural and cosmic forces are more awesome than in the land of the 'shaking earth' (Wolf, 1959). If we know from the end of their history that they were in terror of their world coming to an end like an erupting volcano, and felt bound to propitiate the forces responsible for it with the bloodiest and most brutal sacrifices, then it cannot be so hard to understand how the people of Teotihuacan were prepared to make equal sacrifices of human energy more than a millennium before. If divine kings and priests, with their splendid temples, their gorgeous rituals, terrifying sacrifices and convincing shamanistic trance performances, could convey these certainties, as countless ethnographic examples demonstrate that they could, then the feeding of the multitude of the Teotihuacan populace and the maintenance of public order may become intelligible. Priests, temples, rituals, public festivals, processions and ecstatic celebrations, writing, monumental sculptures and all beautiful unprecedented, inspiring and awesome works of art were means for the communication of new cultural marvels to the members of a transformed and transforming society. As Raymond Williams argued (1980:38–9), the symbolic order permeates production through the hegemonic process of the dominant culture – a central system of practices, meanings and values, organized and lived, a sense of absolute because experienced reality beyond which it is very difficult for most members of society to move. It is the beginning of the inculcation of false consciousness. But as described by Godelier (1978) people brought it upon themselves. They were sucked into the system of glorification and sucked in others. Pyramids, ziggurats, art, architecture and artefacts all were indeed marvels and objects of wonder, calculated to inspire awe, perhaps fear, in any case to generate a condition of over-whelming humility and submission, which the grand cultural communi-cators of the dominant regime, with their institutionalized and cumulative experience of centuries, could channel and manipulate into a willing worship and submission, not so much to human rulers as to the gods themselves, whom they all recognized and abjectly worshipped, in whose name their earthly representatives, mediums and incarnations could harness the large mass of the population into productive work for the glorification of the city, its symbols, its leaders and ultimately, in however small a way, themselves.

The Olmec were the earliest and in some ways the most grandly artistic of all the great mesoamerican civilizations. (Recent reports suggest that La Venta was a city and that Olmec centres such as San Lorenzo reached urban status (Stuart, 1993).) Some writers tend to assume that because the Olmec made colossal statues they must have had colossal kings, but the opposite is the case. Their colossal statues are proof of the labour they were prepared to devote to honouring their great ones, human or divine or as often a fusion of both. The identities of the jaguar, 'shaman of the animal world' were animal, human and divine. The society was deeply and tightly integrated, ritually and symbolically, not politically. Just as Maya rulers slashed their own flesh to promote the harmony of gods, humans and nature, so the Olmec and Teotihuacanos may have been pre-pared to give their uttermost for their city and, in effect, for their own eternal salvation as they perceived it. We cannot hope to penetrate the veil of such far off mysteries completely, but we can strive to avoid intruding twentieth-century biases into situations two, three or four millennia ago, and humbly 'read the remains of the city hermeneutically as a text open to interpretation' (Kurtz and Nunley, 1993).

Implosion, militarism and collapse

In Sumeria, the city-state of Umma may be another variant of implosive expansion, manifested in its sudden, intensive settlement with dense clus-ters of almost adjacent large towns which 'probably were totally absorbed' into Umma before 2500 BC (Adams, 1972:739). Generalizing still further, Adams notes: 'during roughly the first half of the third millennium wide areas of the alluvium were heavily depopulated as the overwhelming majority of their inhabitants were persuaded or compelled to take up residence in politically organized city-states' (1972:742). The city-states thus acquired an almost uninhabited zone of from five to fifteen kilometres in which it is assumed the urban population carried on cultivation. Adams sees the early city-states as artificial creations brought together 'to increase the economic well-being and offensive and defensive strength of a very small, politically conscious superstratum' (1972:743). We are not told by what power this was achieved. We have seen that the lofty, ritual-symbolic uniqueness of divine rulers was an existential necessity of the system, not a political or class phenomenon. This may be a view from rather outside the time and space concerned. Other writers see the Teotihuacan elite as very wide (as lack of evidence certainly suggests), but regard the Maya elite as very narrow, with a huge gulf separating it from the people. But the Mayan elite was of a ritual rather than political nature, even an elite of self-immolation.

One might hypothesize an earlier cultural outburst and over-extension at Uruk, Umma and Teotihuacan, later taking a more military form, and a later politico-military outburst and over-extension at Ur and Akkad. The rapid Sumerian implosion seems to have begun before the political and military development of the city-states was in any way sufficient to enable them continuously to coerce the whole population to move into town. It would seem that cultural processes of attraction and integration must have played a considerable if not predominant part. Some centuries later, the capacity for political and military operations had been greatly expanded by the competitive process of warfare between the city-states. It enabled Ur and Akkad to create their unprecedented empires, but their imperial capacity was an illusion and their empires began to crumble very soon after they were formed. Similarly the military phase of Teotihuacan came late, long after its most spectacular depopulation of the countryside, and led on to its mysterious collapse and abandonment. The most colourful Maya warriorhood and fighting depicted seem often cosmic rather than terrestrial.

3   Greece and Rome

Chapter 3 deals with the city-states of Greece and Rome, variations of the Ancient mode of production, their roots and transformations, ending in decline before the Germanic invaders whose interaction with their heritage generated a new, dynamic mode of production, while a rearguard action of exceptional brilliance was organized at Constantinople.

GREECE

The dialectic of city-states and invaders

The westward spread of urbanization from Asia into Europe involved many ethnic groups, cultures and languages, close to one another spatially and quite limited in distribution, though some expanded over vast areas from small beginnings. The most impressive urban culture to emerge in Europe was that of Crete, at Knossos, Phaestos, Malia, Zakro and other urban sites (Faure, 1973:185), early in the third millennium BC. The island was strategically placed for maritime trade between the earlier mainland urban economies, north, east and south. Besides, it offered a wide variety of opportunities for agriculture and settlement, between rich lowland grain farming; easily defended mountains, pasturing goats and nurturing olives, grapes, figs and chestnuts; rich coastal fisheries and many harbours suitable for their small, shallow draft vessels.

The Cretans built a number of autonomous temple-palace city-states (Cherry, 1986:19, 26) concentrating populations of at least several thousands, with paved streets, tiled conduits, sewers, piped water and densely packed two- and three-storey houses of stone or plastered brick, lit for the first time with many paned windows of some translucent material such as alabaster or oiled parchment, but facing blank walls to the street (Faure, 1973:180–8).

These city-states concentrated on maritime trade enriched by highly skilled craft production, symbolically emphasized in the myth of Daedalus, especially in metalwork, including cire perdue bronze casting, engraving, embossing, filigreeing, milling and encrusting (1973:212). They pioneered the exciting experiments of writing represented by the Minoan linear A and B (1973:30, 32). Their rulers had the attributes of divine personages, symbolized as bulls, ritually re-enacting the process of creation with temple priestesses attired in skin costumes as cows (Graves, 1960, I:293). It was an open civilization with little sign of fortification (Faure, 1973:229). The many chambered temple complexes included pillared halls and altared chapels, baths, kitchens, granaries, wells, water closets, laundries, storerooms and servants' quarters. They had a north-north-eastern orientation in a rectilinear but asymmetrical design, with lines of shops and markets nearby. They were the first emphatically mercantile urban culture, though so heavily ritualized.

The cities of eastern Crete were burnt and abandoned in the fifteenth century BC. Knossos was destroyed in the fourteenth, but later re-occupied. There are signs of severe volcanic eruptions and earthquakes, which probably brought plague, pestilence and famine in their train, and may have coincided with the period of attack by Mycenaean invaders, finding the Cretans weakened by cataclysms and perhaps also by fighting amongst themselves, as in the tradition of attempts by Knossos to subdue the other cities (Faure, 1973:112–18).

Cretan skills and myths echo back to the Near East and on to Classical Greece. The Minoan civilization had already spread to other Aegean island centres, such as Rhodes and Melos, where the incoming Mycenaeans modified and transmitted it to the later Greeks. Cyprus, long famous for its copper, had also mingled Minoan, Egyptian, Phoenician and Anatolian with later Mycenaean culture. The Mycenaean age produced the fortress principalities celebrated in Homeric epic, but no further urban advances. The movement of the various Greek-speaking peoples, Achaeans and Aeolians, Dorians and Ionians, from the north into mainland Greece and Peloponnese, into the islands and across to the Anatolian shores, seems part of the secular pressure of population from the interior of Euroasia which forced Celts (Gauls), Huns and Germans into the Mediterranean world in an age-long succession. This was a turbulent period, about which so little is known that it appears as a Dark Age.

The splendid Mycenaean city-states were overwhelmed and there was a major cultural regression and depopulation. Yet it was an extremely favourable conjuncture for the outburst of Aegean trade and colonization, which followed the invasion and settlement of new populations. Byblos, Tyre and Sidon, pioneers of Mediterranean trade, were fighting one another and fell under Egyptian, Assyrian and Persian control between the ninth and sixth centuries. Crete was the first known island urban culture, followed by the first known archipelagic city system, in Greece and the Aegean. Neither of these would have been conceivable except in reaction to and building upon the earlier urban cultures all around the eastern Mediterranean.

The transition from the Kinship to the Ancient mode of production

Marx explains major transition as resulting from the dialectical contradiction of forces and relations of production (Marx and Engels, 1969a:503–4). There comes a point when the relations of production no longer have a positive effect upon the forces of production but 'become their fetters', so that the forces of production burst out of the old relations of production and new relations eventually develop to accommodate and encourage them. The emergence of the political economy expressing the Ancient mode of production, as illustrated by the transition from Crete and Mycenae to the emergence of Athens and other classical Greek city-states ΠΟΛΙΣ (*polis*) over about half a millennium, can be interpreted in this way, but the migration of peoples, the substitution of one population for another, with its culture, polity, system of production and technology, by gradual incursion or violent aggression and invasion, seems in this and other instances to have been a major instrument whereby both forces and relations of production changed, but especially the latter, as the theory implies. The incoming peoples were, in human form, bearers of the new forces of production bursting the fetters of the old relations of production and generating new relations of production from within themselves, as they developed in interaction with their new environment. They were emerging from the Kinship mode of production (Southall, 1988a:186–8) and changing in reaction to the new ecology and resources they confronted as well as under the influence of the people they met, often in violent conflict.

In the city-states expressing the Ancient mode of production which then developed, the citizens collectively owned the means of production in land and minerals, being collectively responsible for the security of the state against the slave population.

What combination of internal disorder and external attack brought about the downfall of the Cretan city-states and the subsequent Mycenaean collapse is uncertain. But the movement of new populations from the north-west into the Greek mainland, Aegean archipelago and Anatolian shores is clear. Perhaps the crucial century of 'birth' of the new mode of production is a dark age of ignorance, however awkward for theory, but natural enough in the context of disorder, depression of culture and population, breakdown and destruction. There was greater continuity of occupation at Athens than in most areas.

By contrast with the autocratic, divinely sanctioned hierarchy and elaborately detailed administrative control of Mycenae, the incoming groups were relatively egalitarian, with a kin-based structure including warrior leaders, peasant followers and a subordinate labour force enslaved by capture in war or entanglement in debt. The significant forces of production they disposed of were: improved iron technology for cultivation, warfare, mining, construction in wood and stone and ship building. They acquired much of their predecessors' high culture and technology without being able to reproduce their elaborate palace, state and urban structures or luxury crafts. They moved into the distinctive ecology of innumerable islands, deeply indented, craggy, fortress-like coastlines, narrow plains and high mountains, where their own small polities inevitably reproduced themselves in numerous independent settlements. Their productive relationship with land, sea and their varied resources was distinctively self-structuring. The coasts nurtured small-holding fishermen and potential sailors. The plains supported the largest agricultural operations and produced the dominant, wealthy families, who also profited from exploitation of mineral resources such as the silver mines of Laurium in Attica. The foothills and barren, marble rich mountains offered grazing to hardy herders of pigs, sheep and goats, feeding off acorns and other wild products and exchanging meat and milk for cereal, wine and olive oil from the plains.

Successful settlement encouraged population growth which rapidly reached the narrow limits of available productive land, prompting further migration to new areas, especially by sea, leading to more and more maritime exchange of the products of different, or differentially exploited, ecological niches. So arose the famous Athenian trading trinity of pottery, wine and oil. The pots, originally required as oil and wine containers, were also on demand in their own right and developed into the splendid painted vases which brought a new dimension in luxury trade and cultural achievement. Although the elite were not themselves the active traders, they clearly dominated it through their associates, partners, servants and slaves, as they also did the banking system which arose from it. Some might even be encouraged to go to other settlements where, as non-citizens they could trade with impunity. These economic processes led to the development of some two hundred small city-states on or near the coasts, and to the founding of colonies as new towns, at first to secure more land for cultivation and then to extend the range of trading, bringing new products into the network and providing attractive investment opportunities. The growing population was thus tied together by intricate yet far-flung economic relationships, from the Black Sea and Egypt to Spain while remaining atomistically fragmented politically.

The most spectacular and revolutionary development was that the potential for kingship (inherent in the ritual and military leadership of small kinship clusters) atrophied, instead of emulating the great monarchs of the past and was transformed into ritually enhanced magistracies. The economy had become so attractive with its unfolding possibilities that kingship simply became irrelevant. The ruling class became motivated in a different direction. This was truly epoch making. The switch of interests was both marked and fostered by the growth of intellectual culture, based on the acquisition of an improved, Phoenician-derived alphabet and the emergence of written literature.

In the case of Athens and many other settlements, the leading families remained gathered together in their original principal settlement, which grew into a city. They managed their affairs collectively by developing specialized offices to take responsibility for vital public affairs, providing for the incumbents to be elected from time to time among themselves. They gathered together in a great council of notables, which excluded the majority of the common people. But the latter were still able to meet in the assembly of all free citizens, which derived from the informal popular assemblies of primeval times (Vernant, 1982:46 fn. II).

The continuing growth of population and wealth, with increasing differentiation of the economy, led to slave captives, further swelled by the numbers of impoverished peasants, falling into debt slavery, as powerful magnates improved their means of agricultural exploitation. It was easy for the affluent to become increasingly dependent on slave labour and in course of time the slave population grew to rival or even surpass the numbers of free citizens. Slavery became the fundamental basis of production, not only a necessity, but an increasingly menacing threat. The gulf between slave and free became the pivot of the whole political economy and the over-riding basis of class division. The wealthy, powerful and more and more sophisticatedly educated elite were obviously most sensitive to the smouldering slave threat and came to realize that it was essential for the whole free population to stand together in its own defence. However, the free population, though all recognized as citizens, was exceedingly unequal, varying from the large numbers impoverished, on the brink of debt and slavery, up to the effectively ruling elite with their large estates, factories, mines and shipping fleets.

The elite were highly motivated to secure their own position through binding all citizens in loyalty to them and the city, by lightening their burdens and increasing their privileges in access to justice and political participation. All high offices were opened to election, the length of tenure was shortened and all male citizens were encouraged, and eventually paid, to attend the people's assembly and participate in the voting procedure. In this sense all citizens, wherever they primarily lived or worked in the national territory of Attica, were members of the city of Athens. This was Marx's 'ruralization of the city'. It was easy for the wealthy to commute between their rural interests and their urban operations and residences, but it was difficult or even impossible for many poorer citizens. However, the impoverished were increasingly attracted to the city to live on their pay for attending the assembly and on other state perquisites. They formed the urban, citizen mob. They could easily be drafted on to ships or into the army for national emergencies, or seduced into the following of would-be tyrants.

This was the Greek miracle. It was indeed an expression of the progressive dialectical contradiction between the forces and relations of production, but as in other cases, the breakdown and collapse of other productive systems and political economies, accompanied and followed by the moving in of new populations, were crucial aspects.

The ΠΟΛΙΣ emerges, through tyranny and war, to the Golden Age

With the eclipse of kingship the city was centred on the agora, place of public assembly and then market, not upon the palace. Walls surrounded the city itself instead of fortifying the palace (Vernant, 1982:47), and public temples were built in place of the private king's palace. 'Once the city was centred on the public square, it was already a ΠΟΛΙΣ in every sense of the word' (1982:48). These unprecedented changes were in process from about 700 BC onwards. The struggle to retain privilege, on the one hand, or build citizen solidarity, on the other, continued, as a series of public-spirited men, like Draco, Solon and Cleisthenes, sought reform to prevent polarization from destroying the fundamental unity of rich and poor citizens as a slave-controlling class. The floods of gold and silver from Carthage, which controlled the richest mines, are credited with the inflation which caused unrest among seventh-century Attic peasants. The wealthy wanted power and privilege, the masses better living and justice.

Competing factions supported both. Peisistratus was popular from a victory he had won against Megara, but his first two attempts at power failed, so he retired to the north, making a fortune from gold and silver mining and collecting his own army. In 546 he invaded Attica, defeated the Athenians and became tyrant of Athens. He mainly followed the constitution, put up fine buildings, made loans to small farmers and was widely popular. His son Hippias continued after his death, but when he encountered opposition he became repressive, executing his enemies. The opposition called in the Spartans, expelling him in 510. All Athens then expelled the Spartans. Cleisthenes got his reforms passed against reactionary opposition which appealed again to Sparta.

Cleisthenes persuaded the citizen assembly to a radical reform of the constitution, switching the basis of representation from family to locality. Though forced into exile by Spartan pressure, Cleisthenes' reforms were eventually implemented, instituting ten new national constituencies, each including components from the city, the coasts and the interior, supplying armed infantry and cavalry, voting together for one general each year and selecting fifty members by lot for the council, which acquired control over finance, foreign affairs and general government policy and administration. It gave the appearance of participation and responsibility to all, with an aura of divine choice from the lottery system, while tending to exclude the rural population from direct power, giving supremacy to the city, where it was exercised, and preventing domination by one faction, family, region or class, but weakening continuity, which was met by electing generals annually for competence, not by lot, allowing outstanding leaders to dominate the popular assemblies and the city. Inflation reduced the significance of wealth and property qualifications. It was as though Athens had just managed to put its democratic house in order before the peril of Persian invasion threatened to overwhelm it. It was a gorgeous flower which richly suggested all that it might be, but rarely in reality approached it for very long.

The Greek city-state was suddenly thrown into the front line with the Persian onslaught: a cluster of tiny communities facing the greatest empire of the contemporary world. Xerxes was an oriental potentate in caricature, whipping the sea when a storm drove off his fleet. From 490 to 480 the exiguous Greek forces stood up again and again to confront apparently overwhelming numbers. Virtually the whole of Athenian manpower was on the ships at Salamis, their city evacuated, administering a stunning rebuke to the vast forces of the Persian tyrant, with a sublime combination of skill and luck routing a fleet six times their own, sending the Persians home and initiating the decline of the Achaemenid Empire.

Spectacular as this was, revealing some previously unheard-of qualities in the Greek city-states, it was not merely the extraordinary physical prowess and endurance, the unflinching courage and cool calculation, the stark grandeur of Leonidas leading his 300 to heroic death, not just Miltiades and the 10,000 boldly and brilliantly attacking and routing five or six times their number at Marathon. These matchless deeds fired the Greek imagination and became the eternal symbol of sublime courage and heroism in the western psyche. But it was the quality of individual

and collective action which was most unprecedented. No supreme generalissimo, no great charismatic leader, no standing army, no overall hierarchical or bureaucratic structure. Just a few dozen city-states, of varied size
and diverse government, often at enmity, but coming together under a
common threat, their chosen delegates meeting regularly in congress,
voting by majority, electing Sparta to supreme command, abiding loyally
by their life and death decision. The ten elected Athenian generals each
led for one day in turn but all obeyed the decision of their polemarch.
Each performed miracles of valour in his own freely co-ordinated place.
Disunity was a perennial obverse of Greek freedom. In the Persian wars
many were traitors, or switched sides. Athens and Sparta were usually
enemies yet came together for the common good. Sparta gave its best
blood unsparingly and when the war was won they just went home, with
no hegemonic ambition.

The Persian wars were the birth pangs of the Athenian golden age,
when Pericles rebuilt the acropolis which the Persians had destroyed.
Pericles ruled Athens by common consent, elected general year after year.
His ability and intelligence were admired beyond challenge, but when the
vote went against him he went home till the people called for his leadership again. He neglected his estates and did not socialize, spending all his
time on public work. He brought his mistress, Aspasia of Miletus, to live
with him publicly at Athens. Rumour and scandal swirled round her, but
she too was intelligent and able. Athenians could not approve of a woman
in public life, yet she became an accepted fact of life at Athens.

Pericles organized the Delian League to finance common protection
against Persia. Most cities exposed to Persian attack contributed and the
treasury was kept neutrally in the Delian temple of Apollo. Pericles called
a conference of cities proposing rebuilding of temples destroyed by the
Persians and sacrifices to the gods for Greek salvation. In the end the treasury was transferred to Athens and contributed heavily to the rebuilding
of the Acropolis and the Parthenon. Some contributors objected and
withdrew, but Pericles also organized further settlements in League territories. He was borne along by the glamour of the Parthenon project and
the indispensability of his leadership.

Murderous factions, brilliant art and thought

Athenian democracy vacillated between the noblest aspirations under its
greatest charismatic leaders and the most ruthless caprice under the shifting whims of uninformed masses swayed by unscrupulous demagogues.
Such unpredictability brought disaster to the Sicilian Expedition of 413
with huge losses of men and material, and unconscionably executed the

victorious generals who recouped the fortunes of Athens at Arginusae, because they had failed to rescue drowning sailors. The almost total destruction of the fleet by Sparta at Aegospotami in 405 marked the end of Athenian imperial influence. The rightist faction installed the tyranny of the Thirty with the help of Sparta, who likewise established many tyrannies and oppressive oligarchies in numerous other Greek cities. Athenian tyrants secured the execution of large numbers of the democratic faction, while more and more fled into exile, building up an increasingly irresistible force against the tyrants, till they were compelled to negotiate a withdrawal, and the limited democracy was re-established. But Athens had suffered greatly and the population showed a drastic decline. During the imperial epoch from 480 to 431 it had risen rapidly, but from that point, with a probable 35,000 adult male population, the terrible plague of 430 BC, the Peloponnesian War and its accompanying effects of loss of tribute, economic distress and emigration reduced their numbers to 21,000 in the fourth century (Bury, 1889:586; Jones, 1960:8, 78–9). Sparta also suffered from the impoverishment and even enslavement of her increasingly debt-ridden small holders, with no more than some 1,500 male citizens surviving in the fourth century (Bury, 1889:604), while in the third a mere 700 could be mustered for service (Glotz, 1930).

Sparta retained her elitist and ascetic way of life and at Athens the ideal of moderation combined with aesthetic enjoyment still prevailed, but armies had become professionalized and Athenian generals tended to live abroad in luxury, bringing their mercenary troops into service when required. Without her tribute, Athens was all the more dependent on her disfranchised slaves, freedmen and foreign bankers and traders, her hardworking potters and other craftsmen, her peasant and slave cultivators and miners. Commerce and banking flourished and Athens had surpassed the other great trading cities of Corinth and Miletus, but despite the form of democracy, economic inequality was extreme.

The leading mainland cities such as Athens, Sparta, Thebes and Corinth, with the great colonial cities of Syracuse in the west and Miletus in the east, were unable either to live at peace with one another or develop a system which could control or unify them. Greece remained under the threat of Persian domination, which her squabbling cities were not ashamed to invoke against one another, so that their factions were often mediated by the Persian monarch. There was a constant dialectic between the forces of oligarchic tyranny and those of democracy within the restricted elites. In the former democracy of Syracuse, Dionysius gained tyrannical power for thirty-eight years after 405, through constant re-election as general.

The noble dream of total citizen participation in electoral and decision-making processes, with office holding widely spread by the goddess of the lottery, already excluded the majority population of non-citizens, not to mention the whole female population. Even so, by the fifth century, when Athens reached a male citizen population in the tens of thousands, the theory wore thin, despite the huge open air assemblies, and Athens was inevitably run by shifting factions and coalitions of closely interlocking wealthy families, with occasional humbler men of genius and ability accepted and eventually co-opted by them.

As these processes evolved, with the explosion of poetry, ceramics, drama, painting, sculpture, architecture and philosophy in sixth-, fifth- and fourth-century Athens, all kinds of ideas about the nature of society, polity and the city were broached, seemingly for the first time. More exciting experiments for realizing them were made than ever before, though never with full success. The general freedom of thought and action, the balanced cultivation of body and mind, the passion for beauty in life and art have haunted western man ever since. But at Athens even in its heyday these things were paradoxically only for a minority. Less than a sixth of the male population were full citizens, another half were free but of non-citizen status, while over one third were slaves. Only citizens participated in Athenian democracy, which was thus a glorious façade. The only women with any freedom were the fashionable *hetaerae* (companions), who lived alone or several together, cultivating beauty, charm and intelligence. Men could visit them honourably and paid them to entertain at parties and sacrifices. They were wealthy, respected and paid taxes. Otherwise, married women were secluded.

Many other Greek cities besides Athens produced great works of art and artists, dramatists, poets, architects and philosophers, but it was at Athens that the light burned most consistently, in periods of political and economic weakness as well as strength, so that even Dionysius of Syracuse, whose city had been so instrumental in the downfall of Athenian political power, aspired most to have his plays produced at Athens. Most of the great philosophers of the age, like Aristotle, wherever they were born, eventually drifted there. It was at Athens that men first thought comprehensively about the problem of men in city and society, fundamental problems which they could not solve and which we have not yet. Even after its defeat by Macedon Athens remained the cultural magnet. Alexander spread replicas of its political institutions all over western Asia. In the second century, Antiochus IV of Syria built the new temple of Olympian Zeus at Athens and Attalus of Pergamum contributed a new colonnade which became the model for many others. Another astonishing innovation was that the metropolitan cities did not, in principle, retain or even claim political domination over their colonies, although they sometimes attacked and even massacred them. The claims to tribute of Periclean Athens were based on recognition of leadership services, not allegiance from colonies.

The good life: for the few

There was the intoxicating vision of liberated men united in a free society deciding its own destiny, living the good life of integrated mental and bodily delights, walking and talking philosophy in the painted colonnades of the agora, exercising together in the gymnasium, creating or enjoying the finest sculpture or pottery, plumbing the heights and depths of tragedy and comedy in the theatre, governing themselves in public assembly, settling conflicts through shared, rotating judicial institutions, each knowing each at personal, face-to-face level, fighting side by side in defence of their city by land or sea. In reality, however – granted that many poor citizens were supported in a degree of leisure by political attendance payments at councils and assemblies (Jones, 1960:17–18), as well as by the free food which both they and destitute non-citizens could share – a minority group of the relatively wealthy and privileged citizens monopolized power and leisure, ignoring women and despising the disenfranchised merchants who generated most of the wealth, collectively oppressing and taxing the peasants who grew the food and standing on the necks of the slaves who did the menial jobs. The fact that most citizens had to work to earn their living, that slaves could be humanely treated or that the elite could joke about the difficulty of distinguishing slave from free by dress (Jones, 1960:20) cannot alter the basic economic reality.

The city dominated its rural hinterland physically as well as politically. From the acropolis you could almost see it all. The countryside was within easy walking distance. Three-quarters of the citizens were also landowners and many brought their own corn, wine, oil, honey, figs and wool to support their urban existence, the wealthier bringing their rent as well. Apart from this inescapable physical symbolism, of central city surrounded by supporting fields, protective mountains on one side, cliffs and seas on the other, both protection and highway to the world, with citadel dominating city and temples towering over all, Athens had no planned symbolic structure. Apart from the supreme beauty of its monumental buildings, it consisted mainly of flimsy houses on narrow alleys without sewers or latrines. Garbage was dumped in the streets and scavenged by birds of prey. Only the wealthy homes were built of stone, with spacious rooms and enclosed courts. Even wood was scarce and most houses were built of rammed earth or unbaked brick, shared with poultry, pigs and vermin, while the frequent wars created a large population sheltering in makeshift shacks like modern *bidonvilles*.

Classical Greece was hardly innovative in urban planning and amenities as Cretan cities had been. However, the fifth-century architect Hippodamus of Miletus conceived the model of a city with symmetrical institutions paralleled by the symmetry of its rectangular physical plan. His own city was rebuilt according to this gridiron layout after its destruction in the Persian wars, as also was the Piraeus under Pericles, with many other cities influenced by the same design, which became general in the Hellenistic states. It was not entirely a Greek invention, having been anticipated by earlier models in Anatolia, Syria, and stretching back to Mesopotamia, as well as paralleled in the Indus valley and in China. In its Greek form the main streets were widened and straightened, with long colonnaded rows of shops and residential blocks of uniform size. The place of assembly was separated from the market, which was often moved down near to the waterfront with its warehouses, docks and ships. It was this more uniform design, in which strangers as well as natives could easily find their way, that Alexander spread from Asia Minor to India as he founded his seventy new cities along the path of conquest. Pericles' idealistic concept of the pan-Hellenic city, which he invoked in the attempt to resettle Sybaris in 446, again with Hippodamus' design, was also further implemented by Alexander's creation of new cities out of Macedonian and other Greek settlers on equality with other subjects of the conquered Persian Empire.

Neither the technical means nor the resources were as yet available to spread the leisurely elite life of political, intellectual and aesthetic activity more widely. At this stage of human productivity and technology the good life could only be led by a few, living on the backs of the poor. Yet awareness of the problems and contradictions of socio-economic inequality became acute in fourth-century Athens. However, the only solution which they could devise was the palliative of free food, free theatre tickets and increasing payments for political assembly attendance to secure the docility of the poor. Originating in the Theoric Fund for the support of religious festivals, this expenditure came to swallow up all surplus financial resources of the city.

Sparta cultivated a similar vision to Athens of free and equal men working out their destiny together, but they were even more alarmingly outnumbered by their helot slave population. Their whole culture was thereby twisted by brutal self-discipline to attainment of heroic courage, superlative physique and invincibility in war. All artistic beauty or aesthetic pleasure was sternly rejected, apart from some attention to poetry and music. They died in eternal glory under Leonidas at Thermopylae

(480) and saved Greece under Pausanias at Plataea (480) but made little contribution to Greek urban culture. Their city was appropriately austere and unwalled.

The Greeks identified city and state linguistically, with one term ΠΟΛΙΣ (*polis*) for both. *Polis* originally meant acropolis, the high city, walled fortress of king, temple, sacred hearth and tomb, with the settlement of the people below ΑΣΤΥ. But the walls came down to enclose and protect all the people. *Polis* swallowed *astu*. In the case of Athens we can distinguish Attica as a geographical territory including all the city's rural hinterland. But in fact the larger physical entity is conceptually subsumed in the smaller, which is culturally greater and all-encompassing. 'Athenians' includes the whole population of Attica, for they all belong to the city of Athens, not merely politically, but much more importantly socially, mentally and spiritually, wherever they actually reside in town and country. The Greek city-states are the earliest with surviving written records to enable us to know this, but the same was true of Rome and Latium to an even more bizarre extent and much later also of the Yoruba city-states of Ife, Ijebu or Ibadan. Teotihuacan, Tenochtitlan and Cuzco seem also to have subsumed their empires into the metropolitan city in a way that was never true of capital cities in nation states in Europe.

Citizens and non-citizens

The franchise of effective participation in public decision making and in politico-administrative office holding tended to widen by the fourth century BC, but never to include the non-citizen merchant, peasant, serf and slave majority. Despite the virtues of free assembly and public debate for citizens, the fact that many of them were not directly involved in the main wealth-producing activities or in physical labour, tended to make their decisions irresponsible. Popular leaders also came to be drawn from humbler though still citizen backgrounds, such as those dealers and craftsmen in sheep, hemp, leather, sausages, lamps and musical instruments who succeeded the noble Pericles. Although lampooned by Aristophanes as boorish clods, they were doubtless still far above the average wealth.

The greatest contradiction was the exclusion of merchants from citizenship despite the ultimate dependence of all the finest products of Greek culture, material and non-material, on commercial wealth. Even the wealthiest Greek merchants were mainly foreigners, ex-slaves or freedmen. The ex-slave Pasion owned the largest shield factory and ran the greatest bank in fourth-century Athens, bequeathing it to his own ex-slave Phormio who also owned ships trading to Byzantium (Michell,

1957:336). Great profits could be made from loans, although the risk was high, for though 12% was good, it could run to more than twice that. On the other hand, public institutions like the temple of Athena lent to its own city of Athens at only 6% in the fifth century and the treasury at Delos lent at 10%. Moneychanging was even more despised, but at one point the Athenian treasury tried to monopolize it. Ignoble activities often no longer appear so in the hands of the noble. Many noble Athenians of power and wealth were in fact indirectly yet closely involved in trade, owning merchant ships, contracting for great buildings, organizing mines and running banks, but they did this through slaves or freedmen and resident aliens as agents. Many of the latter were Syrians, Cretans and others with generations of experience in commerce and maritime trade. As foreigners they were not permitted to own either land or houses, and therefore had little choice but to make a living from industry and commerce (Jones, 1960:91).

The Greek system can only make sense when seen as a whole. It was essentially a system of cities, sitting on a powder keg of slaves, linked in a dense but very far-flung network under no all-embracing, centralized authority. Since as a respectable citizen you could only prosper as a merchant abroad and not at home, it is easy to see the tremendous force which powered the early migration of Greeks and the founding, growth and flourishing of commercial cities governed by commerce-scorning elites all over the Mediterranean. The main pan-Hellenic institutions were the games: Olympics every four years, Pythian, Isthmian and Nemean every two; and the oracles, with Delphi as the greatest. The Panathenaic festival and games were more obviously aimed at the sectional interests of a single city. The Panathenaea was the annual and later four yearly festival of Athena, the patron deity-protectress of Athens, centred essentially upon the presentation to her of a new embroidered robe. All the dependencies of Athens brought sacrificial animals and a great sacrifice was held. The great procession arrayed Athenian society in proper order before the divinity. Recitation and musical contests also accompanied the festival. There were also the many schools of philosophy, Plato's Academy, Aristotle's Lyceum and the mystery religions, all of which served a parish far transcending the bounds of any one city-state. The games and the oracles all had deep ritual and religious roots, which continued to wield effective sanctions, within which their influence, their decisions and their implementation were manipulated and exploited by the politics of particular cities and individual leaders, who, however, rarely dared to interfere directly with these sacred institutions, which not only provided relatively inviolable sanctuary, but also imposed periods of peace most favourable to trade.

The openly political confederacies of cities, such as the Athenian League of Delos, the Peloponnesian League and the Amphictionic League, all failed except the latter, which had the advantage of focus on the mystical and religious centre of Delphi rather than a politically powerful city, so that Philip of Macedon was able to use it successfully to provide a cloak of legitimacy for his growing dominion over Greece. After the battle of Chaeronea established his military supremacy, in 338 BC, Philip formed the more inclusive Confederacy of Corinth.

Despite political weakness great works of art continued: new styles of sculpture and painting, great theatres and improved acoustics, new and rebuilt temples and wonders of the world: Diana's temple at Ephesus, the Mausoleum at Halicarnassus and the Colossus of Rhodes. It was the time of Demosthenes' imperishable yet politically disastrous oratory; after Plato and Aristotle, the rise of the Cynics, Epicureans and Stoics.

Alexander and the Hellenistic cities

After the assassination of Philip of Macedon in 338 BC, his son Alexander, pupil of Aristotle, carried on his work and Hellenized the east. He founded Alexandria, unofficial capital of the Hellenistic world, in 331. It remained the largest city, supplying Greek culture and manpower to Egypt and exporting huge quantities of wheat. The Øαρος light-house towered above the port and the famous museum and library attracted scholars from the whole Greek world. The north winds blew cool air through the straight north–south streets, ibises ate at the vermin and refuse. The protecting marshes were washed by the Nile Flood. After the model of Athens it had its own laws, courts, magistrates and juries, its demes and local constituency organization and almost certainly its popular assembly and council. Like other city-states it also had its own surrounding territory (Jones, 1966:3).

Although Alexander adopted Persian dress and Persian wives, declaring himself both King and God, marrying off 10,000 Greek soldiers to Persian women at a single ceremony, yet he endeavoured to establish Greek language and culture wherever he went, most of all by the founding of cities – thirty-three other Alexandrias and dozens more – and in them holding games to promote Greek literature, music and drama as well as athletics.

After all the turmoil, Greece was full of landless, workless men, tens of thousands of whom were settled by Alexander and his successors in new Asian cities, with the basic principle of 5,000 men as the complement for a new foundation. Alexander's settlements were definitely cities expressing a cultural ideal, not merely fortresses, though strategic military and political considerations were also bound to be present. Convicts were also used, as in Tsarist Siberia, Botany Bay and many other colonial settlements.

After the ebb and flow of war between Alexander's successor generals, relative stability settled upon their Hellenistic kingdoms in Macedonia, Anatolia, Syria, Babylonia and Egypt. The kings continued to found innumerable cities, many fallacious, mere renaming, or forced amalgamations of existing settlements. They were founded for royal aggrandizement and in the name of the Greek idea, for there was no Hellenistic citizenship other than membership of a particular city. Foreshadowing Rome, they were used as convenient mechanisms of administration, taxation, army recruitment and general exploitation. It pleased monarchs to pay lip-service to the Greek idea of city autonomy and suited the *amour propre* of cities to act as if their freedoms were real (Jones, 1966:95). The Greek spell was pervasive, with games of the god Melkart at Tyre identified with Heracles and Sidon stressing its paternity to Cadmus and hence Thebes, or the Temple of Baalbek where three Syrian divinities were identified with Zeus, Aphrodite and Hermes. Cities were named, or renamed, mainly after Hellenistic rulers or Greek deities. Non-Greeks gradually lost the near equality which Alexander had intended, and economic inequality within the city and between city and countryside increased. The cities came to be run by indigenous, but Hellenized, upper classes, loyally meeting the exactions of the royal bureaucracy through their own exploitation of both the urban and the rural economy.

Cities prospered from the cessation of warfare. Wealth increased, and many slaves were freed and many bought their freedom. Life became more luxurious, for the upper- and middle-class minority, with a turning away from marriage and family life, increasing abortion and infanticide leading to depopulation. From the second century onwards the wars with Rome brought the decline and break up of the kingdoms: Macedon defeated in 197, Syria and Asia Minor in 189, Corinth destroyed in 146, Pergamum handed over in 133. Greece still hated Macedonian domination enough to welcome conquest by Rome, and so passed on the weakened spell of the *polis* to the ensuing Roman world.

ROME

The city-state emerges

The *gentes* were the very foundation of the early city-state of Rome (Fustel de Coulanges, 1956:102–5). It was still an expression of the Kinship mode of production. Archaeology reveals that the city founded by the miraculous hero Romulus (Fustel de Coulanges, 1956:135–9) was a small village of shepherd huts on the Palatine hill. The traditions of Aeneas could reflect early settlement in the vicinity of Rome by bronze age seafarers from the Aegean. The shadowy kings, whether Roman or Etruscan, were essentially ritual figures, with little power except as called upon to lead the people in the city's constant fight for survival. This did not preclude a king from arbitrary acts of brutal oppression on a personal level and getting the kings thrown out, as in the story of Lucrece.

At the level of political economy, the Etruscans may have been expelled in the fifth century because they were already weak and had been defeated by the Greeks at sea. But they had enriched Rome culturally and economically, with alphabet, temples, monuments and walls, making it prosperous through participation in their extensive internal and maritime commercial system. The Romans suffered by cutting themselves off, bringing on inflation, unemployment and popular unrest. The plebeian soldiers returning from a campaign seceded from Rome to the Sacred Mount, forcing the Senate to grant them sacrosanct inviolable tribunes to be elected by them with power (inside the city only) to vet any decisions by the patrician government injurious to them. A tripartite temple of Ceres, Liber and Libera (symbolizing fertility) was dedicated by the consul as a plebeian sanctuary at the foot of the Aventine, matching the Capitol.

In 450–1, with the tribunes' leadership, a further effort towards equal justice was made in the drafting of the Twelve Tables, bronze tablets permanently displayed in public, assuring all of the full enjoyment of their rights. So important was this exercise that the consular system itself was held in abeyance for two years during its completion. Among the *gentes* some were dominant, as if some lineage segments which produced wealthy and powerful persons were able to consolidate their influence over the generations. These were the patricians, the members of the ruling Senate. Every gens had its ancestral cult, traditions and family law, to which it was bound by the strongest ritual sanctions. The Comitium Curiata, which had elected the kings, was divided into three 'tribes', hinting at the tripartite ethnic base of Latins, Etruscans and Sabines, each with thirty *curiae* (sections) analogous to *gentes* headed by a *curio* and holding common meals and sacrifices.

Class struggle and transition in mode of production

The plebeians were not in the *gentes*, as if they were an original servile, composite class (Fustel de Coulanges, 1956:229–33). As soon as Rome emerged from the legendary era of the kings, the class struggle became a recurrent theme, over the next few centuries transforming the Kinship mode of production into the Ancient mode of production. The patricians had contradictory needs, as individuals to maximize their control of land, wealth and power, but as a collectivity to retain the allegiance of the plebeians as the vital source of soldiers to defend the city republic. The citizenship status of the plebeians was ambiguous, but the city could never have survived without their loyal services and they were fully incorporated in the military force by the quinquennial census. From the fifth century they were permitted to marry patricians. Plebeians may even have been eligible to become consuls, but were gradually excluded by patrician pressure until a third-century law provided that one of the two annual consuls must be a plebeian. By then the distinction was becoming blurred and patricians were required to vote together with plebeians by wards instead of property classes as previously. The first plebeian Pontifex Maximus was in 280 BC.

The abiding goal of plebeian class struggle was access to land, which reformist patricians attempted to satisfy for the sake of enlightened self-interest, which was also supported by the idealized notion of a united community of simple, rugged, independent peasants as the solid backbone of a citizen army. However, while potent and enduring, this ideology was increasingly at variance with the real political economy. Plebeians never ceased their struggle to win their share of the *ager publicus* (public land) which was constantly being augmented in huge amounts as Rome's conquests, to which plebeian soldiers made a majority contribution, were continually extended. But the land hunger of senators, commanders and prominent families was insatiable. It was indeed part of Rome's policy to strengthen the state by planting colonies in conquered territory, which usually meant allocating land for settlement to plebeians. After the conquest of Veii in 395 its territory was allocated for settlement. In the third century 60,000 holdings were so allocated.

The Punic wars inadvertently brought a decisive acceleration in the implementation of the Ancient mode of production. During the years of Hannibal's occupation much of Italy was devastated. Apart from loss of life, vast numbers of farmers were dispossessed and their properties destroyed. Large numbers fled to Rome greatly swelling the ranks of the urban mob. For the ruling classes it was a blessing in disguise. They could buy great tracts of land cheap, and slaves were in ample supply from war captives, so they created slave-worked latifundia ranches on a great scale, thus transforming the mode of production and the structure of society.

Bloated wealth and private armies threaten the city

Peasant farmer settlement was in the interest of the state. Multiplication of the slave latifundia was more in the interests of an increasingly bloated ruling class. The greater wealth of the empire, always concentrated at the top, made it possible by the first century BC for wealthy individuals to raise large armies from a nucleus of clients and dependants. It was a good investment paying handsomely. Marius and Sulla led the way, to be followed by the Pompeys, father and son, Mark Antony, Julius and Octavius Caesar. These huge private armies left the Senate impotent to do anything but choose who its next protector would be. The triumphing generals juggled the major offices, making friendship pacts one day and murdering one another the next. The same dual economic mission of the uncontrollable military machine continued: it must reward its veterans with land or gifts after each major campaign, and it must yield booty and slaves sufficient to maintain each commander at the top of the high status game. All the major commanders had violated the ancient rules of play; all merited the death penalty in Rome if once their supremacy faltered. It was triumph or death, therefore the drive to propagate the Ancient mode of production was irresistible.

This was not quite the Athenian ideal of free and equal citizens running the city and its territory in a high state of democratic solidarity against the possibility of slave revolt. But it came to much the same result by a different route. Self-interest forced patricians and plebeians into unequal solidarity of common action in the army, in conquest and slave recruitment, with acquiescent though unequal participation in the hierarchical polity which differentially protected and benefited them all. The city-state could not have survived a continuation of multiple uncontrolled military leadership. The example of Julius Caesar dramatized the tragic futility of supreme destructive power, and his adopted son Octavius was gifted enough to exercise the restraint and tact to foster the peace for which all yearned, the reward for which was the Principate unanimously conferred on him by the Senate. His own favourite, informal, titles were *pater patriae* and the name Augustus itself.

The Augustan miracle

So emerged the politically effective, constitutionally ludicrous fiction, that the commander-in-chief of the winning army should be the Head of State by virtue of his confirmation by the Senate as principal magistrate of the city of Rome; effective because the control of the means of destruction ensured the control of the means of production also (Mazrui, 1972:19). The Roman military system as such could never be challenged internally and never produced any movements of transformation within itself. Its chief, as emperor, had virtually absolute power (Rostovtzeff,1957:138) and the ruthless cruelty and corruption always associated with it was constantly manifest. It was remarkable that the competitive opportunity system of the army threw up so many outstanding rulers committed to transcendent values. Augustan peace and prosperity was deceptive, not only because it required continuous frontier warfare to defend it, but that its vast concentration of wealth, wisely and magnanimously used at first, was bound to corrupt, yet the prize was so glittering that effective competitors were sure to appear, even after decades of chaos. Augustus gave peace and prosperity with secure roads and low customs. Urbanization spread through the provinces.

Rome became a monumentally beautiful city, pioneering many urban improvements and amenities: pure water through gigantic aqueducts and fountains, paved streets, impressive covered drains, baths, theatres, temples, colonnades of shops, triumphal arches and picturesque stone bridges across the winding Tiber. However, the masses lived in high, multi-storeyed, congested tenement warrens, without light, heat, water or any kind of sanitation. The most salubrious and picturesque sites went to the lavish palaces of the top elite. Rome had 1,800 single family residences in the fourth century AD (together with their large, servile establishments) and 45,000 tenements (Jones, 1964:689). Fifth-century Byzantium's 4,388 family residences suggest a larger middle class than Rome, between super wealthy elite and impoverished masses.

Augustus not only beautified the city, but assured its superior standard of living by the revival of trade in the largest area of peace that Rome had ever had, securing the roads, stabilizing the currency and developing a more integrated and unified economy focused on the metropolis. He inaugurated a fire service, police and nightwatchmen for Rome, but by the fourth century these declined. The city was divided into wards and precincts, each under an official and all under the prefect of the city, whose staff was responsible for the banks and bed of the Tiber, the aqueducts, drains and public buildings. Other offices, some of them ancient, were responsible for the food supply, markets, storehouses and harbours, caring for the bronze and marble statues and controlling theatrical shows, actors, actresses and prostitutes (Jones, 1964:691).

There was little further innovation after the fabulous conjuncture of Augustus, but increasing ostentation. The great fires of Nero (AD 64) and Septimius Severus (AD 191) allowed for extensive improvement during rebuilding. The population was at its greatest, though probably less than 1 million, declining after the second century as the centrality of the city itself in the imperial system declined. Expectation of life was very low and in time of plague estimates show up to 200 people dying every day. The city supported some 320,000 people by free grain in 46 BC (Hopkins, 1968:69). Under Augustus there were still over 200,000. In the third century AD free oil and pork were added and the grain was baked into loaves for distribution by nearly 300 huge state bakeries each able to service 4,000 persons daily. Slaves and convicts were supplied as labour, but only the wealthy freedmen operators, owning property worth more than thirty pounds of silver, belonged to the bakers' guild. They started store front bars and brothels to increase their revenue. There was an ever larger number of private bakeries. Rome's food supply as well as the emperor was deified. Even in the fifth century, on the verge of collapse, 120,000 still received free rations. The church continued it after the collapse of the city. Constantine reproduced the same system for 80,000 people in Byzantium (Jones, 1964:696–702). The needs of the mob as well as of the magnates were catered for by the temples, theatres, circuses and baths. Imperial Rome had eleven vast public baths and 830 private baths (1964:705). Byzantium had nine public baths and 153 private baths. Antioch also had baths in each of its eighteen wards.

Commonwealth of self-governing cities

It followed from the structure of early Rome as a city-state that the empire was constructed as a 'commonwealth of self-governing cities' (Rostovtzeff, 1957:49), as the Hellenistic kingdoms had been, since urbanization was the only way known to improve provincial life. It was also a structure of cities surrounded by border armies. Conceptually and administratively the city of Rome eventually subsumed the whole empire into its citizenship.

What would become the European network of cities had developed piecemeal as the Roman Republic extended its conquest, incorporating the ancient cities of the east and the Grecian world and winning control of such urban settlements of significance as existed in the west, as well as founding more and more embryonic cities as they settled veterans' colonies on conquered lands. The latter were especially planted along the route which led through the conquered territory to the main campaigning areas of the legions. Strategic spots if not already ancient settlements were obviously chosen and were treated as potential city-states to be built up, beautified and ruled by their wealthier citizens: Lyons, London, Cologne.

There were some 2,000 cities, run by about 250,000 *decurion* city councillors and office holders, under the supreme command of provincial governors. They elected annual officers for administration, finance and public works, had governing councils, restricted by property qualifications, and general citizen assemblies, voting by wards, not as individuals. Free schools were supported in the west, with higher education more in the east where professors were maintained by cities. Slaves did all the menial work, maintaining baths, sewers and gaols, as well as much skilled, professional work, including the accounts.

All territory was under the jurisdiction of some city. Provinces were groupings of cities with effective autonomy under Roman magistrates in major cities. Provincials were expected to live in and beautify the cities, building temples, baths, theatres, circuses, amphitheatres, monuments, aqueducts, fountains, sewers, markets and houses, supporting them with endowments, festivals and games.

The superiority of Greco-Roman culture had attracted the wealthiest classes, and even rural landlords, to the exciting amenities and pleasures of urban life. Some agricultural workers lived in the city and walked to their fields every day (Duncan-Jones, 1974:260) like the Nigerian Yoruba. The basic finance of cities was the common income from the lands given at their original foundation as colonies, or their own endowments, and the customs duties, port taxes and fees they charged. They paid nightwatchmen, guards and mounted police to hunt brigands. Artificers' guilds acted as fire brigades.

Developing a city-state to be democratically ruled even by a minority was an idea of grandeur and fantastic originality. No wonder the process was not smooth. In Greece, as in Mesopotamia, the growth of wealth and population led to destructive conflict, which the cities were unable to solve until overcome by a superior power. In republican Rome, the growth of wealth and conquest of distant territories had created problems of political control and of public morals in the city government, essentially problems of allowing too many citizens of inordinately disproportional wealth and power, each one wielding power far greater than that of any of the potentially controlling institutions of the city. The city approved and encouraged their achievements and their self-aggrandizement until it was too late to control. The solution in Rome, whose conquests had far outgrown its political capacities, was to turn the city-republic into a peculiar, ill-defined and formally unacknowledged autocratic city-state-empire. The cities truly ruled the empire in a day-to-day sense (as long as the armies held the frontier) but the emperor always had the power to intervene, but at great material and moral cost.

The cultural dialectic lay in the overwhelming and unquestioned political supremacy of Rome and its lasting deference to Greek culture, which the latter accepted as its due. Greek remained the dominant language of the eastern half of the empire and many emperors favoured it. Roman writers almost unconsciously modelled themselves on Greek prototypes, while the context and experience out of which they wrote, as well as the Latin language itself, made their compositions genuinely Roman. The Augustan peace inspired a great surge of writing in tactful tribute to

Augustus himself and the achievements of the age and of the Roman ancestors. The first flush waned and there was a second flow of literature in the Silver Age of the second century, looking back at its own Golden Age rather than at the Greek fount. Indeed, Augustus' immediate successors were less than inspirational, but after the insanities of Caligula and Nero and their confused aftermath, five efficient and sometimes admirable emperors maintained security and prosperity. The endless campaigns, invasions and rebellions on all sides felt far away, so that most of the second century seemed the happiest and most prosperous time for the cities of the empire, inducing a false sense of lasting stability. Abundant writing was encouraged by imperial support of libraries and higher education. It was not superlatively creative, but excelled appropriately in satire. Greek literature also flourished, confirming the cultural divide, while Galen and Ptolemy advanced medicine, geography, astronomy and mathematics.

Antoninus Pius was able to celebrate the 900th anniversary of the city. He and Marcus Aurelius brought a rare note of austerely upright devotion to duty, which the ill-conceived mode of succession could not permit to last. The very conscientiousness of Antoninus and Marcus Aurelius in trying to assure the efficient working of the cities was inevitably an interference, which began to discourage civic initiative. However, the Greek cities flourished as never before, Alexandria and Antioch especially and those of Asia Minor. Their industries grew, with a network of banking, credit and commerce extending from Scandinavia to China. But the trade in spices and luxury goods drained metal to the east, and the silver denarius had to be debased. The grossly inegalitarian slave economy began to suffer depopulation.

The ruthless severity of Septimius Severus (193–211) kept the empire together, with increasing strain, but opened new opportunities by ignoring the Senate and encouraging centurions to become knights by way of the tribunate, after which they could enter the bureaucracy, replacing the previously dominant freedmen. Army pay was raised, soldiers allowed to marry and veterans given land, mostly in Africa and Syria. Italy lost its tax exemption, confiscations increased and provincial cities became more and more part of the administrative machine, effectively losing their autonomy. Gaul, with its rich soil, uncorrupted work force and good river transport began to compete economically with Italy, as did other favoured regions. Italian magnates found their latifundia less profitable and increasingly rented them out to tenants, especially as slaves ran short. The population and level of production of Italy began to dwindle and it lost its previous predominance in wine and oil, the most profitable products.

Rome dissolves in factions and vice

From 211 to 284 some seventeen emperors reigned an average of four years each, all but one made by the army and killed by the army. Some notable victories held back the barbarians. Many usurpations and rebellions shattered the contentment of daily life; many regions were devastated and great cities (Lyons, Antioch, Athens, Byzantium) pillaged or destroyed, with twenty years of plague and population decline. The London–Byzantium trade route to the orient was blocked. Municipal government atrophied, inscriptions and dedications were rare and cities suffering from requisitions of goods and conscriptions to state service withdrew behind reduced walls. Cities had remained prosperous while the wealthiest landowners lived in them. Prices were fairly stable for the first two centuries, but the great inflation of the third century hit their endowments and there were confiscations of temple lands, donated by their forebears.

The city of Rome was losing its grip on the empire. It was no longer the primary site where affairs were decided. It remained the symbolic centre and was still a significant node because the network of great roads crossed there. But it was no longer the unique centre of power and action, which were becoming dispersed. The Senate never succeeded in reasserting its authority. It was less and less invoked, surviving only as rubber stamp and as the grand club of plutocracy, assimilating successful knights and even descendants of freedmen. Emperors stayed more and more in the regions where they were acclaimed, or where they had to fight competitors, rather than going to live in Rome. Now co-emperors and sub-emperors made their regional capitals in Germany (Trier) or the Balkans (Salonae, Nicomedia).

The stern morality of early Rome hardly survived the opulent lawlessness of the late republic. After the fabulous conjuncture of the Augustan age, brutal incompetence alternated with ruthless efficiency over the next three centuries. Yet Augustus did, amazingly, restore a decent public restraint, which lasted well through Tiberius' secluded excesses. The exhibitionist idiocies and vicious crimes of Caligula and Nero shattered it and their successors imposed a pitiless discipline rather than morality. The Augustan estate itself formed a significant part of the whole vast empire. In able hands it could be run as a prosperous business meritocracy, but it was an inexorably corrupting force in the long run, above all through its essential dependence on slaves, the supply of which virtually dried up after the last great conquests of Trajan. The wealth from these conquests had been limitless and lasted into the reign of Hadrian who remitted sixteen years of tax debts and burned the records.

How relevant to the common people were the posturings of the imperial elite far above their heads anyway? The empire was promoted as the rule of the city of Rome and its first citizen, not of an oriental potentate. But the concentration of power and wealth was complete and totally uncontrolled, bound to corrupt the average man. No systematic selection or training put emperors above the average, unless it was eventually the deadly competition for popularity and leadership in the army. Their power resulted in their deification according to Greco-Roman cultural norms, which hardly increased their restraint.

As citizenship was extended, from Rome to Italy, to the whole empire, so military enthusiasm (formerly a valuable qualification) dwindled, and army recruitment came to depend more and more on the very barbarians the army was fighting, while emperors desperately tried to increase its size beyond their capacity to pay. The wholesale de-Romanizing process was reflected in the Principate itself, with the armies choosing the successor from any corner of the empire and the impotent senate complacently rubber-stamping.

The degradation of public and private life

Gone was Roman *gravitas*, from women as well as men. There were noble women, heroic, courageous, ruthless and duplicitous, but irrevocable change was expressed in property relations, family, kinship and descent. Poor women, though free, stayed at home and did not go to market. Only limited occupations such as wetnurse and midwife, hairdresser and dressmaker were open to them. The wealth of the late republic already led to changes of manners, morals and institutions. The strict marriage code changed; the old patriarchal union giving powers of life and death gave way to marriage and divorce by consent. Patrician marriage had been an indissoluble union between descent groups as well as spouses, bride and dowry passing from the power of the father to that of her husband or his father. Then dowries increased and fathers acquired the right to control daughters after marriage, even withholding them and their dowries from their husbands and using them as pawns in the ferocious game of political alliances (Hopkins, 1968:70). With corporate agnatic control violated, divorce became frequent, women began to control property and to divorce their husbands without serious grounds. (Augustus had outlawed adultery.) They competed in dress and expenditure, limiting their pregnancies to control their figures. Depopulation thus began at the top and the centre, with replacement from further and further afield. Sumptuary laws to control extravagance and profligacy proved unenforceable. *Quis custodiet ipsos custodes?* – (who will guard the guards?).

Infants came into the world, or at any rate were received into society, only as the head of the family willed. Contraception, abortion, the exposure of freeborn infants and infanticide of slaves' children were common and perfectly legal practices . . . A child whose father did not raise it up was exposed outside the house or in some public place. Anyone who wished might claim it. (Veyne, 1992:90)

Malformed infants, or those of daughters who had gone astray, were exposed or drowned. Others exposed children they could not feed, or gave them to friends, concentrating on a few to give them a better future.

Thus human life was uniquely cheap and undervalued from the beginning. A man would expose a child he thought not his own. After Nero murdered his mother a child was exposed in the forum with a sign 'I will not raise you lest you cut your mother's throat' (Veyne, 1991:11). Mothers could easily put their children to death. The Massacre of the Innocents was thus a piece of interference rather than a crime. Disowned children were an important source of slaves.

Girls were considered nubile at twelve and could marry and cohabit. Boys continued school and could join the army at sixteen. 'For five or ten years young men chased prostitutes or lived with mistresses. Gangs of youths were known to break down the doors of a prostitute's house and rape her . . . Well-born youths wandered the streets of Rome at night in gangs beating passers by, manhandling women and smashing shops.' A boy of fourteen was legally entitled to borrow money at usurious rates to pay for his pleasure. As soon as a young man donned his adult garb, his first thought was to buy himself the favours of a servant or hasten to Suburra, Rome's quarter for mischief. Or perhaps a woman of good society might take it into her head to initiate him (Veyne, 1992:23–4).

The ramifications of slavery and its evaluations appear ubiquitously in these contexts. In the heart of the family it was devastatingly insidious, dovetailing perfectly with the low valuation of human life, which perhaps it brought about. None but the very poor were without slaves. All infants were reared by them, not their parents. Slaves would humour the slightest foible. Mother love may have survived only among the impoverished outcasts and the slaves themselves. Some noble families sent children to supposedly strict paternal grandmothers in the country. Terror was an approved means of discipline and the distance between parents and offspring was dizzying (Veyne, 1992:16). Slavery distorted stratification, making middle-class activity look pauperized to nobles, since all menial work was done by slaves, who were not seen as human.

The Ancient mode of production was irremediably based on slavery. The resulting distortions in Roman society and culture were more profound and encouraged more outrageous excessses than in Classical Greece because of the enormous centralization of wealth and power in

Rome. Although slaves performed all the most inhuman forms of labour, they were also responsible for a great deal of the basic running of the empire, without ever receiving any credit or respect. They were confined in the lowest stratum of an extremely hierarchical society, segregated from all the most rewarding forms of advancement, wealth and power (as was by no means the case in Islam). The results appeared in economic stagnation, lack of initiative and moral decay. While this cancer worked at the bottom, it was accentuated by conditions at the top, where the colossal wealth that slave labour produced was unconscionably concentrated in the hands of senators, landed magnates and, above all, in the huge imperial establishment, which lived increasingly in careless luxury and vicious excess.

The good emperors who held things together in the second century were moral men, aiming at high standards in imperial duty as they saw it, using power ruthlessly and brutally to that end. But nothing prevented their families, wives and relatives from exploiting their lion's share of wealth and power to their hearts' content, indulging their sensual lusts and sense of intrigue with the encouragement and adulation of venal companions, slaves, page boys, mistresses and lovers. Naturally favourites spread the spoils to their own circles of eager hangers-on, so that the tentacles of corrupt self-indulgence spread very wide.

If the family system encouraged such abuse among the elite and free population generally, it was amply reflected in the public life of the city, where alone many pleasures were available, in baths, theatres and amphitheatres, circuses and chariot races. 'The theatre is lasciviousness, the circus, suspense, and the arena, cruelty' (Veyne, 1992:201). *Panem et circenses* (bread and circuses) were the recipe for keeping the city crowds happy and diverted from subversive thoughts. Some seventy-five great cities (less in the east where athletics were more popular) had gigantic amphitheatres for the entertaining slaughter of men and animals. They were, indeed, the greatest regular display of the common interest of city, people and empire. The emperor and his retinue attended in their special box, surrounded by the vestal virgins, consuls, ambassadors, priests, distinguished guests, senators and knights. Above were the upper-class families and above them again the plebeians, with the top gallery for women. In Augustus' reign 3,500 beasts could be dispatched at a time. Nero added the torture of Christians. Trajan's triumph witnessed the mutual carnage of 5,000 pairs of gladiators. Normally several thousand gladiators and hundreds of wild animals were required.

The celebration could go on for a hundred days. Reaching their grand scale in the second century BC, the performances persisted even after Constantine had abolished them, having enlarged the Circus Maximus to hold 250,000. They are said to have been more deadly in the fourth century, 'when sadism and munificence were at their peak' (Veyne, 1992:245). The whole society, intellectuals, philosophers and all, with rare exception, enjoyed the combats with unembarrassed, passionate delight. 'When gladiators were on display, people flocked to the cities from great distances. The better part of private life was spent in public establishments' (Veyne, 1992:198). 'The gladiators brought Rome a strong dose of sadistic pleasure' at the sight of bodies and of men dying. 'The whole point was to witness the death of one of the combatants or, better still, the decision whether to slit the throat or spare the life of a fallen gladiator' (Veyne, 1992:201). It was a favourite theme in mosaic, painting and sculpture.

The disgusting excesses of the Roman ruling class, bloated with the booty of empire, are notorious, now seeming nauseating and obscene: countless men and animals bloodily torn to pieces for pleasure on every public holiday, eventually taking up half the year, enjoyed with odious delight by all, yet also a conscious, cynical attempt to divert the slaves and the poor (reputedly nine-tenths of the population) from the reality of their oppression and exploitation.

This was the most revolting and disconcertingly tenacious side of the urban life so renowned for its urbanity (Veyne, 1992:186). It was a perpetual undercurrent for half a millennium, which has to be recognized as a major component in the lives of all, necessarily colouring any evaluation. There were some critical, supercilious comments, but not a trace of opposition. Even this opiate could not counter the facts of political economy. Reflection confirms that slavery was the essential determinant of the quality of urban life, empowering its triumphs, embuing its infamies and inexorably working its downfall, in the double sense of corruption at the core, and overall erosion, leaving the economy without its indispensable motive power.

The provincial cities had been an exciting development at first, a fine arena for the display of talent and wealth by any successful citizen wishing for public acclaim and renown. It was an innovative extension of the idea of public service. Wealthy citizens elected one another to rule as an honour, vying amongst themselves to beautify their city. But now the spectacular monuments were already built and the monotony and cost of keeping the city going became burdensome. As municipal administration showed signs of flagging, the imperial bureaucracy had to apply more pressure to get things done. Those left were forced into office and the emperor made direct appointments to fill gaps, or simply sent knights as civil servants to administer, signalling the demise of the city as a responsible, self-governing community. The empire had depended on the voluntary municipal officers for collecting taxes, which became more difficult and unpleasant as they kept rising. They were also responsible for army recruitment, maintaining roads, posts and bridges, furnishing cavalry or ships and administering the countryside. The army was still fighting on all fronts, costing more and more with overall expansion and a higher proportion of expensive cavalry, but bringing in little treasure or slaves. The scourge of ever rising taxes, forced deliveries, compulsory labour and unpredictable confiscations discouraged loyal service and penalized production. Office bearing became intolerable and to be avoided at all costs, by heavy payments and bribes, or by winning exemption as a knight or senator, and later even as a Christian priest, by qualifying as a shipper of state corn or tax farmer. So the top elite was siphoned away to the privileged, effete life of Rome. When the empire collapsed, the survivors would be left to choose their own administrators once more, with increasing assistance from the bishops of the expanding church. After the Council of Sardica (343) every bishop had his seat in a city and every city had its bishop.

Diocletian's draconian reform

Diocletian (284–305) unquestionably rescued the empire from the fairly imminent collapse to which the constant switching from one incompetent emperor to another was leading. He faced a desperate situation. The price of wheat rose to 6,000 times what it was at the beginning of the century (Rostovtzeff, 1957:4). Prices and wages were fixed, with the death penalty for infraction. The roads were infested with bandits and the seas with pirates. The superb discipline of the army had broken down, sapped by constant changes of commanders, each vying for favour with the soldiers by bribes and privileges. The wealthy were reduced to indifference and the poor to despair. Great magnates left the cities and retired to preserve their luxurious way of life in palatial villas. Urban craftsmen lost their market and took to subsistence farming as tenants, marrying peasant women. But they were hunted down, and landowners heavily fined for harbouring them (Jones, 1964:762). After paying rents, taxes and arbitrary exactions, peasants had not enough left to rear children and counteract the high death rate.

The period of chaos caused a catastrophic fall in revenue because not only was production affected by the unsettled conditions, but the tax could hardly be collected by disaffected cities and a disorganized, often leaderless, bureaucracy. The result was feverish attempts to extort more tax than ever, causing anyone who could to escape. The wealthy could buy exemptions, the poor could only flee.

When Diocletian restored government, the inevitable impulse was to try to keep everything in place and prevent further flight.

The wealthy must perform in city government, unless they could escape by finding substitutes and paying two-thirds of their property. Their sons were equally bound. Many therefore preferred not to marry, for their bastard sons were not compelled to succeed them in public office, nor could they claim their fathers' estates, so the latter could use them to buy further exemptions (Jones, 1964:747).

All the dozens of crafts and trades in each city were organized in guilds (Jones, 1964:858). They were expected to spend lavishly, so that only the rich could afford to hold office. They maintained halls and temples and gave feasts and funeral bounties, but had no place in city government, although powerful guilds in Rome and Constantinople were able to make serious grievances known to the emperor. The guilds, too, were frozen into compulsory, hereditary statuses, as were the soldiers and civil servants, the slaves in the mines, mints, posts, arms factories, as well as the rural peasantry and agricultural slaves, all forced to serve in perpetuity. Slaves interbred and came to be treated little differently from the free. Only medicine and higher education were exempt from serving and paying for public office. Barristers were tied to particular courts for life (Jones, 1964:507–8). Forced deliveries were assessed annually on every city, workshop, mine and farm, without advance notice of the amount.

Constantine and Constantinople

On the one hand, all these measures could not be effectively enforced, but on the other, with their death penalties, they were enough to increase the determination of anyone who could to escape or lie very low. Diocletian restored a tyrannical order but not economic prosperity, without which, armies capable of holding back the barbarians could not be maintained. Diocletian tried, vainly, to fix everyone in place and bring back the old religion. Constantine perceived that only a radical break would do, chose the new religion and turned the empire back to front. Holding the empire from its eastern end proved much easier, because the resources to hold the eastern half were handier, while the western half could be allowed to dribble away without open shame, through the subterfuge of the confederates.

It was a conjuncture almost as fabulous as that of Augustus, when history takes a new turn which seems at first for the better. The two men aptly framed the greatness of Rome whose whole history seemed to lead up to Augustus and to end with the rebirth of Constantine's New Rome. There had been hints of an eastward move with Diocletian at Nicomedea, but the boldness and success of Constantine's about-turn were superlative.

At the Milvian Bridge[1] he took the Cross as guarantee of victory, confirming this commitment throughout his life, manifested in the edict of toleration for Christians and restoration of confiscated property. He bestowed the imperial Lateran estate on the bishop of Rome, lavishly endowing St Peter's, building two other great basilicas and conferring fiscal and legal privileges and immunities from civic burdens on church and clergy. His mother Helena made pilgrimage to Jerusalem founding the church of the Holy Sepulchre. The honeymoon was lamentably short, as Constantine's sons were executed and killed by one another or usurpers, leaving only the youngest, Julian, the Apostate, to make a disastrous brief effort to dismantle his father's Christian edifice.

Although the Goths had turned on the Byzantines and killed the emperor in 378, the barbarians were usually more judiciously treated and successfully turned into confederates.[2] It was in the west that the barbarians could neither be resisted nor incorporated without the empire disintegrating in the process. During the fifth century, Angles and Saxons moved into Britain, Franks into France, Visigoths into Spain, Vandals into Africa and Ostrogoths into Italy. In this process much of Europe was laid waste and Rome sacked in 410. Vast amounts of gold and silver were spent in buying off Attila, Alaric and other leaders. Romulus Augustulus, supposed last Roman emperor, was never really emperor, nor Roman, but a pathetic child manipulated by his father.

Constantinople, the geographic pivot of Europe and Asia, where the ancient, medieval and modern worlds met, concentrated the trade of east, west and south, receiving oriental luxuries, jewels and silks from Asia, corn from Egypt and gold from West Africa, generating a vast commerce dominated by the Syrians as age-old experts and citizens of the empire, grew quickly to become chief city of Europe for a thousand years, preeminent in size, wealth and beauty. Its crowning architectural glory was Hagia Sophia, the great domed church built and rebuilt by emperors from Constantine to Justinian and surviving the final downfall as a mosque.

Constantine had restored the crumbling finances by a combination of plundering his rivals' treasuries and the pagan temples, stabilizing currency with the gold solidus and imposing creative taxes on senators and urban merchants and craftsmen. This was augmented in the next century by the arrival of West African gold by camel across the Sahara. The initial policy was open, tolerant of pagans and benevolent towards Jews, despite the sternly Christian foundation, however much brutalities, mutilations, murders and fratricide seemed to belie it. There was high social mobility at first, but the hierarchical, immobilist tendencies of Diocletian soon returned. There was a burst of population growth with plenty of recruits for the army. The growth of the capital stimulated the growth of cities along the routes leading to it. The main arteries were: that from Alexandria through Antioch bringing wheat; the route from the Far East also through Antioch and the sea route to Rome through Antioch's port at Seleucia. The Senate was less entrenched than in Rome, less of a barrier between emperor and people, but hierarchical bureaucracy soon grew to such proportions that the emperors were effectively isolated. It was now recruited from students of law and literature and from humble notaries who read shorthand, a marked contrast to previous military and equestrian sources. But most high officials won senatorial status as *clarissimi*.

By the end of the fourth century the city was bursting out of Constantine's new walls, which already tripled its size. Many nobles had up to twenty houses, with several thousand slaves, ivory doors, mosaic floors, oriental rugs and furniture inlaid with precious metals (wrote St John Chrysostom). Splendid as it was, it was not innovative. There was no creative dialectic of opposition such as developed in the west. It was a well-organized, absolutist, military-backed Christian state, committed to preservation more than originality. It had extraordinary staying power, but its greatest later achievement was the reconquest of much of the empire by Justinian's general Belisarius, only a short, and destructive, alleviation to the centuries' long process of attrition.

Success and failure crowned Justinian in tandem. The Blue and Green[3] factions of the hippodrome became uniquely united in 532 against the urban prefects' severity. They rescued prisoners and demanded dismissal of unpopular officials. Justinian's compliance failed to assuage and in the mass hysteria of the hippodrome they declared his nephew emperor. Justinian (only the nephew of a rude soldier who had seized the throne) was prepared to flee, but the Empress Theodora, a woman of indomitable spirit (who had exhibited herself, according to Procopius, naked in the same hippodrome for geese to peck grains from her private parts), refused to capitulate, so Belisarius was sent to lock the crowd in the hippodrome and slaughter 30,000 of them. The return of bubonic plague intermittently over several centuries wrought even greater havoc in reduced population, lowered activity and general impoverishment. Manpower shortage was accentuated by the monastic demand for celibacy. No new churches were built and forced labour was instituted on vacant lands.

Justinian's most celebrated civilian achievement was the codification of laws. The Christian life also was codified and legislated in exhaustive detail. Urban culture became more formalistic and ritualistic. Bishops were replacing civilian officials, as better qualified. They collected tax, dispensed charity and justice, organized commerce, negotiating adroitly with barbarians and even handling the troops. They became an urban episcopocracy. Many cities were fortresses protecting Christian communities under ecclesiastical leadership. Stupendous as the millennial survival of Constantinople was, it presents the appearance of anomaly, of preservation of excellent components which had their heyday long ago. It preserved some essential characteristics of the Ancient mode of production in a rather hybrid fashion: its considerable slave base; its structure of cities, no longer free, yet accustomed to freedom and largely running themselves, through an increasingly bureaucratic and ecclesiastical elite which yet included many wealthy urban-living landowners. The empire was full of cities of great historic achievement in culture and commerce, still commanding profound respect, but hardly immune from destruction if they fell foul of political upheavals.

The new Rome was in part continuation, in part striking contrast with the old. The Senate was weaker, its lands more scattered, with fewer dependants. It could not block imperial access to the vital sources of manpower and peasant production, as the Senate in Rome had done by posing as their protectors. There was no pope to cancel out imperial power. In Constantinople the emperor was unequivocally head of the church as well as the state. Under his authority and the growing ecclesiastical power he had nurtured, society, art and culture were integrated in a theocratic whole. Power and factional struggles were defined and fought in passionately theological terms. Literary creation of poetry, drama and history appeared as hymns, liturgy and the lives of saints. Music was chants and hymn tunes. Art was icons and mosaics. The Christian ethic as perceived was sternly imposed by the emperor's authority reinforcing the ubiquitous jurisdiction of the ecclesiastical hierarchy.

The knot of corruption was cut. With neither Rome's murderous gladiatorial combats nor Europe's later flamboyant chivalry, the entertainment of the populace and the diversion of the mob depended on the hippodrome, compulsory church attendance and constant ecclesiastical festival celebrations. The icon of Christ accompanied the armies, but war was despised by the urban elite and there was general reluctance to kill, with the bizarre result that mutilation became the commonest punishment: loss of eyes or limbs for major crimes, lopping of ears or branding for lesser offences. Rivals for the throne often put out one another's eyes. Eunuchism reached Rome from Persia via Diocletian and was widely adopted in Byzantium. Eunuchs were useful to guard ladies and act as secretaries and medical attendants. But they also became soldiers, high officers, successful generals and patriarchs. It was no shame to castrate a son to advance his career.

After Justinian the episcopocracy centred in Constantinople retained and even increased its concentration of functions. In the eighth century the provinces were reorganized as *themes*: territorial and population groups under the civilian and military command of landowner–generals.

The southern and eastern parts of the empire (Palestine, Syria, Egypt and Mesopotamia) had fallen to the Islamic Arab expansion, while Avars and Bulgars threatened the north-west. The remaining empire recovered strength in the ninth and tenth centuries and the absolute autocracy of the emperor increased, as Basil II declared himself to be the law. The bureaucracy was enlarged, paid directly by the emperor. The prefect of the city had enormous powers of control. The Senate was abolished. The balance of power swung in favour of the magnates of the *themes*. Their military success increased their influence and they pressed for warrior emperors rather than the civilian candidates favoured by the sophisticated, anti-militarist bureaucracy in Constantinople, who wanted civil service expansion, lucrative offices and grandiloquent titles.

Either way taxes increased, peasants fell into debt, selling out to the landowners and becoming tenants. This undermined the military success based on first sons giving hereditary service to the army while their brothers worked their lands.

This urban–rural conflict of interest came to resemble the antagonism of town and country in the Feudal mode of production in Europe. Emperors tried to prevent this feudalization by forbidding further land acquisition either by military magnates or churches, and by banning further monasteries. But after Basil II (976–1025) came weak and disputed emperors, and empresses, quite unfit for absolute autocracy. Yet the dwindling empire remained remarkably prosperous and the great city culturally brilliant. Damaging attacks continued, by Mongols and Turks from the east and, worst of all, Christian crusaders from the west.

Genoa eventually helped the Byzantines win back Constantinople from the Venetians who had taken it in the fourth Crusade. But Genoese impositions became intolerable so the Byzantines switched back to Venetian aid against them. The city was only a shadow of its former self. The last two centuries were increasingly pathetic and ignominious, as emperors went to beg help from monarchs all over Europe and tried to win papal support by betraying their own orthodox faith, infuriating their own citizenry.

As the Turks finally closed in, it was as if the city of God's vice-gerent, however enfeebled, was itself sacrosanct and immune to siege, so interminable were the delays, as though the Greeks felt that the sultan, by taking the city, must thereby himself become a Christian emperor. They made half-hearted preparations for defence of the ever impregnable city, and when the huge stone cannonballs broke down the gates and towers allowing the soldiers in, the planned pillage, enslaving and removal of the population was a woeful and inglorious anti-climax.

Magnificent triumph as adoption of Christianity and the switch from Rome to Constantinople was, it held no promise for the future, except preservation of the *status quo*. It was programmed for perfecting absolutism and hypertrophy, not freedom. The Prince of Peace who came to set his people free appeared there in his absolutist mode as Christ ΠαVTOKραTWρ (all powerful). It was the largest, richest, most splendid city in Europe, a great pilgrimage centre, to which Viking princes from Scandinavia sailed for the honour of serving, and Anglo-Saxon adventurers displaced by William the Conqueror also took refuge. The priceless relics from the Holy Land, to which the True Cross stolen by the Persians had been restored, were gradually dispersed throughout Europe, in a slow trickle which became a flood with the Crusades. It was the cynosure that other cities strove to emulate but could not reproduce. Yet it was their confused strivings which led to innovative forms of urban life in the west, which held the seeds of unimagined change and progress.

4   Cities of the Feudal mode of production in Europe

Chapter 4 portrays the decline of Rome and the cities of western Europe fol- lowed by the emergence of the Feudal mode of production and its characteristic merchant cities, culminating in the world cities which ushered in the Atlantic Age.

A narrative of city destinies: the self-destruction of Rome, early city-states and cities struggling in ruins

The city of Rome survived the repeated attacks of Huns and Goths, the loss of treasure and of population, as a skeleton. Its elite was cut off from its far-flung landed income. It never died, but dwindled from a million people to a quarter of a million in the fifth century, less than 50,000 in the sixth and less than 30,000 in the eleventh century. Only a quarter of the space within the walls was occupied, the rest reverting to gardens, pas- tures and waste, not fully occupied again until the nineteenth century.

Alaric tired of unkept promises and pillaged Rome for three days in 455. The Romans themselves were stripping the city of building stone and specially marble. During Belisarius' attempt at reconquest the city was besieged three times, its aqueducts were cut and for a while its inhab- itants abandoned it. In 846 it was plundered by the Muslims. Finally in 1527 the Christian Emperor Charles V's armies plundered for eight days, destroying thousands of houses, churches and palaces.

It is said that the Romans bequeathed nothing urban except fortifications and the 'habit of living in towns' (Clarke, 1926:10). Nothing could be more significant than this habit. It kept alive the view that rural areas should be governed by cities and that only cities are civilized. By the end of the sixth century Pope Gregory I had little choice but to take on the administration of the city. Characteristically, he came of a Roman patrician family, grandson of a former pope, son of a Roman magistrate, and had already been prefect of the city before he became pope (Bury, 1889:150–2). For over 200 years the popes were an effective autonomous political force, ruling the shrunken city-state and papal territories, still nominally under the secular protection of the eastern emperors and their now barbarian exarchs at Ravenna. Rome flowed with money from the piety of the faithful, and with people from the lure of sanctity or the hope of profitable sinecures. Even in the fourth century, after the Gothic invasion, Bologna, Modena, Piacenza and other great north Italian cities had wide ruined spaces within their walls (Luzzato, 1961:6). Belisarius' brief reconquest (535–53) brought greater general devastation and within twenty years Italy was over-run by the Lombards, part pagan, part Arian, both equally hostile to the church of Italy and to Roman institutions. Last of the barbarians, they were the first to settle permanently in Italy, dividing it into 'dukedoms' (Latin *dux* = leader). They sometimes recognized an overall king and sometimes did not, remaining autonomous for long periods. The Roman landed class finally disappeared, replaced by Lombard feudal lords. Yet the popes were able to dissuade the Lombards from attacking Rome itself and Ravenna, capital of Italy, was not taken till 739.

Many inland cities were over-run and devastated, but retained a skeleton of ecclesiastical organization, still acting as cultural magnets, drawing and assimilating greater or lesser lords into them as feudal authorities or aristocratic urban residents. Great magnates had a stake, through property ownership, in both town and country. They often resided and participated in the life of several cities, as well as numerous rural estates and castles.

When Byzantine protection through Ravenna lost all reality, the popes turned to the increasingly powerful Frankish kings to counteract the Lombards and inaugurated the extraordinary dual sovereignty of priest with secular power and king with spiritual grace which emerged as the Holy Roman Empire with Leo III's crowning of Charlemagne in St Peter's, Rome, in AD 800. It was a brilliant manoeuvre which suited and strengthened them both at the time, though they quickly became bitter rivals, as manifested long after in the urban factions of Guelf (usually Florence, Bologna, Orvieto, Montepulciano) and Ghibelline (usually Pisa, Siena, Arezzo, Pistoia) favouring pope and emperor respectively.

The Lombard capital, Pavia, prospered, but did not play a prominent part in subsequent events. Ravenna was on a protected island in the swampy mouths of the Po, selected as a refuge by the timid Emperor Honorius. It escaped to house the supreme achievements of western Byzantine ecclesiastical art, but invasions and revolts in the eighth century reduced it to insignificance.

As the Lombards were not seafarers, several southern ports escaped their attentions. Amalfi, Naples, Sorrento, Bari, Palermo and others became independent maritime republics under nominal Byzantine rule.

They developed a flourishing commerce in the sixth, seventh and eighth centuries with Greece, Byzantium and the newly conquered Arab lands, Syria, Egypt and North Africa, where the great Islamic cities of Cairo, Tunis and Kairouan were founded (Luzzato, 1961:20). 'The rise of Amalfi . . . is explained by the port's early privileged contacts with Islam' (Braudel, 1985, II:106). Arab, African and Italian merchants dealt together in its streets (Luzzato, 1961:50). It had colonies of merchants in Constantinople, Antioch, Rome and many Adriatic cities. Squeezed between the mountains and the sea, it was driven to commit itself whole-heartedly to maritime ventures, suffering the misfortune of conquest by the Normans and two plunderings by Pisa in the twelfth century, followed by a devastating tidal wave in the fourteenth.

Palermo throve precariously under a bewildering succession of over-lords: Roman, Vandal, Goth, Arab, Norman, German, French and Spanish, from the fifth to the thirteenth century. It flourished under the Arabs as the capital of the emirate of Sicily and emporium of the profitable trade with North Africa, attracting merchants from all over the Mediterranean. As capital of Norman Sicily from 1072 to 1194 it reached a peak of prosperity and cosmopolitan Latin, Greek, Arab and Jewish culture. Its brilliance continued under the Emperor Barbarossa until his mass deportation of Arabs led to economic and population decline. Palermo still survived through many changes of dynasty, but never again became a free city. Exquisite Arab silk-weaving techniques passed from Palermo to Lucca, which became pre-eminent in silk textiles and passed its workers on to the Venetian silk guild in 1314.

In northern Italy and Gaul most cities suffered a prolonged eclipse between the sixth and ninth centuries. The Roman armies and fleets had gone. The roads were overgrown and pirates infested the seas. The Muslim invasion of the Mediterranean threatened the economic system on which prosperity had depended. Merovingian Gaul was still maritime, trade and traffic flourished, whereas the Carolingian Empire was inland and isolated, as its abandonment of gold coinage demonstrated (Pirenne, 1925:24–5). South Italian cities in touch with Byzantium retained it and the new gold ducats, florins and genovinos of Venice, Florence and Genoa marked the thirteenth-century recovery and Europe's capacity to replace the Muslims' debased dinar (Spufford, 1963:590).

'In Italy social and economic development went on without a break . . . but in Gaul, the Rhineland, the Danube and Spain, Roman municipal organization disappeared' (Ennen, 1967:175), yet the church maintained an ecclesiastical shadow of it (cf. Pirenne, 1925:42). The cities decayed, dwindled and retrogressed, incapable of any significant creativity or innovation. If they were to survive they must defend themselves and govern themselves. 'The town ceased to be an essential organization of the public life of the state' (for often the state was not effectively present), 'and the countryside acquired a political significance of its own' (Ennen, 1967:175). A reversal of the Roman situation. Antagonism of town and country, as Marx said. As population fell and economic life disintegrated, forests took over north-western Europe, leaving most settlements except the struggling remains of cities isolated and small, dependent on local subsistence economy.

Venice, never a Roman city, arose poetically from the settlement of refugees on the nests of seabirds, protected like Ravenna in its tangle of islands, a unique city of water 'with canals instead of streets' (Toynbee, 1967:48). Recognized by Byzantium as a dukedom in the seventh century and active in trade with Constantinople, it achieved independence by the eighth century under its *doge* (duke) elected by the wealthy merchant elite. Landlords, clergy and others fleeing from the Lombards had escaped to the swamps and islands, safe from attack and well supplied with fish and salt. The Rialto became the city centre and seat of government by the ninth century. By the tenth and eleventh centuries merchants of other Po valley towns, Ferrara, Mantua, Cremona, Piacenza and Milan began to participate in the Venetian trade (Luzzato, 1961:59).

Milan had been the Roman capital in the fourth century, devastated by Huns in 452, Goths in 539, maintaining only a thread of continuity through its archbishops, who rebuilt its walls in the ninth century and presided over its resuscitation so successfully that the citizens turned upon the church, winning civic autonomy in 1045. It began to fight for supremacy among its neighbours. When it destroyed Como, the Emperor Barbarossa laid siege and nearly destroyed Milan. After fleeing to the countryside the Milanese rebuilt with the protection of the Lombard League and returned to prosperity after Barbarossa's defeat in 1176. Milan became very strong with its large population, great cloth and arms industries and rich agriculture, yet unable to resist imperial intrusion, or to achieve effective popular institutions, remaining under the despotic Torre, Visconti and Sforza. Lucca won its charter in 1118 with less violence. Pisa and Florence achieved communal independence by force of organization and relentless pressure against bishops and feudal authorities. Many of the Italian city-states excluded nobles from citizenship during the thirteenth century.

Genoa, with an ancient Etruscan and Phoenician as well as Roman background, survived under Byzantine protection as a centre of commerce, until, like Pisa, it fell to the Lombards in the seventh century and lay part ruined till the tenth. Both Genoa and Pisa recovered from Lombard as well as Arab attacks, to sally forth on the seas, rivalling Venice and the southern cities, taking the offensive successfully against the Arabs (Villari, 1895:91; Luzzato, 1961:55) and prospering from the opportunities brought by the Crusades (Villari, 1895:72–3).

Marseilles was founded by Phoenicians, then Ionian Greeks, itself then founding Arles, Nice, Antibes, Agde and La Ciotat as its colonies. Its university was the last centre of Greek learning in the west, but siding against Julius Caesar caused its undoing and it was almost extinct when repopulated in the tenth century, prospering as a transit port for the Crusades. Lyons could not escape its destiny at the meeting of two great rivers, the strategic Rhone–Saône confluence. It became the prosperous capital of Gaul under Augustus. At the end of the second century its Christians were badly persecuted and having backed the wrong emperors, it was sacked and its aqueducts cut, condemning it to a long obscurity. But it remained a prominent archbishopric, scene of thirteenth-century church councils and in 1312 annexed to France. Economic prosperity came only in the fifteenth and sixteenth centuries, when Italian merchant bankers made it a major commercial capital and its silk industry achieved prominence.

The Phoenician and Carthaginian city of Barcelona came under Visigothic then Muslim domination, but was rescued by Charlemagne's successor and prospered under independent counts in the tenth and eleventh centuries, consolidating its hold on the rest of Catalonia. After union with Aragon in the twelfth century, its merchants won the right to elect their own council of a hundred and were rivalling Genoa and Venice in their sea-borne commerce till the fourteenth century, when plague and the Aragonese transfer to Naples caused a decline. Seville on the Guadalquivir (sc. Arabic *wad-el-kebir* Great River) grew as a Roman settlement near Tartessus whose minerals brought Greeks and Phoenicians from the other end of the Mediterranean.

The Rhine was the major boundary of the western empire and Cologne its major city, a Roman colony named after the Emperor Claudius' wife Agrippina who was born there. The secessionist general Postumus ruled Gaul, Britain and Spain from here from AD 258 to 268. Constantine built a castle and a bridge (310). Ceramics and glass were manufactured. There was a Christian community from the second century, with a bishop by 313. Hanging on through the dark centuries, Cologne was made an archbishopric by Charlemagne. The archbishop received many tolls, customs and other payments. His interests and those of the merchants became diametrically opposed. In 1288 the citizens defeated the archbishop, winning full self-government, under exclusively patrician rule until 1396, then a council elected by twenty-two guild branches with power over all internal and external affairs. Cologne was fortunate in highly varied craft production, including textiles, metalworking, goldsmithing, enamel, leather, wine selection, books and university schools where Thomas Aquinas, Duns Scotus and Albertus Magnus all taught.

Worms and many cities of the Rhine and Saxony rose against their bishops in 1073–4. Many bishops never returned, establishing residence elsewhere. Worms won freedom as an imperial city by battle in 1156. Liège won a charter from its bishop in 1195, as did Laon by revolt, but had its privileges quashed by the king of France. Cambrai suffered from many conflicting feudal claims but won recognition from its bishop in 1227 after a long struggle (Pirenne, 1925:127–80).

In the twelfth century (1143) Adolf of Holstein with assistance from Cologne merchants called for settlers from Flanders, Frisia and Westphalia to establish themselves in the island of Lübeck, which grew rapidly into a city dominating the Baltic and Russian trade in furs, fish (herring and cod), butter, copper and iron. Lübeck developed its own self-government, constitution and laws, which in the thirteenth century were granted to over a hundred other cities. Out of this developed the Hanseatic League which made its headquarters at Lübeck. It coordinated merchant interests from the Baltic to the Rhineland and London until the fifteenth century (Braudel, 1985, III:102–6). Many of the German merchants of the Hansa network were members of the same families (Rorig, 1970:36). Lübeck held a territory of 240 villages, and Erfurt 83 villages in 610 square kilometres. The Teutonic Knights, noted for their savagery towards the Slavs, pushed further east founding more towns.

These Baltic traders met the Mediterranean traders at Bruges. Though sea transport was cheap it was an exceedingly long way round, so as roads became safer, routes developed from north to south and west to east. Venice had a monopoly on the Brenner pass to Innsbruck, Augsburg and Nuremberg through to Lübeck. Bruges merchants went east through Cologne, Regensburg and Vienna to Kiev and Novgorod. Lübeck trade and prosperity were disrupted by the Reformation and wars with Denmark, Sweden and the Netherlands. Lübeck lost its position as the Hanseatic League disintegrated and new trading patterns were oriented towards the New World. Lübeck retained a more modest local prosperity.

The greater Italian cities had groups of merchant financiers spread through the network, at London, Paris, Montpellier, Nîmes and Barcelona in the west; Cyprus, Antioch, Constantinople and Alexandria in the east. From their arrival in Bruges, Italian bankers dominated the finances of western Europe for centuries.

Background to the new era: the movement of peoples and mode of production

The destinies of cities unfolded in the context of the movement of peoples and consequent upheavals which swept away the dominant institutions of the old mode of production, leaving a more flexible situation in which the new could develop. Most regular long-distance trade collapsed, luxuries became rare and wealth declined. Wars, raids, famines and loss of hope brought declining populations. People became hermits and retired to monasteries. The cities tried to repair their defences, but became hollow shells without means of subsistence. Invasions rippled on, cresting with the Vikings sailing up every river on the Atlantic and western Mediterranean coasts, plundering every city they found. The towns nearly died in most places and a new type of city struggled through its birth pangs on their ruins or on new sites.

The barbarian[1] invasions offer a historical panorama of evolving political economies: small-scale, kinship-based, agro-pastoral societies from as far as Scandinavia and the steppes of Asia, utterly rural people displaced by misfortune but increasingly attracted by the fabled glamour of a great urban culture. Once egalitarian, possibly peaceful communities, embroiled in long conflict, compelled to become warriors, chose strong leaders and fought for survival. Some succumbed, others won supremacy over larger groupings, turning into kings, with larger shares of booty, making inequalities of wealth and differences of rank, as leaders consolidated their powers, endeavouring to transmit them to their sons and turn elective into hereditary kingship. The barbarians thus developed just those institutions from which Greeks and Romans had escaped. When they were able to stop migrating and settle, land was distributed according to rank. Kings and favoured followers got larger shares and claimed contributions of labour to work them. The happenstance of generations created rudimentary classes of nobles, free commoners and dependants. Commoners owned and worked their lands and herds, contributing to king and nobles in labour or in kind for their services of leadership and protection, while landless dependants worked for others. Fierce fighting with Roman legions, or hostile rivals, intensified social differentiation. None the less the notion of free men banded together under chosen leaders to fight for freedom, land and wealth was tenacious.

Clovis: epitome of the age

The intricate interweaving of city and countryside, Christian and pagan, Roman, Byzantine and barbarian, in the personal networks and individual metamorphoses of human lives is vividly portrayed by Clovis, founder of the Frankish kingdom, grandson of Merovech, eponym of the age. His father Childeric led his band of Salian Franks from the north-east, became accepted as a 'federate' and thus legitimated and appropriated by the Romans, ruling a petty principality from the ancient Roman city of Tournai, effectively controlled by able Gallo-Roman bishops. There were many other sections of Franks. Even the Salians had numerous kings. Clovis, born about 466, set about eliminating these and conquering northern Gaul, by defeating its last Roman ruler, Syagrius, and seizing his treasury, just ten years after the displacement of the last supposed Roman emperor of the west.

Meeting some resistance from the cities, he established his rule at Paris,[2] marrying a Burgundian princess. He was greatly influenced by advice from the bishops of Reims, Tours and Burgundy, invoking St Martin of Tours as his patron, conquering the Visigoths south of the Loire and finally accepting baptism at Reims with 3,000 of his warriors. The distant Byzantine Emperor Anastasius, in a further gesture of appropriation, conferred on him the insignia of an honorary consul of Rome. He called a church council at Orleans attended by thirty-two bishops.

Tournai became one of the great textile centres of Flanders, under the counts from the ninth century, till France recovered it, granting a charter in 1188. It was sufficiently far from the reach of feudal power to become an effectively free, self-governing, city-state.

Three centuries later, Clovis' successor Charlemagne led the Franks to conquer northern Italy and most of Germany, proclaiming a second Roman Empire with support from a needy pope. Despite this long evolution of the political economy, Charlemagne's action could only emphasize how utterly different his empire was from its prototype. For he and all the other invaders lacked the economic and technical resources to maintain an empire of the extent he momentarily achieved, a paid civil service, a money economy, a standing army, a fixed capital city, network of supporting cities administering the rural areas and collecting taxes, a maintained network of roads and communications and a navy. The infrastructure had gone and the level of production was too low. When victorious expansion and booty ceased, neither common soldiers nor nobles were willing to serve in the army, whose campaigns were limited to the summer months. There was no continuous supply of slaves for large-scale, specialized production. Slavery was not abolished but it was not essential either.

Charlemagne attempted a civil service bureaucracy of courts, each attached to a city where one existed. But the norms and culture of civil servant and feudal magnate were hopelessly contradictory. As always, these functionaries tended to become hereditary, despite Charles' intention. This and the obligatory partitioning of each generation precluded the achievement of bureaucratic empire. No personnel capable of creating and maintaining cities in the Roman way existed in Charlemagne's realm. Charles and his nobles wanted the luxury products of cities badly enough, but they would have to be created by those who needed them most and really made them, the merchants and craftsmen.

The barbarians came as mixed farmers, some with a strong pastoral emphasis. They enjoyed communal forms of tenure, giving equal access to arable and pasture, which by the time of Charlemagne had produced the open-field system which became the dominant form of exploitation throughout Europe apart from the Mediterranean areas. In the typical lord's manor, at least half the arable was held in open fields by the free peasants. It was divided into three huge fields, in each of which every peasant owned a strip. Managing the third year fallow for communal grazing and working the heavy plough, which might need up to eight oxen, necessitated working communally as a co-ordinated group. The iron plough which the barbarians brought may actually have been superior to that in use in the Roman Empire, where the Mediterranean areas were often of lighter soil and with their extensive vineyards and olive groves had to be worked in a different way and were sometimes irrigated (cf. Braudel, 1985, I:114; Duby, 1978:189–94).

The transformation

Transformation from the Ancient to the Feudal mode of production was epitomized economically by the passage from large-scale, slave-worked latifundia to the small-scale open-field system run by local peasants in equal shares collectively under the lord's demands. Politically, it was the change from vast territories managed and administered by cities owned and run collectively by their wealthy elites, to the hierarchy of larger and smaller fiefs to which conquerors like Clovis had to devolve their powers of control and exploitation, because they were equipped with no other means of minimally holding on to what they had won. Charlemagne briefly broke through this necessity by his bold attempt at a bureaucratically administered empire, after which Europe relapsed into it again for many centuries. On the other hand, Clovis and his forebears for the previous four or five centuries represent the gradual but radical and revolutionary passage from the more egalitarian Kinship mode of production (Southall, 1988a:184–8) to the Feudal mode.

From the fifth to the ninth century the Frankish kingdom was intermittently unified under Clovis, Charles Martel and Charlemagne, but in the long interludes it was split into four or more kingdoms by the system of equal inheritance among sons, who fought among themselves. After Charlemagne his empire split again and again, with occasional attempts at reviving the imperial title at least nominally, in which the pope joined from time to time. Despite constant splits, the units were still far larger than the Germanic kings had been accustomed to lead at the time of invasion. Successor kings tried to control larger areas by distributing lands to bind faithful followers to them. The units so maintained were still too large for one ruler to administer effectively with the human, technical and organizational resources available to him. He had to give away his powers of exploitation to his supporting magnates also (Duby, 1978:45–6).

The pristine community of the anointed leader with his huge establishment, feeding all his knights and principal followers, all drinking together convivially, had broken up into a feudal hierarchy. Much greater social and also spatial distance separated anointed rulers from fiefholders and the latter from peasants, tenants and agricultural serfs. New techniques of administration, recording and control had been learned from the encounters with the Romans and from the urban bishops, abbots and clerics of the church, itself now the largest landholder. Decentralization enabled the local lord to be more autocratic and exploitative than the early kings could be, reducing the rural population to a state of bondage (Duby, 1978:45–6).

The local lords, lay and clerical, demanded merchants and craftsmen to supply any procurable luxuries. All aspired to live in Roman style, symbolized by bread, wine, oil, marble and gold (Duby, 1978:57). The earliest urban nuclei formed in the lord's great household and later outside the walls of his castle. As merchants and craftsmen became more wealthy, numerous and better organized, they sought greater independence from the lord's establishment and eventually struggled to create urban communities of their own. The lords did not entirely oppose the process, knowing that the greater wealth would benefit them too. It was an endless bargaining struggle, often violent, with taxes and services agreed to in return for franchises and freedoms. In this way towns took over the major economic action from the great estates.

In favourable situations victorious overlords set themselves up in cities, occupied palaces and enjoyed the baths and amphitheatres, at Verona, Pavia, Piacenza, Lucca, Toledo and even the ruins of Cologne and the old Roman towns of England. 'Cities had taken on a country aspect', vineyards were planted, shops deserted (Duby, 1978: 57). Around all towns in Gaul, a ring of monastic foundations had been established a short distance from the fortified nucleus since the sixth century. Rulers established courts in Cologne, Mainz, Trier, Speyer, Worms, Salzburg,

Augsburg and Regensburg. The Vikings founded states round Rouen and York.

Accelerated revival

This urban twilight ended during the tenth and eleventh centuries with brisk development and population growth in the leading economic areas.

Some creative flowerings hardly fit a linear exposition. The Vikings burst out of Scandinavia in the ninth century, supposedly because of overpopulation, to terrorize western Europe by savage raids up every river, the last significant barbarian invasion of the west, barbarians invading barbarians. Credited with accelerating the disintegration of Charlemagne's realm and the development of feudalism, their raiding was potential trading and they could turn from fiercesome attacks to settling farms and building cities with lightning rapidity. Unable to expel them, the king of France bestowed on them the territory of three dioceses, as the emperors had done with the *federati*, making their leader duke of Normandy in 911 and watching while they became Christians and constructed the strongest and best governed fief in France.

Norman Vikings conquered south Italy and Sicily, creating another of the best-governed states in twelfth-century Europe with a splendid capital city at Palermo. As Varangians they sailed up and down the Russian rivers, founding the great trading city-state of Novgorod, organizing the city-state of Kiev and reaching Constantinople to form the emperor's crack Varangian guard.

Normans achieved the greatest architectural feats of the time in the great abbeys and cathedrals of Rouen, Caen, Bayeux, Evreux and Lisieux in France; Durham, Winchester, Ely, Peterborough and many more in England. This florescence led immediately into the astonishing burst of Gothic abbey and cathedral building at St Denis, Reims, Notre Dame de Paris, Chartres, Amiens, etc. Stupendous cultural and material effort occurring in the very heat of the struggle between the kings of France and the Normans, now powerfully based in England, as well as Normandy and Anjou, which culminated in the recovery of much lost territory by Philip Augustus in the thirteenth century.

The superlatively massive, richly carved structures of the Normans aptly symbolized the orderly strength and expertise of their political arrangements, like the Domesday Survey, said to be the most remarkable administrative accomplishment of the Middle Ages, made at formal sessions in each county town.

The king of France sent Abbot Suger to Normandy on diplomatic missions to King Henry I of England, duke of Normandy. He was immensely impressed by the achievements of the efficient Norman government, compared with the chaotic feudalism of France. Suger returned to St Denis and created the new Gothic style of architecture by rebuilding two ancient basilicas into the great abbey of St Denis where all French kings were buried. There followed the breathtaking splendours of Notre Dame de Paris, Chartres and the rest, culminating in the exquisite Sainte-Chapelle, for relics brought by Louis IX from the Crusades (1248).

All these cities of northern France were dominated by their huge cathedrals, capable of holding many times their total populations. They had schools for training clerics, under the authority of their chancellors. That of Paris was the greatest. Here Abelard taught dialectic and theology until disputes caused him to lead his students across the Seine to the Abbey of Sainte-Geneviève. The faculty of arts was divided into four nations: France, Normandy, England and Picardy, each with its own professor and students. Here the residential college of the Sorbonne was founded about 1257. Many universities sprouted from this model, in Oxford, Cambridge and widely in Europe.

Thus urbanization, migration and warfare, political economy, art and architecture, religion and education, subtly intertwined to lay the foundation for the cultural supremacy of Paris for centuries to come, spearheading the general élan of urban revival in north-west Europe, with an ebullient enthusiasm almost beyond what material facts seemed to warrant.

The cities revived with very small populations. At first hardly any exceeded 10,000, but by the fifteenth century Florence, Venice and Milan may have reached 100,000, Paris perhaps 80,000; Bologna, Genoa, Siena, Palermo and Ghent between 50,000 and 60,000; Cologne, London, Barcelona, Montpellier, Verona and Cremona from 40,000 to 50,000. Lübeck and Bruges were never much over 30,000; Augsburg, Nuremberg, Lyons, Marseilles, Rouen, Avignon, Brussels, Antwerp, Lucca, Magdeburg, Worms, Ulm and Brunswick even fewer. 'In Germany as a whole in the late middle ages, 3,000 places were reckoned to have been granted the status of cities: their average population was no more than 400 individuals' (Braudel, 1985, I:482). In the sixteenth century Antwerp may have reached 100,000, Amsterdam 200,000 by 1700 (Braudel, 1985, III:187). All estimates are tentative. The density of the greater cities seems to have been about 200 per hectare (Russell, 1972: *passim*).

The growth of population and of cities between 1100 and 1350 was accompanied by growth of production and trade, but followed by an extremely sharp recession (Braudel, 1985, I:3). The expansion mani-

Plate 2 Périgueux, on the site of a great Roman city and a Celtic capital before that, shows the northwards spread of the Byzantine dome. The cathedral is surrounded by twelfth- to fifteenth-century buildings and market squares of merchants and notables in the old city.

fested the energy of Europe and gave it confidence. The impetus 'must have originated in pressure exerted by the seigneurial power on productive forces', arising from the desire of churchmen and warriors to increase their consumption 'in the service of God or for their own self-esteem' (Duby, 1978:177). Tremendous stimulus was imparted by the 'fantastic adventure of the Crusades, which really launched the trading fortunes of Christendom and Venice' (Braudel, 1985, III:109–10).

The feudal barons, especially from France, ruined themselves to pay their expenses, mortgaging or transferring their estates, but often bringing great booty home if they survived. Giant transport ships were built in the yards of Genoa, Pisa and Venice. Many difficult and uncontrollable knights took off for the east, where large numbers were killed, enabling their sovereigns to consolidate their kingdoms and improve public order. Despite the outpouring of piety, the Crusades were also a series of

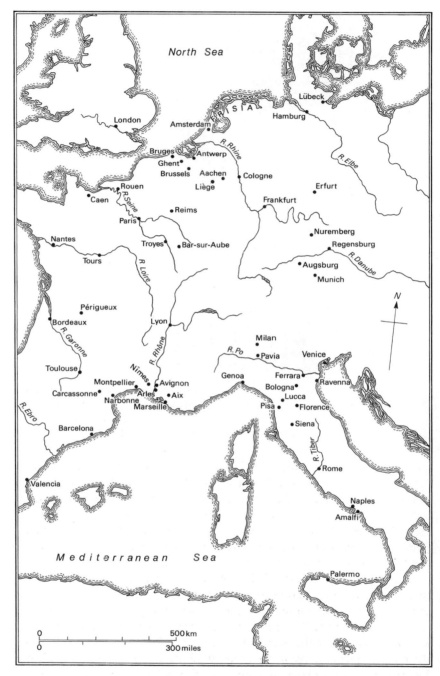

Map 2 Cities of the Feudal mode of production in medieval Europe

fabulously profitable plundering expeditions. The pepper, spices, silk and drugs fed into the Champagne Fairs, making the Italian traders and financiers that much more indispensable, but they also desperately needed the Flanders cities' cloth for their own trade to the Levant.

The Crusades were largely fought by the chivalry of the rural north-west, profitably transported by the traders and ships of the urban south-east, Venice, Genoa and Pisa. The Crusaders achieved the precise opposite of their declared goals. They were pilgrims who had 'taken the Cross', but they pillaged and sacked Jerusalem, which they had gone to save, slaughtering 70,000 inhabitants (Muir, 1896). For three days they pillaged and sacked Constantinople, at whose emperor's request they had gone in the first place.

The fourth Crusade (1202–4) gave Venice effective sovereignty over the coastal areas of three-eighths of the empire, with facilities for churches in every city taken by Crusaders. There had been tens of thousands of Italians at Constantinople, intermarrying at first then bringing their wives, living along the Golden Horn, administered by their own officials, paying homage and large taxation to the emperor (Runciman, 1952:99–101). The Genoese had thirty houses at Antioch and the Pisans a whole quarter in Jaffa, the main centre of trade between Palestine and the west (Luzzato, 1961:73–6). The Crusaders accentuated the demand for oriental products, increasing the profits. The antagonistic elements of the Feudal mode of production were partially reversed, as the flower of rural chivalry from the west went east to conquer and inhabit Hellenistic–Muslim cities. The budding cities of the west were left that much freer to develop by their absence.

The great twelfth-century poles of development had been the cities of Flanders and Tuscany, whose traffic was bound to coagulate at some intermediate point. The plain of Champagne was ideal, because the count was only nominally subject to the king of France and could reap great benefit from giving protection to the fairs. Half a dozen little towns, 'centre of the international commercial activity of the Western World' (Verlinden, 1963:132), kept a sequence of large trading assemblies going, all with their accoutrements, throughout the year. Each fair went through six phases: entry and installation; rapid sale of cloth, sampled and shipped off by professional transporters and business carriers, pack trains over the Alps, carts on the plains; leathers from Muslim Spain (Cordoba, Morocco); spices; a month for bankers settling and closing out; on to the next fair. Jewish merchants and money-lenders were busy. Arras financiers from nearby made great fortunes there until the thirteenth century, when they were put out of business by the more skilful and powerful Italian bankers, from whom they learned a great deal.

It is impossible to find anything – income tax for instance, which did not have some precedent in the genius of one of the Italian republics . . . Everything seems to have been there in embryo: bills of exchange, credit, minted coins, banks, forward selling, public finance, loans, capitalism, colonialism – as well as social disturbances, a sophisticated labour force, class struggle, social oppression, political atrocities. (Braudel, 1985, III:91)

Florence developed cheques, holding companies, double entry book-keeping and simplified maritime insurance (de Roover, 1966:23–7). German cities developed municipal bonds and annuities (Rorig, 1970:163–4).

The thirteenth century was an era of buoyant confidence and growth, the fourteenth century one of malaise, starting with recession and deepening with the general catastrophe of the Black Death. That the psychological moods reflect the economic changes is also recognized, but the theoretical implications are usually disregarded. The harsh conditions of the fourteenth century culminated in the fiercest struggles of the urban workers to win constitutional freedoms and their savage repression by the ruling classes.

While cities and merchant wealth grew, the working class became more differentiated in multiplying crafts, trades and technical specialization, while the poor at the bottom grew in numbers only. 'The state was there to preserve inequality, the cornerstone of the social order' (Braudel, 1985, II:493). Obedience and good behaviour, with resignation to one's lot, were assiduously preached.

The urban poor were always there, the majority, rarely mentioned or noticed. Any demand for change on their part constituted a threat to the whole social order, calling forth the wrath of God and ferocious human retribution. One cannot prove that the poor were much more oppressed or worse off in the thirteenth than in the eleventh century. They were certainly more numerous, because of population growth and the escape of rural destitutes to the cities.

Commoditization and the arrogance of chivalry

Increasing urbanization meant increasing use of money and the commoditization of daily life at least for the city dweller. The extended family was dissolving into separate conjugal families fostering greater personal consciousness and individualism. All this was intensified by the first impact of population decline (combined with local pockets of over-population) and prolonged economic depression, in the fourteenth century bringing a veritable increase in class consciousness. Relative poverty vis-à-vis the ever more luxurious ruling classes raised the problem of inequality to new dimensions. Bad weather and more severe and frequent famines preceded the cataclysm of the Black Death which brought Europe to a standstill, closing off the period of expansion and prosperity. With the loss of half to a third of the population, labour was short, tending to force up wages, bringing draconian measures to force them down, and lengthen working hours, with savage death penalities for transgression, guilt attaching to the employed not the employer.

The brutal sufferings of the poor citizens of so many cities attach a damning stain on the high ideals of chivalry proclaimed by the nobles who remorselessly inflicted them. The mystique of chivalry, 'the dominant order of feudal society' (Duby, 1978:257), flowed from the blessing of the church and its association with the highest aspirations of mankind, always fully exploited as a potent political weapon, often with incalculable consequences. When it launched great armies as soldiers of Christ, 'taking the Cross' in the Crusades, it imparted new vigour to the sense of divine mission in the feudal ruling class (Duby, 1978:164, 167–8). They went on high adventure, seeking salvation and amassing plunder. So it was the holy message of the church transmuted in contact with secular society.

Despite the projected image of the courtly and Christian knight, when feudal chivalry savaged rebellious citizens protesting intolerable oppression, they were only exacting the same abject submission they demanded from their rural peasants. Protesters demanding basic human rights were criminal rebels against God's divinely sanctioned order. The high noble had the legitimate right, ordained by the state and blessed by the church, to claim his peasants as 'his men' from birth, with all their descendants, to sell, give away or punish as he wished, requiring unlimited labour in house and field (Duby, 1978:175). They could not marry without the lord's consent, and owed him part of their inheritance. Under banal lordship he could take everything from a peasant household: cash, crops, livestock and even labour: 'a kind of legitimized and organized pillage tempered only by the resistance of village communities' (Duby, 1978:176). Deprivation of rights in effect deprived the peasant of his humanity. There was no offence against him for which he had the power to hold his lord accountable. This was the monstrous situation from which the cities had partially escaped, to the greater profit and also the displeasure of the lords, who seized opportunities to extort the same inhuman sufferings from townsmen driven beyond endurance (Tuchman, 1979:382–97).

Chivalry felt it was their duty to destroy not produce wealth, to spend on entertainment without thought for cost and to live without turning a finger. The church maintained that work was a curse; for a well-born man to indulge in it could only be an ascetic experience. While economic realities were a secondary consideration and the real world was of the spirit, there was an accumulation of power 'to exploit the expansion of rural production, the profits from which served to support an ever more flamboyant style of living' (Duby, 1978:257–60).

Feudal expenditures constantly increased, with astronomical jumps in wartime. The merchants bore the first brunt, but simply increased their own exactions from the urban labour force. To the ruling class their needs were paramount. Emperors, kings, princes and feudatories were usually in debt to urban merchants and bankers for huge sums. When resources ran out, they felt no pressure to economize, but only to find new victims for borrowing and extortion. When a bankrupt sovereign, in the middle of a war he was losing, wished to celebrate a dynastic marriage alliance, no form of extravagance could be spared. 'The amount the rich could squander in a period of repeated disasters appears inexplicable . . . Where, in the midst of ruin and decline and lowered revenues from depopulated estates and towns, did all the money come from to endow the luxury?' (Tuchman, 1979:244–5). Ostentation and pageantry were expected of princes. 'Now it went to extremes, as if to defy the increased uncertainty of life. Conspicuous consumption became a frenzied excess' (Tuchman, 1979:244–5).

The total disregard for the suffering of those they oppressed complemented the egotistic arrogance of their behaviour in battle. The clash of armour in the shock of attack was the magic moment for which they lived. Whatever the tactics required, the knights refused to be cheated of their opening charge. They would rather cut to pieces their own men who stood in their way. Always over-confident, each insulting the other with braggart boasts, demanding to be first, they repeated their shameful folly at Crécy, Poitiers, Courtrai, Nicopolis, Agincourt and countless other engagements, where dozens of counts and bishops were slaughtered and captured for ransom by the common footsoldiers they despised. Their gorgeous glinting armour was so heavy that, once unhorsed in the mud, they could not get up. It is a tribute to the inexhaustible resources of France that it survived these costly disasters. But it still required rare good fortune for makeshift armies of untrained, poorly equipped urban artisans to prevail against the flower of French knighthood, as they miraculously did at Courtrai and Bruges. More usually they fought with the energy of despair, offered the choice to submit, to starve or fight against hopeless odds. They were butchered in thousands, tortured, hanged and burned alive. When they tried submission, with leading citizens kneeling humbly in their shirts with halters round their necks, offering large sums of money in penitence and crying for mercy, promises of immunity were often revoked on the ground that they had been extorted under pressure. Chivalry and honour did not count where commoners were concerned.

Merchants were the natural leaders in the cities, but their interests were hardly those of the workers. Leadership could not easily be expected from among the workers themselves. Occasionally populist leaders would arise from the merchant class, such as Jacob and Philip van Artevelde in Ghent, or Etienne Marcel in Paris. It took great moral courage for a commoner to stand up alone to the haughty scorn of the ruling class. Despised as a miscreant by the nobility, in an exposed position of mortal danger, preserving a calm and balanced approach was virtually impossible. With no institutional backing and few companions to support them, they drifted into arbitrary and autocratic behaviour, acting rashly in the heat of the moment.

The unquenchable charisma of royalty attained astounding levels. Reared to command from birth, sanctified by the sacred potency of coronation anointing, backed by the weight of generations and bred to secure confidence, Richard II of England could ride out serenely among 20,000 rebelling peasants and win them over to their destruction. The dauphin of France, trembling and cowering in his bed as his two marshals are slain at his feet by the men of Paris, could still summon the people to the Halles, speak to the crowd from horseback and turn it in his favour. No commoner had access to this source of magic success. 'The masses tend to be emotionally responsive to personal leadership' (Weber, 1958:177).

Although proletarian workers shared a vital commitment to the urban community, betrayal by the bourgeoisie often left them defenceless. 'The third estate is always anxious to imitate the nobility towards which it constantly seeks to raise itself, by *unbelievable efforts*' (d'Arcq, 1766:75–6).

The aristocracy was a small percentage of the whole and so were the wealthy merchants. The masses remained always poor, working poor, deserving poor and 'undeserving poor'. The increasing differentiation of society, of which the cities were the main motor, soon became an increasing polarization.

According to Marx, 'the mode in which they gained a livelihood' (1967:82) explains why Catholicism played the chief part although they 'could not live on it'. Could chivalrous monarchs, knights and nobles, decent human beings, as many must have been, live with the extreme hypocrisy of their God-given role of honour, purity and generosity in the face of the stark realities of brutal oppression by which they lived? The church had most land, and feudatories. Catholicism was a constant source of divine legitimacy, the king-pin which enabled them to believe in themselves despite all material appearances. The sublime clarity, or utter confusion, of the complementarily opposed roles in the axis of pope and emperor, on which the whole of Christendom hung, assisted in the delusion. For Christendom was the empire rather than the church. All pre-capitalist realms play upon this axis in one way or another, the Chinese by translating city, state and society into the eternal cosmos, Hindus by the fiction that it is really the sacred Brahmins who stand at the head of society and direct the world, or in the Buddhist reversal, clear-cut in Cambodia, or in Islam, where the ruler is in one way or another assimilated to the divine. Only the Greeks hit upon a pre-capitalist secular formula, as having dispensed with priest kings they were bound to do.

The urban class struggle

The geopolitical siting of Flanders in a fertile plain dissected by multiple waterways, near the North Sea teeming with fish, made it the natural outlet from Germany and northern France to England as well as the convenient intermediary on the sea-route from the Baltic to the Mediterranean. Precocious agricultural, pastoral and textile development in Frisia and the ancient rural subsistence weaving of Flanders attracted the Vikings and stimulated trading in many directions. Frisian cloaks were robes of splendour sent as gifts to Haroun-al-Rashid and the emperor in Constantinople. Merchants and craftsmen settling around the abbeys and the lords' castles from the tenth century began to form the earliest and densest cluster of commercial and manufacturing towns in north-west Europe. Bruges, Ghent, Ypres, Arras, Douai and Lille became the chief centres of wool manufacture, starting with local but later preferring English wool. Wealth from the land, sea and commerce supported a class of burghers who dominated the townsfolk economically and politically, pressing the counts for civil rights and privileges on behalf of all, though their interests diverged from those of the growing body of workers, especially the textile weavers, as much as from those of the feudal lords.

Bruges, Ghent and the other cities suffered centuries of intermittent, violent struggle between a diversity of conflicting interests, in constantly changing patterns of hostile confrontation and factional alliance. The burghers and workers, with their own varying factional subdivisions, were the permanent players, while counts of Flanders and Hainaut, dukes of Brabant and Burgundy, kings of France and England, finally Emperor Maximilian and the kings of Spain played devastatingly on a different dimension. The cities were destined to profit and to suffer, to grow, be destroyed, grow again and finally decline.

The class war centring on the Flemish weavers flared and smouldered through the thirteenth and fourteenth centuries. 'The violence of the conflict between capital and labour was never equalled in modern Europe' (Carus-Wilson, 1952:399). At Courtrai in 1302 the weavers and craft guilds won an extraordinary victory over the arrogant feudal chivalry, taking 700 gold spurs from fallen knights. At Cassel in 1328 the workers and peasants were massacred in thousands. Under the merchant populist leader Van Artevelde the urban militias rose again to defeat the count, who fled to France. The Black Death intervened. In 1379 Louvain killed seventeen nobles in the townhall and Ghent led the revolt against unjust taxes. The count suppressed Ypres and Bruges savagely, with many hanged and burnt to death. Ghent fought on relentlessly through sieges, truces, treacheries, blockades and starvation. Van Artevelde Jr forced the abbeys to release food, and led the militia to defeat the count again, driving him to Lille ignominiously on a mare. Fearing the spread of dangerous anti-ruling class subversion, France mounted a huge expedition, intimidating and humiliating many cities, exacting heavy payments. Artevelde raised a heroic force for a desperate stand, promising independent sovereignty for Flanders. They fought indomitably almost to victory but were taken in the rear by French cavalry. Artevelde and his unflinching standard bearer Big Margot were trampled to death by their own routed force. Still Ghent would not surrender, but clung on for years as pillaging, slaughtering, burning and banishing continued, until by accident of marriage, Burgundy acquired Flanders and wanting to salvage some prosperity concluded the conciliatory Peace of Tournai in 1385.

The weavers who survived were scattered abroad, to the benefit of England and France, and the detriment of Flanders. The struggle for urban freedom continued, Bruges and Ghent rising many times more in the fifteenth century, capturing and imprisoning the Emperor Maximilian in 1482, forced to surrender to his troops but rising again. Bruges was now nearly cut off from the sea and its merchants departed as Antwerp took its place. Ghent rebelled against Emperor Charles V in 1539 and again suffered heavily. It became a Calvinist republic from 1578 to 1584 and rebelled against Philip of Spain, but was forced to surrender. Its Protestant sympathizers emigrated *en masse*. In the ferocity of these encounters there were not only several tangled classes, but two conflicting modes of production, one outdated, the other struggling to be born.

The tragedy of the Flemish weavers cannot entirely dim 'the dazzling fortune of Bruges, . . . centre of a huge trading area, . . . no less than the Mediterranean, Portugal, France, England, the Rhineland and the Hansa . . . In the age of Jan van Eyck (c.1380–1440) and Memling (1435–94) it was unquestionably one of the finest cities in the world and certainly one of the most industrious' (Braudel, 1985, III:99–100).

By the time the count was subdued in 1284 and the fairs eclipsed by competition from the rising cloth industries of Milan and Florence, the Genoese had pioneered the long sea voyage to Bruges (1277), followed by other Italian cities and the Venetian galleys in 1314. Fifteen Italian cities had their palaces on the Place de la Bourse, worshipped in the same churches, established consulates and rode in gorgeous liveries at the ceremonial processions of feudal magnates (de Roover, 1948:14). Splendid as this was, it also displayed Italian superiority (Braudel, 1985, III:40). The greatest merchants of Bruges were foreigners.

The Champagne Fairs, followed by the sea routes, knit together the urban economies of Italy, western Europe and Germany, passing through rather than embedding themselves in France, as the great trading towns were on or over the borders. But Paris and the court drew on the European economy to display the most ostentatious luxury. France was the largest, richest, most populous and successful European state, with immense prestige from the achievements of her greater monarchs, yet allowed herself to become an economic backwater, as 'large scale trade and the capitalism it brought were carried on virtually outside French soil' (Braudel, 1985, II:116), diluting the effect of the twelfth-century renaissance (see above, pp. 100–1).

Meanwhile England was Europe's best organized and most closely integrated state and France's only rival, with the empire fragmented and Spain engrossed in its own liberation. Yet Paris was a great trading city, profiting from the presence of so many businessmen, the unremitting extravagance of the monarchy, the fount of chivalry, its expanding institutions and the building of a wealth of monuments, with the most distinguished university, attracting 'a turbulent horde of students from all over Europe' (Tuchman, 1979:159). The splendour and luxury of the court continued to increase, corrupting even the bourgeoisie, whose plutocrats were bent on imitating and outdoing the luxury around them, copying the highest aristocracy on the eve of revolution (Braudel, 1985, II:493), whereas 'merchants in Toulouse, Lyon or Bordeaux made little display of their luxury' (Braudel, 1985, II:493) and in England, with a less formal court, the Elizabethan peerage already led investment in foreign trade.

City government and guilds

Florence

Florence began as a Roman garrison town below Etruscan Fiesole, becoming a provincial capital and major crossroads with prosperous commerce. During the invasions life continued in the monasteries. The town began to revive and rebuild in the late eighth century. Bishops and counts allowed increasing autonomy as the commune forcefully asserted its independence, supported by the Tuscan League. The city-state of Florence was pre-eminent in industry, banking, the arts and architecture and in the agonizing and abortive struggle for freedom.

After subduing and ejecting aggressive nobles or winning them over to the cause of the city, the wealthy merchants and bankers dominated the city-state government through the public elected offices and the great guilds. Nobles had constructed innumerable urban towers as personal and factional strongholds. As they identified themselves and their prosperity more with that of the city (Villari, 1895:93) – to whose defence they could be useful – the towers were dismantled by the hundreds, in Florence and also in Pisa, Lucca, San Gimignano, Bologna, Pavia, Avignon, Toulouse and elsewhere. 'Town air made men free' but not equal. Rural serfs could take refuge and win freedom if they survived for a year and a day.

Florence had seven major guilds (*arti maggiore*): judges and notaries; Calimala (foreign wool and cloth); Arte della Lana (the great cloth merchants and manufacturers); silk merchants; money-changers and bankers; doctors and druggists; painters, mercers, skinners and furriers. They fought to exclude non-commercial nobility (proclaiming citizens as *grandi* excluded them from the franchise and council membership, as in Siena and Perugia), while trying to prevent the minor craft guilds from winning power. But they did gain in power as their increasing production gave greater wealth to the city, and as they allied themselves strategically to one leader and faction or another, occasionally organizing an uprising, winning an increasing share in councils and powerful offices, with many ups and downs as counter-revolutions and massacres deprived them of their gains from time to time. Growing wealth and population meant a large labour force employed by both major and minor guilds. This urban proletariat also began to make demands, claiming the right to extend guild organization to themselves as the way to power.

Florence enjoyed by turns 'popular' election of ruling consuls, 'monopolised by a few families' (Weber, 1958:130), rule by a 'foreign tyrant' chosen by themselves and her own distinctive rule by a combination of guild officials and civic magistrates. The incessant battles, bloodshed and destruction by the Guelfs, Ghibellines and other factions in Florence caused such distress and despair that the popular election of consuls broke down in the twelfth century as neutral foreign administrators were invited in as podestà. They had to give hostages to the city, but were given a salary and small army, as ceremonial head of the city, with complete civic and criminal jurisdiction, control of taxation, responsibility for foreign affairs and making treaties. They might be from an obscure little town like Gubbio, or be a great feudal figure like the French king's brother Charles of Anjou. Exiles from one city could dominate another. Florence dominated Pistoia by constantly getting a Florentine chosen as podestà and sometimes as captain of the people (Herlihy, 1967:223–4). The podestà might be driven out, or be re-elected and even establish a permanent tyranny. Bologna, Padua, Vicenza and many other cities struggled to prevent the podestà from consolidating absolute power through re-election, yet one after another won freedom from feudal control only to fall witlessly into another tyranny.

The podestà and captain of the people were both elected by the mass *parlamento* of the people gathered in the main square, which might be lined with militia as the notary asked whether a candidate was approved and a few shouted yes (Rubinstein, 1966:48). This seems like a sad parody of popular choice, yet it had been desperately fought for. Perhaps aspirations and ideals ran ahead of power to implement.

When the scrutineers had made up the lists for each post, another group of officials, the *accoppiatori*, put the names in bags and closed them until the lots were drawn. Then the podestà drew the lots in the presence of magistrates and public. Perhaps such a tedious diffusion of responsibilities guaranteed the integrity of the lottery. *Balia*, emergency power, could be voted to yet another council approved for a few months by the *parlamento* for the frequent crises of war, or fear of war. During such emergencies, the *accoppiatori* were sometimes authorized to choose an incumbent for each office from the bags by hand instead of by lot. To qualify as standard bearer of justice a citizen had to get the votes of twelve out of nineteen *accoppiatori* (Rubinstein, 1966:48). It was on these two devices, prolonging emergency powers and authorizing election by the *accoppiatori* instead of by lot, that the Medici relied most to maintain their regime in power. There was a great deal of overlapping membership and apparent circularity. For the statutory Council of the Commune and Council of the People, with several hundred members each, were also chosen by lot every four months (Rubinstein, 1966:14) from names in bags prepared by the same magistrates. The *balia*, after debate, could prolong the life of the *accoppiatori* and authorize them to choose by hand. Of twenty *accoppiatori* more than half were members of the *balia*! But the *balia* had several hundred members. Many of the chief magistrates might also be *accoppiatori*. Despite all the duplication and doubtless all kinds of behind scenes pressuring among small numbers of the dominant elite, it seems that political office was spread widely over time.

The Medici descended from Tuscan peasants who moved into the city in the twelfth century. In 1296 a Medici was standard bearer. In 1378 it was Salvestro de Medici who championed the Ciompi rising of unrepresented workers which the craft guilds also joined, to establish the most democratic regime in Florence's history. Nothing quite equals the dogged determination and heroic courage of the Flemish weavers, but the brief rising of the Ciompi was the high point of the democratic struggle in Florence. They were at the mercy of their employers, paid low wages and forbidden to organize. Factions within the major guilds gave the chance for an uprising in June 1378. Many artisans and small shopkeepers joined in the agitation and petitions were presented to the government of Florence, demanding the right to establish guilds. On 22 July the government was ousted and a government of the minor guilds installed, with a wool carder as standard bearer of justice. The Ciompi were now organized in a guild. During August the major guilds and employers shut out their workers, creating increasing hardship, dividing the interests of the propertyless Ciompi from the artisans, minor guilds and shopkeepers. On 31 August the Ciompi demonstrated *en masse* in the main square, but were routed and dispersed by the forces of the major and minor guilds. Their guild was abolished and dominance of the major guilds was gradually reasserted. The episode counts as the first revolutionary rising of the industrial proletariat in Europe. No feudal authorities were involved. It was a purely Florentine experiment, with no immediate sequel, but an honourable place among experiments of freedom in government in the city-state, whose own freedom of experiment would also come to an end.

Salvestro de Medici was elected standard bearer of the people and head of government by the Ciompi and had to flee into exile when their regime collapsed. His cousin founded the first Medici bank, training distant cousins as partners. The bank made the family the wealthiest in Europe and financed Medici pre-eminence in the city. Its chance had come when the Bardi, Peruzzi and Aciaiuoli houses were broken by Edward III's failure to repay his huge loans. Some twenty members of the family worked for the bank in Florence, Rome, Naples, Venice, Bruges and elsewhere. The Medici arms were composed of the original symbol of the bankers' guild.

Salvestro's championship of the common people was not forgotten but became the confirmed stance of the family in its most glorious days. Cosimo de Medici returned from a year's exile in Venice to lead the bank and establish the unofficial Medici dynasty in Florence in 1434. The chance of the lottery had put in office a clique favourable to him. Seventy-three citizens were banished and many were deprived of civil rights for ten years or so. Many Medici enemies were thus removed, but there was no obtrusive packing of positions of power by the Medici. Rather, a general yet quite unofficial recognition of eight or ten men as chief citizens, with the head of the Medici family among them, all of them in and out of the main offices, for holding one office disqualified from re-election for three years. Cosimo was only three times standard bearer of justice, seven times member of the *balia*, twice among the eight priors and once in the *accoppiatori*, over a period of several decades. Furthermore, the lottery system was intermittently reinstated. It is suggested that the more affluent were heavily represented on the scrutiny lists, while thousands of poor labourers were not even considered (Brucker, 1969:336). 'Cosimo ruled from behind the scenes while preserving the appearances of 'liberty' and constitutional procedure. But no important decision was ever taken against his will or advice. He inspired such awe that his power went unchallenged and no plots were hatched to overthrow his rule' (de Roover, 1966:75). He founded the Platonic Academy and Library in 1459.

Until exiled again in 1494 by the upheaval surrounding Savonarola's inflammatory preaching, his eventual burning alive, and the French invasion, Cosimo, his son Piero, grandson Lorenzo (Il Magnifico) and great grandson Piero, ruled Florence informally without holding any office or receiving any title. Their munificent patronage and largesse, skilled diplomacy, artistic taste and personal brilliance held sway over the illustrious climax of Italy's loveliest city. Lorenzo held Florence spellbound, as poet, patron, host and citizen. The magnates simply came and asked him to take charge.

Over thirty-seven years the Medici spent about fifty-five times the annual income of the city on buildings, charities and city taxes, of which they paid more than any other citizen (de Roover, 1966:29–31, 371). They were learned men, who used their commercial agents to search out classical manuscripts all over the known world, reintroducing Greek scholarship and taste to Italy after a lapse of 700 years. Donatello's David was the first nude since Roman times (Acton, 1967:78). But they remained guild members, refusing noble titles and insisting on their commoner identity, despite supplying two popes and two queens of France and being courted and consulted as sovereign princes. When they dishonoured themselves in returning as dukes by favour of the French king they were more secure and ruthless, but their city was in irrevocable decline, as the focus of European commerce had passed across the oceans.

London

The urban struggle for freedom reflected the structural antagonism of town and country in the Feudal mode of production. It was doomed to failure by the class conflicts within the city, which no leader or movement sufficiently transcended and which drove the merchants to side with the rural nobles. Freedom and representation would stay on the agenda for centuries, until the sources of wealth and power and the mode of production itself had changed. While many smaller cities had a general guild merchant, including artisans as well as merchants – virtually the economic aspect of the civic organization – important cities had guilds representing different kinds of merchants, professions and craftsmen as in Florence. In London civic and guild organization developed within the framework of a powerful state (unlike the situation in Italy or Germany), but where more stable conditions, with peace at home, permitted a less confrontational approach than in Paris or Flanders. There were over seventy guilds: goldsmiths, tailors, mercers, fishmongers, skinners, vintners, joiners, grocers and drapers, with ironmongers, salters and haberdashers added in the fifteenth century. These had about 2,000 members, mostly independent masters. Altogether they were about three-quarters of the citizen body of some 4,000 with 10,000 'foreigners' (non-citizens) and 3,000 aliens from overseas, including the Flemish merchants of the London House of Bruges, who controlled the cloth trade in the thirteenth century, and the Italian bankers who controlled the money market. Some of them later became influential citizens. Edward II's financiers, William Servat of Cahors, pepperer, and William Trente of Bergerac, vintner, became aldermen (Thrupp, 1948:219). The merchants of the Staple were a monopoly established by the king from time to time to run the wool, butter, cheese, leather, tin, lead and other trades. It consisted of prominent alien as well as citizen merchants (Gross, 1890:140), who were called upon to bear much of the risk and profit of the Hundred Years War (Thrupp, 1948:53). The London Hanse of the Steelyard was the branch of the Cologne Hanse which organized all the north German merchants in a powerful monopoly. The king granted them privileges in a Great Charter of 1303, giving them responsibility for the Bishopsgate approach to London Bridge. They paid lower customs than ordinary English merchants and lived an almost collegiate life with their own government and officers (Postan, Rich and Miller, 1963:224).

The twenty-four wards of London each elected one alderman to the council and twelve citizens to an assembly which chose the lord mayor and the four representatives of the city in parliament. There were disputes as to whether the mayor should be elected by the aldermen or the people and on a ward or guild basis. In the fourteenth century a citizen assembly was required to approve the sealing of any document. The seal had six locks, each key kept separately by the aldermen and three ordinary citizens.

The king could suspend the mayor, requiring crushing payments for restoration: 2,000 marks and other gifts to Edward I in 1299 and a loan of £10,000 to Richard II a century later. The king was paid £300 annually for charter privileges. The annual cost of city administration was about £100. The recorder was the highest paid city official, receiving £10 annually (up to £15 in 1310), the town clerk receiving £5 (raised to £10). Fourteenth-century prices were three times higher than in the twelfth century and rose no further till the sixteenth century. Silver coins lost half their value in England and more on the continent. The inequality between rich and poor had greatly increased. A grocer might leave an estate of £300, very few as much as £2,000. However, there were over thirty gentry members of the Mercers' Company in the fifteenth century and the lord mayor was always knighted.

The tortured transition

The calamitous fourteenth century, with the Black Death, Hundred Years War and urban uprisings, all accentuating one another, led to multitudes of displaced persons, beggars and destitutes, vagrants, vagabonds, discharged soldiers and adventurers, coalescing into bands and small armies, under forceful leaders who led them hither and thither, preying on the countryside, seizing castles as headquarters and laying waste roundabout. The villainous captains of these bands were the self-made millionaires of the time, hired by kings and popes to do their dirty work and given the highest honours.

Such was Sir Robert Knollys, grand plunderer worth 100,000 crowns, who burned and sacked from Orleans to Vézelay, controlling forty castles, passing to and fro between brigandage and service under the crown, benefactor of churches, founder of almshouses and charities. Knights and brigands were interchangeable. He became England's most experienced soldier, master of war, who subdued Wat Tyler's rebellion.

The fifteenth and sixteenth centuries with stronger government permitted fewer large bands, but urban polarization of rich and poor increased. Poverty and banditry increased in the sixteenth century and became worse in the seventeenth century. In 1650 it was impossible to hear mass in Florence 'So much was one importuned during the service by wretched people, naked and covered with sores' (Braudel, 1976:735). So terrible was the destitution, poverty, vagabondage and brigandage, reported as worse and worse, one marvels how society survived at all.

Cities were the creation of merchants, which they struggled to defend against the state, creation of kings and nobles. Kings were primarily rural as the vast majority of the subjects were, but town and country were antagonistically fused in Christendom. Cities have always been the centres of innovation, but this was most of all true in the Feudal mode of production where cities and merchants stood for progress, against the *status quo* defended by kings and nobles. The polarity was for a while over-ridden by the new conception of nobility in the city generated by the creative genius of the Italian Renaissance in its intensity of vice and virtue.

Distinction rested not on birth or caste, but on talent, education and achievement. The brigand-mercenary-adventurer-despot-prince was a paradoxical, glamorous expression of the new individualism and freedom from restraint, which the victory of the cities made possible. He might be a bastard, castrating foes, raping maidens, marrying illegitimate princesses, yet his thirst for fame, passion for monumental works, the company of poets, artists and scholars gave him a new legitimacy (Burkhardt, 1944:5). Bastardy, even with Moorish or African blood, no longer barred succession. Nominally celibate popes were procreating dynasties. The condottiere embodied the most admired form of illegitimacy in a heroic and ruthless fashion (Burkhardt, 1944:13). Bloodthirsty ferocity, sacrilege and profanation, profligacy and brigandage, papal simony and nepotism, all came together with the assassins of Galeazzo Sforza praying devoutly in the church before murdering him at mass, and Vitelozzo Vitelli begging the Borgia pope to absolve him of his sins before getting his son to strangle him. The tyrannical Sforza court in Milan was described as the most splendid in Europe. The city-state itself became a work of art, by calculation and reflection (Burkhardt, 1944:2). This flowering of new behaviour and values, flamboyant and monstrous, was brief, as the mania for titles and aristocratic conventions returned in the sixteenth century. The rise of merchants and bankers to political supremacy in the cities, and their subsequent eclipse by or transmogrification into the despotic state power, paralleled the upward curve of innovation and productivity followed by its tailing off.

In the north wars of religion masked social revolutions. But the Mediterranean experienced a 'general and growing malaise' as it passed through 'a lengthy and painful metamorphosis' (Braudel, 1976:755), with appalling violence, suffering, destitution and debauchery in great cities such as Naples, Palermo, Madrid, Seville, Marseilles and also Paris. Riots, assassinations, revolts and reprisals erupted almost daily. An urban underworld seethed with cunning prostitutes, merry widows, ruffians, gamblers, vagrants and vagabonds. The cities were a theatre of a perpetual social war of relentless cruelty, meaningful episodes in the endless subterranean revolution which marked the whole of the sixteenth and seventeenth centuries. However, these cities are more usually lauded for the splendid architecture created for the 'enlightened despots' of the age of absolutism. It was certainly class struggle, but its nature was still not clear to the victims. It was a revenge upon established states in opposition to the vile governments which had succeeded the medieval republics.

Towns were obliged periodically to drive out the poor, the cripples, the idlers, in rage at the constant invasion which they knew would recur. Marseilles expelled vagrants and vagabonds from all its quarters. Seville rounded them up and shipped them to the Straits of Magellan as labourers. Four ships foundered and 1,000 men were drowned. Venice gave free pardon to any brigand who would kill all companions who had murdered more than he. Pirates were abetted by powerful towns and bandits had regular backing from nobles. The rich were extravagantly rich and the poor miserably poor. There was no compassion. The religious Emperor Charles V likened poor soldiers dying to caterpillars. It was no harm if they died. Only property deserved respect. Yet there was an astounding move towards charity in the Catholic world at the end of the seventeenth century. But nothing could bridge the chasm between rich and poor. The Mediterranean even retained slavery, a sign of its attachment to the past despite pretentions to modernity (Braudel, 1976:738–54 *passim*).

Greatly fearing to periodize as a mere artifactual aid to analysis, it is impossible to avoid the conclusion that this was the tortured transition, the cultural and quotidian aspect of the slow transformation from one mode of production to another, which can never occur without accompanying spatial movement. The Mediterranean system collapsed, too closely tied to American silver and Habsburg finance, with its dwindled channels of trade. With the seventeenth century Amsterdam became the centre of the world and the Mediterranean was outside the mainstream of history (Braudel, 1985, III:79).

World cities

Venice

The Flanders–Italy urban axis, with its tentacles growing till the fifteenth century, gave place to an outer sequence of the pre-eminent merchant cities, from Venice to Genoa, Lisbon, Antwerp and Amsterdam as the ancient Mediterranean dominance yielded to the Atlantic. The shameless pillaging of Constantinople in 1204, instead of the infidel, by Crusaders and Venetians, brought Venice priceless treasures, icons and an empire which benefited all the Italian cities, especially when the Mongols, more amenable than the Muslims to the Christians and their missions, opened the overland route to China. The Fondaco dei Tedeschi was established in 1228 to hold the German Hansa merchants in close quarantine by the Rialto to sell their goods and buy only Venetian. Venice and Genoa were always bitter rivals. Genoa destroyed the Venetian galleys at Korcula in 1298, but when Genoa seized the Venetian island suburb of Chioggia in 1379, Venice retook it and destroyed the Genoese fleet, driving them from the eastern Mediterranean for good. Venice retained the best contacts in Syria, Egypt, Germany and central Europe. It took control of its mainland neighbours Padua, Verona, Brescia and Bergamo in the fifteenth century, while Milan took Lombardy, Florence, Tuscany and Genoa, its east and west rivieras. Thus appeared a set of super city-states wealthier than the developing territorial states (Braudel, 1985, III:119–20).

The Venetian city-state income in 1423 was between 7.5 and 15 million ducats, equal to that of Spain and almost that of England and France (Braudel, 1985, III:119–20). The Venetian budget fell less than half as much as those of western European nations in the fifteenth-century recession. At the end of the sixteenth century 2 million ducats of gold and silver were minted every year. To carry Istrian salt, 40,000 horses were brought from Hungary, Croatia and Germany. The city was embellished with splendid palaces lining the Grand Canal. Ships up to 300 tons were chartered by the city to groups of merchants in capitalist trading enterprises. Big business and insurance were conducted on the street, with the Rialto as stock exchange. Most bankers were foreigners, but were not tempted to establish branches outside, as the Florentines did in England and the Genoese in Seville and Madrid. The Venetian population reached about 100,000 in the fifteenth century and 140,000–160,000 in the sixteenth and seventeenth centuries. All but a few thousand of the elite were working with their hands for a living. The entire population was said to be lending money. Unprotected, unskilled workers, 'the proletariat of the sea' (Braudel, 1985, III:133) were porters, stevedores, seamen, oarsmen, dockers and thousands of gondoliers (still 10,000 in 1880, now less than 400) mainly in the service of rich families. Then there were the organized guilds for the glass, leather, wool and silk trades, but also barge helmsmen, tinkers and milk deliverers.

The Arsenal was a state-run enterprise employing some 3,000 workers. No protest movements were tolerated. Venetian wages were high, yet social unrest was remarkably rare. Competition from the mainland and further north led to the decline of Venetian prosperity in the sixteenth and seventeenth centuries. Venice continued to dazzle, but three fatal blows destroyed her pre-eminence. Constantinople fell in 1453 cutting her off from most of her richest markets. Portuguese voyages to the east at the end of the century brought pepper and spices direct to Lisbon, stabbing Venice in the back, all the more as nine-tenths of the consumers were in northern Europe. The Genoese discovered the New World for the Spanish and a vast new volume of trade developed which marginalized Venice.

The logical successor to Venetian centrality would have been Lisbon, but it seems that Lisbon, integrated into its own world network of developing colonial cities, failed to seize the opportunity, while the centre of gravity of Europe had shifted irrevocably north. Lisbon itself sent a shipload of pepper and cinnamon to Antwerp in1510, and as ships from Holland, Spain, Italy, Ragusa, Catalonia, England and Brittany also found it convenient to put in there, Antwerp found itself the new centre of the European world economy almost without realizing it (Braudel, 1985, III:143–8).

Antwerp

Antwerp had already taken the place of nearby Bruges as a better port for larger vessels, but even more than Bruges it was the creation of outsiders rather than of itself. It had only a small fleet and no merchants of international standing. It was governed by aldermen from a tiny landed aristocracy who were not even officially allowed to trade although they were often money-lenders and were themselves under the nominal rule of the duchy of Brabant. In the first phase of Antwerp's expansion (1501–21) pepper from Portugal was the key. In the second phase (1533–57) it was the New World silver from Spain and in the third phase (1559–68) it was 'breakneck growth of industry in Antwerp and the Netherlands' (Braudel, 1985, III:148).

Accompanying changes were: the switch from Baltic honey to Atlantic sugar and from luxury furs to luxury silks as the Hansa presence dwindled; Antwerp also dyed English woollen cloth and distributed it all over Europe; the merchant bankers of Augsburg, who made fortunes from Rhine wine, copper and silver brought these commodities to Antwerp rather than to Venice, doubling the flow of copper there, as it halved in Venice. The spectacular development of Antwerp's tapestry, linen and cloth industry was ruined by the growing religious and political disruption of life and warfare with Spain, culminating in the sack of Antwerp by unpaid Spanish troops in 1576, caused indirectly by the Genoese blocking the gold supply because of a quarrel with the king, and a final conquest and sack of the city by the Spanish commander in 1585, after which nearly half the population left, many merchants going with their wealth straight to Amsterdam, providing a distinguished contribution to a city receiving contingents from every trading city in Europe (Braudel, 1985, III:187), as well as refugees from religious wars and persecution.

Genoa

'Genoa's discreet rule over Europe' (Braudel, 1985, III:164) was of another sort, behind the scenes, yet for a while 'arbiter of the fortune of the whole of Europe' (Braudel, 1985, III:166). Charles V of Spain had relied upon the Fuggers and other merchant bankers of Augsburg, till the Spanish bankruptcy of 1557 ended the arrangement and the Genoese stepped in. They had to guarantee *regular* income to the king out of the fiscal revenues and American silver imports, both irregular. The king's revenues were constantly increasing, as also were his outgoings and consequently Genoese profits. But the whole of their available capital was sucked in. They stopped financing trade between Seville and America in 1568, moving into finance exclusively. They lent to the king at 10%, on gigantic undertakings, some saying they made up to 30%. Galleys laden with *reals* or ingots 'began arriving in fabulous quantities in Genoa in the 1570s' (Braudel, 1985, III:166). Their wealth came from the 'possibility of mobilizing credit' (Braudel, 1985, III:166) more than from gold and silver. Genoese success may have come from realizing that gold was moving up and beginning to invest in it on the Antwerp market, although silver was the recognized means of preserving wealth values. Since the king's ordinance of 1537, bills of exchange had to be paid in gold. The Genoese probably sold the silver they received from the king to traders in Lisbon, Venice or Florence for the Levant trade, which now showed a renaissance. Spices and pepper again poured into Aleppo and Cairo. The silver was bought from the Genoese with bills of exchange convertible to gold in the Netherlands (Braudel, 1985, III:168). Genoa's fortune therefore depended on the American treasure of Spain and the wealth of Italian cities, which all drained towards Genoa. Many of Genoa's great bankers were living in Madrid, 'appearing at court and handling tremendous contracts, acting as advisers and collaborators of the king' (Braudel, 1985, III:168). Below them were thousands of Genoese merchants, shopkeepers, commission agents, clerks, peopling their own city and all cities of Italy and Sicily. Such take-over of an economic zone abroad was a formula for domination, as in Venice's take-over of the Byzantine Empire, Florence's capture of first England then France; and: 'the parallel can be extended to Louis XIV's France and the English colonization of India' (Braudel, 1985, III:169).The inter-continental breadth encompassed by a single city makes Genoa seem like a supra-spatial city anticipating the marvels of the electronic age.

Amsterdam

Holland and Frisia had developed for more than a millennium in battle with the sea, enjoying fish but little land, with very specialized and highly productive agriculture on limited lands ingeniously and arduously protected, feeding the towns as they grew and fertilizing with their refuse, contributing significantly to the country's economic take-off. Born seamen, with abundant fish for sale, they were bound to share in and promote the maritime trading opportunities which developed around them. Holland became the economic dynamo of Netherlands development, though only one of its seven provinces. Its eighteen towns were self-governing with their own system of taxation and justice. The densest and most urbanized part of Europe, with half its population in the towns, quarrelsome and jealous yet forced to co-operate in commerce and industry, they became a closely integrated network of concentrated and co-ordinated forces which peaked in seventeenth-century Amsterdam, with its vast harbour full of thousands of ships from all over Europe. It seems to prefigure some of the most modern objectives, with its decentralization, religious and ethnic diversity, tolerance and individual freedom. Yet it was only narrowly achieved, after bitterly destructive conflicts of often uncertain outcome. It was through or despite these fierce struggles that the Golden Age blossomed, and the painting of the great Dutch masters flourished. Other plastic and performing arts were disapproved. The prevailing Calvinistic morality imposed sober and unostentatious behaviour. But the prodigious wealth of the bourgeoisie began to have its effect in more luxurious habits. By the end of the seventeenth century Dutch economic world pre-eminence had passed its peak and in the eighteenth century the bourgeoisie became bureaucratized, withdrawing from trade and turning their surplus capital to government stocks, finance and credit operations. Already French was the language of culture and Flemish was for ignorant people. Tolerance and individual freedom did not mean justice or equality. Both wages and cost of living were higher than elsewhere. Merchant capitalists would not penalize capital, so taxes were indirect and regressive, bearing upon the consumer and the poor. The tax on two servants was double that on one, but tax on five servants was only 40% more. There were innumerable ways for the wealthy to evade.

Amsterdam shows the final stage of development of the antagonistic city in its struggle for freedom from feudal authority, which was now the state itself. The Middle Ages had passed, and the interest of history turned to the nation-states, but the cumulative thrust of the medieval city-states had one lasting significant contribution to make. This is the concrete narrative, which theory portrays as the dialectical contradiction of forces and relations of production, emerging in a new mode of production, merchant capitalism spawned from the antagonism of town and country in the Feudal mode, with the seeds of industrial capitalism to follow.

The immensity of the European world economy in size, wealth and complexity, with its transatlantic extensions and its expanding monarchical nation-states, made the dominance of a single city-state, in the manner of Venice, Genoa or Antwerp, no longer viable (Braudel, 1985, III:175). In a culmination of the urban form and economy generated by the feudal dialectic, Amsterdam succeeded in a tortured movement of slow transfiguration into the leading city of the new nation-state itself, generating the wealth which financed Dutch victory against Spain and achievement of independent statehood.

The city-states were nimble at manoeuvre compared to the territorial states. The emergent Dutch state organization was a parody, perhaps welcome to Holland, the main archipelago of cities led by Amsterdam, on which the greatness of Flanders devolved. Although the struggle for freedom of the lower orders failed, the city-states were small enough to give even the poor an exciting sense of involvement in the communal struggle. In Genoa 'everyone' was lending money. But one fears that then as now, the neediest were treated as invisible. The significant mass of the population was caught in the enthusiastic thrust of the city's main goals, which brought high wages if not equality. Florence was embellished and St Mark's stolen bones at Venice glorified for the honour of all. This was not so clear in Amsterdam or Genoa. The Italian city-states' formidable achievements in cultural economy were diffused generally throughout Europe and, in particular, through Genoa, which can claim main responsibility for Europe's discovery and exploitation of America, through its transatlantic explorers and the large numbers of Genoese who settled in Seville as a 'second Genoa'.

The world system was one of competitive cities in which the competition of lesser cities fed into the greatness of the leading cities in each major, overlapping archipelago. Genoa's network was almost global, yet based on real agents and contacts in innumerable cities. Just as the achievement of global economic unity (as opposed to world economy) spells the end of the Capitalist mode of production, so the change from Feudal to Capitalist mode was the change from city-state-led (merchant) economic progress, within yet also beyond the asymmetrical parallel framework of landed aristocrat-run states, the relation between the two being savagely contested, involving vengeful bankrupt kings and loss of face. The enmity of cities and states reflected the antagonism in the mode of production (Braudel, 1985, III:91).

Relations with religion and the church were different. Originally count-bishops had fought tooth and nail to deny power to merchants, whom they despised as well as condemning morally, but that contest was largely over. The delicately complementary supremacy of pope and emperor, now superseded, had been worked out symbolically and continued in the political chess game, as the position, size and shape of the board changed and many pieces and their hierarchy and potential changed. For cities, political aims were usually subordinate to economic, as the debate of Doge Mocenigo on the advantages of peace and wealth over war and poverty showed (Braudel, 1985, III:120). Venice's total sabotage of the crusades for its own profit and empire did not disdain war, or suffer from it, because they largely got others to fight for them.

The struggle for democracy in the eighteenth- and nineteenth-century nation-states was in some respects a replay of the city-state experience in the thirteenth and fourteenth centuries, again beginning with restricted franchises, but less tortuous voting procedures. The ultimate contradiction in mode of production was finally resolved in the French Revolution, because the dialectic move forward had been rejected. The *sans-culottes*, assuming the mantle of the Ciompi, again achieved brief triumph, and defeat.

5 Asian cities: Asiatic and Feudal modes of production

Chapter 5 explores the ancient cities of the developed Asiatic mode of production in the Sinic, Japanese, Islamic and Indic regions for their contributions to the overall achievements of human urbanization.

IMPERIAL CHINA: FROM CITY-STATE TO WORLD METROPOLIS

The emergence of the Chinese city

The traditional city remains largely unstudied . . . much of traditional Chinese culture, and particularly its literate aspects, developed primarily in the city . . . where the elite class resided and where decisions of national and local affairs were made. (Ma, 1971)

The world's pre-modern urban history was mainly a Chinese phenomenon' (Rozman, 1973:3). Of approximately 4% of the world's population living in cities of over 10,000 inhabitants in 1800, about one third, or 12 million, lived in China which led the world in economic development until the eighteenth century, when it may have been surpassed by Japan, as well as by western Europe. Some two-fifths of the world's population were in China and Japan, yet 'until now there have been no knowledgeable comparisons of Chinese and Japanese cities with each other or with cities in other countries' (Rozman, 1973:7). The Chinese people emerged from a blending of north and north-western, nomadic and pastoral Turks, Tungus, Mongols and Tibetans, with settled, agricultural Tai, Miao and Yao further south. The blending continued throughout Chinese history and is culturally paralleled by the joint heritage of northern Yangshao (Eberhard, 1960:48; Stover and Stover, 1976:18–24) and south-central Lungshan (Stover and Stover, 1976:24–6). The hand-coiled, white, red and black painted pottery of the former has striking echoes in Turkestan and Caucasus, while their more widespread grey pottery was a local tradition and their chopsticks, double steamers, tripods and woven silk became characteristically Chinese. Lungshan overlapped and succeeded with prototypes of Shang vessels, pounded earth walls, fine techniques of sawing, drilling and eventual bronze-casting and the bringing of rice from South China.

Out of this blending the Shang were developing during the second millennium BC in the deep but fragile loess of the Yellow and Wei river valleys of Honan and Shensi, relatively easy soil to work with bronze age technology. The emergent ruling elite concentrated in mud-walled cities with large, pillared houses, palaces, offices, temples and tombs, served by bronze casters, carpenters and weavers in silk and hemp. The distinctive Chinese writing already employed some 3,000 characters in oracles, records and receipts. Over 17,000 such bone and tortoiseshell documents were found in a single pit. Writing assisted the formidable intellectual achievement of the calendar, co-ordinating elaborate rituals and controlling the vital agricultural operations.

Early Shang polities operated on segmentary principles, as noted in chapter 2, without strictly defined, impermeable boundaries, but rather flexible zones of interaction among themselves and other ethnic groups, including the nomadic and potentially aggressive groups to the north. The Shang realm was held together by the charisma of its divine kingship, routinized and bound in the pervasive, cosmographic symbolism, enacted in ritual and in the very architecture of the city and its arts and crafts, down to the detailed cultural coding of family and individual in daily life.

The city's urbanity was symbolized in altar, temple and palace. As in all segmentary societies, such features were repeated at the cult centres of rulers in the capital city of each segment, as reduced replicas of those in the central capital city of the realm. The early capitals moved a number of times, but by about 1300 BC the capital moved to the site near Anyang (Wheatley, 1971:36–46) where it remained till the end of the dynasty. The fixing of capitals coincides with moving away from primarily ritual and symbolic co-ordination to a more political mode of government. It also presupposes more permanent architectural structures and some mechanism for the disposal of waste. The fixed capital city marks a significant development in states which are expressions of the Asiatic mode of production and are segmentary in form.

As the ritual suzerain endeavours to change into a sovereign (Southall, 1988b:52), extending secular power over peripheral communities, changing their ritual prestations into taxes and trying to increase their amount, opposition to his rule is bound to increase and the realm can only be held together in its larger form by the development of some combination of bureaucratic and military power, as China eventually did. It is the transformation of purely ritual and symbolic centralization into attempts at political centralization. The change from the ritual to the political realm is obviously one of degree. A political realm is far harder to hold together than a ritual realm which is, in a sense, more voluntaristic. A political realm is held together by the willingness to use countervailing force if necessary, to supplement charismatic and hegemonic forces of cohesion.

Extension from the small, original core domain to embrace ritually subordinate but autonomous peripheral communities always reveals a further periphery until rivalry of different political centres leads to the subjugation of all within their reach. Then the victors are tempted to attack and vanquish, destroy or annex one another's territory; and so larger empires may come into being, or else fail and break up again. When the attempt to maintain the centralized political realm breaks down, feudalistic forms of economic and political co-ordination are the only alternative, apart from allowing the component parts to secede from one another altogether.

The Asiatic mode of production may thus be transformed into the Feudal mode of production, as happened in the violent transition from Shang to Zhou. Feudal systems arise in chaos and disorder, often accompanied by tremendous destruction, fall in production and loss of life and population, as happened in the transition from the Ancient mode of production of the Roman Empire to the Feudal mode of production of medieval Europe. But the destruction may be accompanied by innovative opportunities, especially important in the development of cities. The dynamic contrast between the cosmic order embodied in the city of the Asiatic mode of production and the less regulated city of creative opportunity and economic entrepreneurship expressing the Feudal mode of production, or tendency in that direction, is formally analogous with the contrast between simple, linear, orderly systems and complex, chaotic, innovative systems symbolized as Quark and Jaguar (Gell-Mann, 1995).

In the last centuries of Shang, with their capital city permanently fixed and their resources enlarged by increased population, production and exploitation, they began to mobilize large armies and indulge in warlike expeditions. Glorification of the regime reached new heights, with chariot burials and large numbers of beheaded humans, horses and dogs accompanying dead rulers in vast tombs. The divine king was not a war leader, but the nobles formed large armies of thousands of chariots, with peasant infantry auxiliaries. When the Shang thus endeavoured to transform the ritual realm into a political and military force, they aroused an answering political and military confrontation from subordinate segments of the realm, which had not dared to challenge the imperial charisma, nor the validity of the cosmographic structure of the world, but were quite capable and uninhibited in competing with secular organization, mobilizing material resources, manufacturing weapons and deploying armies. It was the rise of competitive warfare, hitherto regulated and restricted by elaborate codes of ritual and military conduct, which allowed the Zhou, advantageously close to supplies of northern nomadic cavalry, to develop their military capacity over several generations until they were able to defeat the Shang and seize the realm (Stover and Stover, 1976:40–1).

The Zhou could conquer, but they were no more able than the Shang to hold the realm together as a politically unified state. Lacking the mystical charisma of legitimate Shang divine kingship, which they continued to revere and tried to appropriate, they had to struggle for political control as best they could, as did the Germanic peoples when they seized the territories of Rome. They could control the large core area round their capital city and place kinsmen and family members in the fortress city capitals of satellite polities all round. Some of these satellites themselves succeeded in expanding and developed satellites of their own.

It is estimated that by the eighth century BC there were some 200 virtually autonomous states, each with its capital city (Wheatley, 1971:114, 195), linked in a loose segmentary hierarchy in the idiom of kinship, with constant usurpations and rebellions. Orders flowed from the capital city through the hierarchy of cities and towns, becoming ever more diluted on the way. Tribute flowed from the lowest level to the top, likewise diluted all the way. The political process and structure of segmentation paralleled the urban segmentation. It was a decentralizing process, eventually allowing more and more states with their capital cities to become largely independent.

In the eighth century the ruler of Zhou was driven out and killed, but a prince was rescued and reinstated. Then the ruler of Wu claimed the Zhou imperial title and seceded. In the seventh century northern nomads over-ran Wei in Honan. Only a few hundred of its city population escaped to flee south (Eberhard, 1960:40). With increasing anarchy the 'Spring and Autumn' period passed into that of 'Warring States' (481–221 BC). Between the eighth and fifth centuries the increasing use of iron greatly improved the efficiency of war and the productivity of agriculture, especially in the luxuriant subtropical south, which was being brought within the Chinese orbit. The conscription of tens of thousands of footsoldiers was superseding the aristocrats' chariots, impractical in the southern jungles and mountains. Weaker polities were defeated and incorporated in stronger polities as large regional states began to emerge.

As Zhou authority waned, the emperor endeavoured to rule by co-opting rulers of powerful segments as ministers and officers. The state of Ch'i in Shantung became powerful and its capital city, Lin-tzu, which first used money in the fifth century, had a court wealthier and more luxurious than Zhou itself, with a probable population of 200,000. Cardinally oriented with east–west walls of 3,000 metres and north–south walls 4,000 metres, it produced much of the salt supply and that of bronze and iron passed through it (Wheatley, 1971:145, 221; Eberhard, 1960:55).

By the Warring States era (481–221 BC), growth of population, production, iron technology and the intense conflict between the various cities and states generated greater political specialization. Rulers in local capital cities felt forced to seek officials and subordinates for merit and efficiency rather than kinship and ritual status. They were driven to experiment with more effective types of political and military organization, reducing Zhou imperial sovereignty to a cypher, deeply revered but much usurped. Duties were more clearly defined and appointments limited in duration to curb political ambition and hereditary tendencies. Civil and military organization were separated.

Confucius, Mencius and the 'hundred philosophers' (fifth to fourth centuries BC) sought solutions to chaos and disorder, emphasizing achievement over ascription. Honour and authority became rewards for virtue and meritorious service, rather than rank. This *literati* scholar class, derived by some from nobles deprived of political position, wandered from city to city and court to court, acquiring an intellectual perspective far broader than that of any particular city they served, as in Renaissance Italy.

Lack of centralized government allowed merchants freedom and opportunity to play off one political interest against another as economic brokers. Political insecurity meant greater risk but higher profits. Merchants even held high office and were not degraded to the low rank they later held, until the Han dynasty.

The regional states fought one another in vain attempts to win supremacy. Qin had advantages from its north-western position, removed from the central arena of conflict, powerful from the combination of intensive Chinese agriculture, with access to the nomad cavalry of the barbarian north from which it also was largely derived. Control of the main trade route through Asia gave it wealth and prosperous merchants, who were assisted by standardization of weights and measures and accorded freedom and high status. It attracted scholar-officials tired of the strife of central China.

Such was Shang Yang, who persuaded the fourth-century Qin ruler to reform his state, with impartial law, meritorious service in place of noble privilege, bureaucratic government and local administration organized in prefectures subdivided into counties. Males not heads of families were doubly taxed, breaking up extended families and establishing nuclear family dominance. Running counter to Confucian values, this was supported by the Legalists, who emphasized absolute supremacy of the ruler.

At his patron's death Shang Yang was killed by the noble faction, yet his system remained intact. The successor claimed the imperial title, challenging the other contenders. Qin power was becoming predominant, outwitting or defeating the main rivals. The last Zhou emperor had already abdicated in favour of Qin, but it had little effect. The stage was set for Shih-Huang-Ti. His ruthless ability seems beyond question, but some characteristic features of 'hero-founder myth' are attributed to him: unorthodox birth to a slave girl, concubine of a merchant, by a Qin prince held hostage in an enemy state. The merchant secured the prince's succession to the Qin throne and that of Shih-Huang-Ti after his death. Shih-Huang-Ti exiled the merchant, executed his mother's lover and, with efficient generals, extensive bribery and espionage, overcame and annexed the rival states one after another, till in 211 BC he could proclaim himself as first sovereign emperor of Unified China.

Shih-Huang-Ti deported the ruling families of the conquered states to Hienyang, capital city of Qin, near Chang'an (Maspero, 1955:312) and sold their land. Hienyang became a huge consumption centre, with great merchant prosperity. The empire was divided into thirty-six military districts. Confucian opponents were executed and their books burned. There was further standardization of language, laws and axle lengths. Roads, canals and fortresses were built and consolidated into the Great Wall.

Shih-Huang-Ti was extremely superstitious, summoning magicians to find him the elixir of life. He made imperial tours of inspection and conducted great sacrifices. His palaces and tomb strictly followed the cosmic design. He became more and more isolated, imprisoned in mistrust. Driven from their grazing, the Hsiung-nu (Huns) had united against him. At his death, uprisings broke out everywhere in eight years of insurrection and chaos. His success was too great, the efficiency of his administration too brutal and burdensome to outlive his own genius, yet allowed a more successful attempt to be made by moderate methods, establishing the long-lasting Han dynasty.

It was Liu Pang, a peasant police officer from Qin turned rebel, who overcame the rest, entered the capital city of Chang'an and proclaimed himself emperor. His dynasty was called Han, after the small western kingdom he had earlier received from a warlord. He was coarse and harsh, but shrewd. He pissed in a scholar-dignitary's hat to show his appreciation for education. But the Confucians returned to influence and the whole empire was brought under civil administration. Rudimentary official examinations were already held. The life of the capital city became increasingly luxurious. Succession was much disturbed by the influence of imperial consorts as mothers, widows and rivals for the title of empress.

Chang'an was the greatest of all Chinese capitals, in the capital district of the Zhou, Han, Sui and T'ang dynasties. Built in 202 BC, the Han capital for two centuries, it claimed 250,000 people, fifty temples and five palaces. Rebuilt by Sui (581–618) and enlarged by T'ang (618–907) it reached a population of 1 million inside the walls and another million outside, the largest city the world had ever seen.

The Han Chinese still form well over 90% of the population of China, named from the Han dynasty which consolidated a territorial state which, with marginal fluctuations, remained the essential China ever after. The formidable brief Qin dynasty was the necessary prelude to this Han achievement. It is a repeated phenomenon in the creation of empires that a ruthless conqueror establishes a tyrannical state which collapses of its own weight at his death, but is recomposed in more tolerant and lasting form by those who come after. Thus were Qin and Han. Sui and Song repeated the theme.

Alternation in urban form and mode of production

No break is ever complete, but the Zhou-Qin-Han break of the third century BC was the most significant break in Chinese development. Shang was clearly a ritual realm (Fox, 1977:41–2), containing the essential roots of the Chinese city, state and culture, though never occupying even half the territory of later China. Such unity as the Zhou realm ever had was also ritual rather than political. Shih-Huang-Ti was the first to create a political state which looked like a complete China, so brittle it soon broke, but reconstituted as the Han China of history, still fragile and fluctuating, often collapsing, with positive as well as negative consequences, but always aimed at and always reconstituted.

Such political or cultural facts are simply stated, but they were the accumulating product of myriads of individual human efforts, to eat, reproduce and realize meaning in life and survival. The underlying material efforts are even more hidden than the efforts at meaning so much talked about. The system of production, of holding and using land, creating and disposing of surplus – the forces and relations of production – were the essential undercarriage moving people on from Shang to Zhou to Shih-Huang-Ti and Han China. We have also characterized this as motion from the Kinship to the Asiatic and Feudal mode of production, and to and fro between these latter. If data and analysis were adequate, there should be some parallel between changes in the city and in the mode of production.

The Shang cosmic city carried the seed of the universal empire, a corollary of the 'symbolism of the centre' which was exclusive not inclusive.

Everything of value is included in the Five Domains and Colours (Stover and Stover, 1976:32, 42). The idea of China was conceived as a universe, not as an expanded universal city in the Roman style, although the city was the indispensable context of civilized life in both. With the Qin-Han achievement of a centralized state it was reified as *Chung-kuo* 'central kingdom', or *Chung-hua* 'Central Cultural Florescence' (Feuerwerker, 1976:vii).

The compelling force of the Chinese system, even in defeat, persisted through the centuries. The fourth-century Turkish Toba kingdom took the ancient eastern capital Loyang, and actually prohibited Toba sur-names, language, dress and customs. The Khitan Mongols made Yenching (Peking) their capital, claimed to be legitimate successors of T'ang and enforced the whole T'ang system. In the thirteenth century the Mongols honoured Confucius and rebuilt his temple, improved civil service examinations and claimed to be a Confucian state. When the Manchu conquered the Ming they imposed the Chinese system even more firmly.

Land

In Shang and Zhou, and even later, the emperor owned all the land in a mystical sense. At first it was possessed by local kin groups, who allocated it to their member families and individuals. Some lost their rights and became slaves, others won power to command the labour of inferiors. As controller of the cosmos, from his cosmic city, responsible for the harmony of nature, the supernatural and the fertility of humans, animals and crops, the ruler with his entourage received the produce of the land in prestations from the people. This was the mandate of heaven. In Zhou the local communal management of land weakened, changing from relations between kinsfolk of different status to those between local lord and subject, the latter rendering labour service to the former, later becoming taxation in kind, precipitating creditor–debtor relations and the imper-sonal link between master and hired hand, or landless labourer.

The contractual relation between the Zhou monarch and the land-holder was neither a promise of fidelity nor the giving of rights of eminent domain in exchange for protection, but the declaration that he and his land entered into the discipline and civilization of China (Granet, 1958:12–13). In the investiture of a high official by the western Zhou monarch, he invested him with a title, granted him land in various local-ities, farm households cultivating the land to serve as his subjects, together with emblems of ritual rank, drums and bells (Granet, 1958:12–13). The context was essentially urban. For if in Europe *nulle terre sans seigneur*, in Zhou, no overlord without a city and no city without an overlord (Wheatley, 1971:175). The propriety and efficacy required of the emperor was 'virtue'. Under the Zhou it was gradually dissipated, as political goals, powered by greater wealth, eroded ritual constraints. Trying to dissuade the emperor from an aggressive policy, a seventh-century noble recalled that 'in high antiquity the populace was kept in tranquillity by virtue' (Wheatley, 1971:162).

The vast majority of city dwellers were also cultivators, going out of the gates in summer daily to work the fields. At first it was a highly self-sufficient local economy, with little trade or exchange, but in later Zhou commerce became increasingly important. Now the **Hsien** city developed as the lowest level of the urban hierarchy and the basic unit of administration in subsequent dynasties (Wheatley, 1971:179–82). The courts of capital cities, very numerous in the segmentary structure of Zhou, and the wealthy in all cities, became magnets for the increase of long-distance trade for luxury consumption.

The weakness of Zhou and the increasing suffering from the competitive warfare of its autonomous segments were unmistakable features of the Warring States climax. But the underlying economic reality was the growing density of territorial settlement, contested by mass armies with more efficient iron weapons, financed by more repressive exploitation of peasant agriculture also made more productive by improved tools and crops, more commercialized landlord and tenant estates and increasing numbers of free, tax-paying peasants. War was a fundamental feature of the economy as well as the polity, tending to monopolize and distort both forces and relations of production. The contradiction of an improving peasant economy increasingly destroyed by warfare was resolved by Shih-Huang-Ti's victory and administrative reforms, followed by the Han lowering of taxation, cherishing the ideal of a totally administrative, theoretically equal division of land among the peasantry.

Mode of production and conflict of duty

This was epitomized in the *ch'ün-t'ien* 'equal field' system (Twitchett, 1963:194), whereby all arable land should be allocated and reallocated every generation, in equal plots to each farming household on a life tenure against tax and service. How far such meticulous regulations could be implemented in such a vast society at the grass-roots level, precisely by those most strongly motivated to subvert them (the village headmen and the lowest echelon of officials) is doubtful, but repeated attempts were made to implement them over a period of at least a millennium and a half. They embody the ideological essence of the strong version of the Asiatic mode of production (Godelier, 1978:241–5) as a redistributive economy in which 'under the whole heaven every spot is sovereign's ground' and as the Book of Rites declares 'lands are not to be sold. One receives them from the state and hence one may not sell them privately for oneself.' But the state and its officials always faced fierce conflict within themselves between their ideologically recognized public duties and their relentless private vested interests. Feudalistic pressures were never absent from the developed Asiatic mode of production, but they were held in check, by military might, state plundering, dispossession of rebels and the weight of value-laden ideological conformity. Vast public works were undertaken (Grand Canal, Great Wall, dykes, city walls, palaces) by mass forced labour. Official monopolies controlled nearly all major commodities. Meritocratic state examinations, in the capital and provincial cities, and mutual surveillance spying teams were instituted. Repressive constraints hampered merchants, who were now prohibited from owning land or riding horses, and were, incredibly, regarded as unproductive and disruptive. In this context, the cities were, necessarily, of the cosmological type.

In the developed form of the Asiatic mode of production, the centralized state endeavours to plan and control the city and the whole economy. In the Feudal mode of production, economic motivation is more individual. Arising essentially from the breakdown of political order, would-be rulers make deals with self-established magnates only a little less powerful than themselves, and so create feudal systems. They offer the possibility of increased scale, and even of better co-ordinated peasant exploitation, by offering titles to land and to honour, in exchange for loyalty, support and service, especially military.

It is essentially this economic motivation, which finds opportunity in situations of breakdown – essentially of land-grabbing – which the Chinese state was able, with long lapses, to control more effectively over the millennia, as it perfected its bureaucratic system. This explains the crucial difference between the histories of China and Europe, and why the Capitalist mode of production emerged in Europe and not in China. For in Europe, those individual economic ambitions, dampened by the Chinese state, were less restrained and led eventually to the birth of capitalism. The Feudal mode of production offered to the powerful considerable opportunity for self-expression, initiative and aggrandizement, which the Asiatic mode of production in its Chinese form strove to discourage and channel into the mandarin way of advancement. I see Max Weber's 'Protestantism and the Spirit of Capitalism' as rooted in this rather than its cause.

The unique historical achievement of the city-based Chinese bureaucracy was, that in 'normal times', when the state was strong, the mandarin's sense of professional duty and moral obligation prevailed over other motivations, although attempts were always being made to satisfy these as well. However, if the state was weak, or breaking down, the temptation to acquire private landed property and personal wealth became irresistible. The mandarin was perfectly placed to realize such ambitions, once the moral restraints failed, and he could even do so with a self-righteous sense of fulfilling Confucian family obligations and honour. The competitive pursuit of such ambitions brings about a situation which is an expression of the Feudal mode of production.

Whenever the centre broke, the state segmented into smaller kingdoms, partially able to carry on the bureaucratic mandarin tradition, but leaving large areas, including all their vast peripheries, for long periods under unstable administration, a situation of *sauve qui peut*, profit who can. It was the army commanders, rebel adventurers and leading families who would for their preservation and profit try to seize power, but above all land, as basis of both power and wealth. Usually this could only lead to forms of the Feudal mode of production.

It was the pressure of invading peoples from the north which precipitated breakdown. Non-Chinese and partly Chinese, they were always culturally Sinicized to a large degree. As with the fall of Rome, they wanted to emulate and profit from China, not destroy it. There could be no question of return to the Kinship mode of production. Any leader who succeeded in taking cities and territories of any size would (after pillage) attempt to consolidate the cities and use trained Chinese officials whenever he could find them, but even these would be in tempting conditions of lax control where the 'landed gentry' option would prevail over the efficient bureaucratic administration option. Private ownership of land, with constant changes of control for consideration amounting to buying and selling, would subvert the duty of administering justice and collecting tax in the name and for the benefit of leaders and would-be rulers whose power was not adequate to enforce this.

Did the Chinese city reflect these alternations and vacillation in mode of production? The alternation was not a simple repetition. The feudalism of Zhou was different from that which appeared in the post-Han breakdown or after the T'ang.

Given that the Chinese state, in its stable periods, was the most centralized, largest and most powerful of all pre-capitalist states, clearly cities would not have much independence during such periods, although it was just then that imperial interests would confer on them their most magnificent visual realization. The greatest cities were the product of political rather than economic initiative, although their siting reflects the influence of the environment through the system of production.

Given that Shang cities were essentially ceremonial centres, representing the early form of what became the 'cosmo-magical symbolism of
the Chinese city in Classical times' (Wheatley, 1971:411), was Zhou
feudalism associated with any change in the structure and function of
cities? In the numerous Zhou capital cities the cosmic plan was actually
further elaborated. Eberhard asserts (1960:56) that 'there were two types
of cities: the rectangular, planned city of Chou conquerors, a seat of
administration; and the irregular shaped city which grew out of a market
place and became only later an administrative centre. Little is known
about these cities, but they seem to have had considerable independence
because some of them issued their own city coins.'

Wheatley mapped out the known urban settlements of western Chou
(Zhou) and shows that 250 years later their number appeared to have
more than quadrupled (1971:165, 169). Although he mentions possible
sources of error, his maps are reproduced by Hsu and Linduff
(1988:272–3) without comment. In the later map, Wheatley distinguishes some thirty state capitals from many times this number of
'other important cities' and an even larger number of 'minor cities'. I am
forced to speculate that the important cities which were not capitals may
have included those Eberhard mentioned as irregular developments from
markets, with considerable independence.

If my hypothesis is correct that Zhou feudalism offered an opportunity
for the development of more independent cities, with a more economic
orientation, then there was the same contrast in Zhou as there was in
feudal Europe between those urban places where merchants and craftsmen were struggling for independence, and other cities under the more
complete dominance of Feudal kings and lords. Both Marx and Weber
stressed the distinctive characteristics of these cities, which led Marx to
give the antagonism of town and country as the distinctive theme of the
Feudal mode of production. This cannot be proved conclusively for the
Zhou, but there evidently was a contrast pointing in that direction. If
Eberhard was under the influence of Weber's monolithic emphasis on the
Chinese city's failure to develop an urban class, and the total dependence
of its commercial functions on administrative officials (Rowe, 1984:5–7),
then Eberhard's insistence on the existence of the second type of Chinese
city is all the more significant.

The creativity of cities in periods of disorder

It was not only the Zhou era of recognized feudalism that permitted
some urban autonomy. After four centuries through most of which Han

rule kept order in unified China, another four centuries of disunity and chaos ensued. Central government was crumbling, armies split into local power groups, banditry thrived and peasant messianic movements proliferated. The Taoist-led Yellow Turbans rebelled against the emperor's tyrannical eunuchs and the cost of vast armies raised to suppress them pushed the dynasty towards collapse. Remembering the contradictory aspects of feudal chivalry in Europe (chapter 4), it is ironic that the bloody warfare at the end of Han was idealized in Chinese literature as an age of chivalry.

Upstart dynasties were so numerous and ephemeral that there was little continuity in government. Local warlords prevented effective control from any established centre. The examination system lapsed and offices were monopolized by great families, who fortified their estates and organized private armies of serfs and clients. Warlords extracting recognition from defeated puppet emperors and claiming imperial rule over vast territories left many cities with few obligations beyond negotiation of bribes and pay-offs. The south-west cities and ports with their increasing profits from oceanic trade and large colonies of foreign merchants were best encouraged as valuable sources of finance and left to carry on as they knew best.

Nanking was a capital city with a rich agrarian economy, but its faction-ridden military regimes exerted only feeble control, so that scholars, poets, artists and philosophers flourished in relative freedom. Political upheaval stimulated intense intellectual questing as scholars sought new ways of thinking in reaction to discredited philosophies.

In these years of continual upheaval and suffering it was cities of this kind, untrammelled by the rigid controls of the strong dynasties, that were able to flourish despite the overall disorder from Han to Sui and T'ang, when Balazs finds (1964 *passim*) the greatest galaxy of intellectual and literary stars. The feudal period of the Warring States had also produced Confucius and Mencius, as well as Lao Tzu and Chuang-Tzu.

The second and third centuries AD not only produced a spiritual renaissance but 'the blossoming of a new kind of lyric poetry and the creation of a magnificent art of sculpture' (Balazs, 1964:188). Although many of the radical thinkers were revolting against the corruption, profligacy, injustice and oppression of the political elite of the capital city of the state in which they were residing, they were themselves very much part of the urban system. Despite yearnings for rustic simplicity and occasional withdrawals into the wilderness as hermits, they were indissolubly bound to the urban elite by kinship, friendship, sophistication and common interest, with the result that they were constantly drawn into high office in spite of their extreme views.

The great poet Ts'ao Ts'ao, 'vile bandit' and 'heroic leader' according to situation and perspective, drew round him the best brains of the age and founded the northern kingdom of Wei with its capital at the already ancient city of Loyang. Another member of the circle was Wang Fu the dialectician, who taught that 'poverty arises from wealth, weakness derives from power, order engenders disorder, and security insecurity' (Balazs, 1964:202), maxims which neatly sum up the long-term experience of Chinese cities. Wang Fu's pupil, the philosopher Tsui Shih, also held office at the capital on the Grand Marshal's staff and later, after a period of dismissal, was made prefect of Liao-tung, but ended his life in poverty as an itinerant vendor (Balazs, 1964:207). His follower Chung-ch'ang Tung in turn was regarded as a 'madman' for his extreme views, outspokenness and unconventional behaviour, yet found himself on the staff of Ts'ao Ts'ao at Loyang devising all kinds of administrative, legal and economic reforms.

As divided, 'feudalistic' China failed to achieve either unity or stability, the urban intellectuals turned in a more nihilist direction, often combined with a despairing libertinism. The 'nudist' circle of the late third century were friends of the highest officials and ministers and accepted important posts themselves 'in order to neglect their duties', intoxicated with abstruse conversation and fine phrases when not actually debauched and drunk. A witty remark in a tavern could start a career for these elegant young men in the 'chic circle at the capital' (Balazs, 1964:248).

As disorder and suffering continued, a great longing for salvation developed, bringing mass adherence to Buddhism when it became influential in the fifth century. The yearning for order was met by turning back to a rethought Confucian orthodoxy, especially marked among the intellectual officials of the southern capital city of Nanking. Fan Chen and his two cousins visited the intellectual salons of both Nanking and Loyang. Fan Chen later became prefect of Ching-chou-fu and then of Fuchou, capital of Fukien, only to be recalled to the chancellery in the capital, banished to Canton in the far south for disrespect to the emperor and at last recalled as Master of the National Academy (Balazs, 1964:260). Intellectuals moved from city to city throughout, whether as wandering scholars, or as mandarins following the vagaries of office.

Bureaucracy, rank and economic status

The gentry-official, scholarly bureaucracy of the Chinese mandarins was the most crucial and significant of all Chinese urban innovations. There was already a recognizable civil service under the Han, recruited by recommendation and sponsorship implying liability. The number of actual officials was small in relation to the vastness of the empire, but they had a large ancillary staff, so that by the end of Han there were over 130,000 officials and secretaries in the capital city alone (Stover and Stover, 1976:66). Candidates for office were already tested by being asked questions, to which they had to furnish written answers. The emphasis was on intelligence and integrity. The memorials of the scholar Tung Chang-Shu to Emperor Wu in 136 BC are credited with the beginning of the examination system and a national system of schools. The Imperial University opened at the capital city in 124 BC with fifty scholars, rising to three thousand a hundred years later and thirty thousand by the end of Han. The script was simplified making administration easier, (but the dictionary of AD 100 contained 9,000 characters and their meanings). Paper was invented in AD 105. Previous writing was on fragile strips of wood and lengths of silk.

National policies were sent for debate by professors and scholars, who thus acted as a kind of national political consultative council. The examination system may not have become regular until the Sui and T'ang dynasties 700 years later. There was a general breakdown of institutions at the end of Han. Expanding bureaucracy involved a large amount of paper work, while writing was so difficult that proficiency in it required a high degree of scholarship, as well as lending itself to the refined art of calligraphy, which explains the gentry-scholar-bureaucrat syndrome. Medieval Europe could use the church for intellectual, administrative and clerical purposes, but the church as an institution was dedicated to other ultimate goals, whereas the mandarins were, in this sense, single-mindedly dedicated to the maintenance of the state.

There were twelve grades of official from ministers at the top with 2,000 measures of grain per annum, to the clerks at the bottom with 100 measures. In theory promotion was possible to the top from the bottom anywhere in the empire. However rarely it occurred it was an exciting and original idea. The three top posts were chancellor, imperial chancellor and commander-in-chief, followed by the nine ministers of state with their departments. They were often in danger of being by-passed by the emperor's private, inner secretariat, which might be staffed by favourite eunuchs rather than regular officials, leading to the threat of the 'White House' syndrome of secret inner government.

The number of provincial commands into which the empire was divided grew from sixteen to eighty-three under the Han, each with a governor and commander, and a civilian supervisor over both, administering from a major regional capital city, while under them in each case were from ten to twenty prefects administering from local walled cities, collecting tax, settling disputes and recruiting for service. Regional inspectors were supposed to supervise the other administrators. Regular mails and posting services kept all administrators in touch, calendars were issued to control seasonal activities and annual counts were made of population. Water clocks, sundials and seismographs were in use, partly for practical, partly for ritual purposes. The Emperor Wu Ti (140–87 BC) had established state monopolies for salt and iron mining, and state agencies for organizing mining, manufacturing and distribution, all of which demanded an even larger bureaucracy to run them. Administrators had to report at the capital every year.

Recruited for merit, knowledge and intelligence by examination in the Confucian and other classics, requiring many years of study, the mandarin bureaucracy acquired a self-perpetuating dynamic of its own, so that whatever natural disasters, political catclysms and foreign invasions occurred, they always remained the indispensable administrators of China. They were firmly entrenched by the regular examinations and expansion of the school system under the strong T'ang administration so that no hereditary aristocracy outside themselves was ever a serious threat to them again. Mandarins in operation were always urban based, though belonging to families deeply entrenched in rural landholding. The urban mandarin constituted the stable corporate peak of power under the emperor, however much the latter might try to build up his own family or ethnic group or his own favourite eunuchs against them. As individuals they were vulnerable to the savage court intrigues the more they neared the top, but as an institutionalized corps they were never seriously challenged. Whatever the abuses, they remained too much an elite of intellect and ability, dedicated to the maintenance of the system, as well as a corps of individuals deeply rooted in landholding all over the empire, for any other category to be able to challenge them.

Confucian ideology saw society, as in a reversed Marxist mirror, as composed of rulers on the one hand and producers on the other. Producers were farmers, while merchants and even craftsmen and artisans were by comparison parasites. But Chinese governments never attempted to deny and exclude the role of merchant altogether, as they did in Japan – though without success. The state perceived its role as all-embracing, with the right to intervene in mining, manufacture, distribution or farming as it saw fit. To the famous salt and iron monopolies were added others for copper, tea, wine, spirits and foreign trade, with state factories for weapons, instruments, silk and porcelain manufacture, state reserve granaries, state distribution agencies and the state farms on the border in which soldiers were supposed to support themselves. But trade and commerce, though despised and officially classed as unproductive, were never deliberately hampered as necessary activities in society.

Rather, they were encouraged, with the state, through the mandarins of provincial cities always retaining the power and right to tax them or take over their operations when it seemed worthwhile.

The supreme goal of official privilege, and the tendency of the elite to spend its wealth on land and real estate for security, or on conspicuous consumption for prestige, was not favourable to economic growth, let alone industrial transformation, yet the excellence, variety and abundance of China's products still proved an irresistible attraction to trade, both Chinese and foreign. Nor could the gentry, even the imperial family, resist the temptation to invest in it through privileged participation. The mandarins and merchants were ideologically and officially distinct and opposed, yet inevitably drawn together by their common interest in gaining wealth and exploiting peasants. They could even belong to the same families, since the gentry traded extensively in their surplus products, and rich merchants always strove to infiltrate the official ranks through bribery and marriage.

Official rank and economic status

The gentry (*shih*), farmers (*nung*), artisans (*kung*) and merchants (big *shang* merchants and small *ku* shopkeepers) were officially ranked in that order (Eberhard, 1960:11). Merchants and their whole families were not supposed to own land, or ride horses, and must wear robes of special colour and materials. Artisans were even more restricted, legally tied to their lord's family, as in Hindu India and early Japan, allowed to sell their surplus but forced to work a certain number of days for the state and moved about by the government wherever their services were required, as when in AD 957 the emperor ordered the carpenters to the capital to build 100 ships in a single year. There were from 200,000 to 300,000 registered craftsmen, each of whom had about five apprentices. In addition there were farmers working at crafts part time and landless farmers, unregistered (and therefore illegal) wanderers, very much at the mercy of the employers for whom they produced. Artisans therefore had no permanent homes until after 1485, when they were permitted to commute their obligations to the state for a monthly payment (Eberhard, 1960:14), out of which the government paid for services. Even below the four official classes there was always a countless, fluctuating mass of landless, destitute or disabled beggars and vagabonds.

In the eleventh century rich merchants were allowed horses, but only with saddles of a special colour. There were moves to let them enter the examinations, their sons were certainly admitted, but it remained difficult without bribery, or marrying into an influential family. In the eighteenth century merchants were allocated a specific but very small quota in the examination. Extremely wealthy merchants, who reached a certain volume of business, were actually granted official rank by the Song.

There was considerable divergence between official rank and actual occupation. At least one member of every gentry family in each genera-tion was expected to qualify as a mandarin in order to retain the family's official gentry status. But families or lineages could be very large, so that many other branches of a gentry family might not be gentry. One family controlled over 334 manors, all of whose population it had to invite to its ceremonies (Eberhard, 1960:204). Poorer branches supplied maids and servants to rich branches. Since gentry families controlled huge estates, although their mandarins always had to live in cities, the disposal of their produce inevitably involved them in considerable business operations, which might be handed over to particular members whose occupation therefore became that of merchant, although legally they were gentry. Family ceremonials themselves involved large-scale entrepreneurship, as indicated by the latter day example of a festival in Taipei in 1960, when over 50,000 came to dinner, consuming 20,000 chickens, 12,000 ducks, 500 heads of hogs, 10,000 catties of fish, 36,000 bottles of liquor, 60,000 bottles of soda and 12,000 packs of cigarettes (Eberhard, 1960:214).

Though mandarins opposed social mobility and changes of social status, as involving onerous paper work and possibly leading to social unrest, mobility may in fact have been as high as in the USA, though very different in complexion, and always higher in periods of weak than strong government (Eberhard, 1960:29). Thus it is estimated that between 1590 and 1684 36% of officials originated in non-official families but only 19% from 1685 to 1780 and 29% from 1781 till 1900, indicating a hardening of the arteries under Qing.

The production syndrome

The rural economy was the essential basis of city life, its development the prerequisite of urban growth, depending on a composite production syn-drome. A mode of production is an integrated combination of forces and relations of production. The forces are essentially land, labour power, technology and other resources and conditions, which form a composite production syndrome. The relations are the property relations, which determine how the surplus is generated and distributed. In the Asiatic mode of production the relations of production assume a predominantly political form, legitimated by ritual and symbolic elements constituting a larger part of the whole in earlier than in later forms. Some see the forces as primary, others the relations (Bottomore, 1983:178–9). It may be that each has predominated in different conjunctures.

The production syndrome from Han onwards included: the fertile land of North China, gradually improved by irrigation, small and large scale, flood control, drainage, dykes and canals, manuring, fallowing and crop rotation, the unremitting toil of the peasantry, motivated by primeval goals and practices, controlled and guided by the state through its local representatives and growing bureaucracy. Both aspects appear in the improvement of technology, agricultural and military, with iron ploughs, wheels, sickles, digging and cutting implements, livestock, draft animals partly replacing human traction and porterage, crop change from millet to wheat, giving higher yields, the adoption and northward spread of rice, dietary switching from mutton and beef to pork and dog, with beans, requiring less space and fodder; with iron spears, helmets, armour, stirrups, bridles, bows and arrows for the military. The military technology may appear more spectacular in operation, but the agricultural is more vital. The inventors are anonymous, but improvements probably issued from the cumulative struggle of the peasantry. Aristocrats were not great inventors, but great rewarders. Writing, paper, money and financial instruments, waterclocks, gunpowder, compasses and gigantic junks, more likely arose from the secular efforts and urban experiments of merchants and scholar-officials.

Thus food production, population, state revenues and bureaucracies all increased, bringing territorial expansion and urban growth, rising density of agriculture, political and military activity, swallowing all intervening space and leading to inevitable conflict. The frontiers of China, as they expanded, met hard resistance in the north and west where aggressive nomads or high mountains were confronted, softer opposition in the south with smaller-scale, more vulnerable, kin-based agricultural groups.

Elements of the production syndrome increased and became more specialized over time, regressing in periods of breakdown, with catastrophic losses, deaths of millions, deterioration of institutions, political structures and resources. Rebel forces destroyed cities, floods and warfare devastated vast areas. Yet the means of production were not irrevocably lost. Population and production expanded again. Cities were rebuilt, new ones founded, the urban network and its hierarchical integration diversified and extended. Much of the production syndrome offers a rural rather than an urban air, but the most fundamental of all necessities to every city, except perversely sited Peking (Braudel, 1979:617–25), were the food and raw materials from its immediate surrounding area (Stover and Stover, 1976:91, 93).

The proverbial fertility and productivity of China was a productivity of land, not persons, based on extreme labour intensity. Peasant output per head may have been no greater in the nineteenth than in the eleventh century. 'In the end the marginal productivity of labour was reduced to practically zero' (Stover and Stover, 1976:13). But the area under cultivation and the density of occupation constantly grew. The intensity of the labour of the Chinese peasant passes belief, amounting to ten or twenty times that of the Indian peasant even in the most intensively cultivated areas (Nair, 1983:26). The double and multiple cropping of early-ripening rice had a prodigious effect on China's food supply and population growth from Song times (Nair, 1983:4).

Philosophers shed tears and mourned for the unspeakable sufferings of the Chinese poor, but saw no solution. The Chinese were more efficient under the final Qing than a thousand years before. Oppression comes more from land:population ratios than from the personality of the oppressor. The supreme contribution of the mandarin was to dampen the development of subversion. For decades workers and peasants somehow struggled on under inhuman conditions of unremitting toil, then a local outburst provided a spark and general rebellion exploded with unimaginable fury. Urban workers and rural peasants were relentlessly squeezed to the bone. Year in, year out, there was little respite for the peasants' grinding toil from dawn to dusk. No *panem et circenses* and public baths as in Rome, let alone free rations, but in the capital and other great cities the obligatory ceremonials of the emperor offered a brief respite but, though human and not slave, endless toil was the appointed lot of most human beings under the mandate of heaven. Cosmic symbolism was no compensation.

Shang and Zhou still occupied the ancient heartland which had been most attractive and rewarding to bronze age agricultural skills, with their use of domestic animals, manuring of fields and improving irrigation techniques. Northern China was already becoming overcrowded during Former Han, but the devastation wrought in the Hsin transition (AD 9–25) was so appalling that millions perished and the Later Han recovery started with more plentiful land, and peasants who survived became more contented. But after the Han breakdown, once again, loss of life, impoverishment and suffering wrought by warfare, flood, famine and general devastation over a long period drastically reduced population pressure by the fourth century AD. However, some areas in the north remained dense, whereas in the south land was plentiful. Renewed devastation led to a major emigration to the south in the seventh century and again in the tenth, while in the sixteenth century under the Ming there was a large flow back north.

The period between the fall of Han and the rise of Sui (AD 220–580) has been compared to the coeval period of the fall of Rome (Elvin, 1973:22 and *passim*), when the Chinese economy, after 400 years of increasing monetization, reverted to local subsistence and barter, although much larger revenues were raised by the cities from the peasants than was the case in Europe (Eberhard, 1960:107–8). None the less, urban populations fell. It was during this period, however, that southern China, less torn by war, was becoming more Chinese, with its population growing towards the critical point where it tipped the balance to quite different economic complementarity of south and north. The Chinese urban system never broke down and reverted to rurality as happened in much of Europe after the collapse of Rome. It is understandable that while in Rome armies hardly ever mutinied or rebelled, in China they constantly did, where soldiers were despised and it was urban bureaucrats who, like Roman armies, provided the real guarantee of imperial unity.

Just when some of the old lands of the north were becoming exhausted, as well as constantly devastated by war, a richer and more complex agricultural economy, including rice, tea and sugar, was evolving in the south. The T'ang restoration of order throughout the empire by the end of the seventh century led to increasing integration as the northern capitals of Chang'an and Loyang required huge deliveries of grain from the south by the Grand Canal. From the tenth to the twelfth century the whole political and cultural centre of China shifted south, as much of the north was lost, and when the Song were driven from Kaifeng in 1127 they made their capital at Hangchow. Already from the seventh to the eighth century the population of the south rose from 23% to 43% of the total. By the twelfth century it reached 65% (Shiba, 1975:16).

The vast T'ang armies had reunified China, carried its authority far into central Asia, brought the empire to the zenith of its power and made its capital Chang'an the greatest city in the world and the ultimate exemplar of the Chinese cosmographic city. T'ang peace lasted a mere 150 years. An-Lushan's revolt lasted eight years and T'ang order was never restored. When the Sui, briefly, and then the Song regained control, the Song founder, though a successfully rebellious general himself, reduced the armies by three-quarters concentrating them on the capital at Kaifeng under firm civilian control, pacifying troublesome generals and neutralizing them with civilian honours. The Song chose material prosperity, civilian values and diplomacy, rather than military might. This made possible their unprecedented achievements and also ensured their downfall. The vicious dynastic cycle could be squeezed, elongated or otherwise distorted, but not broken.

All pre-capitalist empires suffered inherent weaknesses. Highly inegalitarian, class-stratified societies, built by conquest, maintained by ruthless exploitation, nothing could save them from their own temptations, increasing luxury and degeneration. Their religious rituals and symbolic structures were inadequate to the task. Forced to increase military expenditure to defend borders and counter revolution, forced to such extreme levels of extortionate taxation and exploitation that uprisings, banditry, messianic movements and massive popular revolts followed automatically, with famine, devastation, floods and chaos; yearning for peace and order became so desperate that leaders inevitably came forward to start the cycle again, with longer or shorter intervals of 'feudalistic' conditions. The initial Song military restraint and relaxation of controls fostered the Song miracle, but could not defend them from Kublai Khan.

Song achievements

The supporting rural economy further intensified under the Song. Crop rotation replaced fallowing; higher yielding, early ripening rice replaced wheat, even north of the Yangtze, though wheat growing spread on suitable terrain as a winter crop throughout the south, while cotton introduced from Bengal was grown in the summer.

The production of silk, tea and sugar became more specialized. Even the northern elite ate rice and many different kinds were grown both for different types of soil and climate as well as luxury varieties for brewing wine. In the eleventh century dry hill rice was introduced from the southern state of Champa. The Chinese bred from it faster growing, high yielding strains, ripening in 60 instead of 100 days, and drought resistant, so that they could be harvested several times a year on previously unproductive hillsides. Where possible, hillsides were terraced for irrigation. Flooded fields were drained periodically to reduce malaria, and also stocked with fish, ducks and geese, which both increased fertilization and improved diet.

Pigs were even kept in cages on pedestals in fields which they thus fertilized. Processing and applying the manure of one pig entailed immense labour (Nair, 1983:26). As in ancient Mexico, floating fields on lakes further intensified market gardening near the great cities (Eberhard, 1960:199). Green manure, compost, lime and human excrement (in large supply from the cities) were also used, so that many fields could be cropped continuously. Special weeding instruments were invented, and a special float for moving expeditiously in flooded paddy fields. Dozens of different types of boats were developed for transporting different crops in different depths of water over the huge network of rivers, lakes and canals, which spread all over China. More watermills provided power, more and larger locks protected against floods and increased the total supply. Agricultural improvement pushed the overworked peasant towards breaking point. China's failure to discover massive sources of non-human energy other than wind or water was fatal.

On the foundation of this unprecedentedly intensive and productive agriculture many other technical innovations occurred under the Song. They developed the first great Chinese merchant navy for international trade. Ships with multiple decks were propelled by fast, man-powered paddle-wheels. Large junks could carry 600 passengers or 2,000 bushels of rice. Maritime compasses, used long before by geomancers, came into use in the twelfth century. Movable type print enormously increased publication and made books much more widely available.

The ingenuity and artistic refinement of the Chinese craftsmen could not greatly surpass what they had already achieved millennia before under the Shang, but their numbers and the volume of their output were vastly increased and diversified, reflecting the spread of new technological inventions and requiring improvements in productive organization. More sophisticated, elaborate and large-scale methods of buying and selling, supply and distribution, credit and finance, were needed to take account of larger distances and longer time periods in trade, also demanding administrative innovations and currency improvement on the part of the bureaucracy and merchants.

Money coinage had been in use for over a millennium. Coins were made of copper, mined by the state monopolies, and as time went on, the supply was often inadequate. The copper 'cash' were strung in strings of thousands, though the actual number might be less. In later times money values were reckoned by 'strings', whatever the actual coinage or currency might be. The actual strings were bulky and hard to transport in large quantities, so that local shortages were frequent, provoking military governors to prohibit the export of currency, which brought trade to a standstill. By the eighth century AD merchants had evolved a system of depositing the strings of coins and using paper certificates for certified amounts. This first paper currency stimulated the development of banking for wholesale and long-distance trade. The T'ang government took over the system, prohibited its private use, and issued certificates against deposit for a 10% fee (Balazs, 1964:42). This was the first paper currency, which expanded greatly under the Song, to about 10 million strings.

The first century of Song rule, from about 980, witnessed the most rapid economic growth in the history of China. All known economic indicators showed an extraordinary burst of expansion. The acreage of arable land rose from 2.9 to 4.6 million, despite the exclusion of the far north.

It is claimed that the consumption of coal and iron during this period rose faster than in the first two centuries of the industrial revolution in Britain. The production of pig iron in the mid-eleventh century was fourteen times what it had been under the T'ang in AD 800; that of silver thirteen times and copper eight times as great. Such increased production of currency metals inevitably led to price inflation, but the rise in price was actually less than the rise in production, for the national budget only rose seven times, from 20 million strings in AD 1004 to 150 million in AD 1021, against the rise of eight times in copper production, which provided the bulk of the currency, while the luxury and overseas trading currency in silver rose thirteen times. At the same time the monetization of the economy probably proceeded even faster, since in the eighth century only 4% of revenue was received in money, as against over 50% by the mid-eleventh century. In fact, production seems to have more than caught up with price inflation, for the budget of AD 1065 was only 116 million strings as against 150.8 million in 1021. In paper currency there were 10 million strings in circulation by AD 1166. Although the currency was not unified, the capacity to print paper money added greatly to the speed and volume of transactions and the importance of banking. The Song administration also established pawnshops which made loans to peasants.

The annual supply of grain to the capital from the main producing areas of the Yangtze valley averaged 6 million piculs in the eleventh century, reaching 8 million in some years, as against 2 million to T'ang Chang'an 400 years before, 2 to 5 million to Yüan Peking in the fourteenth century and an average of 4 million to Peking throughout the Ming and Qing dynasties.

The Song capital at Kaifeng was easier to provision by the waterways from the south than any other northern capital. The Song did not attempt to reconquer the far north, much of which was devastated, but paid off its Khitan Liao dynasty with an ample tribute which was far cheaper than maintaining huge armies like the T'ang. The number of mandarins administering the empire almost doubled in a few decades from 9,785 in 1016 to 17,300 in 1049.

In the Song era, if ever, China might have taken off into the self-sustaining growth of an industrial revolution. But the powerful intellectual and potentially innovative interests of the urban elite were too narrowly focused in other directions: the acquisition of higher rank and more land. Furthermore, no autonomous urban community capable of promoting energetic and co-ordinated economic development existed. The Song merchant class seemed to be bursting with energy, but dissipated it in diverse personal concerns and never made any attempt to claim civic rights or autonomy and to organize for corporate advance. If they had they would surely have been suppressed. Failure to industrialize was due to the 'indifferent unity of town and country' emphasized by both Marx and Weber. The cities were not discrete, exclusive territorial units, even for bureaucratic administration. 'The Chinese urban dweller legally belonged to his family and native village, in which the temples of his ancestors stood and to which he conscientiously maintained affiliation' (Weber, 1958:81). He was like a temporary sojourner, without effective identification with the city, inhibiting development of an urban class to fight for autonomy and economic transformation (Rowe, 1984:5–7).

Guilds

Here it might be thought that the guilds could have made a strategic contribution. They were certainly very numerous and ancient in Chinese cities. They had great potential, but it could not be realized in classical China. Only in late imperial Hankow did Rowe find 'the rise of a guild-centred, sub-rosa municipal government apparatus, which reached full development only in the political crisis of 1911' (1984:344). Hankow had 179 guilds with halls, and far larger numbers without. Some were vast, containing several temples, assembly halls, courtyards, fish ponds, pleasure gardens and theatres (Rowe, 1984:292). They were religious brotherhoods, dedicated to their patron deities. They staged operatic and theatrical performances to vast crowds. Their magnificent lantern processions and festivals were a 'public burning off of profits' in the economic rivalry between guilds as well as the personal assertion of major benefactors and ritual propitiation (Rowe, 1984:291). They organized schools to prepare their sons for civil service examinations which were, of course, an escape from merchant status.

Guilds had traditionally had nothing to do with city government, which was monopolized by the mandarins, who endeavoured to suppress any resources which could pose the threat of alternative sources of power. There was no chance for guilds, any more than cities, to acquire official charters.

Guilds were always local, to one city and its immediate hinterland at most, for any wider combination would clearly have been a threat, which is doubtless the reason why secret societies have been such a characteristic Chinese product.

Marco Polo found guilds flourishing in thirteenth-century Hangchow. A few of the twentieth-century guilds in Peking seem to date as far back as T'ang, in the eighth or ninth century, but all have been constantly reorganized. Korean guilds, derived from those of China, have retained constitutions more than 1,000 years old. T'ang Chang'an is said to have had 220 guilds, Loyang 120, while Song Hangchow had 414.

Burgess' study of Peking in 1928 estimates that it had 128 guilds then, with at least 128,000 members and probably another 50,000 apprentices, controlling over 5,000 shops. This suggests that virtually all crafts and commerce were under guild control and there are strong reasons for assuming that such had been the case in all Chinese cities for many centuries, so that we are justified in taking this late study as some indication of much earlier institutions.

Guilds were characterized by face-to-face intimacy and high solidarity, with both a kinship and a religious element. Not only in the countryside, but even in small towns with populations of several thousand, there were often considerable and frequently dominant concentrations of persons of the same surname, regarding one another as at least distant fellow clansmen. Sometimes such towns also concentrated on a particular craft or occupation. Thus came about the combination of common occupation and common residence with some sense of common descent, which was reproduced in the wards of the larger cities. Such guilds cannot clearly be distinguished from regional associations, since if rural–urban migrants from the same region settled in the same ward of a city and tended to concentrate on the same occupation all distinctions disappear. It seems that this was usually the case, although at least in the nineteenth-century Treaty Ports there evidently were some regional associations which were not craft or commercial guilds at the same time.

The basic motive for guild formation was protection from exploitation by the bureaucracy. The latter tolerated guilds as convenient and orderly institutions which could in fact be used by officials to collect tax and special levies from members. But the guilds were effective and could usually make a successful stand against an official who tried to exploit them beyond what had come to be recognized as customary limits. Guilds could also strike against employers for higher pay, or boycott intruders, as they even did foreign traders successfully on occasion. Peking guilds were also called upon to serve the imperial court in various customary ways, as when six groups of eight porters were called to take turns carrying the coffin of a royal concubine (Burgess, 1928:81). The absence of any consistent common law in China made guild self-regulation all the more important, including matters such as insolvency, for which there was no recourse to any court of law.

Whether membership was explicitly regarded as compulsory or not, it seems to have been virtually impossible for anyone to practise a craft or trade without belonging to its guild, in view of the boycott as well as violence to which he would have been subjected. Thus guilds exercised local monopolies. Their strength and policy was bound to vary with the state of the economy. In good times they would be more open, in bad times they could simply restrict membership to sons or brothers of those already belonging. They collected dues from all members regularly and effectively, they made comprehensive rules to regulate prices and practices, they organized apprenticeships, usually for three years, and fed, clothed and housed members in need and found jobs for them if necessary. Apprentices were general servants to their masters, having to cook and make their beds for them as well as work at the trade from dawn to dusk. All guilds had appropriate mythical patrons, regarded as ancient ancestors and culture heroes or deities, for whom they performed regular rituals. They also maintained burial grounds, which provided one of their most highly valued services. Their names were not always obvious, thus, Peking Porters' Guild was called the Public Welfare Enduring Righteous Holy Tea Association. The Actors' Guild was called Pear Garden Public Welfare Association, after the garden where a T'ang emperor had called upon their services. The Guild of the Blind was called Three Kings Association and that of Barbers, Beautify the Face Association. Others were more descriptive. Many were highly specialized, thus, there were separate guilds for shoe repairers, sole makers, shoe fastening makers and for those who assembled the different parts of a shoe. An extraordinary range of occupations and socio-economic status seems to have been covered, from the Guild of Bankers to the Guild of Coolies. Guild bonds must also have been highly significant in some, where the range of wealth within the guild could have been very wide. This was partly provided for where only the head of a shop would belong to the guild and not any others of those involved or employed in it.

Representing the Chinese city

Two emphases obtrude: the sublime grandeur and vast expanses of the city's cosmic symbolism, displayed in its physical structure of walls, gates, temples, altars and palaces, enacted in its splendid imperial processions and awesome sacrifices, heavy with ritual, more and more infused with power; on the other hand the ongoing bustle of townsfolk and merchants, the immense variety of goods, the colourful cosmopolitan crowds, the unparalleled richness of exquisite dishes, irresistible aromas, fabled delights and voluptuous pleasures unstintingly offered with sumptuous profusion and enchanting grace. Words fail, for of how many other cities and cultures could such claims be made? But ancient travellers were in accord, acclaiming the marvels of Chinese urban culture, its elaborate cuisine, matchless porcelain, delectable teas, superb silk fabrics, entrancing paintings and calligraphy; the rich displays of the wealthy, the ingenuity of craftsmen and precocity of mechanical devices, and the boisterous gaiety of the overwhelming masses, a kaleidoscope of wonders unrivalled elsewhere.

And what of the tens and thousands of less grandiose and spectacular urban scenes? We can only invoke imagination and indulgence. No statistical representation is worthy or possible. We only offer glimpses of a few distinguished city destinies in time and space (see pp. 152–5).

The early Shang city of **Zhengzhou**, between the later Loyang and Kaifeng, vast in area, with a rectangular pounded earth wall 6,960 metres in circumference, sixty feet wide and thirty feet high, representing 180,000 man years of labour, thought to be a Shang capital because of its grand scale, but there were important regional power centres other than the imperial capital and it could have been the residence of one of the major non-dynastic clans. It housed the ruling family in a thatch-roofed, pillared palace, reminiscent of the Yangshao and Lungshan longhouses, and also the central aristocracy and governmental elite. Outside the walls was a network of hamlets, working in bronze, jade, bone, ceramics, silk and producing food for the city.

Shang city-states were already supplied by trade, direct or indirect, over vast distances, with shells and salt from the eastern sea coast, jade from western Sinkiang 2,000 miles away, tortoiseshell from the Yangtze valley or Malaysia; lead, tin and copper from the south and south-east, the immensely valued, ritually potent, red cinnabar dye from Szechwan and cowrie currency ultimately from the Maldive Islands. That *Shangjen* (Shang man) came to be synonymous with 'trader' indicates the importance of Shang commerce (Wheatley, 1971:30–6).

As a convenient port on the great Yangtze, 200 kilometres from the sea, most central of all China's capital cities, **Nanking** occupied a site of inevitable greatness, but had an erratic destiny. Major gateway for Han expansion to the south-east, capital of a dozen diverse regimes, on and off, but never for long, it was the Ming capital for a bare half century, before they returned perversely to Peking, 1,000 kilometres north in an atrocious climate, just as a sixty mile wall with eighteen gates was being built round Nanking's existing thirty-two mile, thirteen-gated wall. Royal camp indeed! But from the third to the sixth century, with no united China or national capital to overshadow it, Nanking shone as capital of a succession of secessionist dynasties, drawing on the most productive part of China, with booming tea and silk industries and attracting distinguished families fleeing from the north. Here, in this time of flux and disorder, flourished perhaps the most brilliantly original sequence of scholars, philosophers, poets and artists China had seen. Not only did periods of disorder encourage economic and political aspects of the Feudal mode of production, but also favoured the blossoming of intellectual and artistic talent.

Nanking was not cosmographic, but resembled a gourd, indented by lakes, in a scenic setting with the tip north-west and the base toward the river and the foothills of Tzu-shin-shan (Purple-Gold Mountain).

Kaifeng was capital of Wei in the fourth century BC, destroyed by Qin, made commercially important by the Sui Grand Canal link to Hangchow and capital of Northern Song in AD 960. The old rectangular walls were 11.4 kilometres long, with twelve gates, an artificial mountain in the north-east, the old T'ang regional commander's headquarters in the north-west, made into the Song palace, with a ceremonial avenue 300 yards wide running north–south. It acquired a triple ring of walls, twenty-seven kilometres long, twelve metres high and eighteen wide, painted white, with vermilion gates, a moat seventy-seven metres wide and willows on the banks. The population was estimated at between a half and a million inside the walls, 200 to the hectare, and 50,000 more in suburbs outside.

The Song reduced the army to 200,000, half of them stationed round the capital, but by AD 1068 it had swelled to over 600,000, with 200,000 round the capital. The total army including militia was 1.2 million. The numbers of officials doubled from 9,785 in 1016 to 17,300 in 1049, from 2,000 to 4,000 of them in the capital. The royal family numbered 1,080, with over 1,000 kitchen staff and thousands of other servants, guards, eunuchs and concubines.

Merchants flocked to the city as the greatest centre of economic opportunity, but the landless poor also crowded in. The Song imposed no corvée labour on the urban population, making the city something of a sanctuary. Though the unauthorized migration to it of ordinary people was prohibited, the measure could not be enforced.

Markets and stalls spread along the streets, river banks, outside the walls and even along the ceremonial avenue, in a way never previously permitted. Some wealthy officials moved out to live in the hilly suburbs, but may also have kept residences in the city.

Kaifeng was said to have 6,400 shops, as against 4,000 in T'ang Chang'an. Some of its patisseries had over fifty ovens. There was an enormous specialization of products and occupations. The great state arsenals and both state and private iron and steel industries employed large amounts of capital and labour. The city as a whole retained the North Chinese one-storey architecture, but some large inns had several storeys and could accommodate over 1,000 guests. There were 3,000 inns altogether, seventy-two first class, and innumerable brothels, some with hundreds of prostitutes. Between AD 1059 and 1063 Kaifeng candidates took 179 out of a total of 541 advanced doctoral degrees awarded in the national examinations, though Kaifeng had only 1.6% of China's population. Sacrifice was made at the altar of Heaven outside the south gate and of Earth outside the north. After the Song were driven from Kaifeng in 1126 it reverted to a provincial capital and the population declined to a mere 90,000, still larger than any city in Europe at the time.

Hangchow was already a large commercial city and communication centre, southern terminus of the Grand Canal, much admired for its beauty, when the Song reluctantly settled in it as their capital. It soon became the largest city in China and the world, but despite its charm, brilliance and luxury, the emperor and officials still regarded it as *Hsing-tai* (Marco Polo's Quinsay) 'a temporary resting place'. They thought nostalgically of Kaifeng and never gave up hope of recovering northern China. Consequently, most of their buildings in Hangchow were of wood, and devastating fires became frequent.

Some 20,000 high officials, tens of thousands of clerks and 400,000 soldiers had been moved south to Hangchow and the neighbouring cities of Nanking, Su-chou and Chen-chiang. By the lowest estimate, Hangchow's population in the thirteenth century reached 1.5 million: 180,000 families, or 900,000 persons inside the walls, 400,000 persons in the southern and 200,000 in the northern suburbs. Others claim a total population of 5 million.

Hangchow had even less cosmic symbolism than Kaifeng, but it did retain its twelve gates and its ceremonial avenue, more than three miles long and sixty yards wide, with many passenger carriages plying up and down continuously. Many of its buildings in the poorer quarters were of two or three storeys, or more, but still constructed of wood and bamboo. Overcrowding was extreme. Density probably averaged over 100,000 per square mile and over 200,000 in the poorer areas. Appalling fires swept through the city several times a year destroying tens and thousands of houses. As in Kaifeng, fire towers were built every few hundred yards, manned by military detachments with fire buckets. Emperors performed acts of contrition for such disasters, making free deliveries of rice available to the destitute. Huge storehouses, protected against fire by surrounding water and against thieves by guards, were built by the wealthy, including empresses and eunuchs, and rented at high prices (Gernet, 1962:37). Streets were regularly cleaned and garbage transported to wastelands by barge. There were ten principal markets. Water supply came from the lake on the west, vegetables from the east, rice from the north and wood from the south. Canals ran through the city, redug every few years, crossed by thousands of bridges, with constant boat traffic and huge sluice gates protecting from high tides on the river. Luxurious residential suburbs developed, of princes in the north and foreign merchants in the south. Entertainment palaces on islands in the lake had expert catering firms which could provide for hundreds of parties at the same time, with many restaurants serving innumerable dishes, some of them iced, with fish and flesh at the same meal. Littering the lake was forbidden and crowds of pleasure boats plied it constantly.

Luxurious living tended to fuse officials and wealthy merchants together in the same pursuits, marking a sharper break between capital and labour. Something like a cohesive urban wealthy class emerged, blurring the official rank distinction between mandarin and merchant. Official rank was actually bestowed on a few great merchants as a reward for achieving a very large volume of trade. Southern Song teetered on the verge of becoming a capitalist society. But it was still largely supported by a vast, exploited peasantry, although greater attention began to be paid to taxing urban and commercial wealth. It was probably the dominant intellectual ideology of the mandarins which prevented a Chinese industrial revolution from occurring. For many of the necessary technical inventions had already been made, though not fully exploited. The Song intellectual and commercial elite was quite as capable, innovative and rational as those who generated the industrial revolution in eighteenth-century England.

The upsurge of Song commercial prosperity almost coincided with the revival of trade and cities in Italy and Europe, and made an indirect contribution to it through both the ocean and overland routes, transmitted by the merchants of Venice, Byzantium and the crusader connection. The movement in China was on a much vaster scale than in Europe, but also more subject to plundering by the state, yet stimulated by illicit commercial investment through agents of the imperial family, empresses, eunuchs and officials. The excessive plundering of peasants by landowners and merchants and of all by the bureaucratic state led to the usual results of deficit spending for the armies and increasing inflation. The irresponsible pleasures of the Hangchow elite continued unabated till the final siege by the Mongols of Kublai Khan. After the conquest the curfew was reimposed and every householder was compelled to keep a current list of occupants on his door.

Expansion of the urban network

With the southern Song at Hangchow the civilian style of urban civilization reached something of a peak. Oppressive as it was, it was supported by a rural economy which had now become locally specialized, in place of the former self-sufficiency, and with a greatly increased volume of local exchange which brought a new type of small town into existence. Previously, the official urban hierarchy consisted of the national capitals, prefectural capitals and **Hsien** or county capitals below which were the villages (Ma, 1971:51). Centres called **Chen** had been military posts and garrison towns, which by the end of T'ang became commercial nodes also. The Song abolished many military posts and the remaining **Chen** were all commercial centres (Ma, 1971:59–60). They were unwalled and suffered more from bandits, but were placed under civilian officials and varied in size from small towns to tens of thousands of persons, reflected in their paying of trade tax varying from 1,000 to 10,000 strings of cash. In the eleventh century there were 292 capital and prefectural cities, 1,118 **Hsien** cities and 1,810 **Chen** cities. Below this were the small periodic markets, estimated by Skinner (1977:5) at 63,000 in the twentieth century. Under the T'ang every official governing more than 3,000 families had the right to establish and profit from a market and appoint a supervisor. In fact, there was marketing activity far below this level, for 'wherever there is a settlement of ten households, there is always a market for rice and salt' (Shiba, 1975:28).

Port cities grew markedly under the Song. Canton had been important since 100 BC, but it was still the only customs port under the T'ang, whereas the Song had nine. Arab merchants and seamen dominated the eastern seas from the eighth century until the Portuguese arrival in the fifteenth, but Song participation in maritime trade was greatly increased. The Song cash currency became the medium of exchange in Japan. Canton and the great port cities had foreign quarters of Arab, Indian and Persian merchants, with their mosques, temples, cemeteries, and their own organization and leaders, usually outside the south gate of the city. Such leaders had to wear Chinese dress and some even took the examinations and were counted as officials.

Increased flexibility of internal structure

In the walled cities and capitals, the strict local isolation of wards, markets, guilds and occupations came to an end after 1,000 years. The walls of the wards were dismantled and they were no longer patrolled and closed at night then opened in the morning with the beating of the drum. The markets, which had been restricted to specific planned sites, like the east and west markets of Chang'an, were allowed to spring up in other parts of the cities, as well as permitting stalls to mushroom even along the central ceremonial avenues though they were gathered in arcades at the sides, leaving free the central processional way. The different trades, crafts and occupations, with the guilds in which each was organized, were no longer each forced to concentrate together in a single section of the market, but were allowed to spread and mingle all over the city as well as spreading outside the walls. A greater mingling and overlap of classes accompanied this spatial mingling, tending to fuse together the wealthier merchants and peasants.

The Song era not only enjoyed a general opening and relaxing of society (by Chinese standards) which was never repeated, but it achieved the highest ratio of wealth per head of population, the highest combination of national wealth with cultural, aesthetic and literary excellence and the most harmonious point in the relations between great merchants and mandarins. Kaifeng and Hangchow were the largest and most remarkable cities in the world.

The Song lost China to Kublai Khan and the Mongols, who excluded Chinese from high posts, oppressing labour and depressing the economy with vast public works of dubious value. Hundreds of thousands were uprooted to go and build Peking, an unsuitable capital far from the economic heart of the country, requiring more massive forced labour to construct its supply routes from the south, disrupting food production. Reckless spending triggered the usual cycle. The paper money depreciated, unrest was widespread, millions were starving, the cities would not fight and rebels took them over.

The Ming restoration seemed like the return of Chinese prosperity, stable and strong, yet unable to recapture the Song achievement. Nanking was an ideal capital, central to the country as a whole. Its maritime access via the Yangtze encouraged China's greatest efforts at oceanic exploration. Its trading fleets reached India, East Africa and the Persian Gulf. The great opportunity was lost when the rulers moved back to Peking in 1421. 'This choice was decisive. In the race for world domination, this was the moment when China lost her position in a contest she had entered without fully realizing it' (Braudel, 1985, III:32). She would never have another chance.

Ming developed the bureaucracy to the point of involution. Co-ordinators proliferated even at sub-provincial levels. They were imitative rather than original, prescribing the great Song thinkers as orthodox and following Song and T'ang models in literature. Urbanization declined in the cities of the south-east, China's major opening to the world. Emphasis switched from cities and commerce to agriculture. Yet there was no land reform, but only endless official laments for the plight of the common man, while massive estates were given to imperial favourites. Emperors behaved abusively, allowing ambitious eunuchs to displace trained mandarins. The population may eventually have reached 150 million, without matching increase in productivity.

Despite extraordinary rulers, the ruthless surface efficiency of the Qing autocracy was unable to arrest the decline. The level of peasant exploitation reached monstrous levels, as unchecked population raced on to reach over 400 million by 1850, with comparable accentuation of poverty and destitution. As the peasants suffered, China's celebrated urban civilization lost its inspiration and creativity, forfeiting for the moment its chance of contributing to human progress.

I admire the work of Elvin, Rowe and Skinner. None can deny the historical importance of late imperial China. In the severe space restriction of my study, I must end effectively with Song, because all subsequent innovations aimed at survival against mounting overpopulation by ingenious but ultimately counterproductive and intolerably exploitative processes of involution.

JAPANESE INSULAR URBAN DEVELOPMENT IN LONG ISOLATION

The beginnings of Japanese cities and the state

The crucial formation of the Japanese state and its instant capital cities occurred at a very turbulent juncture. Japan had emerged from a hunting and gathering existence little more than half a millennium before, when it acquired the fundamental elements of Chinese material civilization through Korea and Kyushu into central Japan: wet rice cultivation, iron-working, wheelmade pottery, writing and literature (Befu, 1971:19–21). Japan sent many missions to China, temporarily accepting the status of a tributary in return for access to China's heritage of culture, knowledge and technology.

The Japanese village was a 'hierarchically structured union of extended kinship families, living on and working the same land area, sharing the same name and customs, worshipping the same deity' (Yazaki, 1968:10). From this arose associations of villages, 'producing a kind of primitive village state. Extending over admittedly small areas, there were many such village states' (Yazaki, 1968:11). Chinese chronicles mentioned hundreds of small states (Rozman, 1973:20).

The leaders of both village and village state had the title *uji* – 'clan community' – *no-kami* 'deity' indicating divinely constituted rule. In every detail mentioned, these were segmentary states (Southall, 1956a; Stein, 1977), which fought among themselves for several centuries, developing towns at the points of concentration of power and ritual, communications and resources, until the Yamato court in the name of its divine ruler gained dominance over central Japan. Yet, 'the common people were not direct subjects of the state, but were bound to it through their leaders, the *uji-no-kami* . . . the state consists of one large family' (Yazaki, 1968:13).

Japanese rulers have always been personages of divine origin, hedged about by awesome ritual prescriptions which sealed them off from mundane life, so that secular rule devolved upon kinsmen or great commoners, who became nobles as differentiation proceeded. They often married their daughters into the imperial house, so that reigning emperors were grandsons of the secular rulers, whose titles variously signified regent, chief executive, or commander-in-chief.

The segmentary, hierarchical and warlike character of emergent Japanese society might well have led to some kind of Feudal mode of production, but the ruling elite were so completely overawed by the grandeur of T'ang China and the efficiency of its mandarin bureaucracy, that they became obsessed with the necessity of initiating a like system themselves. 'By the seventh century Japan was "ready" to start a civilization, albeit in a small way compared with China' (Befu, 1971:28).

The ruling clique arose from conflict between kin groups, villages and village states, which progressively selected persons of leadership charisma, power and wealth, who secured landed estates in the process and after generations of differentiation became recognizably distinct from the masses as nobles or aristocrats, yet often retaining their positions in the clan structure (Yazaki, 1968:37). They carried within them that respect for divinely ordained rule, on the one hand, and the secular propensity for fierce, warlike self-assertion and aggrandizement derived from the segmentary struggle. Some nobles found the moral authority and formal neatness of the T'ang system irresistible and became determined to implement it. Urban aristocracy at the capital was adopting Chinese styles and dress, house construction and architecture and acquiring the splendid products of Chinese arts and crafts.

The Taika reforms and the building of Nara

The seventh century was filled with tumultuous events. In 603 Prince Shotoku, regent of the Empress Suiko, promoted Buddhism with ardent zeal, giving lectures and writing commentaries. He introduced twelve court ranks distinguished by different coloured caps. His constitution defined the three basic elements of the state as the ruler, ministers and people. He died in 629 and the Soga family exterminated his heir. His students returned from China deeply impressed, adding yet further momentum to the reform movement. In 645 a coup d'état destroyed the Soga family and Prince Regent Tenchi with his powerful chief minister Fujiwara Kamatari began planning centralized government, bureaucracy and absolute monarchy on the T'ang model, with the Taika-Ritsuryo reforms. Private ownership of land (much still in the hands of kin groups) was formally abolished. The state was to parcel all land equally to every family in return for taxation and service, in clear imitation of the Chinese *ch'ün-tien* equal field system (Yazaki, 1968:28; and see p. 133). As in China, this tended to break up extended kin groups in favour of nuclear families.

Cosmographic city and territorial administration were to be established on the same model, which they were convinced was the only correct and divinely sanctioned way to run a civilized state. There now occurred the disastrous expedition to Korea and crushing defeat of Japanese forces under the sixty-seven-year-old Empress Saimei by Korean and T'ang armies. It is only in these early centuries that active reigning queens appear, beginning with the shadowy second-century Queen Pimiko, credited with mediating in a civil war to forge a union of thirty states.

Struggle to found, build and occupy a new capital city, modelled on T'ang Chang'an proved inordinately difficult and devastatingly expensive. By the time the final capital was established at Kyoto in 794 some twelve moves had been made since the exercise began in 645. The imperial residence was then at Asuka, the last of the 'imperial seats' which were 'merely the centre of the association of clans', as the emperor was the high priest *uji-no-kami* of the Yamato Clan (Yazaki, 1968:15, 28), which had frequently been moved from place to place but was now thought to be fixed. However, in 645 the emperor built his residence at Naniwa (later Osaka). The port city of Naniwa, already centuries old, and created for trade with China, had the Chang'an chequerboard pattern, with offices for the eight major ministries and hundreds of subsidiary offices. Residential lots were allocated according to rank. But temples, shrines and powerful clans refused to leave Asuka, so the capital was moved back there after seven years. In 667 Emperor Tenchi and Fujiwara Kamatari tried to move the capital to Otsu, but again failed and had to return to Asuka, faced with the Jinshina rebellion. Unable to leave Asuka, the imperial family built the Fujiwara capital under Empress Jito in 694, on the same pattern. Temples were transferred and markets established, but it was hemmed in by mountains and soon became too cramped, so the capital was transferred to Nara in 710, under Emperor Genmei.

Nara became the first very large city in Japan, with an estimated population of 200,000: 130 high nobles and an aristocratic bureaucracy

of 10,000, about one tenth the size of China's. Nara had a ceremonial
north–south avenue fifty yards wide, crossed by nine streets and paralleled by eight, dividing the city into some eighty blocks, each again subdivided into sixteen small wards, an addition to the Chang'an
prescription, characteristically expressive of the extremely detailed,
meticulous, tightly controlled style of Japanese administration down to
the smallest units. Administratively each block was divided into four
wards, each with its head, under whom every five households were
grouped together in responsibility for registering, taxing, policing, fire-
fighting and public works. Unlike Chang'an, Nara had no walls, though
Kyoto later had. High nobles' plots were one *cho*, lesser nobles a half or a
quarter, commoners one sixteenth and later one thirty-second.

Nara was perhaps even too successful. Factional disputes led to five
further attempts at moving the capital, to escape from the undue
influence of powerful families or overweening Buddhist monasteries. By
now the state was broke, but the decision was made in 794 to move to
Heiankyo (Kyoto) with financial help and gifts of land from wealthy
Chinese immigrant families of weavers. Very few temples were allowed to
move to Kyoto. Nara had been a Buddhist city. The casting of the enormous bronze Buddha in the Horyuji temple was a feat of unbelievable
skill, and became the supreme guardian deity of Japan, to whose creation
the whole people had been called to contribute.

Subversion of the Taika reforms

The effort to implement the Taika-Ritsuryo measures was an attempt to
organize a political economy expressing the Asiatic mode of production,
which soon failed and reverted to a form of Feudal mode of production.
There is quite a gulf between what the Japanese decided on paper and
what actually occurred. The aristocratic enthusiasts and idealists who
devised and promulgated the reforms had no effective means at their disposal for implementing them. They tried to institute the training of
bureaucrats in the mandarin style, but it had taken China many centuries
to achieve. The idea of turning grasping nobles and individualistic
warrior farmers into state bureaucrats, responsible for establishing an
entirely new kind of administration over people who had no idea what was
happening to them, was doomed to failure. A college was established,
with examinations once a year, graded by achievement, but considerations of family and rank were not excluded. It was recognized that the
Japanese emperor was the high priest of the nation in a fuller sense than
the Chinese, maintaining harmony between the human and supernatural
worlds and performing correct rituals. In the central government the

office of deities, responsible for the worship of gods, was of equal status with the council of state responsible for secular administration (Yazaki, 1968:27). The provinces were to be administered by bureaucrats of the central government, but heads of provincial subdivisions were selected from former *uji-no-kami*, essentially sacred, ritual and kinship figures, not civil servants. The counties and villages would be administered by members of prominent local families – absolutely contrary to the mandarin system. In these respects the T'ang model was fatally compromised. The mandarin was still tempted to deviate, even with the weight of centuries of tradition and the prestigious esprit de corps of a great institutional structure to support him. Without these strengths, how could the Japanese bureaucrat, with all the weight of his traditional society pulling against him, including his own personal and family traditions and vested interests, hope to resist the force of deviation? Many continued to behave as if the labour of common people and its produce was their common property. The reforms succeeded for a while in bringing in large amounts of tax and corvée labour to the city for the ruling class, but they could not or would not impose and maintain the equal field system. Traditional kin groups the world over have held on to their land rights with the greatest tenacity until corroded by the spread of the Capitalist mode of production. Enforcing the equal field system would require enormous resources of organization and coercion, far beyond the capacity of an emergent state.

The Taika reforms worked well for the urban ruling class as long as they brought in ample taxes, but implementing them on the ground was not in their interests nor within the capacity of their subordinates. They gradually and surreptitiously seized the lands themselves, as there was no effective government to stop them. The rural masses became impoverished. By the tenth century, young aristocrats or members of junior lines were going out to take up provincial posts, getting control of land and pressing the local inhabitants into their service and arming them, so that conflict became frequent. Out of these contradictions the samurai class of warrior farmers developed. At first they organized small, manor-like estates, out of whatever lands were within their power: former clan lands, equal field allocations or poorly defended private estates. There was no real national administration, or generally supported system of law and order.

With population growth, land became desperately short in central Japan where the Yamato state had developed. All land had officially been made the property of the state, but in 743 it was decreed that all newly cleared land should be the property of the clearer. This led to a frantic scramble by all the aristocracy, temples and shrines, to clear new land, or at least to seize land claiming that they had. It caused a tremendous spread of the Yamato state into areas previously beyond its control. It was the death knell of the equal field programme and of the whole Taika reform, which crumbled, leaving the government shaky. The formal aspects of government continued to be observed but the social reality was increasingly chaotic. The powerful drove the peasants from the land they seized, so that they became roving vagabonds, or tenants on the nobles' or temples' lands, or migrated to the cities.

The building of Kyoto

Kyoto was to be an even more magnificent capital and its ground plan was larger than Nara, but with shortage of funds it took some time before it was fully occupied. As the emperor and his family moved, with all the nobles of the central bureaucracy and their huge retinues, the craftsmen and merchants had to follow, as well as peasants fulfilling labour obligations, or attracted to the city by its lighter taxes.

As at Nara the official buildings were in Chinese style with white, plastered walls, vermilion lacquered pillars and roofing tiles, all other buildings in the simple, austere traditional style. According to the Chinese ritual system the left side (Sakyo) was preferable to the right (Ukyo) in addition to the north–south gradation of rank. Besides, Ukyo was damp, swampy and hard to drain while Sakyo was higher and drier. Many of the large mansions of nobles and the precincts of temples and shrines were attracted to Sakyo, displacing many commoner families. The density of Sakyo remained much higher than Ukyo, where the government asked for parsley and lotus to be grown, since paddy fields were forbidden in the city. There was a correspondingly larger number and variety of shops in Sakyo than in Ukyo market. Government attempts to encourage Ukyo market with monopoly rights failed. These influences, combined with the building of new temples, caused the whole city to creep eastwards over the centuries (as London crept west, or New York north). A hierarchy of provincial and district cities (*kokofu*) was also planned on the T'ang model. A mandarin had to have a walled city.

The structure of the emerging feudal state

Japan spent half a millennium absorbing major features of Chinese civilization, transforming itself from a foraging existence into multiple agrarian, warring, segmentary states, from which emerged the Yamato state with recognized suzerainty over central Japan. For two centuries it struggled to establish a centralized, bureaucratically administered state on the T'ang model. They failed in this but succeeded in creating a huge capital city for their divine ruler. What emerged was a secluded divine ruler in the capital city with his court, while the land-grabbing lords and nobles contested and fought for secular supremacy, spontaneously and necessitously arranging themselves into a hierarchy according to their resources and success. They derived ultimately from those who had been drawn into the court and any adventurers able to find a following among the clans and lineages of the segmentary states, as they were being turned into hereditary fiefs by anyone qualified to seize and hold them. Having reached the top by a mixture of military prowess, kin and clan support, with wealth from land acquired from the clan or from the free-for-all declared in 743, one dominant family could survive for many genera-tions, like the Fujiwara, then Genji, followed by Hoji, Ashikaga and Hosokawa. Whoever emerged supreme was graciously invited by the emperor to become his shogun generalissimo and rule the country on his behalf. This general system continued for over a millennium, till the European powers compelled the Japanese to open their market, causing the shogun's downfall and the emergence of the emperor from seclusion to reign more directly.

This millennium was the era of the Japanese feudal state. The system displayed paradoxically contradictory features: on the one hand a warring free-for-all in which the strongest came to the top at each level in each region and locality, based on the amount of land, wealth and followers which each had; but on the other hand a strongly hierarchical chain of command, with nobles of great power and authority at each major level, exacting total loyalty from those under them while themselves devoting a similar loyalty to those above. (When the chief commander of the victori-ous Oda Nobunaga rebelled against him he committed suicide.) There was nothing to maintain these self-made leaders in authority except the power they wielded. It could be chaotic and often was. At other times the authority of the hierarchy was maintained with undeviating precision and irresistible power.

This combination of chaos and order, voluntary hierarchy and absolute authority, can be clarified by Nakane's model of leadership, based on ver-tical personal relationships in a strict seniority system where Ego has the status of a parent (*oyabun*) to all those vertically below, and of a child (*kobun*) to those vertically above (Nakane, 1970:40–63). The kinship aura in this structure is very powerful, generating awesome authority and unquestioning obedience, embodied in dyadic, asymmetrical personal relationships imbued with loyalty, devotion and conscientious reciprocity and all the empowering and supporting emotions of parent and child. The Authority Loyalty system enabled a family once in power to carry on for generations until internal factions and rival forces overthrew it. High ritual status, acquired by descent, being in power and especially close to the emperor, was insuperable in the short run. When the Hojo achieved supreme power in 1199, they dare not take the title of shogun because of their low status, but appointed Minamoto family members as shogun, generation after generation while wielding the power themselves. The unfathomable reverence for ritual status must have been matched by insatiable yearning to elevate it further, accentuated by Buddhist–Hindu values. So emperors retire into seclusion, sometimes becoming monks, and so do shoguns on occasion, even the victorious first Tokugawa.

If there is no effective, enforceable and enforced national framework of authority and administration, operative in all localities, then, in the absence of any other ingrained system, powerful landholders cannot but be feudal. The breakdown of the centralized Japan of Taika-Ritsuryo gave feudal opportunity just as did the breakdown of Rome or Han China. They copied China as the barbarians copied Rome, with totally divergent results in both cases.

Nakane shows how *oyabun-kobun* shaped and channelled the organization of industrial Japan. It was infinitely more potent in the post-Taika-Ritsuryo period because the feudal system which emerged was little more than an emanation from it, as it had been in the segmentary village states. It derived much of its unshakable stability from Japan's unique record of freedom from any effective invasion since history began. But within each feudal unit the patriarchal *oyabun-kobun* structure enabled the *daimio* (lord) to impose his absolute authority on every aspect of the internal political economy of his domain. This was the major contrast with the feudal structure of Europe.

In a society so structured, cities of merchants and craftsmen struggling for self-governing autonomy could not be tolerated. Feudal magnates were unified by little more than the *oyabun-kobun*-type relationship between them, but within their own domains they were exceedingly powerful and autocratic. They would not allow currency, or markets, to divert and dissipate their power. They tried to exclude free market exchange and the use of money, not wanting there to be any merchants except as their own official agents of collection and distribution. They aimed at purely redistributive economy, in which the peasant paid his taxes in rice, silk or cotton (always growing what he was told by his administrative superiors), the rice being used directly to feed his superiors and their retainers, and eventually to pass on to the capital for its support, while silk or cotton passed to official craftsmen in government factories who spun and wove textiles for government consumption. The purpose of the officially controlled markets was bartering surpluses at each level. However, their very totalitarianism compelled everything to cluster round them and town agglomerations inevitably developed as in Europe. But the urban concentrations of the Japanese castle towns were much greater than their European counterparts. Yet they were never accorded, let alone dared to struggle for, any civil rights. None the less, periods of breakdown did, as in China, offer opportunities for the assertion of autonomy. It was the port cities mainly which were able to exploit this and they usually paid bitterly for their presumption. Osaka, greatest of merchant port cities, was an exception. Marx's aphorism of the feudal antagonism of town and country did appear, and was certainly present in principle, but never allowed to get very far.

Shogun's capital, emperor's capital, and the spread of urbanization

With the shogunate physically established for the first time separate and distant from the imperial capital, Kamakura in the thirteenth century began to grow into a large city at the expense of Kyoto. Its population is thought to have lain between 30,000 and 50,000, to judge from the number of sake bottles consumed and the number of dead buried after an earthquake (Yazaki, 1968:68). It retained an approximate north–south axis with the shogun's residence at the north end of the main street, his chief retainers on the east and its seaport on the south, but it was not systematically constructed according to the T'ang Chang'an design.

The greater political nobles depended upon Kamakura and appointed their own regional governors (*shugo*) who in turn had their own warriors. Temples, shrines and craftsmen were attracted to Kamakura. The shogun appointed a city governor or prefect of the city as in Rome, with almost absolute powers over the administration of the city. He established his own special capital guard, however. He also took steps to have the imperial residence and the temples and shrines in Kyoto repaired. Although Kyoto was no longer the centre of political power (and never was effectively again) it remained the headquarters of the court, the cultural centre of state rituals and of religious life, with its great temples and shrines, the main centre of attraction for the merchants of luxury goods and the most skilled craftsmen creating them. It continued to be in many ways the pivot of the national economy and the largest city in Japan until superseded by Edo (Tokyo) in the seventeenth century. It consumed far more than it produced, so the emperor and court had to rely upon the *daimio* for supplies, although they did directly control their own estates nearby for the partial support of the capital. The capital itself also organized the production of luxury goods, while the great temples and shrines which were attracted there, or founded by the imperial house or the nobles, also constituted important production units both of foodstuffs and craft and art materials. Despite the rules, markets and merchants inevitably increased in such a metropolis, so that with all these resources it did provide a very considerable and highly tempting tax base for the emperor and nobles to exploit. In Kyoto the nobles themselves, and also the temples, employed craftsmen who were able to sell their surplus products, circumventing the official market control system so the nobles could hardly suppress the use of money as they wished. Clusters of shops grew into commercial areas with many pawnbrokers and merchants in foodstuffs and clothing. The great Tokaido route was kept open between Kyoto and Kamakura, with its frequent posthouses supplying lodging, food and horses. Express mail could pass from city to city in four days, though most travellers took a fortnight. Its facilities were strictly meant for official and authorized journeys, but merchants used the route also and inns, tea houses, sake bars, prostitutes, pedlars and shops of all kinds began to line the roads near the posting stations.

Besides Kyoto and Kamakura, smaller urban centres were growing up at seaports, round shrines and temples and at other centres of feudal estate authority, such as Hiraizumi which the Fujiwara had made the main manorial office of their family. Here the lord's mansion was the centre, surrounded by the dwellings of his warriors, with temples on the west towards the hills, merchants on the north and a river giving protection on the east. Instead of the regular grid pattern of streets there were T junctions to confuse and obstruct invading forces – a portent of things to come. However, the town was destroyed by the Genji in 1188 and never rebuilt.

Conflicting pressures in the redistributive economy

The three functional complexes of the temples and shrines, the imperial family and court, and the feudal lords are thought each to have controlled about a third of the estate land. They were closely interlocked, for emperor and court continued despite all vicissitudes to be a focus of attraction both for temples, shrines and nobles. Temples and shrines had to develop their own military forces to defend their lands, their warehouses and their craft production centres and merchant clients. On the one hand monks doubled as soldiers, while in other cases temples were under the protection of powerful nobles. Similarly, nobles founded or attracted temples to their headquarters and gathered merchants and craftsmen to serve their needs as well as maintaining large military forces. All these combinations led to concentrations of power and wealth at particular points of advantage, which became urban centres.

Lords came to demand tax and tribute in coins rather than in kind, for the sake of their flexibility, and they also wanted to control the wealth-producing capacities of the craftsmen, merchants, towns, temples, markets, roads and seaports under their jurisdiction. When the centre was strong feudal lords saw their interest in maintaining and enforcing a strictly redistributive economy, so that they tried to prevent the introduction of money and to restrict merchants and trade except for official exchanges, but when the centre weakened and each local lord had to look to his own interests he had to encourage money, merchants and markets to produce local wealth which he could tax, as well as luxuries which he could enjoy, while trying at the same time to control them. In the long run this proved impossible. In fact, the efficient infrastructure created and organized by the feudal lords stimulated outbursts of spontaneous economic activity, which also proved irrepressible. They also conditioned the structure and volume of urban growth. Thus the values and principles which the ruling elite, as a collectivity, held most dear, were none the less sabotaged by it as individuals.

The weakening central government

Once the Genji set themselves up in Kamakura separately from emperor, court and capital, they established a precedent which led eventually to their own downfall. They were fatally weakened by the threat of Kublai Khan's Mongol invasion in the thirteenth century, to meet which they had to keep huge armies mobilized. This caused a serious fall in the production of foodstuffs since the soldier peasants were withdrawn from the land. Nor was the regime able as in earlier times to compensate itself with spoils of war. Dissatisfied vassals sought to increase their independence. Some estate managers made great fortunes from farming taxes, while warriors on fixed income from land were ruined. Middle level warrior overlords became more independent of their superiors, who were also building up their local power against Kamakura control. This encouraged the imperial court in Kyoto to intrigue for regaining control and restoring the *ritsuryo* system of the centralized and directly administered redistributive economy. They failed in the latter since too many nobles were unwilling to give up their direct control of lands and warriors, but in the fourteenth century the centre of power swung back for a while to Kyoto, eventually under a northern coalition of warrior groups, led by the Ashikaga family who demonstrated the unfailing magnetism of Kyoto by establishing the headquarters of their regime in the Muromachi quarter of the city. They never regained the degree of national control or co-ordination which the Genji had once achieved, but this was a period of very significant developments in the urban arena.

It was a period of local civil wars and still increasing local authority. The organization and security of the official posting routes broke down and bands of robbers marauded with impunity making travel and trade by water safer than by land, except where pirates held sway. Some groups of peasants were strong enough to withhold supplies or to demand and secure cancellation of debts. In a period of decentralization Kyoto none the less remained the acknowledged centre, although the imperial establishment was greatly diminished and decayed, for emperor and court were still able to lead their rather isolated yet prestigeful existence of ritual, artistic and luxurious activities on a reduced scale. But this decline was complemented by two very positive trends. The very weakening of authority gave unprecedented freedom of operation to merchants and craftsmen of all kinds, leading to something more like a self-conscious and self-regulating urban community, filling the vacuum created by the crumbling of the political framework which had always been imposed from above. On the other hand, the whole countryside became studded with a network of castles of greater and lesser lords, the greater of whom attracted growing urban centres around them.

The symbolic north–south axis of Kyoto continued to express itself in the distinction between the Upper (Kamikyo) Kyoto of the emperor, court and military rulers and nobles on the one hand and the lower (Shimokyo) Kyoto of the merchants, craftsmen and middle classes on the other. A large part of the lower class of labourers and service workers was attached residentially as well as occupationally to the establishments of the higher strata rather than in a special quarter of its own.

In a period of increasing anarchy, merchants were really forced to form guild organization for their collective protection, against bandits, pirates and mutually predatory lords, as well as to further their commercial interests: in rice, oil, salt, silk, dyes, fish, metal implements, timber and many other products. Pawnbrokers turned into money-lenders on a grand scale. Kyoto had 400 of the latter, providing financial support to the impoverished court and temples. Some were made collectors, others put in charge of royal warehouses. The merchants of the guild running the rice monopoly became millionaires and helped to finance the imperial family. All these developments were contrary to the officially held traditional interests and policies of the ruling class, but emperor and court, temples and nobles, were left with no option but to barter nominal recognition and protection of guilds in return for their economic support and to grant an unofficial status and influence to merchants which were officially denied them.

Civil war and the rise of merchants and self-governing cities

In the mid-fifteenth century rebellious peasants actually invaded Kyoto, so that temples and citizens' groups had to form their own guard organizations for protection. The Onin War of 1467–78, uncannily coinciding with the Wars of the Roses in England, ended all pretence of Ashikaga central authority. Much of Kyoto was burnt and the whole country was controlled by local warlords for another century. Yet emperor and court were never attacked as such. They continued to survive and merchants continued to thrive, paying off threatening power holders. In Nara, also, organized groups of merchants, craftsmen and other ordinary citizens were left free and permitted by default to administer the city. Most shrine towns and seaports were also being largely administered by councils of prominent citizens, often under the patronage of the local lord. This was the period in which merchants achieved their greatest political power and responsibility, even if it was by default, and cities came nearest to achieving a precarious communal autonomy under their own civilian administration.

The War of Onin not only destroyed much of Kyoto, but destroyed the authority of the shogun's government over the city. It was physically and socially rebuilt gradually from the bottom up, by merchants, craftsmen and dispossessed nobles, with their followings. Ordinary citizens were able to move into previously aristocratic areas and shops sprang up freely. The streets, blocks and wards largely looked after themselves, brought together under the administrative councils, composed of ten representatives selected from each major quarter (the upper, middle and lower sections of Kyoto), with a town manager for each chosen for a month at a time (Yazaki, 1968:111–12). Money-lenders and sake brewers dominated the leadership positions.

The great temples of Nara had always protected it somewhat from the ravages of feudal power. Even in the fourteenth century the market was run by a self-governing council of merchants. But since the latter enjoyed tax exemptions as temple dependants they did not wish for further freedom. Uji-yamada the twin shrine city between Kyoto and Nara was really run by the priests, but had representative administrative councils which secured considerable autonomy.

It was the port towns which achieved the greatest freedom. During the anarchy of the fifteenth and sixteenth centuries they were also free to participate in lucrative foreign trade, especially with China and Annam.

Sakai was the most prominent (surpassed by its neighbour Osaka in the seventeenth century after foreign trade had been prohibited). Its northern and southern sectors were each governed by an assembly of thirty-six men chosen from the various guilds of wholesalers. It maintained strong defences and kept its own army. The Jesuit missionaries compared its freedom and prosperity to that of the free cities of late medieval Europe. Sakai had to play off rival warlords against each other, making huge payments in the process. It successfully withstood the demand of Oda Nobunaga for military tax payments by its merchants in 1568, whereas the port of Amagasaki on the Inland Sea was burnt to the ground for its refusal (Yazaki, 1968:114). Many other smaller ports were virtually self-governing at this time.

Yet the merchants of Japanese cities did not press their advantage to the limit. They continued, ultimately, to assume and depend upon the existence of the politico-military hierarchy to which they had always been inured and subjected. They wanted autonomy and freedom of operation, but they also wanted patronage. They wanted a state government to guarantee their tax exemptions and if possible their monopolies, and they did not expel their court or noble superiors, nor take the final step in establishing self-government.

The castle towns

Meanwhile, local warlords all over Japan were building up a dense network of fortresses, which became the nodes of all political and economic processes. At first they built forts on hilltops for emergency while normally living at the foot of the hill surrounded by their retainers. Later they built their fortresses as themselves the centres of the surrounding urban settlement. With the ebb and flow of warfare, from 200 to 300 major centres of feudal power crystallized out of the fluctuating chain of command between greater and lesser lord, patron and client, in which the great families appointed subordinates from both their close kin and their loyal followers, to exert control over the patchwork of local estates and manors. These major centres developed into the castle towns of late medieval Japan.

They had developed gradually from the twelfth to the sixteenth century. In marked contrast to the consciously planned instant cities of Nara or Kyoto, they were, as a type, the unplanned, unconscious result of multiple forces. But they were not unplanned as individual cities, for like most things in Japan they were the autocratic product of systematic, efficient, politico-administrative design. Little remained of the cosmic plan, except perhaps the tendency in some to construct streets on a rectangular grid when the site permitted, but this was usually countered by the decision to build the streets purposefully narrow and winding, with gates facing on to no major thoroughfare, for defensive purposes. The greater castle towns of the sixteenth century had moats and ramparts, related to natural hills and rivers where possible, and several concentric lines of fortification (Yazaki, 1968:77–9, 85, 107–8). The lord usually lived in the fortress with his family and close retainers. Warriors of the highest status lived close round the fortress; merchants, craftsmen and artisans in a special quarter of their own, and the lowest class of warriors on the periphery to defend the whole (Yazaki, 1968:86, 121). In the earlier castle towns the civilian population was expendable and its quarters might be burnt by the lord to aid defence against an approaching enemy. But the later and greater castle towns aimed at protecting the whole population. Not only did the lord require the residence of his retainers and warriors around him, allocating plots to them according to their status, but he also needed a large labour force and the special contributions of his own merchants and craftsmen. On the other hand, large numbers of landless peasants, poor warriors and enterprising merchants and craftsmen came to the castle town to seek his patronage and protection, as also did shrines and temples, while others were founded by the lord himself.

The reimposition of central power

By the sixteenth century the Portuguese had brought muskets and they were soon being produced locally by Japanese expertise. Warfare changed from individual combat between mounted knights to large-scale battles on the plains between armies of footsoldiers. This led to an increase in scale, combined with the rise in population and in agricultural production, which had occurred in spite of the breakdown of government – or rather because of it – since the peasants had actually been less efficiently exploited and had benefited from greater freedom from interference when not directly engulfed in devastation of actual warfare.

These trends favoured the re-emergence of larger-scale military-administrative authority and three successive dominant figures emerged towards the end of the sixteenth century, first Oda Nobunaga, then Toyotomi Hideyoshi and, finally, Tokugawa Ieyasu. When all the great lords met in 1600 at the battle of Sekigahara, Ieyasu decisively defeated them all. Possessing unchallengeable power, he secured legitimacy as was usual by swearing allegiance to the emperor and receiving appointment as his shogun. He and his hereditary successors made formal and rigid many features of the system which was already being established by Nobunaga and Hideyoshi.

The merchants and craftsmen who had begun to gain so much power and autonomy were 'swiftly disarmed and swept to the bottom' of the official status hierarchy (Yazaki, 1968:115). Their approaches to urban self-government were totally abolished, although merchants were allowed special privileges and some freedom of business operation in Osaka, Kyoto and Edo which became a trinity of specialized capitals, of commerce, court and government, respectively. Nor could they be prevented from gaining yet greater wealth and its accompanying informal influence in personal dealings with great power holders. But the period in which weak central government had, as in Europe, allowed merchants to assert themselves and win freedom and self-government for their cities was definitely at an end.

On the other hand the system of castle towns was made the central pivot of the new structure of government, by an extraordinary seeming paradox, in which the Tokugawa used the feudal system as a mechanism of centralization and adopted the castle towns, which were the product of national anarchy, as mechanisms of total control.

The Tokugawa urban hierarchy

The whole country was systematically divided up into some 260 great domains under great lords (daimios) all of the same basic status, though within this they ranked differentially according to whether they had been hereditary vassals of the Tokugawa family, or the subsequent point at which they had joined in and given it their allegiance, or finally recognized and accepted its overwhelming power. Each daimio was permitted one castle only, in the central castle town of his domain. This meant the demolition of most fortresses which had mushroomed during the period of anarchy. Most of the new, centralized castle towns were founded on old ones, but some were port towns, or temple towns, or highway towns, adopted by daimios and built up as their new headquarters.

From his central castle town each daimio made his domain as self-sufficient and as isolated from all others as possible, endeavouring to restrict the free economy to a minimum. Farmers were told what to grow and prohibited from selling any of their crops. All surpluses above subsistence necessities were to be diverted into the lord's treasury. Farmers were bound to the land and censuses were held to give precision to controls. Indeed, farmers were actually forbidden to eat the rice which they themselves grew as their main crop, their diet being restricted to minor cereals. At first 40% and subsequently up to 60% of their harvest was taken from them in taxation. They were also bound to give labour service, but their rights to land and to work were guaranteed! Yet the system of primogeniture made all but eldest sons a useless burden. Farmers were organized into five family units – like those in city wards – with responsibility for implementing the rigidly oppressive system among themselves, and for reporting any transgression on pain of severe punishment.

The Tokugawa family and their immediate followers and warriors took about one quarter of the total rice yield. In addition they held directly the very productive Kanto region round Edo and a number of cities, ports and mines. The 260 daimios and their families, followers and warriors took another quarter or so of the rice crop. The castle order of society was now strictly defined into warriors, farmers, artisans and merchants, in that order, with outcasts such as the ethnically distinct Eta and the criminal or otherwise outcasted Hina categories even below them. Officially there was to be no marriage or any kind of mixing or movement between castes, or even between domains. Even within castes, every possible aspect of status was made hereditary. The caste regulations even applied to mistresses and *geisha*, for each *geisha* catered only to persons of a specific rank and the number of mistresses a man was allowed also depended on his rank. Warrior status was defined from the shogun and daimio at the top to the lowest ranked warriors by annual salaries in rice. These were hereditary, just as the farmers' land, the artisans' craft and the merchants' trade were all intended to be strictly hereditary and locally segregated.

Levels and directions of production, prices, wages, goods and services were all in theory regulated and distributed without recourse to market or exchange mechanisms. The most obvious paradox was the low status of merchants in contrast to their growing influence. This was further expressed in the fact that the daimio, each within the tightly centralized and controlled economy of his domain, actually encouraged a market in his castle town, as a source of revenue, and in ports or highway towns within his domain, all intended to be strictly under control and regulation. To facilitate this, all weights and measures were standardized and other pre-existing tolls and trade barriers were abolished within each domain.

The Tokugawa harnessed the religious influence and the material power of Buddhist temples and Shinto shrines to back the new order. The daimio compelled major temples and shrines to establish themselves in their castle towns, both to be under their control and also using the strong temple buildings and walled precincts as part of the defensive system round the periphery. Priests had the status of warriors and had always held their own temple lands and farmers and retained their own artisans and merchants. The daimio tried to restrict and control this independent economic power.

The warrior code was more explicitly defined, stressing the total requirements of loyalty from inferior to superior, but also emphasizing refinement, scholarship and cultural accomplishments. Both boys and girls of warrior caste were taught literacy and martial and aesthetic arts, with an aberrant form of Confucian book-learning stressing the Shushigako principle that a person's fate and fortune were determined by birth and could not and should not be changed.

The Japanese population is estimated at 18 million in 1600, rising to 30 million by 1750. From 10% to 15% were living in cities. This was certainly twice the percentage of the Chinese population living in cities (Rozman, 1973:6). The castle towns averaged about 50,000 each, with smaller port, highway, temple and shrine towns. The great cities were Edo, Kyoto and Osaka, numbering by the eighteenth century over 1 million, some 500,000 and 400,000 respectively. About 60% of Edo's huge population consisted of the families, retinue and warriors of the daimio who were required to live there by turns every other year. The male sex ratio in Edo fell from 100 to 181 in the eighteenth century to nearly even by the middle of the nineteenth. Many castle towns had a less extreme male preponderance, while in Osaka with few warriors there was an almost even ratio.

Although the castle town as a form emerged spontaneously in the anarchic period, the selection and building of new castle towns at the outset of the Tokugawa era were purposeful and systematic. Though the cosmic design was abandoned, a hint of the north–south axial orientation remained. The castle tended to be at the north rather than the centre and there was a general gradation in the allocation of space and the type of accommodation permitted almost corresponding to the gradation of caste, with the daimios and higher warriors within the castle, rank and size of accommodation diminishing from the centre, artisans and merchants south of the castle with lowest ranking warriors and footsoldiers beyond, outcaste groups on the southern periphery, temples and shrines on the flanks.

The building of Edo

The building of the city of Edo, and the castle in particular, was a gargantuan operation mobilizing the whole nation. All daimios of 100,000 *koku* annual salary had to supply 1,120 rocks, each requiring 100 labourers to move it and brought to Edo by sea, so that there were 3,000 boats in the harbour at once, each carrying two rocks. The castle occupied 181 acres and could accommodate 80,000 standard bearers of the shogun as well as over 300 mansions of daimios with their families and retinues. The shogun's castle tower had eight storeys, those of daimios in their own castle towns from three to five. While daimios were allocated space to build mansions in Edo, other lesser warriors were housed in barracks with space according to rank. Each daimio also had his own warehouses and his own separate warrior training system. The areas occupied by each caste were segregated. The military occupied some 10,000 acres in Edo, with artisans and merchants occupying only 2,500. Merchants were separated from artisans and shops were prohibited in warrior areas. Temples and shrines occupied another 2,400 acres or so. Merchants' houses lined the streets in continuous two-storey rows, shops occupying the ground floor. Every craft and function had its own quarter. In the back streets there were longhouses each rented out to many poor families.

The terminal stations of the great national routes were now at the outskirts of Edo, with hundreds of shops, tea houses, sake bars and prostitutes' rooms. Every town had to supply hundreds or thousands of horses and labourers every year, according to its size, for official travellers, cargo transport, bearing of palanquins and service to warriors. The main annual supply of Edo was from Osaka, with hundreds of thousands of kegs or bundles of sake, soya and other oils, cloth, salt, firewood and charcoal, coins, and even larger quantities of rice.

At first the daimios had actually tried to break the control of markets, which the merchants had acquired during their pre-Tokugawa period of relative freedom, in order to free trade under their control as a source of greater wealth. There was a continuing and insoluble conflict over whether to break up the merchants' monopolies and guilds for this purpose, or to use and allocate them as controlling and taxing devices. The latter tendency predominated.

This general dilemma haunted and finally broke the Tokugawa regime. While the principles of the system required total control of markets, trade and exchange, individual lords at all levels were constantly forced to grant exemptions to merchants in order to secure more revenue. The merchants of Osaka, Edo and Kyoto became virtually independent of government controls in their operations. By 1615 the Osaka merchants had organized their own express service separate from the official system. The wholesalers of Edo and Osaka banded together in a monopoly for protection against the Osaka shippers. Some contractors and lumber merchants became millionaires and began to lead extravagant and ostentatious lives.

The Meireki fire and the rebuilding of Edo

In 1657, just nine years before the Great Fire of London, the Meireki fire virtually destroyed Edo, with a loss of some 50,000 dead. The city was systematically rebuilt five or six times larger than before (Yazaki, 1968:169–70), with moats, walls, open spaces and regulation for plastering houses with mud as anti-fire precautions. Fire fighting teams were established with observation towers and regular watches, while neighbourhoods were all held responsible for patrolling their areas. New efforts were made to impose the sumptuary laws on civilians – the merchants and artisans – prohibiting three-storey houses, the use of gold, silver and lacquer ornamentation, of silk clothing and extravagant footwear. Yet they were allowed sake, tea and tobacco, not to speak of rice, all of which were forbidden to the officially higher ranking farmers, who were told to divorce wives who pressed too much for tea. After the fire, the main *yoshiwara* of the prostitutes clustered round the pre-eminent Sensoji temple, dating from the seventh century, in the Asakusa quarter. The temple recognized a precinct specially for gamblers (officially illegal) in return for the cleaning and repair of the temple. Kabuki theatres and sake houses multiplied and Asakusa became the great entertainment centre.

The attempt was made to prohibit tiles to civilians, but after 1720 they were allowed tile roofs as a fire precaution. Broad bottomed palanquins had been restricted to the shogun's ladies, senior lords and priests, with ordinary palanquins allowed for senior retainers over fifty years old. In 1700, 300 palanquins were made available for the sick, but this measure was abused by rich merchants, so it was prohibited, then in 1726 palanquins were made free for any who could obtain them. Rich merchants further flouted the laws on extravagant exteriors by indulging in internal luxuries.

Changes in the dominant type of merchant

The dominant type of merchant underwent cumulative change, reflecting the growth of population, the parallel increase of economic density, changes in foreign policy and the opportunities offered by the changing needs of the elite. The despised legal merchant class theoretically defined by the elite included everyone from poor pedlars to merchant princes, but in fact their origins were diverse. Even the anti-merchant daimio barons always required a kind of quartermaster to provision their large establishments, not only with food and craft products but also munitions. It was often a samurai appointed to this post, which carried large potential profit. The more restricted the merchants' role, the more profitable it was for those allowed to play it. Some samurai families thus got diverted to the profits of a merchant career. Their rank was ambiguous and contradictory, but as the generations passed, the distinction between merchants of samurai or other origin became obscured. During the long period of political weakness, culminating in the free port cities of the Sengoku 'Warring Barons' epoch (1467–1568), the greatest profits were in foreign trade, for which the privileged could be licensed.

The prohibition of foreign trade in 1630 brought the great prosperity of these merchants to an end and their position of dominance was taken by a new group of Osaka merchants (Crawcour, 1963:193). They dealt in the surplus rice received by samurai as salary, making a huge central rice market in Osaka. They made loans to daimios at 15% to 20% annual interest. In 1670, just twenty-four years before the establishment of the Bank of England, they established a kind of central banking system, controlled by ten dominant merchant financiers, to handle the financial transactions of the shogunate and supervise the Osaka money market. Money-lending, pawnbroking and sake brewing fed into their wealth. They backed the paper currencies issued by daimios, developed new agricultural land and became great landowners. They counted, paradoxically, as quasi-samurai, almost minor daimios, receiving comparable salaries and the right to surnames and to wear two swords when on official business (Crawcour, 1963:193). They increasingly financed the required residence in Edo by daimios and their families. But they were almost wiped out at the Meiji Restoration, when silver was demonetized, the Osaka gold and silver exchange was closed and the run on their banks forced them to close for good.

By the end of the seventeenth century inter-regional trade within Japan was growing very fast, with the ever growing population of Edo as the consuming centre. Wholesalers in every kind of product flourished, the largest based in Kyoto, Osaka and later Edo. At first competition was fierce, but as monopoly privileges became established during the eighteenth century the spirit of enterprise faded. By this time rural industries were springing up in many areas to avoid the restrictive practices of urban guilds. Prosperous farmers with capital turned into businessmen. Officially disapproved, their success had to be recognized, and like their predecessors their leaders became samurai with the right to wear swords and use surnames. This widespread group strongly supported the Meiji Restoration and promoted modern industrial enterprise, to which they contributed about 40% of the entrepreneurship (Crawcour, 1963:201).

A foreigner's view of seventeenth-century urban Japan

The Dutch consular physician, Englebert Kaempfer, left an extraordinarily vivid description of Japanese cities at the end of the seventeenth century. He found Edo, Kyoto, Osaka, Sakai and Nagasaki the five chief maritime or trading towns in the empire (1906, II:73). Nagasaki was barren and rocky but picturesque with an irregular street layout, conforming with the contours and running up to temples and gardens on the hills above. The town was unfortified, but the foreigners lived outside, 'very narrowly watched and guarded', the Dutch on an island linked to it by a causeway and the Chinese in a walled enclosure on the south.

There were sixty-two temples, some outside the town, with beautiful stone staircases leading up to them, and pleasant gardens, elegant walks, fine apartments and the best buildings in town 'for good air, a sweet situation, a most entertaining prospect over the town', not only sacred to devotion and worship but serving for recreation and diversion (Kaempfer, 1906, II:83).

'My next step shall be, according to the custom of the Country, from the Temples over to the Bawdy Houses, the concourse of people being as great at the latter, as it is at the former' (Kaempfer, 1906, II:83). The quarter of courtesans apparently lay between the town and the Chinese enclosure, and contained 'the handsomest private buildings of the whole Town'. Both Kyoto and Nagasaki were famous for beautiful women, but prostitution was much more profitable in Nagasaki because of the great number of foreigners. The girls were purchased very young from poor parents, for periods of about ten to twenty years. 'After having serv'd their time if they are married, they pass among the common people for honest women, the guilt of their past life being by no means laid to their charge', whereas the Bawds (male owners of establishments) were entirely rejected from respectable society as on the same level as the outcast Eta, or leather tanners and public executioners. From seven to thirty women were kept in each house, and carefully taught 'to dance, sing, play upon musical instruments, to write letters' and doubtless to engage clients in delightfully refined and witty conversation which was lost upon Kaempfer.

The houses of the common people were 'very mean sorry buildings, small, low, seldom above one storey', or if two storeys the second very low, roofed with wooden shavings and with wooden walls, wainscotted within and hung with 'painted and variously coloured paper', the floor covered with woven mats, exceedingly neat and clean, rooms separated by sash-windows and paper screens. Every house had a backyard which, however small, always contained 'some curious and beautiful plants to delight the eyes'. The houses of the wealthy were usually of two storeys with a large courtyard in front and garden behind. Nagasaki was also full of male and female beggars, some in religious orders. There were three governors instead of the usual two, because of the need to watch closely over foreign trade and merchants, with one always resident in Edo and the other two commanding jointly for two years, but presiding alternately every two months, until relieved by the third from Edo. No woman was to be admitted within the governor's residence during his period of command, on pain of banishment or suicide and the ruin of his whole family.

Osaka was the best trading town, with an extraordinarily favourable situation. There were seldom less than 1,000 boats in the river and canal, which had many stately stone bridges of remarkable beauty, railed and adorned with brass buttons (Kaempfer, 1906, III:2–3). The streets were narrow but mostly at right angles except near the curving water fronts (Yazaki, 1968:171), with stone paved sidewalks, and staircases on the steeper slopes. As in all cities each street had its gates, closed at night or at any emergency, and with its fire post and well. Houses were not above two storeys, with the front room at street level occupied by a merchant's shop or craftsman's manufacturing. 'Osacca [Osaka] is governed by Mayors, and the court of Ottona's, headboroughs, or commanding officers of every street. Both the Mayors and Ottona's stand under the superior authority of two imperial governors, who have also command of the adjacent country, villages and hamlets' (Kaempfer, 1906, III:5). Osaka castle was at the north-eastern edge of the city. Even luxuries and every kind of sensual pleasure and entertainment were not only more abundant but cheaper in Osaka.

Yet Kaempfer found Kyoto (Miaco) 'the greatest magazine of all Japanese manufacturers and commodities . . . There is scarce a house in this large capital, where there is not something made or sold' (Kaempfer, 1906, III:21). Every product was made with the greatest refinement and perfection. 'There is nothing can be thought of, but what may be found at Miaco, and nothing, tho' never so neatly wrought, can be imported from abroad, but what some artists or other in this capital will undertake to imitate' (Kaempfer, 1906, III:21). But Kyoto was expensive, for it had the constant demand of the imperial court of 'his holiness the Dairi, or Ecclesiastical Hereditary Emperor' whom Kaempfer thus quaintly distinguishes from the secular monarch (the shogun) at Edo.

Edo was the largest of all, also unfortified, but with many broad ditches and canals, stately stone bridges and high ramparts lined with trees, for fire prevention rather than defence, with the many palaces of the shogun and 'of all the noble and princely families of this mighty Empire' (Kaempfer, 1906, III:75).

Edo, too, was 'a nursery of artists, handicraftsmen, merchants and tradesmen', but dearer than anywhere else because of the great concourse of people, the number of idle monks and courtiers and the difficulty of importing provisions.

Kaempfer's maps show the contrasting designs of these cities very clearly, from the symbolic symmetry of Kyoto to the almost complete lack of it in Edo. As he travelled the great Tokaido route between the cities he was staggered by the throng of people, on 'some days more crowded, than the public streets in any of the most populous town in Europe' (Kaempfer, 1906, II:330). He estimated the train of a great daimio as amounting to 20,000 men taking three days to pass by.

Urban mobility, family size and styles of life

Remarkably high rates of residential mobility prevailed in the pre-industrial urban areas of eighteenth-century Japan (R.J. Smith, 1960, 1973). Distinctive and consciously urban styles of life were already established. Although the tightly organized and closely administered small wards of the cities meant that urban neighbourhood relationships were similar to those of small rural communities in their particularistic solidarity, they were in no sense a rural phenomenon brought into the city, but 'an administrative response to an incredibly high rate of population turnover' (Smith, 1973:165). The majority of renters and tenants stayed for less than five years, while the majority of house owners stayed for less than ten. A study of a ward in Kyoto showed that 70% of all households stayed for five years or less (Smith, 1973:205). Both families and households were of small size, the majority consisting of five persons or less. Twentieth-century studies show households only slightly smaller, with urban households somewhat smaller than rural (Smith, 1973:201).

Commercial and small manufacturing businesses were already in the hands of small households, with small family nuclei made possible by the general practice of single-heir inheritance, well before the time of the Meiji Restoration (Smith, 1973:206). Smith feels that the Japanese kinship terminology, with its flexible bilateral emphasis and limited identification of distant relatives, would greatly have facilitated the adjustment of the family to the changes required at the start of Japan's emergence as a modern state. This terminology owes nothing to western influence or the forces of modernization.

In eighteenth-century Edo, especially, but also in Osaka and to some extent in Kyoto, two distinctive styles of urban living had become established, and identified by the terms *yamanote* and *shitamachi*, referring respectively to the hillside districts which were typically occupied by samurai, and the old downtown area which was dominated by 'townsmen' (Chonin). These townsmen were precisely those owning and operating small businesses, with one or two employees: merchants, independent craftsmen, tailors and restaurant or workshop proprietors. They had the reputation of being lusty and hot tempered, sceptical and anti-bureaucratic. Their taste was characteristically expressed in the *kabuki* theatre, *yose* vaudeville, *geisha* performances and *sumo* wrestling of the bustling entertainment quarters. They were fond of bloodthirsty romances and witty, salacious comedies. They had their own kind of melodious music, and their poetry was cheeky and sardonic. They liked to indulge in conspicuous waste and were not ashamed of their plentiful money. Their women were often fully involved in the family business, and enjoyed more freedom and better status than those of other classes. Within the *shitamachi* style the Edo merchants were stereotyped as manly and impetuous, while those of Osaka were more noted for their integrity and steadiness.

By contrast the *yamanote* style denotes a more aloof demeanour and austere cultural expression in music, literature and theatre, or the extreme refinement of the Noh tea ceremony. After the Restoration *yamanote* was typical of white-collar workers, officials and executives, prudent and bourgeois, speaking politely in standard Japanese, rather than the vulgar dialect of *shitamachi* (R.J. Smith, 1960).

Though in many ways suggestive of the distinction between merchant and aristocrat, these were not class styles, but real alternatives with one or other of which people could identify. They were nothing to do with any distinction between urban and rural, or traditional and modern.

The cities strain the Tokugawa system

Although agricultural productivity increased and much new land was reclaimed, the population also grew. The enormous number of the unproductive military caste in the cities and their even larger army of servants was a permanent strain, accentuated by the huge cost of major disasters like the Meireki fire. The *Sankin-Kotai* alternate year's residence in Edo of the daimios with their retinues, and their families there permanently as hostages, was prohibitively expensive and eventually set in train a momentous sequence of irreversible events.

Although the caste rank of warriors, and even their status within it, was supposed to be defined forever by hereditary succession, and constantly expressed in the quantity of their rice ration, warriors and their families were under pressure to compete with one another in styles and standards of living. There was a momentum built into the system which nothing seemed able to reverse. Warrior indebtedness rapidly became an increasingly serious problem, with repercussions at all levels. Since all daimios and their domains were purposely kept in direct competition with one another by the shogun, they were involved in further heavy expense maintaining liaison agents to the shogun, high officers of state and other daimios, through the private quarters of the palace women. Even in the seventeenth century many domains were already in debt, and there were even instances where nearly twice the revenue of the domain had to be spent in Edo. The problem got worse and worse and by mid-nineteenth century the domain of Nagaoka reached the point of spending nearly three times its annual revenue for a single year's residence in Edo. In fact the interest paid in debts was more than the total revenue, and nearly 80% of expenditure took place through and presumably in Edo (Yazaki, 1968:210).

The shogun's government itself tried to assist hard-pressed daimios with the result that it too began to fall into debt. Debt meant one of several harsh alternatives: borrowing from the merchants, cutting warriors' salaries or grinding out of the farmers a higher proportion of their crop. In course of time, many warriors were so impoverished that they began to sell part of their rice salaries. The commercial agents dealing in warriors' rice cornered the market and became exceedingly wealthy. It became possible for warriors to sell their names and caste status to merchants, at least by adopting a merchant as their heir. Besides, very rich merchants began to buy grants of warrior status from lords whose need for loans made it impossible for them to resist. All these transactions struck at the very heart of the system. Impoverished warriors were forced into other occupations as scholars, priests or even farmers and townsmen. Debts were rarely repaid and in 1784 and again in 1841 all debt payments to merchants were officially cancelled. This meant that poor warriors, having no collateral, could not obtain further loans and were forced to even more desperate expedients. They began to do odd jobs for merchants who took pity on them and so degenerated from warriors into townsmen. Successful merchants in the three main towns became more wealthy than daimios, more than half of whose revenues went on salaries to dependants. The glaring discrepancy between merchants' caste status and wealth led to the illicit adoption of warrior styles of life.

While merchants and craftsmen in Edo, Osaka and Kyoto profited, those in provincial towns suffered from the stranglehold of their monopolies, in which the government was forced to acquiesce as the price of its growing financial dependence. The farmers were so oppressed by tax and labour obligations, intolerably accentuated from time to time by famine, that many gave up in desperation and abandoned their land either to the new category of big landowning farmers which emerged from the process, or to merchants who thus contrary to all caste rules became landowners. Landless farmers flocked to cities to become pedlars and petty traders, again in contravention of caste, or to swell the ranks of beggars and thieves living on their wits, or joining the Hina outcastes, while their wives and daughters became maidservants or prostitutes. Thus the whole system so clearly and consistently planned was distorted and threatened with disruption, becoming a mockery of itself.

All this presupposed and occurred within a completely closed national, island market. The Portuguese had been driven out and their Christian converts put to death early in the seventeenth century. Dutch and Chinese trade was still permitted through the port of Nagasaki, but under such restrictions that the city actually dwindled in size. Thus the Japanese market was completely isolated from the external world and the prices of Japanese products bore no relation to the prices of the same products elsewhere.

It might well be asked why the shogunate, with its apparently absolute power, allowed the Tokugawa scheme for society to be sabotaged. Why did they not systematically plunder, or even execute, the merchants to whom they and other daimios were becoming increasingly indebted, as European medieval monarchs had done? The answer seems to be that, after the initially overwhelming victory of Ieyasu at Sekigahara in 1600, the shoguns increasingly had to maintain their supremacy by the ubiquitous game of playing one force off against another. They tried to ensure rivalry between neighbouring daimios, and through the management of their vast estates, spread in all parts of the country, they prevented the local economy of any daimio from being completely autonomous and self-contained. The increasing indebtedness of daimios was really welcomed as sapping the possibility of revolt and making all the more effective the control exercised through the enforced alternate year's residence in Edo. Debt moratoria were therefore only imposed at moments of extreme crisis. Merchants might be despised, but were none the less convenient weapons against daimios. The weakest point in the whole policy was the assumption that Japan could be secure and cut off from the rest of the world indefinitely.

The ultimate paradox of the Tokugawa was that of a military regime living at peace for over two centuries. Overtaxing and famine brought fairly frequent uprisings, but they were no serious threat to the state. But when, in the nineteenth century, daimios lost confidence in the shogun's regime, perceiving the official rules and contours of society increasingly subverted at every point, the shogun's armies, which had not been involved in major warfare for two and a half centuries, were found to be poorly trained, out of practice and incapable of enforcing his authority.

Despite the intention to keep the great domains unspecialized and isolated from one another, both economically as well as socially, with neither movement nor marriage nor trade or exchange across their borders, many internal pressures broke this down. The military government tried unsuccessfully to prohibit employment across domain boundaries. Some daimios early encouraged specialization, which necessitated exchange across domain boundaries, to increase revenue and taxation. Hard-pressed farmers sought to circumvent the official system of redistribution by direct sales of their products to town populations. Osaka and Edo developed large vegetable markets supplied by rural areas nearby, while specially suited areas concentrated on the production of silk, cotton, oranges, grapes or rape seed. Rural industries developed, producing salt, paper and sugar. Small towns also developed special industries to try and break the central monopolies. Thus while some domains remained isolated, others became more and more involved in an embryonic national exchange economy. More specialized agricultural production and rural industry led to more capitalistic organization and employer–employee relationships not provided for by the caste system. Growth of population and constant pressure on farmers to produce more led to heavy pressure on arable land and desperate need for new areas to be reclaimed. To encourage this the military government actually exempted reclaimed land from taxation and this brought merchants into land investment, or warriors using merchant capital. This further confused caste statuses, as merchants became at the same time large-scale farmers. Thus they also came to control whole villages, as though they were local lords, and were permitted to do so as long as they accepted responsibility for the tax. The area of arable land actually doubled during the seventeenth century but land reclamation withdrew large areas which had been used to produce grasses for fertilizer so that other products such as dried sardines, soy beans, lime and whale fat had to be used as fertilizer, requiring new industries and yet further complicating and extending the intricate network of specialized interdependent exchange.

As government and warrior indebtedness increased the pressure for more taxes during the eighteenth century many farmers gave up in despair and land was actually left desolate. As tax receipts fell tax rates were raised, farmers practised abortion and infanticide, mortgaging their lands and becoming tenants of the few more successful farmers, some of whom grew rich, brewed sake and lent money at interest. In 1790 the government actually provided travelling expenses, free tools and grants of land to persuade peasant immigrants to leave Edo.

The increasing scale and specialization of urban production

By the nineteenth century some provincial towns with special skills and local resources, or even innovative lords, had begun to develop more industrialized forms of production on a small scale in metal casting and forging, lacquer making, dyeing and leatherworking. Some such local developments were of longer standing, as in the case of Kiryu which even in 1687 succeeded in preventing control of their silk sales by the Edo monopoly. They continued to develop their hereditary skills as weavers of silk, profiting from their own market, until they were able to challenge the reputation of the famous weavers of the Nishijin quarter in Kyoto. On this solid economic base Kiryu grew to seven times its size from the mid-seventeenth to the mid-nineteenth century, developing a kind of small-scale factory production with shops of about ten looms and sixteen workers each.

The military government was not unaware of the irreconcilable conflicts in the system and the developing sense of crisis. When a group of scholars advised them in 1841 that prices would fall if monopolies were abolished, they terminated the Edo wholesalers' union, then those of Osaka, Kyoto and Otsu, at the same time remitting the tax contributions which they had made. But the merchants banded together in secret fraternities and prices actually rose, so that, ten years later, the unions were reinstated, but with the requirement that membership should be open. In Edo alone there were 12,000 wholesalers, dealing in ninety-five different commodities. The small merchants had also been organizing in thousands against the big monopolies and they were now for the first time officially permitted to move from place to place. Local administrations also began positively to encourage warriors to defile their rank and establish industries, borrowing merchant capital for such investment. They produced brushes and hats, umbrellas and raincoats, medicines, tobacco and mats, but they took their products to their sales agents at night with masked faces to preserve their honour as warriors. In Sendai the foot-soldiers produced 300,000 paper lanterns a year. Warriors' wives also began weaving fabrics at home and were proud of receiving money themselves, but their honour too was protected by the agents coming to their houses discreetly to collect what they had produced. In Fukui the warriors actually introduced machines for weaving so that their transition was quite gradual when Japan began to industrialize under western influence.

Peasant revolts and urban riots

Increasing pressure on the poor, both urban and rural, led to increasingly frequent peasant revolts and urban riots. Sometimes tenants rose against landowners, but sometimes the peasants were led by hard-pressed landowners against their superiors, always aimed at the relaxation of some burdensome tax or service obligation, or at the particular official endeavouring to exact it. At first the government tried to suppress these with great severity, but towards the end of the eighteenth century there were notable cases where they tried to meet the demands of rebels, remitting tax, allocating land or distributing food. As the mob of unemployed townsmen swelled, urban riots also increased. Locusts created famine in 1732 and skyrocketing rice prices caused rioting in Edo. Famine continued and hundreds of thousands of peasants are said to have died. In Ueda riot of 1761, 5,000 or 6,000 farmers and townsmen destroyed fifty merchants' houses, whereupon the shops served food and sake free and the government distributed rice. In the Aomori riot after a fire in 1783, 8,000 or 9,000 bales of rice were stolen from the port by thousands of townsmen, demanding that reserves should be kept, rice sales freed from controls and secret police abolished. The Fushimi uprising of 1782 succeeded in getting an oppressive town commissioner removed. Wakui Toshiro led the townsmen of Niigata against their commissioner's office with 2,000 men. Wakui was released and made administrator, introducing a democratic system which stabilized prices and made loans available, but he was then again imprisoned and later paraded in public and put to death.

From 1781 to 1787 the price of rice rose six times in Edo as merchants again cornered the market after a famine. The government released 60,000 bales of rice and 20,000 *ryo* of money for relief, but rioting continued and many shops and homes of wealthy merchants were destroyed, until the government shut the gates, patrolled the city and ordered 200,000 *ryo* of emergency rice shipments to the port. Osaka had many riots, the worst in 1837 when Oshio Heihachiro, a scholarly ex-police guard, wrote denouncing the town commissioner and the rapacious merchants and began to collect firearms for an armed uprising. He was betrayed by a comrade and committed suicide after being forced to make a premature attack, which was defeated with difficulty after getting near to Osaka castle, burning many parts of the city and looting gold and silver coins from merchants' shops for distribution to the poor.

The failure of isolation and the Meiji Restoration

All through the nineteenth century external pressure had been building up from European nations to break open the Japanese market. Russian envoys came in 1792 and 1804, British in 1808, and then under pressure from a United States squadron in 1853 the shogun's government realized that it had no weapons which could effectively oppose the aggressive Europeans. The port of Kanagawa, renamed Yokohama, was opened in 1858 and also Fukui, while Nagasaki hitherto open only to Dutch and Chinese was opened to all. Nagasaki's exports soon doubled and so did those of Yokohama, while imports trebled. Yokohama had 99 export firms in 1859, 390 in 1863. Since export prices were five to ten times higher than internal prices the latter rose three or four times from 1859 to 1867, causing huge profits to merchants and even greater distress to the warrior upper caste, with a strong backlash movement to expel the foreigners who had caused it. The eastern domain of Choshu led the drive, but its demonstration in Kyoto was a failure and its army returned humiliated and in desperation attacked Dutch, French and American shipping in their port, which was then forced to surrender by a combined European naval force. Compelled to face external realities, Choshu then turned against the shogun in favour of reorganizing the country under the direct authority of the emperor. The shogun's punitive expedition against Choshu failed, with neighbouring daimios refusing their support, so that the shogun was totally discredited.

The Satsuma domain in the west had favoured the opening of the country all along, but when a Satsuma warrior, true to traditional values, killed an Englishman by whom he felt slighted, Satsuma refused to pay the indemnity demanded and fired on British ships, whose cannon then proceeded to level their capital city of Kagoshima. Satsuma then immediately asked the British for help in importing arms. Other domains in south-west Japan, which had found their economic initiatives blocked by the shogun's rule, had secretly begun to produce their own arms and ammunition, determined to enforce a change of policy.

The balance of power was swinging away from the shogun in Edo, back once more to the imperial court in Kyoto, which was still the enduring fount of ultimate legitimacy. Many lords began visiting there for confidential discussions. The shogun reduced the residence requirement for daimios to only 100 days, but at this stage it only led to further collapse of Edo's economy since the great mansions now stood empty and idle, destroying the consumers' market. Revolts broke out all over the country. When the shogun visited Osaka he was greeted with rioting and destruction of houses, so the government provided boiled rice soup and wealthy merchants distributed rice and money. There was widespread destruction of houses all over Edo. The shogun returned the powers of government to the emperor in 1867, who ordered him to return all his fiefs and retire from office. His loyal troops, refusing to accept the inevitable, then marched on Kyoto but were again repulsed, and the imperial forces, led by Satsuma and supported by more and more domains, attacked Edo castle and the shogun took refuge at a temple in the quarter of Ueno, and then surrendered peacefully, although 3,000 of his die-hard warriors attempted a last stand but were crushed. The emperor took the epoch-making decision to move the imperial capital to Edo, renaming it Tokyo (a phonetic reversal of Kyoto), and occupying its castle as the new imperial palace (Yazaki, 1968:284–5).

Many daimios had left Edo and dismissed their vassals and servants, lesser lords also having to return to their home province unless they could find some petty business to support them. Some started tea houses, with their wives and daughters ignominiously serving customers, others started antique shops with their ancestral furniture, or roasted sweet potatoes and sold them on the street. The warriors' areas fell into decay and were overgrown with weeds. By 1873 the population had fallen by almost half, to 597,905.

Although there had been significant moves in the direction of small-scale industrial production in pre-Meiji Japan, its general industrial transformation came later than that of any of those western nations with which it now competes so effectively. When the western powers began to knock rudely at the gates, the Japanese state still had the organizational and administrative power, and cultural integrity, to transform itself from within, in a way that its great neighbour China, carried by its own huge momentum on a collision course, was unable to do for another century, after much humiliation. In the furious race to catch up the west in production, no factor was more significant than Japan's unique ability to preserve its national autonomy, cultural integrity and continuity despite the onslaught. The implications for the city of Japan's original and momentous, but war-scarred, rise to eminence in the contemporary industrialized world belongs to the account of urbanization in the capitalist era.

ISLAMIC CITIES

The mark of Islam has been impressed on the life and appearance of its cities more indelibly than anywhere else. (de Planhol, 1959)

The life of the dynasty is the life of the town. (Ibn Khaldun, 1958)

Family and political economy in the urban beginnings of Islam

Although sages ancient and modern seem to assume it, the notion of Islamic city, and even of Islamic civilization is contested. But as human affairs are not cut into neat slices or cubes with absolute boundaries, all divisions of human matter are polythetic notions. Strikingly similar sets of characteristics mark most cities through the vast belt from Morocco to central Asia and down through India to East Africa. But the enormous number of cities involved, new and old, of which only a few can be mentioned, coupled with the aggressive speed of Islamic advance, both maintaining initial unity through space yet generating heterodox and reform movements and fanatical sects of great ferocity, the development of four legal schools whose differing precepts offered pretexts for furious battles, all led to an endless mosaic of rich diversity and immense complexity, to which any attempt at a coherent account is liable to do considerable violence, if it manages to avoid unintelligible convolution. The Javanese cities are not included, because they retained a distinctively Indic urban symbolic structure from their pre-Islamic development. 'In Indonesia Islam did not construct a civilization, it appropriated one.' The leitmotifs of Moroccan society, in town and out, 'were strongman politics and holyman piety' sometimes momentarily fused, whereas 'the Hindu-Buddhist Javanese state . . . had cast its roots so deeply into Indonesian society . . . that its impress remained proof not just to Islamization, but to Dutch imperialism' (Geertz, 1971:8–11). The saints 'are the Prophet's flesh and blood. Koranic propriety emanates from their essence, as it were. Islam *is* what they do. They *are* Islam' (Gellner, 1981:40–1).[1]

The new religion of Islam arose through the inspiration of Muhammad in the oasis city of Mecca, which controlled the central Arabian caravan trade in spices, frankincense and myrrh, from the Yemenite kingdoms of Arabia Felix to Syria and Europe. Muhammad was a disadvantaged, orphan member of the dominant Qurayshi group of Meccan traders. As his following grew, so did the apprehensions and harassment of the elite, until in AD 622 he and his companions fled 250 miles north to the city of Yathrib, at the invitation of disputing factions there, which thus came to be known as 'city [Medina] of the Prophet'. Islam emerged with an urban focus in which the importance of merchant, religious and political activity were all emphasized – 'a religion of towndwellers and merchants, propagated by nomads' (de Planhol, 1959:126).

The pre-Islamic city of Mecca was already a dominant shrine city exploited as a political oasis for free trade. It was essentially a merchant city, in which the common interests of urban merchants and nomadic Beduin traders together used their respect for a potent religious force to

sanction peaceful exchange to their mutual advantage. There was a relative absence of the threat of force and no levies were imposed on visiting
traders. However, it was an unstable situation in which the dominant
classes depended ultimately on military force mobilized through interlocking networks of agnatic kinship. Nomadic production and consumption in kin-based communities generated wealth through exchanges
concentrated at Mecca, producing class differences which cut across the
divide between nomad and urban settled traders.

It was a social formation based uneasily on a complex network of cross-
cutting kinship, economic and politico-military bonds and shifting factional alliances. The Prophet's Revelations precipitated new forces of
transformation, accentuated by the political and military movements, and
conflicts accompanying proselytization. As the Prophet's following grew
it increased tensions and aroused growing fear and hostility from the
Quraysh, which inevitably exploded in a crescendo of hostile encounters
culminating in Muhammad's withdrawal to Medina and eventual military supremacy.

The Quraysh lost their merchant dominance but became the military
elite of Islamic expansion, turning into administrators, acquiring estates
and receiving privileged state allowances. The basic forces of production
were significantly transformed as the military and religious leaders swept
rapidly westwards through Iran to central Asia and India. New forms of
social and economic reproduction, distribution and exchange arose of
necessity and from convenience, exhibiting many of the features which
Marx outlined as the Asiatic mode of production (Marx and Engels
1969a:504; Marx, 1973:472–3; Southall, 1988a, 1988b).

The lightning seventh-century military and religious expansion of
Islam swallowed up the very core area of the earliest Old World urbanization in Mesopotamia, Syria, Palestine and Egypt. It established a distinctive type of pre-industrial urban civilization, varying locally according
to the strength of the ancient cultures on which it was superimposed,
founding many new cities, as well as transforming many that were already
ancient, from Mecca and Medina to Jerusalem, Damascus, Aleppo, Tyre,
Sidon, Tripoli, Kufah, Basra, Baghdad, Isfahan, Shiraz, Samarkand,
Bukhara, Kashgar, Alexandria, Fustat and Cairo, Kairouan, Tunis, Fez,
Maknes, Marrakesh, Seville, Toledo, Cordoba and, in the fullness of time,
Istanbul (Constantinople).

The Syrian city of Damascus, already thousands of years old, became
the first major capital of the huge empire under the Umayyad caliphs,
until after the first great revolt, when the Abbasid caliphs founded the
new capital of Dar-es-Salaam at Baghdad in 763. By this time religious
factions, ethnic divisions and sheer geographical separation led many

distant frontier provinces to secede as virtually autonomous states, and the brief political unity of Islam ended for ever.

Many independent capital cities developed and where rival claims to both political and religious leadership coalesced, as with the secessionist Umayyad caliphs in Cordoba, or the Fatimid caliphs in Kairouan and then Cairo, brilliant bursts of cultural creativity occurred.

Mecca was a rare but not unique phenomenon, comparable in some aspects to Tepe Yahya. Its dominant population derived from the agnatic, intermarrying, interlocked groups of nomad Arabs with some ancient traders called forth by the need for long-distance exchange between the fertile, productive areas far to the south and to the north. The nomads themselves could play an important part in exchange as long-distance carriers, caravan protectors and profitable irregular participants in the trade, but they could not organize or co-ordinate it without settling and concentrating as the Meccans did.

The Meccans lived in a transitional phase of the Kinship mode of production (Southall, 1988a) in which the well-known equilibrating mechanisms of its segmentary lineage systems provided adequate order under the powerful supernatural authority of the ancient shrine which was the focus of their city. Its transitional nature showed in the plethora of inspired prophetic outbursts marking the growing inadequacy of the primeval religions of that mode of production, beset on all sides by the insidious beliefs of bigger religions based in ancient urban civilizations of the Asiatic mode of production. Mecca's own prophetic outburst provided a dramatic catalyst, precipitating a sudden transformation in the relations of production. The messianic mass attraction of Islam in the desert context necessitated strong leadership, which that context made inevitably absolute. Nomads became soldiers and left the desert to take control of the great cities of the ancient world. Hierarchies of absolute authority, based on physical force, replaced the egalitarian structures of the segmentary lineage based on primordial kinship values.

All religions that convert large numbers acquire wealth and power. Islam was the only world religion founded by an unrepentant warrior. Only Islam made its empire by open warfare, explicitly sanctifying any campaign against other religions as Holy War, with conversion, death or slavery as the choices. Umayyad and Abbasid caliphs were great and glorious rulers in magnificent world cities, exploiting and plundering much of the world for their pleasure, luxury and excess. But these splendid emperors were religious heads of an exacting faith.

Muhammad reigned serendipitously by charisma. Following him demanded a divine combination of piety and power. It was a propitious conjuncture. Byzantium and Persia had exhausted one another, leaving something of a vacuum in the north. The south Yemen kingdom had collapsed and Ethiopia was threatening invasion. The Quraysh of Mecca, with their great shrine, were the strongest force in central Arabia, but people had lost faith in the old cults and were seeking new inspiration, which numerous prophets rose to provide. The Quraysh sought to enhance the Ka'aba sanctuary, still a great pilgrimage attraction, by adding new idols of other faiths to make an all-Arabian pantheon.

Muhammad had no qualms about encouraging raids on Meccan merchant caravans, from Medina, or leading raids himself, but his stern piety surpassed all other considerations. The consistent force of his message met a widely felt need, gathering more and more adherents, until by his death he had mobilized more of Arabia than any Arab before him. Beduin martial ardour was fired with religious zeal, needing hardly a word to set off on irresistible conquest, continuing for 100 years. There was a driving passion for plunder and above all slaves.

At Muhammad's untimely death the family and the faithful core in shocked consternation chose his father-in-law Abu Bakr, fortunately of Quraysh, as first caliph 'successor'. Many Beduin fell away as the prospect of plunder momentarily dimmed, and the tax demanded by Islam seemed a burden, but Abu Bakr sent expeditions under good Qurayshi leaders to quell outbreaks of 'apostasy' among these recalcitrants, turning Islam into an effective military and political force, while the nomads of the north-east set out on their own to invade Iraq. Abu Bakr on his deathbed nominated another Quraysh father-in-law, Umar, as second caliph. Umar presided over lightning expansion with remarkable skill, supplying much needed organization and co-ordination. He ordained that conquered peoples should live in peace, be protected, keep their own laws and religion, paying less tax than before, but more than converts. Muslim Arabs were to live apart in new garrison towns on the edge of the desert, as a privileged caste supported by the taxes of the conquered, as the Muslims' duty was war and religion. This privilege tended to confine free nomads in a way they resented. Umar was assassinated by a Persian slave.

Uthman of the Umayyad group of Quraysh and a son-in-law of Muhammad was chosen third caliph. Uthman collected an authoritative text of the Quran and continued to appoint relatives to high offices and as provincial governors. Disgruntled warriors of Iraq and Egyptian garrisons murdered Uthman reading the Quran in his house at Medina. These were all old men and now Medina hailed as caliph Ali, husband of Fatimah the Prophet's daughter and adopted son of the Prophet himself, already passed over three times, but Aisha the Prophet's favourite wife, rode her camel with her party of supporters to raise an army against Ali.

Near Basra at the Battle of the Camel, where she is said to have sat on her camel to cheer on her supporters, Ali was victorious, and Aisha banished to Medina.

The Prophet's brother-in-law Mu'awiya, another Umayyad Qurayshite, now the powerful governor of Syria, opposed him more dangerously. They fought indecisively. Mu'awiya stuck pages of the Quran on his soldiers' spears, telling Ali 'leave it to God', and demanding arbitration, which went against Ali for reasons unrevealed. His support weakened and he was assassinated by a Kharijite in 661. Ali's son was proclaimed caliph in Iraq, but bought off with a large pension by Mu'awiya, who won recognition as caliph and founder of the Umayyad dynasty.

This troubled founding of the sacred realm of the Prophet and the Quran, God's Holy Kingdom, seems a tragic story of blood, assassinations and family hatreds, Muslim killing Muslim, kin killing kin, the most sacred laws broken, the Ummah defiled. Kinship, religion and politics clashed in an extraordinarily intense and sudden flood of power and wealth, turning people's heads, poisoning their loyalties. In a society of blood feud, only strong organization and firm command could prevent suicidal killing. Uthman still ran the caliphate from his house in Medina. Ali took it away briefly to his base of support in Kufah. Mu'awiya founded it more formally and appropriately in the illustrious city of Damascus, fought over, conquered and embellished for several millennia.

The problems of guilt and hostility unwittingly aroused by Ali were a permanent legacy to Islam. To the Kharijites, Ali's acceptance of arbitration was sinful, as transgressing the Quranic injunction 'if one party rebels against the other, fight against that which rebels' (49:9). No one ever questioned that Ali was caliph, however much they opposed it. He is highly praised for his diplomatic and administrative, as well as military, skills.

The Sunni caliphate: from Medina to Damascus and Baghdad

Abu Bakr, Umar, Uthman and Ali were all affines of the Prophet, two elderly fathers-in-law and two sons-in-law, Ali being also a cousin. The first three ruled informally from their homes in Medina. Only Abu Bakr died a natural death. The rejection, then hostile acceptance, of Ali, raised the deplorable level of intrafamilial violence, fighting and killing, all forbidden by the Prophet, enforcing much more formality, protection and defence. Mu'awiya, cousin of Uthman and appointed governor of Syria by Abu Bakr, had become the most powerful of the powerful group and when Ali was assassinated he was generally supported as caliph by influential Meccan traders, generals and administrators. Already governing Syria from Damascus, he now made it the capital of the Islamic Empire and of the Umayyad dynasty he founded. Hitherto caliphs had been chosen from 'seniority' among the most capable elder family members, by canvassing support despite deep disagreement. Now Mu'awiya determined on hereditary father–son succession as did most subsequent caliphs. His son Yazid succeeded, to face mounting troubles, reigning only three years, followed by his brother for only a few months, dying childless. Then another Umayyad line was sought and Marwan ibn al-Hakan, a former secretary and adviser to Uthman, was chosen. He was succeeded by his son Abd al-Malik, whose four sons succeeded him, with the interspersion of Umar II, then Marwan's grandson the last of the dynasty, which thus consisted entirely of the Mu'awiya and Marwan families, with a three-year interlude for Umar II, descendant of Umar I and son of the governor of Egypt. He had been made governor of Hejaz in 706, where he beautified the Holy Cities, improved the pilgrim routes and lightened the unjust restrictions on *mawali* non-Arab Muslims, for which he was removed from office. His qualities were so outstanding that Suleyman when dying, passed over his brothers, against family opposition, to nominate Umar caliph. Umar then immediately called off the siege of Constantinople, the last for over 700 years, which had been monopolizing the Muslim armies and fleets to no purpose. Umar gave the *mawali* equal fiscal rights with Arab Muslims, but correspondingly tightened restrictions on Christians and Jews. He alone of Umayyad caliphs was respected by the Abbasids and even Shi'ah. He died after only three years and the caliphate reverted to Abd al-Malik's son in the person of Yazid II, who dropped Umar's reforms, devoted himself to music and the arts and died of grief for a favourite slave girl, it is said.

The Umayyads continued for twenty years, losing Khurasan and Afghanistan to rebels and Turkish invaders for ten years and holding only Kairouan from a Berber revolt in the Maghreb (far west), with Kharijites controlling most of Iraq and even occupying Medina, and the long bubbling Abbasid machinations bursting into open revolt in 747 and defeating the last Umayyad caliph at the Great Zab river near Mosul, to enthrone Abbas-es-Saffar as first Abbasid caliph, deriving his legitimacy from the Prophet's uncle al-Abbas.

Recapitulation

Fifteen Umayyad caliphs had ruled in Damascus for ninety years, three passing almost unnoticed in a single year. Ten Abbasids would rule for 100 years, after which the Turkish slave guard would take over, making and unmaking caliphs, as many as four in a year and the Islamic Empire would gradually fragment into provinces, becoming autonomous states under similar Turkish regimes. Yet the caliphs would remain as essential religious legitimating king-pins, imbued with an inexhaustible if dwindling sanctity, whatever their manners or morals.

In the tenth century the Shi'ite Persian Buyids ruled from Baghdad over a number of emirates in Persia and Iraq while the greater part of the empire continued on its own. In 1055 the Seljuq Turks relieved the caliphs by driving out the Shi'ist Buyids and taking their place. The caliph legitimized them, as he had not the Buyids, because of their Shi'ism, by conferring the title of sultan on their leader, like a Japanese shogun. He married the sultan's daughter, but did not bestow one in return. However, in 1087 Sultan Malik Shah married Caliph Muqtadi's daughter. The Seljuqs[2] founded many sultanates in Iraq, Anatolia, Khurasan and Khwarezm, while the caliphs remained quiescent in Baghdad, idle and relaxed, displaying impressive piety. If the sultans faltered, they became more active.

For the first four caliphs disputes were family disputes. There were no mass attacks or invasions from outside. At this stage, the militant spread of Islam was its own, very material reward and raised few problems between subjects and rulers – as they found they had become – until the non-Arab converts began to demand justice for the social and economic discrimination between them and the Arab Muslims and for the nepotism which filled all desirable posts with the caliphs' kin. From the fifth caliph onwards, the major problems of government arose from among the population, not from within the ruling family, although cases of fratricide and patricide continued to occur.

The capacity of the first four caliphs to adapt to a kaleidoscopically changing situation, improvising a government on the spur of the moment, was totally amazing. The stupendous challenge and opportunity brought Medinans and Meccans together to become an initial ruling class, as ordained by Umar.

The cities of Medina and Mecca were home ground for the Arabs, but when faced with ruling Syria, Egypt, Persia and on and on, east and west, central Arabia was disqualified by geography, ecology, communications and Beduin culture from holding stable sway over such vast distances. Beduin were no longer the core of the army which now relied on Syrian troops supplemented by mercenaries. The highly select group of the Prophet's affines, suddenly proving themselves as rulers of vast populations and huge areas, managed to make the transition, with other Meccans who moved into the rapidly expanding Islamic administration. They learned from the more sophisticated urban culture into which they moved and often married from among them.

With the Umayyad caliphs there was a noticeable increase of scale. The political capital moved from the family urban base in Medina to the ancient metropolis of Damascus, becoming strongly influenced by Damascene and Syrian urban culture, of a different order of complexity from that of Medina or even Mecca. The ethnic dominance of Arabs was tempered by the recruitment of experienced and sophisticated officials of many other nationalities. Even the purity of Arab blood was compromised as Syrian and even Christian women were married. While caliphal candidates with slave mothers were barred at first, they had become acceptable by the end of the dynasty. This mixing of cultures and even religions imperilled the purity and asceticism of the Prophet's way of life. Some caliphs were accused of drinking wine and leading dissolute lives, causing deep offence to more traditional Quraysh and Meccan elders. Many more able lieutenants were required to enable caliphs to meet their vast responsibilities, though hardly yet formalized as vizier or other high official title. Some became extremely able governors and rulers in their own right. Out of confusion in succession arrangements one became the first anti-caliph. Once the nimbus was on, it could hardly be removed.

Islam's first schism became irrevocable when Umayyad troops intercepted and massacred Ali's grandson Husayn and his family, launching the great Shi'ite Ismaili branch of Islam. Power became more naked and despite universal reverence for Islam, its holy commands were violated one by one in the exigencies of political ambition. In place of family feuds, the major concerns of the state were perpetual rebellions in first one then another corner of the empire near and far. Rather than the feuds of leading individuals, the opposition and revolt of large organized movements and groups were now the menace. So weakened were old loyalties that aggrieved Syrian soldiers for the first time plundered the Holy Cities and desecrated the Ka'aba.

With the Abbasid caliphs in Baghdad some of these processes were intensified. Having won power by deceit and fraud, they first had to eliminate the most powerful of those who had set them up. All surviving Umayyads were remorselessly hunted down, except for Abd ar-Rahman who escaped and eventually reached Spain to found the Umayyad caliphate of Cordoba. Even the tombs of the Umayyads were desecrated. Revolts recurred in all parts of the empire.

Set between Persian and Byzantine influence, the Abbasid regime absorbed massively from both. Able Greek and Persian administrators were recruited in large numbers. Their languages were in widespread use and the ideas of Greek and Persian philosophers and theologians began to influence Islamic orthodoxy. This and the steadily penetrating weight of the imperial burden, as well as its concentrated wealth and power, removed the rulers even further from the people, increasingly protected from sight or any physical contact except through lengthy protocol. They recognized the refinement of Persian urban culture and its august imperial and religious heritage. Imperceptibly the caliphs became like oriental potentates, secluded from the public in their palace in the centre of the capital city, deciding a person's fate by a word or gesture. The highest officials and ministers could be ignominiously and capriciously snuffed out. They found slaves and underlings more trustworthy than kin, mercenaries more effective than ethnic militias, so they began recruiting Turkish slave soldiers in large numbers, brave and hardy fighters under their own officers, from central Asia through Bukhara, until they became the most powerful and uncontrollable element in the capital city and the state.

The rulers married fewer Arab wives and more Persians, Greeks and others, till they became themselves unrecognizable as Arabs. Eventually caliphs did not bother to marry at all but simply bred by chance with their innumerable slave concubines from all corners of the empire.

In the ninth century the palace guard became larger and more important. Enlarged to protect the caliph, it began to threaten him. Slaves of Turkish, Berber and Slav origin, their generals began to make and unmake caliphs at will. Some were killed and some blinded. When the Buyids took power in Baghdad, many of the provinces became autonomous. Turkish slave commanders and governors ruled in most places, often becoming independent potentates, frequently assassinating one another, but still recognizing the impotent caliphs with rich gifts. Slave dominion had its own contradictory dynamic, played over and over again in the ruling cities all over the Islamic world. Bukhara enjoyed great prosperity from controlling the central Asian trade in Turkish slave soldiers.

Revolts proliferated and even the strongest caliphs could hardly control distant frontier provinces. The administrative system remained too elementary. The first great slave revolt occurred among the *zanj* (Black) slaves of south Iraq plantations in the ninth century, taking fifteen years to suppress.

Now that extensive conquests were over and tax had to replace booty, governors were appointed to each historic province. They could be arbitrarily removed at will, but given the distances, poor communications and violent, disturbed conditions, the real hold of the caliph and his staff became at best nominal; government over distant provinces was problematic and governors became tacitly hereditary and autonomous, or formally so by agreeing to pay annual tribute. Large areas were already independent: Fatimid Cairo and Egypt, Umayyad Cordoba and Spain.

Many other local rulers paid respect or even tribute to the caliph, but otherwise were totally independent. It is really amazing how potent the mystique was. With the development of the slave armies of Turks, from the eleventh century much of the Islamic world came under Turkish rule. Arabs had lost supremacy and Arabia was a backwater.

The diversification of the west: from Egypt to the Maghreb and Spain

The advance of the caliph's forces through North Africa to Spain from the seventh to the thirteenth century was constantly bedevilled by Berber uprisings, Shi'ite plots and outbreaks of fierce, fanatic zeal. Periods of cultural brilliance and architectural splendour embellished the great cities of Cordoba, Seville and Granada in Spain, Kairouan, Fez and Marrakesh in the Maghreb.

Cordoba is on the navigable Guadalquivir, 200 kilometres from the sea, probably of Carthaginian origin, perhaps the biblical Tarshish famed for its mines. It became a Roman colony, was sacked by Julius Caesar with supposed slaughter of 20,000, nurtured Latin poets, philosophers and Christian leaders who influenced the conversion of Constantine. The Muslims took and destroyed it in 711, Abd ar-Rahman I made it his capital in 756 and the revived Umayyad caliphate was declared there in 929. It was the largest, most cultured city of Europe, excelling in industry (silk, brocade, leather and jewellery), architecture (the great mosque, with its entrancing cusped, inverted and traceried arches), art, literature and scholarship. Its women copyists rivalled the Christian monks. It acquired the refined tastes of Baghdad, developed the Andalusian school of music and was noted for fine wine, horses and women.

Kairouan was founded in 670 on the site of a Byzantine fortress, drawing on Roman as well as oriental inspiration. Further advance was blocked by Berber attacks under both male and female leadership. In the eighth century a force of some 100,000 Arab militia conquered the whole of North Africa, but their greedy exactions in their Ifriqiyah (Tunisia) headquarters led to general revolt, depriving them of everything except the city of Kairouan. In 750 the Abbasids were able to appoint Ibrahim Ibn al-Aghlab as governor, whose descendants continued to send tribute, recognizing the caliph's suzerainty, but ruled as independent sovereigns, even invading Sicily and south Italy, before being overcome by the Fatimids in 910.

In the Maghreb Sharifian Shi'ite descendants of Ali, fleeing Abbasid persecution, winning support from Kairouan and Andalusia, founded the city of Fez at the end of the eighth century, developing a distinctive urban cultural blend during the ninth century. In the tenth century its territory fragmented but the Almoravids unified it in the eleventh century.

The fusion of vengeful Ismaili missionaries with rebellious Berber zeal produced the Fatimid movement, claiming prime legitimacy by descent from the Prophet through his daughter Fatimah and her spouse Ali, aiming at total overthrow of the Sunni Abbasid caliphate at Baghdad. They seized Kairouan from the Aghlabid rulers and built up an army strong enough to invade Egypt and Syria, but never reached Baghdad. Their governor in Kairouan betrayed them, returning to Abbasid allegiance, so the Fatimids sent the wild Bedouin Beni Hilal and Sulaym from Upper Egypt against them. The Bedouin ravaged both cities and countryside, exacting tribute, ruining arable land and forcing sedenterized Berbers back to nomadism. They remained an uncontrollable scourge of the Maghreb for centuries. The Fatimid threat and Abbasid weakness caused the Umayyad ruler of Cordoba to declare himself caliph, avenging the Umayyads against the Abbasids and strengthening his position against the Fatimids.

After the suppression and murder of Ali and Husayn the Shi'ah had usually operated clandestinely and their imam leaders were 'hidden' both for mystical and practical reasons, but their missionaries were scattered unevenly all over the Islamic world, always ready to seize their opportunity.

The Fatimids fulfilled the promise of Amr Ibn al-As' Fustat and Ibn Tulun's Qatay in building their magnificent capital at Qahira (Cairo, Victory City). They made Cairo rival Baghdad as a brilliant centre of culture, learning and grand architecture. Their realm extended from Cyrenaica to Aleppo and down to Nubia and Yemen. After a century of memorable rule they began to fall into the same trap as the Abbasids, supplementing their Berber troops by recruiting Turks and other *mamluks*, then Black regiments from Nubia and Sudan. Caliph al-Hakim (996–1012) was so abnormal and paranoid, declaring himself divine, that the solidarity and credibility of the caliphate was damaged. He persecuted both Sunni and Christians, and destroyed the Holy Sepulchre in Jerusalem, bringing on the Crusades. The different national groups of slave soldiers began to fight one another and the caliphs became puppets of their viziers and generals. There was plague and famine. The Holy Cities turned back to Abbasid Baghdad. There was such disorder that the Fatimid caliphs summoned the able commander Badr-el-Jamali to take control. He executed the slave generals and took power over the three main departments of government as commander of the armies, director of the missionaries and vizier. He was succeeded by his son Afdal, who abandoned the Fatimid claims to universal caliphate. The head of the Ismaili mission in Persia, Iraq and central Asia, now the Assassins,[3] withdrew recognition from the Fatimid caliph and proclaimed his elder brother Nizar, bypassed by Afdal, as rightful imam. The caliph al-Amir (1101–30) was murdered by the Assassins. It was then claimed, in Shi'ah fashion, that al-Amir had an infant son who was now 'hidden' imam. The Yemenites refused to recognize the effete occupants of the caliphal throne, who were so abject that the Seljuq sultan in Baghdad sent the Kurdish officer Saladin to take charge. He allowed the prayers over the dying caliph to be read in the name of the Abbasid caliph, thus ritually terminating the Fatimid caliphate.

Saladin's father had been governor of Damascus under the Seljuq sultans. Saladin restored the Fatimid empire in Egypt, Upper Iraq, most of Syria and Yemen, but he drove the Fatimids and Ismailis out, exterminating all except those in Iran, Yemen and Gujerat (the ancestors of the Aga Khan). He made Egypt the most powerful state in the Muslim world, but before his death in 1193 distributed his territories to autonomous vassal relations. His brother and nephew held nominal power in Cairo till 1250, when the slave armies which had started the trouble became themselves the *mamluk* regime.

After the Fatimids left Kairouan and sent in the Beduin Scourge, other forces appeared in the Maghreb. In the eleventh century the head of a Berber confederation, which had raided and conquered through Mauretania and across the Sahara as far as the river Niger, made pilgrimage to Mecca and brought the scholar Ibn Yasin back with him to improve Muslim piety. Yasin's mission aroused hostility and he called upon the Almoravid Sanhajah military monks from the desert to holy war. From 1054 to 1059 they conquered southern Morocco and founded Marrakesh their capital. Yasin's successor Tashfin led them to victory over northern Morocco, and in response to appeals from Spain crossed to Algeciras and defeated King Alfonso VI in Estremadura in 1086, deposed the ineffective Muslim rulers and, after being held up at Valencia by the Cid until his death in 1099, achieved mastery of all Muslim Spain by 1103. The inquisitorial orthodoxy of the Almoravids aroused yet another fanatical reform movement from the Atlas beyond Marrakesh, which grew and grew until as Almohads (unitarians) they defeated the Almoravids and established a single authority for the first time over the Berbers as a whole. But they could not control the marauding Arabs, nor stem the Christian advance in Spain, where they were finally defeated in 1212. Marrakesh was taken from them in 1269 by another Berber uprising of the Banu Marin (Marinids). Anarchy reigned, with vizier fighting vizier, making and unmaking sultans, but in the fourteenth century the Marinid dynasty established stable rule at Fez which reached a zenith of cultural efflorescence, craft excellence and commercial prosperity.

Extension to the east: Ghazna, Bukhara and Delhi

Among the opportunistic adventurers, mostly captains of rebellious or self-recruited slave bands, or disgruntled scions of already established slave sultanates, encouraged by the effete decadence of the Abbasid caliphs, was Mahmud of Ghazna (998–1060), son of a Turkish slave guard of the Samanid sultans of Bukhara, who raised a huge army, and made his way across India to the Ganges, triggering slave-ruled polities along his route. He always sent lush booty back to the caliphs, receiving grandiloquent titles in return. Holding sway from Persia and central Asia to the Ganges, he was on the brink of expelling the Abbasids altogether to make Baghdad his winter capital.

The rulers of Ghazna attracted splendid court, stimulating fine poetry and painting, creating exquisite buildings and excellent woodcarving. They assassinated the last ruler of Bukhara, their nominal overlord, and were themselves defeated by Seljuq Turks and their cities destroyed. But they influenced artistic development in Iran and Muslim India.

Given the lightning speed of the initial Muslim advance from Arabia, their warlike culture and the untold wealth of the cities of India, it was surprising how long they had been deterred by its hot climate and formidable mountain barriers. Even Babur's troops after many victories demanded to go home because of the heat.

The city of Multan in the Indus valley, conquered by Alexander the Great in 326 BC, fell to the Muslims in AD 712 and remained the outpost of their advance in India, becoming the centre of Qarmatian Ismailis in the tenth century. Muhammad of Ghur recovered Multan and Lahore from the Rajputs in 1192, thus opening the way into India, before being assassinated himself.

One after another, marauders fought and plundered their way over the 2,000 miles across India to Bengal, adding a whole new world to the realm of Islam. Countless ancient cities were captured, many dating from Alexander the Great, founded at the oases and strategic junctions of Transoxania, Hindu Kush and Afghanistan; countless more like Multan and Lahore were wealthy Hindu cities of the plains of northern India, doomed to conquest and Muslim penetration.

Many of these adventurers were lax in religion and obeyed few rules but those of military success, yet the violent acquisition of vast territory and huge wealth imposed inevitable routinization. They were in awe of wandering Muslim holy men and tended to seek God's favour when faced with imminent disaster.

Warrior horsemen were still seduced by the luxuries and delights of urban life and built magnificent palaces, mosques and tombs in the cities they captured or instantly built. All tried to establish hereditary sultanates, but with frequent assassinations, plots and rebellions. Great talents were needed to survive and inspire loyalty, dissolve dangerous factions and effectively exploit the wealth of farmers and traders. Delhi became the capital of the most powerful sultanate, with wildly fluctuating territory from Sind to Bengal, changing hands frequently.

The Mongol Genghis Khan ravaged central Asia in the thirteenth century. In the fourteenth century the Turkish Muslim Timur, also descended from Genghis, ravaged Asia again. He was always in the saddle, continually moving with his court and household, but he wanted his capital at Samarkand to be the most splendid in Asia. It became a centre of scholarship, science and astronomy, with splendid mosques, tombs, *madrasas* and palaces. Timur only spent a few days there before moving back to his huge pavilioned camp outside. His descendant Babur made the final assault upon India which established the Mughal Empire.

'The really large cities must be regarded here merely as royal camps, as works of artifice' said Marx (1973:479) as if he were thinking of Timur. Genghis Khan and Hülegü hardly entered India and although Timur is said to have sacked Delhi, executed at least 50,000 and removed almost everything of value, including all those still living, the sultan only had to move next door to Agra. Even Akbar, the greatest of the Mughals could not resist moving the capital from Delhi to Fatehpur Sikri, returning after sixteen years for lack of water. The site of Delhi itself was moved six or seven times in the thirteenth and fourteenth centuries and Mughal emperors kept switching between Delhi and Agra, whose splendours and delights probably equalled those of the Arabian Nights.

The end of the caliphate, awakening of the Sufi and the last perfections of Islam

As Khwarezm had threatened the caliphs with another unrealistic plan for an Alid Shi'ah imam–caliphate to restore Islamic unity, such as the Abbasids themselves had used to lure the Umayyads to destruction, the caliph was somewhat relieved at Khwarezm's foolhardy defiance of Genghis Khan (in massacring the trade and diplomatic missions he had sent) which brought about their destruction. Genghis laid waste the cities of Khurasan and Transoxania one by one, in blood and flames, withdrawing contemptuously. Yet it is said the experience finally taught him the meaning of cities, which he had never appreciated before.

Within a generation, Genghis sent his grandson Hülegü with an invincible host which in 1258 obliterated Baghdad and the caliphate altogether. This was the definitive end of the unified Islamic caliphate in practice. Religious as well as political unity was lost. The Abbasids had already suffered two major schismatic secessions, which they might have weathered if they had not been so ignominiously snuffed out.

It was a climactic collapse for Islam: Baghdad 1258, Cairo lost to the *mamluks* by the defunct Fatimid caliphate 1250, the caliphate of Cordoba fallen to Castile 1236, the Marinids took Marrakesh 1269. The most expansive Islamic city of the time was Delhi, capital of the Delhi sultanate.

Slave army rule was an easy, individualistic, meritocratic way to run a state. The values were very similar to those of capitalism, although the forces of production were very different. It was an easy way for bold adventurers, or the slave armies themselves as the *mamluks* showed, to make a state. The cessation of marriage meant a parallel '*mamluk*' system in the harem also. The only problem for caliphs and sultans who took this route was that they might themselves become superfluous. It was especially easy given the huge primate cities which concentrated wealth, power, culture and religion. It was only necessary to control these, adding further to their concentration by the tens of thousands of soldiers and their dependants. It was a system which could be elaborated and varied in detail, but was not amenable to any further development, so that the dozens of sultanates scattered across the Islamic world eventually stagnated and marked time until the advance of capitalism overwhelmed them. Their legacy still weighs heavily upon the Middle East. None the less *mamluk* rule, and the cities that took their shape from it, was a highly original invention of Islamic civilization. No Islamic state tried very hard to have a caliph any more, for the problem of the righteous monarch had been solved in other ways.

However, the idea of caliph had become deeply rooted in the minds of Muslims and was not easily abandoned. Without a caliph, Islam was deprived of any central focus. It was a threatening spiritual vacuum. The rise of the Sufi orders, the growing attention to mystical experience and the development of organized cults of saints out of the veneration of holy men, all seem to have occurred at much the same time, as though in some way they helped to fill the gap left by the caliphate. They obviously provided spiritual service of a very different kind, local and largely spontaneous, although the great Sufi orders were very widespread. It was pluralistic and voluntary. Perhaps it gave symbolic and spiritual expression to the realization that the unified earthly empire had created a common consciousness and a constantly changing material framework of interlocking political economies, which enabled and motivated the great scholars to move to and fro from one end of the Islamic world to the other, spinning a web of threads of knowledge and communication, confirming and strengthening the common consciousness. The ecstatic and mystical revelations and communion in the congregations of Sufi orders and saints' shrines did fill the gap left by the caliphs, perhaps in a more valid and effective way than they could ever have done.

That the Sufi preached to the proletariat and to rural people, while their relations with the *ulama* became more amicable, suggested an awakening of awareness of profoundly important aspects of society not dealt with under the caliphs.

Only two achievements approaching perfection appear in the Islamic world after the fall of Baghdad: the perfected slave system of the Ottomans and the surpassing beauties of Isfahan. The Ottoman slave system came close to a perfect and invincible meritocracy, but it excelled in military and less in other directions. Its own forces of attraction were so great that they eventually overcame the human will to maintain it by enforcing the essential restrictions. By the seventeenth century they had broken down and Ottoman invincibility with them.

The latest and perhaps the most exquisite of all the urban creations of Islam was the city of Isfahan. The site is so ancient that some link it to Nebuchadnezzar, others to a fourth-century settlement of the Jewish queen of Yezdegerd I. Arab Muslims captured it in 642, making it capital of the mountain province of Media. It became extremely prosperous in the tenth century under the Buyids, as Abbasid Baghdad declined. Togril Beg the Seljuq conqueror made it his capital and his grandson Malik Shah and his vizier Nizam al-Mulk, the patron of Omar Khayyam, greatly embellished it. But Iran had suffered endless wars, invasions and conquest ever since the ravages of Genghis, Hülegü and Timur. The Safavid movement expressed the Shi'ite yearning to purge Iran from the contamination of Mongol infidels by establishing an Iranian Shi'ite Muslim polity. Their leader won control of Iran in 1502 and the dynasty reached its peak in the reign of Sultan Shah Abbas I (1588–1629). Tabriz and Kazvin had surpassed Isfahan for a while. Sultan Abbas moved the capital back to Isfahan as more central to a united Iran. He replanned and largely rebuilt the city, making it one of the most beautiful in the world. Four stupendous mosques, the great ceremonial square for polo and gladiatorial games, or crammed with merchants' tents, overlooked by the *'Ali qapu* (lofty archway crowned by a huge covered balcony), echoing the

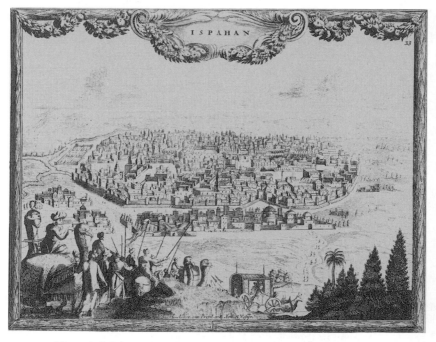

Plate 3 Isfahan: the Great Mosque is perhaps the most exquisitely beautiful of the monuments of Islam, even including the Taj Mahal. It is the product of fusion between the 'unorthodox' Shi'ites and the ancient aesthetics of Iran. The lofty pavilion which crowned the square itself was an innovative feature. The distant view shows the typically sharp contrast between urban and rural which prevailed in most pre-capitalist cities.

Ghaznavid style; gardens, pavilions, palaces, bazaars, fountains, trees; the domes in matchless tiles of heavenly blue, deep peacock green and flowers in rainbow colours, holding the eye spellbound with delight, and besides the tiles, exquisite craft work in silver, copper, brass and pottery, not to mention continued excellence in poetry, music and painting. In the seventeenth century a foreigner recorded 162 mosques, 48 colleges, 273 baths and over 1,800 caravanserais. The political elite and the merchants were well cared for. Even the masses may have proudly enjoyed the stunning beauty of their city, but of their lives we know virtually nothing. The Afghans reduced the city largely to rubble in 1722. Famine and epidemics are said to have killed over 100,000. The beauties of Isfahan were the finest flower of Iranian artistic genius, which maintained its inner strength through so many conquests and dynastic defeats and could display itself in different guises through so many religious changes. The distinctiveness of Iranian Shi'ism came not so much from the drama of Ali's rejection and Husayn's martyrdom but from the unquenchable originality of Iran's deep culture and intellect, which had to submit politically to the victory of Sunni Islam, but were bound to impart an idiosyncrasy to its religion and urban culture still manifest today. In Isfahan, Shah Abbas encouraged weaving and carpet making, brought commercially energetic and industrious Armenians to settle nearby and exercised a silk monopoly, all bringing increased prosperity, but great invasions had ravaged the economy and endless warring military chiefs and puppet princes had exploited and taxed to the limits of endurance. The labour and resources to embellish and adorn the city could ultimately come only from the overburdened peasantry.

The implications of Islam for urban society: basic principles and contradictions

The fundamental paradox of Islam, which imparted a quite special quality to its cities, was the equal prostration of all Muslims directly before God, which discouraged the systematic development of specialized institutions for the organization of society or the well-being and protection of the people (Lapidus, 1967:185). This absolute restriction could never be fully implemented or maintained, yet it had dramatic results. The Prophet's guidance was alarmingly authoritarian and inclusively vague: 'Obey God, and obey the Messenger and the people in authority among you' (Quran, 4:59).

In principle there could be no church or priesthood, no king or royalty, no craft or trade guilds, no formally certified legal profession or judiciary, no distinct local government, no trained bureaucracy for fiscal, financial, industrial, educational, cultural or other purpose (Lapidus, 1967:107). Yet all these roles and institutions appeared in one way or another, as though the essential principles of Islam precipitated a political and institutional vacuum which demanded to be filled.

At the Prophet's death a vaguely defined 'Successor' (khalifa or caliph) was appointed, yet this role acquired some of the aura of divine kingship and was subject to many rival claims in different parts of divided Islam, an aura which attached also to some of the imams of Shi'ah sects, even down to our own day in the case of the Aga Khan (Morris, 1958). Islam, properly speaking, had no saints, yet holy men later sprang up everywhere, with cults and pilgrimages round their tombs. Though not a church, there had to be mosques, which had to be built and organized and kept up somehow. Sultans sought to establish hereditary dynasties, behaving in many ways like kings although crowns were forbidden in Islam (Le Tourneau, 1961:82). There were guild-like organizations of craftsmen and merchants imposed by rulers for their own ends, there were legal experts and judges, also appointed by rulers, and informal schools of law and procedure of adjudication. There was a vast body of functionaries, who were not consistently trained, or specialized, or systematically organized in any co-ordinated whole.

The characteristic results were unrestrained autocracy and arbitrary violence, since only ineffective moral controls were applied to the use of power, and a certain vague and nebulous informality and lack of distinction, since roles were formalized and activities institutionalized only by necessity and improvisation, rather than legitimate design. In this sense, above all, sacred and secular were not distinguished, for the law applying to secular activities was a sacred law, and the house of prayer was also a place of secular assembly, rather than a consecrated shrine. Even 'the police is another religious function' (Ibn Khaldun, 1958, I:457). Islam 'does not divide religion from society' (de Planhol, 1959:126).

Islam could not in fact prevent the emergence of institutions which it seemed in principle to discourage, but it did profoundly affect their nature, co-ordination and functioning. It could not and did not attempt to abolish the state, but was 'unfavourable to the formation of national organisms' (de Planhol, 1959:126). Indeed, the very lack of deliberate institutionalization threw all duties diffusely on the state and made it of overwhelming importance, though its structure and limits were unclear. A further paradox is that the Islamic state is also necessarily religious, yet essentially secular. It must be religious, since the whole life of man and society should be guided in detail by the just and holy teaching of the Prophet, the Quran and Sharia. It 'covers all human activity' (de Planhol, 1959:127). But it is essentially secular in that there can be no mediator between God and man. This is of extreme importance because it stripped, or should have stripped, from both the ruler and the city the whole encrustation of sacred symbolism and ritual which the city had always had, from the very beginning until the time of Greece and Rome in Europe, and elsewhere right up to the time of the Prophet himself. Yet even here ideas of sanctity and symbolism crept in, with the Ka'aba at Mecca and the caliphs' round city of Baghdad perceived as the navel of the world, and the inability of the most powerful rulers to dispense with the nominal figurehead of a caliph, however captive and impotent. Yet, in a profound sense, often overtly manifested in the structure of roles and institutions, the city itself could not be distinguished from the state, although physically and ecologically it often stood out in stark contrast against its surroundings.

Although the Prophet's religion may have been seen as a dangerous rival force by the urban establishment of Mecca, it was in no way a revolt against authority, to the extent that early Buddhism or Christianity were. No other religion so immediately, or so successfully, set up its own great society and great tradition (Redfield, 1956:70) in which city and state were inseparable.

Islamic idealism left the person, and especially the city dweller, at the mercy of arbitrary absolute rule. Because politics is subsumed in religion, and city in state, Islam is politically naive from one point of view, cynically realistic from another. The ruler, of course, more than anyone else, should be the just and righteous servant of God. But in fact absolute power corrupts more absolutely for lack of lower level restraining institutions. The most interesting sociological implication is not only the lack of formal institutions, but the fluidity of roles, which remain highly generalized, overlapping and interchangeable. The absolutism of earthly rule matched and mirrored the absolutism of heavenly rule. As there was to be no mediating institution or role between the divine omnipotence of God and the absolute submission of the obedient disciple, so there was to be no mediating institution or role between the ideal righteous absolutism of the earthly ruler (sultan) and the absolute pious obedience of the earthly subject. The righteousness might falter but the absolutism was relentlessly pursued. Its absolute authority never extended effectively over the whole area of jurisdiction claimed, but it was certainly dominant at the urban centres where the action was concentrated.

The principle of absolute concentration of power inevitably brought an extreme concentration of subjects. That is why, metaphysically, the practice of Islam could only reach perfection in the city, and in the biggest city at that. If the absolutism of the righteous ruler, the caliph, wavered, no other form of absolutism arose to substitute for it, either that of the sultan, a less hallowed form of absolute rule, or the absolute physical force of the slave army leader, the slave of slaves by ultimate reversal, developed most completely by the *mamluks* of Cairo, most elaborately by the janissaries of Istanbul, but increasingly pervasive throughout the empire as a whole from the ninth century, when it first developed in Baghdad. Though never envisaged at the start, institutionalized rule by slave armies became the predominant political institution of Islam for at least three-quarters of its pre-capitalist existence. Given the concentration of power and the concentration of residence, it was also a primary characteristic of the Islamic city, responsible for many other of its secondary characteristics such as unsuppressed violence. The absolutism of the harem and its eunuchs paralleled that of the slave armies, adding its complementary mass to the concentrated population of capital cities. The Kharijites took this to its logical conclusion in declaring death to all sinners. Kharijism was so ultimately fundamentalist that they often came out on opposite sides of the same issue. The injunction to enjoin good and forbid evil meant *vindicating truth by the sword*. Mu'tazilites said if God were to withhold punishment for evil and forgive it, it would be as *unjust* as withholding reward for righteousness. This theme in Islam was very attractive for earthly rulers.

The tendency to slave rule

Mamluk slave rule in Cairo, Damascus, Delhi, Baghdad, Istanbul and other cities was a characteristic product of Islam, which sanctioned slavery in order to minimize its evils. It was a widespread tendency resulting from the general dynamics of the slave household. It was the extraordinary and certainly unanticipated outcome of pressures generated by the rules of the system in the context of local circumstances. It emerged at a particular point in the structural evolution of Islamic society, and came to dominate the political economy of the greatest Muslim cities.

Since Muslims must not be enslaved, it was inevitable that most slaves should be foreigners and either Christian or pagan. The greatest wealth was in the hands of political leaders and it was always tempting to build up support by purchasing slaves and training them as a military force. Many local leaders did so to some extent. The line of distinction between household and army was blurred. Sometimes large numbers of slaves were acquired directly in the course of military operations, especially when great cities were sacked and their inhabitants enslaved. In the early days of Arabian Islam the body of the faithful had been the army at the same time, but this identity could not survive the inevitable process of routinization and sheer growth of scale and distance. Nor was calling upon the warlike proclivities of neighbouring Beduin a reliable basis for a large state. After the whirlwind conquests, the caliphs as religious leaders soon lost political control of the vast empire, but not their aura of sanctity. Local leaders stepped into the political vacuum as ruling sultans, yet always sought ritual confirmation from a caliph. Striving in their turn to establish hereditary succession, they too could become cyphers in the hands of administrators risen by merit.

All rulers face the problem of rivals, among whom kinsmen and trusted lieutenants are the most dangerous. Slaves who in theory and at least at first are powerless strangers without family, kin, friends or any other links or sources of support seem to offer the ideal solution, the most trustworthy and the least threatening. But when carried beyond a certain point, as frequently happened in Islamic society, slaves collectively become the real power holders and take over. Slave systems centred in cities could provide the basis for a remarkably efficient, completely ruthless meritocracy.

The Baghdad caliphs began to recruit Turkish slave mercenaries from central Asia, bought from the Samanid rulers of Samarkand and Bukhara, as a counter force to local factions. They were dressed in splendid uniforms and kept distinct from the rest of the army. They controlled the dangerous crowds of the urban mob by riding fiercely and fearlessly into them, striking to the right and to the left. They plundered homes, attacked women and murdered with impunity, forcing Caliph Mu'tasin to move them and his capital from Baghdad to an entirely new city at Samarra. Soon their leading officers were able to make and unmake caliphs at will, killing them with impunity. They even kept the caliph's appointed viziers as figureheads to work through, but destroyed them pitilessly if they resisted (Wiet, 1971:39, 43).

Slave governments sprang up in many places, taking over from the Samanids themselves, who had bought or captured and supplied them in the first place, and seizing power in many of the successor states which split off from the Abbasid caliphate of Baghdad. It was they who began the Muslim conquest of India and established slave rule from Delhi for most of the thirteenth and fourteenth centuries. The structure and dynamism of this regime paralleled those of *mamluk* Cairo to an extraordinary degree, but Delhi was virtually destroyed by Timur in 1398. The same tendency had also occurred in the far west, where the secessionist Umayyad caliphs of Cordoba bought Slav captives from the Franks, thus supplying the term 'slave' in its English and various European forms.

Types of Islamic city

The distinction between newly founded and transformed old cities, or 'spontaneous and created cities' (Pauty, 1951) was very much a matter of degree and increasingly blurred with the passage of time. Many cities of the early period of military conquest did begin as military camps, like Kufah, Basra and the Fustat period of the agglomeration which later became Cairo, with the local divisions or wards of the city corresponding to the ethnic divisions of the army.

Thus the city of Fustat was originally divided into ethnic quarters which derived from the ethnic divisions of the army camp of Amr Ibn al-As, who conquered Byzantine Egypt in 640. Having taken the fortress of Babylon he founded Fustat, 'the tented city', nearby on the basis of the structure of the army (said to have contained 4,000 men), which initially peopled it. Each commander's troops tended to belong to a particular ethnic group or Beduin 'tribe' and thus formed the basis of an urban quarter. The same held in the early garrison towns of Basra and Kufa, as well as later in Kairouan and Tlemcen (de Planhol, 1959:3). In the absence of stronger, conscious design, such a form inevitably occurred in the initial foundation of military or royal cities, which usually soon amounted to the same thing. The camp of the Almohad general and ruler Abdal-Mu'min, who took Marrakesh from the Almoravids in 1146–7 was of this type, 'un camp où chaque tribu eut sa place, une mosquée et un minaret' (Deverdun, 1959:159). The form of instant camp city appeared as late as the nineteenth century, in the founding of Addis Ababa with its *sefers* (wards), by the Coptic Christian King Menelik (Shack, 1973:255–7). It also appeared as an adjunct or imposition on a much older city, as with the Arab conquest of Damascus. The ethnic character of wards continued as the expression of associated occupational specializations, rather than military units. It is also characteristic of urban processes in the Asiatic mode of production, an expression not of state centralization but of the power of autocratic rulers to mobilize vast human and material resources rapidly.

The palace complex in the capital city was much more than the mere residence of a ruler, yet usually proving inadequate as a complete city. When Egypt was conquered and Fustat occupied by the Fatimid caliphs from Kairouan – a city that started in exactly the same way, beside another Byzantine fortress – they added the new Palace City of Qahira (Cairo) some two miles north of Fustat in 969, on a more monumental scale than they had previously done in Kairouan. A century before, the Turkish general Ibn Tulun had begun the move north from Fustat with his enormous fortress mosque and intermediate city of Qatay. Fatimid

Cairo had one great street, running north to north-east in the direction of the prevailing summer winds, with twenty side streets (de Planhol, 1959:17). The building of Fez Jdid (New Fez) in 1276, 750 yards apart from the walls of Old Fez across a small valley, as the military and administrative palace city of the new Marinide dynasty (Le Tourneau, 1961:12), paralleled the Fatimid creation of Cairo. Twelfth-century Rabat is said to have been modelled on Alexandria (de Planhol, 1959:16) and other Moroccan cities had at least some straight streets oriented eastwards to Mecca with the Qibla of the chief mosque. It is clear that the rectangular Hellenist plan had a diffuse influence, but one which was ineffective in the long run.

Uncontrolled building in the Islamic city began or continued the encroachment on the spacious classic porticos and colonnades of cities like Damascus (Elisséeff, 1970:171), Aleppo and much later Istanbul, turning them into narrow, crooked bazaars and winding alleys. Ancient temples, having been transformed into churches, were again transformed into mosques. But in Jidda and Mecca the movement of huge crowds of pilgrims had to be provided for with a more regular network of open streets (de Planhol, 1959:20–222).

The concentric plan, attributed to early Basra and Kufa and reported in Persian cities by Marco Polo (de Planhol, 1959:10, 17), reached its brief apotheosis in eighth-century Baghdad. Probably influenced by Sassanid Ctesiphon nearby, it was a vast palace complex, but had no lasting influence on the design of Baghdad as a whole. Thus military camp and palace complex made their successive contributions to the basic structure of many Islamic cities, but were increasingly overlaid by more general forces of Islamic urban society.

Baghdad and Samarra

Caliph al-Mansur's round city of Baghdad was 'an enormous palace-complex combining the residence of the Caliph with the administrative agencies of government' (Lassner, 1970:169) and so quite similar in function to the royal city of Fez or Qahira, but it was unique among Muslim capital cities in its systematically circular design, derived from pre-Islamic models at nearby Ctesiphon (Lassner, 1970:132–3), and other Persian cities. Its diameter was just under one and a quarter miles. It had two concentric outer walls and a moat, with four gates (Kufah, Basra, Khurasan and Syria) at the south-west, south-east, north-east and north-west corners. Each gate led into a long passage with fifty-four bays on either side and another circular wall at the inner end, through which the passage opened on the huge central, circular space, with the great mosque and the palace in the centre, with quarters for police and guards. The architects drew a line on the ground with cotton seeds set afire so the caliph on the hill above could visualize the shape, size and site of the city (al-Najim, 1993:346–7). The residences of al-Mansur's children, servants and slaves were round the inner wall (Lassner, 1970:109). At each gate, 1,000 guards were quartered, with another 26,000 stationed outside the walled city. Markets occupied part of the arcades in each gate passage and residential areas the sectors between the gates. No bazaars were allowed. Merchants gathered outside the Basra gate, forming the suburb of al-Karkh. Outside the north-eastern (Khurasan) gate was the pontoon bridge over the Tigris, the palace of the heir, al-Mahdi (father of Harun al-Rashid) and three more suburbs.

This round city, said to have been built by more than 100,000 labourers between 762 and 766, was a failure, for by 774 the markets were transferred outside the city after an uprising and the caliph moved soon after for security reasons to a new palace outside the Khurasan gate, where Harun al-Rashid also later resided. There were large suburbs at al-Karkh south of the round city, al-Harbiyah on the north and across the Tigris on the east bank.

Although it is often felt that the charms and wonders of Harun al-Rashid's Baghdad have been overblown by the hyperbole generated by 1,001 nights' fantasies, there was something distinctively unique and very fleeting about this fairy-tale Baghdad. This circular city, planned to outshine Babylon, Seleucia and Ctesiphon has no counterpart. Occupied in 766, it was abandoned forever in 836. The wealth of the ancient world, ruthlessly extorted, was concentrated and lavished upon it. Harun al-Rashid reigned from 786 to 809 and probably covered the peak years of Baghdad's splendour. His sons, whose orderly future he had planned, quarrelled, the one killing the other. By then the slave guards were terrorizing the city and the caliph withdrew to Samarra. In 896 they moved back, to the eastern suburb of Mukharrin, not to the round city, which was allowed to decay. Despite this confusion, the exceptional brilliance of Baghdad culture probably continued for another century. Scholars from Persia, India and central Asia thronged there, creating the stimulus of many cultures interacting in emulation. It was a golden age of art, literature, music, science, philosophy, astronomy and astrology, supporting Christian and Jewish as well as Muslim culture and learning.

Early Islam had doubted the legitimacy of music for Muslims, except for chanting the Quran, but in eighth-century Baghdad it had a rich flowering. Musicians and poets gathered round the caliph in the gardens, drinking wine despite the law. Harun's strong adherence to religious values excused his great love of life, pleasure and wine. Slave girl singers acquired great renown. They were trained by their owners in music and poetry without inhibition. They were freer than free women to participate in public life and influence the general taste. It was a proud, refined city, contrasting itself with the desert. The Baghdad style showed Persian mannerism and the graceful arrogance of women. The house of wisdom, *Bayt-al-Hikna* was founded for the translation of ancient sciences. Delegations were sent all over the world for books of science to be translated. An observatory was attached to it, with elaborate instruments and an improved astrolabe. Even when the caliphate weakened, the momentum of Baghdad culture and learning continued. The Buyids built the House of Knowledge as a kind of university, in the tenth century (al-Najim, 1993:350; Canard, 1962:286). In the twelfth century there were still some 2,000 baths and eleven cathedral mosques.

For half a century after 836 the caliphs moved to the brand new city of Samarra, sixty miles further north, but the site was very unsatisfactory and the water supply atrocious, so they moved back to Baghdad in 896, not to the round city but across the river to the eastern suburb of Mukharrin. The ruler's move, with his army, was prompted by the wish to escape from the turbulence of Baghdad (Rodger, 1970:129) which the presence of the army further exacerbated. Although Samarra was so consciously founded and immediately built, it had no coherent overall design and straggled along the east bank of the Tigris intermittently for some thirty-five kilometres (Rodger, 1970:124, 145). Palaces, mosques, barracks and other official buildings were, as usual, constructed by forced labour. The magnates had to build for themselves on the concessions allotted to them. As the population grew, with the usual ethnically segregated quarters established, the original advantage of moving there must have been lost. The round city gradually fell into disuse and disappeared, but the much larger unplanned city which grew up around, and eventually over its ruins, continued to flourish for centuries, despite constant political upheavals.

Mamluk Cairo

When the great Seljuk general Zenky drove the Crusaders from the Syrian city of Edessa in 1143, and spared the Christians and their bishop, his own *mamluks* murdered him (Muir, 1896:xx). When in 1247 King Louis of France was captured in his attack on Cairo, but magnanimously allowed to go free by the Sultan Turan Shah, great-great-nephew of Saladin, he too was murdered by his *mamluks* and Egypt was ruled by them from this time. Indeed, the ninth-century Turkish governor for the Baghdad caliphs, Ibn Tulun, had already begun to purchase slaves to make his army independent and set up his own dynasty at Cairo (Qatay), so that it became standard: his son squandered his fortune and managed to rule for twelve years before he was murdered, leaving the regime to fall apart under his heir, and when a new Turkish governor was sent and tried to repeat the process, power fell into the hands of the Abyssinian slave Kafur. The system had begun long before in all but name. Muslim rule in Egypt was chronically unstable. Already in the eighth century Fustat suffered twenty-four governors in twenty-three years under Caliph Harun al-Rashid.

Although the Ottoman sultan of Istanbul conquered Cairo in 1517 and put it under an appointed pasha as governor, it was not long before the *mamluks* regained their hold and the pasha's authority became nominal, until the final massacre of the *mamluks* by Muhammad Ali in 1811 brought to an end their five and a half centuries of domination.

Bought as slave boys from central Asia and the Caucasus, the *mamluks* were trained together in city barracks as an elite military corps, and as the supreme holders of political power, as well as being given the most refined literary education. When they chose Emir Eibek from among themselves as leader, after killing Sultan Turan Shah, Eibek wished to legitimate his position by ruling through Turan's mother, but when the caliph in Baghdad ruled against this as improper he married her. She had him killed later when he married a princess of Mosul, but also perished herself in the fray. Eibek's juvenile son was chosen as sultan, with the *mamluk* Kotuz as vice-gerent, who soon displaced him and seized the sultanate, only to be killed himself a few years later by the *mamluk* Beibars, with whom he had previously campaigned successfully against the Mongols. Beibars found a surviving Abbasid and brought him to Cairo as caliph, swore fealty to him and was invested as sultan by him in turn. Beibars tried to restore the caliph to Baghdad, but he died on the way, so Beibars found another Abbasid survivor and set him up as a puppet caliph in Cairo. This line of puppet caliphs continued in Cairo until the Ottoman conquest of 1517, after which they deserted, and transferred their title to the sultans of Istanbul, who thus acquired their chimerical claim to be caliphs too (Muir, 1896:214).

Before his death, Beibars proclaimed his son Said as successor to the sultanate and married him to a daughter of the *mamluk* Qala'un. At his accession, Said poisons his father's vizier, imprisons a number of his favourite supporters and antagonizes the rest. Eventually Qala'un prevents him from re-entering Cairo after an expedition, forces him to abdicate and seizes the sultanate, though pretending for a while to act as guardian for Said's brother. At Qala'un's death his son Nasir ruled as sultan on and off for fifty years, first as an infant, deposed and several times recalled. Numerous sons and grandsons of Qala'un became sultan, often as infants and for very short periods, until the Circassian *mamluk* Barquq took power in 1382. This sequence of events expresses most of the recurring characteristics of *mamluk* rule: constant attempts of self-made sultans to impose their sons, even infants, as a hereditary dynasty, often with considerable support, and equally frequent usurpation and establishment of a new *mamluk* as victor.

Though mainly a ruthlessly violent opportunity system, there were some surprising moral constraints, such as the need for a tame caliph to sacralize the seizure of power. Though seeming an empty formality, it did give protection against rivals attempting similar claims. Or again, the devotion to hereditary rule, so that virtually every sultan tried to win succession for his son, and though this rarely occurred successfully, there was a certain reluctance of rivals to flout it openly, so that they adopted the subterfuge of posing as guardians or regents before finally seizing power for themselves. If fathers were in this sense devoted to their sons, the latter perhaps understandably cared for their fathers, usually trying to sweep away their fathers' friends and supporters as completely as possible, with hideous tortures, at their fathers' death. But the tie between a *mamluk* and the *mamluk* who purchased him seemed very strong, even lasting for generations and providing the basis for the main factions.

While the original selection of *mamluk* slave boys, and their early allocation within the system, depended upon fallible assessment by leaders of their future potentialities, those who rose to the top and survived must have had outstanding gifts. In principle, those of talent could be promoted to be emirs of ten, or a hundred, or a thousand. But promotion must have been easier, *ceteris paribus*, in a large rather than a small establishment – less if you followed an emir of ten than if you followed an emir of a thousand. Presumably the establishment of the sultan (who was only the chief *mamluk*) was always the greatest. Many sultans bought themselves *mamluks* on a massive scale, running into tens of thousands. *Mamluks* could marry and have concubines, but their descendants were excluded from becoming *mamluks* themselves. It is obvious, therefore, that there was a profound contradiction in *mamluks* who became sultans getting their sons to succeed them. *Mamluks* prided themselves particularly on being *bought* and despised anyone who was not. It suggests that there was a general tendency to regard the position of sultan as an exception to the rules. The succession of a *mamluk*'s son seems a kind of sacrilege, and in fact they were failures in nearly all cases.

Even strong sultans rarely ruled for long, in fact, they were often astonishingly old when their rule began. Thus it is said Qaitbey died at eighty-six years after seventeen years and al-Ghuri at sixty after fifteen years.

Each one of these was, from the perspective of the sultanate, a usurper. Not surprisingly, strong sultans had usually been *mamluks* of a previous strong sultan, that is, they came out of the most advantageous establishment in the opportunity system. Correspondingly, strong sultans who achieved long reigns were usually followed by fierce succession wars.

This extraordinary kind of rule, which at first brought Cairo a period of glorious prosperity, though in the end it seems to have squeezed the system beyond breaking point into a decline by counterproductive exactions, permitted an extreme accentuation of basic features of the Islamic model. All the affairs of the state, the city and society were ultimately at the personal direction of the *mamluks* collectively. The political structure of the state and the city was simply the aggregation of the personal staffs of the *mamluks*. It was one vast interlocking edifice of patron–client chains. So, in a sense, are all societies, but this one was virtually nothing else.

Ottoman Istanbul

The most perfect slave administration was developed by the Ottomans in the fourteenth century (Toynbee, 1934:31–45), enabling them to conquer western Anatolia and the Balkans, finally capturing Constantinople in 1453. Like the *mamluks* of Egypt, they were recruited as children, and picked from raids on central Asia, Russia, Poland and the borders of the Ottoman realm. They were given a lengthy and severe education, both physically, mentally and morally, with harsh discipline and brutal punishment combined with continuous selection for merit, rewarded by high incentive pay, resulting in a fiercely competitive situation of very high risk and virtually limitless achievement opportunity. Not only did they provide the viziers, ministers, even *qadis* and most high officialdom, but also the crack divisions of the army and its officer corps. The sultans ceased to marry, taking slave consorts, and mating their daughters to the slave officials, so that rulers and administrators were united in a uniform slave status. Female slaves were recruited in a separate but similar system of selective purchase or capture and elaborate education and training.

The special slave training schools were in the great cities of Istanbul, Adrianople and Galata. Pupils with the highest achievement scores were taken into the palace to train for the highest offices. Slaves occupying the top positions of vizier, mufti and *qadi* in the fifteenth and sixteenth centuries had Serbian, Dalmatian, Albanian and various Christian peasant backgrounds (Toynbee, 1934:40).

The crucial feature of the system was that no sons of slave officials were permitted to enter the slave bureaucracy. The sultanate itself remained hereditary, but each successive sultan was required to put all his brothers to death at his accession. The great Ottoman Empire was thus paradoxically ruled by slaves who were mostly both of foreign and of Christian origin. So attractive was the system, providing the spectacular opportunity of advancement from peasant origin to grand vizier, that Muslim families actually tried to bribe Christian neighbours to arrange for sons of the former to be taken as slaves. There was great pressure both from slaves in high office and from free Muslim nobles to get their sons accepted into the corps. One exception was made for the elite regiments of Sipahis, and for some of the highest slave officials, to enrol their sons, but not their grandsons. Towards the end of the sixteenth century the restrictions broke down. Up till Suleyman's death in 1566 the janissary corps numbered only about 12,000 and the whole slave household, including boys in training and slaves of slaves, about 80,000. But by 1598 there were 101,600 janissaries and 150,000 unpaid supernumeraries (Toynbee, 1934:45), as all free Muslims other than Negroes came to be accepted as eligible.

Discipline and efficiency slowly decayed. The supernumeraries sullied their profession by trading to make a living, recruitment of Christian boys almost ceased, and European armies began to defeat the hitherto invincible Ottomans. Instead of its salvation, the corrupted janissaries became a menace to the state. Selim II lost his life trying to supplant them in Istanbul and they were finally extirpated there by Mahmud II in 1826, by which time the *mamluks* of Cairo, already weakened by Napoleon's conquest, had also been massacred by Muhammad Ali in 1811.

In Delhi and India the meritocratic, equal opportunity system of slave household as an instrument of government was virtually overcome by the politically weak but invincibly incorporative caste principle. Hindu caste in its formal version, of moral and spiritual values triumphing over political power, was not a concretely realizable idea (Dumont, 1966:93) just as the amorphous theocratic state of Islamic theory was not a concretely realizable ideal, because unintended institutions sprang up to fill the political vacuum. The essential and insidious Hindu inequality of purity and pollution easily overcame the essential but unrealizable Islamic equality.

Islamic urban theory

Much Islamic thought about the city is remote from reality, and much recent scholastic comment on it even more so. I shall mention only two of the greatest, al-Farabi of the tenth century and Ibn Khaldun of the fourteenth. They represent the characteristic diversity of origin of the Islamic, urban, intellectual elite, which maintained a remarkable though entirely unorganized unity, which partly facilitated and partly resulted from the extraordinary mobility with which many of them travelled, in constant peril, from city to city throughout the Islamic world. Al-Farabi was probably the son of a Turk in the caliph's bodyguard at Baghdad, therefore presumably of slave origin. He spent his life mainly at Baghdad, and his last years in Aleppo. He was influenced by Aristotle, on whose works he wrote commentaries, but does not seem to have had access to a reliable text. He studied under the Christian scholar Yohanna.

Ibn Khaldun, on the other hand, though born in the far west, and spending his early life in the cities of Spain and Morocco, came of an Arab family of long noble lineage. His life vividly illustrates both the natural and political hazards, wildly fluctuating opportunities and arbitrary despotism of the time. His father and mother perished in the Black Death of 1349. His whole immediate family of wives, concubines and children were drowned while sailing to Alexandria to join him. He served as a secretary to the sultan of Fez, but after two years fell under suspicion and was thrown into prison, later released, promoted and again lost favour. He was made chief minister of Granada, but was robbed and stripped by nomads while on a punitive expedition. He made pilgrimage to Mecca and in Cairo was made a professor at al-Azhar and then chief *qadi* of the Maliki school of law by Sultan Barquq, whose successor took him to Damascus and left him there under siege by Timur, at whose request he was lowered from the walls by ropes and taken to the Tartar camp, and witnessed the destruction of Damascus. Obtaining safe conduct to return to Egypt, he was again robbed and stripped by nomads, but eventually managed to reach Cairo where he died a few years later.

Ibn Khaldun's somewhat earlier contemporary, Ibn Battutah, was the greatest traveller of all, visiting most of the cities of the Islamic world, from Morocco to Turkestan and India, south across the Sahara to Mali, and down the east African coast to Kilwa. He did not speculate deeply about cities, but left the fullest descriptions of them.

Al-Farabi's tenth-century view of the city from Baghdad and Aleppo is essentially hierarchical. It must be dominated by a chief whom no one else can dominate, just as the body is dominated by the heart. As the heart is constituted first, to be the cause of the existence of all other organs of the body, so that the heart can cure any trouble in other organs, in like manner the chief of the city must exist first, to be the cause of its existence, its parts and their voluntary behaviour and hierarchy, so if any part is troubled the chief can provide what will bring the trouble to an end (al-

Farabi, 1949:79). This seems a pathetically naive faith, in view of the constant daily experience of Muslim cities. Yet perhaps it was realist, as the best belief that an idealist could cling to, hoping against unrealized hope that it could impose some restraint on the exercise of otherwise naked power. Islam provided a set of ideas which definitely discouraged the development of those urban institutions which could protect the populace from arbitrary rule. Perhaps the best Islam could attempt was to stress the responsibility of rulers despite the constant demonstration of its neglect.

There are three perfect and three imperfect societies, according to al-Farabi (1949:76), large, medium and small. All men, the nation and the city within the nation are the three perfect, while the three imperfect are the inhabitants of a village: a quarter, a street or a house. The sovereign good and ultimate perfection can first be obtained only in the city, and not in any less perfect society. The rest of al-Farabi's descriptions of 'the virtuous city' are even more perfectionist and remote from reality.

Ibn Khaldun likewise sees dynasties as prior to towns and cities, which are the product of royal authority (1958, II:235). Men must be forced to build cities by the stick of royal authority, or by rewards which only royal authority can afford. 'The life of the dynasty is the life of the town.' But Beduin life is prior to sedentary and city life. Most dynasties pass within three generations, or 120 years, from the privation of the desert to the luxury and plenty of the city, from a state in which everybody shared in the glory for himself, and from proud superiority to humble subservience, corruption and eventual destruction (1958, II:343–5).

The most important part of the Islamic world was contained in the arid belt, punctuated by mountains, stretching from Morocco to Turkestan. The dialectical interaction of rural nomads with urban populations and the dynamic flow between the two prevailed throughout this lengthy zone. Sedentary settlement and irrigated agriculture was a vital element, closely linked to the centres of urban settlement, over against the nomads. Ibn Khaldun perceived this fundamental relationship with unsurpassed brilliance. Having no obvious predecessor or successor, the foremost social scientist between Aristotle and Machiavelli, he was to Arnold Toynbee the greatest of all philosophers of history. It is hardly surprising that his basic perception was one of an endless cycle of flowering and decay, with only the vaguest glimpse of a larger framework of progressive development.

When dynasties thus become senile, as all do, cities must take care of their own affairs and protection, but they cannot stay free, for a free for all ensues, in which 'everybody vies against everybody else' until one of them achieves superiority and the cycle begins again (1958, II:303). He approves a saying attributed to the sixth-century Sassanian King Khosraw I that

royal authority exists through the army, the army through money, money through taxes, taxes through cultivation, cultivation through justice, justice through the improvement of officials, the improvement of officials through the forthrightness of wazirs, and the whole thing in the first place through the rulers' personal super-vision of his subjects' condition and his ability to educate them, so that he may rule them, and not they him. (1958, II:80)

'The religious law does not censure royal authority as such and does not forbid its exercise. It merely censures *the evils resulting from it, such as tyranny, injustice and pleasure seeking*' (1958, II:391, my emphasis). However, these 'are the concomitants of royal authority' (1958, II:391).

The true caliphate is the supreme expression of royal authority, whose proper exercise 'causes the masses to act as required by religious insight into their interests in the other world as well as in this world' (1958, II:387). But 'in later times' caliphate and sultanate were confused, the conditions governing the institution were disregarded and 'people were forced to render the oath of allegiance to anybody who seized power' (1958, II:388). No wonder the unorthodox Mu'tazilites and Kharijites decided that 'it is necessary only to observe the religious laws' and no caliph or imam is needed (1958, II:391). But for Ibn Khaldun there will be royal authority anyway, bad or good, although some thought that there should not be more than one God. In any case, like all prophetic religions which gain and keep a mass following, Islam soon became routinized and institutionalized despite itself, and the Islamic city was the expression of this.

Islamic urban institutions

While caliphs, sultans and *mamluks* belonged essentially to great cities, they none the less ran the wider states of which these were the capitals. Chief *qadis*, also, though urban based, had jurisdiction running far beyond them. On the other hand, Friday or cathedral mosques, *ulama*, merchants, palaces and huge domestic establishments of the elite, dense quarters of the common people, baths and markets, *muhtasib* controller of markets or 'provost of the guilds,' as well as the guilds themselves, were all more exclusively urban roles and institutions.

The Islamic city is important to the understanding of cities as a whole, not only because Islam has covered and influenced a large part of the Old World and provided the basis for a significant part of its cultural achieve-ments, but because it was an explicitly urban formula, though partly imposed by circumstances. For instance, within a few years of the Prophet's death, Caliph Umar tried to turn the Arab soldiers of the far-flung armies into city dwellers by prohibiting them from owning land anywhere outside Arabia. The good life can only be adequately led in cities, where there is a Friday mosque, bath and market (contrary to the vulgar perception of Muslims as ferocious nomads – who indeed also played their part).

With ecclesiastical organization prohibited, the place of the mosque in the Muslim city is critical. It is characteristic of non-institutionalized Islamic institutions. It must have its caretakers and cleaners, its preachers and Quran readers. It provides space for those who are expert in various schools of Islamic law to expound their wisdom to those who wish to hear. Small mosques may be the spontaneous expression of the piety, contributions and labour of local people, whereas great mosques can hardly be built or maintained except by great political figures. The mosque thus exemplifies the nature of the non-institutionalized institution, which in its building and maintenance, its fabric and furnishing, its servants, leaders and congregations, with its supplying bazaars clustered densely round, represents the largely unorganized, spontaneous efforts of great and small, co-ordinated by a single compelling idea, but motivated by a mixture of piety, selfless devotion, private interest and ulterior considerations as in all religions. Often, as at Fez, the ruler appointed the weekly preacher on the recommendation of the *qadi*, making the Friday prayer of the city an 'act of political significance' (Le Tourneau, 1961:133). The mosque is above all the House of God, yet it is also in part the seat of government, the court of justice, place of assembly, haven of male repose and university. Medieval Christian cathedrals also approached many of these functions, but not nearly to the same extent as the cathedral mosque of the Islamic city.

If the mosque is the most important physical expression of Islam in the city, its most important social manifestation is the elusive *ulama* (Lapidus, 1967:108). No more explicitly defined or clearly bounded than any other element, *ulama* included all those who could successfully claim or were in fact recognized as having a high combination of Islamic piety and learning. They were in no way organized, had no leader or formal membership, nor distinctive property, place of meeting or constitution whatsoever, yet they were the unquestioned authorities on Islamic doctrine and law, hence also the only counterweight to the otherwise naked power of the rulers or *mamluks*. Being educated as Muslims, though often sons of Christian families and not compelled to convert, the latter were more or less subject to the dictates of conscience as enunciated by the *ulama*. As they were not organized, *ulama* were scattered in every kind of occupation and family, yet in a vague way they corresponded to a large extent with the mass of functionaries who administered city and state for the *mamluks*. Though without formal power, the *ulama* were the most revered element in society. *Ulama* could never become *mamluk*, nor *mamluk ulama*, though their descendants, disqualified from *mamluk* status, could. There was, therefore, in the duality of *ulama* and *mamluk*, as well as of caliph and sultan, another version of the ambivalent quest for the solution to the problem of power and righteousness, the hopeless attempt to elevate right above might at least in ideology if it cannot be achieved in practice, as appears in Plato's philosopher king, in the ranking of Brahmin priest above Kshatriya ruler in Hindu India, or the uneasy balance between pope and Holy Roman Emperor.

The anti-institutional influence of Islam could not detract from the importance of the long-distance merchants, especially those in silk and spices from the east, over which the *mamluk* empire in combination with the Venetians enjoyed a virtual monopoly which gave Cairo its greatest wealth. (The loss of this to the Portuguese at the end of the fifteenth century, followed by the Ottoman conquest, was the greatest cause of economic, political and eventual demographic decline in Cairo.) But even here there was a certain blurring, for there was nothing to prevent a merchant also belonging to the *ulama*, on the one hand, while on the other the profits of trade induced *mamluks* to involve themselves in it directly, as well as milking it by taxation and customs.

The Ottoman janissaries held estates collectively, but the *mamluks* of Cairo and Damascus were supported by the allocation of estates to them individually, which eventually came to be treated simply as sources of income to be farmed by urban absentees, rather than as producers of real goods to be organized. Minor *mamluks* were paid for their services directly in grain, sugar and other staples. Either way, *mamluks* became involved in the grain trade, trying to resell their supplies at higher prices, to corner the market and establish monopolies. They were noted for luxurious living and contravening Islamic prohibitions by drinking wine and eating pork. But then, plundering and massacring innocent citizens was equally 'illegal'.

Perhaps the most distinctive feature of the social structure of a city organized in this fashion was that a significant part of its population was absorbed and incorporated in the huge establishments of the most important *mamluks* and the wealthiest merchants, as domestics, armed retainers, eunuchs, harem concubines, entertainers, barbers, butchers and servants of every kind. These were obviously residential units of great size and heterogeneity, but also formed the core of an even larger patron–client hierarchy of dependent and semi-dependent scribes, stewards, craftsmen, suppliers and multifarious agents, some of whom belonged exclusively to one such pyramid while others might serve several, with constant fluctuations between them. Outside these great establishments, which clustered in the centre and also later occupied certain fashionable elite suburbs, were the lesser establishments of smaller merchants, shopkeepers, craftsmen and professionals, and eventually the smaller residential units of ordinary poor folk and finally of the underworld riff-raff of vagabonds, illicit practitioners and criminals, the halt, the lame, the blind, the diseased and half witted.

In the Maghrebine cities three classes were distinguished: the central power elite (El Khassa), often of foreign origin like the janissaries and *mamluks*, or Arabs ruling Berbers; the notables (El-ayan) including *ulama*, rich traders and artisans; the broader urban masses (El amma), small artisans, shopkeepers, pedlars, journeymen, apprentices and petty urban folk, a proto-proletariat despised by the first two and subject to taxes, compulsory gifts and forced labour (Zghal and Stambouli, 1974:1–20). Zghal and Stambouli accuse French Marxists of identifying pre-colonial Maghreb too much with either the Feudal or Asiatic mode of production. They were thinking of the rather rigid analyses of the Centre d'études et de recherches Marxistes. Yet they themselves confirm in nearly all respects the original formulations of Marx in the Preface and *Grundrisse*.

Rejecting an identification either with medieval European towns or classical Chinese cities, they recognize that some isolated towns (Mzab, Tafilelt) were almost 'feudal' in their autonomy resulting from sheer geographical inaccessibility, and that Mogador did conform with the Asiatic mode of Chinese cities, but was exceptional.

While the great and their entourages occupied palaces and suburban villas, and ordinary small traders and craftsmen lived behind or above their places of business, there were extensive areas of very dense population in Cairo where the masses were housed in what amounted to multi-storeyed tenements comparable to those of ancient Rome. They were of five or six storeys (or as much as fourteen according to one account), each building like a fortress.

The Yemenites have constructed their cities as multi-storeyed edifices for several millennia, and certainly multi-storeyed buildings were quite common in Moroccan cities in the far west and those of at least two or three at Bukhara in the east. De Planhol claims that Islam is fundamentally hostile to lofty dwellings, and 'proscribes the house of several storeys', with actual regulations in Istanbul limiting height to about sixteen feet for Muslims and thirteen feet for others (1959:23–4). 'The low built house is characteristic of Islam, in contrast with the lofty buildings characteristic of our cities since the Renaissance' (1959:23–4). This is rather misleading, for he notes multi-storeyed dwellings in Cairo, Fez and North Africa, Jidda and Mecca, as well as Yemen and Hadramaut. In fact nearly all Islamic towns seem to have had dwellings of two storeys or more, and the contrast is much greater with the one-storey dwellings of Java or northern China.

The residential areas were divided into quarters, or wards, running off the main thoroughfare into narrow, winding, branching, blind alleys, each ward forced into a general communal solidarity by the general insecurity. 'The city is a collection of cities living under the haunting fear of general massacre' (de Planhol, 1959:14), 'not yet made into an organized collectivity', as Le Tourneau notes of Fez (1949:42), where, as elsewhere, every ethnic and religious group had its own quarter, making the whole a 'mosaic of cultures and creeds' (de Planhol, 1959:13) as with Antioch's forty-five districts described by Weulersse: aristocratic Turkish agas at the centre, Christians, Greek Orthodox and Armenian, Alawites, not to speak of other Muslims. To this segregated pattern largely correspond the local concentrations of particular trades, crafts, professions and commodities. Jerusalem had forty wards, Damascus seventy, with another thirty in the suburbs of al-Salihiyya, Cairo only thirty-seven, which must have been much bigger, and perhaps further subdivided. Ward populations seem to have varied from about 500 to over 1,000 (Lapidus, 1967:85).

In accordance with the Islamic principle which we have stressed, Muslim cities lacked distinctive corporate definition, structure or constitution, yet in practice the rulers of Egypt always had to appoint a governor of the city of Cairo, as of other cities, and a sheik of every quarter. The roles of these officials were characteristically diffuse and general. They were to do the bidding of their superiors, and could turn their power into profit as long as they could get away with it. They were most of all concerned with collecting taxes, but had the general duties of policing and administration as required.

In addition to this administrative skeleton, the most important urban official was the *muhtasib* in charge of the markets. Of course this official's role and duties varied in different times and places, but the ambiguity and confusion of the literature obviously stems from the same principle already outlined. In Islam it was impossible to circumscribe such an office clearly. Since the whole economy, like any other sphere of life, was *meant* to be regulated by an all encompassing law which was *sacred* in that it came from God, yet *secular* in that it was not to be encumbered, encrusted or corrupted by any ritual or ecclesiastical mediation, there was bound to be ambiguity. The *muhtasib* was inescapably part of the *ulama*, sometimes seen as the second (after the chief *qadi*) or third ranking member of its inevitable yet indefinable hierarchy. He was thus a legal official and therefore held 'court' and settled disputes. Hence inevitable overlap and confusion (in theory but not in practice) with the more purely legal hierarchy of the chief *qadi* and his deputies. Most typically the *muhtasib* was controller of markets, but hence also the 'provost of the guilds' and also overseer of the baths, of prostitutes and entertainers, sometimes even responsible for the upkeep of mosques, of city walls and water supplies. He had many assistants, whose positions and consequent lucrative opportunities at some periods were bought for huge sums.

Of all the formal roles of social control in the Islamic city, the hierarchy of the *qadi* was the most explicit and clear-cut, since they held general responsibility for the interpretation and administration of the law, which was the most explicit definition of Islamic government and society in general. However, there was always some room for legitimate (let alone corrupt and illegitimate) debate as to the exact provision of the law in any specific, empirical situation, especially in Cairo where all four orthodox schools of law were represented. As with all offices, that of *qadi* of Cairo had responsibility for *qadis* outside the city as well.

The extremely personal form which politics and government inevitably take in an anti-institutional system accentuates the exposure of all offices to corruption. In corrupt late *mamluk* times even the office of *qadi* became subject to purchase in Cairo and to use for the farming of revenue. At the best of times *qadis* were compensated by a proportion of the value of property involved in the cases they judged.

The other pervasive Islamic institution which deeply affected urban life was that of *waqf*, the establishment of perpetual charitable foundations. As in other cultures, the harnessing of piety and charity to economic interest had far-reaching implications. The attachment of support for services to mosques, hospitals and schools through *waqf*, motivated by the attainment of religious merit and the salving of conscience by the great and powerful, provided some minimal help to the less privileged of which they were sorely in need. However, *waqf* was very useful to *mamluks* as they could pass on wealth and power to their descendants by appointing them as administrators to such establishments. While *mamluks* were thus constantly motivated in one capacity to extend *waqf* for their descendants, in another they were increasingly frustrated by the greater and greater proportion of urban real estate which was thus fenced off from them and protected by the aura of the sacred law. Pressures upon *qadis* and the learned in the law to devise or fabricate legal pretexts for breaking open *waqf* in the name of the public interest and powerful patrons were often irresistible. The responsibility of *qadis* for the *waqf* became the most explosive attribute and the strongest temptation of the office. In Ottoman Cairo responsibility of *qadis* for the *waqf* was actually taken from the *qadi* and given to the chief eunuch.

Guilds

The question of the existence of craft and trade guilds in Islamic cities is controversial. Obviously, according to the ideal rules there should be none, and in a genuine sense there was none. The political, philosophical and institutional atmosphere was clearly inimical to them, but as in Chinese and Japanese cities the state authorities found control mechanisms over major economic occupations highly necessary. Guilds as self-governing and self-regulating bodies, controlling standards of production, conditions of work and conditions of entry did not exist (Lapidus, 1967:96–8). But the *muhtasib*, on behalf and by appointment of the ruler, was required to control the productive occupations. The only way he could do this was by requiring each trade or craft to propose leaders who could be held responsible. They did this not by election, but rather by elite consensus (Le Tourneau, 1961:96–7). Thus a leader (*amin*) of each was officially recognized, who had to co-operate with the authorities in allocating the duties and taxes required of his trade or craft. The essential contrast with the guilds of medieval European cities was that the latter organized themselves to control the standards and conditions of their work and to fight for their representation in the power structure of the city.

In the Islamic cities this did not and could not occur. Their trades and crafts were organized to allocate the services and taxes required by the ruler through the *muhtasib*. They were not corporations (Cahen, 1970:61–2). But the same principle operated here as everywhere, that when city and state government was weakest, the trades and crafts were forced to organize themselves for their own protection. The contrast with European guilds was real, but the similarities were striking. In the later Middle Ages when the Muslim world was fragmented in innumerable pieces, the guild organizations were that much stronger. In Fez each guild had its own patron saint, whose annual festival it celebrated, just as did the European guilds. But it remained true that Muslim guilds were largely organized against superior powers (Le Tourneau, 1961:96). There may have been many similar but unrecorded instances. However, Fez was perhaps fortunate in that it was not the capital of a very large or wealthy state, sometimes not a capital at all, but even when it was, this function was actually segregated in the separate walled royal city 750 yards across the valley from the walled merchant city, which with its agriculturally productive immediate hinterland, its long-established trade routes and its stable bourgeois population maintained a remarkably prosperous though relatively modest commerce and craft production.

The social and physical structure of Islamic cities

Both the social and physical structure of Islamic cities rather consistently reflects the interaction of Islamic ideals with the constraining necessities of urban life. They were full of splendid buildings: the great mosques, palaces, baths and markets which were by definition essential, and the impressive walls, gates, citadels, schools, hospitals and monumental cemeteries which usually developed. Yet they were distributed in a haphazard, even disorderly, fashion, without any overall plan. Although in a few cases, such as Baghdad and Samarra, rulers regarded the city as a living expression of their glory (Rodger, 1970:154), the general impression was one of looseness and lack of grandeur (Hourani and Stern, 1970:13), with the most venerable religious buildings crowded by the markets in their gloom, noise, smells, dust and swarming humanity (Elisséeff, 1970:176). Even in Samarra the grandiose projects of the caliphs treated the urban population 'as filling material for the new areas they built, as books are bought by some people to furnish rooms with rather than read' (Rodger, 1970:154).

This again reflects the opposition of Islamic principle to any corporate organization within the state, putting the emphasis on the individual, but leaving him at the mercy of arbitrary, absolutist rulers. The net result was chronic insecurity, with frequent massacres as its most alarming manifestation (Elisséeff, 1970:173). The only effective defence for the ordinary townsman was withdrawal into the neighbourhood quarter in the attempt to make a protective sanctuary. As the city had no constitution, so it had no plan, no cosmic design. In Fustat no streets were parallel, nor ever straight for more than ten yards (Rodger, 1970:143). Even narrower and more winding alleys led off these crooked streets into dead-end quarters. It was much the same in later Cairo, and Damascus, Aleppo, Fez, Bukhara and most Muslim cities. At the most one or two main thoroughfares were kept wider, but the *muhtasib* had an almost impossible job preventing private encroachment on them.

The small, irregular shaped quarters, with their densely packed, sometimes lofty and almost fortress like tenement buildings, took their basic solidarity from the pervasive violence and insecurity which threatened everyone, strengthened by ties of common kinship or ethnic origin, religion and occupation. Arabs, Kurds and Turkomans, though all Muslims, tended each to have their separate quarter, as did Jews and Christians.

Some degree of occupational specialization coincided with these ethnic and religious differences, but without any official enforcement.

The coincidence of occupation, ethnic group and ward was not expressed in any clear-cut social ranking, for diverse considerations influenced the status of a craft, with a good deal of change in emphasis from one city to another. Some were honourable because esteemed by the Prophet, or because they had to be sited near the mosque, or because of their wealth and economic importance. Others were despised as dirty or obnoxious, disapproved because in seeming contravention of the sacred law, or feared because of their association with mysterious forces. Nor did the actual status behaviour of townsfolk correspond with the ideal views expressed in the writings of scholars.

Thus 'perfume and milk were thought of as excellent trades' (Lapidus, 1967:83) for the Prophet's sake, and tailors and carpenters similarly respectable. The silver, gold and silk crafts were rated low because usurious, as also money-changers. They were often practised by non-Muslims, especially Jews. The 'forbidden' but ubiquitous wine, pork and hashish dealers were even lower. Scavengers, tanners, drivers, leatherworkers, butchers, barbers and surgeons were all defiled by association with dead animals and waste materials. Prostitutes of both sexes, dancers, entertainers, mourners, cockfighters, were all socially rejected as members of the underworld. Yet in practice these theoretical views worked out in very variable fashion. For example, in Fez, the tanners and leatherworkers were so numerous and so vital to the city's prosperity that they seemed to have enjoyed respect, whereas work in the oil mills was despised and left to foreigners because it was dirty (Le Tourneau, 1961:105). Indeed, one would not expect Islam to impose a clear-cut ranking of occupations, and their status clearly varied with local circumstances.

The wards of Islamic cities were not planned, built, organized, administered, protected or controlled in the systematic and orderly fashion of China and Japan. The maze-like pattern of Muslim cities in Spain also contrasted with the Christian cities there, which retained and adapted the Greco-Roman rectangular design, as well as the concept of a distinct municipal entity. Given the high level of insecurity, it was to be expected, as in so many pre-industrial cities, that residential buildings opened on to interior courtyards, facing blank walls outwards to the street, at least for the lower floors. Market streets were often covered and houses often met across narrow alleys and the 'flat roofs seem to be continuous, so that one might be able to walk all over the town from roof to roof', as Olufsen found in Bukhara (1911:512). Women could visit neighbours after dark across the roofs, without going into the street.

Despite the lack of overall plan, several features recur in similar relationship. At Cairo, Damascus, Aleppo, Tripoli, Marrakesh and Bukhara, there is the citadel on a hill at one side of the city, a great cathedral mosque near the centre, with markets close by, and the ruler's palace to one side. Sometimes these elements were planted separately and linked by later growth. The Fatimids' palace city of Qahira was right outside the existing city of Fustat, and Saladin's twelfth-century citadel was right outside both. At Fez, as we have seen, a royal city for ruler, officials and army was built with separate walls, across a valley from the previous city, which remained the commercial centre.

Urban insecurity: violence and freedom

It was only in times of complete political breakdown, as Ibn Khaldun remarked, that Muslim cities achieved any sort of self-government, and then only very briefly. The cities of Syria and Mesopotamia repeatedly rose against their governors between the eighth and tenth centuries, but never achieved administrative independence. When the Umayyad caliphate of Cordoba collapsed, the city of Seville was for a time governed by a group of local notables, under the leadership of its *qadi*, but soon reverted to a military emirate. A number of other Spanish cities were governed by their *qadis* in the inter-regnum between the Almoravid and Almohad Empires. The same happened occasionally in North African cities when central government weakened, but municipal institutions were never developed. While the periodic break up of the larger Islamic states, from Morocco to India, tends to be perceived as a move towards political chaos, it is also noted that in such periods of political weakness at the top, the quality of life for townspeople may actually have improved.

'Islamic civilization was urban' (Hourani and Stern, 1970:23, 25), and though objective judgements in this field are very hard to prove, the conclusion is irresistible that Muslim cities were more violent and unsafe than those of any other major urban civilization. First there is the initial violent expansion of Islam, but this is common to all empires; then there is the constant warfare with Byzantines, Crusaders, Turks and Mongols. All this affected the cities greatly, especially those of Syria and Mesopotamia. But the internally generated violence of cities, arising from tyrannical rule without restraining institutions, was worse. Of course, unjust and arbitrary violence was contrary to Islamic law and against the conscience of the *ulama*. But precisely because of the constant threat of disorder, the *ulama* usually supported the powers that were, for the sake of 'peace' at any price, that is, however many lives were lost or property destroyed in the course of enforcing it.

One is impelled to ask what could have induced ordinary people to live in such cities. Obviously, for caliphs and sultans, viziers and ministers, *mamluks* and generals, even *ulama* and foremost merchants, the prizes were sufficient to be irresistible. But all these together were a very small minority. A larger number can be explained as soldiers conscripted in the armies, or attracted by the frequency of opportunity for looting and plunder. The huge number of slaves was a further element requiring no explanation, though we must remember that slave status ranged from menials and concubines to viziers, *mamluks*, sultans and sultans' spouses. Then there was the huge, unknowable number of the urban underworld: halt, lame, blind, diseased, crazed; beggars, criminals, rebels, drug addicts and mystics, fused in various combinations.

From the Maghreb to Egypt, Syria, Anatolia, Mesopotamia, central Asia, northern India and south-east Asia, peasant subsistence was not so attractive or secure with half the production often taken in taxes or exactions. The cities were visually magnificent, full of tempting amenities absent from the countryside, above all constant, lavish and wasteful spending of the political elite on public works and entertainments. It is likely that most of the urban masses were tied in to opportunity systems of patron–client linkage, which provided them with beguiling hopes of advancement or enrichment, however unrealistic for the vast majority.

When all is said and done, the truly impressive achievements of Islamic culture in mathematics and philosophy, architecture, medicine and poetry, were the efforts of a very narrow elite, who either lived directly under the tempting but unreliable patronage of political leaders, or had the means to provide themselves with a reasonable degree of residential security. It is from this very restricted group that we know most of what we know about the quality of life in Islamic cities.

Clearly life in Cairo and Baghdad, as was very usual in medieval cities, was highly unpredictable and insecure, but the anti-institutional bias made it even more arbitrary. Sultans and powerful *mamluks* were constantly trying to corner the market in a particular product, to double or treble its price and make an extra fortune by forced sale, or to raise taxes without warning on particular trades or crafts or categories of the populace. The only hope of redress was an uprising of the group involved. Whether they succeeded depended largely on the naked balance of power. If they could mobilize sufficiently widespread support to constitute a serious threat, the authorities would step down, otherwise they were likely to be punished by physical attack, further plundering, or loss of life. Groups of merchants would shut their shops in protest against the enforcement of low selling, or high buying prices. They might either succeed, or find their shops attacked by a detachment of *mamluks*, broken open and plundered. In such recurrent crises the scales could be tipped by support from the *ulama*, or respected individuals among them, or by the market officers, or the sheiks of quarters, or by a powerful rival patron. The sultan kept a Cairo cloth dealer in prison until he renounced a claim to 90,000 dirhams owed to him (Lapidus, 1967:281).

The ruthless attitude of rulers to masses was shown on unforgettable occasions, as when Fustat was burned as possible discouragement to an invader, and its tens and thousands of inhabitants left homeless, if they escaped with their lives. It was the same when Ibn Tulun's Qatay was destroyed in a dispute of ruling factions. The Fatimid caliph al-Hakim simply had the balconies and façades of all houses knocked down which were found to obstruct the passage of a great chandelier which he happened to want taken to the mosque of Amr, right at the other side of Cairo (de Planhol, 1959:29). The same had to be done in 1813 for the parade which followed the marriage of the pasha's daughter (de Planhol, 1959:29).

Factions were so severe, especially when they had a religious basis, as between Muslims and Christians, or even among Muslims, as between Sunni and Shi'ah in Baghdad, that while rulers usually attempted to mediate between them there were frequent occasions when they felt forced to support one against another, even to the point of 'authorizing the looting of the city and the massacre of part of the population' (Wiet, 1971:90).

Doomed to lack of hard quantitative evidence, how can the disturbing violence of the Islamic city be assessed? As an urban civilization, wealthy and splendid in many cultural achievements, it can perhaps be faulted for the deliberate dearth of appropriate urban institutions.

Given the speed and enormous extent of its early expansions and the relatively small numbers involved, it was inevitable that Islamic civilizations should be extremely heterogeneous, both in ethnic and religious composition. This being so, the degree of similarity between them is remarkable. Many had Christian majorities and large Jewish populations. Non-Muslims were of different legal status and subject to different taxes, but in certain respects they could have advantages. It was not so much that they were discriminated against as that they were helpless in the face of frequent and fanatical mob violence, touched off by the most trivial incidents. Rulers often tried very hard to protect them, and even punished their attackers severely, but sometimes popular feeling was so strong that even they had to bow to it (Lapidus, 1967:292). In fact, their efforts to suppress violence often simply added to it. The attacks of Crusaders also prompted vengeful acts against Christians, despite their belonging to different churches at least as hateful to the Crusaders as Islam itself. In Cairo Christians were for a time even driven to pass as Jews (Muir, 1896:xvii).

It may be said that Islam did not discourage violence, but while the Confucian scorn for soldiers and martial valour certainly was a significant factor in China, as Buddhism may also have been in parts of south-east Asia (though never, of course, preventing rulers from warfare), it is quite doubtful whether the peaceful emphasis of Hinduism was at all effective in India, or even Christianity in Europe. Even so devout a Christian as Sir William Muir is horrified at the barbarism, cruelty and treachery which Crusaders matched with their fanatical piety, culminating in their treatment of the city of Jerusalem itself.

The sacred city flowed with blood; the Jews sought refuge in their synagogue, but it was set on fire, and they perished in the flames. Within the next three days, 70,000 Moslems, without respect of age and sex, were put to the sword. Having sated thus their savage passions, the soldiers of the Cross fulfilled their vows, and kissed the stone that had covered Him who said, *My kingdom is not of this world, else would My servants fight.* (Muir, 1896:xvii, my emphasis)

Not only was the *mamluk* system institutionalized violence at a high level, with fewer mitigating factors even than European chivalry, and more intrinsically urban, but at the lowest level also there were many urban groups professionally committed to violence, which, in fact, the *mamluks* sometimes encouraged. In fact, for the common people poised 'between violence and impotence' (Lapidus, 1967:147), mass violence directly reflected the lack of channels for the expression of grievances, or consultation, let alone participation in decision making, for Islam was averse to the 'brutal law of the majority' (Le Tourneau, 1961:41).

The ravages inflicted on the cities by external conflicts and enemies were frequent enough, but internal sources of violence, though sometimes smaller scale, were even more frequent. The obverse of the protection which the face-to-face solidarity of the quarters provided was the hostility they bore one another. Damascus was perhaps the most extreme case of a general phenomenon, especially common in the cities of Syria. But even in the holy city of Mecca the different ethnic quarters fought one another.

In the economic decline of the end of the fifteenth century, with the cities full of unemployed and destitute, the Zu'ar youth gangs of Damascus became extremely active, with many paradoxical functions. They both protected and preyed upon the quarters. Regarded as a rabble of thieves and scoundrels, a lumpenproletariat, they yet included shopkeepers and craftsmen, even a few *ulama* notables. They succeeded in assaulting and even killing tax collectors, *mamluks'* agents and police chiefs, barricading the quarters and attacking the troops. Having no other effective mechanism, the *ulama* even bribed them to attack rampant abuses, while at the same time the Zu'ar also ran protection rackets. Unable to control or subdue them, the *mamluks* tried to co-opt instead,

arming them and enrolling them in the army, cleverly converting potentially revolutionary political violence into mere criminality (Lapidus,
1967:154–63).

Extremely similar were the *ayyar* of Baghdad from the ninth century
onwards: vagrant, plebeian, outlaws and bandits, counting it virtue to rob
the rich. As in Damascus they attacked and killed tax collectors and other
officials, actually controlling the city for years at a time. They were also
linked with secret societies and religious movements, contributing to the
constant battles of Sunni and Shi'ah, the Saffavid revolt at the end of the
ninth century, the *hashshashin* killings (Wiet, 1971:109) and many other
violent outbreaks, as well as being hired as mercenaries. From AD 921 to
932 eighteen uprisings were recorded. Besides this, Baghdad suffered the
great slave revolt of the ninth century, the recurrent battles between rival
armies of sultan and caliph and the final destruction by Timur in 1401,
from which it never recovered. As a much reduced provincial city under
Ottoman pashas it relapsed into *mamluk* control like Cairo, and in the
eighteenth century is said to have enjoyed a relative security (Wiet,
1971:174).

All large cities also had large numbers of beggars (*harafish*) who
roamed the streets and lived in mosques, cemeteries and shacks as best
they could, depending on the alms of sultans, emirs and wealthy citizens.
Some were handicapped, but others able bodied, engaging in unskilled
and menial labour when called upon. They provided much of the mob
which joined in the riots or plunderings of Zu'ar and *ayyar* and were
attracted into the obscure Sufi orders (Wiet, 1971:106, 178–82).

The less important, smaller cities may have been less torn by internal
violence. Fez, with its walled commercial city separate from the royal
capital across the valley seems for certain periods to have been more
peaceful (Le Tourneau, 1961:102–3). Less completely dominated by
arbitrary political leaders in their day-to-day affairs, the craft organizations eventually developed a more guild-like character, with their festivals
and patron saints, while still remaining social rather than technical bodies
(Le Tourneau, 1961:98–9). The fights between young men of different
quarters, though still sometimes violent, had become largely ceremonial
(Le Tourneau, 1961:70–1).

Trading city-states

The innumerable small trading city-states which Muslims founded along
the coasts of Africa and Asia, or on the overland caravan routes, were
more close-knit and integrated as urban communities, with the political
and economic elite overlapping or fused together. There were, however,
frequent battles between neighbouring rival cities.

Given the political disunity and ethnic heterogeneity, the recurrent similarities of physical structure and social life in Islamic cities over the 4,000 miles from Marrakesh and Fez to Bukhara and Samarkand are quite remarkable. The even longer chain of maritime commercial cities from the Persian Gulf and East Africa to Indonesia had similarities of a different sort. Here were no great Islamic empires and no huge metropolitan cities, but small coastal trading ports, with the same ethnic ward structure, but with merchants and rulers virtually fused into a single class, though ritual and symbolic differences might be stressed. The humid tropical forest environment often provided a great ecological contrast to the arid zone. On the rivers of Malaysia and Indonesia, which provided commercial highways to the interior, many port towns were built on wooden piles in the water. Further east still, Muslims usually formed only wards in cities ruled by others. It is said that Canton once had a Muslim majority, but nothing is known of its urban structure at that time.

Although the primary motivation for the foundation of these small coastal city-states must have been mercantile, perhaps sparked off in many cases by the desperate need to escape from threatened danger somewhere else, there was here too the possibility of the gradual emergence of a distinction of emphasis, though not of class, or institutions, or even intercourse, between the main ruling elite becoming more and more associated with property ownership, both rents from urban real estate and produce from slave-worked plantations, over against the body of actively trading merchants. There was usually considerable mobility between the two categories, since a successful merchant house was likely to invest in real estate if it survived for several generations, while ruling dynasties were unstable and constantly changing, so that persons fallen from power may have taken up or reverted to trade. On the other hand, it was possible for such status and occupational differences to approximate to local divisions within the city and to become encrusted with ritual inhibitions and symbolic meaning. However, it was probably more significant for cities in economic decline, as most of them were by the time any recent studies were made of them. The complex diachronic changes of symbolic structure in relation to politico-economic changes have been analysed by El Zein (1974) for the ancient city-state of Lamu on the northern coast of Kenya.

The dialectic of trading profit, real estate wealth and political power can be seen in the case of the city-state of Zanzibar, whose nineteenth-century burst of prosperity was one of the last of its kind. Similar processes had occurred in Mombasa (Kenya) and Kilwa (Tanzania) as they did within different ethnic and cultural frameworks at Malacca, Johore (Malaya), Acheh (Sumatra) or Banjarmasin (Borneo). In other cases rich and ancient cultures of the powerful inland states of Java and

Sumatra enforced more profound political, cultural and even religious accommodations.

The small urban outposts from Africa to the Far East mingled deeply with local peoples and cultures, through intermarriage, concubinage, conquest and slavery, becoming extensively transformed genetically in the process, yet the prestige of Islamic religion and scholarship persisted strongly and often spread widely. The diffuse yet consistent forces of Islamic society were thus expressed in the maritime city-states on a smaller scale.

Conclusion

The Islamic city, as a recognizable though variable type, was thus spread over a huge area of the world, divided among many different independent states and emergent nations, all of which had to submit, in devastating ways, to the political or economic penetration of western colonial nations. None had any appreciable chance to work out its own cultural solution for the adjustment of its urban tradition to the modern industrial world.

Since there is still no coherent, generally accepted statement of how an Islamic state can be ruled, other than by an absolute, just monarch, such as has never appeared, most predominantly Muslim cities and countries today still face the same human and political problems they failed to solve 1,000 years ago, paying lip-service to democracy and making an ugly travesty of it to deceive the people or drive them to cynical apathy alternating with fanatical fury. Consequently, much of the life and ecology of the Islamic metropolis today retains entrenched features of the great caliphal cities. For example, formal institutional deficiencies covered by bloated, inefficient bureaucracy; incurable corruption; ultimate resort to military force; ineradicable urban poverty, escaping to the intricately impenetrable dead-end quarters, where few strangers venture and original, creative coping mechanisms can be worked out in the despotic cultural solidarity of the domestic neighbourhood (Wikan, 1995).

Islamic cities and states expressed the polythetic features of the Asiatic mode of production: the ruler was owner of all land in principle and largely in practice. Estates were given to followers who, as everywhere, tried to make them hereditary, but they could be arbitrarily withdrawn and transferred. The ruler's authority was absolute at the centre, imposed by his army, increasingly composed of slaves, his private property. Towards the periphery, local polities of warlords or traditional groupings were autonomous. Officers were appointed and dismissed arbitrarily. Correspondingly, tax was exacted directly at the centre, farmed further out or exacted as tribute. Cities, especially capital cities, reflected the ruler's arbitrary, absolute authority. They were 'royal camps' (Marx,

1973:479) in that they could be built to vast size almost on the spur of the moment, by mobilization of hordes of forced labour, and equally suddenly abandoned and rebuilt elsewhere, as in the case of Agra and Fatehpur Sikri, or Fustat, Qatay and Qahira (Cairo).

INDIC CITIES

Suppression at the centre and spread to the periphery

Paucity of evidence for the social life and political economy of Indian cities, as a distinct cultural form, results from centuries of Muslim and British rule and mythopoetic, ahistorical emphasis of the Indian genius, constraining us to look first at the rich evidence from the Indianized periphery: Angkor in Cambodia and Bhaktapur in Nepal; then disparate examples from India itself: Varanasi, Broach and Ahmedabad, for hints of the ritual, ecological and economic structure of Indian cities and the organization of guilds. The civilizations of India, China and the west have been distinguished by varying emphases on kinship, caste and club association.

Dominant Chinese ideas and religion were pragmatic expressions of life and problems within the Chinese realm, therefore did not spread strongly beyond it. Indian thought and religion so transcended the realms within which they developed that they spread far and wide, undergoing transformations as they went, with significant implications for the cities that grew within their influence. They expressed the symbolic integration and equivalence of city, cosmos and society architecturally. Cambodia, Laos and Thailand embodied this tradition, with other states peripheral to Indian culture such as Nepal and Bali.

Funan was the earliest and easternmost Indianized state (Coedès, 1968:36 *et seq.*), from which other rulers in Cambodia and Indonesia may have been derived (Provencher, 1975:34). Funan stretched from the lower Mekong to the Gulf of Siam from the first to the sixth century, with its capital city Vyadhapura twenty miles from its coastal port Oc Eo (McGee, 1967:31; Wheatley, 1983:122–34).

In Sumatra, the capital of Srivijaya's trading empire till the eighth century was a city of rafts on the Palembang river (McGee, 1967:34), probably with houses built on piles by the shores, as in Brunei, and Bandjarmasin in Borneo. There were many competing principalities in the fertile irrigated valleys of south central and eastern Java (Geertz, 1966:41–2), from which developed the Sailendra (Provencher, 1975:34), Kadiri and Singhasari kingdoms and the Madjapahit empire of the thirteenth to fifteenth centuries centred near the present Surabaya, each generating its own capital city.

Cambodia

Although tradition suggests that Brahmin traders brought the Indian cultural inspiration as part of a diffuse but lengthy migration, it was necessarily transformed in contrasting directions by markedly different ecologies and local opportunities. The palace-temple-capitals of Khmer kings round Angkor carried the cosmic city idea to an excess, which may have brought its downfall. It was a tribute to the enormous increase in fertility and rice production achieved by channelling and controlling the seasonal fluctuation of rivers in the Cambodian plain.

The richly carved ornamental walls and cloisters of Suryavarman's twelfth-century Angkor Wat extend for 1,700 by 1,500 yards, with three concentric enclosures and nine towers. It is surrounded by huge stone-lined reservoirs with an intricate network of canals. Nearby, the successor, Jayavarman VII, built the even larger Angkor Thom complex of towers, terraces and enclosures, with a further set of moats, reservoirs and canals. The central tower was the mythical Mount Meru, the hub of the universe, the corner towers of the concentric enclosures the four cardinal points. The surrounding waters represented the primal ocean out of which the gods churn the universe into being, with the central tower as churning rope. Within the central tower was the *lingam* (phallus) of Siva (Coedès, 1963:37), with which the vital force and personality of the god-king himself was eventually identified.

Angkor represents a highly centralized vision of society and constituted a highly centralized and concentrated organization of space, of water and of subsistence production, with a similarly centralized mobilization of massive manpower for its construction. It consisted of an accumulation of many, partly overlapping, temple complexes created by successive rulers. It is claimed that all the villages of the Cambodian state were tied in a relationship of service and tribute to specific temples and that the whole city complex of Angkor required the services of over 300,000 persons in 13,500 villages to support its temples. Besides, the king and the royal family, the priests, nobles and administration were obviously very large and, in that highly stratified society, required even larger numbers of personal servants in attendance, over and above those required to bring in basic supplies, not to speak of those involved in the extensive multi-directional trading evidenced by Chinese sources. On this basis, Angkor must have been urban in the size and density of its population as well as in the very nature of its cosmic conception. The Brahmin trader tradition of origin fuses the sacred, ritual and economic sources of city development. The difference of emphasis between sacred cities, based on the rich, rice growing alluvial valleys, and the coastal and riverine trading cities appears in the contrast between *negara* and *pasara* in their varied forms throughout the Indianized world, and provides much of the substance for the abstract distinction drawn by Redfield and Singer between orthogenetic and heterogenetic cities.

This distinction between agrarian-based and trading city-states was far from absolute. Often the agrarian capital controlled trading ports as well, as in the case of Mrauk-u, or a city-state whose power derived from maritime trade gained control of a large agrarian empire, as in the case of Madjapahit. Both were ruled by autocratic kings and nobles, sharply distinct in rank from the merchants, many of whom were foreign, though as elsewhere kings and nobles found ways of participation in profitable trade themselves, as well as taxing the merchants.

Some of the most obvious strategic spots were clearly destined for the domination of trade, such as Malacca (Sandhu and Wheatley, 1982), which easily controlled the straits between the Malay peninsula and Sumatra, through which all ships had to pass between India and China to avoid a very long detour. Such pure trading centres naturally tended to be much more heterogeneous in population than the sacred cities. Malacca was a Malay principality until it adopted Islam in the fifteenth century, but it already had traders from Sumatra, Java, Bengal, Gujerat, Ceylon, Arabia and China. Like most medieval cities its population was small by modern standards, probably not more than 10,000 persons, but it was essentially urban (McGee, 1967:41).

The spread of Islam had itself created many such maritime trading settlements, along the seaways of Arabia itself, East Africa, India and south-east Asia, not reaching the latter region till the fifteenth century, only 100 years before the Portuguese. But they were very widespread throughout the Indonesian archipelago and as far as the Philippines.

Early cities in Hindu and Buddhist India

Hindu India undoubtedly produced one of the great urban civilizations, in view of the number of its cities, their size, age and distinctive culture. It also formulated a distinctive urban design in classical writings such as Arthasastra (Law, 1914; Shamasastry, 1956).

Although the Chinese conception of the city was cosmographical, a symbolic expression of powerful beliefs in whose implementation the city was instrumental, it was sufficiently pragmatic to be embodied in physical form without insuperable difficulty. Temples, palaces and ordinary dwellings, as well as streets, walls and gates could represent mythological realities and stages for their enactment. The Indian conception of the city is so profoundly and intricately mythopoetic, so deeply involved in the symbolic representation of the otherworldly rather than earthly phenomena, that it is better expressed in the architecture of temples than of cities for mundane activity and residence.

The enormous temples of Madurai, Kanchipuram, Mahabalipuram or Bhubaneswar may give the impression of being themselves cities by mere size, but they are religious not secular structures. When Indian anthropological scholars studied the city of Kashi (Varanasi) and its ascetics they could not avoid including poetic and legendary elements. The earliest factual accounts were, significantly, by Chinese travellers (Sinha and Saraswati, 1978:6–7, 12–13). Descriptions of early Indian cities by Indian and western scholars are understandably idealized, revealing more about temples and shrines, religion and philosophy, and the imagined activities of mythical beings, than about empirical urban life (Piggott, 1945; Puri, 1966). Unlikely elaborations of hypothetical institutions compound the confusion (Turner, 1941:748–50). Candragupta Maurya's fourth-century BC capital Pataliputra was described by the Greek ambassador Megasthenes as a parallelogram surrounded by a wooden palisade with arrow loopholes. At Candragupta II's capital 600 years later, a Chinese visitor described the inlaid sculpture of the palace as the work of superhuman spirits. In Kautilya's Arthasastra of similar date, the city appears only as a fortress. Alexander carried Hippodamus of Miletus' rectilinear design as far as north-west India. That of Harappa lay buried further south. Asoka's city of Ujjain was mentioned by Ptolemy and eventually sacked by Muslim invaders in the thirteenth century. In Hindu India the cosmographic impetus spent itself on the temple rather than the secular city. In Cambodia the royal temple city virtually swallowed the secular city. In Indonesia the Kraton palace city as at Jogjakarta had a rectangular pattern more comparable to the Chinese but different in orientation.

The early Indian cities had superbly skilled metalwork and textiles. Great trade caravans plied between them. Crude copies of Greek coins were issued, but the economies of the Indian states were highly redistributive, accentuated by the caste system with its hereditary *jajmani* service obligations. They were ruled by very narrow elites, deploying vast armies and dispensing brutal justice without clear practical codes. From 20% to 60% of the peasants' crop was expropriated for their support. The Hindu merchants' caste was included among the 'twice-born' strata, but as in other autocratic systems, merchants were largely at the mercy of rulers.

Broach was the major port of Gujerat in pre-British times, one of India's greatest ports under Asoka, ruled by Muslims for considerable periods and occupied by Britain in 1777 when it contained about 30,000 people, with perhaps 20,000 in suburban settlements. The walled city covered three square miles, by the Narbada river, eighteen miles from the sea. In 1961 its surrounding district still had 70,000 wooden and only

674 iron ploughs, 51 power driven sugar crushers but 132 bullock driven – a highly traditional, almost unchanged technology. The basic ecological structure of the city had probably altered little.

Four groups of Brahmins occupied the south-east corner, near the river bank, with areas occupied by domestics of ex-slave status, low-caste palanquin bearers conveniently near to the north of them. Further north of them there was a Muslim area just inside the wall, and further west the Muslim administrative area and mosque. West of the Brahmins on the river bank were: a Punjab warrior caste, the collector's office, the gardeners, painters and weavers. Inland from them to the north was the main Banya area, with areas for Jains, artisans and Muslims further west and the customs house near the south-west corner of the wall.

The Parsis had an area just inside the western wall and a larger area outside further west. Oilpressers, fishermen, potters and another Banya area were just outside the west wall, with another potters' area on the east outside the wall and next to the bricklayers. Just to the north of them was the main cluster of seven Hindu temples. Further east still, beyond the north–south railway line were the compounds of several Hindu societies (Patel, Bhrugupur, Pritamngar and of Nanak's temple).

North of the walled city there were more low-caste areas of domestic servants, washermen, printers, butchers, cattle fodder dealers, with untouchables and paddyworkers even further north. There were also a number of cotton mills and ginneries outside the walls to the north, an *asram* and a *dak* bungalow for travelling officials. On the far west side outside the walls was the new British administrative area, with offices, bungalows, padre's compound and gymkhana field.

This ecological arrangement expressed a fairly clear caste gradient punctuated by the placing of some low service castes conveniently near to their masters, and by the intrusion of anomalous new castes, low in ritual rank but high in political power: first the Muslim rulers and their followings, then the British, even more effectively segregated (Desai, unpublished manuscript).

Bhaktapur

The city-states of the Kathmandu valley date from before the time of Christ and changed little until a few decades ago. As national capital, Kathmandu has been totally transformed. The city-state of Bhaktapur was modelled on the ancient Hindu Gangetic kingdoms. The rectangular royal palaces, major temples and squares were at the conceptual centre, with Brahmins, priests, courtiers and rich merchants in spacious three-storey houses adjacent to them. Farmers occupied intolerably congested quarters further out, forming 60% of the urban population, with untouchables on the edge, next to the cremation spots on the river. The urban axis was a ridge, crossed by the ancient India–Tibet trade route marking eastern upper from western lower town.

The clockwise circumambulation at the great festival follows not the edges of the city but its essence, from square to square and house to house of mother goddesses. Thirty-four sets of three types of ritual sites, one for each god and goddess make 102 stopping sites along the route. The serene circumambulation is intersected by a violent ritual drama of conflict. The chariot of Siva, an enormous wooden creation four storeys high, is pulled about by crowds of men in a tug-of-war indicating dissolution of accepted social and spatial orders on nearing the end of time (New Year). Lesser chariots of other deities are crashed together representing and enacting procreative union. The chariot must reach Yagsikhaya square to signal the creation of the Yahsi pole as a sign of New Year victory. Lowering the old pole and raising of the new represents the umbilical centre of the world, the mythic pillar of Indra separating earth and heaven and the erection of Shiva's phallus in his consort's *yoni* re-enacting primal procreation.

The total population of the city is directly involved and engrossed. The reconstruction of the wrecked chariots and repair of shrines goes on throughout the year, expressing the communal political order and devotion of the economic resources of the townsfolk. The whole phenomenon exists also as a map in the mind, realized in a perfectly symmetrical mandala (Southall, 1993:381–5; Gutschow, 1984).

There is a conception, even if it is restricted to the learned, and there is also a static physical representation in the host of actual shrines, goddess houses and porches, which do correspond to the conceptual deities. Most important is the action of the populace, the congregation, the city in the flesh. This mass communal ritual action binds all the sacred places, and hence the ideas which they represent, together into an integrated whole. By contrast, the sixty or more sacred places (churches) in the city of Norwich are not formally linked together in any such way, though all are under the hierarchical authority of the bishop in a way that Hindu shrines are not.

Kashi

The holy city (Varanasi or Benares) is divided into portions: the *pucca mahal* or old city of masonry houses, 'a perfect labyrinth of lofty buildings separated from one another by narrow stone paved alleys' (Sinha and Saraswati, 1978:16). *Kachcha mahal* consists of the interior and lower

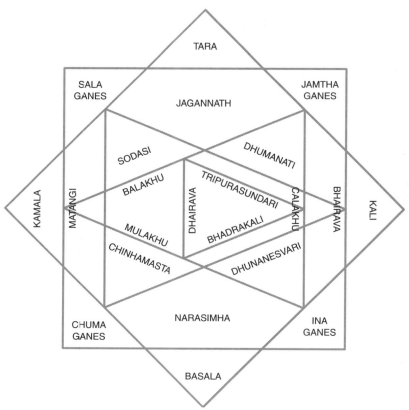

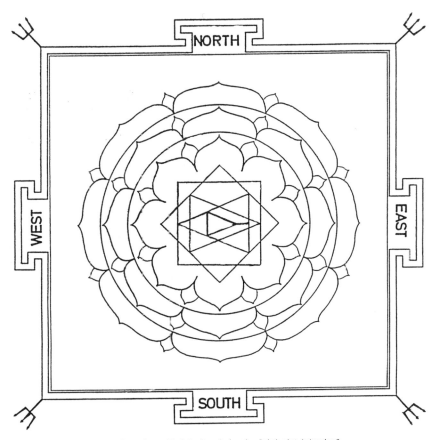

Bhaktapur: the complex mandala, designed as a ritual map by a Brahmin priest. An 'unordered' topographic abundance changes into a symbolic reproduction of reality, with the divine couple (Bhairava and Bhadrakali) and the Ninth mother (Tripurasudari) in the centre. For the initiated there is no contradiction between the idea, the map of the mind, and reality.

Plate 4 Bhaktapur: it must be accepted that such a highly abstract diagram is the representation in the learned mind of the tortuous realism of the still symbolic city.

areas of inferior buildings. The boundary is marked by a path which circles the city at a radius of five miles and is circumambulated reverently by thousands of pilgrims every year. Another circumambulation route between holy places further out extends for 269 kilometres.

Sinha and Saraswati found twenty-seven wards containing 43,865 houses. In the nineteenth century 1,454 temples and 272 mosques were counted. The most important wards and temples are along the banks of the Ganges. The Brahman zone contains the river banks, ritual places and shrines. There are more than eighty 'burning *ghats*' for cremation and immediate salvation. The Vaisya zone is the main business centre of the markets and bazaars. The Shudra zone on the outskirts shelters outcasts, Chamar, Bhangi and Doms. Kshatriyas are not permitted in the city of Visheswara. Even the raja must live on the other side of the Ganges. Kashi is a microcosm of India, with concentrations of people from Bengal, Nepal, Maharashtra, Gujerat, Tamilnadu and Kannada in their own areas. It was visited by the Emperor Asoka and the Buddha himself.

Foreign visitors may be horrified by the brown waters of the Ganges with its corpses floating by and old ladies sipping its holy waters from brass vessels. But 'few cities in India can hope to rival Kashi in the affection and reverence which it evokes in the Hindus of all categories'. On entering

one is overwhelmed by the crowd of pilgrims hustling through narrow stinking lanes infested with dreadful fighting bulls and insidious monkeys, and pursued by rapacious Pandas to small untidy temples. His clothes will be spoilt on being the least bit careless, by reckless spitting of betel juice. But ask a devout Hindu what he thinks of Kashi and you will find in him so much love, such enchantment, so much adoration for this unique sacred city.

The Sanskrit verse says 'in this unreal world there are only four realities – staying in Kashi, the company of ascetics, bath in the Ganges and the worship of Shiva'. 'In all the *puris* if one dies he is reborn but in Kashi he finds salvation once for all, and at once.'

Kashi means light, one can really achieve the merit of Kashi only when he has attained the knowledge of Brahma or the light of Brahma. To a devout Hindu pilgrim the discomforts of the city are no matter. He is not frightened by the fighting or goring bulls; the stinking narrow lanes do not suffocate him and the rapaciousness of the Pandas or the booming and milling crowd does not bother him. Aware of all inconveniencies, exploitations, dirt, filth and stinking garbage he continues to hold the highest regard for this city of bliss hallowed by myth and guarded by tradition. (Sinha and Saraswati, 1978:5)

The standards of urban taste and pleasure have a different dimension in Kashi, mysterious and mystical. It is regarded as the centre of the first created spot on earth, where Vishnu created a *lingam* which shone in glorious effulgence. This was Kashi.

Guilds in Indian cities

Guilds in Indian cities are traced back to 600 BC at least (Hopkins, 1901:167) and their emergence attributed to the rise of Buddhism and Jainism which 'placed the warrior caste before the priest caste and gave unrestricted freedom to the third estate' (Hopkins, 1901:171), that is, the merchants. Buddhism was at its strongest in the third century BC, especially in eastern India, where the earliest Hindu kingdoms appeared, and still the core of the Maurya Empire of Candragupta, who himself became a Buddhist. Here were the great cities of Pataliputra (Patna), Varanasi (Benares) and Allahabad, all in the middle Ganges valley, though the empire also stretched to the Indo-Greek city of Taxila in Kashmir.

Guilds are said to have reached their strongest in the fourth century AD, which was the second period of Indian strength and prosperity under the Gupta emperors, still centred on the central Ganges. Guilds made lavish donations which enabled the finest Buddhist and Jain monasteries and monuments to be built. In the Deccan, kings invested in guilds and gave the interest to Buddhist monasteries. Some guilds could themselves build temples and guildhalls, acted as banks and had strict apprenticeship systems.

These were mainly guilds of merchants, with largely hereditary heads, who could hold very high positions in the city and state. It is said that the hereditary head of the merchant guilds of Benares could be the king's treasurer. Plutocratic ties to some extent cut across caste divisions. Distressed warriors, nominally of Kshatriya status, could at the same time be goldsmiths by profession, which made them practically Vaisya by status (Hopkins, 1901:205). Legal texts indicate that the king must respect the guilds and support their actions, yet he could also restrain them and their disputes were appealed to him. In any case, he could always tax them as he pleased, to the limits of his power. In fact, 'the connection between state officials and the guilds is left to the imagination' (Hopkins, 1901:203) and it is assumed that they strengthened rich guild corporations which, in turn, supported and intrigued for them.

After the decline of Buddhist influence, the Jains still maintained guild power, but as time went on, with the Muslim conquest of north India and the Ganges valley from the thirteenth century, Gujerat became the strongest centre of guild organization. It was not brought fully under Muslim control until the fourteenth century. With its long, almost island coastline it was especially favourable to long-distance ocean trading between Arabia and Europe on the one side and the rest of India and the Far East on the other, with ancient ports at Broach, Surat and Cambay, which later served the new city of Ahmedabad, founded by the Muslim conquerors in the fifteenth century and later surpassing the others in commercial and industrial importance. Broach had Jain kings in the thirteenth century, supporting its guilds and commerce, dominated by the Hindu Banya merchants.

Apart from such general tendencies, similar to those encountered elsewhere, very little is known of the life and structure of these early Indian cities, or of the organization and place of guilds in them. Hopkins' conference with the heads of guilds still alive in Ahmedabad in 1896 was the most informative. Some remained in nearby Bhaunagar and Udaipur. Further north in Jaipur they were weaker still. A few remained in Delhi and Lucknow, but further east in Benares guild titles had become a mere polite courtesy.

As guilds weakened, they proliferated and ended up as mere social clubs, as had already happened in London. Thus Ahmedabad still had forty large guilds, though the number was growing, while Jaipur had over a hundred smaller ones. The head of the guilds had the title of *nagar sheth*, or city chief. He was 'practically the leader of the religious community of the Jains' (Hopkins, 1901:179). But he was also head of the bankers' guild and, together with the head of the clothmakers, dominated the city, at least in religious matters, which in Hindu society were pervasive. In fact, by 1896 Ahmedabad was already transformed from a great medieval textile city to one of industrial cotton mills. The millowners were not favourable to guilds, though they were often former members, and it was a leading manufacturer, not in any guild, who had taken over the title of *nagar sheth*.

As in Europe the most powerful guilds consisted of wealthy merchants, who tried to keep control of the artisans and low-status trades and services. Each merchant guild, and the whole guild merchant if they were organized into one, was called *mahajan*, whereas the artisan, trade and service guilds were called *panch*, or *panchayat*, a term which fails to distinguish them from either caste or village local government committees. Likewise, their heads were called Patel.

The Broach city *mahajan*, or guild merchant, included bankers, money-changers, agents, brokers and cotton dealers, organized like a chamber of commerce, against the artisans. Goldsmiths and silversmiths were the most important crafts, and could form the highest *panch*, or the lowest *mahajan* – certainly the latter if, as often, they were also bankers. Of the other artisans, the tilemakers were the most influential, completely controlling the lower-status potters. While there were several separate guilds in the silversmiths' caste, there were three separate castes in the single confectioners' guild.

There were many cases of rivalry between guilds. In 1878 the Banya merchant guild (*mahajan*) of Ahmedabad levied a tax for religious purposes, which the Brahmin traders refused to pay. The Banyas boycotted them until they had to yield. A banker was unable to get the tiling of his house finished because he had quarrelled with the confectioners, who were able to enforce their boycott on the tilemakers. The banker was forced to come to terms with the confectioners before he could get his tiling finished (Hopkins, 1901:193–4). On another occasion a merchant was boycotted by the carpenters. Or again, a sweeper was insulted by a merchant and all sweepers boycotted him, but the merchant *mahajan* was able to mobilize the grain dealers to boycott the sweepers and they were forced to give in. When the lowly potters tried to enforce a rise in price, the merchant *mahajan* broke them by buying up the rights to clay. It was obvious where power lay. Beyond the guilds were the rulers. In Hyderabad it was the *nizam*, not the guild, who regulated grain supplies in a famine. On the other hand, in the city of Jaipur, the rulers referred trade disputes from their court back to the *mahajan*. But the power of craft guilds was limited and when the handloom weavers struck in Ahmedabad they were replaced by boys. Many strikes were on religious rather than economic issues and the guilds were inevitably involved in quarrels between Hindus and Muslims.

In all this it is obvious that guilds and castes were bound to be confused in Indian cities. Sometimes a local subcaste included more than one guild, or a guild included several subcastes, but very often the organization of a so-called guild must have been indistinguishable from the organization of caste fellows practising the same craft in a particular city. This was a more extreme case than the tendency to approximation of occupation, clan and place of origin in China. Naturally wealth had the greatest power to blur caste and sect lines, so that in Ahmedabad the Hindu Banyas were the most important merchant caste, yet the goldsmiths claimed to be pure Banya, while there were also small merchants of Lohan and Bhatia subcaste, claiming Rajput descent as did most artisans. There were Muslims, Parsee and Jain merchants, as well as Vishnuite Banyas, Vishnuite Brahmans and Sivaite Brahmans, all occupied as merchants and therefore all sometimes loosely referred to as Banyas. There was thus a tremendous overlap, if not confusion, of supposedly strict and potentially pollution-bearing distinctions of caste, sect and occupation. It is claimed that the caste system was more flexible and movement from one occupation to another easier, in the early Hindu cities. But for that period there is practically no empirical evidence for the structure of urban life.

Indian states and city-states did develop legal enactments for the control and even the protection of guilds, at a remarkably early date, in a way that never occurred in Chinese or Islamic cities. On the other hand, there is no evidence of written guild charters such as existed in China and Korea. But in India too there may have been periods when guilds won more power and freedom because state organization was weak, as occurred at certain periods and places in Islam, for a brief period in Japan and for the crucial creative period in Europe. In parts of China which were under secessionist and revolutionary movements for considerable periods, guilds may have had to assert themselves with greater power and responsibility in some cities. The caste rank of merchants was not as low as it was in China and Japan (since they were below farmers in the latter case, but were equal to them in the former). There is no way of knowing whether this significantly affected their economic or political power.

Clearly the European guilds achieved the greatest power, freedom and control of their occupations, most in north Italy, then Flanders and Germany, then in monarchies such as England. Japanese guilds had their brief period of power and responsibility in the fifteenth century. Islamic guilds hardly achieved this even during the period of political weakness in Spain and Morocco, when it was rather the *qadis* who were forced to assume responsibility, nor is there any evidence that the Indian or Chinese guilds ever did.

The place of kinship, occupation and association in the urban structure of India, China and Euro-America

It is a strange paradox that India, apparently somewhat secluded by its seagirt subpeninsula, cut off from the rest of the world on the landward side by the loftiest of all mountain barriers, was constantly invaded, but without the logical dialectic of this process in China, and produced no clear-cut consistent theme or principle of political and urban organization and structure, despite its rich and long continuous culture. Whereas the world of Islam, spread over an apparently exposed and vulnerable, vastly long but narrow corridor, with some distinctive ecological homogeneity of arid lands, relieved by maritime and watered margins and punctuated here and there by fertile river basins, produced a considerable coherency of political themes expressed in similar urban structure. India's dominant socio-political, economic and religious feature was its organization into collective strata defined by ritual caste purity and pollution. But we do not really know how this was expressed in either the structure of the city or the state. It does present a dialectical contradiction, as in another way Islam also did, but we do not know how it was worked out in practice.

The attempt to explain the basic cultural differences between the three urban civilizations of India, China and the United States, by relating them to the key features of caste, clan and club (Hsu, 1962) involves the difficulty of confusing differences of kinship with those of technological level and degree of social differentiation. Clans exist most strongly in stateless societies, although they survive in many states, while castes are only found in state societies, and clubs rarely proliferate outside industrial societies. The functions attributed to Chinese clans were actually performed by locally focused lineages. The Chinese clan, as such, had no functions or common interests because of its vast dispersion, so its unity and harmony cannot be meaningfully contrasted with the divisiveness of Indian caste. The United States and Britain did not lose clan organization, because their kinship and descent background lay in a cognatic and clanless system, which is different, but neither earlier nor later than clan organization.

The reason why particular organizations flourish is not because they are the most virtuous, but because they are the most effective in particular situations. The countries which were the first to succeed in industrializing were only able to do so under conditions which also favoured the club, in the sense of the voluntary special interest association. But we must remember that clubs existed in pre-industrial China as well as pre-industrial England and America, although associations only became the dominant form of organization after the Industrial Revolution.

The industrial transformation, accompanied by the proliferation of the club, was a momentous transformation for Euro-American societies. At the time when it first occurred, no equally momentous transformation had occurred in Asian societies for several millennia. Another such transformation was attempted by Russia in the Soviet Revolution, but the resultant society remained basically of the western club type.

However, clan, caste and club may stand symbolically for the factors of kinship, occupation and voluntary association, each of which still remains fundamental to the structure of cities in industrial societies and cultures in their contemporary experiments. The mistake in western thought was to suppose that kinship could be, or should be, eliminated from the occupational and associational fields. It is now coming to be recognized that selective kinship ties provide one of the indispensable safeguards for keeping urban life in technological mass society tolerably human, but that it will be combined in various forms and degrees with the essential organization of occupations and voluntary special interests.

6   From colonial to Third World cities

Chapter 6 traces the cities engendered by the global expansion of Europe as the collecting agencies for the accumulation of capital which powered the Capitalist mode of production and the industrial revolution. Out of this process came not only the cities of the Americas, which won their independence in the eighteenth and nineteenth centuries and those who did so in the mid-twentieth century, but also the cities of the White dominions whose privileges enabled them to break out of poverty into self-sustaining growth.

IBERIAN COLONIZATION

The founding of cities by the Portuguese and Spanish

The expansion of Europe and beginning of its monopoly position over the rest of the world was dramatically signalled by the voyages, conquests and settlements of the Portuguese and Spanish. Retaking Portugal from the Muslims led on logically to attacking them in Africa, taking Ceuta in 1415. Within a century, stupendous voyages carried Portuguese power round the coast of Africa to Brazil, India, Indonesia and China. The Azores and Madeira started sugar export to Europe, El Mina exported African gold, the Kongo kingdom became the source of slaves, Kilwa dominated the East African coast, Calicut produced calico, Molucca opened the Spice Islands, Hormuz, Goa, Malacca, Canton and Ningpo siphoned all the trade of the east. Soon Macau was secured, and Japan's trade through Nagasaki. So Portugal founded Europe's global urban trading network, extended by Spain through most of the Americas. Dutch, French and British soon picked up the relentless penetration and construction of the fiercely contested network of world trade and embryo cities, without whose products and profits the industrial revolution would not have occurred.

In 1500 Portuguese and Spanish were still dividing all between them. The pope's Tordesillas award gave all to Spain beyond 370 leagues west of the Cape Verde Islands, unwittingly presenting Brazil to Portugal when discovered. But west eventually meets east as Columbus hoped, so when

Spain reached the Philippines to make a route to the Spice Islands, Portugal already blocked the way.

With soldiers, sailors, traders, missionaries and adventurers from small nations spread over vast distances, urban growth was not immediately spectacular, but a framework was set. Tiny posts became great cities: Luanda, capital of Angola, its second city Benguela, composed of 'rene-gades from the Congo, exiles and convicts from Portugal, criminals from Brazil, forced to survive on fishing, farming and trade'. Mozambique Island, fort factory and hospital, greatest station between Lisbon and Goa with a massive fort, cathedral, churches and monasteries, had only 400 men in 1600, but many times this when the fleet came in, and thousands of slaves. Though still in use, it now 'hovers in isolation from its low white coral reef over the peacock sea' (Duffy, 1963:52, 82).

The Spaniards won enormous treasure from the ancient urban cultures they destroyed. The Portuguese completely redirected the most profitable channels of Asian trade. Both were official, royal exercises with clear-cut designs, however modified in practice. In Mexico and Peru the Spanish plundered existing monumental cultures, incorporating parts of the ancient buildings in their plaza-centred cities. They founded cities in the hinterland because of the wealth they found there, whereas Portuguese trading profits kept them on the coast as rumoured wealth inland was at first illusory. When they ventured inland in the Mozambique *prazos* or *bandeira* raids in Brazil it was on private initiative, beyond any royal or colonial control.

The tragic miracle of a mere handful of Spaniards seizing the highly organized city-states of Aztec Mexico and Inca Peru is mind boggling. 'The entire enterprise of the Spanish Conquest seems shrouded in a curious air of unreality' (Wolf, 1959:152). The Spaniards planted a Spanish cultural image on these lands, as the Portuguese did theirs in Brazil, with its sparse and weakly organized Indian populations.

The Portuguese could not establish new urban networks for whole countries as the Spanish did. They had to make strings of posts which could stay in reasonable touch and support of one another, from one monsoon to the next, collecting and storing the most profitable products for export. They chose fine natural harbours, defensible islands or promontories for the fortress-like stations. Profit lay in keeping to the sea with minimum land involvement, not squandering gains on armies defending useless territory. There was simply not enough manpower to occupy hinterland Brazil for several centuries.

Archbishops and bishops were central to the official hierarchy, often second in command on voyages and in cities. The highly functional belief that Portuguese imperialism was a sacred crusade, continuing the attack on infidels from Iberia to Africa and Asia, lent crucial strength and confidence to a shoestring operation. The city-state of Goa became the vice-regal capital of Portuguese Asia, marshalling point of expeditions, trade and administration, an archbishopric and flourishing centre of Indo-Portuguese culture. The city-state of Macao was the archbishopric with ecclesiastical jurisdiction over the whole of the Far East.

The Portuguese had developed the most effective long-distance ocean craft of their day, apart from the Chinese junk. Their cannons and muskets were quite terrifying for indigenous Africans and Americans at first encounter, but less so in Asia where vital parts of the technology had been invented. In the Far East, European intruders were not perceived as very powerful or wealthy. The Chinese always treated them as inferior barbarians come to offer tribute.

After the early Caribbean discoveries, Columbus began slave hunting as a means of support for his settlers, accidentally falling upon the gold of the Maya cities of Yucatan, which led them on irresistibly, with rumours of more to come, until, unbelievably, Cortés found the envoys of Montezuma hailing him as a divine saviour and heaping upon him treasures such as he and his companions had never seen.

The Aztec appeared cruel and bloodthirsty in their religion and warfare, but their pathetic self-deception makes the ruthless savagery and duplicity of the Spaniards hard to stomach. Pizarro, thus inspired, initiated a similar sequence of treachery, plunder, massacre, exploitation and genocide in the Andes with equally profitable results. The chronicles give the Mexican capital a population of 400,000 at the conquest, with a market attended by 60,000 every day. The Aztecs had conquered hundreds of petty city-states and consolidated them into thirty-eight provinces, each with its capital city. The Inca capital of Cuzco was a large and dense metropolitan city at the centre of a vast bureaucratic network of far-flung administrative posts.

Yet both these empires, comparatively recent creations out of long antecedent developments, had in contrasting ways come to an impasse and reached their limits. The Inca had triumphed marvellously over their lack of mechanical transport in controlling enormous stretches of very difficult terrain. The Aztec (Mexica) 'remained little more than a band of pirates, sallying forth from their great city to loot and plunder and to submit vast areas to tribute payment, without altering the essential social constitution of their victims' (Wolf, 1959:149), so that the capture of the Mexican capital of Tenochtitlán was 'less a conquest than it was a revolt of dominated peoples' (Wolf, 1959:154). The factions in the Inca ruling class put them equally at the mercy of a determined invader with a technological advantage. Mexico was probably suffering already from overpopulation and famine. Thousands of victims were immolated annually to

assure the balance of the heavens. The Mexican ruling class had a fanatical obsession with blood and death. Cruel against himself and others, doing battle against doom and yet attracted by it, as its victim succumbs to the fascination of a snake, haunted by omens, the Mexica warrior constituted an extreme among possible psychological types, ever engaged in fulfilling his prophecies of destruction by acting upon the assumption of imminent catastrophe. (Wolf, 1959:145)

'As a society and as a culture, they were doomed to disappear in a holocaust of their own creation' (Wolf, 1959:151).

After mining the temples and palaces the Spaniards set to work on the mines themselves, enslaving or enserfing the Indians for the purpose. They were made to carry loads of 225 to 250 pounds on their backs up exceedingly steep underground ascents (Wolf, 1959:178). After largely destroying the Aztec capital, the Spaniards reconstituted it as Mexico City, capital of the vast vice-realm of New Spain. Cuzco was too inaccessibly mountainous to be the capital of the southern vice-realm, so Lima was founded, with its nearby port of Callao. Two centuries later Bogotá became capital of the new vice-realm of Nueva Granada, Buenos Aires of that of La Plata.

The physical and social structure of cities in Spanish America

Both in concept and practice the Spanish Empire was founded upon a network of cities. Spaniards who emigrated preferred city life and were strongly encouraged to do so by the royal system of centralization and control. All these official cities were laid out, site permitting, on a symmetrical plan which puts them in the category of symbolic cities. It is not surprising that this most recent case of the genre was inspired by the most pious and absolute monarchy of Europe, with its strong Roman urban heritage. In both conception and implementation the colonial design was actually much more consistent than those of most Spanish sites in the homeland, with their long and turbulent history, rugged sites and cramped, cumulatively irregular plans (Wolf, 1959:163). Each city focused on a central plaza, scene of frequent mass ceremonials for religious festivals, as well as of regular and often daily markets. In Mexico City 14,000 Indians were being baptized every day during the early years, and Fra Pedro de Gante baptized hundreds of thousands with his own saliva for lack of holy water (Wolf, 1959:153, 173).

The plaza was surrounded by impressive, monumental edifices: cathedral, governor's palace, treasury, prison, arsenal, provincial and municipal offices. The shops of merchants and artisans lined the rest of the plaza and the main streets leading from it. The whole city was on a rectangular gridiron plan, with the next most central positions occupied by the establishments of the wealthy magnates, very large, composite and heterogeneous, consisting of arcaded buildings round an interior, tree-lined patio. They controlled the labour of large Indian populations, and had as resident members of their entourages priests as chaplains; lawyers and notaries; surgeons, accountants, chamberlains, blacksmiths, artisans, grooms, gardeners, guards, retainers and domestic servants of all sorts, in addition to their own families with the numerous kinsfolk and other clients attracted by their wealth and power. They varied from Spanish relatives and professional men to skilled Indian and Negro craftsmen, unskilled Negro and Indian servants, both slave and technically free, Negro and Indian mistresses and concubines with their increasing progeny of mestizo children, who grew up to occupy many of those roles in turn.

Such large, heterogeneous establishments were characteristic of the centres of most pre-industrial cities, so that persons of a wide variety of statuses and occupations, as well as ethnic origins, were bound together in patron–client chains with some degree of close contact and personal interaction, yet great social inequality, in total contrast with the stereotypical ethnic purity and status homogeneity of the North American suburb. This continues in most Third World cities today, despite changed technology and some reduction in the size of establishments, because of the mass poverty which makes cheap servants readily available to the elite, as well as the prevalence of their own large families. Those of highest status were at the centre – as owners and controllers of these composite establishments – and those of lesser status at the periphery, beyond which again was the forest of poor huts and hovels occupied by Indians either seeking work, or occupied in marginal service jobs, or merely resident temporarily while presenting their annual tribute contributions to their lords. The largest and most central establishments were those of the highest government officials and owners of the labour of Indian communities, but also of the richest merchants, who themselves had their apprentices and employees, their mistresses, domestic servants and slaves as likewise did the pre-eminent artisans, such as goldsmiths and armourers.

Beyond the main urban network the missionary priests established chains of mission stations, centred on great stone churches, which often became primary urbanizing points as well as major forces of acculturation and control. Hence the pioneering of the mission chain of Los Angeles, San Francisco and other stations for thousands of miles up the coast of California in the eighteenth century, and the network which laid the foundation for Spanish penetration of the Philippines.

The political elite consisted of the viceroys, governors, captains-general and direct administrative and military officers of the crown; the members of the *audiencias*, which were primarily councils of lawyers concerned with adjudicating, policing and enforcing the royal rules of the game, and the feudal-like *encomienderos*, landowners controlling the forced labour of large Indian populations. The higher offices received no salary but were sold by the crown to the highest bidder. Resale was permissible on payment of further tax to the crown. They were enormously lucrative and sought after, since all were clearly expected to squeeze all they could from those they ruled. The religious elite consisted of the ecclesiastical hierarchy of archbishops, bishops and heads of monastic houses, all large-scale owners of land and Indian labour, including the rare saints and idealists futilely concerned with protecting the human rights of the indigenous population, causing profound disputes but little effective action.

The economic elite consisted of European merchants and artisans, the most skilled of the latter, in luxury and elite products, also achieving high status and wealth as goldsmiths, silversmiths or armourers. There was also a wide variety of Indian and Negro craftsmen, some in the great establishments, but others working individually at a humble level, or for Spanish artisan masters. The merchants were organized in guilds, and linked in networks often strongly based on kinship ties between brothers, fathers and sons, nephews and cousins. These networks ran especially between Lima, Mexico City and Seville, with branch links to the secondary cities.

The bishop of Guadalajara described the capital city of New Galicia at the beginning of the seventeenth century (Parry, 1948:185) as lavishly laid out on a formal rectilinear plan, which it retains to this day, with two main squares, one containing the *audiencia* buildings, president's lodging, treasury, prison and arsenal, the other municipal buildings and cathedral. There were five monasteries, a Jesuit college and a twenty bed hospital. The Spanish population totalled about 500, half of the men being officials. Domestic service and unskilled labour were mainly performed by Negro slaves while Indians were in more skilled trades and had their own suburb and church. There was a market every five days, and four water mills for grinding corn. Most merchants trading in Guadalajara had their homes and headquarters in Mexico City.

The mining towns of Spanish America, whose contribution was the most vital, grew up more haphazardly than the official cities. The most famous were Guanajuato and Zacatecas in Mexico and Potosi in what is now Bolivia, all established in the mid-sixteenth century. Zacatecas had a long, winding, valley street, with short, steep side branches and small, cramped houses, similar to the Welsh mining towns three centuries later (Parry, 1948:186). Potosi, 13,200 feet up in the Andes, is said to have attained a population of 150,000 in the late sixteenth century, far the largest city in the Americas and equal to Naples or Milan. A Dominican monk described the mines in 1550 as 'a mouth of hell into which a great mass of Indians enter every year and are sacrificed by the greed of the Spaniards to their "god"' (Hamilton, 1977:1, 14).[1] The miners chewed coca leaves to deaden the pain of hunger, fatigue and cold, but the death toll was very high. Yet the great wealth of Potosi brought fine buildings, planning and an outburst of cultural activity. The city had its central plaza bordered by a huge stone mint and other public buildings, with many fine churches and grand mansions. A local school of painting flourished in the seventeenth century, though the peak of economic prosperity was past. The silver refining system included thirty-two man-made lakes, a ten-mile artificial sluiceway, eighteen dams and hundreds of water wheels. However, most mineowners lived in the capital cities, for they were aristocrats whose good fortune it was that mineral deposits lay within the territory they controlled. Later on, in the eighteenth century, Brazil's gold mining Vila Rica (Rich Town) enjoyed an even briefer glory of only a few decades, but it too boomed to a population of perhaps 100,000, sprouting delicate baroque churches, graceful fountains, elegant stone houses, monumental public buildings and fine statuary (Harris, 1956:12–13).

The official centralizing and urbanizing policy penetrated even below the city level, in the attempt to force the Indians of Mexico into nucleated towns, having their fields within a radius of less than half a mile from the central church (Wolf, 1959:164). Such concentration aided infection and increased the appalling death from typhoid, measles, malaria, yellow fever and generally brutal oppression, which swept away six-sevenths of the Indian population by the mid-seventeenth century. All Spaniards kept mistresses, at least before and after regular unions, as well as frequently breeding with female slaves. This was the prime initial source of mestizo population, combining Indian, African and European blood. Wolf (1959:235–47) sees the mestizo as despised by all, belonging nowhere, therefore congregating in the cities, further interbreeding and looking for new sources of power. Discrimination was social rather than racial. Blacks who succeeded economically almost lost their blackness and could achieve moderate social success as well. Indians who spoke and dressed Spanish could change their identity into Ladino, but this was mainly after the Spanish colonies claimed their independence early in the nineteenth century. Under the rule of metropolitan Spain Indians had been forbidden to wear Spanish clothes, or to own horses or guns. In Brazil the coloured population became numerically preponderant by the eighteenth century and no legal line was ever drawn. Most remained despised and desperately poor. But great magnates could send half-caste sons to school and college if they seemed intelligent. Some became distinguished and intermarried with the White elite (Bastide, n.d.:3). Many mulattos passed for White who would have been Black in the United States.

The effect of the new urban network on Spanish society

The New World cities administered, governed, extracted the precious metals and got them to their destinations overseas. The kings of Spain and Portugal officially took one fifth of the gold and silver mined, but a great part was lost to smuggling and enemy attack. Mexican silver was brought to Vera Cruz, Andean silver to Lima, shipped to Panama, carried across and reshipped. Galleons sheltered in the harbour of Cartagena between arrival and departure. The silver fleet massed every year in the fortified harbour of Havana, sailing off together for safety. Another annual fleet of silver ships set off from Acapulco to Manila to pay for the silk and luxury goods brought there by the Chinese fleet. They ran to and fro for over 200 years.

In this highly restrictionist system, the king granted a trade monopoly to the guild (*consulado*) of merchants in Seville, who dealt with their counterpart associates in Mexico City and Lima. Trade was to be kept in the hands of the Spanish and to direct exchange between the colonies and Spain. The colonies were not to produce any goods which might compete with Spain, and, incredibly, were not permitted to trade with one another, so that all trade from Buenos Aires was supposed to pass through Lima, the other side of the high Andes, thousands of miles away. Such an unreasonable rule was circumvented by extensive contraband trading. More serious, the Spanish could not stop the British, French and Dutch from breaking into their trade and plundering their ships, especially in the Caribbean. In 1628 Piet Heyn, director of the Dutch West India Company, captured a Spanish treasure fleet of 4 million ducats in gold and silver, thus financing the Dutch war against Spain in the Netherlands. Worst of all was that Spain had relatively little to offer its colonies in exchange for their silver, gold and primary products. The influx of precious metal did support king, nobles and merchants, and built them palaces and monasteries but caused a terrible inflation which made Spanish exports even less attractive.

Paradoxically, the easily won plunder accentuated features of Spanish society which resulted in the stimulus flowing rapidly through their hands with little positive effect on the economy of Spain, into those of more commercially and industrially minded peoples like the Genoese, Dutch and British. Castile was a poor and arid land, with a backward agriculture. The powerful Mesta sheepowners' guild further ruined the land by moving huge quantities of sheep to and fro for hundreds of miles every summer and winter. They represented the interests of the great landowners, and with the support of the merchants who sold the wool to Flanders, they paid the king to prevent a change of policy. The poor peasants were unable to buy manufactures, so the cities remained small, underdeveloped industrially compared with those of Italy and the Netherlands. Those of Andalusia were larger, but dominated by urban nobles living off the countryside. The only exception was Seville, for which the new colonial trade was reserved by the crown. In 1548, the Cortes (council) actually petitioned the king to prohibit exports from Spain to the Indies, because it would raise prices in Castile. In fact, Castile was forced to import goods from Italy and the Netherlands for export to the colonies, financed by Genoese and south German merchants.

Very little of the treasure was invested in the economy. Most went on court display, imports, war expenditure and German, Italian and Dutch creditors. It encouraged the aristocratic emphasis on fighting, plundering and enslaving as the noblest occupations, hallowed by the illusion of conquering heathendom for Christ. It also encouraged the restrictive merchant emphasis on maximizing rate of profit rather than volume and value. So gold actually swamped the industrial growth of Spain which might otherwise have occurred (Wolf, 1959:159). Official imports of precious metals were estimated at 1 million pesos annually for the years 1526–30, 5 million annually from 1541 to 1544 and over 35 million annually in the peak period from 1591 to 1595, after which there was a steep decline. The Asian and Brazilian trading profits of the Portuguese similarly enriched and maintained an expanding urban elite and aristocracy without transforming the metropolitan economy.

Urban development in Brazil

The Portuguese touched the coast of Brazil in 1500 almost by accident, and claimed sovereignty, but did little to develop it for some time, with all their energies focused in the opposite direction. The future Brazil was therefore divided notionally into fifteen huge latitudinally parallel blocks of territory and sold to twelve great proprietors as feudatories of the sovereign and entrepreneurs nominally obliged to develop it.

The Bay of Guanabara was of such obvious attraction and strategic importance that the Portuguese fought bitterly to keep it from the French from 1565 to 1568 and founded Rio de Janeiro like a medieval citadel at its entrance. The only initial attraction of Brazil was the valuable red dye wood after which the country was named. However, Portugal had pioneered the production of cane sugar for Europe. The vast coastlands of north-eastern Brazil and smaller areas around Rio in the south, with fertile soil and plenty of water for the extraction process provided the necessary supplement to Madeira and São Tomé, making sugar the largest Brazilian export. This led to the growth of a cluster of cities and ports: Bahia (Salvador), first capital of Brazil, with another fine harbour, became the second largest Portuguese city after Lisbon, larger even than Goa, with splendid buildings and winding streets like a medieval city and an estimated 4,000 'hearths' and over 21,000 communicants in 1706. Olinda was 400 miles to the north, with its anchorage at Recife five miles away, and had been the capital city of the territory of Pernambuco for a hundred years and the sugar magnates lived there in great style. The Dutch took and occupied Olinda and Recife from 1630 to 1654, during which time Olinda declined and Recife developed into a strong city of traders, who revolted against Olinda to form a municipality of their own in 1710. Recife superseded Olinda as capital of Pernambuco in 1823 and its twentieth-century industrial growth has swallowed up Olinda within its spread.

The city of São Paulo 300 miles west of Rio was the headquarters of cattle ranchers on a high plateau thirty miles inland from its port of Santos. The settlers of Bahia, Olinda and Recife had hunted far and wide for Indians to enslave as sugar workers, but the more mobile ranchers of São Paulo were the most adventurous, going on long raiding expeditions deep into the interior during which they discovered the gold deposits of Minas Gerais, which with diamonds found three decades later led to a great rush of immigration from Portugal and all over Brazil, and to a spurt of urban growth for São Paulo and Rio (Harris, 1956:14). The sugar boom of the seventeenth and the gold and diamond boom of the eighteenth century led to a huge demand for African slaves, which the Portuguese were only too perfectly equipped to supply from their West African settlements, especially Angola.

São Paulo officially became a city in 1711, having had a municipal council since 1560. The population of Rio rose from 12,000 in 1740 to 24,000 in 1749. In 1763 the capital of Brazil was transferred there from Bahia. The export of gold to Portugal – with much leaking out illicitly on the way – amounted to over 14,000 kilos in 1712, providing major support to the Portuguese economy, paying for imports and ostentatious public works and further maintaining the stimulus to the economy of western Europe as a whole, at a time when the supply of silver from New Spain was only recovering from its seventeenth-century decline. The resulting inflation in Brazil raised the price of slaves, which together with the exhaustion of the sugar lands led to a decline in the whole industry. Its place was taken by the West Indies which had alternative sources of slave labour supply, and as the gold and diamonds were also soon exhausted, Brazil relapsed into ranching as the dominant mode. In 1796 Brazilian exports were only half what they had been in 1760.

The aristocratic values of New Spain were weaker in Brazil. The Portuguese government was already over-extended elsewhere and the plethora of royal, bureaucratic institutions imposed on New Spain were lacking. Brazil was left much more to fend for itself. Its cities had their grandiose churches, monasteries and powerful ecclesiastical offices, their royal representatives and municipal organization, but the clear-cut ideal-istic conception of the city, which the Spaniards tried to implant, was less effective in Brazil. For two centuries there was no spectacular treasure to motivate a heavy investment of metropolitan power and control. There were no cities in the vast interior, except the mining towns of Minas Gerais, which had their brief flurry of a few decades and then relapsed into isolated, poverty stricken stagnation (Harris, 1956:17–19), though retaining their claim to urban gentility. In the vast Amazon region, as in far away Zambezia, there were only a few riverine fortified trading posts, like the one studied by Wagley, which never had a stable urban population of more than a few hundred, yet had its gridiron plan, its public squares, continuous rows of houses and official urban status as a town and municipality (Wagley, 1953:23–5, 42–5).

In the second half of the eighteenth century, foreign minister Pombal, not only banished the Jesuits for their troublesome defence of human rights of the vanishing Indians, but also banned Indian slavery, which was in any case of little significance by that time, encouraged intermarriage between all ethnic groups of Brazil and ordered mission stations to be transformed into towns and villages. More even than in New Spain, the dominant demographic element came to be a mixed population of Europeans and Africans, with a smaller Indian element (Wagley, 1953:32–7). Pombal also prohibited the development of industry in Brazil, which would have dangerously diminished its economic depen-dence upon the European colonial powers thus, paradoxically, inhibiting its own industrial development. In the nineteenth century the British were even to force free trade upon independent Brazil, thus continuing to inhibit the development of Brazilian home industry (Bastide, 1960:409–10; Harris, 1956:13).

To the genetic mixture there corresponded a cultural syncretism. Despite the submerged status of the African slave and the traumatic blow to his culture in captivity, the African gods and rhythms did not die. The influence was naturally strongest in cities such as Bahia and Recife in the region to which the slaves were brought in largest numbers. The great carnivals, particularly renowned in Recife, in seasonal and life-cycle festivals, in music and dance and curative ritual, African gods, rhythms, plastic art forms and values lived on, transmogrified in the rituals of the church and the festivals of the urban masses.

At Bahia, Rio and São Paulo there were Yoruba cults of the *orisha* and Bantu cults of *caboula*, but the *macoumba* cult syncretized African, Amerindian, Catholic and spiritist elements, and introduced Yoruba *orisha* into the Bantu *caboula*. The influence of the great city caused former ethnic and cultural bonds to dissolve in the solidarity of misery in a coloured proletariat, cemented by mystical experience (Bastide, 1960:411). White devotees eventually became as numerous as Black, with Portuguese, Spanish and even Japanese participants. Popular Catholicism also slipped in, the more easily since the Bantu Zambi and Yoruba Orishala had become identified as Christ, and other correspondences of Yoruba *orisha* were Ogun (St George), Shango (St Jerome), Oshossi (St Sebastian) and Oshoun (Notre Dame de Aparecida). Police repression turned the cult from collective to individual forms. The *macombeiro* became a diviner, healing the sick, finding jobs for the unemployed and making and breaking love and marriage (Bastide, 1960:461–7).

Ironically, Brazil had developed little under the Portuguese, most of whose efforts were devoted to brutal and destructive ends, despite its sugar, gold and cattle, until the belated planting of coffee in the state of São Paulo later in the nineteenth century, after it was already lost to Portugal, brought a new prosperity and a new flood of immigrants from all over Europe, who organized new commerce and new industries, turning the city of São Paulo into the greatest metropolis in the southern hemisphere.

Portugal's greatest possession, yet object of the least effort and lost first, inherited a diluted form of Portuguese culture and surpassed the mother country ten times over not only in size but in population, power and wealth. In the orient, Portuguese culture was nowhere implanted on any significant scale. Most of the cities which she founded were either taken over by others, or overtaken in size and importance by those founded by other European nations.

Malacca, which led to the Spice Isles and China, dominating the Malay Straits through which all shipping to and from the Far East had to pass, was held from 1511 till 1641 when it was taken by the Dutch. Founded by Javanese pirates early in the fifteenth century, its ruler became a Muslim and through commercial power and dynastic alliance Malacca was responsible for much of the spread of Islam in Malaysia (Sandhu and Wheatley, 1982). Separate trading communities of Javanese, Indians, Chinese and Malays clustered round the walls of the Portuguese and later

Dutch fortress. By the nineteenth century the Chinese controlled nearly all the retail trade. After 1850 Malacca declined because it could not accommodate the larger steamships.

Macau gave Portugal a continuous if minor share of the Chinese trade from the sixteenth century onwards. But it was the city-state of Goa which really held the slender tentacles of Portuguese interests in Asia together. Under the authority of viceroy and archbishop, a distinctively original social hierarchy emerged, with the Portuguese officials, soldiers, priests and merchants at the top, followed by persons of mixed descent, who were Roman Catholics but ranked according to the Hindu castes of their Indian origin. It remains a culturally distinct enclave in India.

PROTO-CAPITALIST COLONIZATION

Contrasting interactions of colonial cities with indigenous societies

The embryo cities founded from the sixteenth to the seventeenth century grew very slowly. Bombay was exceptional, reaching 50,000 in the seventeenth century, as was Mexico City's half million in 1519, which it could not recover till the twentieth century. In the eighteenth century Calcutta was one of the fastest, exceeding 100,000 (and 300,000 in the 1820s), New York 60,000 (1800), Philadelphia 30,000 (1770) and Boston 16,000 in 1740. Rio de Janeiro grew from 12,000 to 24,000. Québec City had only 8,000, and Cape Town only 200 houses, reaching 2,000 people in 1806. Between Cape Town and Cairo no colonial cities reached large populations till the twentieth century, Lagos having only 41,847 in 1901. Johannesburg grew extremely fast but dated only from 1886.

The typical demographic structure of eighteenth-century colonial capitals was Whites and Others: local people ('natives') and foreigners or non-locals, mainly the trading diasporas, local merchants in India where the city already looked dual: White Town and Black Town.

In twentieth-century Africa the distinctions within Black Town were much clearer, as the Indians of eastern Africa and Lebanese, Greeks, Moroccans and others elsewhere were firmly above 'natives' and clearly below the Whites of the ruling groups, the precise relation depending upon the local political economy of racism and discrimination, involving colour, religion, culture, education and wealth.

In Latin American cities similar distinctions obtained, but acceptance of miscegenation and less virulent race prejudice, despite the near extermination of 'natives', blurred the boundaries.

In the Americas, Africa, Oceania and pockets of Asia, indigenous soci-

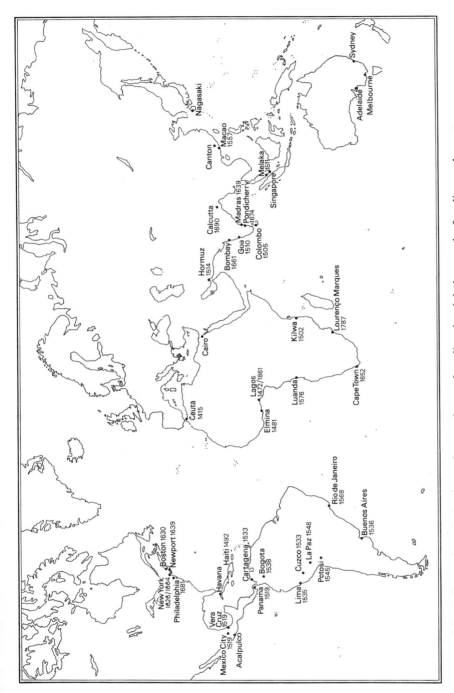

Map 3 Europe's explosion into other continents, founding the global network of trading settlements, forts and future cities

eties were very small, living by the Kinship mode of production, some in Africa and many in America by the Foraging mode of production (Southall, 1988a). Mainland Asia was dominated by large states with diverse hierarchical, monarchical systems, impressive capitals and large merchant cities. Most of the American and many of the African peoples had complex, egalitarian systems of social and political organization, hitherto often misleadingly called tribes. In Asia the invading Europeans could win trading rights by dealing with urban merchants direct, or with the ruler or his local representatives, as happened in India, Burma and Ceylon, Malaya, Java and Indo-China, Egypt and Morocco.

Where there were cities, the Europeans used them as centres for their own import and export, exploitation and consumption. Where there was none they had to found their own. Their object was wealth and raw materials, which had to be obtained by some form of exchange and trade after initial plundering, and all official trade must relate to the European imperial metropoles, requiring a complete reorientation of trade routes. Even if cities existed, they had not been sited or organized with this in view so it was sometimes convenient to found new ones. But Portuguese private merchants traded vigorously between the Asian ports, under the Portuguese naval umbrella, rather than with their metropole, generating high profits while official trading often made a loss.

Dutch and British city life in the east

The Dutch had become the most urban most truly bourgeois people in the world, with a very dense and numerous cluster of cities and a third to a half of their whole population urbanized. In every major way they were exceptionally fitted to participate energetically in the European overseas commercial expansion. Individual entrepreneurs and private companies formed in the different cities were the overseas pioneers, but in 1602 the Dutch East India Company and West Indies Company were formed to fight the Spanish and Portuguese attempt to monopolize world trade routes. Overseas trade and settlement was actively maintained into the eighteenth century, largely in alliance with Britain, but expansion then slowed down and the cities fell under almost hereditary burgher oligarchies, until engulfed in the Napoleonic upheaval, out of which the new nation-states of Holland and Belgium eventually emerged. The Dutch settled in Java before the end of the sixteenth century and in 1619 made Batavia (Jakarta) their headquarters. Java was certainly the most important and strategic base left open by the Portuguese for others to break into the spice trade. This was the early symbolic attraction, together with the vague realization of the fabulous untapped wealth of China.

The spectacular future site of Cape Town, with its safe harbour and good water had often been visited by the Portuguese in the sixteenth century and later by British, French and Dutch. Dutch sailors shipwrecked there in the mid-seventeenth century were so enamoured that the East India Company sent van Riebeek to found a settlement in 1652. Fire patrols, burglar watches and water supply were organized. A representative council decided public affairs and dispensed justice. Company staff could settle as free burghers. Vegetable farming was established in Newlands and vines planted at Wynberg. Most remarkable, in the light of twentieth-century South African *apartheid* was the considerable miscegenation, and actual marriage, with the local Hottentot population, even on the part of van Riebeek's highest officers. Growing rivalry between French, Dutch and British (with the French lending the Dutch a garrison against the British) led to a spurt of building at the end of the eighteenth century, by which time there were 1,000 houses. From 1806 Cape Town was under British rule and reached a population of 20,000 by 1840.

The British arrival in Asia was hard on the heels of the Dutch and their main prize was India. They had already established their first factory in 1612 at Surat, with the consent of the ruler. It was an important textile and shipbuilding town, exporting cloth and gold. Already twice burned by the Portuguese, it was under the remote control of the Mogul, part of the coastline of Gujerat whose capital, Ahmedabad, was one of the greatest commercial and industrial cities of India, also with an ancient textile industry. The British bought Indian textiles for trading to other countries, as they surpassed European textiles in quality and value. Gujerat was very close to the Arab Middle East by sea, and both the Muslim and Hindu Gujeratis were prominent among the overseas traders of India, though in theory Hindus were ritually prohibited from *going* over the sea. The Portuguese had already long been trading nearby at Calicut, as well as Bombay and Goa. In Ceylon they had stations at Galle and Colombo, both ancient trading cities with fine harbours. These stations were taken from them by the Dutch in the mid-seventeenth century.

The Portuguese ceded Bombay to the British in 1668, as dowry for their Infanta marrying Charles II and for British aid against Spain. By then the British had already established their factory and fort at Madras, as they did later at Calcutta in the 1690s. The French likewise founded their settlement at Pondicherry, south of Madras, but their influence in India, with ups and downs, proved minor. The stations on the coast of Gujerat were all subject to possible harassment by the officers of the Mogul and the British felt much more secure on Bombay Island than at Surat, and safer on the left bank of the Hooghly at Culcutta, with the river between them and the Mogul.

The English nabobs of Bombay and Calcutta, with their Dutch counterparts in Batavia and Surabaya, in their necessary interaction with local populations of both high and low status, arrived at sexual, family and household arrangements, urban structures and layouts quite in conflict with the overt beliefs, principles, values and standards they had originally brought with them.

The British governor of Bombay made compacts with particular castes – the Palshikar Brahmins already there and the Banya traders of Surat and Din who were anxious to move there – variously granting them freedom and security in the exercise of religion and trade, promising that no English, Portuguese or other Christian, nor Muhammadan, should be permitted to live within their compound, nor should they be forced to become Christian. The Bhandari toddy tappers and warriors, also early settlers, were granted exclusive rights over production and sale of toddy and other alcoholic drinks. Each caste had its own residential quarter and was governed by its own *panchayat*. Twenty-four castes are mentioned in the early eighteenth century, with Banyas and bankers the most prominent (Rowe, 1973:218–21).

The Dutch set out with the principles of puritan burgher frugality, but tended to acquire elitist oriental tastes for luxury. They tried to reproduce the canals and close-packed lofty merchant residences of Amsterdam in Batavia, but the stuffy heat and lethal malaria drove them eventually to higher ground, with spacious garden villas more reminiscent of the houses of Javanese aristocrats (McGee, 1967:51). As their cities grew, the layout of wide avenues at right angles from a central space borrowed something from the symbolic royal *kraton* model with its four roads radiating from the umbilical centre and the palace in the south facing north and lower ranking dwellings facing southwards to it from the north, as may be seen in Jogjakarta.

The fortress was the first necessity, containing the whole European community, a military-based segregation usually reinforced later by social prejudice, often on both sides, especially in caste-ridden Hindu areas. However, the Portuguese and Spanish begot populations of mixed descent wherever they went. Minimal territorial involvement was the most profitable: 'factory'-warehouse to store trade goods and crops as they accumulated, ready to be picked up when the ships called. They needed to be permanently on the spot to take advantage of low prices especially of local crops at harvest time, otherwise prices were always raised when ships came into port. Further territorial expansion only squandered profits on expensive defence forces, constantly decimated by disease.

For most of the seventeenth century the few British officers of the East

India Company lived collegially in their fortified White Towns, messing together. Later more of them brought their wives and acquired their own residences. Job Charnock, the founder of Calcutta, saved a Brahman widow from the funeral pyre and lived with her happily for fourteen years. Hawkins married the Armenian Christian slave girl given him by Emperor Jehangir. Behaviour in the early period was flexible compared with later rigidity echoing Indian caste.

The British in India adopted turbans and linen shoulder scarves, sitting on the carpeted floor to eat and converse. Besides the chaplain, surgeon and steward, they had British servants, bakers and cooks as well as Indian menials. Though worried about their digestions in the heat they ate many varieties of meat and fowl as well as adopting Indian dishes, drinking *arrack* spirit, tea and water. Men always went on horseback, ladies in palanquins – as also the president of the company on official occasions, with trumpets and ostrich feather fans, standard bearers and guards, like medieval guilds.

British and Dutch religious tolerance proved an attraction contrasting with the Spanish and Portuguese. Slaves were not a significant part of the urban economy or the eastern trade and the British tried to ban their sale before the end of the seventeenth century, though still vigorously capturing them in Guinea. They had judges and courts, but administered a more summary justice to natives than to themselves. The cities were autocratically governed by the senior officials and councils appointed by the Company. The greater colonial cities of the coasts of Asia were virtually autonomous city-states in practice, because of slow communications, though legally under the authority of the Company and the ultimate sovereignty of the metropolitan government.

The Mogul government was completely disdainful of commerce, as were the Javanese aristocrats, but this was not true of the specialized Hindu trading castes, like the Banyas, or of the Arab and Muslim traders. However, the rulers and their staffs welcomed the lavish gifts and revenue from customs, taxes and other levies, which foreign traders provided, and they liked to play them off against one another. The British and Portuguese or Dutch and French, with the various court factions, or rival local rulers, were constantly intriguing against one another in ever shifting alliances. It was the regions where indigenous trade was already most highly developed that were most attractive and profitable for the European traders to tap. They did not start the trade in Asia, but only added extra demand through new channels and some new products and they only took a minor share of the total.

Increasing embroilment with one another and with Indian rulers led to attempts at interior conquest by the French and British in which the latter triumphed during the eighteenth century. The Dutch had a similar inter-action with rival traders and local rulers in Ceylon, Java and Sumatra leading gradually to more extensive conquest. Elsewhere most trading posts were by arrangement with local rulers, or simply formed foreign enclaves in or on the edge of extant cities, not much different from the ethnic quarters which they had always contained.

The Dutch, British and French conquests were less centrally organized state enterprises than the Spanish or even the Portuguese had been. The operations of individual adventurers were co-ordinated within the frame-work of chartered companies, royally favoured and unreliably backed by government policy, but responsible for their own day-to-day operations.

As the Dutch gained control of Indonesia and the British of India, they were eventually faced with the problem of organizing whole vast coun-tries, as the Spaniards had been in America. While governing crucial strategic cities themselves, they were forced to use local rulers as their instruments – the court cities in Java and maharajas and rajas in the cities of the native states of India, into which the Mogul Empire was breaking up. The Dutch were even able to coerce impoverished local princes to act as their produce collectors from the peasantry. Colonial cities assisted many lower- and middle-class Europeans to rise in status and to live in luxury with large establishments of numerous servants in palatial houses, often winning considerable fortunes as a ticket of entry to the gentry, on their return, if they survived the hazards of violence, shipwreck and disease.

The qualities required were a spirit of adventure, rugged health, ambi-tion and perhaps greed, tempered by loyalty to cultural and corporate values, military courage, naval skill, political shrewdness, commercial talent, administrative competence and sometimes proselytizing zeal. Few had all these, but a surprising number among the rather few involved and surviving had many.

The expatriate elites absorbed many quaint features of local culture in a selective and disdainful way, particularly during the period before it was considered safe for White women to join their men folk. Undoubtedly this loose world wide network of brash, new struggling, competitive cities channelled to Europe that extra wealth which brought first Britain, and then the rest of north-west Europe and the United States to the point of development at which industrial take-off became possible. The momen-tous transformation of the American Revolution turned exploited colonies into an exploiting colonial power. The White dominions of Canada, Australia, New Zealand and South Africa were founded as exploiting agencies and were able to maintain this role as they won their independence and joined the ranks of the industrialized nations.

Continental contrasts

Bombay, Calcutta and Madras were all founded by Europeans for this reason, but as Indian trade was already highly developed, the new cities acted as catalysts to which indigenous merchants flocked, in much larger numbers than the intruders, so that the basic development of colonial trade and the cities through which it was organized and channelled were largely in their hands. European and indigenous traders were competitive and could understand one another well. Their incentives were the same, the destination of their efforts different.

The peoples of the New World had no immunity to major diseases of the Old World, to which they quickly succumbed in millions, as well as to the savagery of the invaders. Most Africans and Asians had developed immunities to the major epidemic diseases of the Old World. It was Europeans who were at a disadvantage in the tropics, with no immunity to killer diseases like malaria and yellow fever. Consequently, Europeans faced a labour shortage in the Americas, hence the horrendous traffic in African slaves (the nearest abundant source of poorly protected humanity to the Americas), from the sixteenth to the nineteenth century.

In parts of the Americas first discovered by Europeans, notably the Caribbean, the indigenous peoples were virtually exterminated, partly on purpose, partly by disease, leaving fertile uninhabited areas for easy plantation exploitation once African slaves were brought. These proved the most profitable areas of exploitation anywhere in the colonial world, before the advent of industrial capitalism.

Eighteenth-century Haiti was the most prosperous New World colony, supplying France with slave-grown sugar, coffee, cocoa, indigo and cotton, absorbing two-thirds of all French foreign investment and requiring 700 ships and 80,000 seamen for annual transport. By the nineteenth century the wars of the French and the slaves had completely devastated the country and ruined the economy. The French Caribbean had 20,000 Whites barely controlling 160,000 Black slaves before the Revolution. It promoted urbanization more in France than in the Caribbean. The amount of sugar and coffee refined in Bordeaux, Nantes and Rochefort multiplied ten times between 1715 and 1789. It enriched the planters, Paris bankers and manufacturers of luxury goods to export to the planters in return.

The pre-capitalist states of Asia, with their great cities, hierarchical class structures and complex economies, had advantages in dealing with European imperialism. Their large-scale institutions, organizations and religions could not be eliminated by the new rulers, but were adapted, distorted and used wherever possible. They could still also be used by their literate elites to begin fighting back against imperialism, together with western style associations which they easily adopted.

Africa and Oceania had not needed great states and cities, nor elaborate class structures. In their indigenous system they were less exploited and less unequal. This handicapped them in opposing imperialism. Their economies had mobilized little wealth compared with Asian states, so they were less initially attractive and not seriously colonized till later. The Indian independence movement had already begun before much of Africa and Oceania was brought under effective colonial administration. The innumerable small societies of Africa could not be transformed into strong, united, democratic states, as the formula proposed, after little more than half a century of effective colonial rule, whereas India is respected as the world's largest and one of the few uninterrupted democracies.

Decolonization of American colonies came earlier. The English democratic spirit developing representative assemblies for their kinsmen in America made the bourgeois revolution inevitable. After the French lost their whole stake in North America the New England colonies needed no British protection and the restraints on their trade and customs exactions became intolerable. They protested with amazing loyalty as subjects, but the crown tactlessly insisted on formal submission and the popular forces took over and won independence. The Latin American elites likewise were miscegenated brothers and cousins of the Iberian imperial peoples. Just as they were receiving the infectious influence of the French Revolution, Napoleon removed their distant rulers from power giving them the chance to assert their freedom. Whites retained social supremacy but no legal barriers hindered miscegenation, whereas in the United States south the dominant plantation economy depended on African slaves and rigid racist laws enforced by barbaric lynching.

North America: southern slavery and northern democracy

The southern cities of Virginia and the Carolinas were dominated by the upper-class style of life of their slave-owning merchants and plantocrats – who also kept town houses – breeding a certain indolence and lack of economic enterprise, although the tobacco and cotton grown by the slaves produced great wealth for the cities in combination with their export trade. The long-term adaptive pattern of Charleston's 'nabobs' to the successive threat from small up country farmers, urban Blacks and finally nouveaux riches industrialists has been characterized as 'absorption, predation and suppression' (Fox, 1977:153–7). Charleston had no elected city government, being controlled by twelve commissioners appointed by the state legislature.

The slave owners proved to be against the tide of history. Increasingly bound to the northern economy, as well as tied to the Union, they were unable to determine the urban culture and social system of the whole society, as their counterparts in Latin America did. They had to be carried along until, after the cataclysm of the Civil War and the long intransigence which followed it, they would ultimately boom again, with their previously depressed Black populations providing cheaper labour for new urban industries, if they had not already migrated to the industrial cities of the north.

In the eighteenth century the southern cities of the future United States had Black majority populations. In the nineteenth century the Black population fell below 50% and only one seventh of families owned slaves. Yet to an observer outdoors it seemed that Blacks were doing everything (Wade, 1964:16–17).

The southern city had created a distinct world in which both Black and White, slave and free, became quite different from their rural counterparts (Wade, 1964:27). It was not segregated by neighbourhood, since domestic slaves were housed in brick rooms at the back of the high walled yard behind the mansion, at much closer quarters to their White masters than was the case on the rural plantation. Slavery remained a stable urban institution until about the 1820s but was already disintegrating, with insoluble contradictions, before the Civil War brought it formally to an end (Wade, 1964:3, 246).

Between the New England cities of Boston, Newport and Providence in the north and widely spaced coastal and slave-based port cities of the south such as Richmond, Williamsburg, Charleston and Savannah, lay Dutch New Amsterdam (1653–64), soon to be New York, and Quaker Philadelphia.

The southern cities, despite their advantages of warm climate and long growing season, armies of slave labour and profitable plantation hinterland, remained sluggish, while the cities which grew and prospered at their expense were those of the north, with its short growing season, where the survival of early settlements was only achieved by the most unremitting toil, fortunately quite in tune with their Puritan convictions.

Though they were refugees from oppression, the original constitution of the Mayflower Pilgrims stressed just and equal laws rather than democratic rights. The general emphasis remained on freedom, not equality. Inequality was recognized from the start and increased with prosperity. Though they were cities in a wilderness, pioneers in a largely empty land, they were focused on foreign trade from the beginning, while the farmers of the hinterland, even if they had to survive initially by guaranteeing their

own subsistence, were focused on marketing and export, closely integrated with the cities.

The loose framework of colonial government and slow communication
by foot, horse or sailing ship made each embryonic city a virtually
autonomous merchant republic, almost a city-state, rival to all the rest.
Each must solve its urban problems on its own, by self-help and local initiative. Government and regulations were kept to a minimum, yet constant fires forced them to form volunteer fire companies and to impose
curfews. Personal safety and convenience demanded the prevention of
fast riding through cobbled main streets and prevention of building
encroachments on the thoroughfare. Health hazards required inspection
of ships, quarantine and immigration control, as well as drainage and
grading of streets, building of privies and provision of water supplies. All
men were required to contribute labour for these services, but the wealthy
soon escaped by sending substitutes or simply paying money – they could
not usually send slaves as in the south. The dangers of fire, theft, violence
and attacks of pirates necessitated the organization and payment of con-
stables and night watchmen. Compulsory common effort and financial
contribution were required, despite strongly anti-governmental prejudices.

Although the New England cities like Boston and Newport aired grievances, decided major issues and elected their executive councils of select-
men at meetings of all adult male freemen, the ruling elite of each city
effectively consisted of merchants and religious leaders and voting came
to be restricted to those with property qualifications. By the time that
urban communities emerged they were already informally stratified into
merchants and professionals at the top, followed by craftsmen, small
shopkeepers and innkeepers, with unskilled labourers and sailors below
them and Negros and Indians always at the bottom. These two lower categories, without the franchise, made up about half the population. After
the hazards and rigours of first settlement the little towns grew fast and
both spatial and social mobility was high. By the eighteenth century the
social structure hardened, 15% owning 66% of the property. Widespread
poverty and destitution forced the cities to spend large sums on relief.

Propertyless labourers remained in poverty, but some were able to rise
out of their class, replaced by ever growing numbers of immigrants both
from countryside and overseas. Class divisions were not clearly defined or
fixed, for status depended upon wealth, style of life and education more
than hereditary position. American cities probably provided a better
chance of improvement to a larger percentage of their population than
any other cities in the world at the time, yet the extent of economic
inequality constantly increased. By the mid-nineteenth century a mere

4% of Bostonians owned two-thirds of the wealth and similarly in New York and other cities.

Urban populations could still be counted in hundreds till nearly the end of the seventeenth century, when Boston, the largest of them all, had just 7,000 people, while Philadelphia and New York had about 4,000 each, Newport 2,000 and Charleston about 1,000. In the eighteenth century Philadelphia became the largest but was soon surpassed by New York.

Boston was favoured by the rich fisheries and early dominance in overseas trading supported by a fine shipbuilding industry. Before the end of the seventeenth century its merchant fleet was exceeded only by those of London and Bristol in the English-speaking world. Most of this expansion was achieved in complete independence of any colonial government. When Charles II imposed a British governor in 1660 – thrown out again for a while in 1688 – resentment kept erupting and intensifying until the War of Independence, which hit Boston hard by closing the port. Destitution led to armed insurrection and Boston was actually forced to hire militia men like mercenaries to hunt down rebels.

In the mind of William Penn the founding of Philadelphia in the 1680s was a central aspect of the establishment of Pennsylvania. At the very start he instructed the Quaker immigrants 'to settle a great town'. Before occupation began, the site was purposefully laid out in a rectangular grid design, which the other colonial cities did not then have, but which subsequently became general in the newer cities as urbanization spread ever westward. The free atmosphere, greater tolerance, than New England, great natural and mineral resources and favourable position of Philadelphia as a port led to very rapid growth.

Philadelphia had its charter and city council, but at first its officials were largely appointed by the governor. In New York the freemen of the city won the right to vote for their council in 1731. Philadelphia later got the right to elect its own officials, but the city government remained exclusive and sluggish. None the less these cities of the north-east coast from Philadelphia to New England were the most advanced of their time in the world in progress towards democratic urban self-government.

In the southern states where slaves were numerous, there was miscegenation, but clandestine or discreetly ignored. Officials tried to deny it, while blaming it especially on the cities, where 'any lady is ready to tell you who is the father of all mulatto children in everybody's household but her own' (Wade, 1964:122–3). Negresses were held to protect public morals and the virtue of White girls in the same way as prostitutes did up north. The progeny of slaves were slaves, whether they had a free White parent or not. There were small numbers of freed slaves, who at best achieved respectable poverty as artisans and craftsmen, but most remained in menial jobs. New England cities had small numbers of free Blacks but in very lowly positions. New Orleans being French or, for a time, Spanish, approximated to the Latin American situation. In 1803 it had 4,000 Whites, 2,700 slaves and 1,300 free coloured persons.

In North as in South America indigenous peoples fared badly. The early settlers were often well and hospitably received by them and many treaties of friendship were made. But as the settlements grew, so encroachment on Indian lands increased. When they reacted violently to the violence of some settlers and to persistent lack of redress for broken treaties they were massacred by superior firearms. Decimated by the new diseases, they shrank to a mere remnant. The Massachusetts Indians succumbed to the same epidemic which killed many of the first pilgrims. Their numbers were soon reduced from an estimated 95,000 to only 5,000.

INDIA

Housing and kinship in Bombay

Despite great public and private investment, Bombay housing manages an average of only twenty square feet per person, less than one seventh the United States minimum. Nearly 80% of families occupy a single room or less, in a multi-tenement *chawl*, three- or four-storey block with rooms facing round verandahs sharing sanitary facilities. One building may have eighty families, two or three related families in a single room, one or two latrines and faucets for twenty or thirty families (Clinard, 1970:75). People even have to sleep in shifts for lack of space.

The lack of privacy is deeply shameful and humiliating, threatening caste pollution. Rents are frozen at 1939 levels, discouraging rental building and driving waiting lists and key money sky-high. But there is a higher percentage of housing in permanent materials than in most great Third World cities.

The government encourages suburban extension, granting loans to 60% of building costs for apartment co-operatives of people with less than about $300 a month, 80% to those who will move further, up to thirty miles or more from downtown along the early constructed railway.

Ethnically homogeneous neighbourhoods are impossible to achieve, but caste and language categories keep to themselves, contriving virtual caste and kinship homogeneity in particular blocks, close enough for personal networks to consist of family, kin and castemates. In one case more than twenty scattered families were linked in this way. Networks must be constructed by embracing cognatic uncle, aunt and cousin links on both sides, extended fictively within the subcaste, not sticking to village unilineality. Local endogamy is correspondingly weakened.

One subcaste of Saraswati Brahmins is almost entirely urbanized, so cut off from rural kin that they might be recognized as a distinct subcaste, though visiting village deities for marriage and other rituals. They have caste halls in Bombay. Their utter commitment to caste respectability, with limited income, necessitates mutual aid between kin, affines, sometimes neighbours, who are often also kin. Such collective interdependence generates tyrannical conformity, gossip constantly evaluating the score, also giving tips on jobs, houses and other opportunities lost if not seized immediately.

Men's inescapable duty is to get sisters or daughters married, thereby accumulating social credit and obligations to help brothers to respectable matches. Dowries may take more than a year's salary. The dice are loaded so heavily against love matches that young couples prefer elders taking responsibility, rather than risk the burden of failure, unhappiness and disgracing the whole caste section. It is pointless to economize on the expensive marriage feast by going quietly to the registrar. That only causes lack of patrons and creditors to help in future emergencies. All family activity feeds into a comprehensive account, determining respect enjoyed by the family and the status, wealth and personal attractiveness of brides and grooms to whom its sons and daughters can aspire. Pre-marital chastity reigns, at least for girls. Wives and especially mothers ought to stay at home, but 15–20% now go out to work, mainly teaching, which is acceptable as associated with children. Heavy unemployment of the highly educated turns school into a fierce rat race. For a better chance children are registered at expensive private schools at birth, though the first four years at state schools are free. Such pressure actually forces these couples into contraception, aiming at a son and daughter each, regarding those who cannot control as lower class and bovine. Manual work is considered to be degrading. Shortage of acceptable work makes nepotism a rational necessity. When so many are equally qualified, the only hope is to hear first through your gossip grapevine and patrons, or kin networks.

Convention rules throughout life. Men wear western clothes to work, changing to pyjamas at home. Women should wear saris and not venture into pants, despite the traditional prevalence of women's trousers in North India. Cooking, eating, entertaining and visiting must all be correctly accomplished. The crime rate is very low.

Servants' pay is so low that even these poor families commonly employ them. Wives are proud of running their households, doing their own cooking and cleaning, disapproving of ostentation in the use of servants.

Sweepers, launderers and kitchen aids are often shared among several households. Traditional rules have been relaxed, but great care is essential to avoid serious kinds of ritual pollution, either from low-caste servants or from mixing polluting with other activities, cooked food being the most vulnerable. Their non-local kinship clustering constitutes a form of joint or extended family within which children grow up. Different households in the network cook special foods and children pass freely from household to household, eating at each (Michaelson, 1973).

Joint family in Madras

In Madras, leading industrialists now live in nuclear households with unmarried children. However, seven out of nineteen studied still maintain large joint households. Even if they are dropped as residential groups, they are kept as social groups in countless ways, for marriage, worship and separation of the sexes in eating and visiting. Home and workplace are compartmentalized: English speech, western dress, frequent inter-caste contact, new foods and drinks and the whole panoply of techniques and concepts of modern science and technology at work; speaking Tamil, traditional dress, observing beliefs and practices at home, even if the men are often not there. They convince themselves that they are good Hindus by 'vicarious ritualization', curtailing prayers and absolution, employing domestic priests to perform rituals on their behalf and acquiring merit by religious and charitable donations.

Jajmani

The *jajmani* relationship seemed the most untranslatable Indian institution, but has adapted surprisingly. In the city of Meerut, North India, servants of middle-class families regard themselves as attached to the house rather than its often short-term occupants (Vatuk, 1971:157–8). Servants are paid in cash, clothing, festival food, life-cycle ceremony gifts and left-over meals. A Rajput service station owner in Calcutta claimed he was *jajman* to his Brahman mechanic because both were from Benares and the Brahman's family had served his for generations (Ghitelman, 1975:23).

Calcutta

Palaces and penury also meet, with unspeakable poverty, famine, riot and disease in Kipling's *City of Dreadful Night* echoing with Salman Rushdie's *Midnight's Children* across the subcontinent in Bombay. 'We have not seen human degradation on a comparable scale in any other city in the world, one of the greatest urban concentrations in existence rapidly approaching breakdown in its economy, housing, sanitation, transport and the essential humanities of life', said the 1967 Planning Commission of the 'Petrified Jungle' of Calcutta (Moorhouse, 1983:265).

The palatial grandeur of Chowringhee, White Town (now offices, shops, hotels), always confronted Black Town, 'the city of stinks'. There were 400,000 people at the time of the Black Hole (1857), nearly 1 million in Kipling's day, and 15.9 million estimated for the millennium. Slavery was effectively outlawed by 1845, but the conditions of work were indistinguishable from slavery. Infant mortality and tuberculosis were at world records. In 1961 there were over 30,000 pavement dwellers; 3,000 *bustee* slums housed 189,000 families and 366,000 persons were in institutional shelters; 600,000 units average three per very small room.

If an employer refused to improve wages and conditions, workers surrounded him *en masse* in a *gherao*, perhaps taunting, but not touching him. He could not move without police rescue. If he resisted *gherao* the workers could beat him to death with their fists.

Calcutta and West Bengal were taken over by communist governments in the 1970s, which showed considerable efficiency in administration and reform, but brought fights between chief minister and deputy chief minister. Their Congress and Communist parties brought mass disorder and violence, uncontrollable riots, police outnumbered, couples coming out of cinemas stripped, jewellery snatchings, rapes and bombings, high officials attacked, the French consul's wife hacked to death in bed. The chief minister resigned and the Indian army was called to restore order. Nothing can extinguish Calcutta's pre-eminence as financial, commercial, cultural and intellectual powerhouse.

Untouchables

Untouchables occupied the most segregated enclaves in Indian cities, on peripheries and derelict pockets of wasteland. Scavenging, collecting human excreta and rotting matter, removing dead animals, therefore working with leather, were highly polluting activities and *chamar* leather workers were one of the largest Untouchable groups. Some became contractors for scavenging and dealing in hides, organizing their own associations and claiming Kshatriya descent through a bizarre reinterpretation of myth (Lynch, 1968:215–16). They became conscious of their own identity, acquired education and a genealogy, abstaining from polluting foods and practices according to the Sanskritization process (Srinivas, 1962:57). They made the shoe industry a *chamar* monopoly, protected by its very pollution, and achieved prominent municipal and state offices. But Sanskritization is a very slow process. Dr Ambedkar's All-India Scheduled Caste Federation offered stronger possibilities and in 1956 they followed him into Buddhism as Hinduism had no place or sense for them. They continued to battle against caste, for improvement of slum conditions, extension of opportunities and ending of all harassment and discrimination against Untouchables (Lynch, 1968:225).

Untouchables are the most rejected but not always the poorest. Materially poorest are the shanty towns and pavement dwellers diverse in caste status. The adaptive survival capacity of the latter is extraordinary. In the 1961 census of Bombay, 62,177 were counted, 1.9% of the central city. Of the adults, 80% had been there more than ten years, some born there. Men were nearly twice as numerous as women. Many women also worked, some widowed, divorced or unmarried, others living with husbands on the pavement. Larger families had higher incomes, several members earning small amounts, most from Rs 100–200 ($5–$10 per month). Most single member households earned less than Rs 100, yet 87% of them bought meals outside, but only 15% of larger households. Over half the illiterate households and three-quarters of the women household heads did their own cooking. Some also paid washermen. Their temporary awnings, some with alcoves for a woman to bathe, could be removed in ten minutes in case of a raid. A remarkable 2% had not tried to find accommodation; 11% were not keen to leave (Ramachandran, 1972: *passim*). No other accommodation would be free. They felt the security of being with kin or castemates from their native place. They had convenient earning stratagems nearby. A man could always run across the street if he heard his wives quarrelling. Many were rather respectable though there were some prostitutes, illicit brewers and a runaway intercaste marriage. This was far from the pervasive promiscuity of La Vida (Lewis, 1966b).

Chandigarh

The most idealistic city experiment in India was that of Le Corbusier for President Nehru saying at Chandigarh, 'let this be a new town, symbolic of the freedom of India, unfettered by traditions of the past', Le Corbusier replying 'Chandigarh is a realization not only for Punjab or India but for the whole world.' Le Corbusier's high-rise towers were vetoed. Threatening to resign, he redesigned a square containing a cross axis, with the capitol complex culminating in the north-east axis towards the mountains. A plan arranges organs in order, lungs, heart, stomach, creating an organism. Le Corbusier used a six-foot male figure with one arm raised, a 'modulor' stick, as a standard, organismic measure of human scale, apparently echoing the ancient Indian instruction to draw a mandala on the land as ground plan for construction of a city and temple, including the primeval *purusha* figure, embodying the caste structure, his head the Brahmin, his arms the Kshatriya, his thighs the Vaisya and feet the Sudra. The creation of the world was the sacrifice and dismemberment of the *purusha* and the formation of the components of the universe from his body parts, as in the myth of Osiris. When construction was complete, the architect might be buried under it, literally or symbolically. In an uncanny way, Le Corbusier re-enacted this myth, carrying a miniature 'modulor' in his pocket when visiting the site at sunset. On his return, the modulor was missing, having fallen from the jeep on the soil, never found, therefore buried under the new city. Thus the symbolic design of the Indian city, which we found at first illusorily mythopoeic seems to end in the same vein (Singer, 1984).

The splendour of Le Corbusier's design and the grandeur of the major public buildings, which alone were constructed within the official programme, were progressively overwhelmed by the labourers, artisans, shopkeepers and businessmen, without whom the city could not have been built. They had to have their own city to live in, higher design or not. The plan marked a five-mile and ten-mile radius (like Varanasi pilgrimage circuits) as a controlled area, but by 1984, 40% of the people lived in slums. Planners ordered their removal, but politicians depended on their votes, so a removal resolution was never voted. There were 3,500 violations pending. Makeshift huts became regular colonies. 'In another five years, Chandigarh will be another Amritsar or Ludhiana, with the only saving grace of the underground sewer system, if that does not choke by that time' said the Punjab chief town planner (Singer, 1984). It has been the same story all over the world, from India to Africa, to Brazil and Peru.

AFRICA

Partition

By 1860 France was just recovering from wars and revolutions, Germany moving towards unification, both ready to compete fiercely with Britain in the colonial world. Steamships now reduced time and distance, intensifying rivalry and conflict. The United States Civil War cut off exports from the south, raising the price of cotton to the enormous benefit of Egypt and India. Then the drive to the American west resumed full force with expansion of agriculture, extension of railways, discovery of vast mineral resources and creation of the first fabulous fortunes.

The capitalist nations settled conflicting claims by compromise at the Berlin Conference (1884–5). Almost the whole of Africa was partitioned. Serious road and railway building began, as otherwise exploitation of the interior was limited to slaves and ivory and certainly cities could not develop. Each colonial territory had its capital city and a dozen provincial and district capitals, which grew from their initial single administrator and half dozen police to small towns over the next fifty years, mainly after World War II.

The modernization of Cairo

In the nineteenth century Egypt did not consider herself part of Africa, as she came to do under Nasser's charisma in the 1960s. Cairo has been the greatest city of the continent for a millennium and more, leading the way in growth and innovation. Strangled by loss of empire to the Ottomans and oriental trade to the Portuguese it gradually tumbled down, to a quarter of a million people by the nineteenth century. Now it is twenty times bigger.

Westernization began with Napoleon's expedition, conquest, then defeat and the emergence of Muhammad Ali as ruling pasha. He built the country, finally massacring and driving out the *mamluks*, curbing bandits, imposing peace, reopening canals and irrigation ditches, reorganizing a productive country in support of its capital, strengthening order with a strong police force, clearing the streets of filth, rubbish and rubble (Abu-Lughod, 1971:91–2), less felicitously prohibiting the *meshrebiyya* wooden traceried oriel windows in favour of plain lattice. Glass windows came by 1835. Cairo had thirty wheeled carriages, for the ruling family, after many centuries without wheeled traffic, despite the chariots of the Pharaohs and the Romans. There were only eight avenue throughfares and they were obstructed by stone *mastaba* seats built out of every shop front, which were gradually removed. Walkers carried lights after dark and houses were white-washed.

French influence continued, bringing secular schools, a medical school, an engineering polytechnic and small factories for cotton, wool and linen textiles, an iron foundry and a printing press. Consul De Lesseps won the Suez Canal contract after twenty years' effort.

Ismail Pasha was determined to win acceptance in the circle of European monarchs and recognition for Cairo as a modern capital. Invited to the Paris Exposition of 1867 and deeply impressed by Haussmann's success cutting boulevards through ancient Paris just as he had wished in Cairo, he felt compelled to emulate. He wanted his own White Town. Enriched by doubling cotton sales at four times the price for five years by the American Civil War, water and gas were piped to the city. The canal would be finished in 1869 and a new Cairo must win over the fashionable world at its opening.

New streets had been cut, one reducing congestion for European merchants, one right through the old city. What this cost in human hardship, despite compensation promises, cannot be known. Priceless mosques were destroyed. It was too costly and slow, forcing Ismail instead to create a new Cairo. The Minister of Public Works, with French architects, planners and landscape gardeners began at once. Verdi was commissioned to compose Aïda for the new opera house. Systems of radiating boulevards, Haussmann-like, led westwards to the receding banks of the Nile. The paving, sidewalks, tree planting and framing mansions of the wealthy began and continued through the century. Empress Eugénie opened the canal and drove by carriage with the distinguished guests right to the pyramids, on a new road, over the first bridge across the Nile, hurriedly constructed on boats and later made permanent in iron (Abu-Lughod, 1971:108).

Egypt's dominance of the route to the east was restored after 400 years. Ismail was bankrupt, allowing Britain to buy Egypt's whole share in the canal for £4 million. Ismail's cabinet was reinforced with French and British overseeing ministers. Intolerably humiliated, Ismail tried to dismiss them only to be dismissed himself by the sultan of Turkey under French and British pressure. Ismail's son Tawfiq failed to suppress an army revolt, inevitably bringing the British to his aid. Wolseley's defeat of the rebels at Tel-el-Kebir in 1882 and triumphal march into Cairo completed Egypt's undeclared colonial subjection. Cairo was too big and dense for its ruler to cut streets through it or for British overlordship to penetrate very far. It did not become a western city, but, under the British, Ismail's own plan was achieved.

British control made Cairo very attractive to European investment. As the exploiting centre of a fertile land whose productivity had been restored, Cairo had enormous resources of commerce to tap, besides its winter climate, the mysterious glamour of its ancient past, which made it a fashionable resort and further led to the rebuilding of Alexandria as one of the Mediterranean's greatest summer resorts. Belgian, Swiss, French, British as well as Egyptian private capital flowed into the building of modern shops, hotels and villas to fill out Ismail's plan.

The first twenty-two miles of tramway opened in 1898 before New York had any, soon extended further, carrying 56 million passengers a year by 1911, 93 million by 1925. What could not be achieved by cutting into the old city could be by filling in unnecessary canals. By 1900 the great pharaonic canal from the Nile to the Red Sea, reopened by Trajan and again by Amr Ibn al-As who conquered Egypt in AD 639, was filled in to provide wide dual carriageways with tramlines between, running for the first time right through the ancient city from north to south.

It was the control of the Nile flood by the first Aswan dam of 1902, heightened in 1912, which made it possible both to fill in the old canals of Cairo to provide new transport arteries, and also to make firm banks both sides of the Nile as well as on its previously fluctuating islands. All these river banks made prime residential sites of greatly rising value and further encouraged the westward spread begun by Ismail, till it covered the banks and the islands and encroached west of the river for the first time.

In 1906 mainly Belgian capital built an electric railway out north-west into the desert at Heliopolis. Roads, water, sewage and electricity were supplied to 6,000 acres bought for £1 an acre. The gamble succeeded and Heliopolis grew into a prosperous upper-middle-class satellite town, increasingly self-sufficient as well as partly a commuter dormitory for Cairo. By 1947 it had a population of 50,000, and over 100,000 by 1970.

After the Revolution of 1952 Nasser's government began to build public housing for the poor, as well as imposing extensive rent control. By 1964 some 100,000 persons had been housed in multi-storey buildings of over 14,000 units, averaging seven to a family, 28% in one-room, 54% in two-room, and 18% in three-room apartments – at a cost of nearly £6 million. At 400 Egyptian pounds per unit this is remarkably cheap.

An even larger middle-class community project is under way at Nasr (Victory) City on 20,000 acres of desert between Heliopolis and the old city, designed for a population of half a million over a twenty-year development. On the first 7,000 acres some dozens of very attractive, large, eleven-storey apartment buildings have been constructed, together with shops, schools and all recreational and community facilities. The whole area is fully designed and laid out, much of it for private building within the scheme, villas for high government officials as well as institutional and industrial sites (Abu-Lughod, 1971:232–6).

Although the great size of Cairo puts it in a place apart, more than six times as large as Johannesburg, or Ibadan, three times the size of Lagos, its development suggests lessons for other African cities. To adjust to western influence and new technology it became a dual city, in less rigid White Town–Black Town pattern. All the great pre-industrial African cities which modernized did it this way, as shown by Tunis, Algiers, Rabat, Fez, Marrakesh, Kano or Ibadan. Kampala-Mengo provides the lower end of the spectrum (Southall, 1967). The dual development of Cairo has become well fused. There never were two separate cities to the extent visible in Fez or Kano. There was never any doubt about Cairo having its own culture, language and religion. Indeed, it has become more thoroughly Egyptian through the eclipse and absorption of its Turkish ruling elite. Nor was there ever any real question of racial segregation, despite the strong European influence and presence in the new zones during the colonial occupation. Despite their humiliation, its elite was still too numerous, wealthy and sophisticated for this to make sense. Ethnicity has played a relatively minor part. There were local concentrations of Copts, Jews, Greeks and Europeans, but no one could have drawn a boundary round them.

Cairo is a mass transit city. It acquired its trams and electric trains remarkably early, supplemented by ubiquitous bus services since the 1930s. Subways were also planned, when the city became engulfed in the Middle East War. They were completed in the 1980s. The low incomes of the masses and even middle classes, combined with the high cost of imported cars and gasoline protected it against the automobile until recently. Overpopulated in an overpopulated country, with a sudden access of another million people as refugees from the canal zone after 1967, its buses, trams and trains became unspeakably overcrowded. This is the fate of every great Third World metropolis.

Cairo is a proletarian city. French estimates at the beginning of the nineteenth century suggest that over half the population was a 'lower-lower' stratum of unskilled labourers, domestics, slaves and agricultural workers. It is estimated that in 1877, 57% of the economically active population was still engaged in farming. Succulent pigeons on their roofs and verandahs, make a substantial contribution to the nutrition of an overpopulated city. The size of the contemporary urban working class is not precisely known, but it has been estimated at 60%, with a solid middle class of over 30%. What is important is that Cairo like other North African Arab cities had a full array of experienced urban rulers, religious leaders, professionals, merchants, craftsmen and poor urban workers whose necessary degree of adjustment to new roles and ways of life demanded by the modernization process was not nearly so great or difficult as in most cities of Black Africa, where these mediating classes hardly existed. Urban workers had to adjust from different lives in small-scale, self-contained rural communities and would-be craftsmen, traders, professionals and political leaders had to struggle very hard to acquire new knowledge, techniques, training and positions in the face of discouraging competition from better advantaged foreigners if not actual discrimination. West African pre-industrial cities were better placed than those of the east and south, in their historical practice of both long-distance and petty urban trade and elaborate crafts, but the difference from western cities in scale and specialization was so much greater than in the case of Cairo that their adjustment was more difficult and, for better or worse, they had no urban proletariat comparable to that of Cairo. The result has been that the carry over of craft skills and the survival of their products has been less, so that they have been more at the mercy of mass-produced imported goods.

During the nineteenth century the growth of Cairo was largely from internal reproduction, as improvement of health conditions and services enabled urban and rural populations to rise at about the same rate. In recent decades Cairo has received a heavy immigration, but the previous base was so large that Cairo's immigrant population has never constituted such a high percentage as in Black Africa. The percentage of the Cairo population born in the city has averaged over 60% throughout this century, whereas most cities of Black Africa have the vast majority of their population born outside them. Given the polyethnic character of Black African countries, the migrant stream to big cities is polyethnic too. Some cities may have members of more than 100 ethnic groups converging upon them, as in the case of Dar-es-Salaam.

While ethnic problems were relatively unimportant in Cairo, it revealed many processes common in other parts of Africa and elsewhere (Abu-Lughod, 1961). In the 1947 figures half of the 400,000 migrants to Cairo from the Delta in Lower Egypt were women, whereas four-fifths of the 250,000 migrants from Upper Egypt were men. Many of those from Lower Egypt seem to have been landless and having nothing to lose moved permanently as families, also allowing their women to work, like the South India migrants to Bombay and Bangalore. The Upper Egyptian migrants include many Nubians, who are more conservative, trying to keep their women in seclusion and not permitting them to work. In conformity with this it is mainly men who go to Cairo leaving their families behind. In Cairo they work especially in domestic and personal service and unskilled jobs, living as bachelors or sometimes taking temporary wives. Thus they may work all their lives in Cairo yet keep in close touch with their rural families, visiting and sending them money. In a sense they reject the city, limiting their contacts to fellow villagers. There are many dues-paying, mutual aid, benevolent associations of fellow villagers in Cairo, relieving isolation and assisting with expenses of poverty, unemployment, sickness and burial, meeting at specific coffee houses, often run by one of themselves. The Upper Egyptians in Cairo are encapsulated in a way comparable to the Red Xhosa described in East London (Mayer, 1971:90ff). The major difference is that the latter were reacting to oppressive apartheid which severely discouraged urbanization, whereas the Upper Egyptians reflect the contrast of rich and poor in Cairo, which offers little hope of advancement to the latter.

Surviving in Cairo

An intensive study over a quarter of a century of a snowball sample of seventeen families comprising 100 persons in the back streets of a poor quarter startlingly challenges current assumptions on the possibilities of poor people extricating themselves from poverty, not only in Third World but in First World cities (Wikan, 1995). In 1969 all were tenants, in windowless basement rooms, flimsy sheds on roofs, and some in three-room apartments. In 1994 half the families owned their homes or had bought lots for building. Their average education had risen from 3.6 to 9.8 years. They now eat better, dress better and work less hard because of new domestic appliances and enjoy more leisure with Egyptian television. This has been achieved despite worsening overpopulation and general economic deterioration, but at daunting cost in hardship and human effort.

Family planning has reduced the numbers of children. Fifty-year-old women have borne eight to nine children; thirty-year-old women will probably not exceed three to four by the end of their cycle. This is an extraordinary achievement but still not enough, nor as much as they themselves wish. Some husbands are now actually keener on birth control than their wives, because they are determined to make a better future for their children.

Husbands are responsible for the family income and have to work several jobs, a main, low-paying regular employment and supplementary jobs in the informal sector, endlessly tracked down through the intense gossip and mutual aid network of kin and friends, averaging a sixty-hour week. But wives hold the purse and budget; women are responsible for organizing family improvement, mainly through their savings clubs, which pool the group's resources, giving the whole sum to a different member every month. Enterprising women able to gather members to form a club, get the first allocation, which may make the down payment on a building site, add a floor, pay school fees or any emergency.

Rents are controlled at the level of the original contract, so that parents are paying little but children must pay fifteen times more for a new place. People at different stages of the struggle unite their efforts. One family has a plot but cannot afford to build. Another with no plot but some savings co-operates, paying the first family some years of rent in advance, itself starting construction. The uncontrollable growth of Cairo forces all new building to the periphery, so that young couples get separated from their parental families, on whom they depend for solidarity, confidence and daily mutual aid, by long bus journeys which leave them to walk a further half hour through desolate potholed streets.

Men adamantly exercise their legal right to prevent their wives working, unless they have post-primary education to get a respectable job. So they are left alone in their new flat far from kin and friends, distrusting neighbours and preventing children from any access to the street. Discipline remains very strict. Children must be polite, obedient, respect parents and not mix with children on the street, which risks learning bad behaviour, swearing and fighting. Young mothers block windows so that close but stranger neighbours cannot see in. They huddle in dark inner rooms with only neon lights. This forces them to send children to nursery school and tutoring for escape, costing 200 Egyptian pounds yearly and up to 30% of a monthly salary. Husbands accept this extra burden which they have brought on themselves by confining their wives. With bride payments dropped, they now marry years before cohabitation, satisfying male pride with permanent proprietorship of the wife, without supporting her, retaining the right to divorce at any time, but almost never exercised as the situation now commits them irrevocably to struggle together. Although he supervises his wife's clothes and every detail of her life, he has of necessity become a real partner in a way wives always struggled for but never could achieve. The burdens he assumes to satisfy the imperatives of the male role impose an alarming strain. He works too long hours and gets too little sleep. But for the over-riding goal of making a better future for the children they accept this painful, unending sacrifice together.

It is the astonishing intensity over the long term of generations which makes the unremitting drudgery endurable and pitilessly slow improvement possible. It is assisted by Islam, which does not emphasize suffering, like Buddhism, or ritual elaboration, like Hinduism; it forbids drunkenness and usury, or wasting resources on costly rituals. Government assists with food subsidies, health and education, though overwhelmed in its attempts at other vital services (Wikan, 1995:635–48).

The net results are low crime, without any effective welfare system; stable families with no divorce in this sample; security from eviction and no homelessness, promoting compassionate reception of destitutes; the home as a linchpin of personal identity, powerfully directing energies to future-oriented striving, with surprising stress on material possessions as epitome of status and respect, since you are 'who you appear to be'. Envy and rivalry generate positive effort, instead of witchcraft. Despite poverty, they share a culture with the larger society, embracing values and developing capacities similar to the middle class. The reason this is impossible for Blacks in America's inner cities is racism (Fernea, 1995:649). It is a very old and resilient urban culture. Despite warnings that 'Cairo 2000 may be an ever growing mass of underemployed, disaffected wretches in one of the world's largest slums', it is a mega-city monster drowned in air pollution and congestion but with remarkable human features. 'Mega-city management is more important than mega-city size' (Richardson, 1993:52).

Lagos

The pre-colonial cities of West Africa show interesting institutional adaptations to modern needs. Immigrants who commit themselves fully to urban life in Lagos (acquired by Britain in 1861 by manipulating a succession dispute) try to acquire land and purchase or build houses to accommodate their family and also provide themselves with rental income. As landlords they are eligible, by recent custom, to sit on the landlords' council of their ward, whose chairman ranks as an important chief. These chiefs meet in seven suburban committees, each chaired by a chief with the supreme title of *oba*. The seven *obas* meet to consider the problems of the whole area, as well as furthering their own interests.

In old Lagos the *oba* and chiefs attained their positions by descent and seniority, but now in the suburbs they qualify by achievement, through owning land and by success in bringing opportunities to their clients through their wide networks of influence. They are usually Yoruba from Lagos or any of the other former Yoruba city-states. The social networks of Yoruba kin, friends and patrons keep a stranglehold on the channels of advancement.

Those successfully established formed descent group 'wings', consisting of all those members of their lineage resident in Lagos over whom they are able to exercise control. Such wings could become autonomous descent groups if their members stay in Lagos sufficiently long and successfully. Membership became bilaterally optative rather than strictly patrilineal, to meet the urban need to mobilize diverse networks of kin. So the Yoruba were able to adapt their traditional kingship (*oba*) to modern needs, by broadening the criteria of eligibility and providing patronage services, conflict resolution and lobbying for improved amenities of water, electricity, roads, sewerage and representation.

In a sample suburban area 21% of women and 9% of men were landlords. Most had established and focused upon urban kinship groups. More of the men belonged to hometown associations, more of the women to savings associations. Nearly half of the male landlords over the age of thirty were polygynous, but only 4% of tenants. While 16% of immigrants took one to two years to find a job, 15% took more than two years.

The vast majority of women are traders. Tens of thousands of them sell in the markets or in stalls outside their houses and along the streets. The wealthiest send their sons to university, though they themselves are usually illiterate. They try to keep their daughters in their profession. Both the city and suburbs have leaders of the market, women who are titled chiefs ranking second to the *oba* himself. Under them are the chair-women of each market, each general line of trade and each specific commodity. They are greatly feared by political leaders (Baker, 1974; Barnes, 1986). The market queens were thrust into prominence as pivots of faction fights in which the original Yoruba constantly strove for supremacy over the settlers, masking their attacks with spurious issues to delude the opposition (Barnes, 1986:183–4).

African cities and cultural decay

Some African peoples further from the main routes of invasion and urbanization did not have time to learn western culture sufficiently for effective adaptation before the intensity of capitalist penetration broke upon them. They are left in a pathological condition, their own rich culture decayed and incoherent, no longer capable of securing harmony among them. They say their country is riddled with witchcraft. They fear for the lives of themselves and their children if they stay there. So they go to the capital city and say they will never return. Some still fear and suffer from witchcraft in the city, even high level civil servants in their office lives. But generally the ethnic heterogeneity of the city inhibits witchcraft. It only flourishes where numbers of the same ethnic group are clustered, so that others of the group avoid going to that locality. The only thing that could exorcise witchcraft from their country is an industrial revolution, a very remote prospect. Thus in Africa people abandon the country for the city, while in America middle-class people fear to go to the city centre (e.g. Detroit) because of violence.

LATIN AMERICA

Social relationships in Latin American cities

Latin America benefited in its confrontation with industrial capitalism by having its great port cities, hinterland capitals and state organization (however fragile and subject to military intervention), already established and developing for several centuries. Britain was the main initiator of capitalist development, investment and urbanization in the nineteenth century. The Latin American nations and cities were better able to maintain cultural integrity (having overwhelmed or absorbed the indigenous peoples) than the African nations and cities, which were too recent foreign intrusions. But the Iberian upper-class cultural heritage, contrasting with northern neighbours, was antipathetic to the penetration of capitalism except as pay-offs for themselves.

Latin American cities do not have the extensive kinship of Africa, nor the caste of India, but they embody two to four centuries of Iberian pre-industrial urbanism. Cities were divided between the elite of urban-dwelling landowners, church magnates, bureaucrats, army officers and professionals, and the effectively disenfranchised masses forming about 60% of the population (Leeds, 1964:1326). They were structured by elaborate stratification and mechanisms for manipulating, maintaining and adapting sets and networks of supportive personal ties, emphasizing reciprocal dyadic relationships, notably *compadrazgo* and patron–client relationships.

Contemporary urban *compadrazgo* is less ritualized, formal and church oriented than before. Poor migrants with few friends may choose co-parents from kin, who are usually excluded in the country. In a Mexico City shanty town sample, 150 co-parents were nearby kin, 200 were non-kin neighbours, mainly status equals, to extend the network for mutual aid in general. Men were also strongly tied by *cuatismo* drinking relationships (Lomnitz, 1977). Generally *compadrazgo* links people across classes, providing higher-status partners with followings of clients, conferring prestige and giving practical service. Upper-class men tend to have very many co-parent clients, middle and lower classes fewer. In Lima an Indian worker could find through his home town club a middle-class lawyer otherwise beyond his reach (Mangin, 1970). In Mexico City's huge informal sector 90% of migrants have network support on arrival, increasing their sense of *confianza*, security and trust (Lomnitz, 1977).

A shanty town carpet layer made contact with a carpet dealer who gave him bigger and bigger jobs, so he recruited two brothers, a brother-in-law and two or three neighbours to assist him, thus acting as a broker to the outside world, controlling all deals with his patron directly and paying his assistants just enough to satisfy them. The foreman to a big contractor captained a crew of 200–300 fellow shanty town workers at peak periods, organizing them in gangs led by his co-parents. Countless businesses large and small give similar opportunities to shanty town brokers. There are some 25,000 seamstresses in Mexico City, groups of neighbours, mothers and children, working sixteen to eighteen hours a day, organized by brokers.

Innumerable informal activities provide opportunities, with political bosses, lottery tickets, street vendors, youth gangs, drug syndicates, or garbage collection to feed pigs, turkeys, cows and rabbits for sale to dealers. Life is irregular, fluctuating, often illegal, mobilizing cheap labour, evading wage and union regulations. Formal jobs, better paid, protected and regular, are controlled by the labour aristocracy of the unions for themselves, their families and kin.

Shanty town patrons can become wealthy and build themselves fine houses, but cannot leave the shanty town because success depends upon personal relations with their clients. Like the old American city bosses they show personal concern and help in emergencies. A foreman took over a nightclub sometimes for a week, letting his people enjoy all the wine, food and women they wanted at his expense (Lomnitz, 1977). Hence the wide range of income and status in shanty towns.

Advancement depends on access to influential patrons above, supported by armies of useful clients below and dependable equal networks of family, kin and friends. Personal expertise works better than highly specialized training. The starting careerist must hold multiple jobs, each giving access to different networks, continuously assessed for their potentialities as the operator moves between nominal employment in bureaucratic agencies, universities, managerial structures and public services. Through all his connections, including sports groups and church ties, he develops his *trampolim* springboard to project himself on a successful career. No relationship or occupation is indispensable. All are instrumental, subject to manipulation, or termination, as new possibilities appear. He must attract attention to his name and quality, even by a sequence of contradictory activities calculated to attract notice. He will get himself discreetly invited into a *pañelinha*, 'little saucepan', informal primary group of smart operators, held together by friendship, common goals and interests. The successful *pañelinha* could include lawyers, a customs officer, insurance agents, accountants, bankers and municipal, state or federal deputies (Leeds, 1964:1330–6).

Initial success makes continued projection of an influential public image all the more important, through journalistic, television and radio contacts, purposefully directed gossip and all the panoply of classical techniques celebrated in Figaro's *largo al factotum*. The university rector has journalistic clients who keep him before the public eye to impress his political patrons. Powerful individuals can always arrange to perform symbolic public acts and ensure that they are reported. High-level *pañelinhas* not only make personal links between important businesses and offices, but have branches in all major cities, culminating in the top decision makers of Rio and Brasilia with the president as keystone.

Brasilia

The winning design for Brasilia brilliantly bound together the symbolic conception of the modern and ancient city. The essential elements were the crossing of two highway axes on which is superimposed an equilateral triangle defining the area of the city, two terraced embankments and a platform. The sign of the cross signified the primordial act of founding not only Brasilia but any city, recalling the Egyptian hieroglyphic sign for city. It combined outrage and admiration, almost a joke, sketched on a few cards, yet realized a Brazilian dream going back to the eighteenth century.

Poets and writers enthusiastically celebrated its inauguration, press and politicians of every hue lampooned it as pure folly. It was designed as antidote, not mere antithesis, to the evils of capitalist Brazil: the basic units, huge apartment blocks, all equal, same façade, same height, same facilities, built of the same materials, on columns, with garages; preventing the hateful differentiation of social classes, all families sharing the same life together. The dispersed, homogeneous dormitory settlements, set in a green city with a new system of traffic circulation, would eliminate *the street*, the public space and the urban crowd of traditional Brazilian cities.

But the first generation of Brasilians rejected the defamiliarizing intentions of the design, rejected the negation of familiar urban Brazil. They found the same façades monotonous, producing not equality but anonymity. They rejected the mixing of social classes, as igniting conflicts between irrevocably different life styles and values. Without streets and crowds Brasilia was *cold*. They repudiated the anti-street design by putting their shops back on the street next to the curbs and the traffic. Many upper bureaucrats moved out to build ostentatious houses to display their wealth and negate the modernist aesthetic. The elite found 'the same life together' intolerable and abandoned the intended egalitarian social clubs to form exclusive, class-based private ones. If Brasilia became a travesty of its creators' intentions, its people are still better off than the rest of Brazil. The city is tranquil, convenient and works, free from the congestion, high crime rate, omnipresent misery, lack of urban services, and pollution (Holston, 1989:64–71, 19–27).

Shanty towns

The mushrooming post-World War II shanty towns were a dramatic exposure of the extreme economic inequality and resultant mass poverty of Latin America. The inner city slums, already dense warehouses of the destitute, were quite inadequate to hold the multitude. About 40% of the inhabitants of large cities live in shanty towns. They were often occupied by planned mass invasion of unoccupied public or private land, seized at night or during the weekend, so that when authorities woke up to their

Plate 5 Mathare: Nairobi's Mathare valley illustrates one of the rich variety of squatter settlements in which the poor struggle innovatively to survive, against police harassment, in the shadows of urban luxury.

presence their ramshackle shelters were up and they were in residential occupation. Repeated attacks by police, with many dead and wounded, could not deter them. They were gratuitously branded as revolutionaries, reservoirs of disease, vice and crime. It has been shown that they have a strong law and order bias, somewhat conservative, with less crime, promiscuity and broken homes than central city slums, less alienated, and devoted to hard work and enterprise, slums of hope rather than of despair (Lloyd, 1979), which have vastly increased the stock of proudly owned housing, whereas government schemes have always proved beyond the reach of the poor.

Everywhere in the Third World the urban poor have found pockets of wasteland, swamps, steep slopes and railway reserves. In cities all around the world are big projects aimed at the poor, which either failed or were turned over to the middle class. In well-established shanty towns many houses have been made permanent and respectable. Such settlements have begun to provide or improve water and electricity supplies and garbage collection.

We must praise the courage and initiative of shanty town builders, but they are a blistering indictment of the callous, wealthy elite who control the cities.

CONVERGENCE

The great break of war

The decades after World War I confronted the impact and implications of the Soviet Revolution and the Great Depression. Wars stimulate change, but positive effects were cancelled by the perversely contradictory developments of Soviet Communism, Fascism and Nazism. Italy rushed belatedly to join the sickening colonial powers by a brutal invasion of Ethiopia.

The two wars marked a period of world conflict from 1914 to 1945 when 'the great edifice of nineteenth century civilization crumbled' (Hobsbawm, 1994:22). Colonial development was inhibited, but opposition to empire was stimulated, with independence movements from the Maghreb to Indonesia. Those in subsaharan Africa were sparked in the metropoles, in the dissatisfied class of educated urban Africans and in strikes on the Copperbelt and generally, all gathering force in the post-war era. Attention then focused more seriously on the poverty and neglect of colonies. African cities had received little assistance, growing slowly, some White Towns being attractively laid out as garden cities, whose spacious amenities, after post-war blossoming, would gradually succumb to overpopulation, congestion and poverty after Independence was won. Development plans achieved improvements, with good cash-crop prices in the 1950s and 1960s.

Post-war development

The World Bank and International Monetary Fund, established to tackle economic problems of post-war rehabilitation and reconstruction, turned their attention to the New Nations, defining their problem as development and modernization. Eligibility for assistance depended on calculating need in monetary terms, for the first time categorizing countries universally, prompting the popular characterization of poor countries as Third World.

Development programmes for enriching poor countries and closing the gap between them and rich countries did not work. After fifty years the gap was larger still. Third World countries became an increasingly insoluble problem for the capitalist world. Their cities were becoming clogged with overpopulation and ringed with shanty towns and illegal slum settlements. They were also clogged with multiplying fleets of aid and development vehicles, governmental and non-governmental. Yet all aid must pass through this clogged filter. Much of it never got further, sticking in the hands of the elites and the burgeoning army of expatriates sent to administer it.

This led to an outburst of growth in the smaller capitals of the poorer countries, where the vehicles, equipment, offices and houses brought and built for the army of expatriates created a veneer of prosperity downtown and in new suburbs, while the rural economy and population continued to deteriorate. The indigenous urban elites and skilled intellectual and manual workers benefited at the expense of the rest. The relation of the city to the nation on the one hand, the aid donors on the other, was increasingly distorted; the former counted in millions of impoverished people, the latter in millions of dollars and hundreds of affluent expatriates. Structural adjustment treated countries as if they were business firms made 'lean and mean' to recover profitability. Here it was the mass of the people who got lean and mean.

Intractable urban poverty

Scattered mostly over the southern, warmer and tropical parts of the globe, Third World cities cover a vast variety of situations. They have basic aspects in common, but their range of size is extraordinary and some gross contrasts attach to their different continental positions. As the decades pass, the contrast in size continues, carried to a higher level, but it is more and more their intractable poverty which makes them alike.

We can talk enthusiastically about the richly variegated indigenous cultures of Africa in their thousands; the scarcely less numerous but more populous cultures of Asia; or the Latin American cultures with their common Iberian, African and Amerindian roots, but vastly varied combinations and ecologies, and how these thousands of variables interact with innumerable urban situations. That is both fascinating and relevant, because all these millions are human beings and their cultures and languages and what is happening and will happen to them in these cities is of the deepest moral and personal concern to them. To ignore this is to forfeit all claim to common humanity. Yet the over-riding poverty of their plight demands frank recognition not only for the appalling impact it has on those who suffer it, but because it is now having an increasingly disastrous impact upon ourselves, who are in significant part responsible for it. Few of these situations have been adequately studied, or ever will be, but of those few which have been, some are profoundly illuminating.

Global culture

Furthermore, the thousands of cultures and millions of combinations are all now confronted and being undermined by the spreading global culture, the celebrated syndrome of jeans and teeshirts, Coca-cola and McDonald's, plastic sandals, dark glasses and rock music, irresistibly disseminated, across all cultural and linguistic barriers, by television, cassettes and radio.

This commonplace is very novel. It is not a centrally directed propaganda campaign, but is quintessentially urban and capitalist, by far the finest propaganda instrument for that system of production and the way of life entailed. It is a culture incompatible with peasant farming. Those affected by it are driven to acquire the apparatus of participation, which means going to town because the culture convinces the participant that abundance, stimulation, modernization and progress are in the city. The result is that the countryside loses productive workers and agricultural production falls, while the city gains productive workers for whom it has no employment, so migrants from country to city may suffer even greater hardship and poverty than they did in the countryside.

Since there were no usable cities for Europeans in subsaharan Africa, all the cities are foreign creations. The few important ancient cities in Nigeria, Mali or Zimbabwe were so wrapped up in divine kingship and symbolic structure that they could only adapt to colonial conditions by destroying themselves (Lloyd, 1973; Krapf-Askari, 1969; Southall, 1970b).

Since the Europeans created new cities, they depended on migration of the local population to them. Migration has been vital to all cities, because until the twentieth century they were too unhealthy to reproduce themselves. African cities were created entirely by migration within a few decades. They were all the more migrant based in that most early migrants were male and only stayed temporarily. Some stayed only a few years, some for their whole working careers, yet determined to retire to their rural homes. In the racially discriminatory cities of eastern, central and southern Africa this was legally compulsory. Such a base is very unstable for national cultures which are urbanizing rapidly without having any national culture of their own, because of the dozens of competing cultures of their immigrant components, except the very alien invading global culture, resistance to which is made virtually impossible by the very situation itself. Resistance would in any case provoke charges of traditionalism, 'tribalism' and unacceptable protectionism involving the withdrawal of international aid.

Urban migration

When migrants go to town in large numbers they have to establish mutual self-support networks. If they are divided by poverty, culture and ethnicity or race from the dominant population of the city, they inevitably become enclaves of separate relationship clusters and networks within it. Since they do not, and in many ways cannot, belong to the culture of the city, the culture from which they came remains of paramount importance to them although it is incompatible with that of the city. This is the great incompatibility. There are lesser incompatibilities between the culture of a person or family left in the village or community they came from and the culture and languages of many other communities from which people also migrated to the same city. These contradictions can be relieved and metaphysically resolved and reconciled by symbolic performance in dance, song, mime, gesture and costume on recreational occasions (Mitchell, 1956).

Both the work situation and the leisure situation are strange in the city, so that migrants must rapidly perform and grasp new roles and types of relationships and activities. They must acquire new roles and relation-ships with their associated culture, without losing those they had before, which they will resume and perform again when they go home on vaca-tion or for good. So the same person is equally a cultivator, herdsman, polygamist in the country and miner, labourer or servant, and bachelor, in the city. He cannot be a miner in the country or a herdsman in the city. But if he goes on circulating between town and country, he becomes a changed person and if he finally stays in the city he becomes simply a townsman. Country ways cannot work in the city. Employers who tried to make them eventually failed (Epstein, 1958). One ethnic group may be specially associated with a city which grew up in its area, and derive advantages in land, housing and social support from it. Such people become like hosts to migrants who come from more distant areas (Parkin, 1975:37; 1969: *passim*). Migrants who strongly resisted the foreign city, as in apartheid South Africa, yet had to keep going there for unskilled labour to survive, could for a while encapsulate themselves, at least symbolically in the dress and behaviour of their rural culture (Mayer, 1971), but the protest was shortlived.

The irresistible global cultural invasion engenders a kind of conver-gence in cities throughout the world. Unfortunately their material condi-tions are very different. Migrants to Third World cities now find that their relatives and friends, with all their good-will, simply cannot find them jobs. They may have to scavenge, picking garbage, sorting bottles and cans, salvaging thrown away food.

Urban underclass

The underclasses of Asia, Africa and Latin America meet those of the First World, both momentarily entangled in the same expressive culture of the treacherous global village. It is a chiasmus: they come from different trajectories and they cannot continue along the same road. Although First and Third World poor now seem similar in their degree of deprivation and exclusion, the drug- and crime-ravaged inner city ghettos of the United States are none the less at a distinctly different material level. In an overaffluent society even they always have access to junk cars, or as crime gang leaders or drug dealers to the latest models of newest luxury cars. They spend extraordinary sums of dubiously obtained money on flamboyant designer clothes, cosmetics and hairdos of their own distinctive style, carry stolen money in Gucci bags, affecting sports-gear and footwear from the fashion pages. The slum dwellers of São Paulo and the *bustee* and pavement dwellers of Calcutta can only dream of this. The large-scale dumping of second-hand clothes from the First World in the Third World shows recent progress.

THOSE WHO ESCAPED

White dominions

The cities of the White dominions left after the United States secession escaped the colonial and Third World straitjacket. Despite the celebrated convicts, many probably unjustly victimized, their founding fathers and mothers shared culture, blood and aspirations with those of the first and richest industrial capitalist nation. This connection was of inestimable value in countless unobtrusive ways. Constant kinship links kept their practice and knowledge in step with the mother country, if they did not actually push ahead. Being socialized already in the British culture and values on industrial capitalism saved much of the time, tension and frustration which those in other continents suffered in being painfully acculturated to them. The Australians and New Zealanders were treated benevolently by the mother country, to whom they were unswervingly loyal through two wars. The twentieth-century influxes of European refugees and immigrants, sometimes brilliant intellectuals and scientists, had a stimulating effect as it did in the United States.

Australian cities developed a distinctly original variation in the relation of city and suburb with federal and state government. The federal (com-monwealth) government takes responsibility for costly services such as police, fire, transport, welfare and education. This may make possible a fairer distribution of resources between urban, suburban or rural areas. New York city would certainly have fared better, but not all problems would have been solved.

Sydney is Australia's largest city, capital of the state of New South

Wales, which has an area of 802,000 square kilometres and a population of 5.3 million. The official reports and guidebooks show Sydney with a population of 3.3 million in 344 square miles. Enquiry reveals that the city of Sydney actually has a population of less than 50,000. Like other metropolitan cities it has been losing population, from 95,789 in 1861 to 61,940 in 1971. It is surrounded by extensive suburban areas, organized into twenty-seven municipalities.

Adelaide is capital city of the state of South Australia, which has a population of 1,331,000 (1981) in 984,000 square kilometres. Adelaide's population is given as 952,700. However, the city of Adelaide, with its lord mayor and lady mayoress, aldermen and councillors, has a population of 12,656 in 1,520 hectares, more than half of it parks and squares. The boundaries of urban jurisdictions are determined by state governments.

The Sydney of 3.3 million and the Adelaide of 952,700 have no legal existence. The two cities have no control over and no official relation to the dozens of municipalities around them, which are totally independent, democratically governed entities, though all popularly referred to as Sydney and Adelaide respectively. They have to be recognized as metropolitan Sydney and Adelaide, though having no legal existence. There are hardly any urban concentrations or settlements of any significant size in the whole state of South Australia outside metropolitan Adelaide. But there is considerable and inevitable overlap between the overall control of the city of Adelaide, metropolitan Adelaide and of South Australia itself. All the most important institutions are concentrated in the tiny city of Adelaide and all important people of the state either live or work there. Till recently it was said that the city of Adelaide (and perhaps the state itself) was ruled from the Adelaide club, where decisions had already been worked out before they came to the formal decision-making body of the city council. Comparable situations exist in all the important cities of Australia, which are all state capitals, with the federal capital at Canberra.

Despite its tiny population and small area, the city of Adelaide gives the authentic impression of a metropolis. It has the cluster of high-rise buildings, which stands out from the plain, the only such cluster in the state except the seacoast resort of Glenelg where the initial pre-Adelaide settlement was. It has all the appurtenances of a metropolis, state government and parliament, as well as city government, theatres, cathedrals and churches, banks, hotels, stores, shopping malls and arcades, restaurants, university, medical school and teaching hospital, museums, art galleries, markets, grassy tree lined squares and red light district. It is a swinging place (doubtless Sydney would claim pre-eminence), advertising many female escort agencies with twenty-four-hour service for 'home, motel or hotel', 'all fantasies, tastes and functions catered for', strippers, topless waitresses, 'male escorts, transvestites and trans-sexuals available'.

Melbourne, Sydney's rival, noted as conservative financial centre, follows the same pattern, the metropolitan area having 2.38 million people and the city of Melbourne 75,000. Melbourne was capital of the Commonwealth of Australia from 1901 to 1927 when the new federal capital of Canberra superseded it.

The Second World experiment

The greatest experiment in progressive social change since the capitalist transformation was that of the Soviet Union, transmitted to China, eastern Europe and elsewhere, whose revolutionary dynamic deteriorated from initial euphoria to increasing violence and the horrendous massacres and inquisitions of the 1930s, making it a totally unacceptable model. The largest part of it was colonial until 1917 and is Third World today. Its material achievements were great, creating a new urban industrial system and, as master builder of all time, tripling the number of houses in twenty post-war years as population only doubled (Ward, 1976:77–8).

Between 1945 and 1965 the number of residential units tripled, while population only doubled. Yet gigantic efforts barely provided six square metres per person and only a quarter to a third had piped water, sewerage and central heating. Urban and suburban accommodation was in huge, drab, pre-fabricated apartment blocks of the type abandoned in Euro-America.

Control of urban growth was a key priority, but Moscow proved uncontrollable, soon exceeding its limit of 5 million, and revised limits of 7.5 then 8.5 million, within an eight-mile radius, surrounded by a motorway and greenbelt, with 15 million suburban population spreading thirty or forty miles out. There could be no suburbs in the sense of low density estates of privately built family homes in voluntarily organized communities. Urban planning was understandably pragmatic and its major goals were not achieved. They were stated as dogma: the city will be eliminated as a distinct spacial form (as the capitalist system is inexorably doing), achievement taking the form of ideological necessity, as with the 'withering away of the state'. The achievement of Soviet eastern Europe is wryly characterized as 'the longest and most painful way from capitalism to capitalism' (Szelenyi, 1993:61). The aphorism can be shared by the former Soviet Union, and perhaps by China too, which continues the experiment, without demonstrating any convincing new urban beauties or innovation beyond those of 800 years ago. The degenerate nineteenth-century state provided major capitalist nations with grand profits in the treaty ports, customs and railway concessions.

The most original contribution in urban political economy within the Second World was that of Yugoslavia, which broke free of Soviet tutelage. Events have deprived it of attention or respect, but it was impressive, though brief, so that the urban implications could not be fully worked out. Single men still lived in barracks four to a room, or in more spacious bachelor hotels for $3.20 per month. They were still migrants tied to village homes and families. But urban zoning transcended class. Workers and managers could be living under the same roof. Enterprises were administered by their working staff, electing unpaid workers' councils by secret ballot, which hired, fired, disciplined, decided wages and budgets, chose the executive management board and could remove directors. From 1953 to 1959 GNP rose 10.4% per annum and wages rose faster than productivity, unwisely, but showing genuine workers' control. The value of all economic activity in 1970 was twice that of 1960. All was swept away by gathering ethnic strife and civil war, but it was the most fruitful innovative large-scale experiment in economic organization this century and will surely have to be revised and repeated.

Newly industrializing countries

Korea possessed the Sinic factor of peasant masses millennially inured to unremitting toil and routinized *yang-yin*, with ruling elites skilled at regretful exploitation, accentuated by the harshness of Japanese colonialism, creating an imitative love–hate relationship in which they 'cannot get over their respect for authority'. The Korean war cleared virgin economic and institutional space for constructing capitalism, just as World War II and the devastation of defeat prepared the Japanese and German peoples to recreate the most efficient and productive capitalist economies. Korea and Japan, together with Taiwan, had to become Far Eastern redoubts of the United States against Communism and primary beneficiaries of American and United States financing and protection, which pumped in more than 5 billion dollars between 1948 and 1971. Korean post-war civil-military dictatorship efficiently planned the growth economy, using peasant masses to feed the growing industrial labour force.

Extraordinary entrepreneurial prodigies broke through. The Hyundai patriarch Chang Ju Yung (CJY) left home against his father's wishes. He wanted to go to the city to avoid extreme poverty. Average income was only $60 a year. You worked fifteen to sixteen hours a day with still not enough to eat. He began repairing cars, worked as a stevedore in Inchon and Seoul, carrying stones on his back to build Korea University. He pieced cars together from junk and formed Hyundai construction in 1947. His brother was interpreter to Americans, trying to channel American projects, making airbases with only horsecart transport. CJY's brothers and brother-in-law would do anything. They achieved miraculous success with farmboy workers, anything done wrong being done again congenially (Kirk, 1994). Korea industrialized so late, so fast, it could pick up the heavy industry abandoned by others, with their long hours of low paid, disciplined labour, without unions, minimum wage, or benefits.

Confucianist one man rule in state and economy was widely accepted, with instinctive homage to the man at the top. CJY's sons worked in the firm with abject obedience. All breakfasted together daily, none dared miss. The government planning board experts, combining Korean CIA and FBI, ran the economy under Park Chung Hee, who with the army and Hyundai favoured one another for twenty years. Government borrowed from USAID and funded Hyundai cement (Kirk, 1994). Tariffs protected the giant *chaebol* monopolies, reminiscent of the Japanese *zaibatsu*. There were sixty-one with assets over 500 million dollars each, all with one man at the top. The top ten produce 77.3% of GNP, the top fifty 97.4%. The families own 46.9% of the equity and occupy 75% of the chief executive and managing director positions. Founders hold 65.65% of Hyundai, 58.3% of Samsung, 48.8% of Daewoo and 39.7% of Lucky Goldstar. None can own more than 8% of a bank. The government controls banks. The *chaebol* bargain with the plan what each should do. Hyundai industries generated a city of nearly a million people at Ulsan and Seoul expects a population of some 12 million in AD 2000.

Korea shows the way the NICs, with adequate cultural, human and material resources in favourable conjunctures, could break through the sound barrier of traditional poverty into self-sustaining urban growth, by expanding so fast as to reach a plausible opening middle-class standard, sufficient to encourage transition from the goal of generational quantity to that of generational quality before rapidly rising population could choke them. It appears that Korea and Taiwan have been able to do this in comparably similar ways, as Japan was able to in the first half of the century. We may say, in shorthand, that these countries were able to do it through the Sinic factor which generates cultural capital with a potency lasting several generations, as the White dominions were able to by the Anglo-Saxon factor. Hong Kong and Singapore also achieved it through the Sinic factor, in exceptional conjunctures whereby, as highly concentrated latter-day city-states, they were able to fashion a new role as specialized supranational commercial and financial brokers to the globe. It is not clear that any other Third World country will be able to do this.

Plate 6 Hong Kong: On Hong Kong's spectacular topography, the towers of banks, corporations, hotels and even of poor mass housing, compose many scenes of monumental beauty.

But unforeseeable combinational conjunctures may arise. The oil-rich countries, especially those with sparse desert populations seem exempt from Third World limitations. But depending on an exhaustible resource, they must either emulate the NICs, observing the same conditions of success and changing their culture, working and consuming habits very radically, or they will revert to the situation of other Third World countries. But oil depletion could have catastrophic effects on the First World too.

The cities are the clearest gauges of the transition, marking the contrast between the metropolitan areas of developed countries, which are losing population from the centre, which lowers density as suburban density still grows and spreads, and the metropolitan areas of the less developed countries, caught the wrong side of the sound barrier with the malign combination of the traditional generational quantity goal, with improving health services. As a result, the metropolitan growth rates of the latter are outstripping those of the former, so that the very largest cities of the globe are coming to be those of the greatest poverty, viz. Mexico City and São Paulo, with 24.4 and 23.6 million expected in AD 2000, far outstripping New York, no other western metropolis even half their size. Tokyo's growth continued longer, but its authorities are determined to prevent any further expansion (Hauchler and Kennedy, 1994:115; Kiyotaka Aoyagi, personal communication). Calcutta, Bombay, Shanghai, Teheran, Jakarta and other Third World metropolis cities follow in the tracks of Mexico City and São Paulo, while the First World metropolis shrinks.

7   The transformation of the city: from the Feudal to the Capitalist mode of production, and on to the apocalypse

Chapter 7 traces the process of transformation to the Capitalist mode of production, the pitiless tyranny of the formation of capitalist labour, the factors favouring the transformation in European cities, particularly in Britain, culminating in spectacular take-off at Manchester. It shows the special place of London, the horrors of the slums and the eventual outbursts of civic pride, the reform of urban government, flowering of the bourgeoisie and hazardous progress of the working class. It portrays the urban network in Britain and post-war urban rebuilding. Paris and its history are searched and sketched for the sources of urban charm and its modern travails, the drama of the Paris Commune and the Sacré Cœur, the failures and successes in housing the urban poor in post-World War II Paris. The cultural continuity and post-war reconstruction of German cities are illustrated. Urbanization in the United States is traced from the colonial to the industrial cities, the immigrant flood to the cities, the westward expansion of cities and railways, the failure of industrial slavery; the inter-relations of urban transport, technology and class; immigrants and boss-rule, the ubiquity of violence and corruption, extreme wealth and exponential city growth. The post-World War I city scene of boom and stubborn depression is delineated, the post-World War II baby-boom and prolonged prosperity; the urban strategies of employers and workers, the dialectics of mass Black urban migration, the automobile age, ghettos and suburbs, the unfolding dynamics of suburban life, ethnicity and class, the farce of urban renewal and the difficulties of small towns. The penetration of the media is emphasized, the revolt of urban youth, social and sexual conventions overturned. Interlocking urban scourges are examined: ghettos, gangs, homicide, drugs, AIDS, crime, family breakdown and homelessness. Urban problems become globalized. Can the menace of annihilation by atomic bombs and nuclear terror, overpopulation, pollution, global warming and destruction of the vital environment – can these mortal threats coerce and bully us into a new morality, for the sake of our own survival, reconciling obscene wealth and dire poverty by humane redistribution? Inexorable struggle bars our way to achieving the transcendent city.

BRITAIN

Cities and capitalism: commercial and colonial

The transformation to the Capitalist mode of production resulted from deep and prolonged changes in the forces and relations of production and

306

their interaction, just as did the previous transformations, accompanied by new types of city and forms of urban life. The capitalist transformation, like the others, was long and jerky. Capital accumulation in multifarious forms, from cattle to cash, has appeared from time immemorial, but as a major aspect and goal of human endeavour and central mechanism of economic life it is recent, generated from the increasing attribution of a money price to every human product, quality, act and thought (Braudel, 1985, III:536–42).

The first emphasis was commercial: mobilizing, collecting, exchanging, distributing and concentrating wealth in the great mercantile, seafaring cities: Venice, Genoa, Antwerp, Amsterdam, which blossomed out of the later phase of the contradictory, antagonistic Feudal mode of production. They reached their limits and passed the torch to other cities, better backed by powerful territorial states, with variegated empires, above all London. The colonial cities of the empire marshalled very great accumulations of wealth in their metropoles. It was certainly an invitation to further forms of activity, supporting larger, more educated and enquiring ruling classes, as well as the great corps of merchants themselves, with their seamen, clerks, administering consuls and proconsuls, venturing, learning, governing (fighting, killing, oppressing, exploiting), in a tremendously intense abundance of potentiality.

The Iberians were not ready for advantageous use of the knowledge and wealth they found and plundered. They had to pass it on. Two hundred years later the British were ready. Few networks of kinship, friendship or locality, high and low, were entirely unaffected in this small, seagirt country, whereas in France, larger and more intrinsically powerful, this influence was ineffectively dispersed and dissipated in the land-based concerns of the nation (Braudel, 1985, III:50, 315–25). All other countries were initially disqualified by their lack of predisposing advantages, except from secondary competition and emulation. They also suffered from Europe's wars all through the eighteenth century, culminating in the French Revolution and Napoleon's continent-wide campaigns, which Britain escaped. But Britain also eventually suffered from coming first.

In the transition from the Feudal to the Capitalist mode of production, accumulation from the profits of industry overtook that from trade and exchange. Manchester overtook Amsterdam. At a much later stage in the information age, the distinction would become blurred, as the exchange of information became the dominant form of production. While critical developments thus occur in global contexts, and spread in time and space, they interact dynamically with local conditions, from which dialectic new configurations emerge, as in the American suburb.

Capitalist industrial cities appeared in Britain, Germany, America,

Plate 7 Les Minguettes: the demolition of Les Minguettes in Greater Lyons dramatizes the end of the era of high-rise houses for the poor in the west, whether France, Britain or the United States, as in the blowing up of Pruitt-Igoe in St Louis.

France, Brazil, South Africa, India, or China, recognizably the same in part (all began belching smoke), yet diverging increasingly in appearance, long-term dynamic trajectories and effect. The urban growth which they fuelled likewise varied in quality, behaviour, beauty and horror, political and religious implications: inner cities and ghettos; industrial cities, factory towns, company towns, garden cities, suburbs of contrasting variety; slum tenements, back-to-back houses, *favelas*, *barriadas*, *bustees* and *chawls*; villas, cottages, terraces and towers; Pruitt-Igoe and Les Minguettes. The process was structured by the counterpoint of business cycles and wars. Wars devastate some, stimulate others, often in sequence (Braudel, 1985, III:609–13).

Capitalist labour

In the genesis of the Capitalist mode of production no prerequisite was more indispensable than the adequate supply of suitable labour power. This was the pure power of labour freed from all forms of property or support, helplessly dependent on capitalist wages. The development of such abjectly free labour had in fact been in preparation in western Europe for centuries as though by predestination. The major element in this preparation was the constant hounding of the poor in ever reiterated policies of savage oppression couched in moralistic purpose. Major historical events (plagues, wars, Reformation and suppression of monasteries, man-made or acts of God) all became providential instruments to this process of relentless humbling and chastening. The state was there to preserve inequality, the cornerstone of the social order, with culture and its spokesmen preaching resignation to one's lot. The peasant commune was in perpetual conflict with its oppressors: the state, the landlord, external circumstances, hard times, marauding troops, struggling to protect the village commune 'which was the condition of its liberty'. Driven beyond endurance, the peasants rose up repeatedly in violent insurrection, but their 'furious outbursts regularly failed'; to rebel was 'to spit in the sky' (Braudel, 1985, II:495). States, nobles, bourgeois property owners, even the church and certainly the towns were almost constantly in league against the peasant. The entire world of labour was caught in a vice between low wages and the threat of incurable unemployment, from which it could only break out by violence, but was powerless to succeed against the implacable force of the means of coercion: surveillance, repression, imprisonment and even execution. The town unrelentingly supported the privileged class. The enormous sub-proletariat itself constituted a brake on social unrest. The great division between town and countryside that took place in the eleventh to twelfth centuries had left a

Plate 8 Grozny: the unspeakable plight of the Chechen of Grozny speaks of the continuing, uncertain, always bloody struggle for transformation of the former Soviet peoples. It also speaks of the unspeakable devastation of so many cities in Europe, America, Africa and Asia by civil wars and violent upheavals.

permanent mass of unfortunates unprovided for in the hell of pauperdom, beggardom, vagrancy. In town they were rounded up and expelled, driven out in their vermin ridden rags.

The numbers were staggering and caused terror: 6,000 or more at Venice in 1547; 17,000 at the walls of Paris in 1587; 10,000 permanently in eighteenth-century Lisbon, despite shipments to the faraway penitentiary at Goa. In Stuart England (seventeenth century) from a quarter to a half the population was below the poverty line, in eighteenth-century Cologne the same. In Lille over 20,000 were on permanent aid, in Cracow 30%. The English parliament decided on slavery for vagrancy in 1547 but revoked it because they could not agree on ownership. In Genoa the workhouse closed in 1710, choked with corpses. Paris had 91,000 of no fixed abode in 1776. This was only the fringe of the problem, as vast numbers were absorbed to superfluity in the armies and in domestic service. In sixteenth-century Lyons 19–26% were servants. In 1754 Paris had about a million people (and 12,000 carriages), 200,000 being servants. Besides, many escaped altogether to organize bands of criminals, gangs of bandits whose leaders were often noblemen, and pirates based on cities such as Algiers, Tripoli, Pisa, Valetta, Segna. The 'excrement of cities' could become useful thugs as instruments of power, helping to suppress their fellows. This is hardly the making of a trained, disciplined industrial labour force. That came later. But it did ensure a certain docile adaptability and helpless destitution without choice, unable to refuse the longest hours and the worst conditions, which served well enough at first. The horrors of the industrial revolution seem more bearable against the aimless barbarities. The Capitalist mode of production brought a new sense of meaning and purpose (Braudel, 1985, II:493–508).

In England some additional eventualities swelled the hordes of the poor. With recovery from the disruptions of the Black Death, the emergence of a new nobility after the Wars of the Roses and an efficient restored monarchy, the country was ready to break out of the restrictions of feudal life. More money-minded nobles got together and simply drove 'emancipated' peasants off their lands to make sheep walks for more profitable wool, also disbanding and expelling all the surplus retainers from their mansions. The old proportion of one acre pasture to two to four acres arable steadily rose until three acres pasture to one of arable was considered best, matched by the expulsion of peasants, razing of cottages, enclosures of commons. Suppression of monasteries in the mid-sixteenth century produced a new flood of landless, workless people. Queen Elizabeth found paupers everywhere.

Ruling-class determination to subjugate and exploit labour was primordial. The Statute of Labourers in 1349 already aimed at lengthening the working day and restricting wages. Exceeding the maximum wage met harsh penalties, but twice as severe for the employee as for the employer. From 1530 poverty and vagrancy were criminalized. Bloody beatings at the cart tail culminated in hanging for the third offence. Ears were sliced, hair shaved, head or back branded. Under Edward VI the accuser of a caught vagrant received him as a slave, whipped, branded, chained and finally executed for attempts at escape. Subsidized pauper labour was provided through the workhouse.

Suppression of the Stuart uprising in Scotland was followed by the depopulation of the highlands. Peasants were again driven out for the sake of sheep and finally even they were displaced by wild deer for the cultivated pleasure of super rich aristocrats and their big business recruits. The destitutes were forbidden to emigrate, expected to drift to Glasgow and the manufacturing towns (Marx, 1967:235–45, 255–77).

Aspects of the conjuncture

The culminating transformation of the mode of production in the eighteenth century was the outcome of long unfolding processes: the relative freedom of the medieval and Renaissance European cities, which despite their restrictive guild practices showed the way to economic freedom; the rising productivity of British agriculture, under its more innovative and commercially minded landowners, accompanied by their enclosure of land and movement of surplus population out of the countryside to search for new employment; the improvement of internal communications and facilitation of trade by hard surfaced roads, iron bridges and the building of extensive canal networks; the growing supremacy of England on the seas, a vast empire of ready markets and vital resources, with immunity from the wounds of European land wars and revolutions, leading to a general mood of security and confidence.

Britain could live in greater social order and peace, developing both local and national institutions in greater harmony, despite rotten urban boroughs, 'Peterloo' outbreaks and the suffering of the oppressed poor. Already half a millennium of constitutional development, in the parliamentary direction, had encouraged an extension of the sense of capacity to undertake projects and develop enterprises, as opportunity offered, with less fear than elsewhere of interference or naked plunder by higher authorities and the state. While French or Spanish grandees were encouraged to waste more wealth than they possessed, in glorification and frivolity, or even in disgust to retire and vegetate on stagnant rural properties, the British landed elite and much of the bourgeoisie were freer to develop in more varied directions. Command of the seas and vast territories from which more and more wealth was being extracted, as well as slaves, made them rather buoyant and expansive during the eighteenth century. This does not explain, nothing can (Braudel, 1985, III:ch. 6), but it renders intelligible and meaningful the crescendo of technical inventions, most small, almost obvious, some dramatic, but all together decisive, which suddenly began to build on to and out of the accumulated wealth of commercial capitalism its new, revolutionary, industrial phase, which would roll on to become globally dominant to an unprecedented degree and lead ultimately to the post-industrial, financially driven, computer directed, information media age.

Britain had enjoyed 200 years of fairly continuous economic growth, with an exceptional run of good harvests early in the eighteenth century, so that the rural population was no longer either a peasantry or self-subsistent. Ample coal and iron supplies, the moist Lancashire climate favourable to cotton threads (the most amenable of all textiles to machinery), cheap river and sea transport, intelligently complemented by canals, which would cut the cost of all other contemporary forms of transport by 80%, were all helpful factors, none of them explanatory by themselves since all were present elsewhere without similar results, but only England had them all in momentary optimal combination. Moist climates were common, the great Silesian coal fields produced no industrialization till much later, Roman Catholic Belgium industrialized before Protestant Holland. As in all great transformations in mode of production it was the ripe complementarity of numerous reinforcing factors which was critical.

British society had already diverged from the European model through its deep shake-up in the bourgeois revolution of the seventeenth century (building on the thorough purging of the Wars of the Roses) which no other country shared. British grandees were no longer like their continental counterparts. Even a medium junker had more servants and dependants, for the British had become committed to profit rather than to war or ostentation. They made money commercially and militantly, making war and peace for profit, capturing markets and establishing productive colonies.

Although retailing and polluting industries had low status, merchants had long been able to buy their way into the nobility if they were rich enough. So the eighteenth-century upper class was neither closed nor stagnant, and if any were truly disdainful of trade and industry, other than as a pose, it was probably the lesser backwoods rural squires who were out of touch with the times (those who had not made their fortunes in India), or the more status-aspiring upper bourgeoisie of the cities already irrevocably tainted anyhow. The aristocracy was fully alive to realizing the profits of improved agriculture and land rents, coal mines, canals, toll roads, railways and the increased value from building a new London with stately squares and residential terraces on their West End properties.

Population had been static at about 5 million from the seventeenth century till around 1740 when it began to rise, from a falling mortality rate – after the lethal excesses of cheap London gin (Trevelyan, 1945:341–3; Briggs, 1968:19). After 1770 it began to rise really fast, although there were no really significant medical improvements till the 1850s, doubling from 1780 to 1840 and doubling again from 1840 to 1900. The rise from 1770 began before anyone was aware of an industrial revolution, but it did provide an expanding home market and a necessary extra and cheaper industrial labour force, though in other circumstances population growth can stifle and kill development, as the Third World is finding today.

Flour milling, brewing, coal mining, iron pots and pans, nails, stoves, ploughs, horseshoes and wheel rims constituted industries already stimulated technically by the expanding eighteenth-century market. Iron production rose from less than 50,000 tons in 1720 to about 100,000 in 1788, but for its spectacular rise it had to wait for the demand of industrial and above all textile machinery, armaments for the Napoleonic Wars and the railways.

While the home market grew slowly, the export market was vastly more expandable. The change was most dramatic in the case of cotton cloth, since it had been woollen fabrics which for centuries had been the mainstay of British exports, while most cotton had actually been imported, a great deal of it from India. Exports of woollen goods had even fallen from the 1750s and the cotton trade was still uncertain. Overall production for the home market had risen 7% from 1700 to 1750 and again by 7% from 1750 to 1770. But exports had risen by 76% and 80% in these two periods respectively. It was this latter sudden twenty-year growth, mainly in textiles, especially cotton and mainly for export, which seemed to form the spark igniting the revolution. Exports of cotton cloth multiplied more than a hundred times from 1760 to reach their level of £22 million in 1815. Imports of raw cotton rose from less than £5 million in 1775 (mostly from the orient, some from the West Indies) to £12 million already by 1782, £33 million in 1790, mostly from the West Indies, and £140 million in 1820, nearly half from the United States, so closely was the economic growth of America linked to Britain's industrial revolution.

The production of iron goods was vital to this expansion in a much more diverse way, for making the engines and the new machines, the railroad tracks and bridges, as well as expanding the enormous variety of tools and weapons, not to mention the multitudinous metal trinkets sent from Birmingham all over the increasingly British world market. Pig iron production, which had progressed little for over a century, leapt up more than thirty times, from 30,000 tons in 1760 to 1 million tons in 1800, including 60,000 tons exported. This reflected, stimulated and depended upon cumulative innovations from the early eighteenth century reaching a crescendo in its last quarter, with the development of steam power applied first to the spinning jennies just devised and later to the cotton looms themselves, with parallel innovations in iron production. From 1772 to 1798 British exports to India and to the United States doubled, despite the War of Independence, while those to the West Indies quadrupled. From 1814 to 1832 the export of cotton piece goods to countries east of the Cape of Good Hope (but excluding China and Japan) rose from 800,000 to 57,000,000 yards (Redford, 1934–56, II:112). Thus the availability of the imperial raw materials and the imperial market, with the spurt in textile production, accelerated by mechanical innovation, leading to a transformation of the general infrastructure and especially transport, demanding a huge expansion of coal and iron production, all began to spin together into a fantastic, self-stimulating growth spiral for the first time in human history.

Take-off and spectacular growth

To choose one particular moment, it was, perhaps, when the duke of Bridgewater, typical of those commercially minded aristocrats, linked his coal pits to Manchester by canal in 1762, and when Manchester was further linked by canal to the port of Liverpool in 1776, that the chain reaction began, and the urban industrial revolution was bound to be centred first and foremost on Manchester.

Manchester was only a market town of 10,000 people in 1771, but reached 40,000 in the 1780s, over 70,000 in 1801 and 300,000 in 1851. The first real factories for cotton milling came in the 1780s and by 1800 Manchester was said to be steam mill mad. By 1830 it had ninety-nine mills. The madness spread like wildfire and neighbouring Bradford, known as Worstedopolis (Briggs, 1968:140), which had only one mill in 1801, had sixty-seven by 1841. Birmingham grew from 15,000 people at the end of the seventeenth century to 70,000 at the end of the eighteenth century. Liverpool, the port of Manchester, which had like Bristol for centuries already profited from the West Africa–West Indies triangular trade in manufactured goods for slaves, sugar and spices, similarly rose from 15,000 in 1730 to 78,000 in 1801. London had also doubled to 1 million in 1800 from 1700.

What happened in Manchester and Birmingham was revolutionary from the point of view of urban development, not only because of their dramatic speed of growth, but because they grew from virtually new roots and developed new, unprecedented types of urban social structure. True, Manchester had had its annual fair, its corn and fulling mills and its borough charter for over 400 years, and it had exported woollen cloth through London to Europe in the sixteenth century, and in the seventeenth invented the fustian cloth with a linen warp and *cotton* weft, which really set it on the road to a cotton industry, but it was not one of those great European merchant cities which had won their freedom from local barons and developed their own law, currency, representative institutions and city-state policy. Despite its charter it had no proper urban government of its own, was administered by an antiquated annual court leet under the steward of the lord of the manor and was actually subordinate to Salford, the capital manor of the hundred, with an earlier borough charter, which was just on the other bank of the Irwell river from Manchester and was immediately enveloped by the latter's industrial growth, whereupon the little river between them is said to have become a flood of liquid manure (Briggs, 1968:29). In fact the arrival of Flemish weavers in Salford during the fourteenth century probably marks the beginning of textile manufacture in the area, and Salford anomalously retained its administrative distinctness until 1972.

Manchester established a police force in 1792 and won an elected council in 1838. It symbolically and progressively superseded and over-shadowed Salford in its canals and docks, chamber of commerce, stock exchange, bishopric, museum, football team, university, airport and plethora of distinctive institutions.

Birmingham, likewise, had long been pre-eminent in the production and export of metal and firearms on a small scale but in the eighteenth century it nurtured a cluster of brilliant men, such as James Watt, Matthew Boulton and William Murdock who invented and developed the steam engine and its own revolutionary applications, Joseph Priestley the chemist, James Baskerville the printer, all integrating innovative genius, scholarship, science, engineering and industrial development, just as later on in the nineteenth century Joseph Chamberlain's urban reforms not only increased its general prosperity but brought Birmingham civic fame throughout the world.

With rapid attainment of great wealth by self-made men like Arkwright and the Peels, the new towns established the wealth and supremacy of the manufacturer over the merchant, who in all previous ages had outclassed the manufacturer (formerly the artificer, artisan and craftsman). This had still been the case in 1760 on the very eve of the revolution, when it was estimated that while 13,000 merchants, 7,500 retailers and 2,500 manufacturers had annual incomes over £200, only 100 merchants and *no* manufacturers had incomes over £600, though 150 noble landowners realized over £6,000 per annum (Hobsbawm, 1968:17).

The Manchester cotton industry lent itself to the formation of large enterprises, so that the new phenomenon of the exploiting capitalist owner of the means of production appeared in particularly stark contrast to the worker. In Birmingham the metal foundries remained much smaller and the relationship between master and men correspondingly closer.

The extraordinary fact that all raw cotton was imported while nearly all manufactured cotton cloth was exported sufficiently demonstrates the intimate connection between the industrial revolution and the British Empire. Great Britain was able to destroy much of the competition of rival nations and to capture their markets, as well as capturing or buying millions of African slaves to work on plantations to produce the raw materials for British industry. By the various European nations probably less than 1 million Africans were sold to the Americas in the sixteenth century, 3 million in the seventeenth and 7 million in the eighteenth century. By that time it was becoming more profitable for Britain to move to the next phase in which colonial raw materials would be as well or better produced by legally free but independent individuals. India, which had produced a huge part of all the handwoven cotton which entered into world trade, and most of that used by British overseas merchants themselves, and which was still recognized as of higher quality than British manufactured cloth, was deindustrialized under pressure of colonial administration and fiscal and tariff discrimination. The Indians were condemned instead to produce the raw cotton for British mills to export back to them. It took the Indian businessmen of the great textile city of Ahmedabad just a century to recover sufficiently from the eclipse of handwoven cloth to build their own mills with machinery and technical assistance from Britain. By then the sale of machinery was an interest strong enough to compete with the rival cloth export interests of Manchester.

The British navy tripled in size during the eighteenth century, demanding massive manufacture of guns and accompanying technological improvements. The great industrializer of the iron industry, Henry Cort, had risen as an agent of the navy and Henry Maudslay, the machine tool innovator, gained his experience at Woolwich arsenal. Britain was able to attain a supremacy which itself prevented others following for at least half a century. Indeed it seems likely that the breakthrough of the first industrial revolution could only have been achieved by one nation alone with these multiple and partly fortuitous advantages.

Other European nations were also endowed with many of the enabling factors, as well as the United States and in its own strikingly different way Japan after the Meiji Restoration of 1868. So Britain faced ever fiercer competition during the second half of the nineteenth century and in the twentieth. After pioneering so many winning industries it could be said by the 1950s that there was no single British industry superior to its European, American or Japanese competitor.

While Manchester and Birmingham were the most important cities in the initial industrial revolution, dozens of other cities in the industrial north of England made significant contributions. All were operating within the same general context of factors, but with particular local combinations and situations. Birmingham and Sheffield show a striking contrast, although both were metal towns (Briggs, 1968:36–7). The example of Sheffield demonstrates what very long-term processes established those strongly set values, principles and relationships – urban culture and social structure – which have conditioned a town's reaction to changing situations and opportunities, determining the shape which it has taken, even in the modern age.

Sheffield had a charter, as a tiny market town, from its local lord of the manor, in 1296, which freed it from feudal services and tolls for an annual payment of £3–8–9 1/4 in silver, but still left it otherwise under manorial government until the nineteenth century (Walton, 1952:32). Sheffield cutlery already receives special mention in the fourteenth century, but there were many cutlery centres then, and the greatest were London and York. Sheffield's advantage was to have local material for making grind-stones, plenty of wood, coal and iron, with plenty of little streams falling into the Don valley where it lay. It had its first industrial revolution, which in many ways shaped its second, in the late fifteenth century, when the streams were harnessed to water wheels for grinding blades. Apparently, water wheels had long been used for grinding corn, but no one thought of applying them to other uses. The idea of grinding blades and tools seems to have reached Sheffield from Germany (Walton, 1952:39), where metal industry was already much more highly developed in cities such as Nuremberg.

The first industrial revolution put Sheffield ahead of all its English competitors except London. In the late sixteenth century Sheffield merchants successfully defied their London rivals in selling their wares in the capital. All the lord mayor was able to do was to confine their shops to the Minories, near Leadenhall Street. In 1624, with the help of a knight of the shire in parliament, an act was passed establishing Sheffield's Company of Cutlers, with a master, two wardens, six searchers (of faulty workmanship), twenty-four assistants and a commonalty of master cutlers. Although they were supposed to be elected annually, these thirty-three officers became in effect the company, making and enforcing all rules and decisions, depriving the ordinary cutlers of any power in the organization. However, the company built its own stone hall and held an annual feast.

Seventeenth-century Sheffield consisted of two streets with a dozen or so lanes off them. Most of the houses were thatched, each separate and many with their own gardens and orchards. The town had a population of about 5,000 and half the men were employed in the cutlery trade. Even minor gentry sent their sons to be apprenticed and the pre-eminence of Sheffield was recognized by London. However, the wealthiest cutlers lived outside in the country and were often farmers at the same time. In the Civil War the town supported the Roundheads and became more independent of its lord, who was a royalist. Despite harassment and imprisonment, a Dissenting Chapel was established and nonconformists became a powerful element.

Cumulative innovations began on the eve, but distinctly before, the

industrial revolution. In 1726 the merchants got an act passed to establish
a company which made the Don navigable right up to Sheffield, bringing
the rather isolated valley into much closer and cheaper touch with both
English and foreign markets. A new town hall was built, with the lord of
the manor still bearing half the cost with the burgesses, but its predecessor had been entirely manorial. In 1712 a reservoir was made and in
1737 a chain of dams was constructed, not only controlling the water
power, but bringing piped water to the town. In 1743 Thomas Boulsover
invented the process of plating copper with silver. He only made buttons –
which had a large market with the gentry and the army – but silver plating
became an important and exclusive Sheffield specialization for nearly a
century – until killed by electro-plate – making dishes and teapots, boxes
for snuff, tobacco and money, all with a large foreign market. The Quaker
Benjamin Huntsman, of Dutch extraction, who had been a clockmaker in
nearby Doncaster, moved to Sheffield and invented the improved process
of making crucible steel, but the conservative cutlers failed to adopt the
process until the 1760s after serious competition from French cutlery
made from crucible steel.

Thus Sheffield had a highly specialized metal industry before the
industrial revolution of steam power and large factories. Steam power was
not applied to Sheffield's grinding mills till 1786 and did not overtake
water till 1794 and the grinding process still remained the same. Yet
Newcomen's steam engine had been used nearby to pump out coal mines
since the 1720s. A colliery railway brought coal into Sheffield from 1774,
but it was not linked to the outside world by rail till 1840. The precocity of
Sheffield's long, cumulative industrial development and the renown of its
workmanship somewhat dampened the shock of the industrial revolution
and induced a parochial complacency. But the new big firms like John
Brown's, Firth's, Cammell's and Vickers began to dominate Sheffield,
though many of the old and smaller firms continued. The independent
cutler of former times had sunk to the level of a wage earner by the end of
the eighteenth century and there were serious strikes over wages in 1777,
1787, 1790, 1796.

The crucial difference which made Sheffield development and its
urban way of life contrast with those of Birmingham was that it was a
much more isolated and smaller town, less than half the size of
Birmingham in 1800. Its products were much more specialized than
Birmingham's vast variety. Its most profitable silver plate was cut off from
its main European market by the Napoleonic Wars, while the colonial
outlets of Birmingham and Manchester were little affected and new
markets were won. The small firm of master and apprentices was typical
of both towns till the nineteenth century, but the ordinary Sheffield cutler

was much less fortunate. He was better off, as a skilled craftsman, than ordinary industrial workers, yet he was strangely impoverished, isolated and conservative, inhibited by the once innovative but now archaic and autocratic Cutlers' Company.

The merchants were a separate class and many of them wealthy, though the most successful followed the usual process of turning themselves into gentry. Though many of the big steel magnates of the mid-nineteenth century were local men made good, and prided themselves on the common touch, they were also drawn into major interests outside Sheffield and the kind of solidarity between workers and wealthy businessmen, which so distinguished Birmingham, never developed in Sheffield. It eventually got most of the institutions which expressed civic pride elsewhere, but rather later than in Birmingham or Manchester. A subscription library was formed in 1871, some streets straightened in 1875, and the High Street widened in 1895. The new town hall was opened, as customarily, by Queen Victoria in 1897, and Sheffield was at last made the seat of a bishop in 1914. The Corporation acquired the Water Supply Company in 1887 and that for electricity in 1898, running electric trams from 1899. There were no grandiose or imaginative projects of the kind with which Joseph Chamberlain glorified Birmingham.

London

Because of trade and profits of the empire, London was already expanding markedly by the eighteenth century. Some great landowners built well-planned squares, streets and fine rows of houses west of the City wall, while east of the City the ever increasing shipping, loading and unloading attracted a shifting population of labourers and desperate poor. The population of inner London reached a million early in the nineteenth century. It had lost supremacy in textiles, shipbuilding, metals and chemicals to more specialized cities like Manchester, Birmingham and Glasgow, but central London grew to a colossus of 2.5 million by the 1840s, 3 million by the sixties and 4.5 million by 1900 with a vast growth of suburbs in all directions. It retained its pre-eminence as the greatest port, political, financial and cultural capital, with the greatest and most varied concentration of commercial, light industrial and ever proliferating service activities. This centralization multiplied its power a hundred times. Within the central area of the future county of London lay the ancient square mile of the City, anachronistic in its medieval guild government and pageantry, no longer a residential area, declining in population from 1851, but still housing the financial and commercial operations of the most potent and wealthy elite group in the nation as a whole. Yet it contributed nothing organizationally to the much larger urban area of which it was a part. Lord Brougham confidently assumed in 1848 that the City of London would be reformed within a few months, but it was another forty years before London as a whole would receive a modern government, and even then the City was excluded from it.

The population of London declined from 1901 and outer London by 1951, as the peak population of 8.3 million fell back towards 7 million over the next twenty years, while the population of the south-east region as a whole, London's commuting area, reached 17 million. It was the improving public transport system of underground electric railways from the 1890s and the motorbus services beginning before 1914, which made it possible for even the working class to live in better housing, further from the centre, reducing the extreme population pressure on inner London.

London's slums and poverty were on a scale greater than anywhere else and the exploitation of the poor quite as ruthless. The docks were the largest commercial undertaking of all. 'When the St. Katherine's Dock was built in the late 1820s, eight hundred houses were destroyed and eleven thousand people turned out into the streets' (Sinclair, 1950:245). Of the whole population of London 30% were reckoned to be in poverty. The East End was a separate world of its own, whose inhabitants never visited the West End, though there was concealed poverty there too. It was constantly remarked that the life and people of the East End were as foreign, exotic and unknown to the West End as Tahiti or Darkest Africa.

The first great urban anthropologist found 'no more imposing view' than this 'commercial capital of the world' as he came up the Thames to London Bridge, jammed with ships (Engels, 1975:328). But these were sailing ships and in 1887 he found it 'covered with ugly, sooty steamers'. Engels anticipated the 'Simmel effect' in Londoners 'forced to sacrifice the best qualities of their human nature' to achieve these marvels of civilization, 'becoming a world of impersonal atoms in mutual exploitation, all classes and ranks crowding past one another by hundreds of thousands, in callous indifference, as though they had nothing in common and were not all human beings with the same qualities and power and the same interests in being happy'.

Everywhere he was amazed how the poor were kept in immediate juxtaposition to the rich, yet discreetly concealed from them by the rows of shops along the roads where they constantly passed up and down. Twenty or thirty died of starvation during his stay. Enquiries were held, but the real causes never admitted. Far larger numbers died of sickness and malnutrition. The same appalling conditions were found everywhere: two sexes and three generations crammed in a ten-foot square room, starved and scarred with vermin bites, no change of clothes, some sleeping naked, making a hole in the floor to use as a privy. Heaps of garbage and ash in all directions, filthy streets unpaved, sometimes flooded, no gutters or sewers, full of animal and vegetable refuse, foul liquids thrown out in stagnant pools, sometimes no doors, scarcely a whole window pane, walls crumbling, doorposts and window frames loose and broken. Hundreds of thousands in narrow alleys and courts, close to the houses of the rich; the famous 'rookery' of St Giles in the midst of most populous London, surrounded by broad, splendid avenues where the gay world idles, three- or four-storey houses jammed from cellar to garret for 3 shillings weekly, making a handsome 'tribute' of £40,000 a year for the aristocratic landowner. In Edinburgh, five to six storeys, like Paris, 50,000 people tossing refuse and excrement every night, beyond the capacity of the scavengers. Children die one after another. 'An ass stood in one corner.' Chickens roost on the bedposts, dogs and horses share, swarming with vermin. Yet 'unfit to stable a horse'.

Glasgow, 78% working class, exceeding in abject wretchedness, a dunghill in each court, fifteen or twenty men and women huddled on the floor, clothed or naked, living from thieving and prostitution. In Liverpool more than 45,000 in narrow, damp, dark, badly ventilated cellars. In Birmingham more than 2,000 courts of eight to twenty dwellings each, housing most of the working class, some more recent ones 'tolerably respectable'.

The utterly homeless were even worse off, perhaps 50,000 in London, some getting beds in lodging houses for one or two pence a night, four to six beds to a room and four to six in a bed, mixing the sick and the well, young and old, drunk or sober, men and women indiscriminately, often with strife, blows and wounds, or 'worse if they agree' (Engels, 1975:336). Those without a penny sleep in passages, arcades, or parks 'close under the windows of Queen Victoria'. ' The majority are young girls who have been seduced from the country by soldiers and turned loose on the world in all the destitution of friendless penury, and all the recklessness of early vice', reported the *Times* with horror.

As Burgess decades later in Chicago, Engels accurately noted and mapped the distinctive urban ecology of Manchester, 'the classic type of a modern manufacturing town', which he knew intimately, 'as my own native town, more intimately than most of its natives know it' (Engels, 1975:345). The commercial district at the heart, about half a mile square, with offices and warehouses, no dwellers, but watchmen and police at night with dark lanterns, cut through by main throughfares concentrating vast traffic, ground level lined with brilliant shops, upper floors lively till late at night. The working-class quarters spread round this commercial district like a girdle, about one and a half miles wide. Beyond were the middle bourgeoisie in regularly laid out quarters, and the upper in remoter villas with gardens, fine comfortable homes in free wholesome country air on the breezy heights, passed every quarter or half hour by omnibuses to the city. This money aristocracy takes the shortest road, through all the labouring districts, to their businesses, without ever seeing that they are in the midst of the grimy misery that lurks left and right behind the shops in the middle and lower bourgeois stretches, hiding from the eyes of the wealthy men and women the working-class dwellings and the misery and grime which are the complement of their wealth. Southwards from the centre are mills and warehouses, then second rate shops and alehouses, then less inviting shops, beer houses and gin palaces and entirely working-class shops.

Visitors were scandalized by the appalling physical and social conditions juxtaposed with such rapid creation of wealth: homes of vice and poverty surrounding the huge palaces of industry, but an unbridgeable gulf between rich and poor, civilization working miracles but turning civilized man back into a savage. Manchester's opulent thoroughfares were cleaned weekly, secondary streets fortnightly, third-class streets monthly, but the wretched, filthy alleys and courts of the poorest, needing daily cleaning, never. Concern for the workers was denounced as 'morbid sensibility'. The poor gave more to each other than the rich gave to the poor. Adulteration of food was thought just a form of competition. Depression hit in the late thirties and early forties and the majority of workers in Manchester were unemployed or on short time in 1837, provoking fears of plunder and violence. A famous general was despatched to take command of the troops and restore bourgeois confidence. But consciences were aroused and attention drawn to critical problems long accumulated and ignored, in urban government, as well as poverty, overcrowding, sanitation and water supply, health and the danger of epidemics.

Urban horrors and civic pride

Cholera broke out at York in 1849, at Exeter in 1832 and at the port cities of Liverpool and Newcastle frequently. The power of nonconformists in the new cities meant pressure for removal of religious disabilities, while the new urban interests also demanded free trade and repeal of the corn laws. Reformers were forced to battle on the national level and extension of suffrage was inevitably a first priority for the achievement of any other goals. The industrial cities contributed much of the riots and strikes, as well as powerful political movements – the Chartists and the Anti Corn Law League – which led to the Reform Bill of 1832 and the repeal of the corn laws in 1846. It was widely recognized that if the national government was reformed, the even more inadequate city and small town governments would have to be reformed also.

A whole series of acts of parliament provided the framework within which this became possible in a wide variety of fields: the Municipal Reform Act of 1835, followed quickly by the incorporation of greater industrial cities, the Nuisance Removal Act of 1846, the Public Health Act of 1848, followed by those of 1872 and 1875, the Free Libraries Act of 1850, the Education Act of 1870, masterminded by the Bradford Quaker, Foster, the Cheap Trains Act of 1883 and the Housing of the Working Classes Act of 1890.

The crisis in urban government brought to a head by the explosive force of the new industrial cities drew attention to the contrast between three broad types of English city at the time: the industrial cities themselves and, at the other end of the spectrum, the rotten boroughs, older cities which had lost their former importance and shrunk into insignificance, providing parliamentary seats as family sinecures. In between were the older cities which managed to retain their importance, like Bristol, one of the greatest English port cities for many centuries, Liverpool, already prosperous from the slave trade more than a century before the industrial revolution, and of course London. Dozens of other small cities, now overshadowed by the new giants, carried on much as before, with reduced relative importance. Such were the more important cathedral cities, often at the same time centres of county administration and market places for their whole surrounding region: York the greatest of them, Norwich, Winchester, Exeter, Lincoln and a dozen more.

Despite the horrors of Victorian cities there was at last an outburst of effort devoted to works of civic pride (Briggs, 1968:135–231). Literary and Philosophical Societies were founded by Manchester in 1781, Newcastle in 1793, Liverpool in 1812, Leeds in 1819 and Sheffield in 1822, while Birmingham's Lunar Society, founded in 1766 before them all, failed to survive. The industrial revolution led to a greater proliferation of voluntary interest associations in the cities. It was the age of charity, a gracious expression of class differences which reduced some of the worst evils, and was a form of enlightened self-interest in the long run. Manchester was one of the most unhealthy as well as the most thriving cities in the country (Briggs, 1968:101).

Excessive hours of work, including women and children as well as men, poorly lit and ventilated factories, constant smoke pollution, extreme overcrowding in bad housing without proper sanitation or clean water, all produced very bad health and high mortality. All this was exacerbated by very heavy immigration, such as no city had learned to cope with adequately by that time. Manchester was one fifth Irish by 1840 and Liverpool, through which they all had to pass, was even more seriously invaded. As late as 1884 parts of Liverpool had densities of over 700,000 per square mile, equalling the worst of medieval and modern Cairo, or contemporary Calcutta. Like Calcutta and Bombay today, mid-nineteenth-century London is said to have had 100,000 men with nowhere to sleep, while women and children were found dead of hunger outside hotels they could not afford to enter (Briggs, 1968:86). In the 1840s the average age of death for labourers and their families in Manchester was seventeen years. This was less than half the life expectation of gentry and professionals in Manchester, or even of labourers in the county town of Rutland. Although active health measures were taken in the second half of the century, death rates did not fall significantly until after 1900. There were very energetic men of good will among the urban elites, but it is unlikely that these measures could have passed if they had not progressively extended the franchise to enable the workers to back their demands with legitimate political force, and if it had not been for the constant fear of revolution, kept alive by frequent strikes and riots, and for the growing strength of labour organization. Engels and the aristocratic 'Young Englanders' alike agreed that there never was a more 'feudal' system than that of the mills, for the influence of the factory owner 'went further than that of the Norman baron' (Briggs, 1968:93–4).

The efforts of civic pride were partly for the welfare, working strength and enlightenment of the poor, and to obviate revolutionary tendencies, but more for the glorification of the city and the city fathers whose pride was being expressed. The filthiest areas, out of sight, were never cleaned. Manchester in 1839 was described as the 'chimney of the world' and 'the entrance of hell' (Briggs, 1968:134), just as Potosi had been in the sixteenth century. But there was a long period of prosperity after 1850 and many of the working class voted Tory even with the extended franchise of 1867. The shopkeepers represented a wide range of status from working class to those who mingled with the elite, within which there was a great deal of intermarriage and mutual acquaintance.

Naturally the first spectacular civic monument was the cotton exchange, completed in 1809 and enlarged in 1838 as the largest in Europe. The Free Library was built very soon after the enabling act of 1850. The Free Trade Hall was built for £40,000 in 1856 on the site of the massacre of Peterloo. The Manchester Exhibition of 1851 was visited by the royal family and over 1,300,000 others and led to the establishment of the Halle Orchestra. The huge gothic town hall built from 1868 to 1877 cost a million pounds and was something of an anti-climax.

Bradford had built its St George's Hall in 1851, partly to demonstrate that laymen and nonconformists could provide for the moral, spiritual and cultural uplift of the people as well as the Church of England. Bradford's big neighbour and rival, Leeds, immediately began planning to build a town hall which would also serve the same ends (Bradford also built a town hall in 1873). Leeds town hall was dogged by disputes between the economy faction insisting that nothing should be built for mere ostentation that would not be useful and the culture faction dreaming of giving their 'squalid and unbeautiful town' (Briggs, 1968:162), a symbol of spiritual and cultural aspiration and achievement, proving that their interests were wider than cotton and machinery, vying with the glories of Bruges and Florence. Costs rose as they debated, architect and contractor quarrelled, until the latter went bankrupt. The hall was finished at last in 1858 for £122,000 instead of the £40,000 planned, but it was complete with its magnificent organ and controversial tower, duly opened by Queen Victoria, attended by the aristocracy of the north, as well as the city fathers.

The unusual degree of support by the Birmingham working class for upper-middle-class reform aspirations was already evident in the Birmingham Political Union of 1829. Nonconformist churches had been very influential since the seventeenth century, especially Unitarians, Congregationalists and Baptists. A new town hall was already built in 1835, after pressure from the music festival committee. Yet Birmingham languished through the mid-century with unprogressive civic government, despite its elected council, hampered by the still restricted franchise, which only replaced the former street commissioners with elected but unprogressive tradesmen. The death rate was rising rapidly from 1849 to 1853 yet the appointment of a medical officer was rejected and other services were cut for the sake of economy. Meanwhile 14,000 open middens and ashpits ran into the sewers, which discharged directly into the river Tame, until local landowners secured a court restraining order in 1858. It was against this unpromising background that the age of reform led by Joseph Chamberlain shone so brightly. He was a Unitarian and a very successful businessman of tremendous enthusiasm and drive, who organized the Liberal Association in the 1860s, like an enlightened 'machine', with a branch in every ward and a central caucus which decided on the strategy of each issue and told every branch how to vote in each election. In 1869 he was elected chairman of the Radical and Nonconformists' National Education League, whose greatest strength was Birmingham, and he was elected to the city council in the same year. He was mayor from 1873 till 1876 when he was elected a Member of Parliament for Birmingham, entering the national cabinet as President of the Board of Trade in 1880. Within the space of a few years he transformed the face of central Birmingham and many of its most vital institutions, anticipating 'urban renewal'. He took over the gas works from private interests, for the city, against the opposition of the economizing faction, modernized the plant and improved working conditions, lowered the price and showed an immediate profit.

Birmingham suffered a smallpox epidemic in 1874 and in the following year, 3,000 wells used by 60,000 people were condemned, and the death rate began to fall. In 1876 the waterworks had also been acquired for the city, against bitter opposition in the House of Lords. The new town hall and Council House, comparable to that of Leeds, and projected since 1853 when the site was acquired, had its foundation stone laid by Chamberlain in 1874 and opened in 1879. But Chamberlain's most ambitious and crowning achievement was the Improvement Scheme initiated in 1875, providing for compulsory acquisition of insanitary areas. Forty-three acres were acquired at a cost of £1,310,000. New streets occupied eight acres, greatly increasing site values, and the new main throughfare of Corporation Street, influenced in its conception by Haussmann's Paris, altered the whole topography of Birmingham (Briggs, 1968:228). Given the improved rateable values the scheme probably cost the city only £12,000 annually and although there was an economic depression from 1879 till 1885, by 1892 the accounts of the city showed a surplus. But housing was neglected, as in most other cities, despite the enabling Housing of the Working Classes Act of 1890, and critics argued that the very poor would have preferred new dwellings to the Improvement Scheme.

Chamberlain was a man of destiny in that he appeared at the perfect moment when population growth and economic expansion could make city finances buoyant through good management. His party organization had the autocratic power of a city machine, but opposition and criticism were never stifled, nor was the organization ever seriously accused of corruption. An efficient and honest urban civil service was an essential part of the civil gospel he preached. Much had been achieved, but the dynamism was never recaptured and through the twentieth century it became more and more difficult in most great cities to recruit the ablest men to the arduous and time-consuming, unpaid task of urban politics and government. The lower ranks with still unsatisfied ambitions could be attracted, but most of the more successful preferred to devote their whole energies to business profits, or to transforming their status by the acquisition of country estates.

Towns are always like 'transformateurs électriques' (Braudel, 1979:369) and the phenomenal growth of the new industrial towns became itself a causative factor forcing the greatest transformation of urban life since the Middle Ages; not only throughout England but by its stimulus and example in neighbouring countries too. The new energy of these towns, both physical and human, the power, wealth and unprecedented horrors which they generated, could not be ignored. Indeed, there was an almost worldwide desire to learn the lesson they taught of the need to control and ameliorate the more destructive effects of industrialization on urban life. Meanwhile, under the influence of constantly erupting revolutionary forces, which the rulers sought to defuse by reform, many cities in western Europe were receiving more democratic governments by the 1830s.

The industrial towns burst and finally broke the remaining fetters of the decaying feudal framework. The archaic administrative systems of the localities in which they grew could neither contain nor control them, so that there was an early period of almost anarchic freedom, giving enormous opportunities to the early entrepreneurs. But on the one hand they threw up their own zealous reforming and often nonconformist spirits, and on the other they were forced to fight for parliamentary reform, not only to secure the new measures their new economic interests demanded but first of all because they were effectively disfranchised, in the absence of a complete overhaul of the basis of parliamentary representation.

The first round of parliamentary struggle was won with the Reform Act of 1832, leading quickly to the Municipal Reform Act of 1835, which not only gave elected councils, though still with a limited franchise, to the new towns which had till then no integrated administration, but also to hundreds of older towns still dominated by the 'shabby mongrel aristocracy' (Briggs, 1968:370) of medieval closed corporations.

The most important of the older towns, like Bristol, Derby, Exeter, Leicester, Newcastle, Norwich and Nottingham, were undemocratic, but not necessarily stagnant. Norwich and Bristol had already provided free libraries in the seventeenth century, but the number of literates was then so small that it was hardly more than a service to the elite. Nor were the new councils of the 1830s always progressive. In Exeter the new council remained Tory. Although Nottingham had long been Whig, and its council remained so, it made little progress until its rather late Enclosure Act of 1845 encouraged rapid growth. In Derby it was the old Improvement Commissioners, representing the property owners, who pressed for an improved water supply, while the newly elected council, representing the small ratepayers, opposed it on grounds of economy. But in Leicester and Norwich the new councils meant a real changeover of power.

Some of the older parts of the old towns were even worse than the industrial slums, and so were their riots in the early 1830s. Exeter, York,

Leeds, Newcastle and Liverpool were all having cholera epidemics in the 1830s and 1840s.

Industrial magnates might support repeal of the corn laws for the sake of their workers in the hope that it would enable them to pay lower wages, and therefore support extension of the franchise to get such measures passed. But some of them realized that the process would rebound on them as the increasing working class vote, combined with idealist reformer leadership, enacted measures to curtail their freedom of action, limiting child labour and working hours, imposing more and more controls on working conditions and sanitary arrangements both in factory and home.

Bourgeoisie and working class

The bourgeoisie reached its peak in the staggering economic growth of the 1860s and 1870s, making up more than a fifth of the population and crowning the Victorian age of respectability and snobbery, haunted by hidden sex. The external world was the battlefield of men, while the interior was the haven of rest for the capitalist warrior, where the faithful wife must prove by her vanity and helpless stupidity the husband's power to keep her in idle luxury, a pretty slave, but she must run the large household hierarchy with authority and efficiency, a contradiction which may have spurred the feminist movement. American liberty spilled on to daughters, who shocked Paris boulevardiers by walking unaccompanied with men, by their fathers' consent.

The lush, velvety interiors were cluttered with objects expressing the solidity of wealth and harmonious happiness, stifled in crochet and antimacassars. The secluded women were totally hidden in clothes (red hair must be hidden under black wigs). Secondary sexual characteristics were grossly exaggerated: hair, breast, waist, hips, and false buttocks, complementing the hairy profusion of male beards.

Production and wealth had risen so fast that bourgeois families found it easy to save but hard to spend enough. Abstention and repression of instinct were extolled. Success and enjoyment were incompatible. Despite spectacular fortunes and self-made men, few bourgeois families were of proletarian origin. The family was simultaneously unit of society, of enterprise and property, exchanged through virgin brides and dowries. It was hard to guarantee capable heirs, so marrying daughters to industrialists for fresh blood was attractive. Inherited wealth created *rentiers*. In Cologne they increased from 162 to 600 in twenty years, imitating aristocracy.

Factories stayed small until the 1870s, when Krupp and Schneider built work forces of 12,000 or more. Krupp's palace outshone the junkers', whose titles were spurned. Culture began to replace religion. The bourgeois worked through contacts, 'old boy' networks and private pressure, not the mass politics of the workers. Labour agitation was by definition 'foreign' and abhorred. Strikes and unions were prohibited everywhere but Britain. Bosses convinced that insecurity promoted hard work could not grasp that the best workers were the best organizers.

The world boom in property and urban construction from 1875 to 1900 further swelled the bourgeoisie. Workers began to feel better off, though pay hardly rose till the 1860s. Any loss of job was catastrophic for a family, with no protection from destitution. Wealthy families spun off some intellectuals. Bankers were good parents for philosophers. Thought rose with dividends (Hobsbawm, 1978:316–22).

Metropolis of the world

In 1899 the Tory government created twenty-eight metropolitan boroughs as 'sham municipalities' within the area of the London County Council (LCC) to curb its power (Briggs, 1968:333–43). The LCC with its 118 popularly elected members was a powerful and prestigeful body. One tenth of them were MPs, including some cabinet ministers. However, the outer fringe was already growing ten times as fast as the county area, having increased in population from 400,000 in 1861 to 2 million in 1901. Eighty years later, Tory forces triumphantly abolished the Greater London Council, enlarged version of the LCC, leaving its uncoordinated fragments supreme.

It was the time at which the future Lord Northcliffe founded the *Daily Mail*, and the national press, based in London, began to dominate the great provincial papers which had already been flourishing for several decades. In France the latter continued to dominate. It was an aspect of improved transport and communications, which enabled London to act effectively as the centre of a small, compact nation. Marconi sold his wireless to the post office, the first cinema shows were being put on in the West End and automobiles no longer had to have red flags carried in front of them. London became the great imperial city, with the impressive vistas of Whitehall and its government buildings, Regent Street and Oxford Street with their great department stores. Even to Americans, London was the world's metropolis, 'where the whole world's intellect comes to pay homage' (Briggs, 1968:38). The cities of Great Britain were the most significant in the world for innovative developments in the nineteenth century, but by the end of it there was no doubt that American cities were more vigorous. The economic context of British cities had changed completely. By the last quarter of the nineteenth century the capitalist system was drawing every aspect of production and distribution into a more integrated and interdependent net of greater and greater scale and complexity. As a result, the working classes of the cities were subjected to more and more severe blows of unemployment as the cycle of boom and slump proceeded.

The holocaust of World War I, an essential product of nineteenth-century economic success, its horrors far greater than any of those who brought it upon themselves could possibly anticipate, brought the golden age of Britain's Victorian and Edwardian industrial expansion to a sudden end (Hobsbawm, 1994:22). Of course modern war itself stimulates further technological change, but focused on destruction rather than welfare. It also causes dramatic social changes, like the new kind of female factory labour and the loosening and transformation of restrictive moral codes.

Although the economic exploitation of the newer parts of the empire went on with increasing efficiency for another half century, it was interrupted for almost twenty years, from the economic crash of 1929 until the post-World War II recovery. In the inter-war period Britain was forced to live more and more on the proceeds of past overseas investments to make ends meet. The cost and devastation of World War II liquidated these and left Britain on the verge of bankruptcy, skilfully avoided for a while by the efficiently controlled economy.

The basic foundations of the welfare state were boldly laid by Britain's first powerful Labour government, immediately after World War II. Working-class life was brought to a much higher level of affluence and security, with the gap between rich and poor temporarily narrowed.

The urban network in Britain

The rise of industrial towns in England had exposed the relative stagnation of many older cities but caused a rapid growth of urban areas in general, not only of the coal and iron mining towns, but of the ports and commercial centres, and then the resort towns, retirement towns and residential suburbs for the newly affluent, enlarged middle class, especially round London. So it was also in the other countries which followed England in industrialization. But in the huge new countries of White settlement, the continental United States, Canada, Australia and New Zealand, the industrial process itself was somewhat masked at first by the sheer exigencies of territorial expansion. In the United States it was the railways, rather than industrialization as such, which enabled the whole country to be settled, exploited and integrated within a comprehensive new urban network. Apart from the valuable minerals, this meant mainly a vast expansion of agricultural production, not industrialized, but highly mechanized and rapidly becoming more and more labour saving, far beyond the level of older countries of peasant production. The high farming of Europe which had been imposed on peasants and labourers by progressive landowners, was here practised by the farmer himself in a highly capitalistic, though not at first power-driven, system of production. This huge agricultural expansion caused an enormous growth of cities for the processing, marketing and export of its products, as well as for the servicing of its population.

Europe had only six or seven cities of over 100,000 people at the beginning of the sixteenth century and just twice that at the end of the century as a result of the New World conquests. The seventeenth century was a period of civic and religious wars. There were few new cities, but Madrid and Vienna replaced Antwerp and Messina in size (Weber, 1899:449). By 1850 there were forty-two European cities of over 100,000, by 1870 seventy and by 1895 one hundred and twenty, while the United States had twenty-eight (Weber, 1899:40).

Although all cities came to depend upon industrial technology, they were not all cities mainly characterized by industry as such. Mid-twentieth-century British towns (1961) showed three main groupings: industrial towns, suburban type towns and administrative, commercial and resort towns (Moser and Scott, 1961). The industrial towns included railway-dominated towns like Crewe, Darlington, Doncaster and Swindon; the great ports like Liverpool and Birkenhead, Hull, Swansea and Newcastle, as well as the Black Country towns of Birmingham and Wolverhampton; the textile centres such as Halifax, Leeds, Dewsbury, Bradford, Bolton, Manchester, Nottingham and Leicester; other industrial and mining towns of the north-east and Wales: Gateshead, Sunderland, Merthyr Tydfil and Rhondda; and the newer metal manufacturing towns including Stockton, Middlesbrough, Bootle, Wigan and Smethwick (Moser and Scott, 1961:17).

The suburban type towns included the exclusive residential suburbs like Coulsdon and Purley on the south, and Southgate on the north; older mixed residential suburbs such as Ealing, Hendon, Wimbledon, Ilford, Twickenham, Croydon and Surbiton all around London; Crosby and Wallasey on Merseyside; newer mixed residential suburbs: Chigwell, Orpington, Ruislip, Harrow, Wembley, Merton and Morden on the outer fringe of London; Solihull and Sutton Coldfield outside Birmingham; light and defence industry suburbs including Gosport, Luton, Uxbridge, Watford, Slough and Enfield; the older working-class and industrial suburbs of London: Willesden, Tottenham, East Ham, Leyton, Acton and Stratford; and lastly newer industrial suburbs like Hayes and Harlington, Barking and Dagenham.

The group of administrative, commercial and resort towns included mainly commercial centres with some industry: the old county towns of Norwich, Gloucester, Northampton and York; Cardiff, Bristol, Southampton, Portsmouth and Plymouth; spas and professional and administrative centres all in the south: Bath and Cheltenham, Oxford and Cambridge, Exeter, Bedford and Colchester; and the seaside resort and retirement towns of Worthing, Brighton, Torquay and Bournemouth and Blackpool in the north.

Naturally, London could not be confined within any of these broad categories, nor could Huyton with Roby, a new town to relieve Liverpool which grew ten times between 1931 and 1951 (Moser and Scott, 1961:18). The survey included 157 towns of more than 50,000 people, excluding all the post-war New Towns, which had not yet reached that size, but were likely to develop many of the characteristics of Huyton. The greatest concentration of towns is still that precipitated by the industrial revolution in central Lancashire and adjacent western Yorkshire, with smaller concentrations in the midlands round Birmingham, in the northeast round Newcastle, in South Wales and as always London itself.

The greatest correlation with other factors was shown by social class, classified according to the census as: (V) the unskilled, forming 13.1% of occupied and retired males, (IV) partly skilled 16.1%, (III) skilled 53%, (II) intermediate 14.5% and (I) professional 3.3% (Moser and Scott, 1961:105). The majority skilled group showed little variation between areas. The significant contrasts were between classes I and II combined (18%) and class IV and V combined (29%).

The main factors considered, besides social class, were population structure, housing and household size; percentage of occupations, of male and female, and retail sales; voting patterns, health and education levels. The size of towns as such did not affect the incidence of these factors significantly.

The industrial towns of the north still suffer a much higher level of overcrowding than elsewhere (34%, against 1.7% in Coulsdon and Purley). They are overwhelmingly working class in population, with the percentage in classes IV and V often almost double what it is in most southern, suburban or resort towns, while the percentage in classes I and II is less than half, or even less than a third as great.

There are some middle-class, suburban and resort areas in the north, like Crosby and Blackpool, which do not show these extreme characteristics of the industrial north, but they are few; just as there are industrial areas in the south which, though fewer, resemble those of the north. The real weight of these contrasts appears from the fact that some 45 out of the total of 157 towns are in fact suburbs in the Greater London area. The industrial towns remain the most numerous, after their phenomenal nineteenth-century growth, but the suburban group is nearly as large, overwhelmingly dominated by the Greater London area together with a few other suburbs of northern towns and of two or three in the south. Outside London and the north, excluding both suburbs and industrial towns, and apart from the seaside resorts and spas, most of the administrative and commercial towns are the old cathedral county towns which have managed to add new commerce and services to their ancient cultural and political importance.

The social class criterion, elementary though it is, clearly divides the industrial north from the metropolitan, suburban, resort and professional south, with the few exceptions noted of suburbs and resorts specifically catering to northern industrial areas, and some older and heavily industrialized areas in the south. Towns with 25% or more belonging to classes I and II have fewer children and more old people, fewest young women married, fewest households of six or more, and least over-crowding, with highest provision of sanitary facilities. They are engaged more in service industries and less in manufacture and they commute far more, vote left more rarely, have better health and twice as many in full-time education between the ages of fifteen and twenty-four (Moser and Scott, 1961:54–5). Towns with over 20% belonging to classes I and II, that is the forty-eight towns mainly in suburban London and the south, grew twice as fast as the rest, yet it was actually the latter which had most new houses built, to replace old rather than to expand, over three-quarters of them being built by the urban local authorities themselves, with central government financial aid. This was *real* 'urban renewal'.

Such characteristics are obvious, yet significant. They would be more so if class types within cities could be distinguished, for of course there are very rich people of higher-class status in the north and large numbers of lower-class status in the south. While London's industrial and working-class districts developed primarily round the port, in the East End, with more affluent areas further west, there are a few higher-class suburbs and resorts on the east side of London and catering to it, tending to make Southend a lower- rather than higher-class resort, as also is Blackpool in the north, as opposed to higher-class Brighton and Bournemouth on the south coast. Likewise there are some more industrial and working-class suburbs scattered on the more affluent west side of London.

From a global point of view, the diversity among British towns is not impressive, for standards of health, housing and education are so high in all of them by world standards. British towns with less than 10% belonging to the top two categories show the lowest standards, but this category includes only nine towns. They still have nearly 10% overcrowding, and more than twice the mortality rate from bronchitis compared with the higher-class towns, yet more than 90% have their own internal piped water supply and water closet. Only in a few old mining and industrial towns of the north and Wales, some 30% to 40% of households still have to share the use of a bath or water closet. In Paris at about the same time only 77% of households had their own internal water supply and only 46% also had water closets, gas and electricity (Chombart de Lauwe *et al.*, 1952:114).

Rebuilding post-war London and new cities

Britain and Germany had to rebuild their mutually bombed cities. France, whose social fabric suffered most, did not to the same extent. Britain, with its first strong Labour government, had effectively co-ordinated plans and began rebuilding the vast bombed areas of London, especially in the working-class east. Rebuilding was aided by fall in population. The East End in 1960 had less than half its 1901 population. Large numbers went to houses and jobs in the New Towns. But there was spectacular rebuilding.

The problem of rupturing important kin ties through rehousing was solved rather successfully in the largest of the London County Council schemes, to rehouse 60,000 out of the 100,000 in Poplar, eventually making a Stepney–Poplar New Town for 100,000. The Lansbury Estate created from 1950 onwards successfully revived a sense of community and neighbourliness because 90% were working-class people from the area itself, who were proud of it and felt they belonged. Until then 72% had been without bathrooms and nearly half the families had shared accommodation. They were rehoused in two or three times the amount of accommodation they had before, at two or three times the rent. Rising wages enabled most to manage, with many wives also working. Not only were bombed areas rebuilt, but apartment towers and terraces were interestingly blended.

The Greater London Council bought twenty-five acres of dockland in 1969 at £60,000 per acre, worth £250,000 per acre in 1972, building marinas, hotels, a theatre and a 'village' for 2,000 people; the 1,450-acre, 300-year-old Royal Arsenal of Woolwich was redeveloped for a population of 60,000; the eighteenth-century rum warehouses of Deptford turned into sixty-five flats and a yacht centre; the Barbican bomb site turned into 2,113 flats for 6,500 people, with lake, theatres and restaurants. Last came the Olympia and York colossus at Canary Wharf on the

Isle of Dogs: twenty-six buildings and London's largest skyscraper, 10 million square feet of offices for about 60,000 staff, with shops, restaurants and bars, London's biggest project of the century and largest single business development in Europe, with new rail link to the London underground, soon bankrupt for a while, but rescue in sight. It is gentrification on the grand scale, giving a great boost to employment and to London's place in the global economy. Most of the bombed East End was rebuilt through government local authority projects, with fairly conventional blocks of flats. As elsewhere, they began with towers (but only luxury towers work), later changing to lower, smaller, more harmonious and widely spaced blocks. The Thames was also restored, till swimmers and fish could return.

The other alternative, of moving out, is illustrated by South Oxhey (Jeffreys, 1964:207) seventeen miles from central London, where the LCC built 4,000 dwellings for a population of 17,000 on a 920-acre estate during the 1950s, mainly in two-storey terraced or semi-detached houses. The new residents were 90% working class and 70% manual. They and their estate were greatly resented by neighbouring middle-class communities at first and blamed for all the social evils of the area, but after five years they were gradually becoming accepted, with a lot of joint activity and participation in churches, schools and voluntary associations. There was a fairly high rate of juvenile delinquency at first but it fell later. Some 40% of married women took up full- or part-time work, to help pay the higher rent for their improved conditions. Their children were found to be as healthy, intelligent and well cared for as those of non-working women. Greater loneliness and distress showed in the higher rate of mental admission for women between forty-five and sixty years old. The old and unemployed were the most isolated, having fewest chances of making new friends. But three-generation families were the most stable.

Another large and successful experiment was the building of a cluster of high-rise apartments by the Westminster City Council in Pimlico. About four-tenths of the new tenants were non-manual or professional, the rest manual working class. There were some complaints by the higher-status minority about noise and hooliganism, but most were happy enough to stay. More than half the earners worked in or near Westminster. The estate gave general satisfaction for its fine planning and design, with complete provision of shops, social and cultural services.

On a continuum from the inner slum working class of Bethnal Green, to the suburban working class of Woodford, to the Woodford lower middle class, the residential proximity and social interdependence of mother and daughter and of parents and adult children generally, as well as the segregation of the husband's role and network of relationships, grew less, while the conjugal partnership of spouses, the integration of their social networks, and their dependence on formal voluntary organization for social fulfilment, grew more. This documentation of simultaneously existing situations corresponds with the temporal process through which large numbers of individuals and families are passing in the course of suburbanization (Willmott and Young, 1960).

Suburbanization weakens the close solidarities of the slum both in Britain and America. In the worst American ghettos solidarity is a rare treasure. If poor people cannot be saved from poverty and discrimination, moving them to distant suburbs cannot be a happy solution. As long as they are poor they need coping methods they have devised for survival. The life satisfaction of people in Bethnal Green or Boston's North End cannot be effectively increased by welfare measures or rehousing elsewhere unless there can be a significant improvement in their economic situation at the same time. While this is possible for some, it requires improved education, change of occupation and many other transformations which often seem blocked. Cultural differences are also involved. Italian Catholics find it harder to transcend sex roles than Protestants, subject to frequent divorce.

Britain planned thirty-four New Towns, eight of them ringing London, twenty to thirty miles out, aiming at populations of 80,000 to 100,000. Further out to the north, forty to seventy miles, Milton Keynes (entirely new and fastest growing), Peterborough and Northampton (ancient cathedral and county towns) were to grow, respectively, from 40,000 to 250,000, 84,000 to 185,000 and 130,000 to 230,000. Small clusters of three on Merseyside relieve Liverpool and Manchester, three serve the north-east conurbation round Durham and Newcastle, with two more west of Greater Birmingham. They are the largest experiment of their kind, although they only tackle a small percentage of the new growth of a conurbation like London (Schaffer, 1972).

In all cases they were planned as grouped and integrated communities, with old and new skilfully exploited and blended, as with Peterborough cathedral, and in relation to wider perspectives of job availability, new industries and balanced regional development. With a 19 million stock of dwelling units in Britain, 2 million of them condemned and another 3 million lacking in essentials, the need is astronomically greater, amounting to one New Town of 60,000 every month for thirty years (Schaffer, 1972:257–8).

While the English New Towns have revitalized some older small towns and in the United States, as in other industrialized countries, many small towns have been swallowed by metropolitan and suburban expansion or absorbed into new industrial and commercial development, many of the remaining small towns are left as backwaters harbouring the elderly and unenterprising. They do not appear to offer any practicable solution to the big city problem.

FRANCE

Paris

London and Paris were the two historic western capitals, their rivalry as deep as their millennial entanglement. London is the favourite of many, but for 'hundreds of years, by a process never successfully explained, Paris has radiated an enchantment irresistible to millions around the world, including hosts of people who would live and die without ever seeing the place'. But by the 1970s 'this magical Paris' existed almost 'exclusively in the hearts of believers'. 'Gay Paree' – that honeycomb of breathtaking women and women-taking men, capital of the arts, of *savoir faire* and *savoir vivre* – survives only in scattered, scanty fragments. The naughtiness of French bedroom farces, French cabaret nudity and French yellow-backed novels has long since been rendered innocuous by the 'permissive society' of other rich western nations. The celebrated *cocottes* have become anonymous call girls, the famous *maisons de tolérance* were closed down in 1948, and there remains nothing unique about commercial vice in Paris. Even the practice of amateur dalliance has altered:

'the cinq-à-sept' hours for mistress visiting between office and home has been abandoned . . . In the past, even though life was often brutal for the masses, the little people of Paris seemed as much under its spell as anyone else. The city seemed to bewitch even those whom it devoured, and songs celebrating the joys of Paris bubbled up from the most wretched of corners.

The old buildings, the river boats, the changes of colour reflected by the water, the gardens, and the 32 bridges (many of them handsome) compose one of the world's grandest, yet most enduring cityscapes. Along the river are two of the great set pieces of urban spectacle in the contemporary world. The first sweeps down from the Palais de Chaillot on the right bank, crosses the river to the Eiffel Tower, and continues through the gardens of the Champs-de-Mars to the eighteenth-century Ecole Militaire; the other begins at the Seine and marches up a broad esplanade to the golden dome of the Invalides . . . One of the *enchantements* of the view is that it has all the qualities of *trompe-l'œil* painting into which, extraordinarily, one can walk. (Encyclopaedia Britannica, XIII:1005–8)

We can attribute the enchantment to the intensity of the concentration of France on Paris over the centuries, to the extent to which Paris sucked the wealth and talent out of the nation as a whole, and of course to the French genius itself. Tracing the sources of enchantment involves a brief detour into the past.

After the Viking interloper became the French king's greatest vassal, conquered England, creating the most centralized feudal state, more powerful than that of his suzerain, smaller, but more compact and unified than France would be for many centuries, the strange poker game alchemy of medieval inheritance and marriage settlements transferred more than half of France to England. Both sides built beautiful fortified towns (bastides) across the centre of France. The two capital cities shared and reflected the dialectical rivalry and cultural complementary opposition of the two kingdoms, developing strikingly different qualities. English kings lived outside London, treating it with haughty deference. French kings lived inside Paris assuming total submission, only to move out much later, to Versailles and Fontainebleau, while the English kings moved in as their palaces were swallowed up by expanding London, but were never abandoned for the calm of Windsor. Paris was always more turbulent. Its scholars and the students they attracted internationally brought its earliest distinction as intellectual centre of Europe, and the great body of students, which London lacked till later, was always in the forefront of new movements and upheavals.

By 1450 France had regained most of the territory lost in the Hundred Years War, while England, engrossed in the Wars of the Roses, refocused on new goals. Francis I and Henry VIII vied for glory on the Field of Cloth of Gold (1520), but while *la gloire* became a permanent obsession with the French, the little English 'world set in a silver sea' turned her attention to her natural opportunity for maritime expansion and commerce.

Towns in both countries struggled for freedom and were usually allowed it as long as they were loyal and paid their dues. They were compelled to fortify and defend themselves in the frequently anarchic conditions of France and the continent, up to the nineteenth century, whereas England's peaceful isolation made this unnecessary.

The greed and wisdom of Henry VIII in suppressing the monasteries and making his own independent church saved England from the ferocity of France's religious wars, costing Charles I his head, but reducing the salience of religion as a national issue. Paris contained the primate cathedral, London did not. In religion and politics, France was more centralized than England. In marketing and distribution both showed some concentration, but in Paris it reflected political and cultural more than economic realities. No enemy ever occupied London but Paris suffered multiple occupations by the English and the Germans from the fifteenth to the twentieth century. Internally also, Britain suffered no major wars or upheavals since the seventeenth century, whereas France experienced numerous revolutions and uprisings in addition to foreign invasion.

The centralization of France was partly illusory. It was the first modern nation-state, but a 'mosaic of small *pays* each living primarily on its own resources in a confined space little affected by the outside world' (Braudel, 1985, III:315). It long remained a kind of federal system with peripheral provinces retaining their own powers, customs and languages. Yet France thought of itself as more centralized than England. It was a victim of its size. The Dutch and the English had 'more compact nervous systems and were more easily unified' (Braudel, 1985, III:315).

The enchantment owes something to the glamour and chivalry of Francis I, and the dashing popularity of Henry of Navarre, the 'Green Gallant'. Francis evoked a new sense of unity by his energetic travels all over France, though ending in calamity. He founded the Collège de France, a prestigious focus of national cultural and intellectual endeavours. Henry entered Paris as a mediator between murderous Catholics and Protestants, having to become Catholic himself, for 'Paris is worth a mass.' He attracted the respect of a country tired of senseless and insoluble religious warfare, but was allowed only ten years before assassination. He is credited with encouraging the Parisian theatre, as Louis XIII did its music and Louis XIV its dance, embarking on the rebuilding of Paris as a tasteful, ordered city, a focus of polite society as never before. Brilliant *salons* flourished, associating great nobles, intellectuals, men of letters and distinguished women on terms of unprecedented equality.

Henry got the great Pont-Neuf – 'most painted bridge in the world' – finished to become the first sidewalk of Paris, crowded with street vendors, acrobats, conjurors, medicine men and shops, main street and perpetual fair for 200 years, as Charles Bridge in Prague is today. Henry clearly enchanted the French people with his style and daring in love, war and statecraft. The sumptuous grandeur of the Sun King magnified the effect. An idle court can concentrate on elaboration of charm and enchantment, so the decadence of Louis XV's indolence and Louis XVI's incompetence hardly tarnished the enchantment of Paris, as it descended into revolution, the greatest real life drama ever played on its open air stage. The revolutionaries caused little major damage to the beauties of Paris and the new absolutism of Napoleon added further embellishments, greatly accentuating the centrality of Paris in France.

The intensity of enchantment was further fuelled by the forbidden flowers of evil: the naughtiness of Paris was more than good clean fun, leaving de Sade's ingenuity far behind, as is shown by the recent revelations of the volumes of creative pornography in seventeenth- and eighteenth-century Paris. Contemporary urban fashion fosters not only limitless sex, but unbridled violence, laced with drugs. Parisian pleasure depended largely on only one of these. What redeems French pornography, and allows it an original contribution to Parisian enchantment, is that it contained within it the subversive realization, or fantasy, that 'in the state of nature (that of the courtesan) all men are equal (but the lower classes always outdo the upper; three orgasms of a servant are worth more than eight of a count)' (Darnton, 1994:68). A courtesan can sleep her way from the bottom to the very top of society as Mme du Barry did. The eighteenth-century pornographers used sex to give positive expression to the key ideas of the Enlightenment: nature, happiness, liberty, equality. The differences between men and women were represented as minimal. In this unlikely context, the most subversive – and still unrealized – ideals of sexual equality had a precocious flowering. This ethical value, lurking in illicit sexual excess, was peculiarly equipped to impart an enchanted potency to the creative *libido* informing the cultural practices of Paris.

The enchantment of Paris may have been further preserved by the tardiness of the French industrial revolution. For the great Revolution itself, its menace and its aftermath, the military hyperbole of Napoleonic Empire, the reverberations in 1830 and 1848, pre-empted French attention and energy from the eighteenth to the mid-nineteenth century. It was only with the nostalgic stability of Napoleon III's reign, so vilified by Marx, that the French economy burst into a delayed boom of expansion. Industrial production doubled, railway mileage rose six times, steam power five times, foreign trade three times, as French engineers moved abroad, building railways, docks, bridges, sewerage systems and tackling the Suez Canal. Investment banks multiplied in Paris and Bon Marché became the first department store. Although the lucrative French Caribbean trade had expanded ten times from 1715 to 1789, this was the most significant economic expansion France had experienced. It made France the world's second industrial nation. Numerous Protestants and Jews were among the entrepreneurs.

Behind its charm, enchantment has another face, usually hidden, but appearing in each eruption and always a nightmare presence to the bourgeoisie. 'Red' Belleville in the miserable slums of north-east Paris was its symbol. The Revolution had momentarily brought together bourgeois and working class to purge nobility, church and state from feudal privilege. The *sans-culottes*, once aroused, drove on the Revolution, but even the leftist intellectual revolutionaries remained fearful of giving too much ground to the people. The bourgeoisie vacillated between allying with liberal nobles to defend property against the masses, or uniting with the masses to destroy feudal privilege. The 1791 Constitution gave a very limited franchise based on property taxation. When the insurrection of August 1792 brought universal suffrage, defeating the upper bourgeoisie and Girondins, Lafayette emigrated in disgust. That unprepared universal suffrage of the uneducated was indeed counterproductive showed again in the total defeat of progressives in April 1848, precipitating the June Days massacre of some 1,500 and arrest of 12,000. Britain was sufficiently shocked by the eleven brutal deaths in 1819 at Peterloo (satirically compared to Waterloo) with some 500 injured.

The positive and negative faces of enchantment were fused in Haussmann's transformation of Paris. He added magnificent vistas and great traffic arteries, also facilitating rapid deployment of troops and artillery in any future Red eruption. The enormous sums spent were further proof of Paris' capacity to suck France dry, but they also brought Paris debt charges to over 44% of the 1870 budget. Apart from a large labour force, many thousands were attracted to Paris, whose population rose 4.4 million from 1851 to 1931, while Lyons/St Etienne and Nord rose only 1.8 million and the rest of France fell 1.2 million. As in all urban renewal, vast numbers were displaced, their fate unknown, except to swell the slums still further out of sight. However, Haussmann's blocks, with flats of varied quality and size under one roof, encouraged a wide range of wealth and class status among residents. Wealth concentrated ever more in Paris and wages rose 40% above those of the provinces. As construction was completed, unemployment rose, once again raising anxieties, in ominous anticipation of the events of the 1870s.

Commune and Sacré Cœur

Louis Napoleon wanted to die a hero with his troops, but was ignominiously captured and deposed, leaving France and Paris in confusion, paralysed between those who wanted to resist the Germans and those who wanted to surrender. Guns were placed on the heights of Montmartre for the possible defence of Paris, but Thiers, nervous of how else they might be used, sent troops to confiscate them from the National Guard. The confrontation led to a bloody encounter. The generals were caught and lynched by the mob and violence spread through the city. The Paris Commune was established, with other cities following. The great experiment had not proceeded far before Thiers' forces had grown strong enough to attack. The Communards were beaten back, fighting street by street. The Tuileries Palace and Hôtel de Ville were burnt. In the last stand of Père Lachaise cemetery 20,000 Communards were killed or executed, thousands more deported in servitude. Such a bloodletting purge was good, said Edmond de Goncourt, giving twenty years of peace and deferring the next revolution a whole generation. The bourgeoisie had feared the Reds more than the Germans.

The Communards were beaten but the victory needed symbolic

ratification and spiritual legitimation. The church saw its opportunity. Since Avignon the papacy took French protection as a right and astutely twisted French failure to secure the pope's territorial sovereignty into a source of guilt for the French nation. The church cultivated the mood of remorse and channelled it into the convenient cult of Sainte Marguerite Marie, beatified in 1864 for her 1689 visions calling on Louis XIV to repent. Now her devotees stigmatized the decadent opulence and luxury of Paris and its neglect of the pope's need. The movement crystallized into the goal of building a basilica dedicated to the Sacré Cœur on the very heights of Montmartre where the godless Red commune had been born and where the government now wanted to build a fortress. The archbishop of Paris (his predecessor executed by the commune), persuaded the government that the Sacré Cœur would be better anti-Red defence than a fortress. The glistening white dome in the sky above Paris would be a potent symbol and reminder of the unended struggle. The church organized a demonstration of 30,000 people dedicated to the Sacré Cœur at the tomb of Sainte Marguerite Marie. For laying the foundation stone, the pope declared a day of dedication to the Sacré Cœur for all Catholics world wide, hoping to defuse confrontation. In a further attempt at conciliation, chapels built by subscription were dedicated to Jesus the Teacher and Jesus the Working Man. But a counter reaction was provoked, sending some Catholics among the Reds at Belleville to start Workers' Catholicism. Hatred developed for the Basilica and a demand of amnesty for the deported Communards. In 1873 the city council reversed the law enabling land to be acquired and voted for a work of 'truly national significance', calling the Sacré Cœur 'an incessant provocation to civil war'. In 1880 the council proposed a Statue of Liberty in front of the Basilica, just as funds were being raised for the one in New York. The archbishop had to defend the project before the Chamber of Deputies, now dominated by reformist republicans. The majority feared the problem of compensating the 600 workers on the project and the 8 million subscribers. Anti-clericalism and socialism grew in the 1890s, but the Catholics distanced themselves from the lost cause of monarchy and the pope rededicated the Sacré Cœur to the ideal of harmony among the races, social justice and conciliation. The Basilica opened for worship in 1891, the cross on the dome was blessed in 1899 and the campanile completed in 1912, but the official consecration was postponed by the war and took place after victory with fiery oratory from Clemenceau. In 1976 the Basilica was bombed and one red rose put on Blanqui's grave at Père Lachaise. So echoes and ricochets through time the counterpoint of deeds and symbols, class warfare, spiritual devotion and political machination (Harvey, 1985:230–48).

Growth, war and reconstruction

After Haussmann, deprived of a mayor, Paris suffered a century of neglect. Industrial suburbs of dour tenements grew 'beyond the walls' in the north-east (Aubervilliers, Les Lilas, just beyond Belleville) and south-west (Issy-les-Moulineaux) 'lovely names for ghastly places' (Ardagh, 1990:252) to house the growing labour force, as Parisian dominance continued. World War I decimated a whole generation, with 1.3 million dead and 1 million crippled, leaving France reeling. The most advanced agricultural and industrial areas were devastated, industrial production fell to 60% of pre-war and took a decade of high tariffs to recover. The growth of Paris slowed, but some 80,000 little red-roofed, petit bourgeois *pavillons* cottages of assorted shapes, with gardens, spread in an ungainly rash across the outer suburbs.

The concentric and sectorial pattern established for Chicago (Park and Burgess, 1925; Hoyt, 1933, 1939) can be discerned in Paris. The zones buckle outwards where easy transport like railways extends similar conditions. The sectors formed thus by the east–west distribution of class are superimposed on the concentric zones (Chombart de Lauwe *et al.*, 1952:41–3). Seven zones are distinguished. Zone 1 is the ancient heart at Notre Dame on its isle in the Seine, with the commercial, financial, administrative and cultural centre extending west and north. Zones 2 and 3 are concentric transition zones with proletarian working-class, north, north-east, south-west and south, bourgeois north-west, west and south-west. The average proletarian is shorter in height and lighter in weight, with higher overcrowding, tuberculosis, juvenile delinquency and frequency of civil burial; lower rents, religious observance and newspaper reading. The bourgeoisie are less dense, with more bathrooms, elevators, private cars, lawyers, doctors, dentists, inspectors of finance and technically qualified people. Here also is the mixing and acculturative influence of hotels, bars and cafés, bounded north and south by the Bohemian, artistic quarters of Montmartre and Montparnasse.

The scientific, literary and intellectual Quartier Latin and Saint-Germain-des-Prés are proletarian in character except for the ancient aristocratic quarter of Boulevard Saint Germain. The Romanian quarter was in the east of the proletarian belt and North African settlement scattered through it, with major concentrations. The outer edge on the west has the most luxurious large apartment buildings, bordering the Bois de Boulogne and growing in population, the east being mixed between working-class residence and small to medium sized industries. This is Paris of the twenty *arrondissements*, dating from the revolution and indispensable points of reference.

Zone 4 contains large enterprises, such as Renault, with dense, fast-growing working-class residence, the outer edge bordering on rural areas and suburban towns. Zone 5 is the heavily residential mid-suburban area with many dormitory communities, growing less rapidly than zone 4. Zone 6 is peripheral suburbs, Versailles and Plessis-Robinson, with heavy concentration of the more distant housing estates. Its boundary extends out along main arteries. Zone 7 has few housing estates and few commuters into Paris, by which it is clearly affected, though not integrated with it.

In both the bourgeois west and the proletarian east, residential streets with multifloor apartment buildings have small essential shops: dairy, baker, café, butcher, fruit and vegetable, barber, laundry, shoe repair; but large, terraced cafés, shoe and tailor shops, bookshops, printers, and most butchers, are on larger commercial, bus route and market streets. In the outer suburbs people sort themselves into overlapping networks of relationships in adjacent areas, working class or better off, accommodating different statuses and interests and relating them to different compromises of need and convenience, drawing several neighbourhoods together into small suburban towns and urbanizing the countryside.

Proletarian neighbourhoods show reduced kinship networks but more profound relations with neighbours, strengthened by feelings of solidarity and daily encounters and conversations. Bourgeois keep in touch with larger numbers of relatives, including more distant cousins, with their advantages in wealth, leisure, transport and accommodation. But they keep track and balance out their relationships like an account and rarely meet except on major occasions.

This spatial arrangement and sequence of functions, activities and class, which now characterizes all western metropolitan cities, contrasts with the pre-industrial pattern which still persisted in nineteenth-century Vienna, with the castle of the rulers of its multiple nationalities at the centre, surrounded by the Austrian, Polish, Czech and Hungarian higher aristocracy, the further ring of petty nobility, higher civil servants, businessmen and old families, with further out still the zone of the petty bourgeois and then of the proletariat. These different classes formed separate little worlds, hardly meeting except at the great festivities either in the city centre, or in the park of the Prater on the Danube where 300,000 could give enthusiastic acclaim to the ten top families in their splendid ornate carriages (Chombart de Lauwe *et al.*, 1952:71–2).

Another morally as well as physically and politically destructive war left France less bombed wasteland than Britain or Germany, at least in Paris, but there was a gigantic housing crisis and a growing population, with a virtually new state, constitution, total changeover of personnel, all taking some time to sort out. In 1954 nearly 9% of metropolitan residents still had no regular home; 15% were overcrowded; 18% had no kitchen; 55% no inside WC; 17% were sharing with another family. Yet Paris was still best for industry seeking skilled workers, therefore 'all France' was emigrating to Paris to look for a job.

After the immense housing effort of the 1950s and 1960s the suburban landscape was dominated by *grands ensembles*: large, very dense, high-rise housing estates of 20,000–60,000 inhabitants. They were flung up anywhere cheap, vacant land could be found. That meant no infrastructure services or transport, producing very ugly, gloomy non-communities. Here was housing as a bare means of reproduction of labour power (Castells, 1983:75). Sarcelles was the largest and most notorious. Housing 40,000 people, it had no lycée for fifteen years, or commercial centre. People went to escape unbearable conditions in Paris. Its ugly flat façades were a paradise of fresh air and plumbing for slum evacuees. It was an austere gridiron of grey box-like blocks of five to seventeen floors, a clumsy misunderstanding of Le Corbusier, lacking schools, clinics, transport, post offices, sports facilities. It produced nervous breakdowns, delinquency, boredom and prostitution. The monolithic uniformity aroused general complaint. In 1963 a heating system exploded, killing three people. Lengthy protest and further breakdown were needed to get the system overhauled. In 1967 stairs collapsed causing one death and most stairs were found to be unstable. Raising rents caused demonstrations and refusal to pay. The authority tried intimidation through janitors, threatening individuals with eviction. But the Residents' Council insisted on collective bargaining, eventually winning shared management. The communists and left wingers had started the association, with a broad popular base, which eventually led to some hundred voluntary associations and helped to win Residents' Councils in all *grands ensembles*.

Later extensions were more harmonious, gayer, with balconies, large windows and bright colours. The *grand ensemble* concept of low-cost housing was abandoned in 1972 for smaller estates integrated into extant communities. After thirty years Sarcelles became contented and proud, not beautiful, but lively. The *grands ensembles* mushroomed for twenty years, submerging the romantic images of Paris. From 1973 not a single one was built or replaced. Anything over 2,000 units was forbidden.

The Val d'Yerres project of 6,000 units for 30,000 population was developed from 1966 to 1974 as a desperate attempt to meet the criticism by improving environmental quality and human interaction. After 1960 rent and qualifications were raised so there were fewer blue collar workers and more middle managers and technicians. An old farm house was retained as cultural centre. Rents were higher than Sarcelles, yet it was more open to the working class, as much of Sarcelles was monopolized by big corporations. Units were varied and scattered, none very high, reducing segregation by mingling types. There was a great effort to create a shared community, with help for hobbies, ballet lessons, music, theatre, pottery and crafts and political meetings. Yet it never came to life . Homeowners (48%) wanted segregation from public housing unit children. Immigrants faced racist complaints. Extra police and gun permits were requested, yet the records showed no increase in crime. *Insecurity came simply from juxtaposition of strangers* (Castells, 1983:75–94).

French new cities and new buildings

In the 1980s less than 16% of 10 million Parisians lived within the city limits. Mindful of the British New Towns scheme, the French decided on even larger *villes nouvelles*, five round Paris and others outside Marseilles, Lyons, Rouen and Lille. Each straddling several communes and involved with several ministries, they faced fiendish bottlenecks, until de Gaulle was able to burst through. Disliking British solutions, yet inspired by Swedish and British models, one even hired British consultants. The goal was 400,000 population each, with all amenities, lowered to 200,000 or less, as population growth slowed again in the 1970s. 'Long commuting is not French.' They are part of the Paris conurbation in the new Ile de France Region, with an embryonic green belt. Cergy-Pontoise, twenty miles north-west of Paris, has a fine site and spectacular city centre. Offices and industrial estates brought 40,000 jobs. It aims at 120,000 population. Spaciously spread villas and flats provide attractive housing at half Paris prices. Cergy has been compared with Milton Keynes (Ardagh, 1990:293).

The 1960s boom brought ten new hospitals, and new theatres, colleges, swimming pools and libraries to the suburbs. By 1970 the *périphérique* ring road was saturated and a new one started five miles further out. California-type garden cities sprang up around Versailles, with pools and sun terraces, contrasting with eastern suburbs. The 15-billion-franc Disney project at Marne-la-Vallée, sixteen miles east of Paris, bringing 30,000 permanent new jobs, new motorway and a fast rail extension, was something the defence of French culture was unable to reject. Its programme is 90% as before, only 10% specially European. Like its partner, Air France, it has made heavy losses but is struggling to restructure.

The contradictions of providing housing, jobs and traffic flows while preserving enchantment have been gruelling and unending. The 209-metre business tower of Montparnasse, approved by revered Culture Minister Malraux was widely execrated. Twenty metres was the legal maximum height for buildings in central Paris. Then fifty-eight towers of over eighty metres were approved at Porte d'Italie, with shops, offices and flats for 60,000. The eighty-five-metre blocks downstream from Eiffel Tower were quite harmonious, with well-spaced gardens. Paris was losing its skyline. Giscard later halted the Eiffel scheme. Two miles beyond Arc de Triomphe, across the Seine beyond Neuilly, greater height was tolerable for La Défense, some forty high-rises of over forty floors, the 'largest shopping centre in Europe', with some very original architecture, some towers distinctive, some dull and squat, some 'ziggurat' flats and the ultimate backdrop of the 105-metre-high white marble office tower with the square hole in the middle, which further extends the fabulous vista from the Louvre and Tuileries, along Champs Elysées through Arc de Triomphe on and on to this Arche de la Défense.

President Mitterrand proved to be the greatest adorner of Paris for centuries, but the other face of enchantment is never absent. La Défense cleared a mass of shacks, tenements and seedy workshops, human flotsam driven out to no one knows where. All this slum clearing and rent inflation was so reducing the Paris proletariat that any repeat of 1871 becomes most unlikely. Major corporations moved into La Défense for rents half those of central Paris. Yet only 25% of slums were cleared by the 1960s. From 1968 to 1982 homes without flush WCs fell from 45% to 21.5%, still shocking, but bourgeois ghetto prices were too high for low-cost housing. Between 1975 and 1982 the population under twenty years old fell from 28.5% to 18.5%. Paris' first mayor since the Commune subsidized 2,000–3,000 flats per year and financed the improvement of poorer *arrondissements*. Pompidou's Beaubourg Centre cost 1 billion francs. Three times bigger was the Science Museum and Leisure Complex created by Giscard and then Mitterrand out of the 2 billion franc abattoir at La Villette (NE) made obsolete by freezer trucks. Another billion went for the Bibliothèque de France. The Forum development at Les Halles has some 200 boutiques, ten theatres and cinemas and is a great commercial success. Paris is made more cheerful by rediscovery of the 1852 law making it compulsory to clean façades every ten years. A city with its buildings, people and action can embody the essence of an age, symbolizing critical issues boiling up within it and spreading throughout the land. Paris is now closed down from time to time for air pollution. People are told to avoid going outside if possible.

GERMANY: CULTURAL CONTINUITY AND POST-WAR RECONSTRUCTION

In the end, Germany suffered terrible material damage in World War II: 1 million buildings lost and 8 million homeless, apart from 12 million refugees and a further 3 million later. The German peoples never gave up easily. The enormity of defeat left them no alternative but to start again with enormous energy, determination and their famed efficiency. The Republican government had the good sense and moral courage to translate military defeat into a rejection of war on principle. It built 10 million housing units in twenty years, and in 1966, 87,000 units were built in the biggest cities, averaging 4.8 units per building.

Having grown again miraculously into Europe's strongest, wealthiest economy, Germany makes a striking contrast with the United States. Only 16.5% of city folk live in single-family houses (USA 76% 1960), 44.5% in two-family houses and 39.2% in multi-family houses. Manufacturing employment is 89% in firms of less than ten employees.

Germany decided to reconstruct its historic cities as exactly as possible after the ghastly destruction of the Allied bombing raids. Many ancient traditions, ways of life and economic practices have also retained remarkable vitality. Streets occupy only 9.5% of city space, compared to 15.69% in the United States. They wind in the picturesque way retained from before the destruction and most are less than the minimum width for two cars passing. Hanover, Hamburg, Frankfurt and Saarbrücken did make new inner city thoroughfares conforming to the general pattern. In the 1960s Frankfurt already had 180,000 registered automobiles and 6,500 parking spaces. Munich had 300,000 automobiles and 5,800 spaces. Its autobahns stop at the outskirts and 20 million summer tourists have to find their way through from Austria or Italy.

The urban economy has remarkable continuities: sixty-four registered crafts in 9,345 local guilds run 658,387 shops, employing nearly 4 million staff. The crafts are highly honoured and well integrated with the production system. In Hamburg 14% of firms are small, in Munich 18%. There are 680 market places in 296 cities with 43,000 stalls and frequent weekly and special markets, operated by 9,400 local farmer-gardener sellers, 5,600 salesmen of producers and 24,000 itinerant sellers (Holzner, 1970). Europe's most advanced and prosperous industrial state cannot be called old fashioned. It must be concluded that apartment living, small family business and even narrow congested streets and unmodernized sewer and powerline layouts do not inhibit successful economic progress.

European cities maintained their fortifications into the nineteenth century. Growing population crammed within the walls and overflowed. Cityfolk rent apartments rather than trying to own single-family houses. The nineteenth-century mass of industrial workers were housed in cheap multi-storey apartment buildings. Despite traffic and high density there are forests and gardens within cities. In smaller cities 3% of the labour force is primarily engaged in farming and forestry. The state and public opinion aid and encourage industrial workers to be part-time farmers, binding them to the soil and discouraging revolutionary tendencies. Family houses are rarely rented or sold. Of urban households 28.5% own small allotments and most of the 386,461 small farmers owning half- to two-hectare plots in 1966 were also part-time industrial workers in the cities.

THE UNITED STATES

The emergence of a new urban system

Suffering less material damage in two world wars, while receiving great economic stimulus and competitive advantage from them, recharged confidence in the capitalist free enterprise system and continued technological innovation, providing a context for North American twentieth-century urban experience markedly different from that of Europe. But the capacity to exploit this situation derived from the values and institutions shaped by previous events, even before the industrial revolution.

As the largest and richest urban civilization, the American urban and industrial experience is tremendously influential for the rest of the world, especially for more impressionable poor Third World countries. Coming later, yet foreshadowing the future, it is gazed at ambivalently as an example of desirable goals and ways of fulfilling them, despite fear and hostility to its hegemonic dominance by countries whose political economies and cultural situation in time and space completely disqualify them from such aspirations, and whose cities in their present form were founded and dominated by westerners. The circumstances, dynamics and potentialities of Third World cities are quite different, lacking the crucial advantages earlier enjoyed by Britain or the United States.

The growth of cities in America and their eventual industrialization is the example of a follower able to catch up because of specially favourable circumstances. In following Britain, the United States had the even greater and rarer advantages of having nearly all the natural resources needed within a single territory, which could be turned into an internal market, by the very process of territorial expansion and immigrant population absorption which was a necessary prerequisite and accompaniment of early industrialization. She had a firm cultural, linguistic, intellectual and innovative continuity with the first industrial leader.

From the Mayflower pilgrims to the starving Irish immigrants of the nineteenth century and all the others who followed, significant elements of her population were actually preselected for individualism, enterprise and innovation, by necessity for survival; also for the valuation of status for personal, moral and economic worth, rather than hereditary rank, so that enterprise and innovation were likely to take an economically productive form. If British industrial cities were the first, those of the United States are the greatest. The pre-industrial colonial cities of North America in the seventeenth and eighteenth centuries laid the foundation of this greatness.

The combination of the personal qualities of the population, the huge open territory available for expansion once Indian rights were ruthlessly swept away, and the speed with which it occurred, produced the world's largest and nearest approach to a laissez-faire distribution of the urban network in response to the 'invisible hand' of blind economic forces. As with the south German plain, but on a much vaster scale, this favoured approximation to the prescription of central place theory more than other urban systems (Christaller, 1933; Loesch, 1954; Vining, 1955), and has tended to bias American urban theory in this direction, even with regard to other less appropriate regions.

Philadelphia was only a few years behind England in industrial development, but the critical difference between being first and second showed in the preference for tariff protection, especially tempting in view of the potential size and speed of growth of the internal market. Machine carding and spinning jennies were introduced as early as the magical year of 1776, with steamboats on the river by 1780 and steam pumps for the waterworks by 1798 (Warner, 1966:65–6). But the enormous number of handloom weavers who immigrated, many from England and Ireland, after the War of Independence resulted in the rejection of power looms for textiles and even for carpets, although a mechanized textile industry did grow up outside the city early in the nineteenth century. In 1881 there were 4,000 hand weavers in the city mainly concentrated in a quarter of their own. But with Philadelphia's climate of tolerance, intellectual freedom, scientific tradition and innovation, its ample supply of capital as the banking centre of the country, its strategic situation as a great ocean port with an extensive river and canal system already highly developed, as in England, before the end of the eighteenth century, and its accessible supplies of coal and iron, it produced a highly successful industrial complex producing steam engines, machinery for flour and textile milling and machine tools. Its eighteenth-century Philosophical Society and Franklin Institute recall the similar societies of Manchester and Birmingham, oriented towards intellectual curiosity and scientific innovation with a highly practical, commercial and industrial bent.

By the time that the industrial revolution was getting under way in

England, the urbanization of the North American interior had barely begun. Albany up the Hudson was perhaps the oldest and had several thousand people. Pittsburgh was laid out in 1764 near the fort captured from the French. St Louis was only a fur trading post, not under United States jurisdiction till the Louisiana Purchase in 1803. Louisville was founded in 1780, Memphis in 1819.

But by the end of the eighteenth century a new phase of expansion and urbanization opened further west in the Ohio valley and on Lake Erie, followed by the Louisiana Purchase which brought New Orleans, St Louis and the Mississippi towns into a single urban network. History and geography had produced a potential divergence of interest between the northeastern interior trade network channelled along the Great Lakes and down the Hudson to New York, and the central and southern network focused upon the Ohio valley (marginal to both), St Louis, the Mississippi and all its tributaries, down to New Orleans.

With the accelerating westward expansion Chicago on Lake Michigan became the key. The Erie Canal opened in 1825, joining the Atlantic states to the Great Lakes, shifting the axis north from the Ohio river route, making Chicago the principal western terminus. By 1856 Chicago was the chief rail centre. The St Louis merchants felt secure in their river network and were less aggressively enterprising with railway building than the newly arrived adventurers of Chicago, who first linked themselves to the southern river system by a canal and then from the 1840s began to build railways through to the south as well as the west. St Louis, content with its great river system did not compete with railways till it was too late. The whole continental pattern of trade was tipped in favour of Chicago and confirmed by the Civil War which cut St Louis off from the northeast.

In the huge mid-nineteenth-century westward expansion it was the cities as much as the farmers who extended the frontier, though both were closely interlocked. Embryonic urban settlements were often established before the railway arrived. From the 1840s political oppression and upheaval in Europe combined with famine in Ireland led to greatly increased immigration. Between 1840 and 1890 7.5 million Irish and Germans arrived. This influx swelled the eastern cities and fed westward expansion. More and more of the fertile land of the midwest and the great plains was brought into production, providing both food and trade for the cities, whose own growing population constantly expanded the market. Everywhere there was farming, producing food and raw materials, supporting cities and ports of the east and south, importing from them all the goods needed for production and consumption in the new cities.

Up till 1840 the towns of the north-east had refined sugar, made leather and distilled spirits, in exchange for cotton from the south and grain and meat from the west, as well as running mill towns and making ships, sails and barrels. There was a growing complementary industrial specialization as well, with glass at Pittsburgh, textiles at Louisville, iron at Cleveland, processing and merchanting of meat and agricultural products at Chicago, but until the Civil War urban growth was not so much the product of an industrial revolution as of the huge expanded labour force building the cities themselves and constructing the railways, supporting corresponding expansion of crafts, retail trades and service occupations with their organizing network of merchants, financiers, lawyers and adventurers.

Chicago lots worth $100 in 1832 were worth $15,000 three years later (Chudacoff, 1975:32). Railways ran over 30,600 miles by 1860, many of them meeting there. 'Cities built railroads as much as railroads built cities' (Chudacoff, 1975:85). But in the stagnant south there were no interior cities before the Civil War, as Baltimore, Charleston, Savannah, Mobile, New Orleans, Memphis and St Louis ringed around its periphery on the water fronts of the Atlantic or of the great river.

Urban slavery was highly profitable. It was widely held that slaves could build railroads for a mere fraction of the cost of free hired labour (Wade, 1964:37). But there was a profound and deepening contradiction, for slave labour is necessarily unskilled. Dense population and education, the results of urban living, steadily undermined it. During the nineteenth century fearful urban slave owners began to send male slaves to the countryside, but many of those who remained acquired skills as craftsmen and artisans. Their owners could not resist the profit of hiring them out to work for others, then allowing them to live out as more convenient. They hired rooms or built their own shanties, far from their masters, and inevitably became more independent, supporting their own fervent church congregations and acquiring education. This was alarming enough, but when they could not be stopped from frequenting liquor houses, mixing with poor Whites and participating more and more in the free market economy, perhaps illicitly acquiring weapons, White fears and fantasies of sexual assault, escape and rebellion became uncontrollable and insoluble. All these threatening developments had been fulminated against and legislated against, but all were to the profit and pleasure of influential Whites, despite vociferous public disapproval, so all prohibitions proved ineffective.

After 1840 the urban slave population began to fall rapidly. Only Richmond had even moderate success in developing industry with slave labour. Resentful southern cities were therefore left to watch much of their cotton and tobacco shipped out, and much of their imports shipped in, by New York (Chudacoff, 1975:57). Charleston, Savannah and St Louis felt that only secession could save them. None the less, most southern merchants realized that their long-term interests and those of northern merchants coincided and they opposed the Civil War.

Public schools had been started first in Boston (1818), then New York (1832), Philadelphia (1836) and all cities except in the south by the 1840s, with the explicit object of deterring popular unrest, and turning foreign immigrants into respectable Americans. This could not apply to slaves. The crowds of immigrants brought new ethnic and religious diversity. During the nineteenth century the United States changed from a largely Protestant Puritan to more than half Roman Catholic country. There were riots against Blacks and against the abolition of slavery, and against Roman Catholics and the Irish, who were first regarded as sub-human animals as the Blacks were long to be.

Until the mid-nineteenth century all cities remained walking cities, apart from the wealthy, who had horses and carriages, with no settlement more than two miles' walk from the city centre. Public buildings and high-status families occupied the centre, or an attractively commanding hill, with the lower classes occupying two- to three-storey, multi-family dwellings in the valleys between, or around the docks. There was no specific segregation and high- and low-status residences were to some extent intermingled. Besides, high-status houses were large, containing numerous servants, as well as visiting relatives and friends.

Boston's area of dense settlement extended only as far as a two-mile walking radius from city hall in 1850 when the street railways began. The omnibus had started in 1826 and the steam railway in 1835, but they remained expensive and caused little change. The street railways were still horse drawn up to the 1880s, having spread Boston to a two-and-a-half-mile radius by the time of the Great Depression of 1873 and to four miles by the again booming 1880s. In the 1890s, with Whitney's bought up monopoly of street transport and of the real estate along the way, electric streetcars took over, carrying three times as many passengers twice as fast and spreading Boston to a six-mile radius (Warner, 1962:22). Carriages had long been able to carry the urban elite out to their country estates, but electric streetcars ushered in the middle-class suburb.

The vast continental expansion to the west by individualistic pioneers could not have been contained within the framework of a continuous network of cities from coast to coast without the irresistible pressure of massive immigration caused by extraneous factors far away in Europe, nor without the facilitating railway technology and the integrating cement of a common core language and culture to which immigrants of diverse languages and religions could be at least partially assimilated with the help of public education and common goals. Elsewhere such integration has only occurred, over far longer periods of time, under highly centralized autocratic systems such as those of the Inca and Chinese Empires, or as a result of mass military movements sanctified by the conviction of religious mission as in the case of the seventh-century Islamic expansion of the Arabs. A highly special sequence and concatenation of circumstances allowed and pushed the Americans to accomplish this without the assistance of those autocratic, centralized institutions of government from which they had already fled. Mechanical transport was thus a necessity between American cities long before it became so within them.

The new technology of mechanical transportation and industrial production had already been invented long before in England. America needed the former sooner than the latter. Iron bridges and steam ferries encouraged suburban expansion, so that New York's first great suburb of Brooklyn was already larger than Boston by 1860. The first New York horse omnibus ran along Broadway in 1829 and in all large cities within a few years. Soon they were run on tracks with much greater speed. Cable cars served the hills of San Francisco and most large cities in the 1870s and 1880s but in the 1890s were superseded by electric trolleys (Chudacoff, 1975:73). Subways were constructed in Boston in 1897, New York in 1904.

Horse omnibuses were started by many individuals competing with one another, but rails and tunnels could not possibly be left to open competition, nor be run by individuals, and city authorities were forced to control entry and issue permits for such operations. Given the enormous profits involved and the deep respect for the individual and his private pocket and property, city administrators were forced to issue monopolistic franchises. Distaste for government control was such that those allocating rights and issuing permits were subjected to intolerable pressures from private interests. The old municipal governments of the eighteenth century were not up to this task and in any case these elite families were fast moving out into the suburbs and losing interest in such problems unless their business profits were directly involved. Such a vacuum called forth the city machines to fill it. The crescendo in immigration occurred at about the same time, swamping the eastern cities with millions of newcomers, most of them virtually destitute on arrival, and leading on to waves of similar pressures throughout the urban network to the west. The mass of new immigration itself constituted a new source of profit and prosperity to those already there. They swelled the market for all consumption goods and services and they provided an almost inexhaustible supply of cheap labour just when it was needed to build the infrastructure of the rapid territorial expansion. But they also posed human problems of welfare and control with which the minimal institutions of the 'private' city were totally unequipped to cope.

Machines and bosses met so many convergent needs. They were the quintessential brokers, centralizing decisions and getting things done. The unwilling yet unavoidable expansion of local government activities meant an increase of jobs, but the strong anti-bureaucratic bias meant that city jobs were more likely to be filled by personal selection than by specific training and impersonal competition. They were correspondingly insecure and subject to reallocation with changes in the power structure, so that their incumbents were strongly motivated to make the most of their posts while they held them and amenable to those who would enable them to do so. Expansion not only meant more city jobs but an innumerable variety of contracts, franchises, permits and regulations which had to be allocated and administered. The first immigrant masses, as well as most of the bosses, were from Ireland, where centuries of British oppression habituated them to the necessity of violence and to the game of subverting the government, which they now played in a new form better than ever. Winning contracts and franchises was worth large fortunes, while freedom from permits and regulations was also valuable. The city councils, however ill-equipped or uninterested, had to be elected by a mass of voters increasingly strange to them. The desperate needs of the immigrant masses called the bosses into being to help them find jobs and housing and tide them over emergencies.

In the chaotic jungle of the mushrooming cities, ruthless and impersonal, the bosses provided a saving personal refuge of human assistance, warmth and entertainment, always available, like a chief at his informal court, at a corner saloon, dispensing largesse, giving turkeys for Christmas, attending and if necessary paying for funerals, wakes and weddings, enabling people to forget their mundane problems in flamboyant festivals. Helpless immigrants and the poor and needy in general naturally gave their votes to such benefactors willingly. But they could be paid for them if on occasion necessary. Under these circumstances, American democracy and the party system enhanced the need for and opportunity of bosses, by providing the valuable commodity of the vote in which they could trade so profitably, indeed beneficially. By delivering the votes the bosses could determine who ruled the city, and be suitably recompensed by them, or take over the government themselves. Either way they could influence who got jobs as police, firemen, garbage collectors, janitors and even clerks and sometimes mayors. This greatly strengthened their control of the vote and gave them power over police action as well. They could protect illegal bars and saloons, gambling dens, brothels and criminal gangs, winning a rich recompense. More fabulous gains could be made from the allocation of construction contracts, franchises and monopolies and the general disposal of the cities' business to banks, lawyers, printers and other professionals. Of course, bosses themselves were arranged in hierarchies between local precinct and city hall, more or less united at different times and in different cities. Rivalry as well as loyalty among them could be intense. The fall of one boss could simply lead to the rise of another, without significant change, or might be due to spilling over of resentment and enmities caused by bosses' excesses, giving opportunity to reform movements and a turnover of city government personnel.

Reform movements and victories, however high the principles of some of those involved, were inevitably illusory, because they were necessarily (in terms of the prevailing system) aimed not so much at producing good government as at reducing government to allow freer play to human virtue. This meant a breakdown in the decision-making process and a serious loss of amenity when the poor masses were deprived of the bosses' humanizing touch and solid material assistance. Usually such interludes were brief. Whether the losses or the gains were greater, whether the corrupt diversion and outright embezzlement of funds to the tune of hundreds of millions of dollars, as in the case of Boss Tweed of New York, or the notorious scandals of sewers built to run uphill, was more damaging than the loss of humanity and the services through the breakdown in the entrepreneurial decision-making and allocation systems when the boss was removed, is a calculation hardly possible to make. Reform movements often generate a sharp temporary euphoria but run quickly out of steam and revert to the system as before unless they are able to establish new institutions. This, for the reason stated, they were usually unwilling to do on principle.

The grand excesses of early bosses at the end of the nineteenth century were too flagrant to last, but experience brought more discreet ways of manipulating the same operations. Institutional changes had reduced the feasibility and necessity of vote buying. The desperate days of mass immigration which particularly favoured it had slackened, though comparable loyalties still exist in many voting precincts. Large urban bureaucracies have come into existence, with more professional training and security of tenure, seriously reducing the field for manipulation, but some of the major plums of allocating big contracts for road and bridge building or housing construction and for the supply of innumerable services still exist and are frequently handled in much the same way, as the much publicized convictions of the last few years constantly remind us. Reforming zeal and administrative energy sometimes succeed in curtailing abuses in their existing form, but they usually go underground and reappear modified yet essentially the same.

New and unexpected situations reproduce old opportunities. The wild period of Prohibition in the twenties, when natural appetites inflamed by prosperity broke down the fences which naive idealism and bigotry set up, followed by the destitution and desperation of the Depression in the thirties, reproduced in changed circumstances the favourable opportunities for bosses of the nineteenth century and were followed again after World War II by the explosive opportunities of the Black ghettos, Irish machines, Italian crime syndicates, Black racketeers and new waves of Hispanic and south-east Asian immigration.

The continuity of violence and ubiquity of guns in American cities have also ensured a climate relatively favourable to the perpetuation of illicit and corrupt activities. It is again characteristic that this vice is greatly assisted by another primary ideal virtue of American culture, the sacred right of every man to bear arms, which still guarantees that American cities shall be the most lethally armed in the world.

The cities of the north had grown out of desperate struggle manifested in feverish activity. Without desperate struggle the first settlers could not have survived (as many indeed did not), yet they were powerfully motivated to do so by the excitement of vast untapped, though not over easily tapped, natural resources. As soon as a successful elite of more affluence and leisure had emerged, they were confronted with renewed struggle against imperial exploitation. Wars are the fusion and culmination of long converging processes, yet they bring on a radical break with normal life, relaxing conventions and inhibitions, during which new forces are unwittingly released and change is more unhampered than usual. The War of Independence, the Civil War and the two World Wars (not to mention Korea and Vietnam), first created then vastly enlarged and strengthened the central government, contrary to the cherished values of many who carried it out. The public outcry against politicians and the cynical distrust of central government should not blind us to its still growing strength, especially where cities are concerned, as the case of New York has shown. The energy first demanded for survival, and the rapid change first brought about by the flooding of immigrants into an almost empty continent, have become habitual and enshrined as cultural values. As wars, so fires, like the great fire of Chicago in 1871, while seeming unplanned, unpredictable acts of God, were in the circumstances inevitable, just as the oft recurrent fires of Boston (or London, Hang chow, Tokyo, Kyoto) were, and greatly accelerated processes already under way, hastening the flight of the wealthy from urban squalor and danger to the suburbs and at the same time leaving them free to rebuild the central city, (where they still worked), to their own specification, with little regard for the needs or wishes of the poorer majority of its former inhabitants.

Multimillionaires mushroomed in the far west where capitalism ran riot with railway expansion and mineral exploitation, blessed by absence of government, enjoying private armies and police with little law but force. Cities were built in the wilderness, with hectic entertainment and wild frivolity in saloons, hotels, even opera, all to be deserted a few years later. Politics were to buy, not practise, except for money. Workers found the tyranny of capitalist crooks as absolute as monarchy. Many American ideals and values blossomed in this scandalous golden age, to bear dangerous fruit, haunting the next century (Hobsbawm, 1978:202–6).

By the end of the nineteenth century the major cities were more than ten times as large as when the mass migration began (Weber, 1899:22) (some of them had barely existed), with much greater extremes of poverty and wealth than before. By 1893 New York's tenth ward reached a density of nearly half a million people to the square mile, living in four- to six-storey tenements, many families to a floor, all sexes and ages having to sleep in the same room, many without any light or ventilation from the outside, without kitchen or electric light, large numbers competing for the same water tap and latrine (Clinard, 1970:33–4), an ample, helpless, willing labour force for expanding capitalism. Many worked in sweat shops for wages of two to four cents an hour and for eighty to ninety hours a week, with no compensation for sickness or accidents. Children of three or four years old as well as women worked, or else, lacking parents at home, joined the street gangs despite the public schools. Italians and east European Jews, who had replaced the Irish and Germans as majorities in the latest migration, tried harder to keep their women employed at home (Chudacoff, 1975:113). Yet there was always movement, wages tended eventually to rise and a sufficient number of unskilled workers were able to better themselves and buy their own homes, to convey a sense of upward mobility and hope, maintaining the struggle from within and discouraging any widespread disaffection with the system itself.

Industrialization was now strongly under way and nearly all of it was in the cities. In the 1880s rural population had actually declined, exacerbating urban congestion, but with improved technology and specialized farming, the rural economy recovered, more contented now that railway proliferation brought rural people within easy reach of city lights for leisure and recreation, while mail order houses brought the new industrial products easily to rural families.

Nineteenth-century conditions of poverty, overcrowding, deprivation, disease and high mortality in London or New York were comparable to those of the worst Third World cities today, in Calcutta or Cairo, except that disease and mortality could now be better controlled in the latter, with fateful consequences which exacerbated the situation. Conditions of disease and mortality, especially infant mortality, did not substantially improve in great western cities until the twentieth century.

Boston had been the first large city, dragging the colonies together towards independence. But New York's reach up the Hudson isolated Boston somewhat from the great westward expansion. Philadelphia, with its Puritan yet tolerant outlook and more central seaboard position in the developing nation, overtook Boston in size before itself being overtaken by New York. Geography and railway development gave Chicago dominance over the middle phase of hinterland expansion, while the twentieth-century lure of the west made California the most populous state, relieving the pressure on metropolitan cities of the east and centre, as San Francisco–Oakland, Los Angeles, San Diego and many other western cities grew apace. The continental urban network encouraged huge expansion of both internal and external trade, with further development of industry and technology.

World War I spared America and spurred another outburst of the military-industrial complex, quiescent since the Civil War, destroying European rivals and wasting their wealth, leaving most of the world open to United States trade and investment, cutting off the stream of mass immigration to allow some social and national consolidation. The post-war boom rushed on regardless into the shattering experience of the 1929 crash and the deep depression of the 1930s. Despite reluctance, this enforced the greatest growth and intervention of central government yet. Cities were the scenes of catastrophic unemployment, accentuated by rural bankruptcy driving farmers to seek urban refuge. Blacks also migrated in millions from rural south to urban north, leading to Black majorities and ghetto concentrations in great cities, posing and embittering America's major urban problem, the relation of centre to periphery and suburb, in race and ethnic composition, class, social status and economic opportunity. The Civil Rights movement arose from increasing pressure in southern cities, but moved north and turned into its Black Power phase, followed by the Black capitalist economic struggle in ghetto cities and the capture of urban political power by Black mayors. The success of Blacks, limited as it was, did raise some into the middle class. They moved out of the inner cities like the rest of the middle class (although constantly harassed by suburban Whites and conniving, 'redlining' realtors). It was good for American society, but left the Black masses feeling leaderless and abandoned, precipitating the human catastrophe of the Black ghetto.

The North American network of cities had developed in little more than a century and a half into the largest urban system in the western world, driven by its industrial capitalism which, though not the first, proceeded with unrivalled rapidity. This speed and newness lent itself to strikingly distinctive patterns of urban development.

The colonial cities had been small, face-to-face communities, of relatively humane social interaction, despite considerable differences of wealth, and firm belief in the justice of reward for differential effort. The textile mills of the 1830s and 1840s clustered along New England's rivers, until between 1850 and 1870 coal replaced water power and railways brought mobility. In the many small cities which began to achieve industrial development, the middle class tended to sympathize with the sufferings of the new industrial workers, resenting the intrusive style of pitiless, impersonal exploitation. Their politicians and journalists were even apt to side with workers striking for better conditions. No wonder that manufacture began to concentrate more in the larger port cities, where relationships were becoming more impersonal and allowed, or imposed, greater segregation on the workers. New York, Philadelphia and Chicago all reached over 1 million people by 1900 and their middle classes were much more hostile to the hordes of immigrant workers (Gordon, 1984:34). Strikes were not supported by politicians or the press and often failed to last long. In 1877 striking weavers in New Jersey complained that the mayor, magistrates, press and opinion refused to help them (Hobsbawm, 1978:193).

Industry therefore developed most profitably in these large cities, which also offered increasing economies of scale, proximity to ample labour in close walking distance, easy rail and water access to coal and raw materials, industrial supplies, big city innovations and large consumer markets. New York tenements, Philadelphia row houses and wooden tenements in Chicago and elsewhere concentrated workers at high density. The intolerable overcrowding, noise, filth and stench, belching smoke and rowdy disorder impelled the better off to move out, the middle classes as far as they could afford, the wealthier farther still.

This isolation and concentration of workers favoured the imposition of industrial discipline. But it also began to generate friction. It made it easy for workers to meet and plan protest at their appalling conditions. Speed of growth began to clog transport, increase land prices and create diseconomies. Labour agitation spread and became more political. The strike index rose from 56.8 in 1881–5, 125.8 in 1891–5, 187.4 in 1901–5 (Gordon, 1984:38), concentrated in New York, Pennsylvania and Illinois. Meanwhile, the emphasis of capitalism was passing from its industrial to its corporate phase. After a spate of mergers, the new giant trusts and corporations could aim at a new level of rationalization of production and distribution. By the 1920s they were ready, having consolidated their monopolies, won market control and accumulated capital for rebuilding, to create new central business districts with skyscrapers, moving their factories out, away from the labour trouble. Employers said the strikers marching past were creating a fever among their employees.

Manufacturers became discouraged from investing in the central city. Smaller towns forty or fifty miles outside Chicago were getting new plants. This cut down the contact between different bodies of workers and the communication of ideas between them. Improvements in transport and communication enabled the production process to be separated from administration, letting plant managers run the factories outside, while chief executives saw to their expanding empires from luxury towers downtown. By 1929, 56% of national corporations had their headquarters in New York City or Chicago. Each new skyscraper increased the impact and the reciprocal magnetism of the whole complex of offices, banks, law firms, accountants, advertising agencies and appropriate restaurants, clubs, shows and seductive leisure activities for all of them.

With the factories moved out, the workers moved out into suburbs and the old central working-class districts deteriorated into ghettos. New cities that developed after the era of corporate accumulation began had the great advantage of freedom from the burden of archaic plant and infrastructure, as well as deteriorated neighbourhoods and slums. Their corporate executives' interests were evenly spread over the new metropolitan area, so they favoured annexation by the central city (Tabb and Sawers, 1984:92). The twenty fastest growing cities between 1960 and 1970 more than doubled their land area from 1950 to 1970. These are the cities of the sunbelt.

Suburbs

Suburbs are smaller communities adjacent to a city, still dependent upon it in many ways, but more and more independent the farther and larger they grow from the centre. They reflect nineteenth-century population growth with improvements in transport, eclipsing the walking city, intensified by the automobile. But they are not simply the inevitable results of urban population growth, congestion and the natural, spontaneous reaction of people to escape, as they are usually represented and believed to be. They are an integral aspect of the continuing movement of the capitalist system (Tabb and Sawers, 1984:63–70).

It was not the inanimate motor car, but its human production and use, which above all facilitated the development and expansion of suburbs. As it was North America which achieved the exponential growth of the car, so the North American suburb became *sui generis*, and eventually swallowed the majority of the whole population, generating the epitome of the suburban way of life.

The motor car is the inevitable symbol of this profound and widespread transformation. In 1910 the assembly of a chassis on the Ford production line took twelve and a half hours. In 1914 it took one hour and a half and went on shortening (Ewen, 1977:23). This system of mass production spread throughout American business and industry. It could produce commodities far more cheaply and in undreamed of quantities, provided that both commodities and workers were standardized. They could be trained in a few hours, since only a few, simple, endlessly repeated movements were required of them, through the time/motion studies of F.W. Taylor, parodied as a 'well defined jerk, twist, spasm, or quiver resulting in a fliver' (Ewen, 1977:11).

Earlier production had been mainly for the middle and upper classes, but the vast and ever increasing flow of production necessitated the mobilizing of the whole nation, and eventually the world, as consumers, who were necessarily the worker-producers themselves. The industrial complex advanced from its heavy to its tertiary phase, with the invention and production of a plethora of consumer items which spread down the class structure, and began to generate a homogeneous, basic, material American way of life, differing profoundly at top and bottom, but creating a highly effective, visible illusion of common participation.

Though it is said that Woodrow Wilson before World War I feared the car would cause socialism by causing more extreme envy of the rich, it had the opposite effect. Once cheap models became available in the 1920s they became the most potent force in bolstering belief in the American dream and loyalty to the system. Not only was it the only country in the world where such a large proportion of the population could afford a car, but it seemed a highly visible and beautifully deceptive symbol of equality in enabling everyone to travel in the same way and to participate in a lot of the same activities and be seen to do so, despite the fact that disparity between rich and poor was actually increasing all the time. It enabled a much larger segment of the middle class to follow the rich out to suburbs, which thus got pushed further away from the centre without becoming inaccessible. It produced the huge urban industrial complex centred upon Detroit, as well as large plants with all their ancillaries, work forces and families, which created or expanded many other cities. It dotted the country and lined the interminable urban approaches with gas stations and motels. It contributed to the possible solidarity, or even isolation, of the nuclear family in its own separate house and yard, vastly extended the range of optional activities outside the home and work, also providing an easy escape into anonymity or secrecy for old and especially young, supposedly loosening and breaking sexual inhibitions. It became one of the commonest causes of death and injury, facilitated violent crime and eventually produced acute new problems of noise and air pollution.

Cars and trucks together, through their indirect influence on public policy and spending as well as on individual behaviour, began to eclipse the railways and drive them into bankruptcy. It brought urban traffic congestion to a new pitch and with the resulting construction of urban throughways destroyed large numbers of poor urban dwellings without providing effective alternatives. While at first it made rural existence more viable because less isolated, in the long run this was itself a crucial form of urbanization, since rural dwellers became urban in many of their activities, values, domestic equipment and possessions. Since it also made access to the country much easier for townspeople, the distinction between urban and rural was extensively blurred from both ends.

Domestic life and values were transformed. With refrigerators, washing machines, sewing machines in the home and ready made clothing, canned foods and pre-cooked meals in the shopping centres and supermarkets, the gadgetry of America became the envy of the world and the housewife with her mechanized home was transformed from her age-long producer's role to the relatively idle one of consumer, with the possibility of a new type of white-collar career outside the home. There is a paradoxical relationship between employment and the emancipation of urban women. During the desperate immigration period, as we have seen, large numbers of women with their young children had to work in sweat shops for very long hours at miserable wages. From this they were gradually emancipated after World War I. World War II drew large numbers of women back into factory and clerical jobs, which fell again after the war, but climbed again late in the 1950s till in the 1960s 40% of women were at work including nearly half the mothers with school children (Chudacoff, 1975:244). It became usual for women to work until marriage at age twenty, raise children till thirty, and by the age of forty-six, with all the children grown up, be free for work again for anything up to twenty years. By the 1990s two incomes were becoming a necessity.

Telephone, radio, movies and television transformed family and kinship as well as business communication and filled the new leisure hours with new desires, needs and values, irresistibly promoted by the ceaseless pounding of commercials, as well as by the junk mail and tabloids, which had already tripled their circulation in the 1930s. American movies, in particular, swept the world and continue to dominate all those countries which do not produce and defend their own or attempt specific policies of exclusion. With the relentless development of the consumer mass market, capitalists welcomed huge profits and consumers welcomed low prices, but consumers as workers realized that something was amiss.

The urban worker himself as a person was of less significance. Once the creative maker of a whole article he now made only a small part of one. His skill was so small that he could be taught it in a few hours. Until forced to think otherwise, his employers wanted him to be as much like a mere part of a machine as possible. He was not expected to show initiative, or consciousness of the wider context. To look, think or act differently was assiduously discouraged. Obedience was the greater virtue. Symbolizing equality and classless society in cheery greetings of boss to man was a thin camouflage. Workers were given no voice in the conditions and functioning of their work. Time and motion studies were used to set high production norms, but the wage increases supposed to accompany them were skimped. In the 1920s profits rose four times as much as wages. But ignoring human feelings and motivations did not ensure a mechanical efficiency. It led to irritability, fatigue and neurological damage, with actual declines in quality and productivity.

Elton Mayo's studies from 1924 to 1932 led to the extraordinary conclusion that merely inviting the workers' co-operation in a project, not even directed specifically at their welfare, stimulated a new attitude, made them feel important and raised productivity 25%. The contradictions remained. The organization of work was neither satisfying nor humane. It was notoriously geared to produce colossal fortunes for a few, yet employed workers *were* generally better off except in the traumatic and agonizing years of the depression through the 1930s and the recessions following the great post-war boom.

After the great Ford success in standardizing robot-like workers for a single model, the market was eventually saturated and ready for other models in ever increasing and eventually stultifying variety, in this and all other great industries. The logic required progressive transfer of even the routine movements left to the degraded workman to increasingly smart machines, so that fewer and fewer workers would be needed and those left would increasingly be labour aristocrats supervising largely automated machinery. These were the strong union members of United Autoworkers, or IG Metal in Germany, able to strike and fight for higher wages, pensions, holidays and social benefits, an unwelcome development, which led to moving many of the great plants elsewhere, to southern and south-western states where unprotected labour could not organize, or to countries in far parts of the globe.

Although the number of workers was falling, the labour aristocrats were becoming middle-class aspirants, so that the flow to the suburbs and the commuters' demand for cars did not slacken. Respectable workers, taken in by the deceptive deals, began to buy the new models every year. Newer factories were sited right out in the country so that suburbanites could drive out to work, instead of into town. This created a new demand for road construction as well as maintaining the level of profits. As workers left the city proper, their abandoned accommodation, like the middle-class accommodation abandoned previously, was taken over by the new underprivileged categories, Blacks, Hispanics and recent immigrants, enlarging the impoverished ghetto areas of large cities. The deception in the workplace exactly matched the suburban deception in the homeplace. In the workplace, the development of automation through computer, robots and cybernetics was downplayed as a disappointment till it was forgotten. When the catastrophic loss of employment, foretold long before, actually began, it was masked as 'efficient downsizing to regain profitability and competitiveness'. Moving factories abroad and leaving workers behind was deceitfully euphemized as deindustrialization.

Westlake, California, is quite extreme: developed from a ranch by a notorious multinational on eighteen square miles with an artificial lake in the middle and golf course lit at night. The houses are 'traditional' in wood, brick and plaster (Tudor).

We don't cater to the unmarried, nor older folks. They prefer suburban living, a long way from any ghetto or riot areas. No Blacks [though not banned!], no poor, no advertisements, no TV aerials, works of art, bars, poolrooms, no weeds in the city centre, no vulgarity, or visible sex. Nearer to a daydream of village life in Europe, all unpleasantness removed. A gathering of like minded people with similar incomes seeking the same way of life – family, home and the water. Any deviation from the norm would show. We did not want it to be interesting, stimulating, but a perfect, safe and beautiful rest home cut out from the pain of the world, for healthy people

said the developer. The empirical facts of suburban life are bizarre enough to need no further exaggeration (Davie, 1972:81–3).

The mobile home, mobile village is stimulated by fear and dislike of cities, and is possible because people can afford car and trailer, ready to buy with carpets, furniture, vases and flowers, but have no roots to settle on. Mobile home settlements are advertised all over the country, specialized for 'adults only', 'over 55 senior' and many other restricted, segregating categories.

In southern California it is to the sprawling new suburbs, neither town nor country, that most people are moving, down the coast towards San Diego, or into San Fernando Valley and Irvine (another ex-ranch): aerospace employees, lower and middle technicians, profoundly conservative, threatened by the younger skilled. There are so many Birch Societies. There will only be jobs if things remain the same. There is no community or neighbourhood sense, only churches to belong to, people are nervous of strangers. A new arrival did not take the local conservative paper, or turn on the lawn sprinklers in the evening, or have an American car, or go to church. All the neighbours lied to fabricate a false case against him and he was evicted. The new housing development characteristics are: few Blacks, Mexicans or Chinese, few older people. Most are under twenty years, large households with few women who work, few poor or uneducated. Most are single-family owner-occupiers, all with cars, and blurred, imprecise language (Davie, 1972:88).

In income and schooling small towns are below central cities, which are below suburbs. The old mill town of Putnam had old-style local politics, narrow, immediate and personalized, less prosperous but more satisfied. Bloomfield, transformed from farming village to white-collar suburb had more literacy, conflict and change (Ladd, 1969:55–63, 233). The country divides into 69% metropolitan and 31% macropolitan towns and open country, suffering unemployment, emigration, depopulation and inadequate economic and population base for service and institutions (Tweeten and Brinkman, 1976).

The suburban way of life varies according to wealth, class and life-cycle status, religion and ethnicity, and whether the suburb is primarily a commuter, dormitory, industrial or retirement settlement. A distinctive suburban way of life has been described, but also forcefully rejected, as a myth, or prejudiced stereotype. Yet there is considerable agreement that suburbanites seek to live among people like themselves (in fact, they have little choice) and suburbs encourage this. A certain homogeneity is undeniable and the negative attributes spring from this. Members of a homogeneous community tend to resent dilution by outsiders with other characteristics. There is a danger of complacency making the existing characteristics the preferred standard by which any deviations are negatively judged. Standards of supposed excellence can become a tyranny, imposing the meticulous manicuring of lawns, adoption of similar mechanical gadgets, snowblowers, leaf suckers, automatic garage doors, sitdown lawn mowers and the like, as they are proffered in endless profusion by the irresistible force of daily exposure on TV, the press, glossy coloured brochures in the junk mail or delivered door to door. Those who do not conform in these ways inevitably appear odd and deviant, looked at askance if not feared as potential sources of unknown dangers. The situation is even worse for people cursed with distinctive physical or racial characteristics, for those mentally handicapped or known to have deviant political views. At best, the suburbanites feel kindly and tolerant towards such misfits at a distance, but try at all costs to prevent them from becoming part of their cosy suburban community.

The nice, clean upper-middle-class suburbs outside any American city have been ridiculed as absurdly conventional and suspicious of deviance. The outsider walking in casually is watched apprehensively, police cars cruise by repeatedly, making careful inspection. Housewives and shopkeepers peer out. Yet these are not small-town provincials but sophisticated people, men working in the big city, women with college degrees. The visitor feels no such paranoia in the city, nor in real country, or in a lower-class suburb or even a high-class suburb in a college town. 'It is the business-managerial suburb that can tolerate nothing strange, different, unknown' (Reich, 1972:159).

In the skilled blue-collar, upper-lower- to lower-middle-class newly planned suburb of Levittown many were 'trying to raise their children for middle class careers' (Gans, 1967:23), young families coming to a new community to get more space and to own their own separate, modern home. They were more child centred, with more husband–wife partnership, more permissive, with less physical punishment of children than in the working class. There was great pressure for meticulous lawn maintenance, fences were taboo, as was all public reference to class distinctions. Owners of trucks were prohibited from parking them outside their houses to prevent it looking working class and lowering property values. There was little formal entertaining, or formal associations, with less status striving than in the more individualist, professional, upper middle class. However, Gans argues that the most extreme characterization of suburban life (identical boxes in fresh air slums, with age, income, number of children, problems, habits, conversation, dress, possessions and even blood types identical, driving myriads of housewives mad, intellectually debilitating, culturally oppressive, breeding bland mass men without respect for the arts or democracy) are without adequate empirical foundation (Gans, 1967:xvi).

Suburbs vary considerably, but yet the charges of cultural aridity, limited perspectives, conventional respectability and consumerist monotony have some substance. One is reminded, *mutatis mutandis*, of the airs and pretensions of the Parisian bourgeoisie. Suburbs as spatial phenomena must exist in all urbanized societies, but as social phenomena they have acquired their greatest notoriety in the United States.

There is an extraordinary conjuncture between the standardized homogeneity which industrialists wanted to impose upon their workers as well as on their products, with the same qualities popularly attributed to the suburban way of life. Indeed the conjuncture is even more direct.

Successful mass production concentrated on standardized products for a mass market, which the producers themselves had to create, through their products and their advertisement with the expansion and perfecting of media techniques of seduction and promotion, through the houses and communities which they built, and the roads and bridges, aeroplanes, airlines and airports, in addition to the car itself. The person who must be persuaded to consume all these products was the same person whose behaviour was standardized in the process of their production. With these two forces, operating from both sides, how then could the suburbs and their inhabitants not be standardized?

By the magical alchemy of the individual and the collective, the American middle-class suburb followed the dictates and requirements of corporate capitalism, financed by mortgage mechanisms derived from New Deal prototypes. The individuals and families concerned were persuaded by the building lobby, government propaganda and the media, reinforcing the predilections of their class position and origins, to see themselves as making voluntary choices, to fulfil their ambitions and dreams of rising status, for spacious family housing and good schools in salubrious quasi-rural surroundings, enjoying all the modern amenities of domestic comfort, recreational pleasure and quality health services. Their vast car-borne population movement gave them the pleasurable sense of independent mobility, while it guaranteed the expansion and profits of Detroit's giant auto-industry, as well as the great building corporations and the whole consumer economy. Their pursuit of the rural could only destroy the rural, contributing to the rising menace of ozone depletion, air pollution and undisposable garbage.

No European country enjoyed this combination of factors. Their ancient urban cultures imposed different values and practices. Affluence and obsessive car driving came later. The culture of apartment living and public transport was better established. Urban growth created critical problems everywhere, but they were tackled within this different context, with less reluctant government involvement. In Sweden more than a third of the population is in the three biggest cities, but less than half in individual houses, about half privately built and half by co-operatives and semi-public bodies. Government loans have favoured the latter with 90% coverage of cost while covering only 85% of cost in loans to private building.

The great variety of goods eventually proffered appeared always as the response to popular demand and the will of the people, well saturated by the media avalanche, persuading them that this product is not only good and useful but that it has become the rage with all your neighbours, so that without it you risk shameful embarrassment, loss of face and class prestige. The myth of freedom of choice, unlimited choice and popular choice is thus maintained, while the determining decisions on product style and quality are made according to the dictates of corporate business, always willing to hire the best symbolic promoter if it can be made to pay.

As suburban areas reached a suitable extent and density, they provided perfect market catchments for the great supermarkets, malls and shopping centres, with their vast car parks, drawing more and more business from the shops of city centres, so that the latter became depressed and delapidated like the residential areas around them. The malls and shopping centres carry further the mass standardization of consumer products and their consumers, enlarging and cheapening the profitable market for mass production and distribution industries. When land values in central city shopping and residential areas fall below a certain point, they become profitable investment for developers and urban renewal projects, subsidized by the federal government from taxpayers' money. This was the great fraud of the twentieth century, with the officially stated goal of realizing as soon as possible 'a decent home and suitable living environment for every American family'.

The twentieth-century transformation of urban life and society reflects the further unfolding of the Capitalist mode of production in increasing scale, concentration and eventual monopoly. The motor car and the ever increasing array of consumer gadgets accompanied the moving of half the population into new suburbs, representing a colossal achievement of construction, punctuated by the Great Depression, World War II, the post-war boom and its aftermath, dramatized in spectacular changes in culture and family life, class formation and organization. The story of urban renewal is the story of the Depression and the defeat of the dream of individualistic unregulated capitalism.

The farce of urban renewal

When the 1929 Depression struck, the Republican administration struggled desperately to preserve the business world inviolate from the 'unfair' competition of government interference, trying to cope with rising destitution by appeals to state and city authorities to promote voluntary efforts and by invoking the charity of the rich. Many well-intentioned organizations and programmes were formed and large sums collected, but so pitiably inadequate to the magnitude of the crisis that the Roosevelt administration swept to power in 1933 with a mandate for unprecedented intervention which pervaded most aspects of urban and national life. By the various relief programmes, employing large numbers of unemployed, over 1,000 airports or landing strips were constructed and many parks, swimming pools, sewers, schools, hospitals and water supplies constructed and improved in many cities. But FDR still strove to avoid interference with traditional spheres of business and profit, especially when it came to plums like housing and real estate. Yet the massive private housing construction of the 1920s came to a halt with the Depression. In 1934 Roosevelt started the Federal Housing Authority which spent $4.25 billion in the next six years and provided cheap, long-term mortgages for the first time, enabling thousands of lower-middle-class families to join the flight to suburbs.

Much was spoken of housing for low-income groups but little achieved. The New Deal slum conversion programme of the mid-1930s produced 22,000 dwelling units, but even at $26 a month they were beyond the reach of working-class incomes of less than $1,000 a year and simply drove them on to other slums (Chudacoff, 1975:220). The US Housing Authority built 47,500 units which were more successful in being restricted to those in the lowest third of income levels. Nearly a third of those in urban areas were occupied by Blacks, and their construction costs were 25% lower than those of private industry. Tens of billions of dollars were spent by the Roosevelt programmes, mainly in cities, to the horror of conservatives. Much waste and misdirection occurred but the main object was achieved, of enabling the destitute to survive and eventually beginning to drag the economy out of the Depression, a process which was only completed by the extra demands of World War II, which brought many programmes to a halt, but also brought war factories and mobilization of the whole country.

Many innovations came to stay: food stamps for the dependent, the whole Social Security structure of compulsory insurance for old age and disability, regulation of minimum wages, maximum hours, prohibition of child labour. Trades unions were encouraged and especially the organization and protection of the lowest paid. The CIO came into existence and began to admit Blacks to union organization. Union halls became new centres of support, solidarity and entertainment for the urban working man.

Big business was angered by government encouragement of workers, although the economy was prosperous. These changes weakened the power of bosses and machines. There was no longer the same large stream of helpless immigrants at their mercy and needing their services. Unions provided alternative means of organization, pressure, mutual aid, self-help and friendly solidarity. The spate of federal aid made the bosses' services redundant, but still left them a role in allocation and brokerage, if they were sufficiently adaptable, since in fact the potential volume of job patronage was even greater, as Mayor Daley of Chicago continued to prove until 1976.

The heavy spending special programmes had to bow to relentless business opposition as soon as the Depression began to pass. But World War II soon brought even heavier government spending, on war instead of people. Full employment and the tremendous American production machine achieved new heights. After the war the devastation and breakdown of large areas of the world opened unprecedented opportunities to American exports and overseas employment, largely financed federally under programmes such as the Marshall Plan, followed by various foreign aid and technical and military assistance schemes, all of which would have been unthinkable without the lessons of the Roosevelt era. So a period of great general prosperity and rising incomes – but not reduced inequalities – occurred and it was in this context that renewed efforts to solve the problems of the cities and of housing for the poor took place.

Aims and aspirations were great, achievements often pitiful and contradictory. Whereas private industry built 800,000 houses a year in the 1920s, the 1949 Housing Act promised 800,000 public housing units in four years but took twenty (Chudacoff, 1975:192). So far from concentrating on rehousing the poor it usually ended up tearing down slums to clear valuable land near city centres, both to swell the tax base for the city fathers and to maximize the profits for real estate speculation and big business investment by building shopping plazas, banks and parking lots, together with the occasional cultural centre or theatre and museum, none of which helped the dispossessed slum dwellers, many of them Black, who once again had to move and find or make another slum. The process was further strengthened in the same direction by the 1954 Urban Renewal Act, the effective aim of which was to attract middling- to high-income families and business back to the inner city and so raise values. It is quite astonishing that the Urban Renewal programme which so many happily took to be a sharing of general prosperity with the poor and the raising of slum families to decent housing and standards of living, turns out to have been another bitter hoax and had the opposite effect, causing the net loss of some 2,500,000 housing units to the poor – more than Germany lost from saturation bombing in World War II. The eviction of poor and Black families was essential for changing the image of proud cities from old-fashioned, dirty, industrial cities to gleaming, corporate, modern ones (Kleniewski, 1984:205–20).

The so-called Public Housing programmes left concrete jungles and high-rise slums, while programmes that targeted 'a decent home for every American' destroyed twice as many dwellings as they built (Chudacoff, 1975:258). 'The actual effect has been to keep the poorest of the poor out of rehabilitated areas, in the highest density slums' (Banfield, 1970:16). 'At a cost of more than three billion dollars the Urban Renewal Agency has succeeded in materially reducing the supply of low cost housing in American cities' (Greer, 1965:30). 'Hundreds of thousands of low income people have been forced out of low-cost housing, by no means all of it substandard, in order to make way for luxury apartments, office buildings, hotels, civic centres, industrial parks and the like' (Banfield, 1970:16). 'The FHA and VA programs have subsidized the movement of the white middle class out of the central cities and older suburbs while at the same time penalising investment in the rehabilitation of the run-down neighbourhoods of these older cities. The poor – especially the Negro poor – have not received any direct benefit from these programs' (Banfield, 1970:15; see also Kleniewski, 1984:215–18).

The Office of Economic Opportunity, Job Corps, Head Start, VISTA and other idealistic sounding efforts of Johnson's Great Society era continued the effort, with much waste, good-will and malversation, to improve the training and opportunity of the American poor, especially in the cities and especially for Black Americans. They significantly changed the structure of urban society by generating a new category of highly trained, highly educated, affluent Blacks in business (White and Black, including especially the largest corporations), government (federal, state and city), professions, academia and countless leadership positions.

All the schemes collided and foundered on the same principles and vested interests which have been one of the most unchanging and deeply rooted elements of American culture from its inception. They transgressed the code that private interests and property in business and real estate must be protected from interference or restriction, that unfettered individualistic competition is the American Way, both the most virtuous and the most successful method of maximizing the well being of all, while preserving liberty. Poverty and failure, apart from temporary misfortune, are due to weakness and moral deficiency and can only be solved by greater effort of the victim or by voluntary private charity. It is the age-old ethos of those who have owned the property and made the poor laws for at least the last six centuries. It is the obstructive tradition which has stood against beneficial change and modernity in urban industrial life.

The lion's share of large-scale projects of urban transformation therefore have to be left to corporate capitalist enterprise, with land speculation and windfall development profits enveloped in a determined smokescreen of noble public service protestation. Virtuous calls for popular participation in planning and decision making have failed to involve the poor or the Blacks, for whom the middle-class goals were usually an unattainable mockery.

The attempt to harness national, public and long-term interests with private short-term profit interests involves insoluble contradictions of goals, methods and organization. Cost-benefit analysis is doomed to inevitable inconsistency because no way has been discovered to measure costs fairly or to agree on whose benefits are in question. Consultants face conflicting demands between their personal interests and those of their organization and of the contracting agency. Revitalizing downtown areas *requires* traffic congestion (rather than beltways and bypasses), unless transportation is completely revolutionized; effective planning requires less not more citizen participation (Harvard Research Review No. 5, 1970:14). The logic of science and technology is not that of democracy and in fact the two are hard to reconcile, for the astounding success of high-powered technologies is due to their breaking down ecological complexities by deliberately ignoring the recalcitrant human factor (Mumford, 1961:208–26). Yet the family house has remained the most impervious to technological change of all the commodities touched by the industrial revolution (Abrams, 1970:209–28), partly because local building code jurisdictions are thousands of little kingdoms each having its own way (Harvard Research Review No. 5, 1970:26).

Private entrepreneurs cannot achieve the required volume of new town or satellite city construction because they cannot acquire enough land in the right place, as well as needing huge sums of capital at long term before any return can be expected, and facing the zoning and building restrictions of innumerable local governments (Rapkin, 1966:208–19); therefore the unwelcome prospect of public land acquisition has to be faced. But the federally legislated urban renewal programme enabled business interests to overcome these obstacles.

Mixed public and private projects face difficulties of their own. Three very large private developers and three large institutions (hospital, university and housing authority), with large government financing, held main responsibility for the Douglas Park Community project on Chicago's Near South Side, probably the largest inner-city residential development in the country, with 22,000 residents and a total of 80,000 expected (Suttles, 1972:84). Low-income housing was first developed, but failed to reduce the high level of public danger in the area and the emphasis switched, as often, to middle-class housing. The attempt at co-ordination of public and private efforts did not work well. The vociferous demands of an alert public made private developers feel they were being held responsible for public agencies, so that the representatives of the two interests actually avoided meeting, in order to avoid charges of collusion and conspiracy, which were constantly made, with the result that there was little co-ordination except in face of crisis situations and violent demonstrations. The threat of violence was constant, leading to intense methods of control through police, doormen, custodians, security guards, wire fences, peepholes, television monitors and even at times machine guns on the tops of buildings (Suttles, 1972:97).

The experiment cannot be dismissed as a failure, since it is one of the largest in the country to succeed in creating a new physical community with some racial integration at least at the middle-class level. Yet it bred disillusion and pessimism, providing no model for replication. It drew on highly enlightened groups not readily available elsewhere, yet it was neither fish nor fowl, not a private development on laissez-faire principles nor a centrally developed community with public welfare goals. It is instructive that, in contrast to other areas of Chicago, and to Levittown where it is taboo, talk about class and race is intense, with heightened awareness of conflicts of interest dividing Blacks and Whites and rich and poor (Suttles, 1972:101). This supports the general principle that where hostile groups are forced together, without any desperate over-riding interest to unite them, conflict is intensified.

Large-scale efforts in smaller cities face similar problems. In and around metropolitan Dayton, Ohio, with only powers of persuasion through possible finance for development, over the usual host of parochial, competitive local authorities, the attempt was made to get them to accept integration, through the resettlement of poor and Black families from the inner city in the suburbs, with the construction of inexpensive apartments to receive them. Some movement was achieved, but as in Bethnal Green and Greenleigh, they missed their old friends and kin, their favourite shops and, most of all, their jobs, many of them investing in expensive cars to commute back whence they came: another casualty of public transport failure.

Small towns

There are still some 1,200 small towns in the United States, with a total population of about 12 million. Ideas about small towns are confusing. New England settlements grew into nucleated villages or small towns with rural hinterlands. Most of the country was mechanically laid out in rectangular tracts of vacant land designated townships, which in the south are electoral and administrative districts of counties (Douglass, 1970:50). Springdale is called small town and also rural community (Vidich and Bensman, 1960). Its village is mainly composed of shopkeepers, the town board dominated by farmers (Vidich and Bensman, 1960). The town is exclusively concerned with the country outside the village, although the latter also votes for its officers! Whatever the confusions, small towns are at the mercy of urban mass society and most actually lost population because of the concentrating power of manufacturing industry. In the latest decentralizing phase, industries do not move into older small towns, but rather into suburban fringes or into the countryside, which they proceed to urbanize.

Economic globalization and the mass commoditization of all aspects of human life, even the most sacred and the most aesthetic, leaves little place for relatively self-sufficient small towns of distinctive identity. To survive they must grow, entering the local manifestation of the world system, at least in a disguised, surreptitious fashion. With the demise of the rural farming economy, the small town has no meaning except as a nostalgic idea. The current course of urbanization and suburbanization engulfs small towns also. Many are swallowed and disappear, or acquire official suburban status where cities do not annex suburbs, perhaps claiming the cachet of 'village status' despite dense urbanization. Towns further from larger centres (20–40 miles in Britain, 200–300 in parts of America) seem more authentic, but have to accept dependence on the ubiquitous tentacles of branches of giant corporations, risking the loss of the charms they are trying to preserve. Those in metropolitan regions, or in commuter towns, have more employment alternatives and can escape particular plant closings, so that local taxes and hence services can be maintained, softening class tensions. Such communities can make no pretence of small-town independence, but more distant towns, which seem more authentic, face inevitable class conflict, between maintaining charm and amenity, controlling growth and pollution, or capitulating to the forces of development to safeguard present and future employment, since the bucolic farm economy is no more (MacLennan, 1985).

Working-class families try to remain in the same area, while middle-class families are more mobile, the younger generation moving out to careers elsewhere as others come in (Toth, 1992:26). Local job maintenance or expansion is therefore the prime working-class interest, whereas recently arrived middle-class managers, professors, administrators and retirees want to maintain the quality of life and organize prestigious associations to campaign for it.

When one corporation planned a trucking terminal on the highway and a giant supermarket chain wanted a retail outlet, Carlisle, Pennsylvania, was polarized. A corporation vice-president attending council meetings represented promotion of community jobs and growth to some, but imperious outside interference to others, who feared noise, pollution and traffic congestion. Both corporations appeared to back down at first, but both established themselves eventually nearby where they had planned. In fact the outside forces almost always win, by postponement, changes of name and site, going outside city limits or to a rival community. The small town either suffers an environmental threat or loses potential taxes, jobs and the profits from increased local spending.

Working-class people relax on doorsteps or streetcorners, or in bars and parks, making leisure a family affair, while professional and white-collar middle class take leisure more individually, outside the home but in the gracious calm of private clubs or restaurants. Working-class youth cruise downtown with squealing tyres, backfires, loud radios and obnoxious yelling, offending middle-class sensibilities. The automobile symbolizes financial independence for the otherwise dispossessed, and provides informal, friendly, public competition. They reject the orderly discipline of the City Recreation Department programmes at the YM and YWCAs aimed strictly at the middle class (Toth, 1992:16–17). By virtue of residential area the downtown Junior High is largely working class and the outlying Junior High middle class. The activities of high schoolers are not segregated and both classes are found in all, but clearly preppies are predominantly middle and cruisers predominantly lower class.

Garden City, Kansas, is about the same size as Carlisle. It is far from any big dominant city, but it is totally dominated by two meat packing plants, one the largest in the world (the cost per head slaughtered is only half that in smaller plants). Most Anglo oldtimers feel the quality of life has deteriorated, with increased traffic and crime and less accessible health care. But there is no shortage of work and the town's reception of industrial development has been very positive in expanding water, sewerage and electrical services, new houses and mobile homes, schools, library and bypass to ease traffic problems. The Ministerial Alliance organized and raised funds to help the thousands of south-east Asian immigrants with English lessons, children's camps and cultural awareness projects. Large numbers of south-east Asians were housed in trailer parks, which they could best afford, and naturally kept very much to themselves. There was very little overt discrimination, but false rumours and exaggeration, despite a lot of friendly personal relations. Among the Hispanic Catholic immigrants 30% had married with Anglos between 1950 and 1989.

Small towns, ambiguous as they are, attract less study than larger, more glamorous or historically significant cities. They are far too numerous for anything like a representative sample to be achieved. Public statistics omit the most meaningful data. Boundaries, if present, are very culture bound. The category 'rural area' now conceals more than it reveals. British figures show small towns of less than 50,000 and 'rural areas' growing much faster than larger towns, while all conurbations have lost population – another way of describing flight from centre to suburb (which is not distinguished). 'Rural areas' grew fastest of all (17.9% 1961–71) and this is unquestionably *suburbanization*. United States figures show more than half the population in suburbs. The urban demographic trend therefore is similar on both sides of the Atlantic, granting differences of definition, ecology and density. Many 'rural areas' in the United States could be 'wilderness'. In France also, many small places, as communities, are dying, while those willing to seize opportunities, with all their disadvantages, are growing fast.

Ethnicity and class

The immigrant origins of the United States set it on an ethnic course. Pilgrim Father puritanism fleeing from oppression in England reproduced it with more rigid prejudices in New England towns. They set the dominant tone, though Quakers in Philadelphia had a heritage of tolerance and the Anglicans and Catholics of Maryland also followed that course. Southerners might have shown tolerance, but their economy was class-bound and soon slave-dependent, pushing them irrevocably into prejudice. Each great immigrant tide flooding into the cities was economically welcomed and socially despised. Their ethnic divisions provided a major mechanism for exerting capitalist control. Ethnicity compounded religious difference to make harsh barriers. Early Irish immigrants were treated almost as badly as Blacks, scorned with the same bestial and subhuman epithets. The need of destitute immigrants to cling together for emotional as well as material survival set the template of ethnic prejudice and separatism. Ethnic churches were burned and homes looted in anger at the mid-nineteenth-century immigrants. The even greater influx at the end of the century enormously increased the variety as well as the numbers, providing an urban mosaic of local concentrations based on ethnicity and religion, tending towards similarity of class-occupational status.

The numerous Protestant sects were valuable sources of support and solidarity, providing ready-made boundaries to reinforce the ethnic, giving a vital sense of identity, belonging and coherence in an otherwise chaotic situation.

Even the Roman Catholic church, despite its universalistic stance, could readily be moulded into distinctive Irish, Italian or Polish forms. The church congregation was a core institution in construction of a meaningful local community, ideally regarded as an 'autonomous republic'. Religion, ethnicity and occupation congeal into class status, so that all denominations in a city fell into a class ranking.

Various studies show an approximate order of Episcopalian, Unitarian, Presbyterian, Congregational, Christian Science, Methodist, Baptist,

Pentecostal, then Black congregations and storefront churches, according to the area of town over time and age, wealth, education and race-ethnicity of the congregation and its members (Warner, 1963; Lynd and Lynd, 1929). It is this multifunctional yet monomorphic syndrome which gives the churches the appearance of greater strength in America than in Europe. The American bar like the church congregation is monomorphic: a working-class or upper-class bar, a singles or gays bar, etc., whereas each English public house used to include private, saloon and public bars, so that each person, class and gender could choose its own appropriate milieu.

Women dominate most congregations numerically. Revolutionary experiences secularized the French workers and they departed first, whereas in America some upper-status members were first to leave. Middletown's congregations in the 1920s showed 'unalert acceptance', with bursts of revival for the less sophisticated (Lynd and Lynd, 1937:295). In the 1930s business congregations were older and two-thirds or more women, while working-class churches had a closer relation between pastor and flock (Lynd and Lynd, 1937:298).

The ghetto-like neighbourhoods of big cities began to disperse in the twentieth century. Ethnic neighbourhoods had been structured by churches, clubs, bars, restaurants, shops, newspapers, schools and sports teams, but not stable populations, as people moved at least every few years. Only the Blacks were kept firmly segregated from the rest. Their ghettos grew larger as the flow from the rural south increased. With the move to the suburbs the ethnic tendency remained but less strongly. By now most fellow ethnics were quite well established and needed one another's support less urgently. Their interests more often diverged and anyhow the car could keep ethnic solidarities and networks alive without such residential proximity. Only when bedevilled with racial myths and stereotypes can ethnicity still ruin the lives of millions of Americans and threaten the very structure of society.

The least acculturated are the least mobile. In solidary ethnic groups mobility is regarded as betrayal and causes conflict (Spiro, 1955). Religion resists acculturation more than ethnicity and is more easily dropped than syncretized. Ethnicity inhibited class-based interest groups and as workers had some success in their struggles for higher wages, no strongly sustained socialist working-class movement developed.

Though refugees from the Soviet Baltic, Lithuanians in Los Angeles displayed the stereotypes most desirable to American society: anti-communist, well educated and hardworking. So they have been upwardly mobile, entering mainly professional fields, becoming citizens, voting and participating in the mainstream. Some 15,000 Lithuanians scattered

through Los Angeles have no localized community, but some concentration round the 'parish' church which has a massive Lithuanian Sunday
attendance. Those not keen on church hang out in the Lithuanian tavern
nearby. In early refugee days ethnic intermarriage counted as betrayal,
but may account for half of current unions.

Seeming successfully assimilated, they assert a distinctive identity
proudly, both to one another and outsiders. They maintain a vast network
of associations, a basketball team and a Lithuanian press, striving to
maintain knowledge of their language, use of ethnic names and cherishing of Lithuanian cultural objects. There is great warmth and emotional intensity in the almost mystical 'soul'-like quality of Lithuanian
ethnicity, and strong family life, often with three generations and little
divorce. Yet participation in church and formal associations is falling.
Most are just selectively Lithuanian with friends. But the Los Angeles
community acts as a magnet to further Lithuanian settlement, for many
practical reasons of mutual aid and investment opportunity, as well as
emotional comfort and satisfaction (Baskauskas, 1977).

Achieving satisfactory personal identity is a problem in American
society, but with professional or upper-middle-class status, the knowledge of being nominally Lithuanian may be sufficient, even if most of the
symbols, organizations and distinctive relationships dwindle. Kinship,
concern for the homeland and new immigration may keep them alive. For
the increasing proportion of mixed descent, ethnicity may become
nominal. In Milwaukee, Serbian ethnicity also seemed to become
nominal. Only Sarajevo and Bosnia have shown us how the vicious self-
interest of leaders can fan Serb ethnicity into murderously fierce flame.
Ethnicity is contingent and circumstantial.

Chinese street boys in Boston, caught between two cultures, find they
'cannot accept as self-image any of the existing identities they perceive as
available to them' (Kendis and Kendis, 1976:001). So they have generated a new group with which they can identify. It gives them an acceptable
self-image, enabling them to regard themselves successfully as Chinese
when dealing with Americans and Americans when dealing with Chinese.
For they are beguiled by materialistic American culture and, like most
second-generation immigrants, disaffected with their parents, whom long
hours and hard work prevent from effective contact or control.

In Levittown 'no one paid much attention' to remaining ethnic
differences, although the Lutheran church had a German and the
Catholic church an Irish flavour, while Italians 'maintained their traditional lack of interest in church activities except for Mass' (Gans,
1967:85). But ethnic differences were still something of a barrier between
neighbours. Jewish women were insecure until they had formed or found

networks with other Jewish women. The handful of Japanese, Chinese and Greek families were left rather isolated (Gans, 1967:162).

There is a suburban middle-class culture in which ethnicity is of minor importance for most people. In Atlanta, small groups of fairly recent and mainly middle-class Cubans, Arabs, Japanese, Korean and other Asians and west Europeans are scattered rather than clustered in ghettos. They do not experience disorganization or impersonalization and are beginning to assimilate and depend less on ethnicity, some west Europeans explicitly denying that they are ethnic, though wanting to keep their language (Hill, 1976:333–47; Fennell, 1977:345–54).

Gans suggests 'selective homogeneity at the block level' as a solution to ethnic polarization (1967:172–3). The planners' neighbourhood of several hundred families is socially irrelevant for actual neighbouring, which is based on frequent face-to-face relations between those in groups of no more than ten or a dozen houses. At this level a minimum of homogeneity is required to prevent insoluble conflict, whereas the larger community concerned with services such as schools should be heterogeneous 'because it must reflect the pluralism of American Society' (Gans, 1967:173).

The kinship networks and behaviours of nuclear family members have been studied in the context of class, ethnicity, rural, urban and suburban life. Subsequent events in political economy and culture have so revolutionized this context that, while these studies retain their value and interest, they are of more uncertain relevance to the contemporary situation.

Blue-collar manual workers had a very distinctive life and culture, with a good deal of variation between stable settled families and less successful 'hard livers'. The latter are distinguished by heavy drinking, marital instability, toughness, political alienation, rootlessness, present time orientation and strong individualism (Howell, 1973:263–4). Their cultural and material impoverishment is punctuated by bursts of meaningless affluence. Their overcrowded rooms show slovenly housekeeping and dilapidated furniture, but costly gadgets and appliances, colour TVs and cassette players, multiple cars and guns, electric carvers and expensive mechanical toys.

The blue-collar workers look on the hard livers as lower class, or even white trash, considering themselves middle class although they are blue-collar, for indeed they can earn middle-class incomes and have expensive homes. But they assert aggressively distinct values, they dominate their women and drink at the bar separately leaving them at home where they have glimpsed equality in TV soap operas and the men are terrified of it. The men are highly skilled, highly paid, chauvinistic and racist, but more spontaneous and forthright than middle-class strivers. The younger men, whose long hair and moustaches conflict with the crewcut, clean shaven older lot, may be a little more liberal towards Blacks and women's liberation, some even having been to college (Le Masters, 1975:193–5). Changes in industrial production and technology have changed blue-collar work from its old craft basis to more involvement with big machinery in mass production projects. In both America and Britain the manual working class stressed male dominance as breadwinner and the importance of physical sex, in a largely non-verbal relationship, suggesting the 'restricted code' of the working class (Bernstein, 1975). Wives keep closer to mothers, friends and female relatives than husbands do, especially in Britain.

Urban workers in Greensboro had as many meaningful primary relationships as rural people, but many more segmented, impersonal relations (Adams, 1968:1–3). Of working-class couples 60% had one set of parents in town, but only 45% of the more mobile middle class had. Over half the wives in London's East End visited their mothers every day and 90% did so every week. Less than half the men kept in such close touch, in London or Greensboro. Daughters communicate with parents more than sons. Stable working-class women keep up far more regular visiting, telephoning and mutual aid with their parents than do men. Women express more affection towards kin, maintaining ties to both sets of parents in the middle class, but concentrating on their own in the working class (Adams, 1968:170).

Since the 1970s the self-confidence and pride of the working class has been shattered by deindustrialization, and the youth revolution implies profound changes for the family in the next generation and the class structure. Six European industrial countries lost 7 million jobs from 1973 to the late 1980s, about a quarter of all jobs. Labour in manufacturing settled at about a quarter of civilian employment, in the United States one fifth. Britain lost a quarter of its manufacturing industry from 1980 to 1984. In the slump after 1985 the developing market economies' industrial production fell 10% and international trade 13%. West European unemployment rose from 1.5% in the 1960s to 11% in 1993. Beggars appeared again in city streets and the homeless sheltered in doorways and cardboard boxes. There was a striking growth in inequality.

Class and ethnicity can reinforce one another. North Town, Texas, is a low-income, predominantly Mexican American community. Middle class or working class almost coincided with Anglo or Mexicano. In the 1970s there was considerable social segregation in dating and leisure although both groups played and worked together in the high school, 'Schools are sites for cultural practices that stage or reproduce social inequality' (Foley, 1991:xv). Youth perform their future class roles in sports, youth groups and classroom rituals. Socially prominent youth become adept at managing their images and manipulating adult authorities. These communicative competences in *the art of deceit* prepared them to be future civic and political leaders (Foley, 1991:xv). Working-class lads glorify a macho style emphasizing physical powers, bravery, fighting, drinking, cursing, making fun of authorities and oppressing women and minorities. They have a distinct set of cultural practices in talking, eating, joking, playing, story-telling, singing, dancing and dressing. The counter school culture preserved kids' working-class cultural style and honour and relegated them to school failure and working-class jobs (Foley, 1991:163–7). By the late 1980s the old segregation had crumbled, interethnic-class dating and even marriage was occurring and the churches had opened up. The economic structure was the same, but middle-class Mexicans were making the welfare and patronage systems serve the working class better.

At times of maximum ethnic intensity (after major immigration, or Black migration from the south), much of the class structure flowed through ethnicity and racism, which masked it, although the class position of the established middle class and super-rich was not affected. The post-World War II middle class became larger and more affluent. The power and wealth of the elite rose even more, putting it far outside the middle class (Reissman, 1959:359). There was considerable mobility up to the middle levels, largely choked off above that. The six-class system (Warner, 1963) was an attitudinal statistical construct (Mayntz, 1967:9, 13; Hubbell, 1976:19) analysing overlapping status strivings and strengthening the evasion of Marxist class. In London and the British towns the basic power structure changed little after the war and hardened again after the great Labour Party levelling measures of the 1940s and 1950s.

Intense ethnic chauvinism blurs with racism. The appalling racial prejudices, seeming almost ineradicable in many urban police forces, as time and again in Los Angeles, show the seething strength of hatred still endangering social progress. The rise of Colin Powell to head the American military seems to show considerable transcendence at the very top, while the O.J. Simpson verdict split American society from top to bottom in neatly separate Black and White halves, according to the media. Since the mass migration from the south, racism has become principally an urban problem, applying also to Puerto Ricans, Haitians, south-east Asians and Chinese.

Although classes are not specifically urban phenomena, their structure and function has been decisively evolved in cities. The rural class par excellence, the peasantry, no longer plays a distinctive role in advanced economies. The secular movement has always been away from birth-determined social orders towards those based upon achievement.

Modern class was the product of industrialization. The upper class, which was the aristocracy, has largely lost the attributes which gave it meaning, along with most of its land, and now gets most of its wealth from rents and business investments, prestige directorships or paid performance as nobility. Its titles have no implications beyond rank and ritual. Its unique place in the elite jet-set, fashion-media network of the global world city does give it privileged access to circles and sources of power and wealth if desired. The essential class division is still that of Marx, between those who own and run the economy and those who operate it. All the rest are tied to these in various ways. Intellectuals, writers, artists, performers and professionals are still intercalary, ambiguously facing both ways, irrevocably entangled in the power structure of the large organizations which pay them.

The media age, accelerating from movies and radio to TV, cassettes and computers, introduced new possibilities. The computer brain is so valuable and saleable that its possessor can rocket quickly from middle to top levels of wealth and notoriety. The media array of TV news, talk shows and special features, rental cassettes and glossy weeklies, the whole panoply of global commodity advertising, invading every innocent sphere of human activity, from kitchen to bedroom and toilet, sports arena to race-track, generates a nebulous and heterogeneous yet diversely interlocking layer of stars. Many are ephemeral, not to say worthless or despicable, but add brief glitter to the whole. The layer of stardom overlaps increasingly with the layer of the super-rich, which includes those who run all the large corporations and collectively determine, in a muddled, conflictful, half competitive, half monopolistic way, the destiny of society. The two layers do not work together, and differ radically, but they play together and are fused together by the heat of their common interest in prestige and profit. The media do not run society except as channels and instruments to make or break, but they and those they present and celebrate, together do. Their intense visibility is transparency and deception simultaneously. Some are celebrated because they run society, others are stars because they are celebrated and many manoeuvre to minor roles in running society.

In Marx's day the bourgeoisie owned and ran the multitude of small firms which constituted the capitalist system. They evolved a way of life which is not that of those who run the system today. In Marx's day the upper class was rightfully seen as on the way out, however much glamour and clout it retained, but our initial dyadic distinctions must always be refined into dialectical triads. There is always an upper class on the way in, or out, perhaps both. The irreducible upper class is the *rentier* class of old wealth, who must develop and espouse ways and values symbolically contrary to those who made it and them. Here the effete aristocracies have not lost their force as model. They can perform gracefully in the publicized playgrounds where some of the real wealth makers and power holders join them for brief vacations. American classless squeamishness can only mask these distinctions with its constant celebration of fallacious equalities.

The middle class encroaches on the working class, as those who make the system work as handed to them, without ownership or control and often little responsibility. The working class of skilled manual and blue-collar workers is still very important in numbers, and contribution to production, but dwindling, while the semi-skilled and unskilled drift into the underclass, as major losers in deindustrialization, or robotic-computer-automation.

The western youth revolt

More shocking to White America than even the Black ghetto was the youth revolt of the sixties, which has receded from view but sowed the seeds of today's most intractable problems. American youth of the fifties were the most privileged ever: more urban, especially suburban, more middle class, educated and affluent. Their parents had emerged victorious from World War II to complete their education and take up good jobs in the booming economy. They surged out to new dream houses in the suburbs. Only 19% were willing to live in apartments or 'used houses' (Gitlin, 1987:14), and 85% of all new housing was built outside central cities from 1946 to 1958. America was the greatest and could solve problems. Their war experiences left them few illusions. Having won freedom they would hardly impose strict discipline on their children, but felt the range of their experience should make their guidance acceptable. The Depression still haunted them but their children were fed up with cautionary tales.

America paid for its new hegemony with anxiety. It was lonely and vulnerable at the top. Though income rose 49%, life insurance policies rose 200% in value from 1950 to 1960. Carefree affluence was poisoned by successive alarming events accelerating tension towards panic: first Soviet atom bomb 1949, Sputnik 1957, Bay of Pigs and Berlin Wall 1961, Cuban missile crisis 1962. The country was obsessed with national security. Children were subjected to hours of sudden bomb shelter practice, taking cover and learning about nuclear war, developing nightmares. There was also unrest at home. Sit-ins broke open segregated lunch counters in many southern cities. The great protest marches began, provoking crowd violence, police harassment and killings.

Student youth was intelligent and affluent, with no dominant ideology, religion or purpose. The very freedom was frustrating, challenged by mass produced media images of White youth on the move, with nowhere to go (Gitlin, 1987:29). Intellectuals taunted them with leisure wasted in shallow conformity, charging America with salesman mentality and corporate irresponsibility.

Progressive students got involved in both Civil Rights and Nuclear Disarmament campaigns. They put their bodies on the line in the danger zone, got harassed and beaten up by police and hostile crowds, becoming radicalized. The Vietnam War came to overshadow all other issues. Strong protest organizations developed on campuses from coast to coast, intensely involved with one another as 'the Movement'. The pill spread from 1960, undermining parental control over teenage bodies. Students moved off campus, 'housekeeping without matrimony'. Inter-racial couples became common; copulating with Blacks was a statement. Book censorship ended, letting *Playboy* and Henry Miller add zest to sex, drugs and rock'n'roll. Easy sex felt like freedom at first. Movement leaders recruited staff in bed as serial harems. They were the first youth ever to be allowed and have the money to live on their own together however they liked. As sex lost its virgin magic, violence took its place. The Movement grew in numbers, factions, contradictions, high-minded intentions and ugly results. Big cities and student cities attracted the star events: New York, Boston, Chicago, Ann Arbor, Madison, Berkeley, San Francisco. Anti-war protest got quite personal as draft deferment ran out, and dislike of war turned to fear as the horrors of Vietnam escalated. Drugs increased anxiety, with bad trips, jumping out of windows and acute terror for some. Rape was as common as bullshit on Haight-Ashbury. Sixteen-year-olds were drugged and gang-banged. Minds and bodies were maimed. The Movement could not control the growing lunatic fringe and its growing nastiness. Protest peaked to a crescendo and wilted with nebulous results. Free stew from stolen meat was offered daily at Golden Gate Park. A horse was butchered in protest at a San Quentin execution. Rifle practice was held for urban guerrillas, 'for they got concentration camps ready'. By the time the Movement turned sour and was fizzling out in useless violence, Nixon was bringing the troops home.

The Chicago Democratic Convention of 1968 marked a high point of ugliness and confusion, with Robert Kennedy assassinated and the Prague Spring crushed by Soviet tanks. The anti-war movement planned to disrupt the Convention unless it voted to end the Vietnam War. Mayor Daley refused all permits. Some 25,000 police, national guard, army and FBI agents massed to save, or destroy, Chicago's fair name. For four or five days and nights protesters battled them savagely and bloodily, after they had decided on violence by clearing out the parks with teargas and clubs. Neighbourhood citizens sheltered the wounded, but the Movement had organized infirmaries, fearing police surveillance of hospitals. So many journalists and top anchormen were manhandled that Chicago police brutality was made famous round the world. Spectacular battles were watched by the TV masses.

The protesters felt morally victorious, but the general public hated the anti-war movement, even if they wanted the war ended. The generation gap became harsh, although both were unconsciously bodying the same radical processes of social change. Humphrey denounced the obscenity, profanity and filth as jail-worthy, but he lost their vote and lost the election.

In October 1968 they returned to Chicago for four 'Days of Rage'. Now they did not wait for police attack, but charged into the Gold Coast, trashing cars and windows. Police shot 6 and arrested 250. Cash bail of $234,000 was set for $2.3 million in bail bonds. Seventy-five police were injured. In November they marched on the south Vietnamese embassy, trashing store fronts and fighting police. November the 15th was the largest protest in American history, some three-quarters of a million marching to the Washington monument. McGovern spoke, Pete Seeger sang. The peaceful effect was ruined by thousands of rebels marching on the Justice Department with bombs, getting teargassed. Washington was defiled with gas, fires and barricades. Nixon rejoiced at winning his point. They wanted terror, to rob banks and kidnap.

Despite their numbers, energy and sexual generosity, the women were humiliated by male chauvinistic leadership crowned by the Panthers' assertion 'the place for women in this organization is prone', 'Fuck your woman so hard she can't stand up.' Resentment built up. By the end of the sixties male leadership faltered, floundered and flopped. They had beaten their heads against state power and had them beaten by police and sheriffs to little purpose. Many returned to compete in real life. Women's rage burst out and took over in a wild extravaganza as powerful, murderous, revolting and senseless as anything males had done. They issued a blazing manifesto: men were fucked up, not oppressed; the revolution would have to be made and led by the most oppressed, Black, Brown and White women. It was an agonizing time for men, exhilarating for tens of thousands of women. They had been the cement of the male movement and their 'desertion' completed the dissolution.

In March 1970 Weatherwomen made pipe bombs and nail-studded bombs (Vietnam style) in the West 11th Street townhouse of one of their parents. It blew up killing three. Two women staggered out.

Weatherman sessions were dubbed 'Wargasms'. They felt it must be wonderful to blow up a building or kill a cop. 'We're against everything that's "good and decent" in honky America.' 'All White Babies are pigs' one said (Weathermen were all white!). Weatherwomen wrote articles celebrating the victories over monogamy. 'People who live together and fight together fuck together.' Couples were disbanded by fiat. Everyone was to sleep with everyone else, women with men, women with women, men with men. Having smashed monogamy they turned to celibacy to prove they were 'will incarnate', more powerful even than sex. It was a fitting logical climax. They had made brutally clear the uncomfortable implications of general emancipation. They verbalized and activated the repressed desires of many others, and the scatological terror lives on in contemporary lyrics.

The youth revolts in Europe and America coalesced from diverse sources. The American was sudden, unexpected, without precedent. The French had deep roots in 1871, 1848 and 1796. In Europe also youth became a new class, transnational, communicating worldwide, more ideological, less mindlessly militaristic, but the slogans in Paris: 'to forbid is forbidden' and Italy: 'we want it all and now' (or Thatcher's 1980s' 'there is no society, only individuals') matched the American mood (Hobsbawm, 1994:324, 337).

In America, sales of rock music rocketed from $277 million (1955) to $600 million (1959) and $2 billion (1973). The distribution of sounds and images became worldwide, through student tourism, university networks, the consumerist force of fashion and the panoply of ever improving media devices. Validating youth claims of humanity ending at thirty, their principal idols died young from excess of drugs and alcohol.

In society at large, divorce, abortion, pre-marital cohabitation and homosexuality came to be accepted, legally as well as customarily. The ages of voting and sexual consent were lowered. Living alone became common. Church membership and attendance fell everywhere. In some of the strongest bastions it was remarkably sudden. These changes also meant a general weakening of kinship relations. They affected the status of women most. By the 1980s over 50% of the wives in America were employed, 40% in Europe. They had taken over office and white-collar jobs, nearly half real estate and 40% of bank offices.

Meanwhile deindustrialization was removing manufacturing industry from the countries where it began. In the United States manufacturing declined from 1965, as it was moved abroad, and in Europe by the 1980s, when of a hundred German clothing workers thirty-four were abroad, from only three in 1966. Shipbuilding and iron and steel moved to Korea, Brazil, Spain, Romania and Poland.

In the older stereotype children worked so mother stayed at home.

Now mother worked so children could go to school, and college. Capitalism was based on the assumption that the family and kinship in an ordered hierarchical society guaranteed the reproduction of labour power. The capitalist system could not, or would not, do it. The youth culture demand for the autonomy of individual desire, to do your own thing, despite its origins tinged with idealism, has spread throughout society. The triumph of the individual over society, which the salesman blessed and fostered, allowed the mass consumer society to flourish and run wild, but it rejected the long-established, historical ordering of human relations in society, breaking the threads which once wove human beings into social textures (Hobsbawm, 1994:333–5).

The importance of the urban networks and solidarities of kinship and religion in empowering the exceptional commercial and other achievements of Jews, Quakers, Huguenots, the Chinese and Indian diaspora and even the Mafia cannot be exaggerated. But much of the silent majority remains within the old conventions, enabling society to continue, but creating traumatic insecurity and incomprehension between its polarized parts. It explains the 'two-thirds' society. If one third cannot easily find likeable jobs, they are quite content to sponge on the rest of society, having lost the 'habit of work'. But this fuels the 'enormous, emotionally loaded strength, rational or not of the mass demand of ordinary citizens to *punish* the anti-social' (Hobsbawm, 1994:340–2).

The aftermath flared in the anarchic violence of Bader-Meinhof and the Red Brigades in Germany and Italy, the frenzy of pirate take overs in New York, which abandoned production for pure profit and the many mad movements which have burst out suddenly with mass followings. Youth and especially Black youth were flattered in imitation as rock music, rap and lower-class accents, drugs, long hair and pony tails became chic. This heralded the incorporation of some mobile Blacks into the middle class and the relapse of the majority into new despair, a polarization which nourished the urban scourges.

Urban scourges

The ghetto

Because Blacks have been held down artificially by lack of fair access to education, health, housing, employment and political participation, the vast majority are still trapped in the lowest strata, increasingly called underclass. All other ethnic groups are also represented, but proportionally less, *ergo*, all afflictions which hit the lowest strata most severely, hit Blacks most severely. This makes it hard for large numbers of media-dazed citizens to escape from statistically false stereotypes conveying the impression that Blacks are especially linked with crime, violence, delinquency, poor learning and social failure, drug abuse, AIDS, family breakdown and homelessness. These stereotypes and the fears they engendered served the vested interests of many groups in the past. Scapegoating is a convenient weapon, easily manipulated by the powerful and succumbed to by the weak. But with the advent of deindustrialization and the information age where knowledge is power and wealth, this becomes highly counterproductive and destructive for society as a whole. Many ghetto dwellers, Black and White, have been deprived so long that they are no longer capable of the newer forms of employment. The society which rejected and oppressed them in the past can no longer afford to *warehouse* them unproductively in inner cities and prisons. It is therefore becoming not merely a matter of justice, morality and humanity, but of sheer economic interest and necessity to rescue these outcasts.

Violence, crime, drugs and homelessness have nothing intrinsically to do with Black people, but racism has forced Black people into an intense awareness and common consciousness in which the ghetto and its culture have an indelible presence through parents, siblings and kinsfolk even if not directly. It is *part of the Black experience* in a way that it is not part of the White experience even though in many contexts Whites may be the majority. Hispanics share much of this experience, but they have direct links with other nations and cultures which they regard as their own, giving a foundation to their sense of identity which American Black people have been denied.

All the major scourges of American society come together in the Black ghetto with a special virulence, accentuating one another. The ghettos are the complement of the suburbs, occupying the space the suburbanites left behind. Although Whites are also in the ghettos and may have warm and close relations with Blacks, the Black predominance is an expression of American ethnicity in its racist form. The ghettos have become so deeply embedded in the American political economy that not even the Black mayors of all the metropolitan cities can save them. They combine proximity to downtown with housing so despicably dilapidated as to be worth very little rent. In a situation of desperate housing shortage, much vacant accommodation is too ruinous for occupation.

Unemployment is very high, especially among Black males, who are deeply damaged by it in this society where male pride and self-respect depends upon successful breadwinning. Among sixteen- to nineteen-year-olds, 40.9% of Blacks were unemployed in the early 1980s, 20.3% of Hispanics and 17.4% of Whites (Auletta, 1983:28). New York City lost 600,000 jobs in the 1970s and another 300,000 in the 1981 budget

(Dehavenon, 1993:56). With 'downsizing' and 'deindustrialization' the loss of jobs continues on a massive scale.

In American society as a whole, childbirth out of wedlock, fatherless families and families maintained by single women have risen fast in recent decades. The vast majority of births to Black women are now illegitimate. Indeed, it is difficult for Black women in the ghetto to find husbands. There are two Black women for every Black man in the early twenties age cohort most eligible for marriage (Dehavenon, 1993:62). Among Black males 54% are homeless. They are more liable than Black women to die of seven of the most fatal diseases (Dehavenon, 1993:62). There are 48% of Blacks in prison compared to 12% of the total population. Many are away in the armed forces. Compared to Whites, Black illegitimacy and the female-headed household are simple demographic cause and effect.

Many children have never seen their fathers. Such families are disadvantaged, and hampered in providing for the emotional needs, discipline and habits essential for successful personality development, so that their children are severely handicapped. These are also the poorest families and they are deterred from acquiring a husband or stable male partner because this would disqualify them from the vital welfare assistance they may otherwise obtain.

A single mother and her three teenage daughters in a two-room apartment with three televisions, three videos and two radios all playing together are not exposed to helpful role models of stable family life. She can hardly escape the irresistible media message to aim at a middle-class life and to want the latest product models like everyone else.[1]

Children and teenagers are condemned to street life by the overcrowding, discomfort, noise and tensions of the home scene. Like many others, a ten-year-old boy in Detroit works for a crack dealer. When asked why he is not in school, he pulls out a wad of $10,000 in notes from his pocket and asks 'Why go to school?' He mourns a scholastic brother killed by stray bullets as well as six buddies dead from drug and gang violence. His main anxiety is the price of bullets. He does not expect to live beyond age twenty.[2] Youth in general now consider humanity stops at thirty (Hobsbawm, 1994:324). Violence is now so prevalent among Black unemployed youth that it is said to be the major cause of death. A young man walks into a university office, demands money and for having only $5 in her purse, the victim has her ear sliced. Two teenagers take a forty-five-minute taxi ride out to an affluent suburb. At a stop sign they hold up and hijack a new latest model car and return to the ghetto: the owner always observed security precautions – he avoided streets, used the skywalk downtown connecting offices and business centre with hotels, restaurants, shops and banks, locked his office during working hours and left downtown before six. In a situation of endemic crime the police task is formidable, not to say hopeless, and many police have been unable to avoid entanglement in the temptations which beset every step. Notorious court cases and evidence affirm the frequently deplorable, unsurprising negative and racist attitudes and behaviours of police towards ghetto Blacks. In the media age this feeds into and fuels the racist prejudices, fears and hatreds of the American populace, lamentably fired by the pranks and offences to which idle, resentful, deprived Black youth are inevitably tempted. Such are the daily incidents of the life of ghetto youth, which terms like defective socialization, poor education and juvenile delinquency seem too pale to describe.

It is terrifying alienation, racked with despair between boredom and explosions of violence, relieved only by the delusions of sniffing and injecting mind-blowing drugs and risking the HIV/AIDS infection they bring. The link between the drug lords of the Colombian cartels and the instant wealth, disease and death in the ghetto is devastatingly tight. It is only the huge international army of anti-narcotics agents which keeps the system going, leaving a trail of massive corruption wherever it goes, magnifying the price to the poor Andean peasant for his beneficial age-old crop tens of thousands of times.

It is exceedingly hard for Black youth to escape from the ghetto and its important family ties, obligations and friendships, or if they do, to avoid ever making a false step which will drag them back. The ghetto population is coming to be seen as an underclass, an emotive but indefinable notion varying very widely round an approximate 2 million (Auletta, 1983:27–30). In practical terms, they are no longer required by the American economy, which in the information age is committed to 'downsizing', throwing people out of work as it transfers production plants to Third World countries with cheap wages, no unions and lax safety regulations, concentrating on fewer and more skilled employees at home. The full horror of this 'warehousing', in ghettos, or by consequence in prison, of a substantial part of the national population as useless and unwanted, is so shattering for the future of society that it cannot be explicitly recognized or publicly faced.

Even in such a ghastly perspective, the ghettos are not safe or effective containers, but liable to explode in dangerous conflagrations, as witness the empty wastelands set in the middle of great cities by riots and fires. The ghetto is not a vacuum. The failure of the mainstream institutions in it is made up by its own spontaneous organizations, the Black storefront churches and the youth gangs. The churches perform a gymnastic feat in relating God's message to people in the ghetto and through it channelling emotional and spiritual experience of unimaginable strength and value as well as mutual aid. 'First you feed them. Then you clothe them. Then you save them for the Lord' said Pastor Mamie Roundtree, who spent her life doing this at Little Mount Calvary Whosoever Comes Pentecostal Church, East Harlem, one of seven occupied lots of the forty-one in the block, the rest being razed or abandoned, with seven under renovation (Dehavenon, 1992:35–6, 38). Such churches transcend race, class and age to bring salvation even to drug addicts as few agencies can. It is no irony to find a storefront church with drug dealers occupying abandoned premises above.

Anguish and distress at the hideous wreckage of human life evokes some heroic responses. Brave men and women triumph here and there over fearful odds to stand against drugs and violence, media deception and consumerist infatuation to rescue a few kin and friends from debauchery and ruin. Grandmothers sometimes make a haven of caring and compassion. Steadfast mothers stand by their children. Drug-addled mothers increasingly bear addicted children with HIV/AIDS ready made. Religious oriented groups are formed to save youth from demoralized homes and murderous streets by positive activities and enjoyments, winning them to regular habits, friendly discipline and simple, uniform dress. Black churches offer legitimate diversion and uplift in the sociable joy of collective worship and ecstatic experience. Vivacious choir singing raises the spirits and links with the Black musical genius which has carried many to fame and success. Ghetto rap, blues, rock and dance have made their indispensable contribution to cultural self-worth and survival, apart from being, with Coca-Cola and hamburgers, the American city's most penetrating global export.

Gangs

Youth gangs contribute to organizing otherwise lost and abandoned, anomic youth. Young male groups have been called gangs throughout American history, always linked to anxieties about violence (Cummings and Monti, 1993:318). In the early nineteenth century New York was very dangerous, terrorized by brawling thieving adult gangs up to 1,000 strong, sometimes furiously beaten up by police or engaging them in bloody pitched battles (Asbury, 1970:21–3, 28–45). The city was a very violent, uncontrolled place, with waves of new immigrants adding to the confusion. By World War I these huge gangs were brought under control. Some 300 leaders of the underworld were sent to prison. By contrast with early adult gangs the later youth gangs were 'merely young hoodlums taking advantage of ancient reputations' (Asbury, 1970). After the Civil War the metropolis was infested with bands of professional burglars and bank robbers. Between the wild, brawling adult White gangs of the nine-teenth century and the murderous, drug-maddened Black youth gangs of today's ghetto, the youth gangs of the 1930s and 1950s seem tame and almost respectable. They were highly localized, based on ethnic quarters or ghettos, Italian or Irish, Polish, Mexican, then also Puerto Rican and Negro. They were lower-class corner boys, drawn into racketeering by Prohibition, rarely using guns or drugs, but drinking wine, defending their territory of home streets by occasional almost ritual 'rumbles' with rivals, often planned like scenes of a play, with preparatory drinking, singing, shouting and bragging (Keiser, 1969:50–1). They provided a form of socialization and counter-anonymity for unemployed youth still hoping to enter the world of work successfully, a satisfying means of aiming at dominant values of toughness and manhood and defeating boredom. The Vice-Lords in Chicago had parallel Vice-Lady branches. Relations were tense and sometimes violent, but quite steadily organized. There was still a strong feeling of obligation to marry a girl who became pregnant, whereas in the sociopathic sex of the violent gang, 'fifteen or twenty boys will indulge themselves' on a sometimes disturbed or men-tally handicapped girl, violated by forceful rape and 'banged' perhaps repeatedly over several days (Yablonsky, 1966:193).

Ecological, social context and individual adjustment interpretations are all relevant. Gangs have been more and less violent and violent gangs may be a special type (Yablonsky, 1966:147–63). 'The Murderers' were thirty Polish boys who fought with fists and rocks, not the knives, machetes or zip guns which became standard (Thrasher, 1926:62–3; Yablonsky, 1966:116–17).

Violent gangs reached a crescendo from the 1950s to the 1980s with appalling incidents of savagery: brutal 'wilding' in Central Park and the nightmare raping, smashing, burgling and killing of elderly white women in Ft Worth Rosedale. Violence and drugs came together, not by cause and effect. Race is not of primary relevance. Membership is more local than ethnic.

School violence and drug selling reached such a pitch that school administrations were forced to accept the 'alternative social order' imposed by street gangs (Cummings and Monti, 1993:116–17). Students were stabbed and shot, teachers raped. Half Chicago students do not complete high school. In some schools more than 70% were dropping out. It is a larger, more complex and violent phenomenon than previ-ously, as also in Los Angeles, rich in ceremonial, ritual and symbolic representation with graffiti, tattoos, hair styles, funerals; jackets and T-shirt fashions passed on to the general adolescent culture (Cummings and Monti, 1993:125–37). If the students have shouted at them everyday 'Shut those thick lips! Can't you behave like a human being?' by the teacher, who refers to them as 'wild, crazy animals in a zoo, dopey kids who don't know the difference' (Rosenfeld, 1971:43), one can understand their disaffection. If teachers were raped, students were shut in a metal cupboard in the dark and the sides banged to deafen them (Rosenfeld, 1971:36). Harlem School was a confidence reducing, personality restricting institution. Bad schools lead to truancy, delinquency, violence, unemployment and drug addiction, knitting together many urban scourges.

The Chicago gang nations were renamed Folks (Disciple Groups) and People (Latin King Groups) in the 1980s, with Black and Anglo members. Milwaukee shares the Chicago Folks and People moieties. The Four Corner Hustlers decided they were Vice-Lords, paralleling Chicago, hence also People. 'I don't kill People. I kill Folks.' The Blacks have chiefs of staff, commissioned officers, non-commissioned officers, enlistees and draftees. Chicanos have veteranos, vatos cocos, vatos en la firma, wantables and new vatos TJs. They are near illiterate. They divide by age into Peewees (eight to eleven years), Juniors (twelve to fifteen years), Seniors (sixteen to nineteen years) and Ancients (twenty years and over). They are just groups of friends who sell a lot of drugs, constantly splitting and fractioning. The media exaggerate the size of groups and degree of organization. They are caught 'loitering', become suspect, gaoled for a week or two, therefore learn to do things, and having acquired a criminal record cannot get a job or do anything else. So fighting, stealing and drinking are great fun. It is boring otherwise. Chicanos and Blacks are permanently alienated. Groups can be multi-ethnic up to the Juniors level. The large People and Folks moieties can include Black and Chicano groups, but the former would never join the latter nor *vice versa*. Milwaukee industry has almost completely shut down with deindustrialization. Service jobs pay badly, about the same as welfare. Otherwise gangs decrease with employment. 'Stimulating economic development and training has more impact on the underclass than other policies' (Cummings and Monti, 1993:318).

AIDs, prison, homicide

Drug addiction did not start with gangs, but they are ideally suited to drug promotion. The failure of official attempts at suppression, with the complicity of many people in high places who enjoy the profits, has pushed drug abuses on from the harmless marijuana to the worsening horror of heroin and cocaine in ever more virulent forms. The sharing of drug injection needles, whether from poverty, carelessness or perverted affection, has become a major means of spreading AIDS.

In the contested origins of AIDS, the blossoming of urban homosexual culture in the city of San Francisco holds pride of place. AIDS is yet another serendipitous feature of urban civilization to fit with pernicious perfection into the nexus of the ghetto. Drugs lure poor ghetto youth to their destruction by the easy fortunes they offer to a few but deny to most. Drug craving becomes a major source of theft and violence, with AIDS a horrendous by-product. The combined fruits of these interlocking scourges are crowned for many by homelessness. Those in homeless shelters, on the streets and in prison are particularly vulnerable. 'The prevalence of homosexual rape in prisons, the indiscriminate prostitution that characterizes drug addiction, and the relentless sexuality of college age adolescents' produces complex networks of sexual contacts and sexual practices likely to spread AIDS (Lewontin, 1995:27).

Prison weighs very heavily on Black people and Black families, mainly through their men. With over 1 million in gaol, the United States prison population is relatively far larger than that of any other country and is growing the fastest, with a rate of 455 per 100,000 compared to England 97, Japan 45, the Netherlands 40. The rate of confinement is more than six times higher for Blacks than for Whites. In Baltimore 57% of Black men were in prison, on probation or parole, on bail or sought on arrest warrants. American criminal justice is 'remarkably ineffective, absurdly expensive, grossly inhumane and riddled with discrimination' (Rothman, 1994:34). An eminent criminologist claims that the prison system is rapidly moving in the direction of the extermination camp (Rothman, 1994), with 10 billion dollars' worth of new high security prisons now being built. Reagan and Bush were able to make crime and sentencing procedures an issue that middle-class Americans could use to express their frustrations, not only with unsafe streets but with affirmative action and the cost of welfare. Bondholders see prison as a sound investment, others as a source of employment.

Homicide in the United States is four to five times western Europe, violent robbery four to ten times and rape seven times. It is far higher than in the Calcutta slums and seven times higher than in Birmingham. More than 1 million are convicted and in prison, a rate nearly three times that of apartheid South Africa. It costs more to build a prison cell than a family house and more to keep a prisoner for a year than send him to college. Juveniles commit 23% of violent crime (1977) though only 14.6% of the population. Media, police and public concentrate on crimes against property and violence, the crimes of the underclass, de-emphasizing white-collar crimes such as bank frauds, embezzlement and computer crimes which involve losses hundreds of times greater (Eitzen, 1983:396–401, 431).

America has more guns, less controlled, than other advanced societies, and suspects are often shot to death privately in American cities, without punishment. In 1982 New York city had fifteen such cases, Dallas thirteen, Houston twenty-five and Los Angeles six to eight annually. Texas has a gun mentality, according to police, and property rights are more important than civil rights.[3]

Switzerland provides an extraordinary contrast, as its largest city Zurich has negligible crime (Clinard, 1978:37, 51–2, 70), but experiments with allowing drug addicts in specific localities. This is a severe challenge to the American attempt to impose rigid drug control throughout the world.

Drugs

'Criminal laws create crime and criminals; the rules of society create deviance; systems of justice may be unjust' (Eitzen, 1983:494, 408). The problem of drugs is strategic. Criminalization is recent and began in bizarrely irrational fashion in the United States. California having imported cheap Chinese coolies for railway construction, aroused resentment from organized labour, which found a focus in the 'opium dens' where the coolies consoled their miserable lives. The racist campaign of discrimination secured prohibition of opium in 1875, clearly not for moral or health considerations, but to punish the Chinese. In 1914 opium sellers were required to keep records and pay a fee. The future Narcotics Bureau was established as a division in the Treasury and, without any legal authority, assumed the duty of eliminating drug addiction, harassing addicts and mounting propaganda campaigns against 'drug use and crime', which succeeded in turning patients into criminals, reviled as 'dope fiends' and 'dangerous classes'. It was then the era of Prohibition (1919–33), held to reflect the antagonism of the old, native-born, Protestant middle class to the mostly Catholic immigrant workers, and its determination to reassert its cultural and political dominance. Illegal liquor manufacture and sale continued on a large scale, requiring bootlegging, speakeasies and proliferation of violent, organized crime, with widespread corruption of police, merchants and public authorities, all having a profound and lasting effect upon society. It caused a resurgence of the violent gangs of the nineteenth century, organized under leaders such as Al Capone of Chicago. The experiment led to disillusion and repeal, but a strong reservoir of repressive forces remained.

In the 1960s smoking marijuana became symbolic of youth revolt, rejection of mainstream values and the search for alternative life styles, deemed subversive by conservatives. When marijuana was associated with low-class Mexican immigrants the punishments were very severe, but when it became the rage among White college youth, parents realized the absurdity of legalizing health-menacing drugs like tobacco and alcohol while criminalizing relatively harmless marijuana and even heroin. Attitudes then changed fast, but opposition to legalizing marijuana was still strong in 1980 (70%). Paradoxically it was the poorest and least educated whose opposition was strongest, but those under thirty were moving towards approval. Arrests for marijuana use skyrocketed from 1965 (18,815) to 1973 (420,700). Blacks are disproportionately targeted for arrest, Black juveniles ten times more than White; in Baltimore, Black adults five times more.

The damage and cost to society of drugs and failure to manage them wisely is truly immeasurable. Half the drivers killed in accidents, half those killed by falls or fires, 68% of those drowned are legally drunk at the time (Eitzen, 1983:449–80), as well as most of those involved in homicides and rapes, with $25 billion estimated lost in absenteeism. Smoking is the direct cause of 75% of home, apartment and hotel fires (Eitzen, 1983:479–80). In 1979 medical costs of smoking were between $5 billion and $8 billion. By contrast, the tobacco industry saw its $30 billion wage bill and $22 billion paid in taxes as benefits to the nation. These accidents and offences are primarily committed by urban people and most often in cities.

The drug scourge is also globalized. Long concentrated in the United States, with its distant supply bases in Latin America and south-east Asia, it continues to invade the western world and beyond.

Like all natural sustenance for cities, drugs were rurally produced, until the intensity of the craze impelled the pharmaceutical industry to see irresistible profits in increasing the supply of hallucinogenic substances, to add variety to the menu and fill the gaps. Some elite persons, from Europe to China, have taken hard drugs like opium or cocaine for many centuries without harassment. It was only when non-elite persons, ethnic minorities and rebellious youth wanted the same thing that draconian laws were passed against it and increasingly vast sums and ramifying organizations deployed in the battle. If the smoking of marijuana, which experts consider less harmful than tobacco, had not been criminalized, it might have satisfied the still moderate appetite, and the desperate, suicidal yearning for ever stronger hallucinogens might never have developed into the present uncontrollable scourge. It was probably the inept and insensitive treatment of rebellious youth in the sixties which triggered the epidemic.

The class aspect persists. While it was mainly poor, metropolitan slumdwellers, or low-status migrants in the United States it was a punishable, police problem. When wealthy people became addicted it was a forgivable mental health problem. It is recognized that American attempts at suppression lead to high rates of addiction.

The price of cheaply grown drugs multiplied hundreds of thousands of times under the stimulus of penal sanctions. The habit has spread with American culture, on the wings of American media, round the global village. It is concentrated in the cities and the forces which drive it on and spread it through society are urban derived. Drugs offer untold wealth to urban destitute and homeless people who are outside any bourgeois moral system. Despite incessant hopes to the contrary, the enormous sums of taxpayers' money spent in the 'war on drugs' and the vast waste of civil servants' and public figures' time, including their own frequent corruption by it, have only sparked continuous increase, all the while causing ever more virulent and lethal forms to be devised, enormously multiplying the break up of marriages and families, blighting young careers and amounting to a kind of genocide as it accentuates the violence of the ghettos, where shooting becomes the major cause of death among Black youth. The criminalized drug traffic belongs intimately with those factors causing radical changes in urban social relations, marriage and family life.

It is not the drugs, but the traffic and suppression which are corrupting, softening the edges of the banking system, suborning politicians and financing assassinations, threatening legality everywhere, magnifying support for violent crime and causing wasteful and inefficient spending on prisons, exerting irresistible attraction on all other large-scale criminal activities. The ever rising amount of narco-dollars laundered in the United States and Europe was estimated at $85 billion. In France, after a more recent development, the profit from illegal drugs was 20 to 50 billion francs. These sums are larger than the national incomes of many Third World countries and indicate the havoc which narco-profits can cause internationally. At the base of the system are the many thousands of petty dealers and distributors, as well as the millions of victims. At the top are the international barons, who can threaten national governments and, if captured, establish their own luxurious gaol conditions. Celebrated in the media, even if as anti-heroes, they are constantly advertised, joining the ranks of Superstar Robin Hoods.

In the United States 60,000 addicts are registered and in England 400, Germany nearly 5,000 and other European countries a few hundreds. With a different policy in Britain, addiction remained a minor social affliction. Few countries other than Singapore and Malaysia and some

Arab countries have treated drug possession and use with the severity of the United States. In none of them does the level of addiction reach more than a fraction of the American incidence. The relative freedom of drug use in Scandinavia, the city of Amsterdam and the experiment in the city of Zurich are notorious and widely publicized. Surrounded by a sick world, they have not been completely successful, nor have they caused such widespread ill effects as the United States has suffered. The American attempt to impose drug prohibition throughout the world suggests imperial delusions and has had disastrously ramifying counterproductive effects which will take many years to overcome.

The drug war has sometimes been the driving force and sometimes the pawn of American foreign policy in Mexico and Central America, the Caribbean and South America. It fuelled the peripheral cold war in many Asian countries adjacent to the Golden Triangle. What began as a distinctive weakness of American urban youth culture in the wild sixties became an engine of American foreign policy, asserted through secret agents, narcotics services, police and armed forces in many parts of the world, all of them failing in the goal of suppression, but succeeding horribly in spreading and intensifying corruption and vice in general. For the irresistible profits of drug dealing, which are due to suppression, brought it inevitably into mutually supportive complicity with all the most vile and dangerous vice and crime rings throughout the world.

The soaring personal expenditure on therapeutic drugs, beneficial or otherwise, reflects the gigantic expansion of chemical and pharmaceutical firms and a major revolution in urban life style. Since the 1950s with new tranquillizing drugs, tens of thousands of patients have been released from mental hospitals to greater freedom, but still handicapped by mental problems and poverty which drove many into ghettos, slums and homelessness. Users of these drugs constituted 46% of Americans by the 1980s, requiring 5 billion doses of tranquillizers, 3 billion of amphetamines and 5 billion barbiturates in one year. The public spent $16.5 billion on prescription drugs in 1979, up from $11.6 billion in 1975, bringing pharmacists a 20% return. Then there are the contraceptive pills and the sports drugs. The pressure to use them is unrelenting from parents, friends, doctors, coaches and advertisements, all reflecting capitalist determination to increase destructive consumerism on all fronts at any cost.

Because addicts must steal to get their doses, one can estimate that 100,000 addicts in New York would have to steal goods worth $300 every day to get the $100 they need from 'fences', making $10.95 billion stolen every year. Addicts are so desperate that they are forced into a drug subculture, where they help one another, share information and new techniques, becoming a solidary group, elaborating an ideology justifying addiction, recruiting new deviants and rejecting 'straight' ways (Eitzen, 1983:494). In a dispassionate perspective, repressive drug laws are irrational. They achieve the opposite of their intended goal. They spread corruption through the whole society. They show disrespect for the law, making people cynical about community and public life, as they find high standards and publicly vaunted moral values expressed as masks for the opposite. 'Drug law enforcement and punishment are aimed mostly at minorities and the "war on drugs" is in large part a war on blacks' (Rothman, 1994:37).

As drug taking becomes widespread and commonplace, ordinary people feel increasing need for it, contemporary life seems full of frustrations and dissatisfaction, in families, jobs, schools, institutions and bureaucracies. For the poor, even leisure is frustrating, as they have no money to pay for the relaxations and diversions thrust at them by the media.

Delinquency

Deviant behaviour in general: 'crime, juvenile delinquency, prostitution, drunkenness, drug abuse, mental disorder, suicide, illegitimacy and family maladjustment – have long been associated with slum living' (Clinard, 1970:9). 'There is a direct relationship between conditions existing in local communities of American cities and differential rates of delinquents and criminals' (Shaw and McKay, 1972:315–17). That Chicago rates in areas adjacent to centres of commerce and heavy industry remained relatively constant despite successive changes in ethnicity and place of birth emphatically supports the conclusion that the delinquency-producing factors are inherent in the community.

In low-income areas, attitudes supporting delinquency are so strong and dynamic a social tradition of the local community that they control the development of delinquent careers among large numbers of youth. The tradition is manifested in conduct, speech, gestures and attitudes of people in touch with the youth. Their intimate association with predatory gangs teaches them the techniques of stealing and binds them to their companions in delinquency. A career in delinquency and crime is an option which becomes enticingly attractive to a youth through the promise of economic gain, prestige and companionship coming from people whose esteem and approbation are vital to his security and achievement of satisfactory social status. He is not necessarily disorganized, maladjusted or anti-social *in his social world* where in fact he is highly organized and well adjusted (Shaw and McKay, 1972:316).

Others find that adolescent delinquents have less self-esteem, self-control and social values than others. Non-delinquents get more parental emotional support and are closer to their fathers. According to self-reporting studies, middle-class adolescent offences are in reality as numerous as lower class, and White as numerous as Black. Similarly, ghetto rioters of the 1960s were found not to be 'riff raff' as thought, but a cross section, merely reacting to opportunity. New York city anti-poverty programmes did not lower delinquency (Kalt and Zalkind, 1976:355–7, 394, 443). The most generally agreed cause is family disorganization. The cure is familial love, moral discipline made acceptable by love (Spencer, 1964:4). This does not necessarily require a nuclear family. Policy is obsessed with the individual, for American capitalistic individualism evades social explanations as near subversive. Psychology, the social sciences and their funding reflect this heavy influence.

In higher-status communities, the norms and values of the child's social world are more uniform and conventional, demanding no choice between conflicting systems of moral values. But in low-status communities, although conventional values of family, church and school are still dominant, a powerful competing system of delinquency values confront them. The variation in delinquency rates in different communities of the city corresponds closely with variations in economic status (Shaw and McKay, 1972:315–17). In communities of oriental immigrants, cultural solidarity is sufficient to keep deviance and delinquence at a minimum, because of the close family integration and determination to maintain good repute in American communities. Individual and personality differences also affect the acceptance or rejection of delinquent activities, but do not determine or explain local variations (from ghetto to suburb).

Half a million violent and two and a half million property crimes are committed in American cities every year (perhaps three times that), costing $8 billion, half in damage, half in pursuit, trying and imprisoning (Kalt and Zalkind, 1976:355). Riots are concentrated explosions of violence. In the 1960s Detroit riots 43 were killed, 5,000 made homeless, 700 jailed, suppressed by 5,000 National Guards, 2,700 paratroopers and the local police. The city had 13.9% unemployed, teenagers about 40%. The population fell by half eventually. The city was taken over by a Black mayor, police chief, school superintendent, county sheriff, etc. Black influence was greatly amplified in the 1970s. Violent crime was down 28%. Building projects worth $433 million began. It would be churlish to belittle such changes. But the brute fact is that the cities are part of the American political economy, where the outcome of democratic decision making is that polarization did not stop; the rich continued to get vastly richer and the poor relatively poorer from then until now. Not all the Black mayors, police chiefs and school superintendents (ninety-six cities have them) could do anything about it.

In Brooklyn, Bushwick had 1,300 shops looted in the 1977 blackout. It has over 30% unemployment and poverty is rising. The population is 50% Hispanic, 40% Black and has fallen from 200,000 to 134,000 in flight from fires, crime, fear and alienation. It was refused aid in the 1960s as White and non-poor. Now streets are full of potholes and litter.

Deserts have been created in inner cities by fires, riots, landlord racketeering, neglect and maladministration: 100,000 housing units lost in New York city (1973), 30,000 in Philadelphia, 10,000 in St Louis, 12,000 in Baltimore. Landlords pay gangs to intimidate tenants, drive them out and burn the buildings for insurance when they are abandoned. South Bronx had 12,300 fires in 1974, one third proved intentional. The giant Pruitt-Igoe apartment complex in St Louis became so delapidated, windows broken, elevators failing, stairwells used for rape, that it had to be blown up. At the same time gleaming new skyscraper clusters blossomed in Detroit, Pittsburgh, New York, Chicago, Los Angeles, St Louis, Houston, Dallas, Atlanta, etc., cathedrals of capitalism overshadowing the cathedrals of Christendom, restating emphatically the health, wealth and overwhelming power of the capitalist system, whatever the sufferings of the people.

Homelessness

Homelessness is an integral part of the ghetto syndrome, as many ghetto people are on the margin of it and easily slip into it. Many of those staying with friends or relatives are in fact homeless, subjected to gross overcrowding and humiliated by having to live through other people's belongings, almost lacking personal property of their own in a property worshipping society. In the world's wealthiest economy the persistent growth of homelessness becomes an increasingly shameful scandal.

The numbers of homeless began to rise alarmingly in the 1980s. New ways of treating the mentally ill outside hospitals, the declining rate of marriage, declining welfare benefits of the Reagan era, declining demand for unskilled workers, declining income and the crack epidemic are blamed. Only 1,100 homeless were found in Chicago in the winter of 1958, but twice that number in 1986.

The cheapest accommodation in New York and Chicago was in cubicle hotels, windowless 5x7 foot rooms divided by wire mesh at the top and bottom, therefore noisy, smelling of urine and vomit, sometimes verminous. But in 1958 they cost only 50 to 90 cents a night, less than a six-pack of beer, so that 'privacy was cheaper than oblivion'. They were greatly preferred to the dormitory shelters because of the privacy. Occupants felt more like paying guests than charity cases, and they could receive personal mail. Urban renewal eventually demolished the cubicle hotels for more profitable building. In 1992, only one was left in Chicago, with rents up four times in real terms, so 'oblivion became cheaper than privacy'. Cities had been forced to open thousands of free shelters. Having no choice, unpleasant free shelter with consequently affordable crack and alcohol became acceptable (Jenks, 1994:39). But many preferred doorways, parks, subways and abandoned premises to no privacy. Some 6,000 slept under Grand Central and Penn stations. Another average 12,000 slept in New York's shelters. About 2 million single-parent families now live in another's home. Their only choice is that, the shelter, or the street. Many could find work and pay for housing if the unemployment rate were less than 4%, but this would push inflation to a politically unacceptable level.

Chicago had many empty warehouses that could have been converted into cubicle hotels, but the building code forbade it. Most unmarried adults always lived with someone else as it was cheaper. The number of poor began to grow. In 1979 there were 1.6 million unmarried working age men with incomes below $2,500, but 2.6 million in 1989.

In 1987 there were between 300,000 and 500,000 homeless adults in the United States (Jenks, 1994:41). Roughly half are not in shelters on any given night. For the mentally ill, especially, the lack of privacy and threat of theft and violence in a dormitory shelter is almost unbearable. Low rent control leads owners to abandon their property for demolition. The Department of Housing and Urban Development's financing for subsidized housing fell from $32.2 billion in 1978 to $11.7 billion in 1991. Reagan intended to end all subsidization but was prevented. New York shelters spent $1,500 a month per shelter resident in 1991, over $200 million a year, security services being especially costly. All shelter residents are thrown out on to the streets early every morning. The wretched cubicles required to warehouse the homeless might cost $10 billion to establish. 'Not much in a six trillion budget', it was said. Many citizens would actually oppose such spending because the accommodation is not worthy of human beings. Half the additional income generated between 1977 and 1989 went to the top 1% of American households. The 1980 compensation of corporate chairmen was thirty five times that of the typical worker; in 1990 it was 135 times. Between 1985 and 1990, 7 million Americans were homeless at some time, 5 million of them single adults. The contrast is stark.

GLOBALIZATION

The freedom of deprivation: unused family resources

Given the poverty of ghettos, slums, homeless and unemployed, and the astronomical sums spent on the counterproductive War on Drugs, on endemically racist and pervasively corrupt police forces and even more costly prison construction, not to speak of the homeless shelters and their security guards, questionable training schemes, bloated and uncompassionate welfare staffs, the burning problem of wealth distribution becomes insistent.

Unwarranted wealth perpetuates injustice and frays the essential bonds that strengthen trust and hold societies together . . . There is no reason to suppose that American executives would work less hard if they were paid several thousand dollars a year instead of several million . . . It is grossly unfair that executives receive fifty, one hundred, even two hundred times the average pay of working people who toil away at much less interesting jobs. (Bok, 1993:22–3)

The reason for high salaries derives from status not need. It twists and distorts our fundamental perceptions of what our deserts are and how they should be calculated and recompensed. Media-inflated stars publicly declare conviction that they deserve what they earn. Roosevelt proposed a $25,000 (now over $200,000) ceiling during World War II. Whether redistributing high incomes to the poor would really benefit them is questioned. If the 763,000 declared incomes over $200,000 in 1992 were taxed everything above that figure it would effectively yield $103 billion, providing $2,173 to every family with income less than $35,000 (Hacker, 1994:24). However, this calculation ignored the multiplier, which assuming that these families spent all they received would certainly have a tremendous stimulating effect on aggregate demand. Assume that the payments were made to families with less than $25,000 and a major solution to poverty and the ghetto would be launched. However, only a more imminent threat of nuclear oblivion, global warming and asphyxiating pollution might persuade media-befuddled citizens to vote for such a subversive relative equalizing of incomes. And far more than this will be necessary to end poverty effectively.

The American economy is living an extraordinary contradiction with the dawning of the information age, through brilliant, young, instant millionaire electronic innovators, while the corporate economy pursues short-term profit at any cost by deindustrialization to cheap poor countries, deserting its labour force and abandoning them and the national economy to their fate. It seized the city centres to display its supremacy, leaving the rest to rot. New York city manufacturing jobs have fallen

700,000 since 1961. Yet populist opposition to government intervention in the economic management became so hysterical that freelance militias and uncontrolled violence threatened federal officials, seizing public lands, and federal officials gave up in fear. The ghettos reached extremes of horror in these decades never known before, discarded as unemployable, with no relief but the delirium of drugs and the narcissistic self-defeat of violence. Hitherto, the Dark Ghetto we have glimpsed (Clark, 1967) had an amazing countercultural antithesis of irrepressible revelry and carefree merrymaking which enabled it to survive (Williams, 1981:87–90, 125–7). Deprived of everything, they experienced the ultimate freedom, liberated from the stifling conventions and deceitful hypocrisy of mainstream.

'Genuine' Blacks deny mainstream standards, defile mainstream values and defy social distance among themselves (Williams, 1981:12–18). Mainstream culture is mediated by 'spurious' Blacks who aspire to it without having the necessary resources. Mainstream Blacks achieve the substance, but are still subject to the rites of degradation and ritual race pollution. They subscribe to the values which make victims of them all (Williams, 1981). In the 1960s all Blacks found it fashionable to escape mainstream behaviour, which for a while undermined oppression and the stigma of being Black in America.

The expressive 'genuine' culture demands intense physical interaction from childhood, uninhibited laughter, flamboyant, even shocking body language, loud oral communication, manipulation of the genitals physically in public, symbolically in strong speech, mouth to mouth sharing, wailing for emotional release to soothe one's spirit and others'. To show 'genuine' sophistication some girls go to school in high heels with skirts perilously short; boys adopt the pimp's walk, shape their hair and belong to a gang. Little girls of twelve to fourteen share a quart of wine, discussing last night's orgasms (Williams, 1981:127). The mania for tinsel goods emphasizes the ephemeral present. Symbols are the old Cadillac (for the new is mainstream substance), good liquor, razors and switch blades. 'Genuine' incomes are from dubious and erratic sources: prostitution, gambling and hustling. Bought, when a windfall chance offers, are expensive clothes, furs, rings and entertainment, not stocks, bonds or real estate. The 'king for the day', making a grand entry, throws a thousand dollars on the floor and walks on it. These are the stars of the ghetto (Williams, 1981:10–20).

The workings of Black ghetto family and kinship illustrate another aspect of intensive personal interaction. Domestic functions are carried out by clusters of kin, not necessarily living together, based on the domestic co-operation of close adult females and exchange of goods and services between male and female kin. Separately, no family or person can survive. Parental responsibilities are shared and transferred as children also are exchanged and change households (Stack, 1975:9). Several couples had kin networks of over ninety kin who had come up to midwestern cities over the decades. The family is the 'smallest organized durable network of kin and non-kin who interact daily, providing for the domestic needs of children and assuring their survival' (Stack, 1975:31). It is diffused over several fluctuating, kin-based households. Providing food, cooking and child care are all spread over several households, in which individuals have an adjustable membership.

The strong exclusive Anglo-Saxon father–son relationship is lacking, but parenting is assured by deep affection and shared obligation (as is very familiar in Africa). Domestic networks include friends as well as kin. Childbirth is very highly valued and confers dignity on the mother at whatever age. Sibling groups are large and include a diverse array of parents, greatly extending the network. The custom of sequential swapping of possessions of all kinds deepens the web of interaction and sharing. Those who fail to reciprocate are punished by exclusion and gossip. It is a profoundly creative adaptation to poverty. Most life is shared and borne together, hardly allowing secrecy or privacy (Stack, 1975:43, 90, 101).

Crime, divorce, drug addiction, illegitimacy, single motherhood and female headed households are all higher the larger the city, though Black ghettos are worst of all. The problem of rearing and socializing future generations, in mental and social health and responsibility, capable of bearing the onerous burdens of future citizenship, urgently concerns urban areas and increasingly the whole society, since recent polls and surveys show the nuclear family disintegrating throughout Euro-America. To ensure that coming generations will not consist of skinheads and neo-Nazis, hijackers and bombers, racial fiends and rapists, will require enormous effort and good-will. The collective family network method of parenting developed by Black families demands serious attention. We must blame American slavery for smashing Black family life, but learn humbly from Black experiments in coping which may have relevance for us.

My two children spent most of the daytime hours of infancy and childhood in the hands and tender care of African housemaids. Though they might technically fall into the category of Distant Companions at best, the two principal persons involved were some of the most admirable characters I have ever known: caring, conscientious and devoted. It would be hard to imagine any known form of state or local government providing such services without disaster. But in the future envisaged, occupying leisure time enjoyably, satisfyingly and beneficially will be one of the biggest challenges, which might supply the answer here. Bodies of citizens in the local community could assess, certify and tactfully monitor volunteer (or paid) 'social parents' (female or male) whose aim would be to reach and surpass the achievements of the African nursemaid.

African culture suggests a further possibility. Most African societies had extended family and kinship systems, which also flourished in many other parts of the world. They were very far from being primitive, in any possible sense of the word, but they do not easily fit all the requirements of capitalist labour, though for others they have been very adaptive, as well as providing indispensable flexible strength to the building of mammoth capitalist enterprise, in India, South Korea, Taiwan, Malaysia and even Euro-America. Among contemporary African urban elites, they have had to transcend any localized corporate form, to develop flexible networks with changing, mobile cores.

Siblings all rush to help a brother or sister in trouble, wherever in the world they may be. More important, the deep love and sense of responsibility for children is such that the loss of a parent, temporarily or permanently, is much more easily and adequately made up than is the case in the west. To reproduce consciously what has occurred spontaneously is one of the most valuable forms of social development. The more nuclear families break up, and the smaller sibling groups become, the more possible and necessary it is for adult family members, consanguine, affinal or extended, to develop the profound, generalized African capacity for parental love and caring. It is in such ways that break up and disintegration may be turned into freedom and self-development, for the caring and the cared, rather than personal breakdown and family catastrophe.

City magnetism, pollution and welfare: technological contradictions

Despite the vicious violence and poisonous racial hatreds, scandals of poverty and homelessness, mental disease and chronic illness uncared for, perils of personal attack, traffic congestion, noise and air pollution, the great city still exerts magnetic attraction. The increasing numbers of super-rich can escape most of the scourges, putting them out of sight and out of mind, by occupying well-guarded luxury apartments and travelling in well-equipped limousines and helicopters to and from their country mansions and exotic vacations. Millions of people simply carry on doggedly with their daily obligations, still proud of the city where they were raised. Crowds enjoy the profusion of museums and art galleries,

theatres, opera and ballet, concerts, restaurants, balls and gala performances, festivals, temples and cathedrals, sports events and even the
somewhat by-passed cinema. These are perhaps the most enduring
residue of the urban experience. But the insidious advance of the media
threatens all of these, seducing many to private electronic enjoyment at
home, increasingly isolated with small numbers of family and friends or
alone, malignly reinforcing less inhibited attitudes towards AIDS –
threatening erotic experiments and porno-video-induced orgies or drug
sessions.

Media magic has created a world of make-believe in which the majority
spend much of their time, ceasing to think, read or write, obfuscating
their structurally opposed class position and voting for their class
enemies. But a majority often do not vote, so that media bombardment
ensures the political control of the exploiting class and the super-rich,
with the paradoxical but explicable support of significant numbers of
resentful poor. This might seem a providential recipe for Orwellian social
harmony, were it not based upon a grand deception, capitulating to insatiable and unsustainable consumerism, fatally undermining efforts to
reform the capitalist system before it destroys us.

The urban industrial civilization of capitalism now threatens to destroy
us by polluting the air we breathe and endangering the very existence of
the earth's atmosphere in which we live. The problem of pollution is
formidable indeed. The carbon emission rate is still growing at a pace
which could make the earth uninhabitable in the twenty-first century.
Already 150 million people in the United States breathe badly polluted
air. Depletion of the ozone layer now requires people in Australia to wear
protective glasses and, if not halted, will spread skin cancer increasingly in
human populations. Three-quarters of America's huge and diverse tropical forests which protect the atmosphere and our biogenetic inheritance,
will have gone by 2000 AD. Global warming may lead to melting ice and
rising seas permanently flooding homes of hundreds of millions of people
in coastal cities by 2100 AD. The United States is far ahead in its emission of the 'greenhouse' gases responsible for global warming, producing
more than six times as much as western European countries, nearly eight
times as much as Canada (Kennedy, 1993:117). The main culprit is the
car.

The rich countries are the greatest polluters, but are trying to impose
controls, while the poor countries now pollute on a massive scale which
they have absolutely no resources to control and which will increase in
intensity for decades to come. As their overpopulation increases both
pollution and poverty, there is no hope of pollution control until population can be controlled. The demographic transition and the pollution

transition have to go hand in hand. Nor can rich countries save themselves and let the rest go to perdition, for their pollution will kill our grandchildren as surely as their own, unless we help them with all we have to give and more. Even if the rich countries are transformed from selfish hoarders of wealth and wasters of resources into generous good samaritans, it will take all that they can muster. Wars enormously accelerate pollution. Unless they can be eliminated, whatever justifications are claimed, there can be little hope of survival.

Sophisticated technology can smooth frictions of increasing mobility for rising population. But the purpose of this is not entirely clear, since global survival necessitates stabilization and *gradual reduction* of world population. Much sophisticated technology is already potentially available or easily within reach if the necessary resources were devoted to it. But none of it makes sense unless the population and the inequality problem, which are essentially aspects of the same intractability, are solved first or at least being altered in the right direction.

One rail line can carry forty times as many people per hour as automobile lanes occupying the same space. Sophisticated tunnels could be developed to shoot people between New York and Los Angeles in minutes rather than hours. The trouble is that such astronomically costly projects would themselves enter our delusory official statistics as increased productivity and GNP per head without increasing genuine well-being for anybody, including those subjected to the unnecessary stress of such journeys. For the same reason space travel and space stations are dangerous. The research they require may involve some increase in useful knowledge as a byproduct, but it remains to be proved that life in outer space can be as pleasurable and delightful, let alone morally helpful, as life on earth. It remains to be demonstrated that the physical, mental or spiritual delights of life on earth can be fully reproduced, improved or substituted in space. Trips into space might be made available to the public as a thrill, just as trips in aeroplanes were arranged at fairs. If certain technical processes beneficial to humanity could be better achieved in space, that also could be provided for. But space travel has made no progress in revealing new sources of energy and the very energy wasted in flights to space increases atmospheric pollution and threatens ultimately to destroy the base from which such flights are launched, so that the whole exercise seems naive and illogical. We could regard such efforts as planetary exploration, nuclear fusion and reduction of human population as parallel possibilities of human betterment, but by the latter criterion only the last is certain, the second desirable and the first a high stake gamble, so that they should be prioritized accordingly. Nations or societies which have solved problems of their inner cities could spend more on space research. At present the amount of resources wasted on useless or dangerous projects is so astronomically impressive that it provides its own justification, mesmerizes the public and defies rational consideration. The automobile is certainly the major culprit in endangering the atmospheric environment, but ever increasing intensity of air travel in addition to space rockets obviously constitute an additional danger, founding the most essential link in modern luxury life on a fast wasting resource (Kennedy, 1994:32, 97).

The first phase of globalization is marked by crystallization round the three supreme centres which now vie for economic growth, America, Europe and Japan. In the 1970s Japan and America both struggled to develop robots, but America, having fallen behind, mysteriously gave up, so that by 1988 Japan was using five times as many industrial robots as the United States and nearly four times as many as western Europe. The FANUC plant near Mt Fuji was producing c. 6,000 motors a month with 108 workers and 32 robots before 1982, and after redesign producing 10,000 motors with 60 workers and 101 robots, per month, as an interim step towards full automation (Kennedy, 1994:88).

America's loss of interest in robots was represented as part of a sophisticated move towards efficient, lean, mean, plants through the laying off of millions of workers in the US and the transfer of plants to receptive Third World countries with the perfect combination of low-paid, skilled labour, no unions or effective safety regulations, low taxation and allowance for repatriation of profits. This was deindustrialization, removing polluting industries to Third World countries better able to tolerate their pollution and its effects. Some even moved to 'Third World' areas of the United States like Alabama and Mississippi.

America's urban elite was regaining mastery of the world economy by moving forward to the information age of knowledge and services. But it was the central feature of America's increasing indebtedness, weakening currency and intractable unemployment. In 1987 it imported $550 billion in services (Kennedy, 1994:298), exporting only $57 billion. Having become the world's largest debtor nation, the American deficit forces foreign interests to buy up the American economy bit by bit. This is humiliating for patriots, but it is arguable that distinct national economies are out-moded. 'As almost every factor of production – money, technology, factories and equipment – moves effortlessly across borders, the very idea of an American economy is becoming meaningless, as is the notion of an American corporation, American capital, American products and American technology' (Reich, 1991:3–4, 8–9).

America was in many ways fated to pursue this course. The nation was created from continuing immigration, attracting lovers of freedom, victims of oppression, with brilliant brains, as well as impoverished refugees. Here were great strength and some weakness. America does not suffer from a lack of cheap labour, but from unwillingness to train and use what it has. It has long led innovation in production, so giving up on robotic automation may be losing ground impossible to recover. It was neo-industrialization rather than de-industrialization that was required.

America found manufacturing increasingly unprofitable, dirty and pol-luting, threatened by powerful unions demanding higher wages and benefits, squeezing profits unacceptably. It was easier to be un-American and ship manufacturing abroad to poor countries defenceless against pollution and labour exploitation. The Structural Adjustment pro-grammes imposed by the International Monetary Fund and the World Bank compel the poor countries to abolish tariffs, maintain freely convertible currencies, abolish food subsidies, cut medical, educational and social services and balance their budgets whatever the poverty and ill-health inflicted thereby, to welcome the polluting and labour exploiting industries from the rich de-industrializing countries. The corrupt politi-cians and generals who run these countries get lavish pay-offs and have no interest in protecting either the environment or the people. Their interest is in secret Swiss bank accounts and escape to palaces abroad when the going gets tough.

Japan's phenomenal success in developing its own internal economy, a complete *volte-face* imposed by World War II defeat, led to a labour short-age which cried out for automation, which reinforced her concentration on high technology in information and media development as well as industry. This policy could create an economy supplying (by production and exchange) all its people need, at a very high standard of living, with no need for unemployment or any poor population. Social justice and equality would be a feasible goal, whether pursued or not. Japan has had severe currency and debt problems but they are insignificant for the long term. Her trade surplus with the United States resulted from this success and caused financial adjustment tensions. By some reckoning United States restrictions on Japanese imports are much higher than those of Japan on her (Chomsky, 1994b:16).

The Japanese option in its future potential does not require increasing poverty and destitution in the rest of the world. The current American option does. The most revered intellectual of the foreign policy establish-ment warned in 1948 against unreal objectives, human rights, rising living standards, democratization, altruism and world benefaction, which would make it impossible 'to maintain the position of disparity that separ-ates our enormous wealth from their poverty' (Chomsky, 1994b:121). He did not mention that the latter aim can only be achieved under a convincing mask of the former values. With the productive potentials of current technology this invidious choice is unnecessary. The Japanese option seems to offer the possibility of controlling population, pollution and environmental damage while achieving a high and more equitably distributed standard of living. Whether or not such goals are effectively pursued, it is an example of enormous significance. There are other pointers.

Fewer people wish to live at very high density, whether vertical or horizontal, except as one of several options available to the very rich. The inner cities continue to rot, without major expansion, as some devastated areas become plums for speculative private development with state subsidy. The suburbs continue to grow, but as rising density defeats their purpose, people move further out, so that the smallest places and the areas classified as rural show the highest recent population increase, both in America and western Europe (Wallman, 1993:62).

Citizens now demand a level of publicly provided education, health care, welfare services and retirement benefits which cost far more than they are willing to pay in taxation, since the rich are allowed to retain most of their vast wealth. This is because the latest health and welfare technology and treatment are designed and invented at ever greater cost for the super-rich who alone can afford them. But the media-thrust demonstration effect guarantees that polls and votes will register a demand which no government can pretend to satisfy without gross deception. Given capitalist fiscal policy this spells speedy bankruptcy, already threatening, or a reversal from alleged democracy to firmly imposed inequality. Only massive economic growth would answer, but this is impossible since private business works for profit not for productivity and is unwilling to expand production to provide employment. The contradiction is sharper in the United States where despite a favourable situation of maintained growth and controlled inflation, the middle class, of which both parties' voters are composed, has not benefited from recent growth. Its purchasing power stagnates or even falls, reflecting the two speeds, where income is distributed more and more unequally. Even in Sweden where socialist governments for over half a century have successfully built a model welfare state, in the end voters have revolted against paying 50% of their incomes in taxes for it, although they are still very comfortably off.

The supurban transcendence of the city

Robotic automation, biotech, computers and the whole information age syndrome tend to put productivity in fewer hands. Fewer hands would also be very good for the earth, but would they spell greater equality or more elitism? The fundamental point is that fewer people would be needed to produce the goods and services for any reasonable standard of living for the whole global population. It sounds elitist at present because it is so new, but there is no insurmountable reason for access to be limited to a few. It is simply that, as the transformation proceeds, it would be vital for populations to adjust their reproduction over the generations, to bring numbers down to a level which could secure so many advantages. The present threat to the environment and to continued human existence could be slowed and brought to an end. Productivity would be so high and necessary drudgery of menial tasks so greatly reduced that work and leisure would change their meaning. The necessary hours of productive work would fall and much of it would be stimulating or even enjoyable. The problem for people and society would be to occupy new leisure time with new forms to enable everyone to enjoy leisure with more fulfilment, especially because it could help to meet many non-material needs of both oneself and others.

We are at a very complex conjuncture. Many menacing problems defy solution. Yet in fact a few measures would solve them all, the only barrier to their adoption being human selfishness and greed. Redistribution of wealth would create a surge of prosperity. Pursuing an all-out policy of productive expansion would create abundance, allowing a high standard of living for all. The problems of unemployment, of destitute single mothers, of ghetto crime and drug addiction would be alleviated. Expenditure on police, prisons, courts and justice would be enormously reduced. Fewer hours of work would be required, increasing leisure time, which would demand new forms of education, partly voluntary and co-operative, to ensure its beneficial use. Many would wish to spend some time helping or amusing handicapped people, or playing with children of working mothers. At every point there is a reduction of the need for and cost of bureaucratic welfare services. Health would be greatly improved and medical costs lowered.

If we persist mindlessly pursuing our individual profit and pleasure as before, none of the problems which face us can be solved and our days on earth are numbered. The fear of slow extinction may ultimately compel us to change our ways. For we are forcing ourselves, by the blunt cumulation of our historical action, to confront the stark alternative of slow physical destruction and permanent obliteration, or else change, in what amounts to a fundamental moral reform, individual and collective, whether phrased as Kantian imperative, the perennial philosophy or Christian love. We should be forced to give everything we can possibly spare, to those we have despised, exploited and oppressed, for the selfish reason of our survival.

Futurists try to intoxicate us with visions of ever increasing speed and ephemerality. This is a kind of alienation which can only perceive the vulgar aspects of technology. The worst problems of our situation are those which refuse to budge at all. There is no problem of speed. We are told that we shall face a collision with the future, that it will be painful for most of us to keep up with the incessant demand for change. What we find in fact is an extraordinary obdurate resistance to the changes necessary for survival, such as consuming and polluting less and devoting more resources to bridging the gap between ourselves and the poor of our own country and the rest of the world. It is largely we ourselves who are creating and often compromising our future. The only speed that electronic devices bring us is mental speed which we can use to speed towards disaster as at present, or turn towards the making of a new world of freedom and plenty for all.

Boulding's view of the city (1963, 1971)

Not without long reflection, I find that Boulding's 'The Death of the City: A Frightened Look at Postcivilization', over thirty years old, which he avers is pure fiction, but a way of keeping up with the news, is many streets ahead of the various more recent best-selling futuristic views of the city and humanity, even more plausible today than in 1963. So short an article cannot be complete. It skates poetically over some major subliminal problems. Others have only since become burningly inescapable.

The classical city civilization is a well-integrated organization with defined boundaries, he says, supported by political exploitation, production and trade; insanitary so that the death rate is high, not self-reproducing but dependent upon immigration. Urban and rural culture are sharply differentiated. The national state is frequently only an extension – or a colony – of the capital city (Boulding, 1971:537). But now the city is defenceless because of the diminution in the cost of transporting violence, rendering cities pitilessly vulnerable. The necessity of concentration has gone. Los Angeles is the first post-civilization urban agglomeration, created and poisoned by the automobile. It cannot be called a city in the classical sense. The tentacles of its water supply threaten to strangle the whole west. California is the first 'state-city', an urban agglomeration that is statewide. Part-time farmers, commuting long distances to work in the city, nearly equal full-time farmers blurring the distinction between town and country. As a distinctive subculture within society, rural life disappears. The city has embraced almost everything, so it is more a city than ever before, just when it ceases to have any distinctive existence or meaning. The city is destroyed by its own success, yet it is a rhetorical hyperbole to call it death. It is the dialectical urban subsumption of society.

Civilization and the city are passing away in that we might become spread evenly over the Earth as in pre-civilization. Yet Boulding sees probable a United States consisting essentially of three or four loose, sprawling megalopolises separated by small stretches of largely empty countryside. If post-civilization technology becomes based on the oceans with the depletion of terrestrial raw materials, there will be some manufacturing concentrations round the shores of the world, constituting some exception to the even spread. Furthermore, the classical city could be revived as a 'stage-set' arising out of the freedom and luxury of society, not its necessity, for people to enjoy walking and face-to-face communication, since inequality of income will be reflected in the poor driving vehicles and the rich walking.

Post-civilization will be as destructive to civilization as civilization was to pre-civilization, says Boulding. This borders on the anthropological temptation to see the salvation of the world as the recapture at a higher level of the values of the Foraging mode of production: peace, personal freedom and equality in harmony with an ample, respected nature (Southall, 1988a).

Boulding sees the 'mile-cube' city as the only practicable way to have 20 million people living together. However, both Mexico City and São Paulo are expected to contain about 24 million people within four years' time by uncontrolled horizontal spread (Hauchler and Kennedy, 1994:115). Boulding envisages the possibility of the poor-civilized countries of rampant overpopulation regressing to lower and lower levels of civilization till the death rate rises again or they succeed somehow in population control. However, it will not be possible for rich post-civilization 'post-cities' to sit and watch this process because it will be accompanied by massive pollution and environmental havoc destroying the planet as a whole. One is shocked to hear complacent development and banking experts talking glibly about the megacities of the Third World learning to cope with their situation, when it is manifestly out of control. In 1963 Boulding did not realize the imminence of the accelerating cumulative threat to life on earth from combined effects of pollution and environmental degradation.

We still have to assume that peoples and politicians will come to their senses in time to realize the seemingly impossible miracle by accepting the fundamental measures necessary: to maximize production by automation, robotics and all the accelerating technological advances of the information age, realizing a super-abundance enabling generous sharing with poor countries on the absolute condition of implementing effective population control. It would necessitate equalization by redistribution of incomes and redistribution of work, increasing salaries and lowering hours of work, providing new forms of education and training for the enjoyment of increased leisure, including voluntary contribution to welfare services. With increased leisure there will be a need for significant and meaningful voluntary work, both for therapy and self-fulfilment. The result would be that ghettos would be raised from their squalor and despair, unemployment would be reduced to manageable proportions and the exorbitant costs of welfare services themselves would fall to reasonable levels.

Apocalypse

Suppose we are all living scattered happily over the 'countryside', or, rather, 'natureside', in constant touch with all our dearest friends by video-phone, fax, E-mail, Internet and great future technical improvements of these. Shopping is electronic. Meetings are by teleconferencing. So long as we stay happily apart, conflict and crime will be minimized. Only spouses, lovers and children can abuse one another. Entertainment is, of course, by video and other increasingly varied and sophisticated electronic devices. Chess, bridge, poker, Monopoly, dominoes and Scrabble will all be electronic, whether solo or in groups electronically linked. Will group laughter and wit be satisfactorily intimate and immediate by satellite? Shall we demand physical greetings and occasionally boisterous back slapping? Sport is televised and non-participatory. For those unrestructured traditionalists who insist on actually playing soccer and baseball, cricket, basketball, tennis, wrestling and relay racing, there will presumably have to be major recreation centres scattered at appropriate intervals, or informally organized *ad hoc*.

Government will be on a small and local, experimental scale but just how the necessary levels of co-ordination should be achieved is unclear. Courts, prisons and police should be on greatly reduced scale, as already in Switzerland, but parliaments raise the same brute questions of how rarefied personal interactions can be and remain effective.

Production of all needs, food, clothes, housing, furniture and upholstery, transport systems, laundry, courier and delivery services, tooth paste, soap and condoms, television and computers themselves, all demand serious production, requiring enormous supervision and co-ordination however much automated, electronified and concentrated in small, physically scattered yet electronically linked units. Sex and worship, dealing with life crises, illness and death seem above all to be intrinsic aspects of human existence where proximity cannot be dispensed with. Therefore hospitals and clinics, schools and universities, have to be envisaged in some form after all allowances are made for lightening of the load and reduction of the scale. The total relationship of the eye, face and expression, mouth and taste, ears, hearing and bodily movement, taken in their infinite variety and miraculous co-ordination, cannot conceivably be adequately substituted electronically. Recognizing such ultimate limitations seems to drag us back from dispersion to indispensable points of concentration of many kinds. The clue must lie in the judicious combination of dispersion and concentration allowing for choice, between individuals and over space and time. Despite the increasingly intolerable evils spawned by the city in the grip of capitalist consumerism, there are some livable, lovable cities like Copenhagen or Prague, and the indubitable treasures of the world cities, with cathedrals, temples, mosques, museums and libraries, theatre, opera, ballet and concert music, which many will not allow to be reduced to mere electronic transmission. For the media messages are ultimately derived from these roots and despite their seemingly infinite capacity for creative fantasy, they would ultimately languish without the physical source.

And who will mediate and neutralize the media, the chief villains of the piece, who will be most difficult of all to resist and control? Where will they be? They can too easily be dispersed in activity, but how can they be dispersed in ownership and control? The financial markets seem already to display a less than ideal model.

I have to assume that the poverty problem of the Third World will be solved and the population bomb defused before retribution overtakes us, but it will take billions in compensation, education, interreflexive enculturation and mutual moral reconstruction. The current ethnic massacres, burgeoning conflicts and nuclear fears may ridicule any ultimate optimism, but I insist that it is such events and fears which should drive home the threat overshadowing us all. It is becoming apocalyptic. Those who dismiss it as maverick gloom and doom will only accentuate and accelerate the global dangers and difficulties. There are so many hopeful even if minority signs, that this would be terribly tragic.

The best contribution that 'the city' can ultimately make, that is to say, the attitudes of those who perceive the city as an extant reality, is to develop and diminish it into a global network of uplifting centres of cultural, aesthetic and inspirational performance and experience, almost a glorified museum piece, not a centre of production, nor even primarily of residence as at present. Such future post-cities would still require a formidable amount of care, maintenance and services, but as the electronifiable aspects of all these activities are gradually subtracted from specific space, the remainder will assume its proper place in the mosaic of human effort. As global population stabilizes and ultimately sinks again to the level local populations deem they want and can support, the recreational areas once regarded as rural counterpoint to the city, the forests, prairies, mountains, rivers and seas will recapture their pristine beauties and restorative forces.

Notes

1 'WRITING THE CITY UNDER CRISIS'

1 Such an orientation is unsympathetic to the postmodernist trend, whose emphasis is ephemeral.
2 Hong Kong and Singapore are noteworthy exceptions.
3 'The town is in fact already the concentration of the population, the instruments of production, of capital, of pleasures, of needs' (Marx and Engels, 1976:64).
4 Mastery of the immediate environment has always caused problems with the larger environment.
5 Sewers and water supplies seem humble, drains revolting, yet there was grandeur in the Cloaca Maxima, the drains of Mohenjodaro, the Pont du Gard, the Grand Canal.
6 'Homo sum: humanum nihil a me alienum puto.'
7 Fox, 1971:3–11. Wolf, 1982: ix: 'the insights of anthropology have to be rethought in the light of a new, historically oriented political economy'. Saunders, 1986:184: 'The structure of the city can be said to epitomise the pattern of society at large.' Wheatley, 1983:2: 'concentrating the institutions that establish and maintain order within the subsystem of society'.
8 'It is a definite relation between men, that assumes in their eyes the fantastic form of a relation between things' (Marx, 1967:71). Some see the doctrine of original sin as the story of man's alienation and link it to the Old Testament concept of idolatry (Bottomore, 1983:10). 'The greater your *alienated* life, the greater is the store of your estranged being' (Marx, in Marx and Engels, 1975:309).

2 PRISTINE CITIES

1 More recent excavations suggest that the 'tower' could have been the platform for a temple and the wall could have been a ditch to divert seasonal mud-slides. Such reinterpretations fit our general perspective. Other sites comparable to Jericho and even larger have been appearing, indicating that this era witnessed a general and quite widespread cultural advance.
2 The Zhou dynasty (1122–1221) came after Shang and before Qin and Han.
3 Yu the sorcerer, one of the legendary dynastic founders, walked with the set-square in his left hand, concealing and producing the compass from his right, part of the labyrinthine, cosmic yet quotidian symbolism of city and state; earth

and sky; time, body and life, male and female ever generating opposites out of one another.

4 Recent work shows Maya cities such as Tikal and Copan to have been more densely urban than was realized, as the flimsy structures of mass settlement came to be identified. There was also more intensive agriculture in swamp fields of maize and cacao.

5 Adams' basic comparison was between Sumeria and Aztec cities. Unfortunately the latter were obviously not pristine, so this aspect of comparison is not useful here (1966: 33–6).

3   GREECE AND ROME

1 Milvian Bridge (near Rome). It was here that Constantine confronted the critical battle of his career. Tradition avers that he saw a lighted cross in the sky the night before, had it painted on his soldiers' shields and proceeded to victory, declaring himself a Christian thereafter.

2 Confederates. The *federati* or confederates were 'barbarian' groups whom the Romans, unable to subdue, appropriated as subjects, nominally contracted to occupy and defend certain territory.

3 These two factions ramified throughout the social and political life of the city. No candidate for office could succeed without backing from one of them. There were originally White, Red, Green and Blue factions representing the four seasons, like the four seasonal colours in the Chinese quincunx (Gibbon, 1987:66–7; see above, pp. 40–42). Such symbolic factional dualities were pervasive in the pre-capitalist world, as with Guelfs and Ghibellines in Italy.

4   CITIES OF THE FEUDAL MODE OF PRODUCTION IN EUROPE

1 Enshrined in usage, the term has no theoretical exactitude. Its use by those whose ancestors they are can hardly amount to prejudice and may cause less misunderstanding than 'Germanic' or 'German'.

2 Actually at Lutèce, the defensible Ile de la Cité in the Seine, which Julius Ceasar found occupied by Parissi, who had their own golden coinage.

5   ASIAN CITIES: ASIATIC AND FEUDAL MODES OF PRODUCTION

1 No doubt this properly represents Gellner's fieldwork and scholarly impression, but the cult of saints was not an original element of orthodox Islam and had little prominence during the early centuries.

2 The Seljuqs' immense but ephemeral conquests are, like a number of others, referred to as an empire, but it is quite clear from the details of its composition and history that it was not.

3 The Assassins were a secret society of Ismaili terrorists, devoted to the downfall of the Abbasid caliphate, called *hashishi* because thought to take hashish during their strikes. They established a network of cells in fortresses all over Iran and Iraq, commanded by a grand master in a hillfort near Kasvin. Successfully eliminating many high officers and even caliphs, they were swept away by the Mongol invasions.

7   THE TRANSFORMATION OF THE CITY: FROM THE FEUDAL TO THE
CAPITALIST MODE OF PRODUCTION, AND ON TO THE APOCALYPSE

1 Personal communication and ethnographic fieldnotes, Detroit, 1991.
2 Personal communication and ethnographic fieldnotes, Detroit, 1991.
3 *New York Times*, 21 November 1982.

References

Abegglen, J.C. (1958) *The Japanese Factory: Aspects of its Social Organization*. New York: Free Press.

Abrams, Charles (1964) *The City is the Frontier*. New York: Harper & Row.

(1970) *Home Ownership for the Poor: A Program for Philadelphia*. New York: Praeger.

Abu-Lughod, J.L. (1961) Migrant Adjustment to City Life: The Egyptian Case. *American Journal of Sociology*, 67:22–32.

(1971) *Cairo: 1001 Years of the City Victorious*. Princeton: Princeton University Press.

Abu-Lughod, J.L. and R. Hay (1977) *Third World Urbanization*. Chicago: Maaroufa Press.

Acton, H. (1967) Medieval Florence. In Toynbee.

Adams, B.N. (1968) *Kinship in an Urban Setting*. Chicago: Markham.

Adams, R.M. (1966) *The Evolution of Urban Society: Early Mesopotamia and Prehispanic Mexico*. Chicago: Aldine.

(1972) Patterns of Urbanization in Early Southern Mesopotamia, 735–749. In Ucko, Tringham and Dimbleby.

al-Farabi (1949) *Idées des habitants de la cité vertueuse*, trans. R.P. Jaussen *et al.* Cairo: Imprimé de l'Institut Français d'Archéologie Orientale.

al Najim, Wadia Taha (1993) Baghdad: The City of Learning and Pleasure. In Nas.

Anderson, E.N. (1972) Some Chinese Methods of Dealing with Crowding. *Urban Anthropology*, 1, 2:141–50.

Anderson, N. (1959) Urbanism and Urbanization. *American Journal of Sociology*, 65, 1:68–73.

Anderson, W.L. (1906) *The Country Town: A Study of Rural Evolution*. New York: Baker and Taylor.

Ansari, G. (1995) Calcutta: Transformation from Metropolis to the City of Slumdwellers. In G.E. Karpinska (ed.), *The City Today, Yesterday and the Day Before*. Lodz: University of Lodz.

Ansari, G. and P.J.M. Nas (1983) (eds.) *Town Talk: The Dynamics of Urban Anthropology*. Leiden: E.J. Brill.

Apter, A. (1992) *Black Kings and Gods: The Hermeneutics of Power in Yoruba Society*. Chicago: University of Chicago Press.

Ardagh, J. (1990) *France Today*. Harmondsworth: Penguin.

Arlington, L.C. and W. Lewisohn (1935) *In Search of Old Peking*. Peking: H. Vetch.

424   References

Asbury, H. (1927, 1970) *The Gangs of New York: An Informal History of the Underworld.* New York: Capricorn.

Ashton, T.S. (1955) *An Economic History of England: The Eighteenth Century.* London: Methuen.

Asia Yearbook (1978) *Far East Economic Review.*

Aubin, J. (1970) Eléments pour l'étude des agglomérations urbaines dans l'Iran médiéval. In Hourani and Stern.

Auletta, K. (1983) *The Underclass.* New York: Vintage.

Bairoch, P. (1985) *De Jéricho à Mexico: villes et économie dans l'histoire.* Paris: Gallimard.

Baker, P.H. (1974) *Urbanization and Political Change in Lagos 1917–67.* Berkeley: California University Press.

Balazs, E. (1964) *Chinese Civilization and Bureaucracy: Variations on a Theme.* New Haven: Yale University Press.

Banfield, E.C. (1970) *The Unheavenly City: The Nature and Future of our Urban Crisis.* Boston: Little Brown.

Banton, M.P. (1957) *West African City: A Study of Tribal Life in Freetown.* London: Oxford University Press.

(1966) (ed.) *The Social Anthropology of Complex Societies.* London: Tavistock.

Barnes, S.T. (1986) *Patrons and Power. Creating a Political Community in Metropolitan Lagos.* Manchester: Manchester University Press.

Bascom, W. (1955) Urbanization among the Yoruba. *American Journal of Sociology,* 60:446–54.

(1969a) *Ifa Divination: Communication between Gods and Men in West Africa.* Bloomington: Indiana University Press.

(1969b) *The Yoruba of Southwestern Nigeria.* New York: Holt, Rinehart and Winston.

Basham, R. (1978) *Urban Anthropology: Cross-Cultural Study of Complex Societies.* Palo Alto: Mayfield.

Baskauskas, L. (1977) Multiple Identities: Adjusted Lithuanian Refugees in Los Angeles. *Urban Anthropology,* 6, 2:141–54.

Bastide, R. (1958) *Le Candomblé de Bahia (rite Nago).* Ecole Pratique des Hautes Etudes, VIe Section, Le Monde d'Outre-Mer Passé et Présent, Première série: Etudes V. Paris and The Hague: Mouton.

(1960) *Les religions africaines au Brésil: vers une sociologie des interpénétrations de civilisations.* Paris: Presses Universitaires de France.

(n.d.) *Sociologie du Brésil.* Université de Paris, Institut des Hautes Etudes de L'Amérique Latine, Centre de Documentation Universitaire, 5, Place de la Sorbonne, Paris Ve.

Bastie, J. (1964) *La croissance de la banlieue parisienne.* Paris: Presses Universitaires de France.

Beals, R.L. (1951) Urbanism, Urbanization and Acculturation. *American Anthropologist,* 53, 1:1–10.

Befu, H. (1971) *Japan: An Anthropological Introduction.* San Francisco: Chandler.

Bell, D. (1973) *The Coming of Post Industrial Society: A Venture in Social Forecasting.* New York: Basic Books.

Bernstein, B.B. (1975) *Class, Codes and Control.* London: Routledge & Kegan Paul.

Bernus, S. (1969) *Particularizmes ethniques en milieu urbain: l'exemple de Niamey.* Paris: Institut d'Ethnologie, Musée de l'Homme.

Berry, B. J. L. (1973) *The Human Consequences of Urbanization: Divergent Paths in the Urban Experience of the Twentieth Century.* New York: St Martin's.

Betts, R. (1971) The Establishment of the Medina in Dakar, Senegal 1914. *Africa*, 41, 2:143–52.

Beyer, G.H. (1967) (ed.) *The Urban Explosion in Latin America.* Ithaca: Cornell University Press.

Blanton, R.E. (1976) Anthropological Studies of Cities. *Annual Review of Anthropology*, ed. B.J. Siegel.

Blumberg, P. (1968) *Industrial Democracy: The Sociology of Participation.* London: Constable.

Blumenfeld, H. (1971) *Transportation in the Modern Metropolis.* In Bourne.

Blumenthal, A. (1932) *Small-Town Stuff.* Chicago: Chicago University Press.

Bok, D. (1993) *The Cost of Talent: How Executives and Professionals are Paid and how it Affects America.* New York: Free Press.

Bombay Civic Trust & Yusufu Meherally Centre (1968) *A National Policy for an Orderly Development of Indian Cities.* Bombay.

Bott, E. (1971) *Family and Social Network. Roles, Norms and Extended Relationships in Ordinary Urban Families.* New York: Free Press.

Bottomore, T. (1983) (ed.) *A Dictionary of Marxist Thought.* Cambridge: Harvard University Press.

Boulding, K. (1963) The Death of the City: A Frightened Look at Postcivilization. In O. Handlin and J. Burchard (eds.), *The Historian and the City.* Cambridge: MIT Press.

(1968) The City as an Element in the International System. *Daedalus*, 97, 4:1111–23. Reprinted in Walton and Carns, 1973.

(1971) The Death of the City: A Frightened Look at Postcivilization. In A. Trachtenberg, P. Neill and P.C. Bunnell (eds.), *The City: An American Experience.* New York: Oxford University Press.

Bourne, L.S. (1971) (ed.) *Internal Structure of the City: Readings on Space and Environment.* New York: Oxford University Press.

Braidwood, R.J. (1960) The Agricultural Revolution. *Scientific American*, 203:130–41.

Braidwood, R.J. and G. R. Willey (1962) (eds.) *Courses Toward Urban Life: Archeological Considerations of Some Cultural Alternates.* Chicago: Aldine.

Brandel-Syrier, M. (1971) *Reeftown Elite: A Study of Social Mobility in a Modern African Community on the Reef.* London: Routledge & Kegan Paul.

Braudel, F. (1973) *Capitalism and Material Life, 1400–1800*, trans. M. Kochen. London: Weidenfeld & Nicolson.

(1976) *The Mediterranean and the Mediterranean World in the Age of Philip II*, vol. II. New York: Harper and Row.

(1977) *Afterthoughts on Material Civilization and Capitalism.* Baltimore: The Johns Hopkins University Press.

(1979) *Civilisation matérielle, économie et capitalisme XVe–XVIIIe siècle. Les structures du quotidien. Le possible et l'impossible.* Paris: Armand Colin.

(1985) *Civilization & Capitalism 15th–18th Century*, vol.I, II and III. London: Fontana (Harper).

Breese, G. (1966) *Urbanization in Newly Developing Countries*. Englewood Cliffs: Prentice Hall.

(1969) (ed.) *The City in Newly Developing Countries: Readings on Urbanism and Urbanization*. Englewood Cliffs: Prentice Hall.

Briggs, A. (1968) *Victorian Cities*. Harmondsworth: Penguin Books.

Brucker, G.A. (1962) *Florentine Politics and Society, 1343–78*. Princeton: Princeton University Press.

(1969) *Renaissance Florence*. New York: Wiley.

(1977) *The Civic World of Early Renaissance Florence*. Princeton: Princeton University Press.

Brumfield, E.M. and J.W. Fox (1994) (eds.) *Factional Competition and Political Development in the New World*. Cambridge: Cambridge University Press.

Bruner, E. M. (1973) Kin and Non-Kin. In Southall.

(1974) The Expression of Ethnicity in Indonesia. In Cohen.

Burckhardt, J. (1944) *The Civilization of the Renaissance in Italy*. London: Phaidon Press; Allen & Unwin.

Burgess, J.S. (1928) *The Guilds of Peking*. New York: Columbia University Press.

Bury, J.B. (1889) *A History of the Later Roman Empire, from Arcadius to Irene (395 A.D. to 800 A.D.)*. London: Macmillan.

Butterfield, D. (1962) A Study of the Urbanization Process among Mixtec Migrants from Tilantogo in Mexico City. *America Indigena*, 22:257–74.

(1977) Selectivity of Out-Migration from a Mixtec Community. *Urban Anthropology*, 6, 2:129–39.

Cahen, C. (1970) Y-a-t-il des corporations professionnelles dans le monde musulman classique? In Hourani and Stern.

Calhoun, G. M. (1926) *The Business Life of Ancient Athens*. Chicago: Chicago University Press.

Cambridge Economic History of Europe. H.J. Habakkuk and M. Postan (eds.), vol. VI, parts 1 & 2 (1966). Cambridge: Cambridge University Press.

Cambridge History of the British Empire. J.H. Rose, A.P. Newton and E.A. Benians (eds.) vol. I (1929), vol. II (1940); H.H. Dodwell (ed.), vol. IV (1929). Cambridge: Cambridge University Press.

Canard, M. (1962) Baghdad au IV siècle de l'hégire. In *Baghdad. Volume spécial publié à l'occasion du mille deux centième anniversaire de la Fondation*. Leiden: E.J. Brill.

Carneiro, R.L. (1987) Further Reflections on Resource Concentration and its Role in the Rise of the State. In L. Manzanilla (ed.), *Studies in the Neolithic and Urban Revolutions*. BAR International Series 349.

Carus-Wilson, E. (1952) The Woollen Industry. In Postan and Miller.

Castells, M. (1972) *La question urbaine*. Paris: Maspéro.

(1983) *The City and the Grassroots*. Berkeley: University of California Press.

Castells, M. and F. Godard (1974) Monopoleville: l'entreprise, l'état, l'urbain. Paris and The Hague: Mouton.

Central Intelligence Agency (1975) Research Aid. *People's Republic of China. Handbook of Economic Indicators. A (E.R.) 75–72*.

Chambre, H. (1965a) Urbanisation et croissance économique en URSS. *Economie appliquée*, 17, 1:5–109.

(1965b) L'urbanisation en USSR. In H. Carrier and P. Laurent (eds.), *Le phénomène urbain*. Paris: Aunbier-Montaigne.

Chandler, T. and G. Fox (1974) *3000 Years of Urban Growth*. New York: Academic Press.

Charles-Picard, G. and C. (1968) *The Life and Death of Carthage: A Survey of Punic History and Culture from its Birth to its Final Tragedy*. London: Sidgwick & Jackson.

Chavannes, E. (1895) *Les mémoires historiques de Sema-Ts'ien*, vol. I. Paris: Ernest Leroux.

Checkland, S. G. (1964a) The British Industrial City as History. *Urban Studies*, 1, 1:34–54.

(1964b) *The Rise of Industrial Society in England 1815–1885*. London: Longmans.

Cherry, J. F. (1986) Polities and Palaces: Some Problems in Minoan State Formation. In Renfrew and Cherry.

Childe, V.G. (1950) The Urban Revolution. *Town Planning Review*, 21:3–17.

Chombart de Lauwe, P. H. *et al.* (1952) *Paris et l'agglomération parisienne Tome I. L'espace sociale dans une grande cité*. Paris: PUF.

Chomsky, N. (1994a) *Keeping the Rabble in Line*. Monroe, Maine: Common Courage Press.

(1994b) *World Orders Old and New*. New York: Columbia University Press.

Christaller, W. (1933, 1966) *Die Zentralen Orten in Sud Deutschland*. Jena: G. Fischer. Trans. C.W. Baskin, *Central Places in Southern Germany*. Englewood Cliffs: Prentice Hall.

Chudacoff, H.P. (1975) *The Evolution of American Urban Society*. Englewood Cliffs: Prentice Hall.

Clark, K.B. (1967) *Dark Ghetto: Dilemmas of Social Power*. New York: Harper Torch.

Clarke, M.V. (1926) *The Medieval City State: An Essay on Tyranny and Federation in the Later Middle Ages*. London: Methuen.

Clinard, M.B. (1970) *Slums and Community Development: Experiments in Self-Help*. New York: Free Press.

(1978) *Cities with Little Crime. The Case of Switzerland*. Cambridge: Cambridge University Press.

Clinard, M.B. and D. J. Abbott (1973) *Crime in Developing Countries: A Comparative Perspective*. New York: Wiley.

Coe, M.D. (1961) Social Typology and the Tropical Forest Civilizations. *Comparative Studies in Society and History*, 4, 1:65–85.

(1965) A Model of Lowland Maya Community Structure. *Southwestern Journal of Anthropology*, 21, 2:97–114.

Coedès, G. (1963) *Angkor: An Introduction*, trans. E.F. Gardiner. Hong Kong: Oxford University Press.

(1968) *The Indianized States of Southeast Asia*. Honolulu: Eastwest Center.

Cohen, A. (1969) *Custom and Politics in Urban Africa: A Study of Hausa Migrants in Yoruba Towns*. London: Routledge & Kegan Paul.

(1974) (ed.) *Urban Ethnicity*. London: Tavistock.

Cohen, A.P. (1992) Self-Conscious Anthropology. In J. Okely and H. Callaway (eds.) *Anthropology as Autobiography*. London: Routledge.

Constantinescu, M., *et al.* (1974) *Urban Growth Processes in Romania.* Bucharest: Meridiane Publishing House.

Cornuau, C., *et al.* (1965) *L'attraction de Paris sur sa banlieue: étude sociologique.* Paris: Les Editions Ouvrières.

Crane, R.J. (1955) Urbanism in India. *American Journal of Sociology,* 60, 5:463–70.

Cranmer-Byng, J. L. (1962) *An Embassy to China: Being the Journal Kept by Lord Macartney during his Embassy to the Emperor Ch'ien-lung, 1793–1794.* London: Longmans.

Crawcour, E.S. (1963) Changes in Japanese Commerce in the Tokugawa Period. *Journal of Asian Studies,* 22, 4:387–400.

Creel, H.G. (1936) *The Birth of China.* London: Jonathan Cape.

Cucu, V. (1975) Romania. In Jones.

Cummings, S. and D.J. Monti (1993) *Gangs: The Origin and Impact of Contemporary Youth Gangs in the United States.* Albany: State University of New York Press.

d'Arcq (1766) *La noblesse militaire.* Quoted Braudel, III:62.

Darnton, R. (1994) Sex for Thought. *New York Review of Books,* 41, no. 21.

Davie, M. (1972) *In the Future Now. A Report from California.* London: Hamish Hamilton.

Davis, K. (1969) *World Urbanization 1950–70,* vol. I. Institute of International Studies. Berkeley: University of California Press.

Davis, W.G. (1973) *Social Relations in a Philippine Market: Self-Interest and Subjectivity.* Berkeley: University of California Press.

Deane, P. (1965) *The First Industrial Revolution.* Cambridge: Cambridge University Press.

Deane, P. and W.A. Cole (1967) *British Economic Growth 1688–1959: Trends and Structure.* Cambridge: Cambridge University Press.

Dehavenon, A.-L. (1992) The Holy Women and Homeless Men of East Harlem. A Brief Look at the Underclass Concept. In H. de Soto (ed.), *Culture and Contradiction: Dialectics of Wealth, Power and Symbol.* Festschrift in honour of Aidan Southall. San Francisco: E.M. Texts.

(1993) An Etic Model for the Scientific Study of the Causes of Matrifocality. In J.P. Menchen and A. Okongwu (eds.), *Where Did All the Men Go? Female-Headed/Female-Supported Households in Cross-Cultural Perspectives.* Boulder: Westview Press.

Delouvrier, P. (1972) Paris. In Robson and Regan

de Roover, R.A. (1948) *Money, Banking and Credit in Medieval Bruges; Italian Merchant-Bankers, Lombards and Money-Changers: A Study in the Origins of Banking.* Cambridge, Mass.: Medieval Academy of America.

(1966) *The Rise and Decline of the Medici Bank, 1397–1494.* New York: Norton.

Desai, R. unpublished manuscript.

Descola, J. (1968) *Daily Life in Colonial Peru 1710–1820,* trans. M. Heron. New York: Macmillan.

Deverdun, G. (1959) *Marrakech des origines à 1912.* Rabat: Editions techniques Nord-Africaines, 22 rue du Béarn.

Diamond, W. (1941) On the Dangers of an Urban Interpretation of History. In E.F.

Goldman (ed.), *Historiography and Urbanization: Essays in American History in Honour of W. Stull Holt.* Baltimore: The Johns Hopkins University Press.

Djilas, M. (1957) *The New Class: An Analysis of the Communist System.* New York: Praeger.

Dodwell, H. H. (1929) *The Cambridge History of the British Empire*, vol. IV: *British India 1497–1858.* Cambridge: Cambridge University Press.

Dore, R. P. (1958) *City Life in Japan: A Study of a Tokyo Ward.* London: Routledge & Kegan Paul.

—— (1967) (ed.) *Aspects of Social Change in Modern Japan.* Princeton: Princeton University Press.

—— (1971) *Japanese Industrialization and the Developing Countries: Model, Warning, or Source of Healthy Doubts?* Occasional Paper no. 8. Singapore: Institute of Southeast Asian Studies.

—— (1973) *Japanese Factory, British Factory.* London: Allen & Unwin.

Douglass, H.P. (1970) *The Little Town.* New York: Arno Press.

Dow, L. M. (1977) High Weeds in Detroit: The Irregular Economy among a Network of Appalachian Migrants. *Urban Anthropology*, 6, 2:111–24.

Doxiadis, C.A. (1968) *Ekistics: An Introduction to the Science of Human Settlements.* New York: Norton.

Doxiadis, C.A. and J.G. Papaioannou (1974) *Ecumenopolis: The Inevitable City of the Future.* New York: Norton.

Dubois, J. A. (1906) *Hindu Manners, Customs and Ceremonies*, trans. H. K. Beauchamp. Oxford: Clarendon Press.

Duby, G. (1978) *The Early Growth of the European Economy. Warriors and Peasants from the Seventh to the Twelfth Century.* Ithaca: Cornell University Press.

Duffy, J. (1963) *Portugal in Africa.* Baltimore: Penguin Books.

Dumont, L. (1966) *Homo Hierarchicus: The Caste System and its Implications*, trans. M. Sainsbury. London: Weidenfeld and Nicolson.

Duncan-Jones, R. (1974) *The Economy of the Roman Empire: Quantitative Studies.* Cambridge: Cambridge University Press.

Dunn, S. (1982) *The Fall and Rise of the Asiatic Mode of Production.* London: Routledge and Kegan Paul.

Dwyer, D J. (1975) *People and Housing in Third World Cities: Perspectives on the Problem of Spontaneous Settlements.* London: Longmans.

Early China (1975) Society for the Study of Early China, Institute of East Asian Studies, Berkeley: University of California.

Eberhard, W. (1960) *A History of China.* Berkeley: University of California Press.

Edwards, J.R., E. Leigh and T. Marshall (1970) *Social Patterns in Birmingham: 1966 A Reference Manual.* University of Birmingham: Occasional Paper no. 13, Centre for Urban and Regional Studies.

Ehrenberg, R. (1963) *Capital and Finance in the Age of the Renaissance: A Study of the Fuggers and their Connections*, trans. H.M. Lucas. New York: Augustus M. Kelley.

Eisenstadt, S. N. (1963) *The Political Systems of Empires.* New York: Free Press.

Eitzen, D. S. (1983) *Social Problems.* Boston: Allyn & Bacon.

Elisséeff, N. (1970) Damas à la lumière des théories de Jean Sauvaget. In Hourani and Stern.

Elvin, M. (1973) *The Pattern of the Chinese Past*. Stanford: Stanford University Press.

Elvin, M. and G.W. Skinner (1974) (eds.) *The Chinese City between Two Worlds*. Stanford: Stanford University Press.

El Zein, A. (1974) *The Sacred Meadows: A Structural Analysis of Religious Symbolism in an East African Town*. Evanston: Northwestern University Press.

Encyclopaedia Britannica (1974) Chicago: Encyclopaedia Britannica Inc.

Engels, F. (1975) *The Condition of the Working-Class in England, from Personal Observation and Authentic Sources*. in K. Marx and F. Engels, *Collected Works*, vol. IV. Moscow: Progress Publishers.

Ennen, Edith (1967) The Different Types of Formation of European Towns. In Thrupp.

Epstein, A.L. (1958) *Politics in an Urban African Community*. Manchester: Manchester University Press.

(1964) Urban Communities in Africa. In Gluckman.

(1967) Urbanization and Social Change in Africa. *Current Anthropology*, 8, 4:275–84.

Ewen, S. (1977) *Captains of Consciousness. Advertising and the Social Roots of Consumer Culture*. New York: McGraw-Hill.

Ezekiel *The Book of the Prophet Ezekiel*.

Fabian, J. (1983) *Time and the Other: How Anthropology Makes its Object*. New York: Columbia University Press.

Faure, P. (1973) *La vie quotidienne en Crète au temps de Minos (1500 avant Jésus-Christ)*. Paris: Hachette.

Federal Bureau of Investigation, Department of Justice. *Crime in the United States 1976. Uniform Crime Reports*. US Government Printing Office.

Felber, J.E. (1974) *The American's Tourist Manual for the People's Republic of China*. International Intertrade Index, Box 636, New Jersey: Newark.

Fennell, V. (1977) International Atlanta and Ethnic Group Relations. *Urban Anthropology*, 6, 4:345–54.

Ferman, L.A., J.L. Kornbluh and A. Haber (1965) (eds.) *Poverty in America*. Introduction by M. Harrington. Ann Arbor: University of Michigan Press.

Fernea, R.A. (1995) Comment. *Current Anthropology*, 36, 4:649.

Feuerwerker, A. (1976) *State and Society in Eighteenth-Century China: The Ch'ing Empire in its Glory*. Ann Arbor: Centre for Chinese Studies, University of Michigan.

Field, A. J. (1970) (ed.) *City and Country in the Third World: Issues in the Modernization of Latin America*. Cambridge: Schenkman.

Flerovsky, A. (1978) Sumgait: A Young Industrial City. *Soviet Life* (May).

Foley, D.E. (1991) *Learning Capitalist Culture: Deep in the Heart of Tejas*. Philadelphia: University of Philadelphia Press.

Foligno, C. (1910) *The Story of Padua*. London: J.M. Dent.

Foucault, M. (1980) *Power/Knowledge: Selected Interviews and Other Writings 1972–1977*, ed. C. Gordon. New York: Pantheon.

Fox, R.G. (1969) *From Zamindar to Ballot Box: Community Change in a North Indian Market Town*. Ithaca: Cornell University Press.

(1970) (ed.) *Urban India: Society, Space and Image*. Monograph no. 10,

Program in Comparative Studies on Southern Asia. Durham: Duke University Press.

(1971) *Kin, Clan, Raja and Rule: State–Hinterland Relations in Pre-industrial India*. Berkeley: University of California Press.

(1977) *Urban Anthropology: Cities in their Cultural Settings*. Englewood Cliffs: Prentice Hall.

Fraenkel, M. (1964) *Tribe and Class in Monrovia*. London: Oxford University Press for International African Institute.

Freidel, D. (1992) *Religion, Power and Legitimacy in Maya States*. Cleveland State University: Segmentary States Conference.

Freidel, D., L. Schele and J. Parker (1993) *Maya Cosmos, 3000 Years on the Shaman's Path*. New York: William Morrow.

Friedmann, J. (1961) Cities in Social Transformation. *Comparative Studies in Society and History*, 4, 1:86–103.

Fryde, E.B. and M.M. Fryde (1963) Public Credit, with Special Reference to North-Western Europe. In Postan, Rich and Miller.

Fukutake, T. (1967) *Japanese Rural Society*, trans. R.P. Dore. Tokyo: Oxford University Press.

(1974) *Japanese Society Today*. Tokyo: Tokyo University Press.

Fustel de Coulanges, N. D. (1864, 1956) *The Ancient City: A Study on the Religion, Laws and Institutions of Greece and Rome*. Garden City: Anchor, Doubleday.

Gakenheimer, R.A. (1967) The Peruvian City of the Sixteenth Century. In Beyer.

Gamble, S.D. (1921) *Peking, a Social Survey*. New York: G. H. Doran.

Gans, H.J. (1962a) *The Urban Villagers: Group and Class in the Life of Italian-Americans*. Glencoe: Free Press.

(1962b) Urbanism and Suburbanism as Ways of Life: A Reevaluation of Definitions. In A. Rose (ed.), *Human Behaviour and Social Processes*. Boston: Houghton Mifflin.

(1967) *The Levittowners: Ways of Life and Politics in a New Suburban Community*. New York: Random House.

Geertz, C. (1963a) *The Social History of an Indonesian Town*. Cambridge: Massachusetts Institute of Technology.

(1963b) *Peddlers and Princes: Social Change and Economic Modernization in Two Indonesian Towns*. Chicago: Chicago University Press.

(1966) *Agricultural Involution: The Process of Ecological Change in Indonesia*. Berkeley: University of California Press.

(1971) *Islam Observed. Religious Development in Morocco and Indonesia*. Chicago: Chicago University Press.

Gell-Mann, M. (1995) *The Quark and the Jaguar: Adventures in the Simple and Complex*. New York: W.F. Freeman.

Gellner, E. (1991) *Muslim Society*. Cambridge: Cambridge University Press.

Gernet, J. (1962) *Daily Life in China on the Eve of the Mongol Invasion 1250–1276*, trans. H.M. Wright. London: Allen & Unwin.

Ghitelman, S. (1975) Family and Kinship in Urban India. Unpublished manuscript.

Ghosh, A. (1968) *Calcutta, the Primate City*. Office of the Registrar General, India, Ministry of Home Affairs.

(1973) *The City in Early Historical India.* Simla: Indian Institute of Advanced Study.

Gibbon, E. (1987) *The History of the Decline and Fall of the Roman Empire*, vol. V: *Justinian and the Roman Law.* London: The Folio Society.

Gilbert, A. and J. Gugler (1982) *Cities, Poverty and Development: Urbanization in the Third World.* New York: Oxford University Press.

Gillion, K.L. (1968) *Ahmedabad: A Study in Indian Urban History.* Berkeley: University of California Press.

Gitlin, T. (1987) *The Sixties: Years of Hope Days of Rage.* New York: Bantam Books.

Gladney, D.C. (1994) *Purity and Authenticity: Hui Muslim Identity and the Problem of Ethnicity in China.* Cambridge: Cambridge University Press.

Glass, D.V. (1954) (ed.) *Social Mobility In Britain.* London: Routledge and Kegan Paul.

Glass, R. (1964) (ed.) *London: Aspects of Change.* London: MacGibbon & Kee.

Glotz, G. (1930) *The Greek City and its Institutions.* London: K. Paul, Trench, Trubner.

Gluckman, M. (1964) (ed.) *Closed Systems and Open Minds: The Limits of Naivety in Social Anthropology.* Chicago: Aldine.

Gmelch, G. (1977) *The Irish Tinkers: Urbanization of an Itinerant People.* Menlo Park: Cummings.

Gmelch, G. and W. Zenner (1988) (eds.) *Urban Life: Readings in Urban Anthropology* (2nd edition). Prospect Heights, Ill.: Waveland Press.

Godelier, M. (1978a) Infrastructure, Society and History. *Current Anthropology*, 19:763–71.

(1978b) The Concept of the Asiatic Mode of Production and Marxist Models of Social Evolution. In Seddon.

(1981) D'un mode de production à l'autre: théorie de la transition. *Recherches sociologiques*, 12, 2:161–93.

Goodwin, E.A. (1953) (ed.) *The European Nobility in the Eighteenth Century: Studies of the Nobilities of the Major European States in the Pre-Reform Era.* London: A. & C. Black.

Gordon, D.M. (1984) Capitalist Development and the History of American Cities. In Tabb and Sawers.

Gordon, M. (1965) *Sick Cities: Psychology and Pathology of American Urban Life.* Baltimore: Penguin.

(1973) (ed.) *American Family in Social-Historical Perspective.* New York: St Martin's Press.

Gordon, M.M. (1964) *Assimilation in American Life: The Role of Race, Religion and National Origin.* New York: Oxford University Press.

Gottmann, J. (1961) *Megalopolis: The Urbanized Northeastern Seaboard of the United States.* Cambridge: Massachusetts Institute of Technology.

Gough, K. (1981) *Rural Society in Southeast India.* Cambridge: Cambridge University Press.

Gould, S. J. (1986) Cardboard Darwinism. *New York Review of Books*, 25 September, 54.

Granet, M. (1958) *La féodalité chinoise.* New York: Meridian.

Graves, R. (1960) *The Greek Myths*, vols.I and II. Harmondsworth: Penguin.

Greer, S. (1965) *Urban Renewal and American Cities.* Indianapolis: Bobbs-Merrill.

Gross, C. (1890) *The Gild Merchant: Contribution to British Municipal History.* Oxford: Clarendon.

Gugler, J. (1988) (ed.) *Urbanization of the Third World.* New York: Oxford University Press.

Guldin, G.E. and A.W. Southall (1993) (eds.) *Urban Anthropology in China.* Leiden: Brill.

Gulick, J. (1963) *Urban Anthropology: Its Present and Future.* Trans. New York Academy of Science. Series II, 25, 445–58.

(1974) Urban Anthropology. In J.J. Honigmann (ed.), *Handbook of Social and Cultural Anthropology.* Chicago: Rand McNally.

(1975) The City as a Microcosm of Society. *Urban Anthropology,* 4, 1:005–015.

Gutkind, E.A. (1964) *International History of City Development,* vol. I: *Urban Development in Central Europe.* New York: Free Press.

(1965) *International History of City Development,* vol. II: *Urban Development in the Alpine and Scandinavian Countries.* New York:Free press.

(1967) *International History of City Development,* vol. III: *Urban Development in Southern Europe: Spain and Portugal.* New York: Free Press.

(1968) *International History of City Development,* vol. IV: *Urban Development in Southern Europe: Italy and Greece.* NewYork: Free Press.

(1970) *International History of City Development,* vol. V: *Urban Development in Western Europe: France and Belgium.* New York: Free Press.

(1971) *International History of City Development,* vol. VI: *Urban Development in East-Central Europe: Poland, Czecho-Slovakia and Hungary.* New York: Free Press.

Gutschow, H. (1984) Bhaktapur: The Urban Symbolism of a Traditional Nepalese Town. Workshop on the Meanings of the City, Wingspread, Wisconsin.

Guttentag, M. (1976) Children in Harlem's Community Controlled Schools. In Kalt and Zalkind.

Habermas, J. (1979) *Communication and the Evolution of Society.* Boston: Beacon Press.

Hacker, A. (1994) Unjust Deserts? *New York Review of Books,* 3 March, 20–4.

Haeger, J. W. (1975) (ed.) *Crisis and Prosperity in Sung China.* Tucson: University of Arizona Press.

Hagen, E.E. (1962) *On the Theory of Social Change: How Economic Growth Begins.* Homewood: Dorsey.

Hamilton, J.M. (1977) *The Glory that Was Once Potosi.* New York Times Travel Section 29 May.

Hammel, E.A. (1969) *The Pink Yo-Yo: Occupational Mobility in Belgrade, ca. 1915–1965.* Research Series No. 13. Institute of International Studies. Berkeley: University of California Press.

Hance, W.A. (1960) Economic Location and Functions of Tropical African Cities. *Human Organization,* 19, 3:135–6.

Hannerz, U. (1969) *Soulside: Inquiries into Ghetto Culture and Community.* New York: Columbia University Press.

Harris, C. D. (1970) *Cities of the Soviet Union: Studies in their Functions, Size, Density and Growth.* Association of American Geographers. Chicago: Rand McNally.

Harris, M. (1956) *Town and Country in Brazil.* New York: Columbia University Press.

Hartwell, R. (1961–2) A Revolution in the Chinese Iron and Coal Industries during the Northern Sung, 960–1126 A.D. *Journal of Asian Studies,* 21:153–62.

(1982) Demographic, Political and Social Transformation of China, 750–1550. *Harvard Journal of Asiatic Studies,* 42, 2:356–442.

Harvard Research Review No. 5 (1970) *Technology and the City.* Program on Technology and Society. Cambridge.

Harvey, D. (1973) *Social Justice and the City.* London: Edward Arnold.

(1985) *Consciousness and the Urban Experience: Paris 1850–70.* Oxford: Blackwell.

(1990) *The Condition of Post Modernity.* Oxford: Blackwell.

Hauchler, J. and P.M. Kennedy (1994) *Global Trends. The World Almanac of Development and Peace.* New York: Continuum.

Heath, D.B. and R.N. Adams (1965) (eds.) *Contemporary Cultures and Societies of Latin America and the Caribbean.* New York: Random House.

Herlihy, D. (1958) *Pisa in Early Renaissance: A Study of Urban Growth.* New Haven: Yale University Press.

(1967) *Medieval and Renaissance Pistoia: The Social History of an Italian Town, 1200–1340.* New Haven: Yale University Press.

Hertz, E. and O. Hutheesing (1975) At the Edge of Society: The Nominal Culture of Urban Hotel Isolates. *Urban Anthropology,* 4, 4:317–32.

Hill, C.E. (1976) Adaptation in Public and Private Behavior of Ethnic Groups in an American Urban Setting. *Urban Anthropology,* 4, 4:333–47.

Hobsbawm, E.J. (1968) *Industry and Empire: The Making of Modern English Society, vol. II: 1750 to the Present Day.* New York: Pantheon; Random House.

(1978) *L'ère du capital.* Paris: Fayard.

(1994) *The Age of Extremes. The Short Twentieth Century 1914–91.* London: Michael Joseph.

Hoffman, M.A. (1970) Culture History and Cultural Ecology at Hierakonpolis from Palaeolithic Times to the Old Kingdom. PhD dissertation. Madison: University of Wisconsin.

Holston, J. (1989) *The Modernist City. An Anthropological Critique of Brasilia.* Chicago: University of Chicago Press.

Holzner, L. (1970) *The Role of History and Tradition in the Urban Geography of West Germany.* Annals of the Association of American Geographers, 60, 315–39.

Hopkins, E.W. (1901) *India Old and New.* New York: Scribners.

Hopkins, N.S. (1968) *Popular Government in an African Town.* Chicago: Chicago University Press.

Hoselitz, B.F. (1955) Generative and Parasitic Cities. *Economic Development and Cultural Change,* 3:278–94.

Hourani, A.H. and S.M. Stern (1970) (eds.) *The Islamic City.* Oxford: Oxford University Press and Philadelphia: University of Pennsylvania Press.

Howell, J. T. (1973) *Hard Living on Clay Street.* New York: Double Day/Anchor.

Hoyt, H. (1933) *One Hundred Years of Land Values in Chicago.* Chicago: University of Chicago Press.

(1939) *The Structure and Growth of Residential Neighbourhoods in American Cities.* Washington, DC: Federal Housing Administration.

Hsu, Cho-Yun (1965) *Ancient China in Transition: An Analysis of Social Mobility, 722–222 B.C.* Stanford: Stanford University Press.

Hsu, Cho-Yun and K. Linduff (1989) *Western Chou Civilization.* New Haven: Yale University Press.

Hsu, F.L.K. (1962) *Clan, Caste and Club.* Princeton: Van Nostrand.

Hubbell, L.J. (1976) Class Structure Self-Perceived: A Methodology for Discovering Native Models of Stratification Systems. *Urban Anthropology,* 5, 1:19–34.

Hucker, C.O. (1975) *China's Imperial Past.* Stanford: Stanford University Press.

Hunt, G.M. and N.H. Azrim (1976) A Community-Reinforcement Approach to Alcoholism. In Kalt and Zalkind.

Huxtable, A.L. (1978) Paris's Défense Cluster: Coup of Drawing Board Style. *New York Times,* 11 June.

Ibn Khaldun (1958) *The Muqaddimah. An Introduction to History,* 3 vols., trans. F. Rosenthal. London: Routledge and Kegan Paul.

Inkeles, A. (1966) The Modernization of Man. In Weiner.

Inkeles, A. and D. H. Smith (1974) *Becoming Modern: Individual Change in Six Developing Countries.* Cambridge: Harvard University Press.

International Criminal Police Organization – Interpol. General Secretariat 92210 Saint-Cloud. *1973–4 International Crime Statistics.*

Jackson, B. (1968) *Working Class Community: Some General Notions Raised by a Series of Studies in Northern England.* London: Routledge and Kegan Paul.

Jacob, J. (1974) *Fun City: An Ethnographic Study of a Retirement Community.* New York: Holt, Rinehart and Winston.

Jacobs, J. (1965) *Life and Death of Great Cities.* Harmondsworth: Penguin Books.

Jacobson, D. (1973) *Itinerant Townsmen: Friendship and Social Order in Urban Uganda.* Menlo Park: Cummings.

Jeffreys, M. (1964) Londoners in Hertfordshire. In R. Glass *et al.* (eds.), *Centre for Urban Studies Report,* no. 3. London: MacGibbon and Kee.

Jenks, C. (1994) The Homeless. *New York Review of Books,* 21 April, 20.

Jesus, C.M. de (1962) *Child of the Dark: A Diary of Carolina Maria de Jesus,* trans. D. St Clair. New York: Signet.

Johnson, E.A.J. (1970) *The Organization of Space in Developing Countries.* Cambridge: Harvard University Press.

Jones, A.H.M. (1937) *The Cities of the Eastern Roman Provinces.* Oxford: Clarendon Press.

(1960) *Athenian Democracy.* Oxford: Blackwell.

(1964) *The Later Roman Empire 284–602: A Social, Economic and Administrative Survey,* vols. I and II. Norman: University of Oklahoma Press.

(1966) *The Greek City from Alexander to Justinian.* Oxford: Clarendon Press.

Jones, R. (1975) (ed.) *Essays on World Urbanization.* London: George Philip and Son.

Jugoslavije (1977) *Statick Godisnjak.* Belgrade.

Juppenlatz, M. (1970) *Cities in Transformation: The Urban Squatter Problem of the Developing World.* Brisbane: University of Queensland Press.

Kaempfer, E. (1906) *The History of Japan: Together with a Description of the Kingdom of Siam 1690–92*, trans. J.G. Scheuchzer. 3 vols. Glasgow: J. Maclehose.

Kahl, J. A. (1970) *The Measurement of Modernism: A Study of Values in Brazil and Mexico.* Austin: University of Texas Press.

Kalish, J.A. (1970) In Harvard Research Review.

Kalt, N.C. and S.S. Zalkind (1976) (eds.) *Urban Problems: Psychological Inquiries.* New York: Oxford University Press.

Kandell, J. (1978) Amsterdam Halts Decay in Centre but Prices Workers out of the Area. *New York Times*, 11 June.

Karpat, K.H. (1976) *The Gecekondu: Rural Migration and Urbanization.* Cambridge: Cambridge University Press.

Keightley, D.N. (1979–80) The Shang State as Seen in the Oracle-bone Inscriptions. *Early China*, 5:25–34.

(1986) Kingship and Kinship: The Royal Lineages of the Late Shang. *Early China. Supplement I*, 65–8.

Keiser, R.L. (1969) *The Vice-Lords, Warriors of the Streets.* New York: Holt, Reinhart and Winston.

Kendis, K.O. and R.J. Kendis (1976) The Street Boy Identity: An Alternate Strategy of Boston's Chinese Americans. *Urban Anthropology*, 5, 1:1–17.

Kennedy, P. (1993) *Preparing for the 21st Century.* New York: Vintage.

Kenyon, K. M. (1957) *Digging up Jericho.* London: E. Benn.

(1981) *Excavations at Jericho*, vol. III: *The Architecture and Stratigraphy of the Tell*, ed. T.A. Holland with contributions by R. Burleigh. London: British School of Archaeology in Jerusalem.

Kerr, C. *et al.* (1960) *Industrialism and Industrial Man: The Problems of Labour and Management in Economic Growth.* Cambridge: Harvard University Press.

Kertzer, D. (1978) The Impact of Urbanization on Household Composition: Implications from an Italian Parish 1880–1910. *Urban Anthropology*, 7, 1:1–24.

Kirk, D. (1994) *Korean Dynasty: Hyundai and Chang Ju Yung.* New York: M.E. Sharpe.

Kleniewski, N. (1984) From Industrial to Corporate City: The Role of Urban Renewal. In Tabb and Sawers.

Kracke, E. (1975) Sung K'ai-feng: Pragmatic Metropolis and Formalistic Capital. In Hager.

Kraeling, C.H. and R.M. Adams (1960) (eds.) *City Invincible: An Oriental Institute Symposium.* Chicago: University of Chicago Press.

Krapf-Askari, E. (1969) *Yoruba Towns and Cities: An Enquiry into the Nature of Urban Social Phenomena.* Oxford: Clarendon Press.

Kroeber, A.L. (1963) *Configurations of Culture Growth.* Berkeley: University of California Press.

(1966) *An Anthropologist Looks at History.* Berkeley: University of California Press.

Kurtz, D.V. and M.C. Nunley (1993) Ideology and Work at Teotihuacan: A Hermeneutic Interpretation. *Man*, 28, 4:761–78.

Ladd, E.C. (1969) *Ideology in America: Change and Response in a City, a Suburb and a Small Town.* Ithaca: Cornell University Press.

La Fontaine, J.S. (1970) *City Politics: A Study of Leopoldville 1962–63.* Cambridge: Cambridge University Press.

Lamberg-Karlovsky, C.C. and M. Lamberg-Karlovsky (1973) *Urban Interaction in the Iranian Plateau: Excavation at Tepe Yahya 1967–73.* London: Oxford University Press.

Lapidus, I.M. (1967) *Muslim Cities in the Later Middle Ages.* Cambridge: Harvard University Press.

Laslett, J. (1973) The Comparative History of Household and Family. In Gordon.

Lassner, J. (1970) *The Topography of Baghdad in the Early Middle Ages.* Detroit: Wayne State University Press.

Law, N.N. (1914) *Studies in Ancient Hindu Polity (Based on the Arthasastra of Kautilya).* London: Longmans, Green.

Lawrence, J. E. S. (1976) Science and Sentiment: Overview of Research on Crowding and Human Behaviour. In Kalt and Zalkind.

Leacock, E.B. (1971) (ed.) *The Culture of Poverty: A Critique.* New York: Simon and Schuster.

Leeds, A. (1964) Brazilian Careers and Social Structure: An Evolutionary Model and Case History. *American Anthropologist,* 66, 1, pt 1:1321–47.

   (1967) (ed.) *Social Structure, Stratification and Mobility.* Washington: Pan-American Union.

   (1980) Towns and Villages in Society: Hierarchies of Order and Cause. In T.W. Collins (ed.), *Cities in a Larger Context.* Southern Anthropological Society Proceedings 14, Athens: University of Georgia Press.

Leeds, A. and E. Leeds (1970) Brazil and the Myth of Urban Rurality: Urban Experience, Work and Values in the 'Squatments' of Rio de Janeiro and Lima. In Field.

   (1973) Locality Power in Relation to Supralocal Institutions. In Southall.

Leemans, W.F. (1950) *The Old-Babylonian Merchant: His Business and His Social Position. Studia et documenta ad iura orientis antiqui pertinentia.* Leiden: Brill.

Le Masters, E.E. (1975) *Blue Collar Aristocrats: Life-Styles at a Working-Class Tavern.* Madison: University of Wisconsin Press.

Lerner, D. (1958) *The Passing of Traditional Society: Modernizing the Middle East.* Glencoe: Free Press.

Le Tourneau, R. (1949) *Fès avant le Protectorat: étude économique et sociale d'une ville de l'occident musulman.* Casablanca: PIHEM, SMIE.

   (1961) *Fez in the Age of the Marinides.* Norman: University of Oklahoma Press.

Lewis, J.W. (1971) (ed.) *The City in Communist China.* Stanford: Stanford University Press.

Lewis, O. (1952) Urbanization without Breakdown: A Case Study. *Scientific Monthly,* 75, 1:31–41.

   (1953) Tepoztlan Restudied: A Critique of the Folk-Urban Conceptualization of Social Change. *Rural Sociology,* 18, 2:121–34.

   (1966a) The Culture of Poverty. *Scientific American,* 215, 4:19–25.

   (1966b) *La Vida: A Puerto Rican Family in the Culture of Poverty.* New York: Random House.

Lewontin, R.C. (1995) Sex, Lies and Social Science. *New York Review of Books,* 42, 7:24–9.

Liebow, E. (1967) *Tally's Corner: A Study of Negro Streetcorner Men*. Boston: Little Brown.

Lipset, S.M. and A. Solari (1967) (eds.) *Elites in Latin America*. New York: Oxford University Press.

Lipton, M. (1977) *Why Poor People Stay Poor: Urban Bias in World Development*. Cambridge: Cambridge University Press.

Lloyd, P.C. (1973) *The Yoruba: An Urban People?* In Southall.

(1979) *Slums of Hope. Shanty Towns of the Third World*. Harmondsworth: Penguin.

Loesch, A. (1954) *The Economics of Location*, trans. W.H. Woglom and W.F. Stolper. New Haven: Yale University Press.

Lomnitz, L. (1977) Mechanisms of Articulation between Shantytown Settlers and the Urban System. Paper prepared for Burg Wartenstein Symposium No. 73, Wenner-Gren Foundation.

Lopez, R.S. (1952) The Trade of Medieval Europe: The South. In Postan and Miller.

Luzzato, G. (1961) *An Economic History of Italy: From the Fall of the Roman Empire to the Sixteenth Century*, trans. P. Jones. London: Routledge and Kegan Paul.

Lynch, K. (1960) *The Image of the City*. Cambridge: Massachusetts Institute of Technology.

Lynch, O. (1968) The Politics of Untouchability: A Case from Agra. In M. Singer and B. Cohn (eds.), *Structure and Change in Indian Society*. Chicago: Aldine.

Lynd, R.S. and H.M. Lynd (1929) *Middletown: A Study in Contemporary American Culture*. New York: Harcourt Brace.

(1937) *Middletown in Transition: A Study in Cultural Conflicts*. New York: Harcourt, Brace & World.

Ma, L.J.C. (1971) Sung Urban Change 960–1279. Ann Arbor: *University of Michigan Geographical Publication*.

McGee, T.G. (1967) *The South East Asian City*. New York: Praeger.

(1971) *The Urbanization Process in the Third World: Explorations in Search of a Theory*. London: G. Bell.

McIntosh, S.K. (1995) (ed.) *Excavations at Jenne-Jeno, Hambarketelo and Kaniano (Inland Niger Delta, Mali): The 1981 Season*. Berkeley: University of California Press.

McIntosh, S. and R. McIntosh (1995) *Jenne-Jeno*. Berkeley: University of California Press.

MacLennan, C. (1985) Political Response to Economic Loss: The Automotive Crisis of 1979–82. *Urban Anthropology*, 14:21–57.

Macneish, R. S. (1973) The Origins of New World Civilization. *Scientific American*, 211, 5:29–37.

McPhail, C. (1976) Civil Disorder Participation: A Critical Examination of Recent Research. In Kalt and Zalkind.

Magubane, B. (1971) A Critical Look at Indices Used in the Study of Social Change in Colonial Africa. *Current Anthropology*, 12:4–5.

Mangin, W. (1967) Latin American Squatter Settlements: A Problem and a Solution. *Latin American Research Review*, 2, 3:65–98.

(1970) (ed.) *Peasants in Cities: Readings in the Anthropology of Urbanization*. Boston: Houghton Mifflin.

Margoliouth, D.S. (1907) *Cairo, Jerusalem and Damascus, three Chief Cities of the Egyptian Sultans.* New York: Dodd, Mead and Co.

Marshall, L.S. (1940) The Emergence of the First Industrial City: Manchester 1785–1850. In Ware.

Marx, K. (1967) *Capital,* vol. I. New York: International Publishers.

(1973) *Grundrisse. Foundations of the Critique of Political Economy.* New York: Vintage.

Marx, K. and F. Engels (1969a) *Selected Works,* vol. I. Moscow: Progress Publishers.

(1969b) *Selected Works,* vol. II. Moscow: Progress Publishers.

(1970) *Selected Works,* vol. III. Moscow: Progress Publishers.

(1975) *Collected Works,* vol. III. Moscow: Progress Publishers.

(1976) *Collected Works,* vol. V. Moscow: Progress Publishers.

Maspéro, H. (1955) *La Chine antique.* New edn, revised by P. Demiéville. Paris: Imprimerie Nationale.

Mayer, P. (1971) *Townsmen or Tribesmen: Conservatism and the Process of Urbanization in a South African City.* Cape Town: Oxford University Press.

Mayntz, R. (1967) Methodological Problems in the Study of Stratification. In Leeds.

Mazrui, A. A. (1972) *The Lumpen Proletariat and Lumpen Militariat: African Soldiers as a New Political Class.* Seminar Paper DSP/6/72–3. Makerere University: Department of Political Science.

Mellaart, J. (1967) *Çatal Hüyük: A Neolithic Town in Anatolia.* London: Thames and Hudson.

Meuriot, P. (1897) *Des agglomérations urbaines dans l'Europe contemporaine: essai sur les causes, les conditions, les conséquences de leur développement.* Paris: Belin Frères.

Michaelson, K.L. (1973) Class, Caste and Network in Suburban Bombay. PhD dissertation. Madison: University of Wisconsin.

Michell, H. (1975) *The Economics of Ancient Greece.* Cambridge: W. Heffer.

Middleton, D.R. (1976) The Growth of a City: Urban Regional, and National Integration in Ecuador. *Urban Anthropology,* 5, 2:125–41.

Millon, R. (1973) *Urbanization at Teotihuacan, Mexico.* Austin: University of Texas Press.

Miner, H. (1953) *The Primitive City of Timbuctoo.* Princeton: Princeton University Press.

(1967) (ed.) *The City in Modern Africa.* New York: Praeger.

(1973) Traditional Mobility among the Weavers of Fez. *Proceedings of the American Philosophical Society,* 117, 1:17–36.

Mingione, E. (1977) Territorial Social Problems in Socialist China. In Abu-Lughod and Hay.

Mintz, S.W. and E.R. Wolf (1950) An Analysis of Ritual Co-Parenthood. *Southwestern Journal of Anthropology,* 6:341–68.

Mirot, L. (1906) *Les insurrections urbaines au début du règne de Charles VI 1380–83 leurs causes, leurs conséquences.* Paris: A. Fontemonig.

Mitchell, J.C. (1956) *The Kalela Dance.* Rhodes-Livingstone Papers, 27. Manchester: Manchester University Press.

(1966) Theoretical Orientations in African Urban Studies. In Banton.

(1969) (ed.) *Social Networks in Urban Situations: Analysis of Personal Relationships in Central African Towns.* Manchester: Manchester University Press.

(1973) Distance, Transportation and Urban Involvement in Zambia. In Southall.

Moore, B. (1958) *Political Power and Social Theory.* Cambridge: Harvard University Press.

(1966) *Social Origins of Dictatorship and Democracy: Lord and Peasant in the Making of the Modern World.* Boston: Beacon.

(1970) *Reflections on the Causes of Human Misery and upon Certain Proposals to Eliminate Them.* Boston: Beacon.

Moorehouse, G. (1983) *Calcutta: The City Revealed.* Harmondsworth: Penguin.

Morris, H.S. (1958) The Divine Kingship of the Aga Khan: A Study of Theocracy in East Africa. *Southwestern Journal of Anthropology*, 14, 4:454–72.

Morse, H.B. (1909) *The Guilds of China with an Account of the Guild Merchant or Co-hung of Canton.* London: Longmans, Green.

(1913) *The Trade and Administration of China.* Shanghai: Kelly and Walsh.

Moser, C.A. and W. Scott (1961) *British Towns: A Statistical Study of their Social and Economic Differences.* Edinburgh: Oliver and Boyd.

Mueller, W. (1961) *Die Heilige Stadt: Roma quadrata, himmlisches Jerusalem und die Mythe vom Weltnabel.* Stuttgart: W. Kohnhammer.

Muir, Sir W. (1896) *The Mameluke or Slave Dynasty of Egypt 1260–1517.* London: Smith and Elder & Co.

Mumford, L. (1961) *The City in History.* Harmondsworth: Penguin Books.

Nabokov, P. (1992) *Native American Testimony. A Chronicle of Indian–White Relations from Prophecy to the Present.* New York: Penguin.

Nair, K. (1983) *Transforming Traditionally: Land and Labour Use in Agriculture in Asia and Africa.* Maryland: Riverdale Company Publishers.

Nakane, Chie (1970) *Japanese Society.* Berkeley: University of California Press.

Nas, P.J.M. (1993) (ed.) *Urban Symbolism.* Leiden: E. J. Brill.

Nash, J. (1979) *We Eat the Mines and the Mines Eat Us: Dependency and Exploitation in Bolivian Tin Mines.* New York: Columbia University Press.

Needham, R. (1975) Polythetic Classification: Convergence and Consequences, *Man*, n.s. 10, 3:349–69.

(1973) *Right and Left: Essays on Dual Symbolic Classification.* Chicago: University of Chicago Press.

Olufsen, O. (1911) *The Emir of Bokhara and his Country: Journeys and Studies in Bokhara.* Copenhagen: Gyldendalske Boghandle, Nordisk Forlag. London: Heinemann.

Origo, I. (1960) *The Merchant of Prato.* London: Jonathan Cape.

Ouroussoff, A. (1993) Illusion of Rationality: False Premisses of the Liberal Tradition. *Man*, 28:281–98.

Owusu, M. (1978) Ethnography of Africa: The Usefulness of the Useless. *American Anthropologist*, 80, 2:310–34.

Park, R.E. and E.W. Burgess (1925) *The City.* Chicago: Chicago University Press.

Parkin, D.J. (1969) *Neighbours and Nationals in an African City Ward.* Berkeley: University of California Press.

(1975) (ed.) *Town and Country in Central and East Africa*. London: Oxford University Press for International African Institute.

Parry, J. H. (1948) *The Audiencia of New Galicia in the Sixteenth Century*. Cambridge: Cambridge University Press.

(1949) *Europe and a Wider World 1415–1715*. London: Hutchinson.

(1971) *Trade and Dominion: The European Overseas Empires in the Eighteenth Century*. New York: Praeger.

Parsons, T. (1952) *The Social System*. London: Tavistock.

Pauty, E. (1951) *Villes spontanées et villes créés*. Annales de l'Institute d'Etudes Occitanes. Toulouse, IX, 52–75.

Petit-Dutaillis, C. (1974) *Les communes françaises, caractères et évolution, des origines au XVIIIe siècle*. Paris: A. Michel.

Piggott, S. (1945) *Some Ancient Cities of India*. London: Oxford University Press.

Pirenne, H. (1925, 1956) *Medieval Cities: Their Origins and the Revival of Trade*, trans. F.D. Halsy. New York: Anchor, Doubleday.

Planhol, X. de (1959) *The World of Islam*. Ithaca: Cornell University Press.

Plotnicov, L. (1967) *Strangers to the City: Urban Man in Jos, Nigeria*. Pittsburgh: Pittsburgh University Press.

(1985) Back to Basics, Forward to Fundamentals: the Search for Urban Anthropology's Mission. In Southall, Nas and Ansari.

Polo, M. (1928) *The Travels of Marco Polo*, trans. M. Komroff. London: Jonathan Cape.

Postan, M.M. and E. Miller (1952) (eds.) *Cambridge Economic History of Europe*, vol. II: *Trade and Industry in the Middle Ages*. Cambridge: Cambridge University Press.

Postan, M.M., E.E. Rich and E. Miller (1963) (eds.) *Cambridge Economic History of Europe*, vol. III: *Economic Organization and Policies in the Middle Ages*. Cambridge: Cambridge University Press.

Power, E. (1942) *The Wool Trade in English Medieval History*. London: Oxford University Press.

Provencher, R. (1972) Comparisons of Social Interaction Styles: Urban and Rural Malay Culture. In Weaver and White.

(1975) *Mainland Southeast Asia: An Anthropological Perspective*. Pacific Palisades: Goodyear.

Puri, B.N. (1966) *Cities of Ancient India*. Meerut: Meenakshi Prakashan. Qur'an.

Ralston, R.D. (1975) *Xhosa Cattle Sacrifice 1856–57: The Messianic Factor in African Resistance*. MS Department of History, University of Wisconsin.

Ramachandran, P. (1972) *Pavement Dwellers in Bombay City*. Deonai. Bombay 88: Tata Institute of Social Sciences.

Rapkin, C. (1966) *The Private Rental Housing Market in New York City, 1965: A Study of Some Effects of Two Decades of Rent Control*. New York City: Rent and Rehabilitation Administration.

Rasmussen, S.E. (1960) *London, the Unique City*. Harmondsworth: Penguin Books.

Redfield, R. (1950) *A Village that Chose Progress: Chan Kom Revisited*. Chicago: University of Chicago Press.

(1956) *Peasant Society and Culture: An Approach to Civilization*. Chicago: University of Chicago Press.

Redfield, R. and M. Singer (1960) The Cultural Role of Cities. In Kraeling and Adams.

Redford, A. (1934–56) *Manchester Merchants and Foreign Trade*, 2 vols. Manchester: Manchester University Press.

Reich, C.A. (1972) *The Greening of America*. New York: Bantam/Random House.

Reich, R.B. (1991) *The Work of Nations*. London: Simon and Schuster.

Reissman, L. (1959) *Class in American Society*. Glencoe: Free Press.

Renfrew, C. and J. Cherry (1986) (eds.) *Peer Polity Interaction and Socio-Political Change*. Cambridge: Cambridge University Press.

Richards, G. R. B. (1932) *Florentine Merchants in the Age of the Medici*. Cambridge: Harvard University Press.

Richardson, H. (1993) Efficiency and Welfare in LDC Mega-Cities. In J.D. Kasarda and A.M. Parnell (eds.), *Third World Cities: Problems, Policies and Prospects*. Newbury Park: Sage.

Robson, W.A. and D.E. Regan (1972) (eds.) *Great Cities of the World: Their Government, Politics and Planning*, 2 vols. London: Allen and Unwin.

Rodger, J. M. (1970) *Samarra: A Study in Medieval Town Planning*. In Hourani and Stern.

Rorig, F. (1970) *The Medieval Town*. London: Batsford.

Rosenfeld, G. (1971) *'Shut Those Thick Lips': A Study of Slum School Failure*. New York: Holt, Rinehart and Winston.

Rostovtzeff, M.I. (1957) *The Social and Economic History of the Roman Empire*. Oxford: Clarendon Press.

Rostow, W.W. (1978) Central Planning Is Mandatory, *New York Times*, 21 May.

Rothman, D.J. (1994) The Crime of Punishment. *New York Review Of Books*, Feb., 34–8.

Rowe, J.H. (1963) Urban Settlements in Ancient Peru. *Nawpa Pacha*, 1, 3:1–28.

Rowe, W. (1973) Caste, Kinship and Association in Urban India. In Southall.

Rowe, W.T. (1984) *Hankow: Commerce and Society in a Chinese City, 1796–1889*. Stanford: Stanford University Press.

Rozman, G. (1973) *Urban Networks in Ch'ing China and Tokugawa Japan*. Princeton: Princeton University Press.

Rubinstein, N. (1966) *The Government of Florence under the Medici (1434–1494)* Oxford: Clarendon Press.

(1968) *Florentine Studies: Politics and Society in Renaissance Florence*. Evanston: Northwestern University Press.

Runciman, S. (1952) Byzantine Trade and Industry. In Postan and Miller.

Runciman, W.G. (1966) *Relative Deprivation and Social Justice*. London: Routledge & Kegan Paul.

Rushdie, S. (1981) *Midnight's Children*. London: Jonathan Cape.

Russell, J.C. (1972) *Medieval Regions and their Cities*. Bloomington: Indiana University Press.

Rykwert, J. (1989) *The Idea of a Town: The Anthropology of Urban Form in Rome, Italy and the Ancient World*. Cambridge, Mass.: MIT Press.

Safa, H.I. (1964) Shantytown to Public Housing. *Caribbean Studies*, 4, 1:3–12.

(1965) The Female Based Household in Public Housing: A Case Study from Puerto Rico. *Human Organization*, 24, 2:135–9.

Sahlins, M.D. (1958) *Social Stratification in Polynesia*. Seattle: University of Washington Press.

Said, E. (1978) *Orientalism*. New York: Pantheon.

Sandhu, K.S. and P. Wheatley (1982) (eds.) *Melaka: The Transformation of a Malay Capital c. 1400–1980*, vol. I. Kuala Lumpur: Oxford University Press for the Institute of Southeast Asian Studies.

Sansom, Sir G. B. (1958–63) *A History of Japan*, 3 vols. Stanford: Stanford University Press.

Santos, M. (1975) *L'espace partagé: les deux circuits de l'économie urbaine des pays sous-développés*. Paris: Editions M. Th. Genin. Librairies Techniques.

Saunders, P. (1986) *Social Theory and the Urban Question*. New York: Holmes & Meier.

Schaffer, F. (1972) *The New Town Story*. London: Palladin.

Seddon, D. (1978) (ed.) *Relations of Production*. London: Frank Cass.

Shack, W. (1973) Urban Ethnicity and the Cultural Process of Urbanization in Ethiopia. In Southall.

Shamasastry, R. (1920) *Evolution of Indian Polity*. Calcutta: University of Calcutta.

(1956) *Kautilya's Arthasastra*. Mysore: Mysore Printing and Publishing.

Shaw, C.R. and H.D. McKay (1972) *Juvenile Deliquency and Urban Areas*. Chicago: University of Chicago Press.

Sherring, M.A. (1868) *The Sacred City of the Hindus: An Account of Benares in Ancient and Modern Times*. London: Trubner.

Shiba, Y. (1975) Urbanization and the Development of Markets in the Lower Yangtze Valley. In Haeger.

Shils, E. (1971) Tradition. *Comparative Studies in Society and History*, 13:122–59.

Simic, A. (1973) *The Peasant Urbanites: A Study of Rural–Urban Migration in Serbia*. New York: Seminar Press.

Simmel, G. (1950) *The Sociology of Georg Simmel*, trans. and ed. K.H. Wolff. Glencoe: Free Press.

Simpson, G.E. (1968) *Assimilation*. International Encyclopedia of the Social Sciences. Glencoe: Free Press.

Sinclair, R. (1950) *East London: The East and Northeast Boroughs of London and Greater London*. London: Robert Hale.

Singer, M. (1966) The Modernization of Religious Beliefs. In Weiner.

(1968) The Indian Joint Family in Modern Industry. In M. Singer and B. Cohn (eds.), *Structure and Change in Indian Society*. Chicago: Aldine.

(1984) A Semiotic of the City. (Unpublished paper.) Presented at Workshop on Meanings of the City, Wingspread, Wisconsin.

Sinha, S. and B. Saraswati (1978) *Ascetics of Kashi, an Anthropological Exploration*. Varanasi: N. K. Bose Memorial Foundation.

Sjoberg, G. (1960) *The Pre-Industrial City*. Glencoe: Free Press.

Skinner, E.P. (1974) *African Urban Life: The Transformation of Ougadougou*. Princeton: Princeton University Press.

Skinner, G.W. (1957) *Chinese Society in Thailand: An Analytical History*. Ithaca: Cornell University Press.

(1958) *Leadership and Power in the Chinese Community of Thailand*. Ithaca: Cornell University Press.

(1965) Marketing and Social Structure in Rural China. Reprinted from the *Journal of Asian Studies*, 24, 1, 2 and 30. Tucson: University of Arizona Press.

(1977) (ed.) *The City in Late Imperial China*. Stanford: Stanford University Press.

Smith, M.G. (1960) *Government in Zazzau 1800–1950*. Stanford: Stanford University Press.

Smith, R.J. (1960) Preindustrial Urbanism in Japan: A Consideration of Multiple Traditions in a Feudal Society. *Economic Development and Cultural Change*, 7:241–57.

(1973) Town and City in Pre-Modern Japan: Small Families, Small Households, and Residential Instability. In Southall.

Snyder, P.Z. (1976) Neighbourhood Gatekeepers in the Process of Urban Adaptation: Cross-Ethnic Commonalities. *Urban Anthropology*, 5, 1:35–52.

Southall, A.W. (1956a) *Alur Society: A Study in Processes and Types of Domination*. Cambridge: Heffer.

(1956b) Determinants of the Social Structure of African Urban Populations. In C.D. Forde (ed.), *Social Implications of Industrialization and Urbanization in Africa South of the Sahara*. International African Institute for UNESCO.

(1961) (ed.) *Social Change in Modern Africa*. London: Oxford University Press for International African Institute.

(1966) The Concept of Elites and their Formation in Uganda. In P.C. Lloyd (ed.), *The New Elites of Tropical Africa*. London: Oxford University Press for International African Institute.

(1967) Kampala-Mengo. In Miner.

(1970a) The Illusion of Tribe. *Journal of Asian and African Studies*, 5, 1 and 2:28–50.

(1970b) The Impact of Imperialism upon Urban Development in Africa. In V.W. Turner (ed.), *Profiles of Change: African Societies and Colonial Rule*. Cambridge: Cambridge University Press.

(1973) (ed.) *Urban Anthropology: Cross-Cultural Studies of Urbanization*. New York: Oxford University Press.

(1975a) From Segmentary Lineage to Ethnic Association: Luo, Luhya, Ibo and Others. In M. Owusu (ed.), *Colonialism and Change: Essays Presented to L. Mair*. The Hague: Mouton.

(1975b) Forms of Ethnic Linkage between Town and Country. In Parkin.

(1988a) On Mode of Production Theory: The Foraging Mode of Production and the Kinship Mode of Production. *Dialectical Anthropology*, 12:165–92.

(1988b) The Segmentary State in Africa and Asia. *Comparative Studies in Society and History*, 30, 1:52–82.

(1993) The Circle and the Square: Symbolic Form and Process in the City. In Nas.

Southall, A., P. Nas and G. Ansari (1985) (eds.) *City and Society: Studies in Urban Ethnicity. Lifestyle and Class*. Leiden: Leiden Development Studies, 7.

Spencer, J. (1964) *Stress and Release in an Urban Estate: A Study in Action Research*. London: Tavistock.

Spiro, M.E. (1955) The Acculturation of American Ethnic Groups. *American Anthropologist*, 57:1240–52.

Spufford, P. (1963) Coinage and Currency. In Postan, Rich and Miller.

Srinivas, M.N. (1962) *Caste in Modern India, and Other Essays*. Bombay: Asia Publishing House.

Stack, C.B. (1975) *All Our Kin: Strategies for Survival in a Black Community.* New York: Harper.

Stein, B. (1977) The Segmentary State in Medieval South India. In R.G. Fox (ed.), *Realm and Region in Traditional India.* Durham: Duke University Press.

(1980) *Peasant, State and Society in Medieval South India.* Delhi: Oxford University Press.

Steward, J. H. (1955) *Theory of Culture Change: The Methodology of Multilinear Evolution.* Urbana: University of Illinois Press.

Stover, L.E. and T.K. Stover (1976) *China: An Anthropological Perspective.* Pacific Palisades: Goodyear.

Strickon, A. and S. M. Greenfield (1972) (eds.) *Structure and Process in Latin America: Patronage, Clientage and Power Systems.* Albuquerque: University of New Mexico Press.

Stuart, G.E. (1993) New Light on Olmec. *National Geographic*, 184, 5:88–115.

Stull, D.D. (1990) (ed.) When the Packers Came to Town: Changing Ethnic Relations in Garden City, Kansas. *Urban Anthropology*, 19, 4:303–20.

Suttles, G.D. (1968) *The Social Order of the Slum. Ethnicity and Territory in the Inner City.* Chicago: University of Chicago Press.

(1972) *The Social Construction of Communities.* Chicago: University of Chicago Press.

Szanton, M.C.B. (1972) *A Right to Survive: Subsistence Marketing in a Lowland Philippine Town.* College Park: Pennsylvania State University Press.

Szelenyi, I. (1993) East European Cities: How Different Are They? In Guldin and Southall.

Tabb, W.K. and L. Sawers (1984) *Marxism and the Metropolis: New Perspectives in Urban Political Economy.* New York: Oxford University Press.

Tambiah, S. J. (1974) *World Conqueror and World Renouncer: A Study of Buddhism and Polity against a Historical Background.* Cambridge: Cambridge University Press.

Taussig, M.T. (1980) *The Devil and Commodity Fetishism in South America.* Chapel Hill: University of North Carolina Press.

Tax, S. (1953) *Penny Capitalism: A Guatemalan Indian Economy.* Washington DC: Publication 16, Institute of Social Anthropology, Smithsonian.

Tenhouten, W.D. (1976) The Black Family: Myth and Reality. In Kalt and Zalkind.

Thompson, E. P. (1978) *The Poverty of Theory and Other Essays.* New York: Monthly Review Press.

Thrasher, F.M. (1926) *The Gang.* Chicago: Chicago University Press.

Thrupp, S. (1948) *The Merchant Class of Medieval London 1300–1500.* Chicago: University of Chicago Press.

(1961) The Creativity of Cities. *Comparative Studies in Society and History*, 4, 1:53–64.

(1963) The Guilds. In Postan, Rich and Miller.

(1967) *Early Medieval Society.* New York: Appleton-Century-Crofts.

Todd, I.A. (1976) *Çatal Hüyük in Perspective.* Menlo Park: Cummings.

Toffler, A. (1971) *Future Shock.* New York: Bantam Books.

Toth, J. (1992) Doubts about Growth: The Town of Carlisle in Transition. *Urban Anthropology*, 21, 1:1–44.

Toynbee, A.J. (1934) *A Study of History*, vol. III. New York: Oxford University Press.

(1967) (ed.) *Cities of Destiny*. London: Thames and Hudson.

(1970) *Cities on the Move*. New York: Oxford University Press.

Trevelyan, G.M. (1945) *English Social History*. London: Longmans.

Tuchman, B.W. (1979) A Distant Mirror: The Calamitous 14th Century. Harmondsworth: Penguin.

Turner, J.F.C. (1966) *Uncontrolled Urban Settlements: Problems and Policies*. Pittsburgh: United Nations Seminar on Development Policies and Planning in Relation to Urbanization.

Turner, R. (1941) *The Great Cultural Traditions: The Foundations of Civilization*, vol. II: *The Classical Empires*. New York: McGraw-Hill.

Tweeten, L. and G. L. Brinkman (1976) *Micropolitical Development: The Theory and Practice of Greater Rural Economic Development*. Iowa: Iowa State University Press.

Twitchett, D. (1963) *Financial Administration under the T'ang Dynasty*. Cambridge: Cambridge University Press.

Ucko, P.R., R. Tringham and G.W. Dimbleby (1972) (eds.) *Man, Settlement and Urbanism*. London: Duckworth.

Valentine, C.A. (1968) *Culture of Poverty: Critique and Counterproposals*. Chicago: University of Chicago Press.

Van Werveke, H. (1963) The Rise of the Towns. In Postan, Rich and Miller.

Vatuk, S. J. (1971) *Kinship and Urbanization: White Collar Migrants in North India*. Berkeley: University of California Press.

Verlinden, O. (1963) Markets and Fairs. In Postan, Rich and Miller.

Vernant, J. P. (1982) *The Origins of Greek Thought*. Ithaca: Cornell University Press.

Veyne, P. (1992) (ed.) *A History of Private Life, vol. I: From Pagan Rome to Byzantium*. Cambridge: Harvard University Press.

Vidich, A.J. and J. Bensman (1960) *Small Town in Mass Society: Class, Power and Religion in a Rural Community*. New York: Anchor, Doubleday.

Villari, P. (1895) *The First Two Centuries of Florentine History*, trans. L. Villari. London: T.F. Unwin.

Vining, R. (1955) Spatial Aspects of an Economic System. *Economic Development and Cultural Change*, 3:147–95.

Vogel, E.F. (1969) *Canton under Communism 1949–68*. Cambridge: Harvard University Press.

Wade, R.C. (1964) *Slavery in the Cities: The South 1820–1860*. New York: Oxford University Press.

Wagatsuma, H. and G. DeVos (1967) The Outcast Tradition in Modern Japan. In Dore.

Wagley, C. (1953) *Amazon Town: A Study of Man in the Tropics*. New York: Macmillan.

Wallman, S. (1979) (ed.) *Social Anthropology of Work*. London: Academic Press.

(1993) Reframing Context: Pointers to the Post-Industrial City. In A. P. Cohen and K. Fukui (eds.), *Humanising the City? Social Contexts of Urban Life at the Turn of the Millennium*. Edinburgh: Edinburgh University Press.

Walton, M. (1952) *Sheffield: Its Story and its Achievements*. Sheffield: The Sheffield Telegraph and Star.

Walton, J. and D. E. Carns (1973) (eds.) *Cities in Change: Studies on the Urban Condition*. Boston: Allyn & Bacon.

Ward, B. (1976) *The Home of Man*. New York: Norton.

Ware, C. F. (1940) (ed.) *The Cultural Approach to History*. New York: Kennicat Press.

Warmington, B. H. (1960) *Carthage*. London: R. Hale.

Warner, S. B. (1962) *Streetcar Suburbs: The Process of Growth in Boston, 1870–1900*. Cambridge: Harvard University Press.

(1966) *Planning for a Nation of Cities*. Cambridge: Massachusetts Institute of Technology.

(1968) *The Private City: Philadelphia in Three Periods of its Growth*. Philadelphia: University of Pennsylvania Press.

(1972) *The Urban Wilderness: A History of the American City*. New York: Harper and Row.

Warner, W.L. (1949) *Democracy in Jonesville: A Study of Quality and Inequality*. New York: Harper.

(1963) *Yankee City*. New Haven: Yale University Press.

Watson, B. (1958) *Ssu-ma-ch'ien, Grand Historian of China*. New York: Columbia University Press.

Watson, W. (1964) Social Mobility and Social Class in Industrial Communities. In Gluckman.

Weaver, T. and D. White (1972) (eds.) *The Anthropology of Urban Environments*. Southern Anthropological Association, monograph II.

Weber, A. F. (1899, 1968) *The Growth of Cities in the Nineteenth Century: A Study in Statistics*. Ithaca: Cornell University Press.

Weber, M. (1958) *The City*, trans. D. Martindale and G. Neuwirth. Glencoe: Free Press.

(1968) *Economy and Society*, trans. and ed. G. Roth and C. Wittich. New York: Bedminster.

Weiner, M. (1966) (ed.) *Modernization: The Dynamics of Growth*. New York: Basic Books.

Weisner, T. (1970) One Family, Two Households: Rural Urban Kinship Networks in Nairobi. San Diego: 69th Annual American Anthropological Association.

(1976) The Structure of Sociability: Urban Migration and Urban–Rural Ties in Kenya. *Urban Anthropology*, 5, 2:199–223.

Werveke, H. van (1963a) The Low Countries. In Postan, Rich and Miller.

(1963b) The Rise of Towns. In Postan, Rich and Miller.

Wheatley, P. (1963) What the Greatness of a City is Said to Be. *Pacific Viewpoint*, 4, 2:163–88.

(1971) *The Pivot of the Four Quarters: A Preliminary Enquiry into the Origins and Character of the Ancient Chinese City*. Chicago: Aldine.

(1972) The Concept of Urbanism. In Ucko, Tringham and Dimbleby.

(1978) *From Court to Capital: A Tentative Interpretation of the Origins of the Japanese Urban Tradition*. Chicago: University of Chicago Press.

(1983) Nagara and Commandery: Origins of the Southeast Asian Urban Traditions. Chicago: University of Chicago Department of Geography Research Papers Nos. 207–8.

Wheeler, Sir M. (1968) *The Indus Civilization.* Cambridge: Cambridge University Press.

Whiteford, A. H. (1964) *Two Cities of Latin America: A Comparative Description of Social Classes.* Garden City, New York: Anchor Doubleday.

Whiteford, M. B. (1976) A Comparison of Migrant Satisfaction in Two Low-Income Housing Settlements of Popayan, Columbia. *Urban Anthropology,* 5, 3:271–84.

Whyte, W.F. (1943) *Street Corner Society: The Social Structure of an Italian Slum.* Chicago: University of Chicago Press.

Wiet, G. (1971) *Baghdad: Metropolis of the Abbasid Caliphate,* trans. S. Feiler. Norman: University of Oklahoma Press.

Wikan, U. (1995) Sustainable Development in a Mega-City. *Current Anthropology,* 36, 4:635–48.

Williams, M.D. (1981) *On the Street Where I Lived.* New York: Holt, Rinehart and Winston.

Williams, R. (1977) *Marxism and Literature.* New York: Oxford University Press.
(1980) *Problems in Materialism and Culture.* London: Verso and NLB.

Willmott, P. and M. Young (1960) *Family and Class in a London Suburb.* London: Routledge and Kegan Paul.

Wilson, M. and A. Mafeje (1963) *Langa: A Study of Social Groups in an African Township.* Cape Town: Oxford University Press.

Wirth, L. (1938) Urbanism as a Way of Life. *American Journal of Sociology,* 44:1–24.

Wittfogel, K. (1957) *Oriental Despotism: A Comparative Study of Total Power.* New Haven: Yale University Press.

Wolf, E.R. (1956) Aspects of Group Relations in a Complex Society. *American Anthropologist,* 58:1065–78.
(1959) *Sons of the Shaking Earth.* Chicago: Chicago University Press.
(1982) *Europe and the People without History.* Berkeley: University of California Press.

Workers' Educational Association (n.d.) *A Social Study.* Basingstoke: Workers' Educational Association.

Wright, H.T. (1969) *The Administration of Rural Production in an Early Mesopotamian Town.* Ann Arbor: University of Michigan Museum of Anthropology, Paper No. 38.

Wright, H.T. and G.A. Johnson (1975) Population, Exchange and Early State Formation in Southwest Iran. *American Anthropologist,* 77:267–89.

Yablonsky, L. (1966) *The Violent Gang.* Baltimore: Penguin.

Yancey, W.L. (1976) Architecture, Interaction and Social Control: The Case of a Large-Scale Public Housing Project. In Kalt and Zalkind.

Yazaki, T. (1963) *The Japanese City: A Sociological Analysis.* Tokyo: Japan Publications.
(1968) *Social Change and the City in Japan: From Earliest Times through the Industrial Revolution.* San Francisco: Japan Publications.

Yuan-li Wu (1973) (eds.) *China: A Handbook.* New York: Praeger.

Zghal, A. and F. Stambouli (1974) La vie urbaine dans le Maghreb précolonial. *Revue tunisienne des sciences sociales*, 11, 36–9:221–42.

Zorbaugh, H.W. (1929) *The Gold Coast and the Slum: A Sociological Study of Chicago's Near North Side*. Chicago: University of Chicago Press.

Zuidema, R.T. (1964) *The Ceque System of Cuzco: The Social Organization of the Capital of the Inca*, trans. E.M. Hobykaas. Leiden: E.J. Brill.

Index